THE ARDEN SHAKESPEARE

THIRD SERIES
General Editors: Richard Proudfoot, Ann Thompson,
David Scott Kastan and H.R. Woudhuysen

KING RICHARD III

THE ARDEN SHAKESPEARE

ALL'S WELL THAT ENDS WELL	edited by Suzanne Gossett and Helen Wilcox
ANTONY AND CLEOPATRA	edited by John Wilders
AS YOU LIKE IT	edited by Juliet Dusinberre
THE COMEDY OF ERRORS	edited by Kent Cartwright
CORIOLANUS	edited by Peter Holland
CYMBELINE	edited by Valerie Wayne
DOUBLE FALSEHOOD	edited by Brean Hammond
HAMLET, Revised	edited by Ann Thompson and Neil Taylor
HAMLET, The Texts of 1603 and 1623	edited by Ann Thompson and Neil Taylor
JULIUS CAESAR	edited by David Daniell
KING EDWARD III	edited by Richard Proudfoot and Nicola Bennett
KING HENRY IV PART 1	edited by David Scott Kastan
KING HENRY IV PART 2	edited by James C. Bulman
KING HENRY V	edited by T.W. Craik
KING HENRY VI PART 1	edited by Edward Burns
KING HENRY VI PART 2	edited by Ronald Knowles
KING HENRY VI PART 3	edited by John D. Cox and Eric Rasmussen
KING HENRY VIII	edited by Gordon McMullan
KING JOHN	edited by Jesse M. Lander and J.J.M. Tobin
KING LEAR	edited by R.A. Foakes
KING RICHARD II	edited by Charles Forker
KING RICHARD III	edited by James R. Siemon
LOVE'S LABOUR'S LOST	edited by H.R. Woudhuysen
MACBETH	edited by Sandra Clark and Pamela Mason
MEASURE FOR MEASURE	edited by A.R. Braunmuller and Robert N. Watson
THE MERCHANT OF VENICE	edited by John Drakakis
THE MERRY WIVES OF WINDSOR	edited by Giorgio Melchiori
A MIDSUMMER NIGHT'S DREAM	edited by Sukanta Chaudhuri
MUCH ADO ABOUT NOTHING, Revised	edited by Claire McEachern
OTHELLO, Revised	edited by E.A.J. Honigmann, with an Introduction by Ayanna Thompson
PERICLES	edited by Suzanne Gossett
ROMEO AND JULIET	edited by René Weis
SHAKESPEARE'S POEMS	edited by Katherine Duncan-Jones and H.R. Woudhuysen
SHAKESPEARE'S SONNETS, Revised	edited by Katherine Duncan-Jones
SIR THOMAS MORE	edited by John Jowett
THE TAMING OF THE SHREW	edited by Barbara Hodgdon
THE TEMPEST, Revised	edited by Virginia Mason Vaughan and Alden T. Vaughan
TIMON OF ATHENS	edited by Anthony B. Dawson and Gretchen E. Minton
TITUS ANDRONICUS, Revised	edited by Jonathan Bate
TROILUS AND CRESSIDA, Revised	edited by David Bevington
TWELFTH NIGHT	edited by Keir Elam
THE TWO GENTLEMEN OF VERONA	edited by William C. Carroll
THE TWO NOBLE KINSMEN, Revised	edited by Lois Potter
THE WINTER'S TALE	edited by John Pitcher

THE ARDEN SHAKESPEARE

RICHARD III

Edited by
JAMES R. SIEMON

THE ARDEN SHAKESPEARE
LONDON • NEW YORK • OXFORD • NEW DELHI • SYDNEY

THE ARDEN SHAKESPEARE
Bloomsbury Publishing Plc
50 Bedford Square, London, WC1B 3DP, UK
1385 Broadway, New York, NY 10018, USA
29 Earlsfort Terrace, Dublin 2, Ireland

BLOOMSBURY, THE ARDEN SHAKESPEARE and the Arden Shakespeare logo are
trademarks of Bloomsbury Publishing Plc

This edition of *Richard III* by James R. Siemon, first published 2009
by the Arden Shakespeare
Reprinted by Bloomsbury Arden Shakespeare 2010, 2011 (twice), 2012, 2013 (twice),
2014, 2015, 2016 (twice), 2017, 2019 (twice), 2020 (three times), 2021, 2022, 2023

The general editors of the Arden Shakespeare have been
W. J. Craig and R. H. Case (first series 1899–1944)
Una Ellis-Fermor, Harold F. Brooks, Harold Jenkins and
Brian Morris (second series 1946–82)
Present general editors (third series)
Richard Proudfoot, Ann Thompson, David Scott Kastan
and H. R. Woudhuysen

A catalogue record for this book is available from the British Library.

A catalog record for this book is available from the Library of Congress.

ISBN: HB: 978-1-9034-3688-2
PB: 978-1-9034-3689-9
ePDF: 978-1-4081-3451-2
eBook: 978-1-4081-4512-3

Series: The Arden Shakespeare Third Series
Printed and bound in India

To find out more about our authors and books visit www.bloomsbury.com
and sign up for our newsletters.

The Editor

James R. Siemon is Professor of English at Boston University. He is the author of *Word Against Word: Shakespearean Utterance* (2002) and *Shakespearean Iconoclasm* (1985); he is the editor of Christopher Marlowe's *The Jew of Malta* for the New Mermaids Series (1994).

For Alexandra, Johanna, Rosalie, Anna and Julia

CONTENTS

LIST OF
ILLUSTRATIONS

GENERAL EDITORS' PREFACE

The earliest volume in the first Arden series, Edward Dowden's *Hamlet*, was published in 1899. Since then the Arden Shakespeare has been widely acknowledged as the pre-eminent Shakespeare edition, valued by scholars, students, actors and 'the great variety of readers' alike for its clearly presented and reliable texts, its full annotation and its richly informative introductions.

In the third Arden series we seek to maintain these well-established qualities and general characteristics, preserving our predecessors' commitment to presenting the play as it has been shaped in history. Each volume necessarily has its own particular emphasis which reflects the unique possibilities and problems posed by the work in question, and the series as a whole seeks to maintain the highest standards of scholarship, combined with attractive and accessible presentation.

Newly edited from the original Quarto and Folio editions, texts are presented in fully modernized form, with a textual apparatus that records all substantial divergences from those early printings. The notes and introductions focus on the conditions and possibilities of meaning that editors, critics and performers (on stage and screen) have discovered in the play. While building upon the rich history of scholarly activity that has long shaped our understanding of Shakespeare's works, this third series of the Arden Shakespeare is enlivened by a new generation's encounter with Shakespeare.

THE TEXT

On each page of the play itself, readers will find a passage of text supported by commentary and textual notes. Act and scene divisions (seldom present in the early editions and often the product of eighteenth-century or later scholarship) have been retained for ease of reference, but have been given less prominence than in previous series. Editorial indications of location of the action have been removed to the textual notes or commentary.

In the text itself, unfamiliar typographic conventions have been avoided in order to minimize obstacles to the reader. Elided forms in the early texts are spelt out in full in verse lines wherever they indicate a usual late twentieth-century pronunciation that requires no special indication and wherever they occur in prose (except where they indicate non-standard pronunciation). In verse speeches, marks of elision are retained where they are necessary guides to the scansion and pronunciation of the line. Final -ed in past tense and participial forms of verbs is always printed as -ed, without accent, never as -'d, but wherever the required pronunciation diverges from modern usage a note in the commentary draws attention to the fact. Where the final -ed should be given syllabic value contrary to modern usage, e.g.

> Doth Silvia know that I am banished?
> (*TGV* 3.1.214)

the note will take the form

> 214 **banished** banishèd

Conventional lineation of divided verse lines shared by two or more speakers has been reconsidered and sometimes rearranged. Except for the familiar *Exit* and *Exeunt*, Latin forms in stage directions and speech prefixes have been translated into English and the original Latin forms recorded in the textual notes.

COMMENTARY AND TEXTUAL NOTES

Notes in the commentary, for which a major source will be the *Oxford English Dictionary,* offer glossarial and other explication of verbal difficulties; they may also include discussion of points of interpretation and, in relevant cases, substantial extracts from Shakespeare's source material. Editors will not usually offer glossarial notes for words adequately defined in the latest edition of *The Concise Oxford Dictionary* or *Merriam-Webster's Collegiate Dictionary*, but in cases of doubt they will include notes. Attention, however, will be drawn to places where more than one likely interpretation can be proposed and to significant verbal and syntactic complexity. Notes preceded by * discuss editorial emendations or variant readings from the early edition(s) on which the text is based.

Headnotes to acts or scenes discuss, where appropriate, questions of scene location, Shakespeare's handling of his source materials, and major difficulties of staging. The list of roles (so headed to emphasize the play's status as a text for performance) is also considered in the commentary notes. These may include comment on plausible patterns of casting with the resources of an Elizabethan or Jacobean acting company and also on any variation in the description of roles in their speech prefixes in the early editions.

The textual notes are designed to let readers know when the edited text diverges from the early edition(s) or manuscript sources on which it is based. Wherever this happens the note will record the rejected reading of the early edition(s), in original spelling, and the source of the reading adopted in this edition. Other forms from the early edition(s) recorded in these notes will include some spellings of particular interest or significance and original forms of translated stage directions. Where two or more early editions are involved, for instance with *Othello*, the notes also record all important differences between them. The textual notes take a form that has been in use since the nineteenth century. This comprises, first: line reference, reading adopted in the text and closing square bracket; then: abbreviated reference, in italic, to the earliest edition to adopt the accepted reading, italic semicolon and noteworthy alternative reading(s), each with abbreviated italic reference to its source.

Conventions used in these textual notes include the following. The solidus / is used, in notes quoting verse or discussing verse lining, to indicate line endings. Distinctive spellings of the basic text (Q or F) follow the square bracket without indication of source and are enclosed in italic brackets. Names enclosed in italic brackets indicate originators of conjectural emendations when these did not originate in an edition of the text, or when the named edition records a conjecture not accepted into its text. Stage directions (SDs) are referred to by the number of the line within or immediately after which they are placed. Line numbers with a decimal point relate to centred entry SDs not falling within a verse line and to SDs more than one line long, with the number after the point indicating the line within the SD: e.g. 78.4 refers to the fourth line of the SD following line 78. Lines of SDs at the start of a scene are numbered 0.1, 0.2, etc. Where only a line number precedes a square bracket, e.g. 128], the note relates to the whole line; where SD is added to the number, it relates to the whole of a SD within or immediately following the line. Speech prefixes (SPs) follow similar conventions, 203 SP] referring to the speaker's name for line 203. Where a SP reference takes the form e.g. 38+ SP, it relates to all subsequent speeches assigned to that speaker in the scene in question.

Where, as with *King Henry V*, one of the early editions is a so-called 'bad quarto' (that is, a text either heavily adapted, or reconstructed from memory, or both), the divergences from the present edition are too great to be recorded in full in the notes. In these cases, with the exception of *Hamlet*, which prints an edited text of the quarto of 1603, the editions will include a reduced photographic facsimile of the 'bad quarto' in an appendix.

INTRODUCTION

Both the introduction and the commentary are designed to present the plays as texts for performance, and make appropriate reference to stage, film and television versions, as well as introducing the reader to the range of critical approaches to the plays. They discuss the history of the reception of the texts within the theatre and scholarship and beyond, investigating the interdependency of the literary text and the surrounding 'cultural text' both at the time of the original production of Shakespeare's works and during their long and rich afterlife.

PREFACE

While editing any Shakespeare play can and should constitute an educational experience, editing *Richard III* for the Arden series has provided an extended intellectual and emotional challenge beyond anything I could initially have imagined. Although working on this edition sometimes demanded long hours spent far from family and friends, I have never felt lonely. Firstly, there was the extended Arden family of passionately devoted editors and lovers of Shakespeare who stood ready, anywhere, nearly anytime, with support, encouragement and, not least, criticism. Secondly, old friends rose to the occasion, and new friends appeared wherever I went. I may sometimes have bored unsuspecting strangers with discourses on derivative Quarto variants or printing by formes, but friends learned what to expect from me, and hung on nonetheless; over the years I got to know a world of people who cared deeply about Shakespeare. Finally, the challenge made me feel connected with generations of other editors. How they accomplished so much in the years before photocopies, interlibrary loan, microfilm, email, EEBO and JSTOR is beyond me. The list of collated editions in the present volume begins to suggest its indebtedness, but no list sufficiently conveys the feelings of personal relationship that the struggle to edit Shakespeare elicited. I came to look forward to seeing what Theobald had made of an opaque line, what Johnson saw in an obscure reference or what Furness would do with rival interpretations. Whether I agreed or not, I always learned from these encounters.

I am grateful to the extended Arden family, and especially to Richard Proudfoot, who embodies the Arden commitment to scholarly excellence and does so with inspiring graciousness. My heartfelt thanks to David Scott Kastan, who personally talked me through countless revisions, cheering me on (and up) with unfailing humour and gentle reminders that the struggle was worth it. Grateful thanks also go to George Walton Williams for many thoughtful suggestions and corrections. Thank you, as well, to Jessica Hodge, Margaret Bartley and Anna Wormleighton for all manner of aid and encouragement; and to the very helpful proofreader, Jocelyn Stockley, for her acute attention to detail. Finally, and especially, I thank Jane Armstrong, without whose unflagging devotion to clarity, order and accuracy, to, in effect, editing the editor, this edition could never have hoped to aspire to Arden standards.

Then, my thanks go to colleagues from many institutions who shared insights, asked pointed questions, cajoled, challenged and provoked: Leeds Barroll and Susan Zimmerman, Emily Bartels, David Bevington, Peter Blayney, Keir Elam, Ed Gieskes, Andrew Gurr, Andrew Hartley, Diana Henderson, Jeff Henderson, Peter Holland, Jean Howard, Lauren Kehoe, Maydee Lande, Kirk Melnikoff, Cynthia Marshall, Joseph Navitsky, Lena Orlin, Gail Paster, Val Wayne and Robert Weimann. There were those who generously shared their own work and work-in-progress with me: M.C. Aune, Gina Bloom, Clara Calvo, Richard Dutton, Lukas Erne, Andrew Gordon, Andreas Hoefele, Alex Huang, Nina Levine, Barbara Mowat, Patricia Parker, Marie Plasse and Stuart Sillars. I owe special debts as well to those who read, listened to, published, consulted and commented on the work as it grew: especially Bill Carroll, Kent Cartwright, Pete Donaldson, Steve Esposito, Wes Folkerth, Marta Gibińska, Paul Hammer, Mick Hattaway, Jean Howard, Hugo Keiper, Roslyn Knutson, Bob Levine, Bruce Smith, Boika Sokolova, Alden and Ginger Vaughan, Paul Yachnin and Paul Werstine. I thank the Shakespeare Association of America, the International Shakespeare Association, the Shakespeare Theatre of New Jersey and the Shakespeare Theatre Company of Washington, DC, for opportunities to try out my ideas in formal ways. I am grateful for financial assistance from Boston University and its generous Humanities Foundation, the Folger Shakespeare Library and the Arden Bursary. I am delighted to acknowledge the vital aid of librarians at Boston University (particularly Linda Carr), the British Library, the Shakespeare Centre Library, the Bodleian Library, the Public Record Office, the National Archives, the Harvard Theatre Collection, the Library of Congress and, especially, the Folger Shakespeare Library, where Betsy Walsh, Georgianna Ziegler and the dedicated staff make scholarship a joy.

I thank my students from many years of Shakespeare courses and seminars at Boston University for their numberless insights. Finally, and above all, for inspiration and sustenance, emotional and intellectual, I thank Alexandra Siemon, who never lost patience, and the four other brilliant interlocutors named in the dedication and always present in my thoughts. Where would I even begin? Thanks, not least, for the laughter: who would ever have imagined that Anna Siemon, Julia Siemon and Rachel Nolan could transform the rigours of proofreading into raucous competition?

James R. Siemon
Brookline, Massachusetts

INTRODUCTION

THE PLAY

Though it is easily the most performed of Shakespeare's histories, there is no consensus about the rank of *Richard III*, about what sort of play it is or about what to make of its unique 'crook-backed' villain protagonist. The earliest critical response cites the play as support for putting Shakespeare among the best for 'tragedy' (Meres, sig. Oo2^r). With no clear genre of 'history play', Francis Meres accepts the self-designation of the first edition, published in 1597 (Q1): '*The Tragedy of King Richard the third. Containing his treacherous Plots against his brother Clarence: the pittiefull murther of his innocent nephewes: his tyrannicall usurpation: with the whole course of his detested life, and most deserved death*'. The 1623 First Folio (F1) shows less certainty, placing the play as the last of the first eight histories but titling it, uniquely among them, a 'Tragedy'.[1] One thing is clear: it went through a remarkable number of early editions (see p. 423) and has remained a steady theatre favourite.

Subsequent responses debate merit as well as genre. In the early eighteenth century, Charles Gildon pronounced Richard 'shocking' and 'not a fit Character for the Stage', calling the histories failures of 'Tragic Imitation' lacking 'Design' or 'unity' of action and time, and describing them as suggesting a puppet

---

1   The Folio running title – *The Life and Death of Richard the Third* – suggests biography (Anderson, 111). It is unlikely that the plays were conceived as a group or in Folio order; they were probably never performed before the nineteenth century in chronological order (Mary Thomas Crane, 'The Shakespearean tetralogy', *SQ*, 36 (1985), 291–5; Kastan, *1H4*, 92–3), but some audience members for *Richard III* had probably seen the *Henry VI* plays.

show (Vickers, 2.245, 249). Eighteenth-century editors Lewis Theobald, William Warburton and Samuel Johnson ranked the play 'middling' or 'Class II' (Vickers, 2.459, 3.226). Johnson added 'deservedly', since 'some parts are trifling, others shocking, and some improbable' (Vickers, 5.134). Later sentimentalist and Romantic writers debated Richard's 'character' and his relation to tragic protagonists such as Macbeth (see Donohue). Twentieth-century scholarship placed Richard among his stock theatrical forerunners, the Vice (Spivack, Weimann) or the Machiavel (Charnes, Maus).[1] Genre and relation to Shakespeare's other histories remain debatable: is *Richard III* part of a unified national epic (A.W. Schlegel; Ulrici, 2.283), a moral history and the culmination of the first tetralogy (Tillyard, *History Plays*), a retro-political history imposing providential religious order upon Machiavellian political chaos (Rackin) or a paradoxical comic history treating the values of the earlier plays ironically (Rossiter, 22).[2] Taken by itself, is it melodrama (Wilson, xl; Van Laan, 146–7), tyrant tragedy (W.A. Armstrong), romance (Kastan), a conflicted combination (Brooke, 79; Wilks) or satire, religious or political (Birch, 199; Simpson; Campbell, 321–34)?[3] Finally, after centuries of their omission, truncation or dismissal, what is to be said of the play's prominent, but problematic, female characters?[4]

Over the years, interpretation has assumed neoclassical, sentimentalist, Romantic, Victorian, modernist and post-modern inflections, but attention has consistently returned to the play's unusual protagonist, its highly patterned language and action, its female roles and its religious, historical and political implications.

1 Robert Weimann, *Shakespeare and the Popular Tradition in the Theatre* (Baltimore, 1978).
2 A.W. Schlegel, *Lectures on Dramatic Art and Literature*; trans. John Black (1900), 419; Phyllis Rackin, *Stages of History: Shakespeare's English Chronicles* (Ithaca, NY, 1990), 65.
3 W.A. Armstrong, 'The influence of Seneca and Machiavelli on the Elizabethan tyrant', *RES*, 24 (1948), 19–35; David Scott Kastan, *Shakespeare and the Shapes of Time* (Dover, NH, 1982), 132–3.
4 See Howard & Rackin; Nina S. Levine, *Women's Matters: Politics, Gender, and Nation in Shakespeare's Early History Plays* (Newark, Del., 1998).

Woven through these considerations are different reactions to its pervasive, multiform ironies and comic elements.

In plain sight: Richard

In Jasper Fforde's novel *The Eyre Affair*, *Richard III* appears as an interactive cult ritual modelled on *The Rocky Horror Show*. Performances begin with the audience chanting, '*When* is the winter of our discontent?', to which the stage Richard, chosen nightly from among audience volunteers, responds, 'Now is the winter of our discontent.'[1] Although the premise is that *Richard III* might still resonate with 'our' discontents 'now', Richard's first line is, and always has been, distantly historical. When the play opened in the 1590s, it was about events already over a century past, and 'our discontent' refers to troubles of the York family. Richard's line is only the first of many to invoke grievances that pre-date the play itself. Yet Richard's speech is also about something immediately in our faces. Uniquely for Shakespeare, *Richard III* begins with the protagonist's soliloquy about *his* discontent. Elizabethans thought they already knew about Richard. From the early sixteenth-century narratives of Polydore Vergil and Sir Thomas More, the malformed bogeyman, whose crimes – real, imputed, intended or imagined – included regicide, fratricide, infanticide, uxoricide, incest and ecclesiastical corruption, had appeared not only in Shakespeare's immediate sources (Edward Hall's *Union*, Raphael Holinshed's *Chronicles* and *The Mirror for Magistrates*) but in sermons, ballads, plays, rhetorical exercises, satires, state propaganda and invective. In keeping with early modern clichés about the body expressing the soul, Richard was rendered hunchbacked, lame of arm, crabbed of feature and natally toothed. As far as I know, the limp begins with Shakespeare.[2]

---

1 Jasper Fforde, *The Eyre Affair: A Novel* (New York, 2002), 183. Lois Potter's 'Shakespeare performed: English and American Richards, Edwards and Henries', *SQ*, 54 (2004), 450–61, called Fforde to my attention.

2 Readers are invited to correct this claim.

No one before had made so much of Richard's bodily
challenges: love is out because he is too crippled to dance; dogs
bark as he halts by. Everyone else merrily pairs off, making love
not war, capering and ambling, while he limps and grumbles:

> But I, that am not shaped for sportive tricks,
> Nor made to court an amorous looking-glass;
> I, that am rudely stamped, and want love's majesty
> To strut before a wanton ambling nymph;
> I, that am curtailed of this fair proportion,
> Cheated of feature by dissembling Nature,
> Deformed, unfinished, sent before my time
> Into this breathing world, scarce half made up,
> And that so lamely and unfashionable
> That dogs bark at me as I halt by them –
> Why, I, in this weak piping time of peace,
> Have no delight to pass away the time,
> Unless to see my shadow in the sun
> And descant on mine own deformity.
> And therefore, since I cannot prove a lover
> To entertain these fair well-spoken days,
> I am determined to prove a villain
> And hate the idle pleasures of these days.
>
> (1.1.14–31)

He speaks to himself, and also for us, Freud realized, for Richard
provides something anyone can identify with.[1] Here, too, we
encounter something to resist, interpret or share, an intellectual,
kinetic and vocal energy that demands response (Sprague,
Actors, 136; R. Berry). And he is funny. No Elizabethan would
have expected that.

Easily dominating text, performance and criticism, Shakespeare's Richard has prompted extreme responses. There have

---

1 Freud takes Richard for 'an enormously magnified representation of something we
can all discover in ourselves. We all think we have reason to reproach nature and our
destiny for congenital and infantile disadvantages; we all demand reparation for early
wounds to our narcissism, our self-love' (Freud, 4.322–3; cf. Garber).

been attempts to 'humanize' him on the stage, from Garrick to Branagh, and in sentimentalist commentary from the eighteenth and nineteenth centuries, but other responses downplay 'inwardness' or 'subjective density' (Charnes, 93) to stress personification or monstrosity. He has been taken to embody 'genius' (Charles Lamb, in Bate, *Romantics*, 122), 'intellect' (Coleridge, in Bate, *Romantics*, 145–6), discredited Yorkist rule (Horace Walpole, in Donohue, 198), self-love (Freud, 4.322–3), civil violence (Tillyard, 208), capitalism (Siegel, 80) and masculine discursivity (Sanders, 193). He has been seen as a theatrical property: Punch (G.B. Shaw, in Sprague, *Actors* 135), Vice (Spivack), actor (Rossiter, 16–17), cartoon (H. Bloom, 66), Tudor 'bugaboo' (Budra, 82), or stage Machiavel (Charnes, 47–54).[1] Each designation merits attention; each needs qualification.

In its universality, Freud's figure of wounded 'self-love' that 'we all feel' parallels a relevant theological construct. The spinal curvature Thomas More added to Richard's alleged scapular inequality, whatever its relation to Tudor scapegoating of dynastic competitors, expresses a spiritual deformity that Christians thought 'we all' share as creatures bent and turned from God.[2] Not merely an ugly version of all of us, however, Richard embraces his symptom. Announcing himself 'determined to prove a villain' (1.1.30), he punningly accepts divine predestination to damnation and simultaneously chooses reprobation for himself.[3] Let us descend, as the play does, from pathology and theology, to specifics.

---

1 Paul N. Siegel, *Shakespeare's English and Roman History Plays: A Marxist Approach* (Rutherford, NJ, 1986); Eve Rachel Sanders, *Gender and Literacy on the Stage in Early Modern England* (Cambridge, 1998); Harold Bloom, *Shakespeare and the Invention of the Human* (New York, 1998).

2 On humanity as 'curvatus', see e.g. Augustine's *Ennarationes* (on Psalm 37) in J.-P. Migne.

3 Richard lacks assurances of God's love, such as those William Perkins urges the Christian to remember: God 'created me a man, when hee might haue made me an vgly Toade' and made me 'of comely bodie, and of discretion whereas he might haue made me vgly, and deformed, franticke, and mad' (Perkins, *Treatise*, 113^r). Rejection of brotherhood defines Richard as a reprobate: 'he that loueth not his brother' (Perkins, 'A Case of Conscience', *Works* (1592; STC 19665.5), sig. B3$^{r–v}$).

Deep tragedian or formal Vice

More calls Richard a 'deep dissimuler' and compares public life to playing upon a 'scaffold', but never calls him an 'actor' (*CW*2, 8).[1] *The Mirror for Magistrates* likens existence to a performance before God (*Mirror*, 'Buckingham', 43–9), but does not associate Richard with theatre. In *3 Henry VI*, however, Richard describes himself in terms that recall Elizabethan anti-player polemic – seductive mermaid, gaze-attracting basilisk, orator, deceptive Ulysses, treasonous Sinon, changeable chameleon, shape-shifting Proteus, murderous Machiavel (*3H6* 3.2.186–93).[2] *Richard III* surrounds him with theatrical self-references. Though such vocabulary is not unusual for Shakespeare or for his era, Richard gives these allusions particular resonance when he discusses acting techniques or likens himself to the stage figure polemic had warned theatre-goers they might become: 'you will learne to playe the vice' (Stubbes, L8ᵛ).[3]

Richard's self-comparison to 'the formal Vice, Iniquity' and self-announced wordplay – 'Thus . . . I moralize two meanings in one word' (3.1.82–3) – invoke a stock character and his verbal tricks.[4] Besides his exuberantly stagey wit, Richard also shares the Vice's double relationship to the dramatic action, outside as commentator and inside as participant. He introduces the play with commentary on his appearance, plans and nature. He introduces action already under way: 'Plots have I laid, inductions dangerous' (1.1.32), he says; cue victim number one: Enter Clarence.

1 More's Latin *History* comes closer: '[Richard] could assume whatever mask it pleased him to wear and he played the part he had chosen with the utmost diligence' (*CW*2, 8; cf. *CW*2, 168).
2 *The Anatomie of Abuses* claims theatre teaches one 'to play the Hipocrit: to cogge, lye, and falsifie', to 'play yᵉ Sodomits, or worse', to 'become a bawde, vncleane, and to deuerginat Mayds, to deflour honest Wyues . . . to murther, slaie, kill . . . to rebel against Princes, to co[m]mit treasons' (Stubbes, sig. L8ᵛ). Henry VI invokes the Roman actor 'Roscius' when confronting Richard in his death 'scene' (*3H6* 5.6.10).
3 On Elizabethan theatrical terminology, see Righter, 89–95.
4 'Iniquity' is the Vice in *Nice Wanton* (1560; STC 25016) and *King Darius* (1565; STC 6277). Cf. Inclination's reversal of sense (*Trial of Treasure*, 1561; STC 24271, sig. D4ᵛ).

Such an induction is unparalleled in Shakespeare, but well-anticipated elsewhere. The figure of Dissimulation opens Robert Wilson's *Three Ladies of London* (1584), explaining his disguise as an 'honest' farmer, boasting of his aspiring mind, clever plans and sophisticated amorality, while bragging that everybody, 'men women and children', knows him by his grotesque 'powle [head] and beard painted motley' (sigs A2ᵛ–A3ʳ). We share a secret that is no secret: everyone knows Dissimulation to be dishonest, just as everyone, with the possible exception of 'simple, plain' Clarence and his children, knows Richard to be villainous. External signs – motley beard or twisted body – and frequent soliloquies (five in Richard's first three scenes) should keep us focused.[1] We know what he is, and the other characters should too.

The Vice's particoloured head, like the 'notorious identity' blazoned by Richard's bodily disproportions, invites us to 'epistemological self-assurance'.[2] We laugh with these figures as they name, expose and manipulate the weaknesses of others. This makes seduction scenes irresistibly ridiculous. Still wearing his goofy beard, Dissimulation woos Lady Love in the sequel to *Three Ladies*, even though she recognizes him as the 'monster' and 'Deuill' who has caused her 'sorrowes' (R. Wilson, sigs D2ʳ–D3ᵛ). No matter, the seducer protests, because 'the griefe / that I thy friend sustaine for thy distresse' is great, and they move straight into wit combat:

> Dis. In thy affections I had once a place:
> loue. These fond affections wrought me foule disgrace,
> Dis. Ile make amends, if ought amisse were done:
> loue. Who once are burn'd, the fire will euer shun.
>
> (sig. D4ᵛ)

---

1   On the placement of Richard's early soliloquies and later asides, see MacDonald & MacDonald, 59–60.
2   Concerning audience self-assurance, see Maus, 54; on Richard's 'notorious identity', see Charnes, 20–70.

Sound familiar? The two lengthy wooing scenes in *Richard III* (1.2, 4.4) are wholly invented history but heavily derivative drama (S. Thomas, *Antic*, 30). Richard and Dissimulation share visual stigmata, extra-dramatic commentary, dissembling and witty dialogue. They also share topical functions. Dissimulation mocks contemporary pieties, for example, by calling his evil intentions 'inward zeale' (*Three Ladies*, sig. A3ʳ), invoking a buzzword associated with hotter Protestants that Buckingham uses in praising Richard's own 'right Christian zeal' (3.7.102). We are far from done with seduction or satiric topicality.

Murderous Machiavel

The Richard of the two early versions of *3 Henry VI* names villains he will outdo: 'murderous *Macheuill*' or 'aspiring *Catalin*'. The Roman Catiline, as Ben Jonson's play *Catiline, his Conspiracy* confirms, conjures up ambition pursued by factional politics. 'Machiavel' derives from Niccolò Machiavelli (1469–1527), notorious for the *realpolitik* analyses of *The Prince* (published 1532) and *Discourses* (published 1531) and object of countless denunciations.[1] The name 'Machiavel' furnished a catch-all for any devious foe, and embodied anxieties about religious and social disorder (Maus, 47).

Richard shares characteristics with this figure of the polemical imagination and the popular stage. Above all, he acts out in *Richard III* the ruthless, self-interested ambition implied in his earlier renunciation (*3H6* 5.6.80–3) of roles ascribed by family and society. A self-professed hypocrite, he mocks authority, holds conscience in contempt, treats religion as a functional tool and delights in strategic manipulation. While some of Richard's attitudes and practices are related to the rationalized power

---

1 Editions printed in England include John Wolfe's false-imprint Italian printings in the 1580s; Latin and French editions were available. Many Elizabethans acquired their opinions from Innocent Gentillet's *Discours . . . Contre Machiavel* (1576). See Meyer; Catherine Minshull, 'Marlowe's "Sound Machevill"', *Renaissance Drama*, 13 (1982), 35–53; Peter S. Donaldson, *Machiavelli and Mystery of State* (New York, 1982); N.W. Bawcutt, 'The "Myth of Gentillet" reconsidered: an aspect of Elizabethan Machiavellianism', *MLR*, 99 (2004), 863–74.

politics of Machiavelli's works, his more immediate ancestry appears in contemporary polemic and drama.[1] For instance, the Elizabethan divine Henry Smith imagines Machiavel's followers, his 'apes', pervading England with what Katherine Maus calls their 'sinister interiority' (Maus, 40):

> Oh, if Machauil had liued in our countrey, what a Monarch should he be? to what honour, and wealth, and power, and credite, might he haue risen vnto in short time, whether he had been a Lawier, or a Courtier, or a Prelate? me thinkes I see how many fingers woulde poynt at him in the streetes, as they doe at his apes, and say, there goeth a deepe fellowe, he hath more wit in his little finger then the rest in their whole bodie. You talke of Sectaries how fast they growe, and how fast they breed; I warrant you where any Sectary hath one sonne, Machauil hath a score, and those not the brats, but the fatlings of the Land, which if they had but a dram of religion for an ounce of their policie, they might goe like Saints among men.

> (Smith, *Sermons*, 420)

Machiavels frequented the stage in the early 1590s: Richard is anticipated in Kyd's Lorenzo (*The Spanish Tragedy*) and Marlowe's Barabas (*The Jew of Malta*).[2] All express the alienation of Richard's 'I am myself alone'. Kyd's Lorenzo proclaims, 'Ile trust my selfe, my selfe shalbe my freend' (*Spanish Tragedy*, 3.2.125).[3] Marlowe's Barabas announces, '*Ego mihimet sum semper*

1 On the figure's Machiavellian roots, see Margaret Scott, 'Machiavelli and the Machiavel', *Renaissance Drama*, 15 (1984), 147–74.
2 Henslowe records performances of *The Spanish Tragedy* in spring 1592 and of *The Jew of Malta* between February and June 1592 (Henslowe, 17, 170). 1591 also saw a play called 'Matchevell' (i.e. *Machiavel*) on Henslowe's stage. Jonathan Bate traces 'a direct line' from Marlowe through Aaron the Moor of *Titus Andronicus* to Richard III (Bate, *Tit*, 87–8).
3 Cf. *R3* 1.4.140–2, where the Second Murderer describes the man who would 'trust to himself'.

9

proximus' (*Jew of Malta*, 1.1.188).[1] All kill underlings, profess dissembling and boast of their politic strategy (*Jew of Malta*, 5.2.26–46, 110–23; *Spanish Tragedy*, 3.4.46).[2] Despite initial successes, all three come to confusion. However, Barabas and Richard differ from Lorenzo in the religious nature of their hypocrisy, in their revelation of systemic social corruption, in the sheer size of their roles and in their capacity to incite laughter.[3]

Barabas and Richard repeatedly invoke the Bible, lecture others on religious principles and offer 'counterfeit profession' of piety (*Jew of Malta*, 1.2.291–2), while mocking conscience (*Jew of Malta*, 1.1.118–20; *R3* 5.3.309–11) and charity (*Jew of Malta*, 2.3.29; *R3* 1.2.68–9). They also reveal faults in others: the brutality of Christian anti-semitism in *The Jew of Malta* (1.2.106–28) and the self-serving amorality of courtly culture in *Richard III*. Their humour, self-ridicule and ironic detachment differentiate them from truly Senecan villains (S. Thomas, *Antic*, 17). They revel in exaggerated performance, in speeches riddled with audience asides and in antics stretching to grotesque farce, as when Richard plays 'jolly thriving wooer', or Barabas a French musician, complete with lute, silly accent and poisoned flowers.

Deep tragedian

Richard III raises another theatrical option. As Richard and Buckingham plan to deceive the Londoners, they consider playing the 'deep tragedian':

RICHARD

> Come, cousin, canst thou quake and change thy colour,
> Murder thy breath in middle of a word,
> And then again begin, and stop again,

---

1 Adopted from Terence, *Andria*, 'I am always nearest to myself'. Edward Meyer calls this 'the very pith and gist of all Machiavelli's teachings' (Meyer, 33).
2 Cf. *1H6* 5.3.74, where the phrase 'notorious Machiavel' suggests treachery, and *MW* 3.1.91, where the name denotes being 'politic' or 'subtle'.
3 Kyd's grotesque humour does not centrally involve the Machiavel.

As if thou were distraught and mad with terror?
BUCKINGHAM
    Tut, I can counterfeit the deep tragedian,
    Speak, and look back, and pry on every side,
    Tremble and start at wagging of a straw,
    Intending deep suspicion. Ghastly looks
    Are at my service, like enforced smiles,
    And both are ready in their offices,
    At any time to grace my stratagems.

                      (3.5.1–11)

Does this passage evoke deportment truly appropriate to tragedy, or does it comment on the coarseness of the speakers or the naivety of their intended audience? Does it mock overacting or recommend melodramatic exaggeration?

Contemporary texts mock the overacting 'tragedian' who 'swell[s] / In forcèd passion of affected strains' (Marston, *2 Antonio and Mellida*, 2.3.109–10) or mimics Tamburlaine's 'high-set steps, and princely carriage', filling his 'wide-strained mouth' with 'Big sounding sentences, and words of state' (J. Hall, 8). Hamlet denounces 'overdone' word and action and the player who 'out-Herods Herod', that ranting figure of medieval drama (*Ham* 3.2.1–34). Heywood warns against 'oueracting trickes' (Heywood, *Apology*, sig. C4ʳ). Yet Shakespeare does take emotive signifiers seriously: Clarence's murderer has a 'pale' face and eyes that 'menace' (1.4.169; cf. *AYL* 4.4.168–70). Folio stage directions demand that characters '*start*' at news of Clarence's death (2.1.80 SD). Are Buckingham's prescribed histrionics so different from breast-beating or lip-gnawing (2.2.3, 4.2.27)? Vergil records Richard's lip-gnawing as habitual (227), though More describes him counterfeiting agitation by 'knitting the browes, frowning and froting and knawing on hys lippes' (*CW*2, 47). Othello gnaws his lip and rolls his eyes (*Oth* 5.2.38, 43); Wolsey 'bites his lip, and starts, / Stops on a sudden' (*H8* 3.2.113–14). So in theory Richard and Buckingham advocate suitably 'tragic' action; yet their sheer enjoyment in contemplating the performance suggests the play's oddly close conjoining of tragedy, melodrama and self-irony.

The Mirror for Magistrates articulates a relevant paradox concerning feigned emotions. Rivers should have known Richard false, since 'counterfayte' emotions inevitably overdo the 'naturall mean' to convey 'depe' feeling (*Mirror*, 'Rivers', 410–20). But Richard's performative inventiveness expressed in 'so many a fals device' (*Mirror*, 'Rivers', 424–7) overwhelmed Rivers's scepticism. The victims of Shakespeare's Richard similarly recognize his hostility, duplicity and artificial emotion, but suffer entrapment anyway. Richard's behaviour may be stylized 'performance' and recognized as such, but this does not preclude his successes or mean the play lacks depth, only that depth resides elsewhere than within the 'deep' subjectivity of character.

Some early defenders of the stage claimed that a player could create the convincing illusion of being 'the person personated' (Heywood, *Apology*, sig. C4^r). Similarly, some critics have judged *Richard III* 'the drama of consummate *acting*', asserting that 'Except to the audience, [Richard] is invisible' (Rossiter, 17–18), or that his roles are 'completely successful . . . manag[ing] to deceive virtually everyone' (Righter, 97).[1] In fact almost no one is completely fooled (Ornstein, 70–1; D.G. Watson, 102).[2] Consummate performance, however, need not be equated with illusionistic personation. In 1793 George Steevens praised the role of Richard for its dizzying variety, as 'perhaps beyond all others variegated' and comprehending 'a trait of almost every species of character on the stage. The hero, the lover,

---

1 Van Laan calls Richard a 'magnificent actor', but claims he offers 'melodrama' rather than a convincing portrayal of saintliness (Van Laan, 145, 135, 147).

2 Queen Elizabeth recognizes 'interior hatred' from Richard's 'outward action' (1.3.65–6). Margaret assesses him (1.3.220). His mother discusses his deceptions (2.2.27–32). Hastings recognizes risks in attending him (3.2.27–9). Buckingham wisely deserts (4.2.119–20); the princes scorn him (3.1.120–35); citizens judge him dangerous (2.3.27).

the statesman, the buffoon, the hypocrite, the hardened and repenting sinner &c.' (Vickers, 6.594). Actors have agreed with this assessment, but an early modern account of the historical Richard as 'playing' various roles also deserves attention. Sir Walter Raleigh's *History* defines Richard's 'playing' as ensemble work, enlisting others into his play through manipulation of their 'affection' and self-interest:

> Richard *the Third, the greatest Maister in mischiefe of . . . all that fore-went him: who although, for the necessity of his Tragedie, hee had more parts to play, and more to performe in his owne person, then all the rest; yet hee so well fitted euery affection that played with him, as if each of them had but acted his owne interest. For he wrought so cunningly vpon the affections of* Hastings, *and* Buckingham, *enemies to the* Queene *and to all her kindred, as hee easily allured them to condiscend, that* Riuers *and* Grey, *the Kings Maternall Vncle and halfe brother, should (for the first) be seuered from him: secondly, hee wrought their consent to haue them imprisoned, and lastly* [(] *for the auoyding of future inconvenience) to haue their heads seuered from their bodies.*
>
> (Raleigh, sigs A4^v–B1^r)

Raleigh represents Richard working on desires, circumstances and agencies provided by his social world. This Richard is suggestive for Shakespeare's. Consider the wooing of Anne, a scene often taken as demonstrating either Richard's deceptive 'acting' or Anne's deficient 'character'.

Jolly thriving wooer

Responding in 1779 to neoclassical strictures about the 'vulgarity and even indecency' of the wooing scene, William Richardson defends it as an 'imitation . . . of Nature', given Anne's 'character'. Richard's 'perfect knowledge of her disposition' recognizes her weak principles, and 'vanity' as her 'over-ruling passion' (Vickers, 6.208–9). Such a reading (or its modern variants) focuses on the couple themselves, but in fact, as often, other characters awkwardly share the stage. These others also fall before Richard's onslaught, and not because they are immoral, vain or female.

In a play so dominated by Richard's body, that living symbol of period commonplaces about (mis)proportion and (dis)-order on the social, personal and species levels, the wooing reveals a remarkable disjunction between the body social and the body physical. Fresh from pronouncing himself physically disempowered, Richard proves prodigiously powerful when he – alone, lame, with a withered arm and a single sword – halts a heavily armed procession and disarms a halberdier whose weapon points at his chest:

RICHARD

> Villains, set down the corse, or by Saint Paul,
> I'll make a corse of him that disobeys.

GENTLEMAN

> My lord, stand back and let the coffin pass.

RICHARD

> Unmannered dog, stand thou when I command!
> Advance thy halberd higher than my breast,
> Or by Saint Paul I'll strike thee to my foot
> And spurn upon thee, beggar, for thy boldness.
>
> (1.2.36–42)

This is not 'acting' – Richard could hardly convey a physical capacity to strike down and spurn the lot of them – but it is performance. As such it recalls unarmed Talbot suddenly revealing his corporate 'substance' by summoning his hidden troops (*1H6* 2.3); but Richard's strength lies in the power of hierarchy and religion, not in armour or troops.

Richard and the halberdier replay a nightmare version of a scenario moralized in contemporary polemic. To explain why multitudes have 'humbled themselues' before Queen Elizabeth, a 1589 tract adduces her miraculous control over her 'big bodied Holberders'. Any minute, they might 'bende euery man the point of his Holberde at her', but 'the Religion of the land' causes a 'sweet harmonie of peoples harts that remaine faithful and flexible to the shaking of her princely finger' (*2 Pasquill*, sig. B1^{r-v}). No simple piety, or not simply piety, disarms Richard's opponents, since they appear initially bound to Anne's own religious undertaking before they give in. But give in to what? Richard is greater in substance than simply his own muscle or an armed company would suggest. Onstage he kills no one, no armed cohort supports him, except dubiously at Bosworth, where mental 'shadows' prove more powerful than the 'substance of ten thousand soldiers' (5.3.216–18). Rather, he manages to enlist, almost magically, the power of the legitimate social order's demands for obedience and deference to hierarchy even while ruthlessly violating such demands himself. The moral 'villain' here shamelessly performs his own status, reducing Anne's troupe to social '[v]illains', 'beggar[s]' (1.2.36, 42) and finally lackeys who try to anticipate his desires (1.2.228–9). Fittingly, Richard invokes Saint Paul, the apostle identified with 'obedience to authority' (*STM*, 2.3.101; cf. *R3* 1.2.36n.).[1] No one need be completely duped to become 'Grossly . . . captive' (4.1.79) to the powers his performances enlist.

'Captivation' provides an approximate term for this process, but the powers Richard wields are not simply matters of hereditary status, religion or faction. Clarity of motive empowers him. When he has the sheer nerve to literalize the hoariest Petrarchan cliché by kneeling and '*lay*[ing] *his breast open*' to his lady's fatal blow (1.2.181 SD), he offers 'revenge' but 'in terms that render it farcically irrelevant' (Neill, 104). Killing would only grant the abject lover his wish. Anne 'falls to Richard precisely because she is *not* deceived, because (as he intends) she

---

1 Romans, 13.1–5, commanding subjection to authority, is frequently invoked; cf. Perkins, *Works*, 48.

is bowled over by the nerve, the *sprezzatura*, of that performance itself' (Neill, 104). She never takes back her epithets – devil, minister of hell, villain, murderer – and submits with 'Arise, dissembler' (1.2.187). It is not that 'Richard's amorality matters little to her' (D.G. Watson, 104), because in fact, it does matter; it is his *morality* that matters little. Michael Neill's 'ostentatious theatricality' and 'compelling staginess' seem appropriate, but there is more to say, even if Anne never says it, about the social bases for his successes.

Richard '*so well fitted euery affection that playd with him, as if each of them had but acted his owne interest*' (Raleigh, *History*, sig. A4^v). Anne never articulates her '*owne interest*', but Queen Elizabeth defines the fearful position of a noble woman without a husband and clarifies the (unremarked) security Richard offers: 'If [Edward] were dead,' Elizabeth demands, 'what would betide on me? . . . The loss of such a lord includes all harms' (1.3.6–8).[1] Systemic female vulnerability surely contributes to Richard's power. So does faction: Richard played upon the '*affections*' of Hastings and Buckingham as '*enemies to the Queene and to all her kindred*', Raleigh writes. Self-alienated from his own family, Richard, himself alone, measures exactly how others intersect and interact as families and groups. Thus his pious rebuff to Margaret – 'God, not we, hath plagued thy bloody deed' (1.3.180) – instantly enlists bitterly divided opponents into a supporting chorus, suddenly united, like Anne's armed entourage, behind him.

Finally, the play develops one other factor in Richard's power: religious hypocrisy. When he lays open his breast, whatever his (unspoken) sense of Anne's (unacknowledged) vulnerability as unprotected female or as disempowered family

1   Cf. Camille Wells Slights, *The Casuistical Tradition in Shakespeare, Donne, Herbert, and Milton* (Princeton, NJ, 1981), 75. Concerning the basis of the historical union, see Kendall, 105–9 (love); C. Ross, *Richard*, 27–8 (status and wealth); the Crowland Continuator (in J.L. Laynesmith, *The Last Medieval Queens: English Queenship 1445–1503* (Oxford, 2004), 70) (property interests). In 1474 the Italian Christofforo di Bollato reports that Richard wed Anne 'by force' (Laynesmith, 70).

member, Richard counts on her having limits and being ignorant of exactly where those limits lie. He routinely flouts eternal damnation by blasphemously invoking Christian virtues and transgressing Christian commandments, while others, to varying degrees, appear subject to limits.[1] Anne can no more kill a disarmed kneeling suitor than, for similarly unspoken reasons of latent principle or repugnance, Buckingham can kill the princes. Lesser agents undertake or subcontract such unspeakable acts, but the warrior elite of the *Henry VI* plays does not furnish their number. Times have changed since the days of bloody Clifford, and ultimately Richard enacts a micro-version of the historical phenomenon known as bastard feudalism, paying clowns, boys and marginal hangers-on to get the dirtier jobs done – offstage. One stabbing (1.4), one severed head (3.5) and one death in battle (5.4) are nothing to the mayhem of earlier histories; instead, this play abounds in complicitous nobles and clerics who are, like Anne, passively compromised. Their motto might be her self-exculpating formula, 'To take is not to give' (1.2.205) – as if acquiescence did not entail volition and, ultimately, accountability. For the smaller fry who take what Richard has on offer – the bishops, the Mayor, clerics like Dr Shaw and others – Brakenbury provides a rationale: 'I will not reason what is meant hereby / Because I will be guiltless from the meaning' (1.4.93–4). So would we all, if life or this play allowed. Here too resides a source of Richard's power.

Richard's performances are highly theatrical, but the nature of their taking power is under-articulated. We are prompted to marvel at his sheer audacity, his clarity of motive, his ruthless exploitation of the factional and ideological limits that constrain others, his watchful alertness among half-conscious sleep-walkers, egotists, blinkered factionalists and time-servers. Richard may halt, but his social command is deft. The Scrivener puts it succinctly: 'Who is

1 With the possible exception of Margaret. For Richard's relation to the forms he flouts, see William C. Carroll, 'Desacralization and succession in *Richard III*', *Deutsche Shakespeare Gesellschaft West*, *Jahrbuch* (1991), 82–96.

so gross / That cannot see this palpable device? / Yet who so bold but says he sees it not?' (3.6.10–12).

Tell-tale women and tender babes

Well, some do speak up. Female characters, including the unhistorical Margaret, speak approximately twenty-two per cent of *Richard III* (Howard & Rackin, 217–18). Prominence does not simply equate with empowerment, of course, but the words 'mother' and 'children' (and cognates) are more numerous than in any other Shakespeare play, and that suggests something important. Sometimes desired, the women are more often resented, mocked, manipulated and marginalized. Janet Adelman finds Shakespeare's first history plays move women 'from positions of power and authority to positions of utter powerlessness, and finally moves them off the stage altogether' (Adelman, 9). Phyllis Rackin observes that the active female characters are negatively depicted, while 'The more sympathetically depicted female characters, such as the victimized women in *Richard III*, never go to war, they play no part in the affairs of state, and they seem to spend most of their limited time on stage in tears' (Rackin, 75–6; cf. Howard & Rackin, 98). These otherwise accurate assessments fail to link female tears to railing, lamentation and cursing, utterances that indeed constitute 'affairs of state'.

The females of *Richard III* appear more choric than active. Margaret, who was boldly erotic, political and military in Shakespeare's *Henry VI* plays, becomes a mouthpiece for passionate exclamations. Margaret Beaufort, who historically furthered both her son's marriage to Elizabeth of York and his English campaign, appears only in references to Richmond's 'mother' or the 'wayward' or sick 'wife' whom Stanley excuses (1.3.20–9) and to whom he must 'look' (4.2.91). The notorious Jane Shore is the unseen object of snide jokes (1.1.93–102) and ridiculous accusations (3.4.67–74). Finally, scenes that could have sympathetically represented female emotion are often treated ironically or omitted (contrast *CW*2, 41), contributing to the play's general avoidance of pathos (A.W. Schlegel, in Bate, *Romantics*, 506). But if 'tenderness of heart' and 'effeminate remorse' are mocked and debased (3.7.209–10), lament, denunciation and curse comprise a powerful female idiom of bitter tears (G. Bloom, 92–4).

Initially, female lamentations, curses and denunciations are isolated, ineffective, even laughable. Anne's laments and curses so quickly change to murmured submission that Richard's delight at female fickleness (1.2.230–2) and her shame at her 'woman's heart' (4.1.78–80) seem validated.[1] It is difficult to resist laughter when Richard's wisecracks cause Margaret to breathe her own 'curse against [herself]' (1.3.230–9). Queen Elizabeth and the Duchess of York become blackly comic as they contest for pre-eminence in grief, only to be rebuffed by Clarence's insolent orphans (2.2.62–5). Yet ultimately, female outbursts convey compelling truths, and the women themselves bond in something larger than self-interest. Even Margaret wins grudging respect.

In a remarkable moment of unity despite factionalism and self-interest, Anne, Queen Elizabeth and the Duchess of York join to denounce Richard, affirm love for the princes and demand their mutual right. Under an expanded definition of 'mother' they oppose Richard's representative:

QUEEN ELIZABETH
    . . . I am their mother. Who shall bar me from them?

DUCHESS
    I am their father's mother. I will see them.

ANNE
    Their aunt I am in law, in love their mother.
    Then bring me to their sights. I'll bear thy blame
    And take thy office from thee, on my peril.
                                            (4.1.21–5)

---

1   Though Anne's curse upon any woman who might marry Richard (1.2.26–8) would register prophetically, if not quite accurately in details, with the audience, as it later does with her (4.1.73–84).

Here for the first time motherhood combines rather than divides; being a mother, even if only in feeling ('in love'), trumps self-interest.[1] Affirming this bond empowers an activism that contrasts the women with those who would remain 'guiltless from the meaning' of the wrongs they allow and perpetrate: Brakenbury (1.4.94), the First Murderer (1.4.167), the Cardinal (3.1.57), the witnesses of Hastings's assassination (3.4.78).[2] The women embrace the consequences of doing what is right. Nor is their act of *speaking* negligible.

In this light, Margaret's attainment of one title denied by her mockers acquires particular importance. She never resumes the title 'Queen', but words win her another title. Instead of 'witch' or 'frantic curs[ing]' madwoman (1.3.163, 246), Margaret is ultimately validated as 'prophetess' (1.3.300, 5.1.27) of God's justice (5.1.20). This might appear small consolation, since 'the politically astute Margaret of the early play becomes "poor Margaret . . . prophetess". The curse of the scold is feared . . . as the records of the witch-trials remind us, but it achieves nothing.'[3] Yet the play opens with the deadly effects of 'prophecies, libels and dreams' (1.1.33) and concludes with an armed tyrant shaken by a 'prophet', a dream and a libel (4.2.94–105; 5.3.177–206, 303–5). The roles of 'prophetess' and 'mother' may have power against murderers and tyrants; even dreams may count.[4] A mother's curse could be terrible, as James I warned his son: 'the blessing or curse of the Parents, hath almost euer a Propheticke power ioyned with it' (James I, 44). Nor is it clear that a 'scold' necessarily 'achieves nothing'.

---

1 Nicole Loraux, *Mothers in Mourning*, trans. Corinne Pache (Ithaca, NY, 1998), 3. See also Doris Märtin, *Shakespeares 'Fiend-like Queens'* (Heidelberg, 1992), 71–82.

2 Cf. Madonne M. Miner, '"Neither mother, wife, nor England's Queen": the roles of women in *Richard III*', in Carolyn Ruth Swift Lenz, Gayle Greene and Carol Thomas Neely (eds), *The Woman's Part* (Urbana, Ill., 1980), 35–55.

3 Lisa Jardine, *Still Harping on Daughters* (Brighton, 1983), 118; cf. Marcus, 94; contrast Kathryn Schwarz, *Tough Love: Amazon Encounters in the English Renaissance* (Durham, NC, 2000), 104.

4 'Dream' (with cognates) also occurs more often in *Richard III* than in any other Shakespeare play; see Marvin Spevack, *A Complete and Systematic Concordance to the Works of Shakespeare* (Hildesheim, 1968–80).

Margaret's authority should not be overstated. True, she resembles Richard in her imposing, extra-dramatic, solo pronouncements: compare her 'induction' and entry prompt 'now' (4.4.1–8) with Richard's opening (1.1.1–40; cf. Hodgdon, *End*, 107–8). Yet despite her eerie appearances and disappearances – manifesting herself invisibly, pronouncing judgement, engaging, then 'withdraw[ing]' (4.4.8, 125) with impunity from a world that others traverse or escape with difficulty – and despite the preponderant accuracy of her predictions, Margaret speaks neither for God nor for Tudor history, at least not entirely. Her prognostications are only absolutely accurate when they concern the violent ends of violent men and the 'course of justice' (4.4.105). Any Elizabethan would have recognized the accurate dooms she pronounces for Richard and his cronies, as well as her general homiletic orthodoxy. But Elizabethans would also have perceived her glaring errors. Above all, Queen Elizabeth will *not* end up childless (1.3.203–8), and her child will wed Richmond, a figure Margaret apparently knows nothing about, to found the Tudor dynasty (Brooks, 'Unhistorical', 727). Margaret also wrongly predicts that Richard's most fearful dream will be (as in the sources) a 'hell of ugly devils' (1.3.226). Her foresight is limited to commonplace notions of divine retributive justice and earthly mutability: the violent shall die violently (5.1.23–4), the mighty shall fall (3.4.95–100), the evil shall torment one another here (2.1.14–15) and be tormented by devils hereafter. She is no mouthpiece for Tudor providentialism, nor does she recognize the power of empathy. Any ethical or political vision transcending feudal clan loyalties and competitive grudges lies beyond her. She may eerily anticipate the new king's words for Richard, 'The bloody dog is dead' (4.4.78, 5.5.2), but she perceives neither the power of hope that Richmond embodies (5.2.23–4, 5.3.173) nor the power of victims who curse, frighten or bless.

Attributing power to victims is not mere sentimentality. More claims that after the princes' deaths Richard 'neuer hadde quiet in his minde, hee neuer thought himself sure' (*CW2*, 87) because the murders caused political insecurity. Killing competitors and claimants was hardly unusual, but 'having Hastings, Rivers, Vaughan and Grey put to death in 1483 was not usual late fifteenth-century violence' (Gillingham, 13; cf. Bellamy, 215).[1] Child murder carried particular stigma.[2] Early chroniclers compared the princes to the innocents slaughtered by Herod, a biblical analogy fraught with peril for perpetrators; rulers apparently postponed judgement and execution of underage pretenders and rebels until they were old enough no longer to be perceived as innocent children (Gillingham, 14; Pollard, 136–8). The treatment of the death of Rutland (historically seventeen years old) as the murder of an 'innocent child' (*3H6* 1.3.8; cf. *R3* 1.2.160–1, 1.3.176–93, 4.4.45) reflects an assessment of violence against children as being so heinous as to cause 'Tyrants themselves' to weep and all men to 'prophe[sy] revenge for it' (1.3.184–5).[3] Richard's crime against the 'little souls' prompts his own mother to regret not having aborted him (4.4.192, 138). Historically, the degree of Richard's guilt mattered less than the political significance of evident facts: 'Because he had deposed his nephew, usurped his throne, shut him and his brother in prison in the Tower and took no steps whatsoever to demonstrate to the world that they were still alive, Richard was believed to have killed them. Because they were innocent children, not adults who had offended, his crime was judged to be even worse' (Pollard, 138). Across multiple lines of alliance and antagonism, continental contemporaries expressed condemnation (Gillingham, 16–17). In London men wept openly (Mancini, 93).

1   John G. Bellamy, *The Law of Treason in England in the Later Middle Ages* (Cambridge, 1970).
2   The princes were eleven and thirteen in 1483; the play accentuates their youthfulness (4.1.97–102); cf. 'tender' George Stanley (5.3.95).
3   Cf. the 'pretie innocents' murdered in Robert Yarington's *Two Lamentable Tragedies* (1601; STC 26076) by hired killers who fall out like the murderers of Clarence (1.4), and the ballad 'The Children in the Wood' (Stationers' Register, 15 October 1595; Var, 611–17). Cf. Wiggins, 116–21.

Such public outbursts were political. They could crystallize opinion, incite violence or prompt powerful figures to capitalize on them. Richard rightly fears that citizens might 'wail [Hastings's] death' (3.5.61), as in other plays rulers fear similar outbursts (*Tit* 4.4.1–26; *Ham* 4.3.4–7; *R2* 1.4.24–36). Without a standing army or professional police, Richard's authority, like that of subsequent Tudor monarchs, depended on a widespread conviction of his sanctity and power.[1] Thus denunciations, prophecies or curses were actionable. If three or more people publicly joined in an outcry, furthermore, the complaint could be construed as riot, a term which, William Lambarde suggested, 'signifieth to braule, or scolde' (Lambarde, 175). Passionate outcries directed at a monarch constituted grounds for prosecution as treason.[2] Although Tudor regimes repeatedly modified fourteenth-century definitions, enactments until the early seventeenth century included 'treason by words', which embraced name-calling – 'calling the king (or his heirs) a heretic, tyrant, schismatic, infidel or usurper' – and 'prophecies foretelling the future, whereby the king's death, deposition or incapacity were predicted'.[3] The name-calling and prophecies of the play's women constitute treasonous acts (4.4.136–96). This is hardly domestic 'scolding', but women who did 'Rail on the Lord's anointed' (4.4.151) were partly shielded by a gendered presumption.[4]

Were they not female, the railing mothers would be risking death alongside those men who balk even slightly at Richard's tyranny. However, his petulant responses to 'tell-tale women',

1   See Carole Levin, '"We shall never have a merry world while the Queene lyveth": gender, monarchy and the power of words', in Julia M. Walker (ed.), *Dissing Elizabeth: Negative Representations of Gloriana* (Durham, NC, 1998), 79.
2   For public outcry and mourning by Londoners, see Archer, 33.
3   See John G. Bellamy, *The Tudor Law of Treason* (1979), 51–2.
4   So, for example, one woman punished for publicly ridiculing a bishop in the Vestiarian controversy of 1566–7 was set upon a cucking-stool, but continued rejoicing in her 'lewd behavior' (Martin Ingram, '"Scolding women cucked or washed": a crisis in gender relations in early modern England?', in Jennifer Kermode and Garthine Walker (eds), *Women, Crime and the Courts in Early Modern England* (Chapel Hill, NC, 1994), 61).

ordering flourishes and drums to drown their 'impatience', bluntly refusing to listen, mocking his mother's emotional 'condition' while urging his own martial affairs, suggest comic trivialization, as if it were all merely female temper, best dealt with by condescension and getting on with more important business (4.4.149–80). This refusal to take women seriously resembles the treatment historically accorded female agency, but presumptions of reduced agency could also lessen criminal culpability. William Lambarde criticizes the legal ambiguity surrounding indictment of women for breach of the peace without a person of 'discretion' – i.e. an adult male – to blame for instigating their actions (Lambarde, 179; Houlbrooke, 182).

The prominence of female 'prophets' and 'petitioners' in public outcries directed at authority from the time of Henry VIII through to the time of the English Civil War suggests a potential strength in presumed weakness. Some action consisted of quietly pursued resolution, as in recusant women's refusal to participate in prescribed worship (Willen, 154); other acts were public and/or collective. Women participated in a range of causes, from confrontation with Anne Boleyn in 1531 (Capp, 138–9) to grain and anti-enclosure riots in the early seventeenth century (Houlbrooke, 176–83).[1] Religious controversy prompted public demonstrations: in assemblies during the Vestiarian controversies of the 1560s (Collinson, *Puritan*, 93; Houlbrooke, 176) or in distributing the Marprelate tracts in the 1580s (Willen, 146). Individuals spoke out, as did Margaret Lawson who confronted Bishop John Aylmer, aided the Hackett conspirators in 1591 (Walsham, 34) and, for 'the immodestie of her tongue' (Cooper, 39), became notorious as the muse of Marprelate's invective (*Almond*, sig. B1ʳ), 'the shrew at Pauls Gate / and enemie to all dumb dogs and tyrannical prelates' (Marprelate, *Epistle*, 9–10). In the 1640s collective female petitioning and prophecy became

---

1 Bernard Capp, 'Separate domains? Women and authority in early modern England', in Paul Griffiths, Adam Fox and Steve Hindle (eds), *The Experience of Authority in Early Modern England* (New York, 1996).

major political phenomena.[1] Such evidence complicates gendered limits: Phyllis Mack has argued that the socially attributed 'female' qualities of passivity, irrationality and passion which justified exclusion from authority could sometimes confer a power of their own in public outcry or prophecy.[2]

Ever so briefly, female agency in *Richard III* assumes collective form; female public outcry against Richard differs from the actions of the individual women warriors, witches and seductresses in the *Henry VI* plays. Their 'woman's war', directing the 'bitter clamour of . . . eager tongues' (*R2* 1.1.48–9) against Richard, constitutes more open resistance than anyone else manages before Richmond's invasion. In *Richard III*, as Gilles Deleuze says, 'the women do battle for themselves'.[3] Their outburst contrasts with the silence of common Londoners (3.7.3), of clerics (3.4) and of nobles such as Stanley (4.4.491–3). Their 'complaint' adapts the medieval '*ubi sunt*' ('where be?') mutability trope to demand temporal answers. A lyrical form expressing passive loss becomes public indictment.[4] They name names and irritate, even frighten, the killer before his own men (4.4). Nor do their demands for accountability stop at missing relatives: even 'kind Hastings' gets remembered among the disappeared (4.4.148). There is more.

Sustaining the emotional momentum of this joint outcry, Richard's own mother calls down the guilty memories that will vex his ultimate dream, cursing him with a tormenting vision very different from the demons that Margaret or the sources predict (4.4.191–4).[5] Not devils, but innocent victims

1 See Keith Thomas, 'Women and the Civil War sects', *Past & Present*, 13 (1958), 42–57.

2 Phyllis Mack, 'Women as prophets during the English Civil War', *Feminist Studies*, 8 (1982), 19–45.

3 Gilles Deleuze, 'One manifesto less', in Constantin Boundas (ed.), *The Deleuze Reader* (New York, 1993), 205.

4 Cf. the identification of the play's female utterance with Ovidian complaint (Bate, *Ovid*, 66–7).

5 The 'images like terrible diuels, which pulled and haled' Richard, go back to Vergil, and appear in Hall, Grafton and Holinshed (see 5.3.117.1n.); cf. Stephen Batman, *The Doom Warning all Men to the Judgement* (1581; STC 1582), 281.

and 'friends' will haunt him. Furthermore, Queen Elizabeth manages, unlike Anne, to overrule a 'woman's heart' (4.1.78) and, contradicting the sources, says 'not now' to Richard's proposal while meaning 'never', despite his perverse appeals to her as his 'mother' (4.4.315–17).[1] To dismiss these female accusations and negotiations is to underestimate the strength and strategic cunning necessary to resist a tyrant. That Queen Elizabeth accuses and temporizes with the devil himself while avoiding cursing is also revealing. Her resolute critique logically deprives Richard of grounds for oaths and eventually gets him, in frustration, to curse himself (Birney, 36–42; 4.4.399–405n.). Her careful treading marks this scene as different from all other encounters with Richard.

Unlike Shakespeare's Lucrece, whose laments and curses this scene echoes, Elizabeth acknowledges words as means of aggression and self-consolation (4.4.116–17, 130–1) rather than as pointless wind (*Luc* 1027, 1330); she does not curse the tyrant with 'Himself himself' confound (*Luc* 998), but cleverly allows Richard his 'Myself myself confound' (4.4.399). Violated Lucrece, in keeping with the popular genre of female complaint, lyrically expresses the lonely pathos of self-punishment; she submits to the definition of pollution determined by the male order, leaving death her only 'remedy' (*Luc* 1028–9). If political implications are to be drawn from her suicide, men must draw them, or, as nearly happens, not draw them (*Luc* 1730–855).[2]

By contrast with Lucrece, Joan and the Margaret of the *Henry VI* plays, Elizabeth and the Duchess neither kill themselves, lead armies nor direct campaigns. But they turn the stereotypes allotted them – as impatient (1.3.1) 'indirect and peevish' (3.1.31),

---

1 For reactions to Queen Elizabeth's supposed co-operation with Richard, see 4.4.426–31n.

2 On the political implications of female literary complaint in the 1590s, cf. Hallett Smith, *Elizabethan Poetry* (Cambridge, Mass., 1952), 102–30, with Heather Dubrow, 'A mirror for complaints: Shakespeare's *Lucrece* and generic tradition', in Barbara K. Lewalski (ed.), *Renaissance Genres: Essays on Theory, History and Interpretation* (Cambridge, Mass., 1986), 399–417.

petulant in 'condition' (4.4.158–9), 'lunatic' (1.3.253), 'frantic' (1.3.246), 'wayward' (1.3.29) or 'shallow, changing' (4.4.431) – to use against the tyrant. An analogous use of advantage appears in the right of childish outspokenness that the princes exercise in 'taunt and scorn' described as 'all the mother's' (3.1.153–6). This mother (whom Richard will perversely urge to be his own 'mother'), his biological mother and Margaret Beaufort, Stanley's 'wife' and Richmond's 'mother', do what they can with the licence allowed them, even if, like Stanley, they cannot do what they will (5.3.91). If, unlike Stanley, they openly oppose tyranny, the likelihood of their being 'put to silence' (*JC* 1.2.285) is lessened by gendered attitudes.

Finally, it is important to note an agency falsely attributed to the women. The charge of witchcraft against Queen Elizabeth and Jane Shore is laughable (*R3* 3.4.67–71; More *CW*2, 48). But the historical Richard officially accused Elizabeth of witchcraft, and the earlier histories portrayed 'real' conjurers, spirits, witches and witchcraft (*1H6* 5.3; *2H6* 1.4). Margaret's 'charms' *mostly* come to pass.[1] Does this make her what Richard calls her?

Thomas Cooper puts the positive case: 'When a bad-tongued woman shall curse a party, and death shall shortly follow, this is a shrewd token that she is a witch' (K. Thomas, 512). However, Reginald Scot sceptically dismisses 'witch' as a social slur based on the appearance and characteristic utterance of lonely, enfeebled old women, the guilty consciences of the community and the inevitable misfortunes of earthly circumstance. Those called witches, Scot claims, are 'commonly old, lame, bleare-eied, pale, fowle, and full of wrinkles; poore, sullen, superstitious, and papists' (Scot, sig. C3ʳ). Their 'chief fault', Scot maintains, 'is that they are scolds' (sig. E1ᵛ). Responding to abuses and slights real or imagined, the characteristically accusatory utterances of the 'scold', much like Margaret's own, could sound like or

---

1 For the charge against Elizabeth, see the 1483 Parliamentary text 'Titulus Regius' accusing her of bewitching Edward into marriage (*Rotuli Parliamentorum*, ed. J. Strachey (1776–7), 6.240–1).

become in fact curses. Denied respect, aid and sustenance 'the witch waxeth odious and tedious to hir neighbors' until 'in processe of time they haue all displeased hir, and she hath wished euill lucke unto them all; perhaps with curses and imprecations made in forme. Doubtlesse (at length) some of hir neighbours die, or fall sick' (sig. C4ᵛ).[1] It takes a community to make a 'foul, wrinkled witch' – or a tyrant. If ever a community deserved a Margaret or a Richard, it is the England of this play.

CO-TEXTS: INVECTIVE, SATIRE, LIBEL

Along with 'dream', 'mother' and 'children', which appear more frequently in *Richard III* than in any other Shakespeare play, the word 'news' occurs many times – in frequency second only to its appearance in *2 Henry IV*. Understanding of the play can be enhanced by considering not only its pre-history in sources and analogues and post-history in reception and performance, but also its co-history of articulation in the early 1590s. Literary and ideological 'backgrounds', 'sources' or 'origins' (Tillyard; Churchill; Jones, *Origins*) scarcely exhaust the discursive environment of its shaping.

Richard III shares its language and protagonist with a vast tide of contemporary polemic and invective (Simpson; Campbell, 321). The historical Richard provided material for mudslingers of every stripe. The texts involved include the most widely known of the period. *Leicester's Commonwealth* (*The Copy of a Letter Written by a Master of Arts of Cambridge*) (1584), for example, a benchmark character assassination, invokes Richard to denounce the Earl of Leicester. Similarly, the work popularly termed *The Papists' Commonwealth* (*A Treatise of Treasons*) (1572), which troubled the Privy Council for decades, devotes twenty pages to 'infinit resemblances' between Richard's

---

1   For disputes concerning the 'scapegoat' theory of witchcraft, see *Witchcraft in Early Modern Europe*, ed. Jonathan Barry, Marianne Hester and Gareth Roberts (Cambridge, 1996), 1–45.

England and the 'Machiauellian State' under Elizabeth I's chief counsellor, William Cecil, Lord Burghley, an 'vnknowen Traitour ... taken for the chiefe and most lawful Gouernour' (*Treatise*, 'Preface', sig. 121ʳ). The incendiary classic *A Conference about the Next Succession* (1595) cites the deposing of Richard to urge Englishmen to determine royal succession (Parsons, pt 1, 61). There is much more.

Anti-Cecil discourse peaked dramatically in 1591–2, the years of the elevation of Burghley's son to the Privy Council, with the text called *Burghley's Commonwealth* (*A Declaration of the True Causes of the Great Troubles*) (1592) and *An Aduertisement Written to a Secretary* (1592). Both attack Burghley for the anti-Catholic Royal Proclamations of October 1591.[1] Furthermore, over the following twenty years, manuscript libels compared Robert Cecil to Richard, demanding: 'Richard, or Robert, wch is the worse? / A Crooktback great in state is Englands curse' (Bod. Tanner MS 299, fol. 13ʳ). Richard's ambition, strategic villainy and bodily configuration suggested comparison with a younger son who rose despite physical limitations to vast power and authority amid factionalized politics.[2]

Richard also appears in anti-Catholic works such as George Whetstone's *The English myrror* (1586), which compares the Pope, 'the Archtyrant of the earth', to 'our arch tyraunt', Richard III, 'manifest monster' and 'sonne of the diuel' (Whetstone, 96, 116–17, 9). Furthermore, just beyond direct reference, various texts levy charges of ambition, factional manipulation, religious hypocrisy and physical deformity in vocabulary and in style

1 *Tudor Royal Proclamations*, ed. Paul L. Hughes and James F. Larkin, 3 vols (New Haven, Conn., 1964–9), 3.86–95. On the affair and on Robert Parsons's Latin *Responsio*, see Victor Houliston, 'The Lord Treasurer and the Jesuit: Robert Persons's satirical *Responsio* to the 1591 Proclamation', *Sixteenth Century Journal*, 32 (2001), 383–401.

2 The most widely known of relevant Cecil materials, Bacon's 'Of Deformity', does not invoke Richard III, but its treatment of the strengths, advantages and strategies incumbent upon disability is revealing (see Bacon, *Works*, 6.480–1; cf. James Siemon, 'Sign, cause or general habit: toward an "historicist ontology" of character on the early modern stage', in Hugo Keiper, Christopher Bode and Richard J. Utz (eds), *Nominalism and Literary Discourse: New Perspectives* (Amsterdam, 1998), 237–50.

shared with the play. Pre-eminent among these are the pro- and anti-Episcopal writings of the Marprelate controversy (1589–90), which in turn shaped the 'prophecies' and 'libells' of the Hackett rebellion (July 1591) on behalf of reformers imprisoned by Archbishop Whitgift, and which ultimately anticipated the Elizabethan satirical vogue.[1] Furthermore, the contemporary 'invention' of the stereotypical 'Puritan' also casts light on aspects of Shakespeare's play and protagonist.

Excellent grand tyrant of the earth or lump of foul deformity

Any Elizabethan would know the 'deformed and ill shaped' Richard III for a 'cruell murtherer, a wretched caitiffe, a moste tragicall tyraunt, and blood succour [sucker], bothe of his nephewes, and brother' (Rainolde, sig. D1ʳ). The first theatre-goers might have been surprised by *how* 'ill shaped' Shakespeare's Richard is and by *how much* everyone carries on about it. They might also have been surprised to find that, amid the play's 'violent and vituperative speech' (Chambers, *Shakespeare*, 1.302), Richard himself weeps, sighs, 'play[s] the saint', meekly endures insults and quotes scripture. The violent abuse directed at Richard and his own hypocritical piety and arch foolery carry contemporary polemical resonance.

On the one hand, insults inflate Richard to cosmic dimensions; on the other, they reduce him to subhuman triviality. As 'grand tyrant of the earth' he shares epithets with world-class enemies like the Pope or Philip II of Spain; all three are declared a scourge of God to punish sinful humanity, or even the Antichrist himself – a figure who, it is prophesied, will end creation with 'tyranny and all-embracing persecution, and ... a mocking and counterfeit religiosity'.[2] Identifying Richard with this

---

1   For the Hackett rebellion, see Walsham. On the nine figures imprisoned around London, see Collinson, 412–31. The imprisonments were 'so taken to heart; amongst the reforming and zealous brotherhood' as to threaten armed reaction (Bancroft, *Positions*, 146), 338

2   See Stuart Clark, *Thinking with Demons: The Idea of Witchcraft in Early Modern Europe* (Oxford, 1997), 338.

satanic charlatan goes back to John Rous (Hanham, 123–4). But the play's 'devil' (1.2.45), 'cacodemon' (1.3.143) 'hell-hound' (4.4.48), hell's 'minister' (1.2.46), 'son of hell' (1.3. 229), hell's 'factor' (4.4.72), 'hell's black intelligencer' (4.4.71) and 'God's enemy' (5.3.252) is also reductively called 'dog' (1.3.215, 4.4.49, 5.5.2), 'spider' (1.3.241), 'abortive, rooting hog' (1.3.227), 'wolf' (4.4.23), 'toad' (4.4.81), 'Fool' (5.3.192), 'Vice' (3.1.82), 'villain-slave' (4.4.144) and 'lump of foul deformity' (1.2.57). This polarized lexicon has antecedents in treatments of Satan in the Bible or medieval drama, but it also echoes contemporary polemical usage.

Protestants attacked both the Pope and the King of Spain as 'Archtyrant of the earth' (Whetstone, 96; *Declaration*, 76), but also, reductively, compared 'Antichrist' to a 'cocke, w^t neuer a feather on her back' or a mouse-like abortive fetus (Whetstone, 121, 123, 159–60). Philip, 'Tyrant of Spayne', father of 'Monsters', 'horrible and hiddious', begetter of 'ignorance, malice, deceit, guile, hypocrisie, robbing, theft, incest, feigned Religion, all kinde of execrations, murder sacrilidge and parracide', is also an 'olde Foxe' with a 'mishapen masse or lumpe' of followers.[1] Catholics attacked Burghley – 'the *Archpolitike*', the 'tyra[n]t *Nero*' and '*Machiauill*', master of 'actors', instigator of 'defamatorie libells' (*Declaration*, 43, 52–3, 33) and a 'Cataline' who has 'diuided [England] into factions' – as merely a spoiled child, 'weeping and whining, like a boye and a babe' (*Treatise*, fols 119^r, 166^v, sig. i2^v). However, for sheer sensationalism nothing exceeds the polarized invective that Protestants hurled at one another in 'the biggest scandal of Elizabeth I's reign'.[2]

Between two bishops

In 1589 Bishop Thomas Cooper complained that since the Armada, English Protestants had turned to warring over the

1   *The Masque of the League and the Spanyard discouered* (1592; STC 7), sigs B1^r–B4^v, C4^v.
2   See *The Collected Essays of Christopher Hill* (Amherst, Mass., 1985), 1.75.

office of bishop (Cooper, 33–5; cf. Bancroft, *Sermon*, 52; *Almond*, sig. A4ʳ). This stage of England's ecclesiastical controversies came to be known for the pseudonymous 'Martin Marprelate', whose name with those of his followers appeared on publications between October 1588 and September 1589 and in counter-attacks by officially sponsored writers.[1] This affair contributed to the factionalizing of Elizabethan politics in the early 1590s (Hammer, 390), to the decade's vogue for satire and to the stereotype of 'the Puritan'.[2] Marprelate's innovation was to mix multi-form humour and burlesque piety with religious critique and bitter invective; the mix would have been inescapably familiar to the first audiences of *Richard III*.

Government spokesmen rightly claimed that the Marprelate authors derived their abusive terms from Presbyterians (Rogers, *Sermon*, 13); this vocabulary also overlapped with anti-papal invective (and the charges aimed at Shakespeare's Richard): satanic ambition, tyrannical usurpation, bestiality, hypocrisy and gross deformity. However, terminology was the least of it. The polarities are familiar: the bishops are 'vsurping Antichristes' (Marprelate, *Epistle*, 8), 'the Lords scourge' (*Theses*, sig. D1ᵛ), but also merely 'Hogges, Dogges, Wolues, Foxes' who render the Church a 'deformed bodie' (Bancroft, *Positions*, 63; Rogers, *Sermon*, 8). John Whitgift, Archbishop of Canterbury, 'Pope of Lambeth', 'cruell persecutour' and 'tyrant', bears 'the cursse of God' and is warned to expect 'a fearefull ende' (*Theses*, sig. D3ʳ⁻ᵛ).[3] But a new ingredient renders the Marprelate texts 'impudent in the hiest degree' (Rogers, *Sermon*, 13). Whitgift is also jokily represented as bumbling 'nunckle Canterbury' (*Theses*, sig. D3ʳ⁻ᵛ)

1 On the main and peripheral Marprelate materials, see Joseph Black, 'The rhetoric of reaction: the Martin Marprelate tracts (1588–89), Anti-Martinism, and the uses of print in early modern England', *Sixteenth Century Journal*, 28 (1997), 707–25.

2 Patrick Collinson, 'Ecclesiastical vitriol: religious satire in the 1590s and the inven-tion of Puritanism', in John Guy (ed.), *The Reign of Elizabeth I: Court and Culture in the Last Decade* (Cambridge, 1995), 150–70; cf. Kristin Poole, 'Facing Puritanism: Falstaff, Martin Marprelate and the grotesque Puritan', in Ronald Knowles (ed.), *Shakespeare and Carnival: After Bakhtin* (Basingstoke, 1998), 97–122.

3 Cf. Lake & Questier, 513, on this rhetoric.

and warned with a story about saucy dogs who might treat a bishop's regalia as disrespectfully as Shakespeare's Richard says they treat his limping gait:

> [T]he B[ishop] did sweat (you must think he labored hard ouer his trencher) The dogg flies at the B. & tooke of his corner capp (he thought belike it had bene a cheese cake) and so away goes the dog with it to his master. Truely my masters of the cleargie / I woulde neuer weare corner cap againe / seeing dogs runne away with them.

(Marprelate, Epistle, 43)

Marprelate recasts Antichrist as a sweating trencherman, his idolatrous headgear as cheese cake, his violent rule as pet-wrestling. Similar funny stories abound, such as the one about the preacher who, having once acted the 'vice in a playe', cannot resist running off abruptly mid-service to join passing revellers while mumbling his liturgy.[1] Furthermore, Marprelate narrators mix attack with self-deprecation, adopting the persona of a childlike dunce or 'Plain Percevall', a hunchbacked rustic who admonishes readers, 'thinking belike to ride vpon my Crupshoulders: I am no Ape Carrier'.[2]

Once the bishops stopped huffing, they turned to professional writers to return similar abuse and similar jokes. Of course, Marprelate is Satan's 'intelligencer' or Antichrist, who lamely limps, but leads followers with his name 'on their foreheads' to hell (*Almond*, sigs B2^v, C2^v). Or he is a 'Dunce', 'dogge', 'hogge' or 'abhortiue childe' (*Almond*, sigs D3^v, C2^v, B1^r) mouthing *'tinkers termes'* and *'iestes first* Tarleton [put] *on the Stage'* (*Mar-Martine*, sig. A4^v). Comical images of bishops are countered with comical representations of 'Puritans' as hypocritical cheapskates who quote scripture with sham 'zeal'. One such, for example, when asked by his 'good Ladie' to repay

---

1 Martin Marprelate, *Hay any Worke for Cooper* ([Coventry,] 1589; STC 17456), 3–4.
2 *Plaine Percevall, the Peace-Maker of England* (1590; STC 12914), 12.

a loan, 'began to storme, and said, he thought her not the child of God, for they must lend, looking for nothing againe; & so to acquite himself of the blot of vsurie, he kept the principall' (*Pappe*, sigs C4ᵛ–D2ʳ). Another, to save funeral costs 'tombled his wife naked into the earth . . . without sheete or shroude to couer her shame, breathing ouer her . . . Naked came I out of my mothers wombe, and naked shall I returne againe' (*Almond*, sig. B1ᵛ).

A perverse eroticism with a special interest in widows constitutes a significant element in the anti-Marprelate polemic and associated anti-Puritan discourse (cf. Jonson, *Bartholomew Fair*). *Almond* attacks Martin (and his 'puritane perusers') as a 'wretched seducer, that vnder wolues raiment deuourest widowes houses' (*Almond*, sigs B1ᵛ, F3ᵛ); compare Richard's attempts on widows Anne and Elizabeth. The paradoxical image of the seducer outwardly wearing a wolf's raiment rather than sheep's clothing may be a misprint, but it suggests oxymoronic qualities in 'Puritan' and Ricardian seduction.

Puritans, though monsters of 'ambition', 'male-con[ten]ted mela[n]choly' and 'seditious discontent' (*Almond*, sig. D2ʳ), are also associated with harsh moralism, blasphemous mocking, material self-interest and hyper-seductiveness. Thinking 'to carrie all away with censoricall lookes, with gogling the eye, with lifting vppe the hand, with vehement speeches', the 'Puritane[s]' purvey 'rayling & reuiling Pamphlets' (*2 Pasquill*, sig. B4ᵛ). But these 'seducers' are like 'mermaides' hiding sinfulness with 'faire speeches' (Bancroft, *Sermon*, 5–6). 'Hypocritically,' they act 'as though all they said proceeded of meere love and Christian charitie', with 'great sighes and grones . . . with a heavy countenance, with casting downe their heads, and with a pittiful voice' (Bancroft, *Sermon*, 92). References to such performance pervades an erotic sub-genre. Puritans may 'seduce' male followers, but *most labour hath bene bestowed to win and reteine towards this cause them whose iudgements are commonlie weakest by reason of their sex*'; women are '*apter through that naturall inclination vnto pittie*' (Hooker, 17–18). More explicitly, women are positively mad 'to follow men precise', their intense desires making the Puritan woman a '*holy whore*' or '*Pruritane*' (*Mar-Martine*, sig. A2ʳ⁻ᵛ). Piety is a special turn-on: praying women scan the room '*The purest man to see. / The purer man, the better grace*' (*Mar-Martine*, sig. A2ʳ). This often obscene polemic presumes 'hote' sexual drives perversely compounded by piety, stern moralizing or sighing meekness.

It was not all funny. The war on dissent led to imprisonment and investigation of prominent reformers between 1589 and 1593, the execution of John Penry (1593), and the only Elizabethan Parliament Act (1593) directed exclusively against Protestant sectaries (Collinson, *Puritan*, 412–31), but the '*laughing libells*' (*Mar-Martine*, sig. A1ᵛ) and 'Satyricall immodestie' (Hooker, sig. A5ʳ) even generated stage representations. A July 1589 tract denounces 'stage-players' for serving 'Dick Bancroft' before 'many thousand eie witnesses' (*Theses*, sig. D2ᵛ). The nature of such stagings is uncertain, but by autumn 1589 the Star Chamber and the Lord Mayor acted to control representation of 'partes and matters . . . unfytt and undecent to be handled in playes, both for Divinitie and State' (Chambers, *Stage*, 1.295, 4.306–7; cf. *Pappe*, sig. D2ᵛ; *2 Pasquill*, sig. C3ᵛ; Nashe, 4.465, Lake & Questier, 557–8).[1]

Given this incendiary atmosphere, what to make of the 'never-ending procession of churchmen' (Honigmann, *R3*, 32) who enable Shakespeare's hypocritical tyrant? An archbishop promises sanctuary (2.4), but a compliant cardinal aids Richard in violating it (3.1); the Bishop of Ely hurries to fetch Richard strawberries (3.4). Lesser clerics, including the notorious Shaw, preach on his behalf (3.5.103–5); a chaplain conceals the princes' bodies (4.3.29); bishops appear 'aloft' with him (3.7). How would these ludicrous 'props of virtue' strike Elizabethans who

---

1 With a character called plain Honesty who denounces 'pure precisians' (344) for 'mocking the divine order of ministry' (1856), *A Knack to Know a Knave* (performed in 1592) is relevant here.

heard bishops defended as 'especiall pillers and ornamentes of [Elizabeth's] state' (*Almond*, sig. C2ʳ)? This is all 'history', of course, and Milton assumed Richard's religious hypocrisy to be historical (Milton, 361–2). However, 'historical' parallels served contemporary purposes; just associating Bishop Barlowe with Dr Shaw registered utter contempt.[1]

Bishop Bancroft claimed in 1588, 'a man can scarcelie speake any thing . . . but he shall seeme to pointe at and describe the factions of these daies' (Bancroft, *Sermon*, 14). The depiction of May Day 1517 in *Sir Thomas More* occasioned official warnings about possible analogy with tensions of the 1590s (*STM*, 17–19). The months surrounding the printing of *Richard III* (Stationers' Register 20 October 1597) saw other Shakespearean 'histories' embroiled in disputes about topicality. Sir John Oldcastle was renamed Falstaff for the *1 Henry IV* Quartos of 1598 (Stationers' Register, 25 February 1598).[2] Religion was not the only flashpoint.

Drunken prophecies, libels

Richard employs 'prophecies' and 'libels' (1.1.33), but no known source implicates him for the prophecy about 'G' (cf. Hall, *Edward IV*, fol. ccxᵛ).[3] However, playing on a letter appears prominently in a 1592 attack on Burghley invoking a 'prophecie . . . that one who had two c. c. in his name should be the destruction of Ingland' (*Aduertisement*, 39). Other 1592 polemic accuses Burghley himself of instigating 'prophecies' and 'libells' (*Declaration*, 74–5), as if he were responsible 'for the vain and fond pamphlets and ballads of every idle fellow' (Bacon, *Works*, 8.200). By making Richard the causer of such libels, a lofty intimate of a monarch, a hidden threat and an apparent

1 John Donne, *The Courtier's Library*, ed. Evelyn Mary Simpson (London, 1930), 37, 52.
2 See Kastan, *1H4*, 51–62.
3 Henry Howard's *Defensative against the Poison of Supposed Prophesies* (1583; STC 13858), sigs Hh3ᵛ–Hh4ʳ, anticipates Shakespeare in blaming Richard for authoring the prophecy.

ally of his victims, the play parallels his story with anti-Cecil conspiracy polemic.

The Cecils endured smear campaigns until Robert's death in 1612 (Croft, 'Reputation', 46; cf. SPD 12/180/23). Bacon's 1592 defence of Burghley marvels at the sheer variety and 'number of libellous and defamatory books and writings' (Bacon, *Works*, 8.147–8). These libels consistently attack a 'monopolistic figure' who manipulates the monarch, court factions and the nobility.[1] Many, like the 1584 *Copy of a Letter*, employ terms Richard uses to describe himself in *3 Henry VI*: 'Machauel' (*Copy*, 103; *Declaration*, 53), 'Catiline' (*Copy*, 184; *Treatise*, fol. 118ᵛ), 'Syren' or Sinon (*Treatise*, fol. 132ʳ). They describe 'hyred murders' (*Treatise*, sig. i2ᵛ), 'Libelles and Pamphlets' (*Treatise*, fol. 121ʳ), 'Shawes' (*Treatise*, fol. 124ʳ; cf. *Copy*, 124), 'spies and intelligencers' (*Copy*, 79; *Declaration*, 43), all serving Burghley, 'the *primum mobile* in every action' (Bacon, *Works*, 8.198), who 'so cuningly dispos[es] . . . his affaires, into the handes of other principall actors . . . that very ofte[n] tymes, his owne plottes & inuentions have seemed the practizes of others' (*Declaration*, 52). Burghley feigns piety while 'laughing at other mens simplicity' (*Aduertisement*, 61). Physical handicap enters this polemic with Robert Cecil's rise in the early 1590s.

Amid curses calling for 'vengeance of heauen and earth' upon the Cecils, the *Declaration* mentions a work recalled in 1591 for its anti-Burghley implications, Spenser's '*mother Hubberds Tale*', with its 'false fox and his crooked cubbes' (*Declaration*, 68–71). Robert Cecil's body, 'so il shapen and crooked', prompts the *Declaration*'s recourse to the satirical grotesque. After lecturing Queen Elizabeth for having forgotten the 'Philosopher' who warns against 'such so marked by nature, in these woordes: *Caue ab his, quos natura signauit*', the attack shifts into '*Macaronicall* verses' warning 'to beware of such

---

1 See Simon Adams, 'Favourites and factions at the Elizabethan court', in Ronald G. Asch and Adolf M. Birke (eds), *Princes, Patronage and the Nobility: The Court at the Beginning of the Modern Age, c. 1450–1650* (Oxford, 1991), 273.

deformed creatures, saying in admiration. *O Deus, a[b]guerzis, Zoppis, gobbisq[ue] cauendum est / Nulla fides gobbis, mancum mihi credite Zoppis. / Si . . . guersus bonus est, inter miracula scribam'* ['O God, one must beware of the Guerzi, Zoppi, and Gobbi. There is no trust in Gobbis, believe me, there is something wrong with the Zoppis. If a Guerzo is a good man, I will record that as a miracle.'].[1] After this conjuration of lame, cross-eyed and hump-backed dwarfs come jokes about Cecil's back, birth and function: 'yf her Matie had bene disposed to prefer him . . . to haue made him a writer vnder some clerck or officier of the courte, had bene very conuenie[n]t for him, because as a courtier told her, he was fittest for such purpose, for that he caried his deske on his back' (*Declaration*, 71). From bitter accusations and passionate curses, the attack descends to grotesque caricature worthy of Nashe. Such tonally volatile combinations characterize the manuscript invective.

Robert Cecil's elevation in May 1591 as the youngest ever Privy Council member occasioned rumours that he would soon fill the powerful post of Secretary, which had been vacant since Walsingham's death in 1590.[2] Speculation also ran high that he would inherit the reversion to the Court of Wards held by his father (SPD 12/239/159). In fact he obtained neither till 1596 and 1599 respectively, but his proximity to such power encouraged comparison with Richard. Manuscripts of various dates call him a 'Dissemblinge smothfacd dwarfe' (Bod. Don c. 54, fol. 20), 'Little Cecil' or 'the Littell one it self', 'his fathers instrument' (SPD 14/71/16). Even Queen Elizabeth addressed him 'under her sporting name of pygmy'.[3] Comparisons with humped beasts abound: like a dolphin and camel, a 'Toad' (Croft, 'Reputation', 47), like a spider, his 'Crookebacks spider shapen' (Bod. Don c. 54, fol. 20) or like an 'Ape / Of crooked fame and

1   *Declaration*, 70; translation thanks to Wolfgang Haase, Steven Esposito and Ron Bogdan.
2   Conyers Read, *Lord Burghley and Queen Elizabeth* (New York, 1960), 465, 477.
3   P.M. Handover, *The Second Cecil* (1959), 57.

crooked shape' (BL Egerton 2230, fol. 33ʳ). Insults infer sexual promiscuity – as, for example, 'Robert Cicil, Compos'd of back and pisle' (BL Add. MS 25348, fol. 9ʳ) – and falsely attribute his death to syphilis:

> Heere lieth Robbin Crooktback unjustly reckond
> A Richard the third, he was Judas the second.
> In their lives they agree, in their deaths somewᵗ alter,
> The more pity the poxe soe cousend the halter.
> Richard, or Robert, wch is the worse?
> A Crooktback great in state is Englands curse.
>
> (Bod. Tanner MS 299, fol. 13ʳ)

The similarities include their 'Machiuillian skill' at 'curb[ing] the Peeres', employing 'faction', 'vile detraction' (Bod. Don c. 54, fol. 20) and pious hypocrisy in 'fained religion, & zealous affection' (Bod. Tanner MS 299, fol. 11ʳ).

PREPOSTEROUS ANTICIPATIONS: THE RICHARDS OF *2* AND *3 HENRY VI*

The protagonist who opens *Richard III* is new to the stage, though aspects of himself and of other, alternative, selves had appeared in the *Henry VI* plays.[1] Some are retained or expanded: bodily shape first. The Quarto version of *2 Henry 6* (*The Contention*) announces his bit-part as 'crook-backe *Richard*' (*Contention*, sig. H1ᵛ) and appropriate insults follow: 'foul indigested lump, / As crooked in thy manners as thy shape' (*2H6* 5.1.157–8) or 'Foule Stigmaticke' (*Contention*, sig. H2ʳ; *2H6* 5.1.215). This emphasis remains in the mix, as do religious hypocrisy, bloodthirstiness

---

1   My analysis is indebted to Pearlman, who refutes claims that Richard's characteristics are implicitly similar (Tillyard, 195; M.M. Reese, *The Cease of Majesty: A Study of Shakespeare's History Plays* (1961), 204) or his character unchanging (Spivack, 388; Larry S. Champion, *Perspective in Shakespeare's English Histories* (Athens, Ga., 1980), 82) in the three plays. Pearlman also complicates arguments about Oedipal change (Pierce, 83). On Richard's metamorphosis, see also David L. Frey, *The First Tetralogy: Shakespeare's Scrutiny of the Tudor Myth* (The Hague, 1976), 42; Smidt, *Unconformities*, 33–4.

and status consciousness, but these elements are modified. Taunting his enemies, early Richard burlesques Christian values by preaching, 'Fie, Charitie for shame, speake it not in spight, / For you shall sup with Iesus Christ to night' (*Contention*, sig. H2^r; *2H6* 5.1.213–14), while to himself he declares, 'heart, be wrathful still: / Priests pray for enemies, but princes kill' (*2H6* 5.2.70–1). Yet the religious hypocrite and ruthless Machiavellian 'prince' are wholly subsumed in the partisan Yorkist warrior; nothing yet suggests the sneaky, ambitious, anti-family, anti-everyone *isolato* who suddenly emerges late in *3 Henry VI*, nor the witty showman who will open *Richard III*.

Richard opens *3 Henry VI* with a grotesque pantomime that wins him the title 'best' son. Holding up a severed head, he bids, 'Speak thou for me, and tell them what I did', and shakes it for emphasis: 'Thus do I hope to shake King Henry's head' (*3H6* 1.1.16, 20). Wit? Subtlety? His subsequent speeches sometimes seem randomly assigned. The taciturn head-shaker channels Senecan rant, lusting, like Richard of *True Tragedy*, for 'lukewarm blood' (*3H6* 1.2.33) or threatening to resurrect an enemy insufficiently railed at: 'If this right hand would buy two hours' life, / That I in all despite might rail at him, / This hand should chop it off, and with the issuing blood / Stifle the villain' (*3H6* 2.6.80–3). 'Revenge' is his theme (*3H6* 2.3.19, 2.4.3). Alternatively, he waxes Marlovian, lyrically enthusing, 'How sweet a thing it is to wear a crown, / Within whose circuit is Elysium / And all that poets feign of bliss and joy' (*3H6* 1.2.28–30; cf. Marlowe, *1 Tamburlaine*, 2.7.28–9). These Richards will not make it to *Richard III*. In Act 3 of *3 Henry VI*, however, the new model Richard, our Richard, 'theatrical, scheming, wicked, ironic' springs to life (Pearlman, 416) in Shakespeare's longest soliloquy (71 lines in F, 28 in Octavo *3H6*). For the first time he expresses an attitude toward his body, and admires himself as if his physical appearance does not matter.

Richard begins by wishing his brother Edward 'wasted, marrow, bones and all', rather than about to marry and put him further from the throne. Frustrated, 'Like one that stands upon a promontory / And spies a far-off shore where he would tread' (*3H6* 3.2.135–6), Richard briefly considers an alternative goal – to 'make my heaven in a lady's lap' (3.2.148). But his body – an arm 'like a withered shrub', 'an envious mountain' on his back, 'unequal' legs and 'disproportion . . . in every part' (3.2.156–60) – rules this out. Turning back to the crown, Richard suddenly reconceives his body 'not as the insignia but the cause of his depravity' (Pearlman, 421). *Because* he cannot be loved, domination offers the only compensation:

> Then, since this earth affords no joy to me
> But to command, to check, to o'erbear such
> As are of better person than myself,
> I'll make my heaven to dream upon the crown
> And whiles I live t'account this world but hell,
> Until my misshaped trunk that bears this head
> Be round impaled with a glorious crown.
>
> (*3H6* 3.2.165–71)

The hideous image of his 'trunk' somehow rounded with a crown captures the centrality of his body to Richard's logic: the crown becomes a 'heaven' to be entered in compensation for the inaccessible 'heaven' of love. Here is the Richard who will introduce himself as 'I, that am not shaped for sportive tricks' (1.1.14). But how could he possibly get inside the crown?

Frustration returns, compounded, in the image of enveloping thorns enclosing him in a desperate, self-defeating struggle between desire and impossibility, 'like one lost in a thorny wood, / That rents the thorns and is rent with the thorns, / Seeking a way and straying from the way, / Not knowing how to find the open air' (*3H6* 3.2.174–7).[1] Will he 'free' himself, or flail about with a bloody axe? Surprise, again; as it turns out, neither: 'Tut', he announces, he is already free, and on

---

1   The image develops a commonplace shared with *Mirror*, 'Buckingham', Induction, 512–14.

his way. In a stunning reversal, *3 Henry VI* takes what Elihu Pearlman calls a 'step backward' from psychic 'realism' to an archaic, symbolic or supernatural mode. With no pretence of dramatic preparation or continuity of 'character', a new creature announces himself, claiming a whole bag of hitherto concealed tricks and weapons. And he knows how to use them:

> Why, I can smile, and murder whiles I smile,
> And cry 'Content!' to that which grieves my heart,
> And wet my cheeks with artificial tears,
> And frame my face to all occasions.
> I'll drown more sailors than the mermaid shall,
> I'll slay more gazers than the basilisk,
> I'll play the orator as well as Nestor,
> Deceive more slyly than Ulysses could,
> And, like a Sinon, take another Troy.
> I can add colours to the chameleon,
> Change shapes with Proteus for advantages,
> And set the murderous Machiavel to school.
> Can I do this, and cannot get a crown?
> Tut, were it farther off, I'll pluck it down.
>
> (*3H6* 3.2.182–95)

Really? Nothing has previously suggested he can do any of these things, but from now on he talks much like this – right into his own play. Here, for the first time, Richard sounds mostly like Richard. No longer dynastic 'Dickie . . . with his grumbling voice' (*3H6* 1.4.76), but a 'creature of indirection, irony and dissembling' (Pearlman, 422) with a link to the Prince of Darkness. The 'historical' or 'tragical' Richard of the sources and analogues appears transfused with the energies and attributes of the morality play Vice.

The new model Richard boldly assumes a multi-abled, supernatural flexibility of identity, like that of the Vice Haphazard, 'a Scholer, or a scholemaister, or els some youth.

/ A Lawier, a student or els a countrie cloune / A Brumman [broom-man], a Baskit maker, or a Baker of Pies'.[1] Consummate dissembling comes from the Vice, too. Richard's pride in multi-tasking, smiling and murdering or crying content while suffering, recalls Skelton's Collusion boasting, 'I can dyssemble, I can bothe laughe and grone'.[2] Weeping at will, while secretly laughing, like Ambidexter in Preston's *Cambises*, he also claims the right to boast about it to us, and also like Ambidexter and others, the possession of a dominant quality, sin or tendency. Here, two-faced 'Machiavel' becomes Richard's true name, but in the final act of *3 Henry VI* he claims an identity of biblical proportions. Stabbing King Henry, Richard invokes hell and renounces love itself:

> Then, since the heavens have shaped my body so,
> Let hell make crook'd my mind to answer it.
> I have no brother; I am like no brother.
> And this word 'love', which greybeards call divine,
> Be resident in men like one another
> And not in me: I am myself alone.
>
> (*3H6* 5.6.78–83)

Affirming the sin of sins by renouncing St Paul's primal '*band of perfection*', Richard adopts the 'cognisance of the diuell', marking the 'Apostata'.[3] He embraces the 'inward war' that Thomas More had ascribed to the historical tyrant: 'For whome trusted he that mistrusted his own brother? whom spared he that killed his own brother? or who could parfitely loue him, if hys owne brother could not?' (More, *CW*2, 71). Rejecting likeness, he refuses the very basis of friendship; and in the Octavo line – 'I have no father, I am like no father' – he further renounces paternity, ascribing to

1   R.B., *A New Tragical Comedie of Apius and Virginia* (1575; STC 1059), sig. B1ʳ.
2   See Wolfgang G. Müller, 'The villain as rhetorician in Shakespeare's *Richard III*', *Anglia*, 102 (1984), 47–8.
3   Smith, *Sermons*, 353–7; cf. William Perkins, 'A Case of Conscience', *Works* (1592; STC 19665.5), sig. B3ʳ⁻ᵛ.

himself Aristotle's definition of monstrosity: 'he who does not resemble his parents'.[1]

3 Henry VI concludes with a Richard anything but the Richard of any previous play and all but the Richard of *Richard III*. Violent, ambitious, cunning and demonically isolated, Richard affirms self-denominations – Proteus, mermaid, chameleon, Sinon, basilisk and Machiavel ('*Catalin*' in O1 *3H6* sig. C8ᵛ) – fully functional as epithets in any number of early modern invective contexts. However, he has yet to manifest his primary gifts as a performance artist: brazen religious hypocrisy, callous manipulation and bullying seduction. Above all, he is not yet funny or engaging. That surprise awaited playgoers who were probably amazed, at the opening of the next play, to be invited up, at least figuratively, to the scaffold to join in Richard's version of what More calls king's games. We call it *Richard III*.

NOW: DATE OF COMPOSITION, PERFORMANCE AND COMPANY

We know virtually nothing certain about Shakespeare from 1585 until references to him as a London actor and playwright appear in 1592. We do not know which acting company he was with until 1594, when unequivocal evidence connects him with the Chamberlain's Men (George, 305). *Richard III* was written after 1587, when the second edition of Holinshed's *Chronicles* was printed, and before 20 October 1597, when the First Quarto (Q1) was entered in the Stationers' Register (Arber, 3.25). The 1597 title-page announces the play as 'lately Acted by the Right honourable the Lord Chamberlaine his seruants'. Within those ten years, suggested dates of composition range from 1590–1 (Honigmann, *Impact*, 88), 1591 (Hammond, 61), 1592 (Jowett, 7), after June 1592 (Taylor, *TxC*, 115), mid-1592 to 1593 (Lull),

---

1 Cf. *Coriolanus* 5.2.80, 5.3.36–7. On classical friendship, see Shannon, and Aristotle, *On the Generation of Animals*, 4.4, cited in Marie-Hélène Huet, *Monstrous Imagination* (Cambridge, Mass., 1993), 4.

to 1594 (Bate, *Tit*, 79).[1] Everyone agrees on the early 1590s, and though evidence cannot eliminate either extreme, the dates can be narrowed with probability to 1592–3. Debates about the nature and history of London acting companies during the years 1592–4 preclude certainty about Shakespeare's own affiliation, though features of *Richard III* have suggested possible ties to Pembroke's and Lord Strange's Men.

Richard III builds on the characters, language and action of *3 Henry VI*, later published anonymously 'as . . . acted by . . . the Earle of Pembrooke his seruants' in the 1595 Octavo version (*The True Tragedy of Richard, Duke of York*). Performance of *3 Henry VI/Richard, Duke of York* can be approximately dated by the mockery of one of its lines in *Greene's Groatsworth of Wit* – 'Tiger's heart wrapped in a player's hide' (parodying 'O, tiger's heart wrapped in a woman's hide' (*3H6* 1.4.137). Since *Groatsworth* was entered in the Stationers' Register on 20 September 1592 (Arber, 2.292^v), the play that dramatically precedes *Richard III* had been written and probably staged – if the allusion were to be recognizable to readers – before 23 June 1592, after which the London theatres were closed due to unrest and kept shut due to plague until 27 December 1592 (only to be closed again in February 1593).[2] This timing coincides with Philip Henslowe's mention of a '*harey the vj*', marked 'ne' (used to indicate new, newly licensed or otherwise 'marketably new')[3] and performed fifteen times at the Rose theatre between 3 March and 19 June 1592 (Henslowe, 15–19). It is not certain which *Henry VI* play this entry refers to, but Henslowe usually listed initial plays of a sequence without a numerical marker.[4] When

1 Hammond's dating relies on ambiguous influences and shared commonplaces among *Richard III* and Marlowe's *Edward II* and *Faustus* (Hammond, 61); cf. *TxC*, 116. Against Honigmann's 'early start' hypothesis, see Sidney Thomas, 'On the dating of Shakespeare's early plays', *SQ*, 39 (1988), 187–94.
2 For the June 1592 closing, see Chambers, *Stage*, 4.310–11.
3 Knowles, *2H6*, 112; Roslyn Lander Knutson, 'The repertory', in John D. Cox and David Scott Kastan (eds), *A New History of Early English Drama* (New York, 1997), 467.
4 Roslyn Lander Knutson, 'Henslowe's naming of parts', *N&Q*, 228 (1983), 157–60.

coupled with Thomas Nashe's exactly contemporary reference to the onstage death of 'brave Talbot', Henslowe's listing suggests that Part 1 of *Henry VI* was being performed in early 1592, with the likelihood that Parts 2 and 3 had been performed previously (Burns, *1H6*, 5; Knowles, *2H6*, 113, 116).[1]

This evidence does not firmly date *Richard III*, but it would seem likely that composition would have been under way while the Henry VI plays were still being performed, sometime in early 1592. The plays are closely related verbally to *Richard III*, and the close of *3 Henry VI* leads directly into the opening of *Richard III*.[2] When *Richard III* was 'completed' is by definition unclear, since any play would be subject to ongoing modification according to playhouse practice and to the vagaries of performance. It was probably tinkered with right up to printing as Q1 in 1597 (and beyond that, for performance), but my guess would be that a longer substantial draft (FMS) would have dated from the months that followed the closing of the London theatres on 23 June 1592. A second, shorter derivative version (QMS) would have followed sometime before Q1's printing in 1597. This would date some form of *Richard III* as nearly contemporary with *Venus and Adonis* (Stationers' Register 18 April 1593) and *Rape of Lucrece* (Stationers' Register 9 May 1594), *Titus Andronicus* (Stationers' Register 6 February 1594) and *Comedy of Errors* (performed at Gray's Inn in December 1594).[3] Since the two poems alone run to 1194 and 1855 lines (together equivalent to about one and a half plays (George, 320)), it seems likely that Shakespeare did not tour during the intermission of 1592–3, but stayed put and wrote.

1   Arguments that champion sequential composition of the three parts of *Henry VI*, such as those by Hanspeter Born, Emrys Jones (*Origins*, 130–7), Andrew Cairncross and Michael Hattaway (*2H6*, ed. Michael Hattaway (Cambridge, 1991), 2, 61) oppose Kristian Smidt and J.D. Wilson concerning nonconformities among the plays (see Knowles, *2H6*, 113).

2   To be fair, arguing against connection is easy enough; see Smidt, *Unconformities*, for discrepancies.

3   Taylor finds the play's rare vocabulary closest to the *Henry VI* plays, *Titus* and *Comedy of Errors* (*TxC*, 116).

46

If *Richard III* had not been performed in London by June 1592, then it could not have been staged there before December 1593. This does not rule out performance outside London during the interrupted season of 1592–3. The reasons for thinking it had not been performed in London before the closing of the theatres in June 1592 are derived from Henslowe's relatively complete records for the period and from contemporary polemic.[1] The first responses to any Shakespearean play appear in 1592. *Greene's Groatsworth* attacks an 'vpstart' for penning plays instead of reciting lines written by others. Evidently confronted by those who understood these remarks to attack Shakespeare, Henry Chettle, the editor/author of the book attributed to Robert Greene, apologized.[2] Chettle's *Kind-Harts Dreame* (Stationers' Register 8 December 1592) treats Shakespeare as new on the scene, at least as writer rather than actor. Admitting that he had not been acquainted with Shakespeare before the publication of *Groatsworth* (September 1592), Chettle adds that since then, 'my selfe haue seene' Shakespeare's 'demeanor no lesse ciuill than he exelent in the qualitie he professes', and Chettle's sentence suggests that the 'profess[ion]' to which he refers is acting.[3] Chettle, a stationer and author with a hand in the theatre, thought of Shakespeare as only very recently a writer of plays in 1592.

In August 1592 another book was entered in the Stationers' Register that may also bear on the dating of *Richard III* by failing to mention it explicitly. No one is *au courant* if not Thomas Nashe. *Pierce Penilesse* (Stationers' Register 8 August 1592) defends playing by paying tribute to actors and roles, courts a potential patron associated with theatre and, uncharacteristically, forgoes a wonderful rhetorical opportunity – if Shakespeare's *Richard III*

1   Henslowe records Sussex's Men performing a '*Buckingham*' at the Rose in the December 1593–January 1594 period; no evidence suggests this is *Richard III*.
2   For authorship and allusion, see *Groatsworth*.
3   Chettle adds what he has heard 'reported' about Shakespeare's writing: 'Besides, diuers of worship haue reported, his vprightnes of dealing, which argues his honesty, and his facetious grace in writting, that aprooues his Art' (sig. A4ʳ).

had already been staged. Plays, with their subject matter 'for the most part . . . borrowed out of our English Chronicles', enable 'a rare exercise of vertue', Nashe asserts, and he praises a play that rescues from 'Oblivion' the 'braue *Talbot*', a role recently (and probably exclusively) portrayed in *1 Henry VI* (Nashe, 1.212).[1] Nashe also claims that the stage may dissuade audience members from particular evils:

> In Playes, all coosonages, all cunning drifts ouer-gulyded with outward holinesse, all stratagems of warre, all the cankerwormes that breede on the rust of peace, are most liuely anatomiz'd: they shew the ill successe of treason, the fall of hastie climbers, the wretched end of vsurpers, the miserie of ciuill dissention, and how iust God is euermore in punishing of murther.
>
> (Nashe, 1.213)

With the exception of military 'stratagems', virtually every element Nashe mentions is prominently represented in *Richard III*. An invocation of hypocritical, usurping Richard among hasty climbers and their just deserts would have nicely balanced the tribute to Talbot's virtues.[2] Elsewhere in *Pierce Penilesse* there is a possible glancing allusion to the Richard of *3 Henry VI*, but there is none to *Richard III*, where so many of Nashe's named evils are anatomized.[3]

Pierce Penilesse also appears to miss another rhetorical opportunity – if *Richard III* was already known. Apparently

1 Current estimates support Nashe's claims about large attendance for *Henry VI* at the Rose theatre in spring 1592; cf. Burns, *1H6*, 9. For a compelling argument concerning Nashe's own contribution to Act 1 of *1 Henry VI*, see Brian Vickers, 'Incomplete Shakespeare: or, denying coauthorship in *1 Henry VI*', *SQ*, 58 (2007), 311–52.

2 Hammond assumes that 'cunning drifts ouer-guylded with outward holinesse' refers to Richard (Hammond, 61). *Richard III* and *Pierce Penilesse* share the phrase 'dispaire and die' (*R3* 5.3.120; Nashe, 1.157), but this may reflect shared debt to *Faustus* (see *Doctor Faustus A- and B-texts (1604, 1616)*, ed. David M. Bevington and Eric Rasmussen, Manchester, 1993).

3 Nashe describes an ambitious man without 'comliness' who would swell to a 'mountaine', employing 'stratagems' to resist 'destine' and renouncing 'Father or Brother' (Nashe, 1.176); cf. *3H6* 3.2.124–95.

dedicated to Ferdinando Stanley, Lord Strange, *Pierce Penilesse* praises the star actor of Lord Strange's Men, Edward Alleyn (Nashe, 1.215), while lauding Lord Strange's ancestor Talbot (called 'Lord Strange of Blackmere', *1H6* 4.4.177) (Born, 324). If *Richard III* was then in existence, Nashe missed an opportunity to praise another ancestor of Strange's, since the play gives Thomas, Lord Stanley, later Earl of Derby, special prominence as a victim, defangs possible criticism of him and concludes by having him crown yet another Stanley ancestor, Henry of Richmond, as King Henry VII.

If *Richard III* was not performed in London before 1593, this would make it likely that it was initially staged there – exactly as Q1's 1597 title-page reports – by the Lord Chamberlain's Men, first formed in 1594 and incorporating players from Strange's and Pembroke's Men. After the closure in June 1592, London theatres were open only for five weeks in late December 1592 and January 1593 before plague shut them down again, and Henslowe's records for Strange's Men during this brief period are relatively complete (Rutter, 68–9). The London companies travelled (Strange's Men) or broke up (Pembroke's Men) or both (Queen's Men). Strange's Men are last seen as a company playing at Caludon Castle in Warwickshire on 5 December 1593. Two days later their plays begin to be entered for publication in the Stationers' Register (Arber, 2.303).[1] The theatres re-opened for a brief period on 27 December 1593, but it was not until June 1594 that the newly reorganized London companies began 'a season of unprecedented stability' that ran until March 1595 (Rutter, 84).

A first London performance in 1594 also accords with early references associating Richard's part with Richard Burbage and not with Edward Alleyn, who had probably played 'brave Talbot' in 1592. The twenty-eight-year-old Alleyn, famous as

1 Cf. Lawrence Manley, 'From Strange's Men to Pembroke's Men: *2 Henry VI* and *The First part of the Contention*', *SQ*, 54 (2003), 253–87.

Marlowe's Tamburlaine and Barabas, and since October 1592 son-in-law and business partner of Henslowe, did perform with Strange's Men for an indeterminate time, but by 1594 he was at the Rose with the Lord Admiral's Men; he would exit the stage in late 1597.[1] Burbage, twenty-six in 1594, was an experienced player who, having performed in London since at least 1590 (Chambers, *Stage*, 2.307), rapidly assumed prominence in the Lord Chamberlain's company (continued in the later King's Men), and eventually became one of the three men from his London life who Shakespeare remembered as his 'fellows' in his will.[2] Burbage is the only virtuoso actor of the period besides Alleyn who is known to have undertaken such enormously lengthy and demanding roles as Richard.[3] The play's initial London performances would then probably have been at the Theatre in Shoreditch, which was owned by Burbage's father, James.

Such dating also fits facts of publication. The anonymous Queen's Men play, *The True Tragedy of Richard III*, was entered in the Stationers' Register on 19 June 1594 – the very month that London theatres reopened.[4] *True Tragedy* is by most assessments older, and to be numbered among the Queen's Men plays – *The Troublesome Raigne of King John* (1591), *King Leir* (Stationers' Register 1594) and *The Famous Victories of Henry V* (Stationers' Register 1594) – that inspired Shakespearean versions.[5] Its

1   See S.P. Cerasano, 'Edward Alleyn', *ODNB*, vol. 1, 846–9.
2   Mary Edmond, 'Richard Burbage', *ODNB*, vol. 8, 716–18.
3   In March 1592 Alleyn probably portrayed Barabas in Marlowe's *The Jew of Malta* at Henslowe's Rose theatre. On large roles in Elizabethan public theatre plays, see Scott McMillin, *The Elizabethan Theatre and The Book of Sir Thomas More* (Ithaca, NY, 1987), 62–3.
4   Taylor suggests that this publication was an attempt to exploit the success of Shakespeare's play (*TxC*, 115), but the conjectured timing makes this unlikely (Roslyn Knutson, personal communication). It could have been an attempt at financial survival by the remnants of the Queen's Men. Between December 1593 and May 1595 the initial registrations of public playbooks peaked at twenty-seven publications, compared with three between January and November in 1593 and four from June to December 1595 (Blayney, 'Publication', 385). *The Jew of Malta* was entered on 17 May 1594.
5   For an opposing chronology, see Honigmann, *Impact*.

printing may have encouraged Q1's scrupulous licensing, since the entry for *True Tragedy* enumerates elements that, with the substantial exception of the 'lamentable end of Shores wife', broadly correspond to those of *Richard III*.[1] The financial risks in publishing a work of roughly similar content that might be judged to impact negatively the sale of another were substantial (Blayney, 'Publication', 399).

It has been suggested that *Richard III* was originally staged by Pembroke's Men and that Q1 represents a version staged on provincial tour during the months that the London theatres were closed.[2] John Jowett points to the prominence given both Stanley and Pembroke in Q1 and decides that the play was written 'as if for Strange's Men' but 'given finishing touches towards its close that make it suitable for the new Pembroke company'. This is plausible; however, Jowett adds that there are a good many 'ifs' in any such hypothesis (Jowett, 7–8).[3]

UPON RECORD? MORE'S *HISTORY*: 'PEACE . . . NOT MUCH SURER THEN WAR'

Richard III gets its plot and characters from the same historical compilations that furnished material for the three *Henry VI* plays. *Richard III* differs from them in being based on portions of Edward Hall's *Union* and Raphael Holinshed's *Chronicles* that come from Sir Thomas More's *History of King Richard III* (in slightly

1 '*The Tragedie of RICHARD the THIRD wherein is showen the Death of EDWARD the FFOURTHE with the smotheringe of the twoo princes in the Tower / . with a lamentable end of SHOREs wife / and the Coniunction of the twoo houses of LANCASTER and YORKE*' (Arber, 2.309ᵛ).

2 See Andrew S. Cairncross, 'Pembroke's Men and some Shakespearian piracies', *SQ*, 11 (1960), 339–40; Karl Wentersdorf, '*Richard III* (Q1) and the Pembroke "Bad" Quartos', *English Language Notes*, 14 (1977), 257–64; cf. Jowett, 'Derby', 8.

3 Gurr finds positive references to the Stanley family through all the Henry VI plays, but suggests Shakespeare's presence in a Pembroke's company at the Theatre in 1592–3 (Gurr, *Companies*, 262, 271). Some of the staging details Gurr enlists to support Shakespeare's presence in the company could have originated with sources such as *Mirror*.

differing versions). The contrasts between *Richard III* and the earlier history plays in form, characterization and language appear to be related to this difference in origin. *Richard III* follows More in focusing on a single character to whom other characters react. This concentration contributes to the play's claim to be among Shakespeare's first 'tragedies'. Other features of the play also come from More's vituperative, complexly ironic *History*.[1]

Whatever actually happened to bring Richard Plantagenet, later Duke of Gloucester and penultimately Lord Protector, to rule, and whatever occurred during his two-year reign (July 1483 to August 1485), More's usurping tyrant had established himself as 'history' before Shakespeare appropriated him via Hall and Holinshed.[2] Other accounts existed, but Shakespeare is unlikely to have known them, with the possible (insignificant) exception of Robert Fabyan's *Chronicle*.[3] More's *History* – written between 1513 and 1518 in English and Latin, unfinished, and unpublished in his lifetime – shares elements with other accounts, especially that of Polydore Vergil, the Tudors' royal historian.[4] More, supplemented by Vergil's *Anglicae historiae* (Basle, 1534), dominates all subsequent writing about Richard.

1 'More's authorial irony no less clearly anticipates Shakespeare's dramatic departures from the Tudor myth proper than the orthodox line which More's history in its "finished" forms did so much to establish' (Kinney, *Tyrant*, 53).

2 The extreme assessments stress either More's impressive accuracy (Sylvester, in *CW2*, lxxviii–lxxix) or his 'gross inaccuracies . . . willful distortions . . . bias . . . [and] positive virulence' (Kendall, 500).

3 G.B. Churchill's overview remains important. Early accounts of Edward IV had been recorded in a *Historie of the Arrival of Edward IV* by a Yorkist 'servaunt of the Kyngs' (1471) and in John Warkworth's additions to the *Chronicle of Brut* (*c.* 1484). Two Latin *Continuations* of the *History of Croyland Monastery* (1486) describe events up to Richard's deposing and death. Robert Fabyan produced *The new Chronicles of England and of France* (1516; editions in 1533, 1542, 1559), placing Richard within English and French history from the first century. The story to 1486 is recounted by John Rous (d. 1492), whose *Historia Regum Angliae* (published 1716, 1745) originates details of Richard's difficult birth and physiognomy. Other early accounts include the *History of Henry VII* (1500–3), by Bernard André, Henry VII's poet laureate (*Vita Henrici VII*, in James Gairdner (ed.), *Memorials of King Henry the Seventh* (1858)); the *Memoires de Philippe de Commines* (written 1488–1504), by a French counsellor of Charles the Bold and Louis XI; and the notes of Dominic Mancini, which remained in manuscript until 1936.

4 For textual history, see *CW2*, xvii–lix; also *CW15*.

The English *History* was first published when William Rastell, More's nephew, brought out the *Works* in 1557 (the Latin edition was published in Louvain in 1565). However, a version of More, supplemented by Vergil, had already appeared in Richard Grafton's addition to Hardyng's *Chronicle* (1543) and had been incorporated nearly verbatim, along with material from Commines, into Edward Hall's *Union* (1548). Another version of More, incorporating the material added to Hall, went into Holinshed's *Chronicles* (1577, 1587). More's material was invoked by sixteenth-century humanists and inspired literary works such as *The Mirror for Magistrates* (1559–1610), Thomas Legge's Latin university drama *Richardus Tertius* (performed 1579), the anonymous Queen's Men play, *The True Tragedy of Richard the Third* (1594), and at least one (lost) ballad (1586; Arber, 2.210^v). Each retelling adds and subtracts, framing Richard's story within different designs.

Roger Ascham lauds More's *History* for avoiding 'flattery and hatred' while providing 'causes cou[n]sels, actes, and issues' along with 'wisedome' for the future. He extols its temporal unity, characterization (providing not only 'the outward shape of the body' but also the 'inward dispositio[n] of the mynde') and linguistic decorum – it varies its language, as had Chaucer, 'higher and lower as matters do ryse and fall' (Ascham, 126). Modern detractors have criticized More for bias against Richard, whom Tudor apologists took to embody the previous dynasty, baronial ambition and factional discord. But More was no simple admirer of Henry VII, Richard's Tudor successor (the play's Richmond), and his claims are often corroborated by others, such as the Italian visitor Mancini.[1] Few would dispute Ascham's other assessments. More's narrative treats its material 'dramatically' and 'only secondarily as a repertory of morals or

1 See Antonia Gransden, *Historical Writing in England*, 2 vols (Ithaca, NY, 1982), 2.300–7; Mancini, 1–26; Hanham, 65–73. Mancini's reliability has been qualified (Horrox, 90–4).

a mere series of events' (Tillyard, 40).[1] Ascham's claims about antecedents also ring true: like Chaucer's *Canterbury Tales* or the mystery plays, the *History* mixes elevated tone, serious matter and noble characters with non-aristocratic figures and language, theology with jokes, 'historical' characters with caricatures. Its form traces the 'ryse and fall' pattern of 'tragedie' that Chaucer derived from Bocaccio as 'The harm of hem that stoode in heigh degree, / And fillen so ther nas no remedie' (Chaucer, 'Monk's Tale', ll. 1991–3).[2]

More provided a tightly focused sequence, with a centre of attention, interrelated characters and an overall shape. Beginning with the death of King Edward, proceeding through Richard's ruthless rise and rapid loss of control, the *History* closes with anticipations of the tyrant's destruction. Unlike Vergil, More does not place Richard's story within all of English history, nor does he embed Richard, as Hall does, in the Wars of the Roses. Richard and his brief tyranny provide dramatic scenes: King Edward's deathbed attempt to reconcile hostile factions (2.1); Buckingham's sleazy sophistry (3.1); Hastings's betrayal (3.4); the commoners' scepticism (3.6); Buckingham's failure to manufacture public support (3.7); Richard's staged reluctance to rule (3.7); his break with Buckingham (4.2); and his commissioning of Tyrrel to murder the princes (4.2). But the *History* also provides more.

More adapts precedents from Tacitus' Tiberian Rome to construct Christian providential interpretations of Richard's England (*CW*2, xci–xcii). Tacitus writes of Tiberius, proud of his 'ability to dissemble' (Tacitus, *Annals*, 4.71; cf. 6.50), More of Richard, 'a deepe dissimuler' (*CW*2, 8). Both stories chart factional politics amid omens, dreams, prognostications and sorcery (cf. *Annals*, 2.43, 6.22, 1.65, 12.22). Both tyrants violate kinship bonds: Tiberius kills 'his daughter-in-law, his brother's

---

1 Cf. Stuart Gillespie, *Shakespeare's Books: A Study of Shakespeare's Sources* (2001), to which my account is indebted.
2 *The Works of Geoffrey Chaucer*, ed. F.N. Robinson, 2nd edn (Boston, Mass., 1957).

son, his grand-children . . . fill[ing] his whole house with blood'
(*Annals*, 6.24); Richard kills brother, nephews, wife and family.
Surrounded by mourning widows and orphans (*Annals*, 3.1),
they suffer 'anguish of . . . heart' (*Annals*, 6.6) or '*inward
troubles*' (*CW2*, 87).

Both Tacitus and More appreciate ironies, but Tacitus'
reflections on the 'mockery of human plans in every transaction'
(*Annals*, 3.18) are not funny. Contrast More's treatment of
Jane Shore's humiliation. More opposes her pathos as a kind-
hearted, beautiful adulteress to Richard's repulsiveness as a
hard-hearted hypocrite, but her touching story ends with a
joke.[1] Unable to convince anyone that she has bewitched him
(see *R3* 3.4.66–71), Richard denounces her for lechery, and this
prompts More's ridicule. Her lechery was a thing that 'al yᵉ
world wist', More grants, yet 'euery man laughed . . . to here it
then so sodainly so highly taken, yᵗ she was nought of her body.
And for thys cause (as a goodly continent prince clene & fautles
of himself, sent oute of heauen into this vicious world for the
amendement of mens maners) he caused the bishop of London
to put her to open penance' (*CW2*, 54). This sarcastic caricature
of 'highly taken' priggishness anticipates the exaggerated piety
of Shakespeare's Richard.

However, More never permits us to laugh *with* Richard.
Even when Richard makes sardonic jokes, urging Rivers that
he 'should be well inough' just before having him executed, he
is always undercut. Rivers tops him by responding that such
greetings would be better sent to his nephew since the poor lad
is, alas, under Richard's protection (*CW2*, 20). Here is material
ripe for dramatic exploitation, but Shakespeare reserves almost

---

1 Shore might seem, More writes, 'to sleight a thing' to merit inclusion (*CW2*, 56),
   but she was a popular subject in the 1590s (see Esther Yael Beith-Halahmi, *Angell
   Fayre or Strumpet Lewd: Jane Shore as an Example of Erring Beauty in 16th Century
   Literature*, 2 vols (Salzburg, Austria, 1974)). For Shakespeare's failure to write about
   Shore, see Richard Helgerson, 'Weeping for Jane Shore', *South Atlantic Quarterly*,
   98 (1999), 451–76.

all the laughs for Richard while largely denying his victims wit or pathos. Hastings's demise makes a related point.

The downfall of Richard's Lord Chancellor attracted countless moralizers. Even Mancini, who seldom moralizes, reflects on Hastings's destruction 'not by those enemies he had always feared, but by a friend whom he had never doubted. But whom will insane lust for power spare, if it dares violate the ties of kin and friendship?' (Mancini, 90). Vergil emphasizes retributive justice, explaining that 'the law of nature wherof the gospell speaketh (what soever you will that men do unto yow, do you so also unto them) can not be broken without punishment' and reminding us of Hastings's role in killing Prince Edward (Vergil, 181).

Vergil's Hastings appears scarcely more than an embodied gospel moral. More puts him in a chain of circumstances that implicate his character and an entire mode of life. After recounting Stanley's dream about a violent boar on the eve of Hastings's betrayal by Richard, whose insignia is the boar, More's Hastings pronounces himself 'sure of the man' (*CW*2, 50; cf. *R3* 3.2.66–7). This foolhardy confidence persists despite repeated omens. His horse stumbles, 'a token often times notably foregoing some great misfortune' (*CW*2, 51). Then an anonymous figure inquires why Hastings speaks with a priest, having 'no nede of a prist yet', to which More adds, 'as though he would say, ye shal haue sone'; but Hastings 'so little mistrusted, that he was neuer merier nor neuer so full of good hope' (*CW*2, 51). According to the 'blindnes of our mortall nature', such confidence inevitably anticipates downfall, but Hastings was never 'so mery, nor neuer in so great suerty' (*CW*2, 51–2). In sum: 'Thus ended this honorable man, a good knight and a gentle, of gret aucthoritie w^t his prince, of liuing somewhat dessolate [dissolute], plaine & open to his enemy, & secret to his frend: eth [easy] to begile, as he that of good hart & corage forestudied no perilles. A louing man & passing wel beloued. Very faithful, & trusty ynough, trusting to much' (*CW*2, 52).

Trusty enough, trusting too much, More's mortal Everyman also embodies martial culture: a 'good knight' is uncalculating, openly hostile to enemies, loyal to friends, sexually dissolute but of 'good hart & corage', easy to beguile since he 'forestudied no perilles'. Hastings is the polar opposite of the strategy-obsessed, dissimulating, priggish Richard, but he also contrasts with More himself, the Christian humanist and political analyst, in embodying a chivalric honour culture that above all prizes loyalty to 'friends' and indifference to calculation.[1]

Thus More's *History* reveals a three-fold perspective: religiously, it portrays the insecurity of 'our mortall nature'; politically, it depicts a particular social order 'vnarmed' by factional 'deuision and discension'; and individually it represents characters whose 'demeanours' enable (Hastings), exploit (Richard) or endure (Jane Shore) this systemic failure. Richard's 'demeanour', his relentless 'desire of suerayntee', constitutes the 'whole matter' of the *History* (*CW*2, 5–6).

Although More does not follow John Rous (d. 1492) in comparing Richard to the Antichrist, he amplifies features from Rous that also appear in Vergil (Hanham, 123; Buck, 286–7). All three represent Richard's body, birth and behaviour as befitting one who breaks 'al the bandes . . . that binden manne and manne together, withoute anye respecte of Godde or the worlde' (*CW*2, 5–6). More inflates his reputed scapular inequality into literal 'croke backed' disability.[2] Richard was:

> little of stature, ill fetured of limmes, croke backed,
> his left shoulder much higher then his right, hard
> fauoured of visage, and suche as is in states called

1 On honour culture and calculation, see Mervyn James, *Society, Politics and Culture: Studies in Early Modern England* (Cambridge, 1986), 308–415. For humanist objections that warfare needed calculation, see Steven Marx, 'Shakespeare's pacifism', *RQ*, 45 (1992), 49–95. For the topicality of Erasmus and More, see Dominic Baker-Smith, '"Inglorious glory": 1513 and the humanist attack on chivalry', in Sidney Anglo (ed.), *Chivalry in the Renaissance* (1990), 129–44.

2 See Vergil, 226–7; Buck, 287. Rous's pro-Yorkist Roll extols Richard; his later, post-downfall writings render him the familiar monster (T.D. Kendrick, *British Antiquity* (1950), 21–2).

warlye, in other menne otherwise. He was malicious, wrathfull, enuious, and from afore his birth, euer frowarde. It is for trouth reported, that the Duches his mother had so muche a doe in her travaile, that shee coulde not bee deliuered of hym vncutte: and that hee came into the worlde with the feete forwarde, as menne bee borne outwarde, and (as the fame runneth) also not vntothed, whither menne of hatred reporte aboue the trouthe, or elles that nature chaunged her course in hys beginninge, whiche in the course of his lyfe many thinges vnnaturallye committed. None euill captaine was hee in the warre, as to whiche his disposicion was more metely then for peace. Sundrye victories hadde hee, and sommetime ouerthrowes, but neuer in defaulte as for his owne parsone, either of hardinesse or polytike order. Free was he called of dyspence, and sommewhat aboue hys power liberall, with large giftes hee get him vnstedfaste frendeshippe, for whiche hee was fain to pil and spoyle in other places, and get him stedfast hatred. Hee was close and secrete, a deepe dissimuler, lowlye of counteynaunce, arrogant of heart, outwardly coumpinable [companiable] where he inwardely hated, not letting [refraining] to kisse whome hee thoughte to kyll: dispitious and cruell, not for euill will alway, but ofter for ambicion, and either for the suretie or encrease of his estate. Frende and foo was muche what indifferent, where his advauntage grew, he spared no mans deathe, whose life withstoode his purpose.

(*CW*2, 7–8)

Even Richard's generosity amounts to bribery, his bravery an estate-specific knightly socio-pathology and his friendly gestures Judas-like. To this monster of calculation, More adds, crucially, that he a 'long time in king Edwardes life, forethought to be king' (*CW2*, 8; cf. Churchill, 122).[1] Shakespeare's Richard will start planning his rise before his play begins, despite multiple claimants ahead of him.[2]

But More's treatment of this 'long forethought' is maddeningly (and typically) elusive. 'Some wise menne' claim Richard helped eliminate Clarence five years before King Edward's death, and 'Menne constantly saye' that Richard 'slewe with his owne handes' King Henry VI, but 'of al this pointe, is there no certaintie, & whoso diuineth vppon coniectures, maye as wel shote to farre as to short' (*CW2*, 8–9).[3] More follows Tacitus in warning against anonymous reports (see *Annals*, 3.16), but More's sceptical rhetoric nevertheless invites readers to follow a chain of tenuous likelihoods. The credence granted More's account, notwithstanding such disclaimers, speaks for itself. Despite isolated resistance, such as George Buck's *History of King Richard the Third* (written before 1623), John Stow's qualifications, Sir William Cornwallis's ironic *Essayes* (1601) or Horace Walpole's *Historic Doubts on the Life and Reign of Richard III* (1768), More's hunchbacked, pre-meditating murderer has passed as history for five centuries.[4] This success in creating the effect of truth, despite or even because of disclaimers, suggests a rhetorical paradox of Shakespeare's play.

Could it have been More's seductive, insinuating narrator who inspired Shakespeare's novel treatment of his protagonist? More the master of rhetorical turns, with his engaging rhetoric of self-disabling admissions, pious admonitions, homely proverbs and lurid revelations, is a character we know far more intimately

1 For More's originality, see *CW2*, lxxix.
2 See *3H6* 3.3.124–195.
3 On the difficulty in tracking the multiple voices More employs, see Annabel M. Patterson, *Reading Holinshed's Chronicles* (Chicago, 1994), 110.
4 For Stow's reservations, see Elizabeth Story Donno, 'Thomas More and *Richard III*', *RQ*, 35 (1982), 445; D.R. Woolf, '"The common voice": history, folklore and oral tradition in early modern England', *Past and Present*, 120 (1988), 37. Stow reprints More in his own history (Buck, cxvii).

than his Richard.[1] The effect of More's entertaining verbal insinuations constitutes a rough analogue for the effect of Shakespeare's master of ceremonies, Richard, on virtually all audiences. Despite moral qualms, we are drawn, at least at first, to Richard's side.

We *ought* to disapprove. Visibly embodying 'vnnaturall' alienation from kin and kind, incarnating primal human evil, Shakespeare's Richard is 'curvatus', as biblical and patristic commonplace says sinful humankind is, bent away from the heavenly Creator.[2] Yet this limping caricature seduces characters and audiences. By contrast, More's Richard is neither attractive nor intimate with us. More invites no sympathy, never presents the world as Richard sees it, gives him no memorable speeches. Furthermore, the *History* omits crucial events. We hear nothing of Elizabeth of York, nor of the battle of Bosworth, nor of Richmond's marriage and coronation. These come to Hall, Holinshed and hence to Shakespeare, largely from Vergil, along with seductions, laments and histrionics.

More hereafter: Holinshed, Hall and The Mirror for Magistrates

By contrast with More's 'vnnaturall' monster of long 'forethought', Vergil's Richard is innocent of Clarence's death and lacks royal designs until Edward IV dies (Vergil, 173, 167–8). However, by the time of Hall's *Union* (1548) and *The Mirror for Magistrates* (1559), his guilt and forethought are presumed. If Shakespeare had only read these two texts he might have missed some of More's self-irony, but Shakespeare also read Holinshed, who retains more of the original's mixture of affirmation and scepticism.

Holinshed offered a combination of More with Hall and minor bits from others. Aside from the crucial factor of its stylistic

---

1   Shakespeare transfers 'More's alert sense of irony to Richard himself' (David Riggs, *Shakespeare's Heroical Histories: Henry VI and Its Literary Tradition* (Cambridge, Mass., 1971), 144).
2   See e.g. Augustine's *Ennarationes* (on Psalm 37), in Migne.

contributions, his *Chronicles* also provided some specifics: the bleeding of Henry VI's corpse (1.2.56; cf. Churchill, 216; Holinshed, 3.690–1); the punning prophecy of Richard's death (4.2.101–5; only in 1587 Holinshed, 3.746); the rewards promised to Buckingham (from More's Latin version) (3.1.195–6; Holinshed, 3.721), and the mistaken claim that Richmond had been brought up at his 'moothers meanes' (5.3.324; only in 1587 Holinshed, 3.756). Hall, drawing his More from Richard Grafton's 1543 Continuation of Hardyng's *Chronicle*, sometimes curtails More's rhetorical self-qualifications. For example, Hall repeats the claim that Richard acted on his own in murdering Henry VI but omits More's qualifiers concerning hearsay, giving the very words of the murderer.[1] By the 1550s it had become accepted fact that Richard saw to the execution of Clarence after having 'secretly stirr[ed] up Edward's suspicion and wrath against him while publicly pretending to intercede for him'.[2] *The Mirror for Magistrates* agrees (*Mirror*, 'Clarence', 332–47) and presumes his long 'forethought' (*Mirror*, 'Richard of Gloucester', 297).

Hall's *Union* casts Richard as the evil product of the 'vnnatural deuision' between York and Lancaster and as the opponent to its resolution in the marital 'vnion' that produced the Tudor succession. This holy conjunction is compared to the joining of 'Godhed to manhood' in the Incarnation (Hall, *Introduction*, fol. i^(r–v)). This stress on marriage is especially relevant to *Richard III*. Richard's murders are bad, Hall's Richmond admits, but attempting to marry his niece Elizabeth renders Richard 'a tyrau[n]t more then Nero, for he hath not only murdered his nephewe beyng his kyng and souereigne lorde, bastarded his noble brethern and defamed the wombe of his verteous and womanly mother, but also compased all the meanes and waies

---

1 See Hall, *Edward V*, fol. iˢ; for Commines, Fabyan, the Great Chronicle and Rous on Henry VI's death, and qualifiers about Richard's involvement, see Buck, 288.

2 A.R. Myers, 'Richard III and historical tradition', *History*, 53 (1968), 183. Rainolde makes Richard the physical perpetrator (Rainolde, fol. xiiiʳ).

yᵗ he coulde inuent how to stuprate and carnally know his awne nece vnder the pretence of a cloked matrimony' (Hall, *Richard III*, fol. lviʳ).

This nightmare rape/marriage of a York by a York would have prevented the grand wedding march of Hall's history, and the centrality of marriage to Tudor historical narratives explains other features of his account.[1] Hall exceeds Vergil in denouncing Elizabeth's mother for complying with Richard's desires, and he makes seduction a pervasive metaphor. Queen Elizabeth agrees to the 'vnlawfull and in maner vnnaturall copulacion' of uncle and niece that 'all men and the mayden her selfe' abhorred (Hall, *Richard III*, fol. xlixʳ). Vergil had denounced her female 'mutability' (Vergil, 210), but Hall fulminates against this surrender to Richard's 'will and pleasure' and her violation of every kinship bond, as if she were a female Richard.[2] Queen Elizabeth 'promised to submyt & yelde her selfe fully and frankely to the kynges will and pleasure. And so she putting in obliuion the murther of her innocente children, the infamy and dishonoure spoken by the kynge her husbande, the lyuynge in auoutrie [adultery] leyed to her charge, the bastardyng of her daughters, forgettyng also yᵉ feithfull promes & open othe made to the countesse of Richmond mother to yᵉ erle Henry, blynded by auaricious affeccion and seduced by flatterynge wordes' delivered her daughters to Richard as lambs to 'the rauenous wolfe' (Hall, *Richard III*, fol. xlviiiʳ; followed by Holinshed, 3.750).

Metaphors of seduction and forgetful 'obliuion' permeate Hall's account of the master dissembler's effects upon often complicitous victims.[3] The imagery of seduction even occurs in

1 Hall's Buckingham acclaims the marriage of Elizabeth and Richmond as inspired by 'the holy ghoste' (Hall, *Richard III*, fol. xxxvᵛ).
2 Holinshed allows that fear may have contributed, but 'women are of a proud disposition' (Holinshed, 3.750).
3 Queen Elizabeth is 'auaricious of affection'; Hastings and Buckingham 'easie to kyndle' with factional hatreds (Hall, *Edward V*, fol. vᵛ); Tyrrel 'nothing straunge' to Richard's manipulations because he is 'kept vnder' (Hall, *Richard III*, fol. xxviiʳ).

reference to Richard himself. Hall's Richard, like Vergil's and Grafton's (Vergil, 214; Hardyng, *Richard the iii*, fol. xcixʳ), falls prey to mortal 'security', but Hall describes him as 'seduced and deluded by hys craftie taletellers' into a 'golden slepe' (Hall, *Richard III*, fol. xlixᵛ; as Holinshed, 3.752). Hall's Richard is a seducer seduced, and he is also implicated, unlike More's (or Vergil's or Grafton's) tyrant, in three other themes relevant to Shakespeare's play: confession, self-exculpation and lamentation.

Hall's Richard actually publicly confesses his crimes, lamenting and blaming others for seducing him into seeking the throne. He admits that 'I being seduced & prouoked by sinister cou[n]sail and diabolical temptacio[n] did commyt a facynerous and detestable acte. Yet I haue with strayte penaunce and salt teryes (as I trust) expiated and clerely purged thesame offence, which abhominable cryme I require you of frendship as clerely to forget, as I dayly do remember to deplore and lament thesame' (Hall, *Richard III*, fol. livʳ⁻ᵛ; as Holinshed, 3.756). Nothing like this public confession appears in More, nor in Shakespeare's play, but in *Richard III* mock penitence and seduction are enormously elaborated in two wholly invented wooing scenes, while self-exculpation becomes all-pervasive, with virtually every character blaming others for his or her own problems and shortcomings.

Confession, contrition and lamentation permeate another of the play's sources, *The Mirror for Magistrates*. Lamentation constitutes the very substance of the *Mirror*, but Hall anticipates this tonality.[1] Expanding Vergil's account of responses to the deaths of the princes, Hall adds his usual tropes of seduction and obliviousness, but elaborates on the open weeping of 'all the people' in 'euery towne, streate, and place' and the 'lamentable crienge' of Queen Elizabeth herself:

> she was so sodainly amasyd with the greatnes of yᵉ
> crueltie that for feare she sounded [swooned] and fell

---

1   For More's single reference to lamentation, see *CW*2, 21.

doune to the ground, and there lay in a great agonye like to a deade corps. And after that she came to her memory and was reuyued agayne, she wept and sobbyd and with pitefull sighes she repleneshyed the hole mancion, her breste she puncted, her fayre here she tare and pulled in peces & being ouercome with sorowe & penciuenes rather desyred death then life, callyng by name diuers tymes her swete babes, accomptyng her self more then madde that she deluded by wyle and fraudulente promyses delyuered her younger sonne out of the sanctuarie to his enemye to be put to death thinkynge that nexte the othe made to God broke[n] & the dewtie of allegiaunce toward her childre[n] violated, she of all creatures in that poyncte was most seduced and disceaued. After longe lamentacion, when she sawe no hope of reuengynge otherwyse, she knelyd downe and cried on God to take vengeaunce for the disceaytfull periurie, as who saide that she nothyng mystrusted but once he would remember it. What ys he liuyng that if he remember and beholde these .ii. noble enfantes with out deseruing, so shamefully murthered, that wil not abhorre the fact, ye & be moued & tormented with pitie and mercie. And yet the worlde is so frayle and our nature so blynde that fewe be sturred with suche examples, obliuiouslie forgettynge, and littell consyderyng, that oftentimes for the offences by the parentes perpetrate and committed, that synne is punished in there lyne and posterite.

(Hall, *Richard III*, fols xxviii^v–xxix^r;
cf. Vergil, 189–90)

Here is the lamentation and complaint that pervade *Richard III*, but here, too, there is another side to the story.

The object of complaint is not the ultimate cause of the loss that is lamented; Hall's Richard merely represents a cog in the great wheel of divine judgement. Following Vergil, Hall treats the deaths of the princes as transgenerational payback for the sins of their father. Even Richard's means, his 'disceaytfull periurie', replays Edward's own crime: the princes die 'because king Edward . . . promised and sware one thing by his worde thinkyng cleane contrarie in his harte as after dyd appere. And afterward by the death of the duke of Clarence his brother, he incurred (of likelyehod) the great displeasure toward God' (Hall, *Richard III*, fol. xxix^r; following Vergil, 189–90).

As the wheels of justice turn, some of Hall's characters foresee the process. Hall invents Margaret the suffering prophet with futile foresight:

> she muche lamented, and bewailed the euill fate and destenie of her husbande, whiche eminently before her iyes, she sawe to approche she accused, reproued, and reuiled, and in conclusion, her senses were so vexed, and she so afflicted, and caste into suche an agony, that she preferred death before life, rather desiryng soner to die, then lenger to liue, and perauenture for this cause, that her interior iye sawe priuily, and gaue to her a secret monicion of the greate calamities and aduersities, whiche then did hang ouer her hed, and were likely incontinent to fall and succede (whiche other persones, neither loked for nor regarded[)]
>
> (Hall, *Edward IV*, fols ccxviii^v–ccxix^r; not in Holinshed)[1]

Suffering grants an 'interior iye' to see the future, but Margaret's own pains amount to punishments for earlier sins. Mortals take note.

Hall's inevitable divine retribution, accompanied with copious accusation and lamentation, anticipates *The Mirror for*

---

1 See W. Gordon Zeefeld, 'The influence of Hall on Shakespeare's English historical plays', *English Literary History*, 3 (1936), 317–53. Hall also depicts Margaret mourning the 'losse of Prince Edward her sonne' (Hall, *Edward IV*, fol. ccxxi^v).

Magistrates.[1] In minor specifics, the *Mirror* probably provided Shakespeare with the punch-line about Clarence being 'new christened' (1.1.50; see *Mirror*, 'Clarence', 370–1) and Richard's relations with his mother (Jones, *Origins*, 217). No one before Shakespeare says the Duchess reviled Richard (*R3* 4.4.137–96); however, the *Mirror*'s lame 'Claudius' (who married his niece) reports maternal abuse in lines anticipating Richard's opening soliloquy: 'me a monster oft she namde, / Vnperfect all, begun by nature, but begot / Not absolute, not well, nor fully framde. / Sith thus my mother often me defamde' (*Mirror*, *Additions*, 'Claudius', 8–12; cf. *R3* 1.1.19–21).[2]

More importantly, the *Mirror* anticipates another verbal aspect of *Richard III*. Amid predictable generalities about fickle fortune, the *Mirror* models its world on courtly existence, where the main sins are ambitious scheming and climbing and the likely end a sudden plunge into ruin (Jones, *Origins*, 193). Shakespeare's Hastings, who compares the 'momentary grace of mortal men' to precarious elevation above the deep (3.4.95–100), would be completely at home. But the *Mirror* also provides intensely emotional representations of interiority unparalleled in More, Vergil, Grafton, Hall or Holinshed. Hall leaves Richard's inner workings 'to God whiche knewe his interior cogitations at the hower of his deathe' (Hall, *Richard III*, fol. lix^r; cf. Holinshed's expansion, 3.761). The *Mirror*'s Richard merely reports his evil nature and deeds, but other Ricardian figures suggest a greater contribution to Shakespearean characterization.

Thomas Sackville's famous 'Induction' and 'Complaint of Buckingham' turn generic signs of grief – torn hair, rent cloak, broken voice and tear-filled eyes – into dramatic means (*Mirror*, 'Induction', 533–53). Buckingham's language derives from formal complaint, a generic resource exploited in the *Henry*

---

1 The *Mirror* was first published in 1559 with three relevant complaints; the 1563 edition added six others (Bullough, 3.229). It was further expanded in 1587.

2 Richard's reference to premature birth contradicts Rous's two-year gestation (C. Ross, *Richard*, 139) and the Duchess's claim at 4.4.163–4.

VI plays. Calling down vengeance on his betrayer Banister, Buckingham curses himself, the hour, the time, the place of meeting, the sun, moon and stars, earth and air ('Buckingham', 638–51).[1] But finding invective insufficient, he confronts the question that plagues the victims of Shakespeare's Richard, asking 'Howe shall I curse . . . what shal I say?' (656, 664; cf. *R3* 4.4.117). As the women demand that the earth split (1.2.65, 4.4.75), invoking despair (1.2.84–6) and family destruction (1.2.21–8, 1.3.198–200), so Buckingham wishes the earth 'rent in twaye' (657), urging that Banister 'despayer' (673), that he 'wayle the daye, and wepe the night' (675), that his children die (691–705) while he 'live in death, and dye in lyef' (710).[2] His curses also suggest ironies relevant to Shakespeare's play, as one betrayer curses another with a curse – to 'live in death, and dye in lyef' – that articulates the end that will come home to the curser himself (see 719).

The *Mirror* might also have influenced *Richard III* in another, related matter. No matter how formulaic, Jane's Shore's curses on Richard (*Mirror*, 'Shore's Wife', 330–6) are revealing in a historical sense and significant for a consideration of Shakespeare's railing women. Amid pathetic self-accusations and exculpations, she alone actually curses the tyrant king.[3] Her verbal attack registers a highly relevant gendered asymmetry in the historical treatment of abuse directed against a monarch.

UPON SCAFFOLDS: MORE, HOLINSHED, LEGGE, *TRUE TRAGEDY*

A two-way relationship between Richard's narrative and the stage begins with classical metaphors likening life to a play. Sir Thomas More and the sources dependent on his *History* develop

1 Cf. *3H6* 1.4.111–68; Baldwin, 2.335.
2 The fates he wishes on Banister's children are those Hall says befell Buckingham's own offspring (Churchill, 255).
3 See Mary Steible, 'Jane Shore and the politics of cursing', *SEL*, 43 (2003), 1–17.

this trope. By the early 1590s two dramatic works – in addition to *2* and *3 Henry VI* – had staged Richard: Thomas Legge's Latin drama *Richardus Tertius*, performed at Cambridge in 1579 and widely circulated in manuscript, and the anonymous *True Tragedy of Richard III* (Stationers' Register 19 June 1594), 'playd by the Queenes Maiesties Players'.[1] One other performance, a 1559 London pageant recorded in Holinshed's reprint of Richard Mulcaster's account, deserves attention.

The *theatrum mundi* image comes to More with a history.[2] It appears in its traditional form in *The Mirror for Magistrates*, which compares human existence to a performance played before God and the audience of history (e.g. *Mirror*, 'Buckingham', 43–6). However, More turns cosmic metaphysics to social satire. Calling Richard's Guildhall bid for citizen approval a 'mocckish ellection', More invokes 'Kynges games, as it were stage playes . . . plaied vpon scafoldes', and likens social rituals to stage performance. Social life demands that ordinary people 'forget' mundane identities to sustain assigned public roles and observe their limits – or risk the consequences. More offers an important illustration: 'menne must sommetime for the manner sake not bee a knowen what they knowe. For at the consecracion of a bishop, euery man woteth well by the paying for his bulles, y^t he purposeth to be one . . . And yet must he bee twise asked whyther he wil be bishop or no, and he muste twyse say naye, and at the third tyme take it as compelled ther vnto by his owne wyll' (*CW*2, 80–1). While they here exemplify public rituals, kingship and episcopacy were historical institutions of particular concern – for More, and for Shakespeare and his first audiences. Representing a monarch or a bishop on the theatrical scaffold, or posing questions about their social magic, could earn a one-way trip to another scaffold.

Historians have debated the extent of early modern censorship, but sensitivities about potential official reactions were a factor in textual production, in performance and in oral communication

---

1 See Arber, 2, fol. 309^v.
2 More translates Lucian's *Menippus*; see More, *CW*3, 25–43.

in the late 1580s and early 1590s.[1] By November 1589, well into the furious Marprelate exchanges about the office of bishop, the Privy Council fulminated that 'players take vppon them to handle in their plaies certen matters of Divinytie and of State unfit to be suffred' and instructed the Archbishop of Canterbury, the Lord Mayor of London and Edmund Tilney, Master of the Revels, to appoint someone to scrutinize plays performed in London.[2] Michael Hattaway has argued that the *Henry VI* plays show either Tilney's censorship or the players' self-censorship.[3] In March 1591 Spenser's *Complaints* (Stationers' Register 29 December 1590), with its *Mother Hubbard's Tale* suggesting allegorical reference to Lord Burghley and his son Robert Cecil, was called in (Peterson, 10). By the end of the decade, the 1599 Bishops' Ban would insist that 'noe English historyes be printed excepte they bee allowed by somme of her maiesties privie Counsell' and 'noe playes bee printed excepte they bee allowed by such as have aucthorytie' (Arber, 3.316).[4]

Despite official sensitivities, historical persons and events furnished the material for public pageants as well as for the numerous stage representations that make the late sixteenth century the golden age of the history play. Holinshed's *Chronicles* preserves one officially approved staging relevant to *Richard III* in Mulcaster's account of a pageant that had greeted the young Queen Elizabeth on the way to her coronation at Westminster Abbey in 1559:

> Upon the lowest stage was made one seat roiall, wherein
> were placed two personages, representing king Henrie
> the seuenth, and Elizabeth his wife, daughter of
> king Edward the fourth . . . king Henrie the seuenth

1 See *Literature and Censorship in Renaissance England*, ed. Andrew Hadfield (Basingstoke, 2001).
2 *Acts of the Privy Council, 1524–1604*, ed. J.R. Dasent (1890–1907), 18.214–15.
3 Hattaway, *Companion*, 15; cf. Janet Clare, *Art Made Tongue-Tied by Authority: Elizabethan and Jacobean Dramatic Censorship* (Manchester, 1990), 39–43, and Cyndia Clegg, *Press Censorship in Elizabethan England* (Cambridge, 1997).
4 Even the *Mirror* evidences official disapproval (Budra, 22–3).

proceeding out of the house of Lancaster, was inclosed in a red rose, and ... queen Elizabeth, being heire to the house of Yorke, inclosed with a white rose, each of them roiallie crowned, and decentlie apparelled, as apperteineth to princes, with scepters in their hands, and one vawt surmounting their heads, wherein aptlie were placed two tables, each conteining the title of those two princes. And ... the one of them joined hands with the other, with the ring of matrimonie perceiued on the finger. Out of the which two roses sprang two branches gathered into one, which were directed vpward to the second stage or degree, wherein was placed one representing ... king Henrie the eight, which sproong out of the former stocke, crowned with a crowne imperiall, and by him sat one representing the right woorthie ladie queene Anne, wife to the said king Henrie the eight, and mother to our most souereigne ladie queene Elizabeth that now is ... From their seat also proceeded vpwards one branch, directed to the third and vppermost stage or degree, wherein likewise was planted a seat roiall, in the which was set one representing the queenes most excellent maiestie Elizabeth, now our most dread and souereigne ladie, crowned and apparelled as the other princes were. Out of the fore part of this pageant was made a standing for a child, which at the queens maiesties comming declared vnto hir the whole meaning of the said pageant ... And all emptie places thereof were furnished with sentences concerning vnitie, and the whole pageant garnished with red roses and white. And in the fore front of the same pageant, in a faire wreath, was written ... The vniting of the two houses of Lancaster and Yorke. This pageant was grounded vpon the queens maiesties name. For like as the long warres between the two houses of Yorke and Lancaster then ended, when

Elizabeth daughter to Edward the fourth matched in
marriage with Henrie the seuenth, heire to the house
of Lancaster: so sith that the queenes maiesties name
was Elizabeth, & for somuch as she is the onelie heire
of Henrie the eight, which came of both the houses,
as the knitting vp of concord: it was deuised, that like
as Elizabeth was the first occasion of concord, so she
another Elizabeth, might mainteine the same among
hir subiects, so that vnitie was the end wereat the whole
deuise shot, as the queenes maiesties name moued the
first ground.

(Holinshed, 3.1173)

Here history is staged along with current events and future
hopes 'concerning vnitie'. Even the location in 'Gracious'
(Gracechurch) Street may have borne topical significance, since
Elizabeth's mother, Anne Boleyn, had there witnessed a pageant
for her own coronation.[1] Men must sometimes forget what they
know, More might say, since in 1559 Anne appears represented as
an honoured queen and mother of the new Queen Elizabeth and
not as disgraced, divorced and doomed. The onstage Elizabeth
of York confronts 'another Elizabeth' in the audience, her royal
granddaughter, who herself also appears replicated elsewhere on
the stage. This 'history' obviously depends on a highly edited
past. It omits Yorkist kings, other wives (or heirs) for Henry VIII
and other claimants, while implicating an immediate, offstage
present.

The warring Houses and the 'chair of estate' for which they
contended are woven into a peaceful arbour. The White Rose
of York and the Red Rose of Lancaster conjoin in the union
of Elizabeth of York with Henry of Richmond, the first Tudor
monarch, and grow upwards towards Henry VIII and Anne,
who produce Elizabeth I. The conjugal handclasp and 'ring
of matrimonie . . . on the finger' of Elizabeth of York must

1   A. Kinney, 20; Mulcaster's pageant appears in the same volume.

have put pressure on the new Elizabeth, who witnessed herself portrayed as the sole uncoupled figure. Perhaps eager to appear the antithesis to her late sister Queen Mary, whose reign (1553–8) had seen persecution of Protestants, marital alliance with Philip of Spain and the loss of Calais (A. Kinney, 20), the new Queen expressed no umbrage at this representation. In a few years, such pointedly topical history would have been very risky. Later Elizabethans would lose their freedoms, limbs and even lives for venturing stage advice about matrimony, succession or Church government.

This highly edited royal flow-chart proclaims from the scaffold that 'ciuill warre, / and shead of bloud did cease, / When these two houses were / vnited into one' (Holinshed, 3.1173); offstage, political life, like family life, proved more complicated. Issues that would trouble the later sixteenth century haunt Mulcaster's mid-century account. The dynastic rose-bush was extensively filiated, giving the authors of polemics such as *Leicester's Commonwealth* (1584) a reason to worry and providing guerilla genealogies, such as Robert Parsons's *Conference* (1595) with a dozen or so budding royal alternatives. Then there is religious division. Just steps beyond the signs urging 'concord', other pageants demanded that 'religion true' should 'break Superstitions head' and quash 'rebellion' (Holinshed, 3.1174). Protestant and Catholic, Protestant and Protestant would continue at odds throughout the century. The years immediately following the Armada of 1588 saw the Marprelate controversy concerning ecclesiastical government, Archbishop Whitgift's vigorous repression of Puritans – and Shakespeare's first plays. Reading about the hopeful pageants of the 1550s might remind Englishmen of the 1590s that Queen and Church would not end divisiveness, even amongst family.

A Londoner of the 1590s might have registered an irony in the 1559 pageant when the gift of an English Bible prompts Elizabeth to turn for assistance to Sir John Perrot, her reputed bastard half-brother. In 1590 Perrot was removed from the

1 Family tree from Edward Hall, *The Union of the Two Noble and Illustre Families of Lancastre and Yorke* (edition of 1550)

Privy Council and sensationally tried for treason. Among other charges, it was alleged that he had protested the ignominy of serving 'a base bastard piss-kitchin woman' (Howell, 1.1321). Perrot's meteoric fall, dramatic trial, notorious imprisonment – first in Burghley's home and then in the Tower – and his death in September 1592 were 'the speache of the Towne' as Shakespeare composed *Richard III*.[1] So much for family unity. Furthermore, though 'treason' provided the official explanation for Perrot's fall, an alternative narrative claimed that he had been betrayed by Burghley, suggesting new levels of brutal factionalism within Elizabeth's government and enlarging public awareness of internal divisions (Hammer, 398). Sound familiar? Dire divisions and subtle deceptions, nasty family infighting and abrupt, contrived downfalls pervade *Richard III*. More's *History* lent itself to such themes, although dramatic treatments could be highly various, as in Legge's Latin *Richardus Tertius* and the anonymous public stage play *The True Tragedy of Richard the Third*.

Richardus Tertius was widely known despite its language, length (some 4,700 lines), single academic performance and its remaining in manuscript until modern times. The 1579 staging at St John's College, Cambridge, constituted 'perhaps the most ambitious dramatic performance ever attempted in England (before or since)'.[2] On successive nights, one Actio of the play's three was performed with the same lead actor and a cast of over one hundred men and boys. It included a coronation scene, battlefield gunfire and a horse to bear Richard's corpse.[3] The text circulated widely in multiple manuscripts. In 1591 Sir John Harington, who may have witnessed the performance, recalled the play's ethical power, saying it 'would moue (I thinke) *Phalaris* the tyraunt, and terrifie all tyranous minded men, fro[m]

---

1 See Thomas Tresham's letter of March 1591 (Peterson, 22).
2 Nelson, 61.
3 Nelson, 61; citing *REED*, 1.918–19, 944–6; see also 847; cf. *Richardus Tertius*, xiii; 4588.

following their foolish ambitious humors, seeing how [Richard's] ambition made him kill his brother, his nephews, his wife beside infinit others; and last of all after a short and troublesome raigne, to end his miserable life, and to haue his body harried after his death'.[1] Harington's ethical defence is interesting, since the actor who portrayed Legge's Richard was the first to be implicated in the claim that the role negatively affected his offstage existence.[2] Anecdotes connecting scaffold and life would dog stage Richards from Richard Burbage (see p. 83) to John Wilkes Booth (Wood, 164).

Scholars disagree about Legge's influence on *Richard III*.[3] Some shared elements appear coincidental: Norfolk obtains postponement of Lord Strange's execution; Richmond interviews Stanley and citizens react to England's troubles (*Richardus Tertius*, 2649–706; Bullough, 3.235). Other elements might reflect Legge's influence on *True Tragedy*. Strikingly, however, Legge and Shakespeare emphasize female roles and provide two major wooing scenes unparalleled in *True Tragedy*.[4]

Legge twice portrays wooing by Richard or his proxy. As in *Richard III* (1.2, 4.4), only one attempt succeeds. Lovell, at Richard's direction, induces Queen Elizabeth to hand over her daughters so that Richard can bestow 'splendid marriages' on them (*Richardus Tertius*, 3901–4206). Stichomythic exchanges balance her recriminations against Lovell's testimony that Richard's 'face is wet with weeping' for having murdered her two sons and his insinuations of profit and protection for her surviving son; Elizabeth accepts the bargain. The second wooing scene contradicts Legge's sources to represent Richard

1 'An Apologie of Poetrie', in *Orlando Furioso* (1591; STC 746), sig. ¶vi^r. Francis Meres includes Legge among 'our best for Tragedy' (Meres, sig. Oo3^{r–v}).

2 Thomas Fuller writes, he 'had his head so possest with a Princelike humor, that ever after, he did what then he acted' (quoted in *REED*, 1.286).

3 Churchill and Bullough find parallel divergence from sources; Brooks and Hammond attribute these to Seneca (Bullough, 3.234–7; Brooks, 'Unhistorical', 721–37; Hammond, 82). Cf. Robert J. Lordi, 'The relationship of *Richardus Tertius* to the main Richard III plays', *Boston University Studies in English*, 5 (1961), 149–53.

4 In *True Tragedy* Lovell reports Richard's suit positively received by Queen Elizabeth and her daughter. Richard woos neither in Heywood's *Edward IV*.

personally wooing Elizabeth of York; this scene draws on Seneca's *Hercules Furens*, and for one detail – Richard's drawn sword – Seneca's *Hippolytus/Phaedra*.[1] A sword will play a pivotal role in Shakespeare's – similarly unprecedented – depiction of Anne's seduction (1.2).

Shakespeare may have been directly influenced by Seneca. Neither Legge nor *True Tragedy* makes female lament as pervasive as does Shakespeare, but Seneca's *Troades* brings together three generations of women, 'each with its own memories and griefs' (Bullough, 3.236). The Duchess of York's claim to be the mother of all 'parcelled' griefs (2.2.80–1) parallels Hecuba's claims: 'Whosesoever woes thou weepest, thou wilt weep mine. Each feels the weight of his own disaster only, but I the disasters of them all' (Seneca, *Troades*, 1060–2). However, *Troades* lacks a central tyrant, and it amply conveys pathos that Shakespeare avoids, including the taking of a child, Astyanax, from the arms of his weeping mother (Seneca, *Troades*, 786–812).

Although generally following chronicle sources, Legge makes Richard neither very deformed nor especially strong. The single reference to his withered arm occurs in the well-known plot against Hastings (*Richardus Tertius*, 1679); otherwise, his body prompts neither self-reflection nor ridicule. Although Richard's lust for power is characterized as disease, madness, murderousness, guile and hypocrisy (*Richardus Tertius*, xviii), he is not More's strong, resourceful character. Instead, he is fearful, declamatory and directed by others (Churchill, 376–9). Catesby appears initially more Ricardian than Richard, with personal reasons for resenting Hastings and a design to dupe Richard into acting at his direction (*Richardus Tertius*, 1425–37, 1533–70).[2]

Legge's dramatic innovations consist of his close adherence to historical record in a drama that incorporates Senecan elements – bloody tyrant, stichomythic dialogue, choric observers, *nuntius* figures and animating supernatural spirits – within a trilogy

1 See Whitaker, 66.
2 Cf. the blame heaped on 'Lawyer Catesby' (*Mirror*, 'Rivers', 456–62).

(*Richardus Tertius*, 269–72; cf. Hodgdon, *End*, 238). Seneca's tyrant and focused action are recast within a format 'vastly larger and more complex in structure and in narrative scope than a Senecan tragedy' (*Richardus Tertius*, xv). Shakespeare need not have read *Richardus Tertius* for its form to have suggested historical tetralogy. There is no doubt he did know – though we are unsure by when – a work indebted to Legge, *The True Tragedy of Richard III*.

True Tragedy and *Richard III* share features that have prompted debate about priority and influence.[1] Their strongest connection is the resemblance between 'A horse, a horse, a fresh horse' (*True Tragedy*, 1984) and 'A horse, a horse, my kingdom for a horse!' (*R3* 5.4.7).[2] Their differences are more revealing.

True Tragedy's prologue describes Richard as 'ill shaped, crooked backed, lame armed, withall, / Valiantly minded, but tyrannous in authoritie' (*True Tragedy*, 57–8), but his physical limitations occasion little comment and provide no motivation. As in Legge, Richard blames Jane Shore for his 'withered arme' (946). The only other reference occurs in a patch of Senecan rant: 'this verie day, I hope with this lame hand of mine, to rake out that hatefull heart of Richmond, and when I haue it, to eate it panting hote with salt, and drinke his blood luke warme' (1978–81). Similar rhetoric, foreign to Shakespeare's play, permeates *True Tragedy*.[3] In their self-direction, the two Richards resemble one another more than Legge's manipulated figure. But the great dissimulation is missing from *True Tragedy*'s Richard, who suffers recurrent

---

1 Contrast Hammond, 83, with Churchill, 398; see also Bullough, 3.237, and J.D. Wilson, 'Shakespeare's *Richard III* and *The True Tragedy of Richard the Third, 1594*', *SQ*, 3 (1952), 299–306.

2 George Peele's *Battell of Alcazar* (1594; STC 19531, sig. F3ʳ) has a fleeing character cry, 'A horse, a horse, villaine a horse'. Neither Hall's nor Holinshed's Richard loses a horse, as Shakespeare's does (5.4.4), but both refuse one offered as a means of flight, as do the Richards of *True Tragedy* and *Richard III* (Hall, *Richard III*, fol. lviiiʳ; Holinshed, 3.759–60). For another similarity see 3.1.84–8. In *Edward III* (Stationers' Register 1595) Prince Edward refuses a horse for flight before battle (*E3* 4.4.88–99).

3 *True Tragedy* includes lines that Hamlet parodies: 'The screeking Raven sits croking for reuenge. / Whole heads of beasts comes bellowing for reuenge' (1879–93).

bouts of conscience (Churchill, 472–3) and is no seducer. He neither woos Anne, nor attempts to win over Queen Elizabeth or her daughter Elizabeth. Nor do female figures have extended laments and accusations, although the treatment of Elizabeth of York is suggestive.

The title of *True Tragedy* promises the 'coniunction' of York and Lancaster, and Elizabeth of York appears at Bosworth to agree to wed Richmond, prompting a messenger to declare: 'Thus Gentles may you heere behold, the ioyning of these Houses' (2164–5). That settled, the play concludes with Tudor genealogy and an encomium to Elizabeth I. Because Elizabeth I's Protestant piety and Tudor family values have 'put proud Antichrist to flight / And bene the meanes that ciuill wars did cease', the audience is enjoined: 'Then England kneele vpon thy hairy knee, / And thanke that God that still prouides for thee' (2206–7).[1] Legge similarly concludes with thanks for 'our mighty sovereign Elizabeth' (*Richardus Tertius*, 4695–6). Both plays express concern about the future.

In 1579 Legge praises the 46-year-old Queen as 'a virgin who overcomes the hoary locks of age', and prays, 'May the thunderer hold His hand over her and make long her life' (*Richardus Tertius*, 4696–701). A decade later, *True Tragedy* proclaims that Elizabeth ought 'to liue for aye', but adds anxiously, 'if her Graces dayes be brought to end, / Your hope is gone, on whom did peace depend' (*True Tragedy*, 2220–3). At the conclusion of Shakespeare's *Richard III*, Richmond invites the audience to consider England's prosperity under his descendants, but this, the play's only straightforward political speech (Campbell, 333–4), neither wishes Elizabeth I eternal life nor denounces ambition and tyranny. Richmond prays for 'peace' and warns against 'treason' and 'traitors':

> That would reduce these bloody days again
> And make poor England weep in streams of blood.

1   RP suggests 'hairy' is a misprint for 'harty'.

> Let them not live to taste this land's increase
> That would with treason wound this fair land's peace.
> Now civil wounds are stopped; peace lives again.
> That she may long live here, God say amen.
>
> (5.5.36–41)

Charges of 'treason' against Richard and followers had historical precedent, and *True Tragedy*'s Richmond proclaims 'traytrous Richard' shall be 'drawne through the streets of *Lester*, / Starke naked on a Colliers horse' – 'a traytors due reward' (2153–7).[1] The physical details come from Hall, but not the terms. Hall's Richard concludes a 'caytiue' whose crimes are 'ambicion tyranny and myschiefe' (Hall, *Richard III*, fol. lix^r).[2]

Whether seen as a 'history' of the years 1483–5, a timeless 'tragedy' or a mixture of the two, *Richard III* also addresses the 1590s. Its quasi-epilogue warning against treason registers extra-dramatic concerns; its quasi-prologue, uniquely for Shakespeare spoken by the protagonist, conveys others. A misfit soldier without a war, a 'deformed' malcontent younger brother, an ambitious 'villain' sowing faction by 'plots', 'prophecies, libels and dreams', a pious hypocrite, 'seem[ing] a saint' when most he plays the devil, a 'determined' reprobate – this patchwork nightmare limps right out of late Elizabethan anxieties.

UPON STAGES

Since the rich stage history of *Richard III* has been the subject of several books, what follows is a mere sketch.[3] Its worldwide heritage as most popular of the histories in languages other than English lies largely beyond this brief survey.[4]

---

1 On historical charges of treason against Richard's forces, see Chrimes, 63.
2 Richard is not called traitor in the equivalent passage in Holinshed, 3.760.
3 See Wood, Hankey, Colley, Hassel, Richmond and Day.
4 For popularity, see Hoenselaars, 110–11. For international productions 1949–84, see *Shakespeare Around the Globe*, ed. Samuel L. Leiter (New York, 1986).

Beginnings to 1642

The 1597 First Quarto claims itself 'lately Acted by the / Right honourable the Lord Chamber- / laine his seruants'. The first documented performance is recorded as having been given in 1633 at St James's Palace on Queen Henrietta Maria's birthday (Chambers, *Shakespeare*, 2.352). The play still belonged to company repertory, the King's Men having formed from the Lord Chamberlain's Men in 1603, and evidently remained interesting after nearly forty years. When the theatres reopened after the Civil War, its popularity is briefly unclear. After 1700, it appealed widely, whether in the adaptation by Colley Cibber (from 1700), in translation or eventually as, mostly, itself – in England, in pre-Revolutionary America, black New York in the 1820s, King Kamehameha IV's Honolulu court in the 1850s, Italy in the late nineteenth century, Germany in the 1930s, eastern Europe in the 1970s and France in the 1980s and 1990s.[1]

Richard III also ranks among the most frequently printed Elizabethan plays (Blayney, 'Publication', 388).[2] It is undeniably the first of Shakespeare's very long plays; it appears to have been the longest single stage play ever written in English, and remained so until Q 1604 *Hamlet*. Either it was abbreviated for staging, or its performance took more time than the Elizabethan average.[3] Its later history consists of abbreviations and compromises,

1 *Richard III* was performed in America in 1750 (New York), 1751 (Williamsburg), 1752 (Annapolis) and 1753 (Philadelphia); with *Hamlet* and *Twelfth Night* it was the first American publication as a single play (Boston, 1794) (James G. McManaway, 'Shakespeare in the United States', *PMLA*, 79 (1964), 513–18). It was performed for visiting Cherokee 'chiefs' in 1767 (*New York Journal*, 17 December 1767). On black New York and Nazi Germany, see pp. 95, 104–5; on Edwin Booth's performance for King Kamehameha, see Wood, 159. For Italy, see Tempera, 124–9; for eastern Europe in the 1970s, see Alexander Shurbanov and Boika Sokolova, 'Shakespeare's history plays in Bulgaria', in Hoenselaars, 178–86. On French popularity and adaptations, see Fayard, 137–9.

2 Scholars debate whether plays went into print after losing stage popularity (or when a company had financial trouble), or accompanying revivals or responding to demand created by revivals (see Blayney, 'Publication').

3 See Hart, 147, Hammond, 66. Its length results in reviews with titles like 'The perfidious king dies at 2 a.m.' (Tempera, 129).

but its original length is especially remarkable given its other features.

Many plays of the 1590s, especially 'history' plays, stage parallel plots involving several main characters. Richard, however, like Marlowe's protagonists, dominates even when (briefly) offstage. Onstage for fifteen of twenty-five scenes, Richard speaks more lines (1,145 in F) than any other character in a single Elizabethan play (Barabas in Marlowe's *Jew of Malta* has 1,138) except Hamlet (Wood, 57; Jowett, 73n.). A third of the play's lines are his. Yet his contribution lacks the 'high astounding terms' and fierce declamation of contemporary tragic protagonists. Instead, Richard specializes in puncturing pretension with a suprisingly colloquial tone and a timing 'calculated to bring down the house' (Colley, 6) rather than to convey grandeur or evil machination. The character who in *3 Henry VI* echoed Marlowe's Tamburlaine with 'How sweet a thing it is to wear a crown, / Within whose circuit is Elysium / And all that poets feign of bliss and joy' (*3H6* 1.2.28–30) and vowed on his father's corpse to 'venge thy death / Or die renowned by attempting it' (*3H6* 2.1.87–8), sighs, weeps and simpers 'I thank my God for my humility' (2.1.73), hints at self-deprecation with references to a 'tardy cripple' (2.1.90) and vows to hire 'a score or two of tailors' (1.2.259).

Furthermore, *Richard III* largely eschews combats, processions, ceremonies and the violence of contemporary tragedies or history plays, even Shakespeare's own. A single onstage stabbing and one, silent, combat hardly compare to the mayhem of *Titus Andronicus* or to the eight scenes from five battles in *3 Henry VI*. Nevertheless, the play is hardly decorous by the standards of Horace's Renaissance followers. With a body and demeanour recalling deformed Herods, shifty Vices and ad-libbing clowns, Richard banters with children (3.1.81), mimes a preposterous invasion (3.5.1–30) and snidely mocks a mother's blessing (2.2.109–11).[1] Marlowe's Barabas approximates such outrageousness in looks, speech and action, but Richard is a historical tyrant, not a stage-caricature Jew, so his snarky, self-parodic, shamelessly hypocritical portrayal must have been surprising.

Nevertheless, in 1598 Francis Meres cites *Richard III* to claim Shakespeare 'the most excellent' for 'Tragedy' (Meres, sig. Oo2ʳ). In 1600 Robert Allott's *Englands Parnassus* mines it for poetic utterances. Neither work shows knowledge of performance, but other plays suggest that its subject-matter remained interesting, and in 1606 Barnabe Barnes refers to 'that which is yet fresh in our late Chronicles; and hath been many times represented vnto the vulgar upon our English Theaters, of *Richard Plantagenet*'.[2]

Three other early references may imply performance. An epigram of *c.* 1594–5 (printed sometime between 1595 and 1599) echoes Richard's opening soliloquy:

> I am not fashioned for these amorous times,
> To court thy beutie with lascivious rimes.
> I cannot dally, caper, daunce and sing,
> Oyling my saint with supple sonneting . . .
> Not I by Cock, but shall I tel thee roundly,
> Harke in thine eare, zounds I can (   ) thee soundly.
> (John Davies, 180; cf. Davies & Marlowe, 'Ignoto')[3]

The speaker's combination of self-deprecation, preachy morality and surprising aggression is pure Richard, and becomes strikingly stagey when the poem enlists us to fill in the parentheses. The

1 For Richard Tarleton's joke about parental blessing, see Siemon, 'Power'.
2 C.M. Ingleby, L. Toulmin Smith and F.J. Furnivall (eds), *The Shakespere Allusion Book*, 2 vols (1909), 1.162. Thomas Heywood's *2 King Edward the Fourth* (1599) includes Richard, though less centrally. Ben Jonson was commissioned in 1602 to write a Richard Crookback (R.C. Evans, 'More's *Richard III* and Jonson's *Richard Crookback* and *Sejanus*', *Comparative Drama*, 24 [1990], 97–132); Henslowe records a Buckingham play in 1599; Robert Chamberlain mentions a '*Richard* the third' that can be neither *True Tragedy* nor *Richard III* (*A New Book of Mistakes* (1637; STC 4944), sig. D1ᵛ).
3 John Davies, *The Poems of Sir John Davies*, ed. Robert Krueger (Oxford, 1975).

sexual aggression also resonates with an anecdote about the actor who *became* Richard, Richard Burbage.

Years after Burbage's performances, Bishop Richard Corbet records the identification of actor with role, claiming that his guide to Bosworth field 'mistook' the 'Player for a King, / For when he would have said, King *Richard* dy'd, / And call'd a Horse, a Horse, he *Burbage* cry'd'.[1] Similar conflation of actor and role grounds John Manningham's famous 1601 diary entry:

> Vpon a tyme when Burbidge played Rich. 3. there was a citizen greue so farr in liking wth him, that before shee went from the play shee appointed him to come that night vnto hir by the name of Ri: the 3. Shakespeare ouerhearing their conclusion, went before, was intertained, and at his game ere Burbidge came. Then message being brought that Rich. the 3d. was at the dore, Shakespeare caused returne to be made that William the Conquerour was before Rich. the 3. Shakespeares name willm.[2]

There are many interesting things here.[3] Above all, the woman's desire for Burbage 'by the name of' Richard III (and failing to object to someone else taking the part) suggests attraction to the role itself. While the anonymous city female, interchangeable males and final twist recall *fabliaux* or joke books, erotic power is suggestively attributed to Richard elsewhere as well.

John Weever's *Ad Gulielmum Shakespear* (1599) includes '*Richard*' among Shakespearean characters who have heated 'thousands' with 'Their sugred tongues, and power attractiue beuty'.[4] Echoing Richard's boast, Weever praises characters who 'Say they are Saints althogh that Sts they shew not' (cf. 1.3.337).

---

1 Richard Corbet, *Iter Boreale* (1647), 12.
2 Reproduced in Evans, 1960.
3 The entry suggests physical proximity between audience and actors; Shakespeare's presence at performance; rivalry between actor-playwright and star; Shakespeare's first name specified, as if it were not known; the woman's 'citizen' definition; and the bed-trick format.
4 *Ad Gulielmum Shakespear* in *John Weever*, ed. E.A.J. Honigmann (New York, 1987).

His *Faunus and Melliflora* (1600) depicts Faunus attempting to seduce his 'Sweete Saint' (908) with Richard's question to Anne, 'Are you not then the Autresse of this sinne?' (928; cf. 1.2.120–4).[1] Yet Burbage's Richard must have been ugly. *2 Return from Parnassus* (1601) portrays Burbage and Will Kempe auditioning destitute scholars for stage roles. Kempe spots one for 'a foolish Mayre or a foolish iustice' (1809–11), but Burbage recognizes him for a Richard, telling him, 'I like your face and the proportion of your body for *Richard*, the 3'.[2] Although Burbage also portrayed Romeo, Hamlet, Othello and Lear, the joke depends on his Richard's ugliness of 'face' and 'proportion'.[3]

Burbage's Richard may have influenced offstage behaviour. In 1599 Samuel Rowlands mocks London 'Gallants', who '*like* Richard *the usurper, swagger, / That had his hand continuall on his dagger*'.[4] Dagger-handling appears in sources and other plays, but only Shakespeare's Richard suggests swaggering. Following More, *True Tragedy* interprets Richard's dagger-grabbing to express '*The out & inward troubles of tyrauntes*' (*CW*2, 87), the guilty insecurity that troubles him after murdering the princes.[5] Following Vergil, Hall and Holinshed make it a distracted tic.[6] Only Shakespeare's Richard suggests the Elizabethan 'behavioral genre' of swaggering when he faces down Anne's

1 On the similarity, see *Faunus and Melliflora*, ed. Arnold Davenport (1948), 17n. Citations are from this edition.
2 The scholar starts to recite Richard's opening lines (*Parnassus*, 1835–42).
3 Burbage played the erotically violent Tereus in 'Lechery' from *2 Seven Deadly Sins* (Greg, *Documents*, 2.II); cf. Mark Eccles, 'Elizabethan actors I: A–D', *N&Q*, 236 (1991), 43, and Andrew Gurr, *Playgoing in Shakespeare's London* (Cambridge, 1987), 69.
4 'To the Gentlemen Readers', from *The Letting of Humours Blood in the Head Vaine* (1600), in *The Complete Works of Samuel Rowlands* (Glasgow, 1880), 1.3.
5 See 4.1.84n.
6 Following Vergil (227), Hall writes: 'when [Richard] stode musyng he woulde byte and chaw besely his nether lippe, as who sayd, that hys fyerce nature in his cruell bodye alwaies chafed, sturred and was euer vnquiete: beside that, the dagger that he ware he would when he studied with his hand plucke vpp and downe in the shethe to the middes, neuer drawing it fully out' (Hall, *Richard III*, fol. lix^r; cf. Holinshed, 3.760). Even Edwin Booth's restrained, elegant Richard of the 1870s sheathed and unsheathed his dagger (Wood, 160). For an early seventeenth-century image of Richard prominently featuring a dagger, see Fig. 2.

750 **King Richard the third.**

Another Argument.

Through nights darke shadowes from the house of bale,
The tyrants ghost comes vp to tell his tale.

Orror pursues the homicides sad soule,
Feare hunts his conscience with an hue and crie,
That drinkes the blood of men in murders bowle,
Suspitious thoughts do rest in life denie,
Hate seldome suffers him in peace to die,
By heau'ns inuiolate doome it is decreed,
Whose hands shed blood, his heart in death should bleed.

I was to noble *Yorke* the yongest sonne
Of foure, which he begot in lawfull bed,
First *Edward* was, the next place *Edmund* wonne,
Rutlands yong Earle by *Cliffords* hand strooke dead,
Clarence the third, to death vntimely lead:
I was the last; of all the foure the worst,
By heau'n and nature in my birth accurst.

When my sad mother in her fruitfull wombe
Bore me a painfull burthen to and fro,
Then the babes infant bed had been my tombe,
Had not keene rasors to her paine and woe
Cut me a way, vnto the world to goe:
Nature did grudge to think, that from her wombe
A man-like monster to the world should come.

When

King Richard the third. 751

When first I came into this worlds huge vast,
My birth was not as others wont to bee;
First did my feet come forth, as if in hast
The child of discord had been then set free,
To cause the wretched world to disagree,
Heau'n at that time told b'inauspitious starres
Nations far off of Englands ciuil warres.

As hunger-steru'd to flesh my iawes in blood
I readie toothed came, as who would say,
Nature by signes vnto the world hath show'd
How fiercely he shall bite another day,
That in his mothers wombe well toothed lay,
And maruaile t'was, seeing viper-like he came,
He was not borne by death of his owne damme.

If like a cunning painter on a frame
My shape vnto the world I could descrie,
And with a curious pensell paint the same
In perfect colours, each spectatours eie
Would by my lookes into my manners prie:
The bodies ill-shapte limbes are oft defin'd
For signes of euill manners in the mind.

Little I was, and of a small compact,
My left side shoulder higher then the right,
Both crooked were, and therewithall contract
Into my backe, so that in all mens sight
I did appeare a most mishapen wight:
And hard it was to iudge, if that my soule
Or limbes ill fashion'd feature were more foule.

The deeds of noble *Yorke* I not recite,
Done in those fatall daies of miserie,
Nor tell th'euents of euery speciall fight,
As at Saint Albones, Bloreheath, Banburie,
Northhampton, Barnet, Wakefield, Teukesburie,
Seeing they are often spoken of before,
By those, that heere their wofull falles deplore.

Th'

2 Richard in armour with a dagger in one hand, from *A Mirror for Magistrates* (1610)

armed entourage (1.2.33–42).[1] Nevertheless, Richard remains among the most widely variegated roles in Shakespeare; there is little opportunity for swagger in later acts.[2]

Pre-Restoration evidence suggests that a child played Richard: Thomas Heywood's Red Bull 'Prologue and Epilogue' (published 1637) are spoken by '*A young witty Lad playing the part of* Richard *the third: at the Red Bull*' who apologizes for being a '*Richard* the

1 For swaggering, see George Chapman, *Achilles Shield* (1598; STC 13635), sig. B2ʳ, and *2H4* 2.4.70–107. On 'behavioral genre', see V.N. Vološinov, *Marxism and the Philosophy of Language*, trans. Ladislav Matejka and I.R. Titunik (Boston, 1986), 20–1, 91–7.

2 After Richard wins Anne, says Stephen Daedalus, 'the other four acts … hang limply from that first' (James Joyce, *Ulysses: A Reproduction of the 1922 Edition* (Mineola, NY, 2002), 203).

third ... shrunke up like his arm'.[1] Heywood's own Richard play, *2 Edward IV* (1592–9?), echoes *Richard III* but makes no reference to a withered arm. Children eventually played Richard again in the nineteenth century (Wood, 112).

Restoration

The theatres closed in 1642 and remained shut under the Commonwealth and Protectorate. The Restoration of Charles II in 1660 brought reopened theatres, but evidence survives for only two productions before Shakespeare's play became – for a hundred and fifty years – Colley Cibber's.

A 'Prologue' from the 1670s for a Theatre Royal performance survives, as does a cast-list for a production *c*. 1690. Though lack of other evidence suggests scant performance in the Restoration period (Lull, 24), the play's 'Tudor' elements – fickle fortune, blind pride, emulous faction, cunning usurpation, cruel tyranny and restored legitimacy – proved pliable to reinterpretation. The Prologue claims, 'Tyrants ... / Puft up with pride, still vanish in despair' unlike 'lawfull Monarchs ... preserv'd by heaven'.[2] Denouncing 'Usurpers' and evoking 'giddy Fortune', it likens Richmond to Charles II and warns audience members against hastily 'joyn[ing]' sympathy with Richard or his contemporary equivalents, because 'liberty' means 'Loyalty'. The 1690s cast-list includes Betterton, who was thought to carry stage traditions from Shakespeare's contemporaries, and Sandford, a type-villain who influenced Cibber's Richard.[3]

---

1 Thomas Heywood, *Pleasant Dialogues and Drammas* (1637; STC 13358), sig. R4ʳ. For dating, see George Fullmer Reynolds, *The Staging of Elizabethan Plays at the Red Bull Theater 1605–1625* (New York, 1940), 21. Chambers calls this, 'probably, and certainly if the play was Shakespeare's, some quite exceptional performance' (*Stage*, 2.448).

2 See *Covent Garden Drollery: A Miscellany of 1672*, ed. G. Thorn-Drury (1928), 13–14.

3 See James G. McManaway, '*Richard III* on the stage', *TLS*, 27 June 1935, 416; Montague Summers, *The Playhouse of Pepys* (1935), 223–5; Philip H. Highfill, Jr, Kalman A. Burnim and Edward A. Langhans (eds), *A Biographical Dictionary of Actors, Actresses, Musicians ... London, 1660–1800*, 16 vols (Carbondale, Ill., 1973–99), 2.75.

Two adaptations reveal a bit about reception.[1] John Caryll's *The English Princess, or the Death of Richard the III* updates the play for 1667 audiences (Wood, 72). Set at Bosworth, the adaptation deprives Richard of humour, but retains his renunciation of conscience and his ghost scene. It moralizes against *popular* tyranny, fearing that Richard may infect the audience.[2] John Crowne's *The Misery of Civil-War* (1680) incorporates elements from *2* and *3 Henry VI* and *Richard III* to admonish against 'Religious Brawls', and brings on the ghost of Richard II to curse Henry VI for his grandfather's role in deposing him, while 'Spirits' reassure Henry of heaven – once he dies for his grandfather's sins.[3] Along with generational payback, Crowne also retains the Shakespearean theme of sexual hypocrisy; his Richard, forced to acknowledge his own 'poor Whore' and 'tawny Bastard', apologizes for censuring royal lust (sigs F4ᵛ–G1ʳ). Colley Cibber's *Tragical History of King Richard III* (1700) retains a good deal more Shakespeare.

Cibber

From 1700 to the late nineteenth century the stage play is Cibber's, though after 1741 Richard himself becomes as much Garrick's as Cibber's or Shakespeare's. Despite the appearance of the first scholarly editions, contemporaries acclaimed Cibber's version for its 'compactness', 'plain, simple introduction' and heightened 'spirit' in the final acts.[4] In 1793 the great editor George Steevens acclaimed Cibber's 'reformation', demanding: 'what modern audience would patiently listen to the narrative of Clarence's Dream, his subsequent expostulation with the murderers, the prattle of his children, the soliloquy of the Scrivener, the tedious dialogue of the citizens, the ravings of

---

1   John Wilson's *Andronicus Commenius* (1663–4) adapts 1.2 but otherwise follows Gibbon.
2   John Caryll, *The English Princess* (1667; Wing C744), fol. 65ᵛ.
3   John Crowne, *The Misery of Civil-War* (1680; Wing C7395), sigs K2ʳ–K3ʳ.
4   Francis Gentleman, 1.3–4; cf. his notes to *King Richard III* for Bell's *Shakespeare* (1774), 3.42n. On the play as 'criticism' of Shakespeare, see Sprague, *Histories*, 136.

Margaret, the gross terms thrown out by the Duchess of York on Richard, the repeated progress to execution, the superfluous train of spectres, and other undramatick incumbrances . . . ?' (Vickers, 6.594–5). None of these 'incumbrances' have escaped cutting in modern – 'Shakespearean' – productions (Colley, 19). The stage life of Cibber's text, as itself, as the basis for acting editions and as a continuing influence, registers more than historical oddity.

By 1740 Cibber's *Richard III* had been staged eighty-four times, playing virtually every season, sometimes in two or three houses.[1] The play won praise for clarified exposition and focus, speedier playing time, simplified casting and action that builds to a rousing final battle. For audiences unlikely to know Shakespeare's earlier histories, it provided scenes from *3 Henry VI*, a device still evident in Ian McKellen's 1995 film *Richard III*, which opens with a caption – 'Civil war divides the nation. The King is under attack from the rebel York family, who are fighting to place their eldest son, Edward, on the throne. Edward's army advances, led by his youngest brother, Richard of Gloucester' – followed by Richard killing Prince Edward and Henry VI. Cibber would have approved.

Richard dominates Shakespeare's play, but Cibber cut Margaret, Clarence and his children, the two Murderers, Hastings, King Edward, the Citizens and more, reducing the play by about half and making it 'completely the star's own' (Sprague, *Histories*, 126). Richard gets some seven new soliloquies (editions differ) and speaks 39.9 per cent of the lines (he has 31.2 per cent in F).[2] By pitting Richard against 'a smaller range of innocent victims whose pasts have been wiped clean' (Jowett, 85), Cibber eliminates 'history coming home to roost' but also reduces confusions arising when characters harangue each

1 Colley, 18; Colley Cibber, *The Plays of Colley Cibber*, vol. 1, ed. Timothy J. Viator and William J. Burling (Cranbury, NJ, 2001), 331.
2 Christopher Spencer (ed.), *Five Restoration Adaptations of Shakespeare* (Urbana, Ill., 1965), 27.

other about events that pre-date the play (Hankey, 28; Colley, 4). Remaining characters are helpfully identified in dialogue (see Cibber, *Richard III*, 2.2.14–15). Even today, productions virtually always cut the cast and resort to narrative summaries, genealogy charts or colour-coded clothing to identify factions and families. Margaret is now generally back, but Olivier's film, McKellen's film and Antony Sher's touring *Richard III* did without her. Clarence's children, the Citizens and Queen Elizabeth's extended family still frequently go missing.

Cibber added passages from *3 Henry VI*, *Richard II*, *Henry V* and *2 Henry IV*, hundreds of new lines, new incidents, new pathos and new emphases (Sprague, *Histories*, 123–4). His Richard abuses Lady Anne, fights an extended combat, delivers a rousing death speech and enjoys a eulogy.[1] Ambiguities disappear. Queen Elizabeth explains herself as 'seemingly' complying with Richard's suit (4.4.428–9) 'to let my Child escape' (Cibber, *Richard III*, 4.4.114–16). Richard's obscure mock wager, his 'dukedom to a beggarly denier' (1.2.254), becomes a crude boast, 'My Dukedom to a Widows Chastity' (Cibber, *Richard III*, 2.1.266) – a dumbed-down translation that Laurence Olivier kept. With a curtailed cast, Cibber's Richard can no longer be the game-player who twits the Queen and family, the pious pitier of Margaret or the conniving trapper of Hastings (Hankey, 28). He loses aristocratic haughtiness, trading his brags about high birth (1.3.262–4) for self-pity and worries about being unloved and misunderstood.

Though Cibber read Shakespearean sources and preserved Shakespearean text (printing Shakespeare's lines in italics and paraphrases within inverted commas), his Richard is indebted to the theatre.[2] Samuel Sandford, who had once played Shakespeare's Richard, provided inspiration.[3] His 'low and

---

1   The princes even die onstage, at least in the first version (Donohue, 227).

2   For sources, see Albert E. Kalson, 'The chronicles in Cibber's *Richard III*', *SEL*, 3 (1963), 253–67.

3   Cibber's apparent ignorance of the performance suggests the play was not well known on the Restoration stage (Lull).

crooked person' and limited range constituted an antithesis to the multi-faceted Burbage.[1] This caricature perhaps inspired Cibber's wooing scene. Where Shakespeare's decisive Richard, proud of 'close' intents (1.1.149–59), pops up abruptly, faces down armed men and bowls Anne over, Cibber's Richard mopes about, commenting and eavesdropping. He screws up enough courage to approach Anne, only to 'retire' and listen in on her laments before – finally – moving towards her, consoling himself that though 'perhaps' his form 'will little move her', his 'Tongue shall wheadle with the Devil' (Cibber, *Richard III*, 2.1.53–66). Initially, he reacts rather than acts, but Cibber's Act 4 is another story, and most thought it better than Shakespeare's.

Cibber remade Richard with Sandford's qualities; but an entirely different order of actor became 'the' Richard (Donohue, 225). In Cibber's earlier acts, David Garrick evinced nuances that still haunt today's Richards who emphasize uncertainty, vulnerability, self-pity and pained self-awareness. From Cibber's final acts, Garrick constructed a hero who dies grandly, and Richards would continue doing so even when translated back into Shakespeare's less supportive play. Cibber's Richard neither forgets himself, strikes his messenger (4.4.440–56, 507–8) nor drinks (5.3.63–74); his 'stern Impatience' permits little time for conscience, pity, love or self-hatred (5.3.177–206).[2] At Bosworth, he 'starts' awake, proclaims, 'O Tyrant Conscience! how dost thou afflict me!', but instantly resolves: 'No, never be it said, / That Fate it self could awe the Soul of *Richard*. / Hence, Babling dreams, you threaten here in vain: / Conscience avant; *Richard's* himself again' (Cibber, *Richard*

1 See Colley Cibber, *An Apology for the Life of Colley Cibber*, ed. B.R.S. Fone (Ann Arbor, Mich., 1968), 77. Sandford was round-shouldered, meagre-faced, spindle-shanked, splay-footed, sour of countenance; Charles II called him 'the best Villain in the World' (Anthony Aston, *A Brief Supplement to Colley Cibber, Esq; His Lives of the late Famous Actors and Actresses* (1748), 11).

2 Only the ghosts of Henry VI, the princes and Anne '*rise*', and only to Richard. The second tent would not reappear until 1845 (Hankey, 59).

III, 5.5.82–5).[1] He dies declaiming: 'let one spirit of the First-born *Cain* / 'Reign in all bosoms', and Richmond laments his 'aspiring Soul' (Cibber, *Richard III*, 5.9.15–17, 21–6; cf. *2H4* 1.1.157–8). Garrick made the pathetic wheedler of Cibber's first acts more sympathetic; his concluding heroics evoked high Romanticism.

Mid-eighteenth to mid-nineteenth centuries: from Garrick to Phelps

On 19 October 1741 Garrick's *Richard III* changed Cibber's play – and Shakespeare's – forever (Colley, 37). This Richard was only the first of over one hundred that Garrick would undertake over thirty-five years. Praised for replacing 'ranting, bombast, and grimace' with 'nature, ease, simplicity, and genuine humour',[2] Garrick's Drury Lane performances doubled normal house totals and made *Richard III* a popular staple; acting texts till the twentieth century derived from his performances (Colley, 39; Donohue, 224). Garrick refused to revive Shakespeare's play (Sprague, *Histories*, 128). His suffering protagonist suited period demands for 'sympathetic imagination' and emphasized 'fluctuation of mind'.[3] Garrick conveyed that 'Kings themselves' by their 'sympathizing Souls . . . were *Men*, and *felt* like the rest of their Species'.[4] His Richard, 'galled and uneasy' about a deformity that 'hurts him',[5] prompted Elizabeth Griffith, who rejected 'chearful' villainy as impossible, to admit that evil might originate with jealousy and to admire the play for arousing 'compassion for

---

1 William Hogarth's painting portraying Garrick became the most frequently engraved theatrical image of the century (see Jonathan Bate, 'The Shakespeare phenomenon' in Jane Martineau *et al.* (eds), *Shakespeare in Art* (2003), 12). Besides Hogarth, Francis Hayman, Henry Fuseli, Nathaniel Dance, Thomas Bradwell and Philippe de Loutherbourg painted Garrick's Richard (see Stuart Sillars, *Painting Shakespeare: The Artist as Critic, 1720–1820* (Cambridge, 2006)).
2 Thomas Davies, *Memoirs of the Life of David Garrick* (1808; rpt. New York, 1969), vol. 1, 43–5.
3 See Walter Jackson Bate, 'The sympathetic imagination in eighteenth-century English criticism', *ELH*, 12 (1945), 159–60.
4 J.G. Cooper, *Letters Concerning Taste* (1755), 109 (quoted by Donohue, 230).
5 Thomas Wilkes, *A General View of the Stage* (1759), 237.

the misfortune, even while . . . raising an abhorrence for the vice, of the criminal' (Griffith, 317, 312).

Garrick's final scenes, melancholy and grand, foreshadowed the nineteenth century's Byronic Richards (Colley, 41; Donohue, 276). His 'sublimely horrible' tent and death scenes made Fanny Burney shudder, even as she 'glow[ed]' with moral 'indignation'.[1] To convey 'the Terrors of an Imagination distracted by conscious Guilt', Garrick added pauses and gestures: arising from bed, grasping a sword, he boldly began 'Give me another Horse: . . .'; paused midline, coming forward to cry again, with dismay on his face, 'Bind up my wounds!'; then dropped to his knees on 'Have mercy, Heaven'.[2] This is not Cibber's Richard – or Shakespeare's, either – but generations embraced it.

After Garrick, three Richards dominated into the early nineteenth century: John Philip Kemble, George Frederick Cooke and Edmund Kean. All three left legacies. The Covent Garden and Drury Lane theatres, both rebuilt first in the 1790s and again in 1808–9, were much enlarged, rendering subtleties hard to convey. Garrick's Drury Lane had permitted suppressed smiles, passionate glances and whispers, but in 1826 'extravagant gesture' and 'excess of rant' were demanded (Hankey, 43). Cooke and Kean provided excess and extravagance; Kemble their austere opposite.

Kemble's restrained Richard influenced Macready, Phelps and Edwin Booth (Colley, 43), and his scholarly productions promoted period setting and costume. Garrick had engaged the artist Philippe de Loutherbourg, whose Bosworth designs suggest a sublime landscape (Hankey, 36), but typical pre-Kemble sets amounted to 'architecture of no period' (Wood, 111). Kemble

---

1 See *The Early Diary of Frances Burney; 1768–1778*, ed. Annie Raine Ellis, 2 vols (1913), 1.186.

2 Roger Pickering, *Reflections Upon Theatrical Expression in Tragedy* (1755), 50–1; Sprague, *Actors*, 103–4. Andrew Erskine depicts '*Richard* near his tent': 'He shudd'ring starts, convulsive shakes, / He heaves, he turns, he leaps, he wakes, / Each feature seems with wild amazement hung, / The sudden pray'r to heav'n drops fault'ring / from his tongue' (*Gentleman's Magazine*, 33 (1763), 196).

attempted late medieval costumes and backgrounds (Wood, 111–12; Colley, 46). Until the end of Garrick's era, Richard alone had regularly worn period garb: Hogarth portrays trunks and hose, ruffs at neck and wrists and a short, sleeveless, fur-edged coat revealing the puffed sleeves of a tunic (see Fig. 3; Wood, 108).[1] Richards retained this look up until Olivier.

Kemble's '*gentleman*', with 'ambition' his 'sole impulse' and 'stern valour' his demeanour, downplayed Richard's livelier aspects (Colley, 44; Hankey, 41; Kemble, 167–8). He abandoned traditional clowning in 3.7 (Sprague, *Histories*, 134; Wood, 119), but he tossed aside a prayer-book after the Mayor and men had gone, business that suited Cibber's Richard, left alone onstage, but that survived even when actors returned to Shakespeare's play (Sprague, *Histories*, 134). Critics faulted Kemble's 'uniform' manner.[2] Supporters lauded his 'sublimity' and 'moody defiance', pronouncing it 'impossible not to glory in such a sovereign, by whatever means he gained the title'.[3] Amoral admiration permeates responses in the years that follow.

George Frederick Cooke first appeared as Richard in 1800; he took the role to America in 1810. Cooke, like Kemble, read Shakespeare to prepare for acting Cibber (Hankey, 41; Colley, 55). There the similarities end. In Cooke, Lamb saw 'hypocrisy . . . too glaring'; not wit but 'coarse, taunting humour'; not the 'joy of a defect *conquered*' but '*distaste* and *pain*' (Bate, *Romantics*, 503). Opposing 'musical declamation', Cooke wrote out his lines in prose (Hankey, 42, 45). His energetic Richard, haunted by self-revulsion, influenced Edmund Kean, whose Richard exploded onto the London stage in 1814.

1 On dressing Richard alone in the habit of the times, see Gentleman, 1.10. Remarks of 1801 note Richard's 'fancy cap and feather' (Hankey, 44). The Oxberry 'New English Drama' (1818) describes Kemble and Kean: 'Gloster. 1st dress. Scarlet doublet, trunks, hose, hat, cloak and russet boots. 2nd dress. Black, ditto, ditto, trimmed with gold, crimson velvet robe, white hose, shoes, and plush hat. 3rd dress. Armour body, and hat' (Wood, 119n.).
2 *Remarks on the Character of Richard the Third as Played by Cooke and Kemble* (1801), 24; on Kemble's 'iron and undeviating austerity', see 11.
3 Henry Martin, *Remarks on John Kemble's Performance of Hamlet and Richard III* (1802), 36.

3   William Hogarth's portrayal of Garrick as Richard in his tent, reproduced in an engraving *c.* 1850

The 'quintessential Romantic actor', Kean had writers to appreciate *his* Richard's 'genius, his mounting spirit, which no consideration of his cruelties can depress' (Colley, 61–2; Hankey, 46). Byron enthused: 'He is a soul! . . . Richard is a man, and Kean is Richard' (Wood, 115).[1] In 1814, Thomas Barnes proclaimed that his 'daring and comprehensive intelligence' gave Kean's Richard 'the grasp of a giant', a 'towering superiority' prompting 'awe' as he pursues 'his purpose careless of ordinary duties and ordinary feelings'.[2] Hazlitt called him 'towering and

1   Byron presented a snuff-box with a boar motif to Kean; Kean adopted the boar as his crest (J.F. Molloy, *The Life and Adventures of Edmund Kean Tragedian* (1897), 150). Byron wove Kean's stage business into his portrait of Napoleon (Hankey, 48). On Byron's positive recasting of Richard's disability (and his own) by aligning it with universal forces in his play *The Deformed Transformed*, see Sharon L. Snyder, 'Transforming representation', in Carrie Sandahl and Philip Auslander (eds), *Bodies in Commotion: Disability and Performance* (Ann Arbor, Mich., 2005), 271–83.
2   Reprinted in *Specimens of English Dramatic Criticism, XVII–XX Centuries*, ed. A.C. Ward (1945), 97.

lofty; equally impetuous and commanding; haughty, violent and subtle; bold and treacherous; confident in his strength as well as his cunning' (Hankey, 47). This sublime 'giant' is hardly Cibber's wheedler or Shakespeare's joker. Contemporaries uneasily noted the moral distance separating such adoration from earlier reservations.[1]

Kean triumphed as Richard in America (1820 and 1825) and France (1828); it became his most often performed role and prompted imitation and expansion by, amongst others, two actors very influential in America, J.B. Booth, who transplanted some of Kean's qualities to America in 1821, and the American Edwin Forrest, who played Richard in England and America. Booth performed alternate nights in Kean's style and in his own.[2] Elsewhere in New York that year the African Theatre Company staged *Richard III* for their first production, with James Hewlett as Richard (see Fig. 4). The company included the young Ira Aldridge, who later toured the globe for decades as Richard.[3]

Back to Shakespeare: Macready and Phelps to Irving

In 1821 William Charles Macready tried combining Shakespeare and Cibber. The result was only staged twice. Audiences were confused without passages from *Henry VI*. Macready reintroduced Hastings's entrapment, Clarence's dream and Margaret's curses, much abbreviated since 'the cause of her grief, being so very remote' prevented commiseration (Downer,

---

1 James Boaden (*c*. 1790–1) notes the 'immoral effect' of Richard's 'triumphant villainy' upon the audience: 'their proper sympathy with his victims is blunted by the *certainty* of his success, and the daring intrepidity with which he hurries them on from one atrocity to another' (*Memoirs of the Life of John Philip Kemble*, 2 vols (1825; rpt. New York, 1969), 2.59).

2 See Arthur Kincaid, 'Junius Brutus Booth' (*ODNB*).

3 See George A. Thompson, *A Documentary History of the African Theatre* (Evanston, Ill., 1998); also Michael Warner *et al.*, 'A soliloquy "Lately Spoken at the African Theatre": race and the public sphere in New York City, 1821', *American Literature*, 73 (2001), 1–46. Cf. Carlyle Brown's play, *The African Company Presents Richard III* (New York, 1998). Aldridge performed *Richard III* in England in the 1830s and around the world for four decades (Errol Hill, *Shakespeare in Sable* (Amherst, Mass., 1984), 17–18).

M.ʳ Hewlett
as Richard the third in imitation of
M.ʳ Kean.
Off with his head so much for Buckingham *Act.3.S.2.*
I am myself alone.

4 James Hewlett as Richard, a role he played in New York's African Theatre
   Company production (1821) as well as in later theatrical imitations of famous
   actors in the role

86). Objecting to the 'bombast' of Cibber's 'Off with his head! so much for Buckingham' and 'Conscience avant!', Macready nevertheless retained them as acting 'points ... traditional from Garrick' (Macready, 71, 169–70). Such 'points' grounded critical evaluation, and some live still: I heard 'Off with his head' bring down the house in 2006.[1] Macready rejected a 'moody' Richard (Downer, 87); his witty strategist influenced generations of clever plotters (Colley, 82). The popularity of his and Kean's 'Rival Richards' led to competitions; other rivalries followed, not always peacefully (see Fig. 5 and Macready, 145).[2]

In 1845 and 1849 Shakespeare's *Richard III* was performed for the first time in over 150 years, although Samuel Phelps cut radically to allow time for processions and spectacle, while adding lines from *2* and *3 Henry VI* for pre-history. The 'new' role of Margaret won acclaim, but – despite remarkable scenic effects (barges floated the aldermen onto the stage, all the ghosts rose at once, and for the first time since 1700 both Bosworth tents appeared) – Phelps failed to drive Cibber from the stage. Pressure for Shakespeare had grown, but Charles Kean, son of the great Edmund, resisted it (Colley, 93–7). Calling *Richard III* 'less fitted in its integrity for representation on the stage than almost any other generally acted' Shakespeare play, Charles Kean performed Cibber for decades from the 1830s. His spectacular productions anticipated Irving, and even cinematic Shakespeare; in 1854 he employed arches and towers, pillars, painted drops, a functional bridge, showers of arrows and scores of players (72 for the wooing of Anne, 119 for a final tableau) (Colley, 89–92). Still, audiences wanted more Shakespeare; Irving and Edwin Booth

---

1 I heard laughter, however, rather than the 'tremendous rounds of applause' that halted Vandenhoff's 1837 Covent Garden performance (Charles Rice, *The London Theatre in the Eighteen-Thirties*, ed. Arthur Colby Sprague and Bertram Shuttleworth (1950), 21).

2 For depiction of Kean competing against J.B. Booth, see Colley, 101. The rivalry between Macready's and Forrest's nationalist partisans culminated in the Astor Place Riots of April 1849 (Colley, 104–6; Foulkes, 20–2).

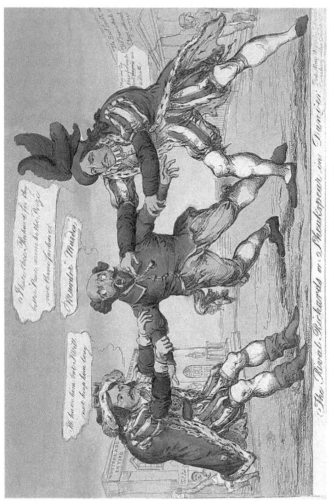

5 'The Rival Richards or Shakespear in Danger'; cartoon (1814) by William Heath, showing Edmund Kean and Charles Mayne Young, one of the Kemble school of actors, tearing Shakespeare between them

responded in the 1870s. Meanwhile, A.W. Schlegel's arguments about the unity of Shakespeare's histories prompted the play's performance within the historical tetralogies; in 1864 Franz Dingelstedt mounted both tetralogies in Weimar (in German) over eight days.[1] English performance of the tetralogies awaited Frank Benson's 1906 Stratford production.[2]

Away from the theatres that featured the dignified Macready, the antiquarian Kean and the melodramatic Forrest and their imitators, popular entertainments provided other perspectives on *Richard III*. Alternative 'Shakespeare' in parodies, burlesques and other strange offerings began another tradition that serves a wide range of popular, topical and frequently comical uses.[3] In 1855 Theodor Fontane witnessed theatricals that featured onstage murder of the princes (played by women) and wife-beating. An equestrian performance in Southwark offered 'Bosworth Field THE BATTLE! And Death of "White Surrey"'.[4] Some burlesques mocked both Cibber and scholarly Shakespearean editions.[5]

Victorian Shakespeare: Irving to Benson

Contemporary performance history of Shakespeare's play begins with Henry Irving in 1877. Cibber remained on London stages up until Barry Sullivan's 1876 production, and would continue

1 See Robert K. Sarlos, 'Dingelstedt's celebration of the tercentenary: Shakespeare's histories as a cycle', *Theatre Survey*, 5 (1964), 117–31. For German productions, see Hortmann, 96–8. *Richard III* was almost continuously in the Vienna Burgtheater repertoire from the 1850s until 1917 in adaptations (Draudt, 196).

2 See Knowles, *2H6*, 5.

3 See, for example, *Monty Python*'s Richard III Ward in the 'Hospital for Overactors' skit (Season 2, episode 25); the *Blackadder* first series, set in the reign of Richard IV; *The Good Bye Girl*'s parody of academic gender analysis; and Julien Temple's documentary *The Filth and the Fury*, in which Johnny Rotten admires Olivier's Richard. Cf. Pierre Pradinas's staging of *La Vie criminelle de Richard III* (1994) with zombies and mechanical dogs (Fayard, 187–8).

4 See Theodore Fontane, *Shakespeare in the London Theatre 1855–58*, trans. Russell Jackson (1999), 10–17; for the playbill, see Foulkes, 56.

5 Cf. Richard A. Schoch, *Not Shakespeare: Bardolatry and Burlesque in the Nineteenth Century* (Cambridge, 2002). F.C. Burnand's 1868 *The Rise and Fall of Richard III; or a New Front to an Old Dickey* jibes at Cibber in a mock footnote justifying interpellated lines from *Macbeth* (n.d., 42).

in America into the twentieth century despite experiments by Jarrett and Palmer (1871) and Edwin Booth (1878) (Sprague, *Histories*, 131; Wood, 161). After 1877, Cibber never returned to London production, at least not entire (Hughes, 151). Irving influenced performers into the twentieth century: Barrymore remembered Irving in his 1920 *Richard III*, and Irving's voice and business influenced Olivier's mid-century portrayals.[1] Irving omitted nearly 1,600 lines: Margaret appeared only in 1.3 in 1877, although she was largely restored in 1896. The deaths of Rivers, Grey and Buckingham (3.3, 5.1) and the Scrivener's soliloquy (3.6) were cut. Clarence lost his discussion with the Murderers (1.4).[2] Irving enhanced his historically appropriate sets and costumes with lowered house lighting, employing the stage pictorially (Colley, 128). In 1877 twenty-two monks and men-at-arms escorted Henry VI's corpse (1.2); in 1896 innumerable extras formed a composition derived from a painting (Hughes, 156–9).[3]

Irving retained Kean's heroics in the later acts – glaring or flinging his gauntlet (Colley, 139) – but he was more character than Titan, and his two Richards (young in 1877, old in 1896) differed substantially. The first he called 'a Plantagenet with the imperious pride of his race, a subtle intellect, a mocking, not a trumpeting duplicity'; his slight deformities prompted him to demonstrate superiority to better-shaped men (Hughes, 153). He expressed pathos in his isolation and in the 'varying changes of his face' (Hughes, 153; Colley, 134). Contemporaries contrasted his 'refined, fascinating' Richard with Barry Sullivan's 'coarse, loud, swaggering bully'

---

1 For stage business, see Hughes, 154; cf. 3.1.130–2. For Irving's voice, see Colley, 170. Irving's 1888 recording of *R3* 1.1.1–24 survives (*Great Historical Sound Recordings*, Naxos Audiobooks CD, NA 220012, 2000); cf. Wes Folkerth, *The Sound of Shakespeare* (2002), 1–10.

2 Edwin Booth's 1878 Shakespeare revival made similar cuts, eliminating Clarence's children (2.2), the women at the Tower (4.1) and one third of Margaret's lines in 1.3 (Colley, 108–9).

3 Irate viewers of Barrymore's 1920 production expected Anne's entourage to number '70 to 80' (Sprague, *Histories*, 138).

(Sprague, *Histories*, 133). In 1896 Irving made himself up to look even older than his own fifty-eight years, and expressed obvious delight in his own intrigues (Colley, 141). Henry James dismissed both conceptions: faulting the 'pauses and lapses, without a hint of the rapidity, the intensity . . . necessary for carrying off the improbabilities of so explicit and confidential and so melodramatic a hero' in the first (Colley, 130) and condemning the second for attempting 'plausibility' in such 'a loose, violent, straddling romance'.[1]

Under Frank Benson, who kept largely to Shakespeare and avoided many traditional acting points, the Memorial Theatre in Stratford-upon-Avon saw thirteen productions of *Richard III* over thirty years, starting in 1886. Minor roles became important: playgoers were astonished to see the First Murderer acted with 'sincerity and fervour' (Colley, 145–6). Benson's performances survive piecemeal in the first film version of *Richard III*, a 1911 silent produced in the Memorial Theatre.[2] Like half of Benson's productions, the film opens with the battle of Tewkesbury and Henry's murder. Benson, showing little hump or limp, suggests mesmerism by moving his hands behind Anne like a puppet-master. The princes are murdered on camera, and one killer kisses the body he bears to the cellerage. The other very early film rendering is the 1912 James Keane and M.B. Dudley *Richard III*.[3] Shot against painted flats and in outdoor locations, the film is full of action. Frederick B. Warde's mature Richard is not very hunched but grows increasingly stooped in later scenes. Warde, a veteran touring actor, concludes the film in modern dress, bowing to us as if at one of his public lectures.

1 Gamini Salgado, *Eyewitnesses to Shakespeare: First-Hand Accounts of Performance, 1590–1890* (1975), 104–5.
2 See *Silent Shakespeare* (British Film Institute, 1999). On early films, see Robert Hamilton Ball, *Shakespeare on Silent Film: A Strange Eventfull History* (1968); Kenneth Rothwell and Annabelle Henken Melzer, *Shakespeare on Screen: An International Filmography and Videography* (New York, 1990).
3 See *Richard III* (Kino on Video, 2001).

The 1920s: psychology and politics

1920 saw historic productions in America and Germany that anticipated future developments. John Barrymore's Broadway *Richard III* looked far more traditional than Leopold Jessner's Berlin expressionist production. Barrymore, prompted by Arthur Hopkins, one of the first directors influenced by Freud (Morrison, 72), approached Richard through character psychology. Jessner directed Fritz Kortner in a performance that treated 'men and women as rhythmic exponents of driving forces' (Hortmann, 57).

Barrymore's *Richard III* was a great success.[1] To portray Richard's psychological development, a third of the scenes were taken from *3 Henry VI*. Barrymore rejected the 'roaring caricature' of Robert Mantell for Edwin Booth's intellect and introspection.[2] His Richard aged 'from questioning youth to bitter old age' (Colley, 155), an approach indebted to Richard Mansfield. Attributing the difference between the lively joker of the first acts and the later embittered king to the historical passage of fourteen years, Mansfield aged into physical and moral corruption, while indicating remorse far earlier than other Richards ever had (see Fig. 6). Awaiting news about the princes, Mansfield shuddered in dismay at a ray of red light falling on his hand (Colley, 113–17). This stress on internal development anticipated subsequent psychological characterizations.

Sigmund Freud's own brief psychoanalytic interpretation of Richard had appeared in a 1916 essay, but character was of little interest to the 1920 Berlin Staatliches Schauspielhaus production.[3] Leopold Jessner's *Motivtheater* rendered Richard merely one element in a pageant of power and political corruption enacted in stylized movements, spare gestures and abruptly changing vocal rhythms (Kennedy, 88; Hortmann, 61).

1 It ran nearly five hours, and closed after twenty-seven performances because of Barrymore's exhaustion (Colley, 151–2). William Luce's play *Barrymore* (1996) portrays the alcoholic star struggling to recall his stage success as Richard.

2 See Gene Fowler, *Good Night, Sweet Prince: The Life of John Barrymore* (New York, 1944), 194; cf. Colley, 154. On Booth, see Colley, 111; Morrison, 110.

3 Freud's essay referring to *Richard III* first appeared in *Imago* (1916); cf. Garber.

6   Richard Mansfield as Richard, showing him holding a book (1889)

Jessner directly influenced Bertolt Brecht's *The Resistable Rise of Arturo Ui*; his famous stage steps provided Jan Kott with the central metaphor of *Shakespeare Our Contemporary* (published in France in 1963), which, in turn, inspired Peter Hall's *The Wars of the Roses* (1963) (Barton & Hall, xi; Lull, 33). In New York, Barrymore's designer, Robert Edmond Jones, influenced by Edward Gordon Craig and Max Reinhardt, incorporated an ominous 48-foot-high hexagon, complete or in part, into every scene (Morrison, 84). In Berlin, Emil Pirchan (also inspired by Craig and by Adolphe Appia; Kennedy, 83–7) put two stone walls across Jessner's stage, the second rising to a terrace. The walls were transformed into a dungeon, a street, a cloister and a throne room surmounted by a pyramidal flight of red steps that rose from the proscenium to the lower wall. The first three acts kept to horizontal movement within the walls; the last two acts proceeded vertically, up and down the stairs. Richard trod the *Jessnertreppen* in Act 4, descending affably, ascending angrily, as others rose and fell. He descended to die. Red was everywhere: in Richard's scarlet robes, the stairs, a crimson sky and blood-red lighting that cast enormous shadows from the actors (Colley, 159; see Fig. 7).

Germany claimed to stage more Shakespeare than the rest of the world combined (a single year, 1937, saw 320 productions; Strobl, 18–19), and the Nazis, taking Shakespeare as ideologically safer than Lessing, Goethe and Schiller, even adopted Richard as a symbol for the failure of Nordic potential (Strobl, 17–19; Habicht, 115). However, Jürgen Fehling's 1937 *Richard III* dressed Richard's bodyguards as Nazi stormtroopers and in Werner Krauss's Richard suggested a resemblance to the club-footed Josef Goebbels. The Scrivener (3.6) directly addressed the audience, who responded with spontaneous applause or uncanny silence. Richard fell at the mere raising of Richmond's sword, according to Fehling, 'because the divine order claims to be re-established'. House lights went up as Richmond's soldiers knelt to sing a *Te deum*. Shakespeare's histories were officially

7   Richard and his courtiers robed in scarlet, atop the red *Jessnertreppen*, above
them a blood-red sky; from the Berlin Staatliches Schauspielhaus production
of 1920

suppressed by Goebbels in 1941 (Hortmann, 137–9; Habicht, 117).

Although continental stage innovations influenced Terence Gray's 1928 Cambridge production, with its focused spots and exaggerated shadows, and its cubes, drums and cylinders arranged on a turntable with steps (Kennedy, 115–16), melodrama and character psychology prevailed over expressionism on the English stage. Baliol Holloway, the first Richard to follow Frank Benson's thirty years at Stratford-upon-Avon, was 'a ranting tragedian of the old barn-storming school, playing straight at the audience all the time, and "asking for it" . . . in every gesture'. Foot firmly on the 'loud pedal', Holloway's Richard was 'Punch' (Colley, 160). Psychological approaches produced a first in George Hayes's 1928 insane Richard. Exuding cherubic innocence, he betrayed signs of malignant intellect, keeping his back to others or reading while they spoke. This type anticipated the many 'lunatic-asylum Richards' between 1953 and 1981 (Colley, 162–3).

Elsewhere in Europe, resistance to naturalism continued. In France, Charles Dullin's 1933 presentation of André Obey's version enjoyed great success. Within a set dominated by two massive portals and the dungeon of the Tower, Richard appeared as physically repulsive but sexually exciting, engaging in whirling dances of exultation and ending in a stylized battle beneath a huge lance.[1] Accounts compare Dullin to 'one of Hokusai's warriors'.[2]

Olivier and after

During the 1930s Cibber's *Richard* concluded nearly two centuries as the most popular play in North America (Wood, 134–50). While some of Cibber's spirit lived on in the most notable mid-century *Richard III*, Laurence Olivier's Richard also needs relating to the 1942 portrayal by Donald Wolfit. Although Wolfit followed the blood and thunder of Edwin Forrest and Barry Sullivan (Colley, 167; Sprague, *Histories*, 132), he recognized the play's topical potential as a treatment of despotism (adopting a forehead cowlick to suggest Hitler (Wolfit, 205)), and he grasped the centrality of its female roles.[3] Wolfit deemed 4.4, with the 'women in black whom [Richard] has so grievously wronged', the 'core of the play' (Wolfit, 206) – a point Olivier failed to appreciate.[4]

Olivier first appeared as Richard in 1944, toured in Europe (1945), Australia and New Zealand (1948), and revived the production in London (1949) before starring in the inescapable

1 On the set, see Fortunato Israel, '*Richard III* sur la scène française' in Dominique Goy-Blanquet and Richard Marienstras (eds), *Le Tyran: Shakespeare contre Richard III* (Picardie, 1990), 154.

2 See Robert Speaight, *Shakespeare on the Stage* (Boston, Mass., 1973), 193–4.

3 Irving had omitted the mourning queens from his first production, reinstating them in the second. Mansfield and (sometimes) Benson omitted Margaret (Sprague, *Histories*, 139, 132).

4 Margaret was in 1.3 in Olivier's stage versions (Colley, 176), but disappeared from the film.

1954 film. Cibber provided some lines – including 'Richard's himself again'. Roles disappeared, action was rearranged, traditional points were observed with gestures going back to Kean and vocal echoes of Irving (Richmond, 56–7; Colley, 170), costume and haircut followed the Garrick tradition and the usual pre-Benson focus stayed on Richard. Olivier's film Richard combines unflagging energy, menace, cynicism and caricature. His nose from Disney's Big Bad Wolf, his voice a donnish treble, his soliloquies and asides are shared directly with us in strategic close-ups, and other roles are reduced. We enter the film with him, slyly invited to appreciate the conflict he has exacerbated. Ignoring 'motive and remorse', Olivier's 'sheer theatricality' set a standard (Richmond, 60–5; Hankey, 68–9). Olivier wanted to win the audience to Richard's side with his 'wit, his brilliantly wry sense of humour', with 'acting for acting's sake' (Colley, 177).

Olivier's popularity resulted in other actors being found wanting: Alec Guinness's 1953 Richard was less accomplished in sneering; Marius Goring's 1953 Richard was less dominating (Lull, 32); Christopher Plummer's 1961 Richard lacked Olivier's diction; Ian Holm's 1963 Richard was a 'pocket Olivier' (Colley, 229). No Richard would so dominate until Antony Sher's 1984 portrayal. Even before his film, Olivier's stage presence loomed so large that Stratford-upon-Avon did not see a *Richard III* until the 1953 Goring–Glen Byam Shaw production (Richmond, 64).[1] Goring's Richard was understatedly mad (the first post-war lunatic), with long red hair suggesting vulnerabilities to offset his soldier's demeanour (Day, 101–2). In a variant of Richard's dagger-play, Goring opened with his sword casually across his shoulder, lowered it as a walking-stick at 'Grim-visaged War hath smoothed his wrinkled front' (1.1.9), placed his heavy-booted foot on the forestage to emphasize his being 'rudely stamped' (16),

---

1 The next would not be for eight years, with Christopher Plummer in William Gaskill's 1961 production.

and then moved the sword to his claw-like left hand on 'Deformed, unfinished' (20) (Day, 101; Richmond, 67). A motif of circulating court documents suggested that war had given way to bureaucracy – no great stretch of imagination for post-Second World War England (Day, 108–9).

Among the most innovative productions with an insane Richard, Peter Hall and John Barton's 1963–4 adaptation set *Richard III* within a half-length first tetralogy, *The Wars of the Roses*. An 1870 commentator had predicted that putting the play in the tetralogy context would expose 'the guile and selfishness, second only to [Richard's] own, by which he was surrounded, and the dreadful circumstances (the consequences of civil war and dynastic ambition) which alone made such a character and such actions possible' (Hankey, 83). To this moral–political mix, Hall and Barton added ingredients from Jan Kott and E.M.W. Tillyard. Hall affirmed Kott's 'staircase' (Kott, 45) as the timeless model of the histories and their 'mechanism of power' (Barton & Hall, xi). Programme notes invoked Stalin, Hitler and Mussolini (Colley, 225). Hall also accepted Tillyard's stress on stable social degree and on the 'curse' upon the House of Lancaster, claiming that 'The bloody totalitarianism of Richard III' was 'the expiation of England' for the deposing of Richard II (Barton & Hall, x, xiii).[1] This conception gave Margaret renewed prominence, though the other women's parts remained reduced (Colley, 228).

Ian Holm's Richard of that year was Kottian but un-Tillyardian. Neither melodramatic nor tragic, Holm portrayed a diminutive, 'likeable juvenile, open-faced and friendly' (Colley, 226). Helmeted, black-clad toughs tramped about in unison with him, as he betrayed madness with blinkings and twitchings, drooling and giggling at secret jokes (Colley, 225, 227). Holm died neither gloriously like Kean, nor desperate like Irving, but gibbering inside a visored helmet through which Richmond stabbed

---

1 On combining Kott's pessimism with Tillyard's Tudor providentialism, see Hodgdon, *End*, 118.

him (Colley, 229). His reduced size, clownish behaviour and final faceless death ultimately derived via Kott from a 1960 production with Jacek Woszczerowicz (Kott, 46; Hankey, 72), which had made 'superman' a 'super-clown' who is 'smaller than all the other characters . . . a figure of fun' (Kott, 47). The production suggested a paradoxical alliance between 'buffoonery' and tyrannical impersonality imputed to world historical figures. The comedian Richard is ultimately replaced by another one: as 'rows of bars are lowered from above', Richmond 'speaks of peace, forgiveness and justice. And suddenly gives a crowing sound like Richard's, and, for a second, the same sort of grimace twists his face' (Kott, 48–9).

Kott's influence permeated the 1970s, and was compounded by the impact of Peter Weiss's *Marat/Sade* (1964). Weiss's allegory of oppression and revolution, set in a grim asylum where the players are mad and the madmen are players, influenced Barry Kyle's 1975 Stratford production with Ian Richardson (Colley, 204). The actors were attired to suggest mental patients or concentration camp inmates. Margaret served as stage manager, emerging to blow her whistle and curse, to blindfold Richard's victims or to articulate his mother's curses (Colley, 206; Day, 166). Bosworth was a pillow fight. The loose invocation of insanity and the political futility of the gulag and the implied similarities between Richard and Richmond may beg enormous questions (Colley, 207), but also missing were the collusions that tyranny demands and encourages from dupes, time-servers and the oppressed, a theme explored in an adaptation that made a huge impression despite performance in a language largely unknown to English audiences.[1]

The 1979–80 performances of the Rustaveli Company of Tbilisi, Georgia, directed by Robert Sturua, boldly recast text

---

1 Cf. Lin Zhaohua on his landmark (but financially disastrous) 2001 Beijing production: 'those who lack vigilance against murderous schemes are the conspirator's accomplices' (Li Ruru, *Shashibiya: Staging Shakespeare in China* (Hong Kong, 2003), 228).

and action. Antony Sher recalled Ramaz Chkhikvadze's Richard as a 'giant poisonous toad' (Sher, 28). Evoking Hieronymus Bosch, Miriam Scvelidze's set put a circus tent above a gallows, with a hell gate to either side, peopled by tyrants and subtyrants – even the citizens became oppressors (Tarsitano, 70, 72). Sturua acknowledged Mikhail Bakhtin's concept of the carnivalesque, with its 'gay relativity' and combinations and inversions of high and low characters, physical elements and themes (Stříbrný, 122; Tarsitano, 70). The white-faced Margaret, brandishing the text, prompted the actors, while a jester accompanied Richard, parodying his actions (unseen by Richard), winking and mocking his successes (Tarsitano, 71–3). Richmond provided Richard's primary audience and understudy. In the final moments the jester stared directly at the audience while Richmond gazed at the crown as earlier Richard had looked at it; the jester's motions in removing his hat were mimed by Richmond who, as though copying him, put on the crown (Tarsitano, 74–5).

Julie Hankey argues for Sturua's justice to Shakespeare's non-naturalistic elements, implacable forces and rigid ironies. For example, 'Buckingham taunts the condemned Hastings with the words "we know each other's faces, for our hearts . . ." and is in turn taunted with the same words when his execution falls due. The device of repeating words in a new context is Shakespeare's' (Hankey, 76). Simultaneous staging emphasized the insecure 'security' that pervades Shakespeare's play: Clarence dreams while Richard orders his assassination; Hastings asserts Catesby's loyalty while Buckingham instructs Catesby to double-cross him (Hankey, 76–7). The production made a deep impression on the century's next great Richard.

Antony Sher in the 1984 Bill Alexander RSC production struck many as 'the most impressive Richard since Olivier' (Hassel, 145). Sher combined 'unassuming tones' (Colley, 237) with spectacular physical deformities (see Fig. 8). With draping tunic, Sher resembled a six-legged spider from the front and a vulture from the side; his snake-like tongue flicked in and out

8   Antony Sher's Richard (directed by Bill Alexander, RSC, 1984)

relentlessly. In the first half of the play, despite a grotesque hump and splayed legs, he moved with incredible agility on black elbow-crutches that performed as feelers to rub together when mentioning doing 'naught' with Mistress Shore (1.1), swords to cow the bearers of King Henry's corpse (1.2), a phallic appendage to lift Anne's dress (1.2), a sceptre to 'knight' Buckingham and scissors for Hastings's neck. A world of stylization separates Burbage's swaggering dagger-drawing or Kean's hand-rubbing and peeks beneath Anne's veil from this. From his coronation onwards, Sher abandoned crutches to stagger weakly, to be carried, or to support himself on the sceptre, a sword or a mace (Day, 208; Cerasano, 623).

One further element harked back to Kean – Sher's emphasis on pacing. A distinctive bodily 'rhythm' expressed his inner distortion from the very first moments (Sher, 90, 144; Cerasano, 621): Sher initially appeared rear centre between imposing tomb-like structures, a dark figure seemingly unhobbled, slowly, sweetly evoking 'glorious summer' until 'But I . . . ' (1.1.14), when the crutches flew out into view and he hurtled to the edge of the stage, causing audiences to draw back in alarm (Colley, 239; Hassel, 'Context', 631). Such astonishingly abrupt movement, repeated in gestures and mood swings, put audiences in the position of the courtiers, fascinated, repelled and off balance, unable to anticipate Richard's next move (Colley, 240–1; Hassel, 'Context', 631). Until he was crowned; then Sher's Richard, like Shakespeare's, lost his dominance as things go wrong (Day, 207).

The power of the mourning women became clear in 4.4 where Richard was humiliated and outmanoeuvred by his mother (Yvonne Coulette) and Queen Elizabeth (Frances Tomelty). Sher's progress, on a litter, was interrupted by their verbal attacks which left his bearers unable to escape; his mother seized his hand and forced him to endure her curses (Day, 208). Queen Elizabeth granted him her daughter, but her self-assured seat on the throne and a surprising kiss on his lips as he tried to kiss her hand suggested more ambition than Richard had bargained for (Day, 203). This was not the woman denounced by Shakespeare's sources, but nor was she the desperate, improvising survivor that Shakespeare provides.[1]

Sher's Richard's own breakdown was most powerfully evident in his pre-battle oration (5.3.314–41). Despairing, his voice broke on 'runaways' and 'paltry fellow' (5.3.316, 323), while his followers menaced the audience (Hassel, 'Context', 638). His death enacted a 'sacrificial' elimination (Hammond, 72–3; Hassel, 'Context', 638–40; Day, 216). Kneeling, Richard offered up the crown to God, as the golden, visored Richmond pinned him with a cross-like sword, executing the judgement of providence.

This proved a hard act to follow. Nevertheless, 1988–90 saw an explosion reminiscent of the years of Macready, Kean and J.B. Booth (Colley, 249). Two adaptations appeared within abbreviated trilogies: Adrian Noble's *The Plantagenets* (1988), with Anton Lesser as Richard, and Michael Bogdanov's English Shakespeare Company *The Wars of the Roses* (1988), with Andrew Jarvis as Richard. Stand-alone productions included Derek Jacobi's 1988 *Richard III* at the Phoenix Theatre, directed by Clifford Williams. The year 1990 brought Ian McKellen to the National Theatre, directed by Richard Eyre. Other productions were mounted in New York (Denzel Washington as Richard) and at the Folger Theatre in Washington, DC (Stacy Keach as Richard).[2] Two of these took the play to affective regions it had never before seen.

Despite a prosthetically hooked nose and jet-black, matinee-idol hair, Jacobi went for laughs with a 'roguish effeminacy, pitched half-way between Olivier and Frankie Howerd' (Colley, 250). Richard opened giggling, lying on his back and gleefully

---

1 At 4.4.206–13 Shakespeare's Elizabeth initially appears to believe that Richard wants to kill, rather than wed, her daughter, and shifts her responses on the spot (see Jones).

2 For Keach's *Richard III*, see a review by Miranda Johnson-Haddad, *SQ*, 42 (1991), 473–6.

kicking his legs in the air while imagining his plots. He closed without a battle, but laughing, laid the crown before Richmond before being neatly dispatched. The jokester emphasis would figure prominently in the Richard of David Troughton. Ian McKellen provided a tight-lipped alternative.

McKellen's stage (1990) and film (1995) performances bracketed the two early 1990s Royal Shakespeare Company productions, Sam Mendes–Simon Russell Beale (1992) and Steven Pimlott–David Troughton (1995). McKellen's National Theatre production evolved into the film (directed by Richard Loncraine). His 'granitic' onstage demeanour was like no other (Jowett, 107). Set in an imaginary England of the 1930s, Richard's rise appeared upon Bob Crowley's spare set as the grim undertaking of a stiffly military figure, killing his way to the top of an order he detested and ending as a black-shirted tyrant (Colley, 260). Any spinal curve was hardly apparent; his arm was unobtrusive, but McKellen performed mechanical wonders with his 'good' arm. Lois Potter describes his opening soliloquy as spoken 'in a dry, old-fashioned, upper-class accent which negates any possibility of making friends with the audience' (Colley, 258). If Sher is the Kean of the recent era, then McKellen's stage Richard is the stately, measured Kemble (Colley, 261).

McKellen's film is another story. The heavy cutting, recast lines and opening recall Cibber. Margaret disappears, and Richard is funnier (and more viscerally repulsive) than he was onstage: his first soliloquy in a men's room is classic. His relationship to his mother (Maggie Smith) provides a subtext. McKellen assesses her 'disgust at his physique', speculating that from her 'Richard learnt how to hate so fiercely' (McKellen, 236, 274). The final moments allude to *White Heat* (1949), in which Jimmy Cagney's gangster, engulfed in flames, shouts, 'Made it, Ma' (Loehlin). As Richard falls into flames, grinning, Richmond 'usurps Richard's privilege and smiles into the camera', to pose 'unsettling' questions about England's future (McKellen, 286). Why there should be questions is unclear, but recent productions generally reject England's purgation and Richmond's innocence.

Richard's capacity to engage the audience with humour, irony and evil, though, is alive and well in Al Pacino's 1996 'home-movie', *Looking for Richard*. Interweaving play scenes with interviews, investigations, exhortations, criticism and brainstorming, the film depicts Pacino struggling with the role (Hodgdon, 'Replicating', 210).[1] Despite its dismissal of scholarship, it is filled with insights. The wooing scene has a demonic intensity that demonstrates how Richard can both repel and project erotic power.

While the Loncraine–McKellen film created a 1930s England that might have been, anachronistic eclecticism prevailed in the 1992–3 Sam Mendes–Simon Russell Beale *Richard III*. In Tim Hatley's spare set, cigars, bowler hats and balloons mixed with armour, ermine-trimmed robes and sweaters. Beale's swollen body and shaven head contrasted with McKellen's austere officer, or any other previous Richard. He indulged in Punch-like 'wide-eyed goggling' in campy disbelief at gullible dupes, or broke into psychotic ruthlessness, his fury only barely restrained as little York jumped onto his back (see Fig. 9). He exuberantly thrust a walking-stick into the brown paper parcel containing Hastings's head (Smallwood, 358–60). Margaret (Cherry Morris) appeared to reiterate the curses of 1.3 as victims met execution (Day, 160–1). She marked the time before Bosworth, tapping as if to the rhythm of the ghosts' curses or the seconds passing (Smallwood, 361; Day, 172–3). Downplaying her derision, she turned revenge to a shared purpose with the other women (Day, 169). There were no tents at Bosworth: Richard and his followers sat at one end of a long table, Richmond and company at the

---

1 On Pacino and McKellen, see Hodgdon, 'Replicating'; Herbert Coursen, 'Filming Shakespeare's history: three films of *Richard III*', and Barbara Freedman, 'Critical junctures in Shakespeare film history: the case of *Richard III*', both in Russell Jackson (ed.), *The Cambridge Companion to Shakespeare on Film* (Cambridge, 2000), 97–115, 47–71.

other, with the ghosts eerily appearing in between, toasting Richmond and cursing Richard. Countering the Garrick–Kean tradition, Beale's waking soliloquy conveyed little emotion. The intercut battlefield orations either made tyrant and liberator 'interchangeable' (Smallwood, 361–2) or treated Richmond as welcome relief.[1] Richmond's difficult, dirty victory in a peat-filled pit depended on Margaret's grant of dominance; Stanley casually tossed the crown in the dirt for him to pick up and hold aloft, in exhaustion (Smallwood, 362).

This *Richard III* employed a device traceable to Garrick, Edmund Kean and Irving: the micropause – even between syllables. Players have frequently commented on what Hankey calls the play's 'relentlessly iambic' verse. McKellen mentions keeping rhythm with his breath in his gas mask; Troughton remarks on a steady 'de-dum'. Garrick hesitated in order to convey the subtleties of sympathetic imagination, Kean and Irving to express their romantic agonies. This production interpellated pauses to register political struggles as hesitations and resistance.[2]

By contrast, the Steven Pimlott–David Troughton 1995 *Richard III* went for meta-theatre rather than political conflict (Day, 195). Troughton opened by recalling Richard Tarleton, the Elizabethan clown who could bring down the house by protruding his head into view and grimacing. Non-representational clowning continued as Troughton hobbled forward, took a deep breath, mouthed the letter 'N . . .' and froze, interrupted by giggling courtiers on a ledge above him. He scuttled off to return with a jester's cap and bells and bauble, ready to entertain this onstage audience, only to switch back to engaging the theatre audience when he lunged forward on 'But I, that am not shaped for sportive tricks' (1.1.14).

---

1 Peter Holland, *English Shakespeares: Shakespeare on the English stage in the 1990s* (Cambridge, 1997), 116.
2 See James N. Loehlin, 'Playing politics: *Richard III* in recent performance', *Performing Arts Journal*, 15 (1993), 80–94; Siemon, 'Between'.

9 Simon Russell Beale as Richard, with Kate Duchêne as Prince Edward and
   Annabelle Apsion as York (directed by Sam Mendes, RSC, 1992–3)

Instead of scaring audiences senseless as Sher had done, Troughton invited them to laugh with him as he deceived the frozen onstage characters (see Fig. 10).[1]

True to Shakespeare in breaking the representational frame, Troughton's jester still endured physical suffering and a troubled maternal relationship. These strands came together in Richard's altered relation to the audience in the second half of the play. From the failed bid for popular adulation (3.7.20–4), when the audience were encouraged to laugh at rather than with him, a rift widened as he displayed ineptitude, conscience (4.2.63–4) and despair. Troughton chose Q1's 'I and I' over the Folio's 'I am I' (5.3.183) for Richard's dream soliloquy to mark this split – the first 'Richard' being the audience and the second the man (Troughton, 95). Beset by censure, Richard despaired and, in effect, killed himself. As the intercut battlefield speeches grew weaker and stronger, Richard laid down sword and crown and walked to the ghosts' side of the stage to applaud – weakly – Richmond's final speech (Day, 218–19), an ironic conclusion perhaps recalling Sturua.

Whatever the uncertain significance of this end, 'the complete absence of any motherly love' was the presumed origin of Richard's suffering (Troughton, 87). Contemporary productions may not trust heroes or providence, but they take mothers seriously. Assessing the crown as a 'substitute' for love, Troughton removed it in 4.4 to curl up in a foetal position with his head in his mother's lap (Troughton, 88). Contemporary productions that ascribe tyranny to thwarted maternal relationships or make Margaret the universal time-keeper certainly contrast with the androcentric hero–villain shows of earlier centuries. Whether or not blaming his mother for Richard or granting Margaret cosmic authority resolves questions about accountability is debatable.

1   Robert Smallwood, '*Richard III* at Stratford', *SQ*, 47 (1996), 327. The bauble had Troughton's face on one side, a death's head on the other (Day, 198; Jowett, 108).

10   David Troughton as Richard with cap, bells and bauble (directed by Steven
      Pimlott, RSC, 1995)

A similarly logical development of naturalistically conceived
character appears in the 2002 Michael Grandage–Kenneth
Branagh presentation of a Richard driven by the pain and stigma
of disability. On a mostly bare stage, Branagh opened naked
except for white underpants, stretched out as if Leonardo's
Vitruvian man were forced to fit an apparatus with weights and

pulleys. Unable to stand erect without a corset and leg calliper, he collapsed into a heap upon 'But I, that am not shaped for sportive tricks' (1.1.14).[1] Another anti-Sher, but in his evident difficulties also an anti-McKellen; once upright, he could pass for convivial, announcing, like a music hall MC, 'The new-delivered Hastings' (121), but he displayed suddenly changing capacities. He could force a kiss from Anne, but the princes knocked him down, pulled off his brace and clambered onto his back, causing a roar of pain. He hurled Buckingham away at 'I am not in the giving vein' (4.2.114), but laid his head weeping in Queen Elizabeth's lap (4.4).[2] Branagh's Richard conveyed inner misery and self-hatred to portray not the demonic Antichrist, but a trauma victim, a wounded animal, not a 'nice, vulnerable Richard on the inside'.[3]

The next logical step would be actors with disabilities playing Richard, or, conversely, physically imposing actors playing against type. Three New York productions fill these bills. In 2004 Peter DuBois directed Peter Dinklage, standing 4 feet 6 inches, and accepting dwarfism as a strategic asset that kept other characters from taking him seriously.[4] In 3.4 Richard leaped atop the council table to walk to Hastings. In 2007 Heidi Lauren Duke directed Henry Holden, an actor who regularly employs arm-crutches. Richard's role was split between Holden, who spoke Richard's lines when alone, and Andrew Hutcheon, who read Richard's dialogue while Holden mimed his actions. Instead of a 'wink-wink' villain, Holden portrayed 'a normal guy who has had enough', his story that of 'any disabled' person.[5] Finally, the Classic Stage Company's 2007 Richard, Michael Cumpsty (co-directing with Brian Kulick), dominated everyone except the crazed Margaret (Roberta Maxwell) with his tall, handsome,

1 Alastair Macaulay, *Financial Times*, 23 March 2002.
2 Stephen Brown, *TLS*, 5 April 2002; Matt Wolf, *Variety*, 31 March 2002.
3 See Brown; contrast the 1987 Viennese *Richard III*, directed by Claus Peymann, which gave Richard Hitler hair but portrayed him as 'never loved . . . lonely . . . a poor pitiable man, worthy of compassion' (Draudt, 205).
4 Charles McNulty, *Village Voice*, 7 September 2004.
5 *New York Times*, 21 July 2007.

surprisingly able-bodied presence and mordant humour through the third act. Brutal yet charmingly comic ('Chop off his head' was followed by a pause, giggle and 'just joking' tone on 'something we will determine' (3.1.193)), Cumpsty, aided by Buckingham and a laughably corrupt Mayor, enlisted the audience to wave little white boar pennants and to answer Richard's 'Will you enforce me to a world of cares?' (3.7.222) with an enthusiastic 'Yes!' The audience cheered, 'Long live King Richard!'[1]

The early twenty-first century also saw *Richard III* again appear in a cycle. Motifs throughout the tetralogy directed by Michael Boyd emphasized moral failings and political infighting across generations.[2] In 2001 Fiona Bell doubled Margaret and Joan la Pucelle, so the same actor who waved a severed arm at its loser in *1 Henry VI* returned with the bones of her murdered son, tipping them out of their sack and reassembling the skeleton to confront the court (see Fig. 11).[3] Keith Bartlett doubled Talbot (*1H6*) with Stanley, turning him into a virtuous figure working within Richard's inner circle (Day, 186). Aidan McArdle's Richard appeared puckish, capable of saying 'I, as a child, will go by thy direction' (2.2.153) without irony and kissing Buckingham's hand. This gesture returned ironically when promise of the earldom of Hereford (3.1.194–8) prompted Buckingham to attempt shaking hands, only to be given Richard's kingly hand to kiss (Day, 181). Richard died cursed by his mother and father, who together removed his crown. The ghostly blessing of Richmond added lines from *3 Henry VI* commending 'mildness' and 'mercy'. This uplifting conclusion, countering recent ironic

---

1 For similar cheering, see Michael Dobson's review of the British all-female *Richard III* directed by Barry Kyle at the Globe Theatre ('Shakespeare performances in England 2003', *SS* 57 (2004), 277).

2 The appeal of the tetralogies also registered abroad in Luk Perceval and Tom Lanoye's *Ten Oorlong* (1997), a cycle including a cannibalistic Richard figure; see Ton Hoenselaars, 'Two Flemings at war with Shakespeare', in Hoenselaars, 244–61.

3 Benedict Nightingale, *The Times*, 27 April 2001.

11   Fiona Bell's Margaret spilling out the bones of her son Prince Edward, with
     Elaine Pyke as Queen Elizabeth (directed by Michael Boyd, RSC, 2001)

tendencies, was complicated by Richard's resurrection, as if he
were ready to begin the conflict again (Day, 188–90).

This cycle was revived in 2006–7 with Jonathan Slinger's
superbly deranged Richard. Short, scruffy and clumsy,
smirking, spitting while speaking, Slinger appeared 'a casualty
first, a sadist second – his life story a runt's revenge' among

12   Jonathan Slinger as Richard (directed by Michael Boyd, RSC, 2007–8)

'smooth operators'.[1] Having concluded *3 Henry VI* by addressing the newborn prince in his arms with the single word 'Now
. . .' as the stage went black, Slinger, now hairless, opened *Richard
III* rocking himself spasmodically while holding what appeared
still to be the swaddled prince but turned out to be his empty
drool napkin (see Fig. 12). Then, taking his nephew's hand, he
began his soliloquy, only to send the boy off before confiding to
us his determination to prove a villain.[2]

1   Kate Kellaway, *The Observer*, 28 January 2007.
2   Benedict Nightingale, *The Times*, 25 January 2007.

KING
RICHARD III

LIST OF ROLES

KING EDWARD IV
DUCHESS of York   *mother of King Edward IV*

PRINCE Edward, *later King Edward V* ⎫
          Richard, Duke of YORK ⎭   *sons of King Edward IV*

George, Duke of CLARENCE ⎫   5
RICHARD, Duke of Gloucester ⎬ *brothers of King Edward IV*
later KING RICHARD III ⎭

QUEEN ELIZABETH   *wife of King Edward IV*

Anthony Woodeville, Lord RIVERS   *brother of Queen Elizabeth*

Marquess of DORSET ⎫   10
          Lord GREY ⎭   *sons of Queen Elizabeth*

Sir Thomas VAUGHAN

GHOST of KING HENRY VI

QUEEN MARGARET   *widow of King Henry VI*
GHOST of PRINCE EDWARD   *son of King Henry VI*   15
Lady ANNE   *widow of Prince Edward,*
          son of King Henry VI, and
          later wife of Richard, Duke of
          Gloucester

William, Lord HASTINGS   *Lord Chamberlain*
Lord STANLEY, Earl of Derby
Henry, Earl of RICHMOND   *stepson of Stanley, later*
          King Henry VII

Earl of OXFORD ⎫   20
Sir James BLUNT ⎬
Sir Walter HERBERT ⎬   *Richmond's followers*
Sir William Brandon ⎭

Duke of BUCKINGHAM ⎫
Duke of NORFOLK ⎪ 25
Sir Richard RATCLIFFE ⎪
Sir William CATESBY ⎪ *Richard, Duke of Gloucester's*
Sir James TYRREL ⎬ *followers*
Sir Francis LOVELL ⎪
Thomas, Earl of SURREY ⎪ 30
Two MURDERERS ⎪
PAGE ⎭

CARDINAL Bourchier   *Archbishop of Canterbury*
ARCHBISHOP of York
Bishop of ELY   35
Sir CHRISTOPHER Urswick   *a priest*
John, a PRIEST

Sir Robert BRAKENBURY   *Lieutenant of the Tower of*
London

KEEPER of the Tower
Lord MAYOR of London   40
SCRIVENER
PURSUIVANT
SHERIFF
TRESSEL ⎫
BERKELEY ⎬ *gentlemen attending Lady Anne* 45
Three CITIZENS

BOY ⎱ *children of George, Duke of*
DAUGHTER ⎰ *Clarence*

Lords, Bishops, Gentlemen, Aldermen, Citizens,
Halberdiers, Soldiers, Attendants, Messengers   50

LIST OF ROLES not in Qq, F; first provided by Rowe.

1 KING EDWARD IV Edward Plantagenet (1442–83), son of Richard, Duke of York, and Cecily Neville, won the crown during the Wars of the Roses from the Lancastrian Henry VI. He was secretly married in 1464 to Elizabeth, daughter of Richard Woodeville and widow of John Grey, alienating the powerful Earl of Warwick (see *3H6* 3.3). In 1471 he defeated the forces of Warwick and Queen Margaret, capturing Margaret at Tewkesbury after killing her son Edward (see *3H6* 5.5).

2 DUCHESS of York Cecily (née Neville, 1415–95), granddaughter of John of Gaunt and Katherine Swynford, mother of Edward IV, Clarence and Richard, grandmother of the play's little princes and their sister, Elizabeth

3 PRINCE Edward Edward, Prince of Wales (1470–83), elder son of Edward IV. Taken under the control of Richard of Gloucester while on his way to London after his father's death on 9 April 1483, he never had his scheduled coronation as Edward V and is presumed to have died in the Tower of London. By 22 June 1483 Ralph Shaw had publicized Richard's claim to the throne, and on 26 June Richard III began his reign. By September 1483 Richard's opponents had apparently given up hope of ever seeing Edward alive and transferred their support to Henry, Earl of Richmond.

4 YORK Richard, Duke of York (1473–83), younger son of Edward IV. He is presumed to have been killed along with his brother in the Tower of London, although in the 1490s a figure claiming to be Richard Plantagenet (also identified as Perkin Warbeck) appeared at the centre of a Yorkist rising against Henry VII.

5 CLARENCE George Plantagenet (1449–78), created Duke of Clarence (1461) by his elder brother Edward IV; married to Isabel Neville, elder sister of Lady Anne Neville, Richard's queen. Clarence fought on the Lancastrian side with the Earl of Warwick against

his brothers in 1470 but rejoined them in 1471 (see *3H6* 4.1, 5.1). He was later imprisoned by Edward IV in the Tower of London, executed and attainted (see 1.1, 1.4).

6–7 RICHARD . . . KING RICHARD Richard Plantagenet (1452–85), created Duke of Gloucester (1461), later King Richard III; fourth surviving son of Richard, Duke of York, and Cecily, Duchess of York. He was named Lord Protector of his nephew Edward V in 1483, but was himself crowned as Richard III two months later. He was defeated and killed at the battle of Bosworth in August 1485.

8 QUEEN ELIZABETH Elizabeth Grey (née Woodeville, *c.* 1437–92), daughter of Richard Woodeville, 1st Earl of Rivers, and his wife, Jacquetta, dowager Duchess of Bedford. In 1456 she married Sir John Grey, who was killed in 1461 fighting on the Lancastrian side at the second battle of St Albans, leaving her with two sons, Thomas (later Marquess of Dorset) and Richard Grey. Married to Edward IV secretly in 1464 (see *3H6* 3.2), Elizabeth was 'the first subject raised to the throne of England as the wife of the reigning sovereign' (Thomson, 100).

9 RIVERS Anthony Woodeville (or Woodville, Wydeville) (*c.* 1440–83), 2nd Earl Rivers, later Lord Scales, having taken the title by right of his wife, heir of Lord Scales, in 1462; brother of the play's Queen Elizabeth. Having fought for Lancaster in 1460, Rivers later aided Edward IV against Clarence and Warwick and in Edward's victories over the Lancastrians in 1471, and served as mentor to the young Prince Edward. Taken captive by Richard of Gloucester while accompanying Prince Edward to London in April 1483, he was executed at Pontefract for treason on 25 June (see 3.3).

10 DORSET Sir Thomas Grey, Marquess of Dorset (1455–1501), elder son of Queen Elizabeth and her first husband, Sir John Grey. Dorset fought for Edward IV at Tewkesbury and supposedly participated in the murder

of Prince Edward, son of Henry VI (though not in Shakespeare's portrayal; see *3H6* 5.5). He was a bitter opponent of Lord Hastings; historically, he supported Buckingham's abortive rebellion against Richard III in 1483 and joined Richmond in Brittany. He proved an unreliable ally and was left prisoner in France as security for a loan, not participating in the invasion of 1485.

11 GREY Sir Richard Grey (d. 1483), younger son of Queen Elizabeth and Sir John Grey. Arrested by Richard of Gloucester at Ludlow in April 1483, along with his uncle, Anthony, Earl Rivers, he was imprisoned and executed with Rivers and Thomas Vaughan at Pontefract on 25 June (see 3.3).

12 VAUGHAN Sir Thomas Vaughan (d. 1483) was for many years in the service of the Yorkists, rising to become chamberlain and councillor to the young Prince Edward, son of Edward IV. One of those accompanying the prince to London for his coronation in April 1483, Vaughan was intercepted by Richard of Gloucester and the Duke of Buckingham and executed at Pontefract on 25 June (see 3.3).

13 GHOST of KING HENRY VI Henry Plantagenet (1421–71), descended from John of Gaunt, Duke of Lancaster, and only child of Henry V; his troubled reign, beset by rivalries between the houses of York and Lancaster, is the subject of Shakespeare's *1, 2* and *3H6*. Henry's death in the Tower of London in 1471 is portrayed by Shakespeare as a murder by Richard of Gloucester (see *3H6* 5.6).

14 QUEEN MARGARET Margaret of Anjou (1430–82), married to Henry VI (1445). Margaret is prominent in *2* and *3H6* as queen and warrior on Henry's behalf; her son and her husband are murdered in *3H6* by the York brothers (Edward, Richard and Clarence) (see *3H6* 5.5, 5.6). Imprisoned after her defeat by Edward IV at the battle of Tewkesbury in 1471, she was exiled in 1476 to Anjou, where she died the year before Richard III's accession.

15 GHOST of PRINCE EDWARD Edward Plantagenet (1453–71), Prince of Wales, only son of Henry VI and Margaret of Anjou; married to Anne Neville (1470). Shakespeare portrays his death as occurring at the hands of Richard, Clarence and Edward IV before the eyes of Margaret, his mother (see *3H6* 5.5)

16 ANNE Lady Anne Neville (1456–85), younger daughter of the powerful Earl of Warwick (Clarence's wife Isabel was her elder sister). She was first married to the son of Henry VI, Prince Edward, who was killed at the battle of Tewkesbury in 1471 (see *3H6* 5.5). In 1472, at the age of sixteen, she married Richard of Gloucester, and in 1483 was crowned Richard's queen.

17 HASTINGS William, Lord Hastings (*c.* 1430–83), a trusted companion of Edward IV, descended from a family of Yorkist allegiance. Hastings was the most powerful and prominent of the non-royal nobility who owed advancement to the favour of Edward (C. Ross, *Richard*, 39). Made a peer, Knight of the Garter and Lord Chamberlain following the battle of Towton in 1461, as Lord Chamberlain he thereafter controlled access to the king's person. Although he had married King Edward's cousin Katherine Neville in 1462, he was bitterly at odds with the Neville family at the time the play begins. He was notoriously betrayed and then beheaded by Richard in 1483 (see 3.4).

18 STANLEY Thomas, Lord Stanley (d. 1504), later Earl of Derby (1485); councillor and steward of household to Edward IV. In 1482 Stanley married Margaret Beaufort, Countess of Richmond and mother to the play's Richmond by her first marriage. He was imprisoned at the time of Hastings's execution in 1483, but was later named Constable by Richard. He held back on the field at Bosworth, and was subsequently created Earl of Derby (as he is frequently called in Shakespeare's play) (Sutton & Hammond, 399).

19 RICHMOND Henry Tudor (1457–1509), Earl of Richmond, afterwards King Henry VII. Richmond was the posthumous son of Henry VI's half-brother Edmund Tudor and his wife, Margaret Beaufort, great-great-granddaughter of Edward III through John of Gaunt and his mistress and (later) third wife, Katherine Swynford. He is the stepson of the play's Lord Stanley. Supposedly prophesied to become king by Henry VI in 1470 (see *3H6* 4.6), he fled to Brittany the following year with his uncle Jasper Tudor, Earl of Pembroke, and lived at the Breton court from 1476. He was proclaimed king during Buckingham's abortive revolt of 1483, but his invasion fleet was scattered by storms and he returned to Brittany, vowing to marry Elizabeth of York. In 1485 he invaded England with support of France, landing in Wales on 7 August; he gathered forces from around England and defeated Richard on 22 August at Bosworth, where he was crowned on the field (see 5.3–5).

20 OXFORD John de Vere (1442–1513), Earl of Oxford, a Lancastrian partisan, escaped imprisonment in Calais in 1484 to join Richmond and commanded Richmond's vanguard at the battle of Bosworth.

21 BLUNT Sir James Blunt (d. 1492), a soldier, having been an esquire of the body to Richard III, left England for France to join Richmond in November 1484. He was knighted by Richmond in 1485 at his landing at Milford Haven, and subsequently rewarded with land forfeited by Richard's allies.

22 HERBERT Sir Walter Herbert, second son of Sir William Herbert, a Yorkist supporter (see *3H6* 4.1.129). Hall and Holinshed report that Richard III initially trusted Walter Herbert to halt Richmond's progress towards Bosworth. He appears prominently among the supporters of Richmond in 5.2 and 5.3.

23 **Brandon** Sir William Brandon (d. 1485), Richmond's standard-bearer at Bosworth (see 5.3), killed there by Richard III according to Polydore Vergil

24 BUCKINGHAM Henry Stafford, 2nd Duke of Buckingham (1455–83); married (1466) Katherine, sister of Elizabeth Woodeville (the play's Queen Elizabeth, wife of Edward IV). A member of the royal family by right of his illegitimate Beaufort descent from John of Gaunt (shared with Richmond), and of direct descent from Thomas of Lancaster, second youngest son of Edward III, Buckingham was head of one of the wealthiest and longest-established of English magnate families. Appointed Lord High Steward of England under Edward IV (1478), he was subsequently excluded from offices and responsibilities. Under Richard III he held the offices of Constable of England and Lord Great Chamberlain. He led an unsuccessful rebellion against Richard in 1483 and was executed on 2 November 1483 (see 4.4, 5.1).

25 NORFOLK John Howard (*c.* 1430–85), created 1st Duke of Norfolk (28 June 1483), was loyal to Edward IV and later to Richard III (C. Ross, *Richard*, 38). He carried Richard's crown at his coronation, and was presented with one of Richard's former titles, Lord High Admiral, and with nearly as many manors as Buckingham (Seward, 138–9). He died leading Richard's vanguard at Bosworth.

26 RATCLIFFE Sir Richard Ratcliffe (d. 1485), younger son of a family from the minor gentry, served Richard of Gloucester from 1475; he was created knight and banneret by Richard on the Scottish campaigns of 1480–2. Ratcliffe, the 'Rat' in William Collingbourne's famous rhyme (see 27n.), was one of Richard's most trusted confidants, and presided over the execution of Rivers, Vaughan and Grey in 1483 (see 3.3). He appears to have died at Bosworth, fighting for Richard.

27 CATESBY Sir William Catesby (d. 1485), councillor under Edward IV, knighted by Richard III and named Chancellor of the Exchequer in 1483, replacing William, Lord Hastings, his

close associate. He became Speaker in Richard's parliament in 1484, and was executed after the battle of Bosworth (1485). Catesby is notoriously remembered as the 'Cat' in William Collingbourne's couplet: 'The Cat, the Rat and Lovell our Dog / Rule all England under the Hog' (Horrox, 222).

28 TYRREL Sir James Tyrrel (d. 1502). Tyrrel is associated with the murder of the children of Edward IV in Polydore Vergil. Thomas More characterizes him as a man of 'right goodlye p[e]rsonage' led astray by Richard III, who exploited his high ambition. He served Richard as Master of the Horse and Master of the Henchmen (Seward, 140). Historically, Tyrrel prospered under Henry VII until his execution in 1502 for favouring Edmund de la Pole (Sutton & Hammond, 407).

29 LOVELL Francis Lovell (*c.* 1457–*c.* 1488) was one of Richard of Gloucester's closest friends, and with wide estates in Lincolnshire and Yorkshire was one of the wealthiest barons beneath the rank of earl. He served under Richard in the Scottish military campaigns of 1480–2, was knighted by Richard (1481), made viscount (1483) and two days after Richard's assumption of the throne became the king's chamberlain, an office implying constant personal contact with the king. He is 'our Dog' in William Collingbourne's rhyme (see 27n.). Sent to guard the south coast against Richmond's invasion in 1485, he may not have been at Bosworth. He participated in later rebellions after Richmond's victory.

30 SURREY Thomas Howard (1443–1524), a supporter of Edward IV and of Richard of Gloucester. He helped arrest Lord Hastings at the Tower of London on 13 June 1483, and was created Earl of Surrey fifteen days later. He remained close to Richard III, helping to suppress Buckingham's rebellion, and was wounded and captured fighting for Richard at Bosworth. After three years' imprisonment in the Tower of London he served Henry

VII and was restored as Earl of Surrey in 1489.

33 CARDINAL Thomas Bourchier (*c.* 1411–86), Archbishop of Canterbury (1454), Lord Chancellor under Henry VI (1455), and Cardinal (invested 1472). He crowned three kings, Edward IV, Richard III and Henry VII, and married Henry VII to Elizabeth of York (1486). He was involved in persuading Queen Elizabeth to surrender her younger son to Richard of Gloucester (see 3.1).

34 ARCHBISHOP Thomas Rotherham (1423–1500), Archbishop of York, Keeper of the Privy Seal for Edward IV; arrested along with Hastings (and John Morton, Bishop of Ely) in the Tower in June 1483 (C. Ross, *Richard*, 42)

35 ELY John Morton (d. 1500), Bishop of Ely and later (1486) Archbishop of Canterbury. Morton's early and close association with Margaret of Anjou and the Lancastrian court led to his imprisonment after Edward IV seized the crown. He escaped and joined Queen Margaret in France, serving as Keeper of the Privy Seal to Henry VI. Pardoned by Edward IV in 1471, he eventually became one of his counsellors. He was arrested by Richard on 13 June 1483 at the same council meeting that led to Hastings's execution, and placed in the custody of the Duke of Buckingham. Morton eventually aided Buckingham's abortive rebellion and escaped to Flanders to serve Richmond, first as a diplomat and later as a member of the king's council and Chancellor. A patron of Sir Thomas More, he may be one source of More's account of Richard III.

36 CHRISTOPHER Sir Christopher Urswick (*c.* 1448–1522), a priest and supporter of the Stanleys, was chaplain to Lady Margaret Beaufort and involved in negotiating the marriage of her son, Richmond, to Elizabeth of York (see 4.5). He joined Richmond in France and accompanied him to Bosworth in 1485.

38 BRAKENBURY Sir Robert Brakenbury (d. 1485), appointed Lieutenant of the

Tower of London by Richard III in 1483 (i.e. years after the imprisonment and death in 1478 of George, Duke of Clarence, depicted in 1.1 and 1.4), died fighting on Richard's side at Bosworth.

40 MAYOR Historically, the Lord Mayor of London depicted in the play was Edmund Shaa (or Shaw) (in office 1482–3; d. 1488). He served on a commission to inquire into treasons within the City in December 1483 (Sutton & Hammond, 394). His brother Raffe (or Ralph) delivered a notorious sermon claiming the bastardy of Edward IV's children (see 3.5).

47 BOY Edward Plantagenet, Earl of Warwick (1475–99), the only surviving son of George, Duke of Clarence, and Isabel Neville (d. 1476), orphaned in 1478; he was imprisoned in the Tower by Henry VII, found guilty of conspiring against Henry with Perkin Warbeck (see 4n.) and executed in 1499 (Hammond & Sutton, 385).

48 DAUGHTER Margaret Plantagenet (1473–1541), daughter of George, Duke of Clarence, and Isabel Neville, married to Sir Richard Pole by Henry VII (not by Richard as claimed in 4.3) in 1487; she was executed by Henry VIII on charges of treason.

KING RICHARD III

1.1   *Enter* RICHARD, Duke of Gloucester, *alone.*

RICHARD

Now is the winter of our discontent
Made glorious summer by this son of York,

1.1 location: 'The COURT' (Pope) or
'London: *A Street*' (Capell); references
suggest proximity to the Tower of
London. After Irving, a street scene
became the norm. The play's earliest
texts seldom name specific locations
for scenes (but see 3.3.0.3), usually
allowing the dialogue to establish location whenever specificity is required.
Editors have generally tried to aid
readers by suggesting locations for
the action.

0.1 *Enter* Richard is the only character to
open a Shakespeare play with a soliloquy; Cibber's version opened with
the imprisoned Henry VI and discussed the struggles between York and
Lancaster. Kemble and Cooke entered
majestically, Edmund Kean 'hastily –
head low – arms folded' (Colley, 66–7).
Junius Brutus Booth used delay to
enormous effect (Matthews & Hutton,
111). Simon Russell Beale's cane
tapped his way onto the dark stage
(de Jongh).

alone Cf. Queen Margaret's entry at
4.4.0.1 ('*sola*' Qq).

1 SP *Richard's first speech lacks a SP
in F, Qq. Richard is usually '*Glo.*' in
Qq SPs – until his crowned entrance
in 4.2; thereafter he is '*Ki.*', '*King.*'
or '*King Ri.*' In F he is '*Rich.*', '*Ric.*'
or '*Ri.*' until 3.1.63–180, where he is
'*Glo.*' He then becomes Richard again
until 5.3. From 5.3.49 on, he is usually
'*King.*' but otherwise '*Rich.*'

1 Now Dramatic rather than historical
chronology: Holinshed has Edward IV
enter London on 21 May 1471, victorious
over the house of Lancaster; Henry VI
was killed that day (by Richard, according to Holinshed) or died soon after
(from melancholy displeasure, according to writers 'fauoring . . . the house
of Yorke'), in the Tower of London.
Clarence was killed in February 1478
and Edward IV died in April 1483. The
first two acts span 12 years.

1–2 winter . . . summer Metaphors of
seasonal transformation are ubiquitous
in Tudor poetry (e.g. Sidney, *Astrophil
and Stella*, 69), but Richard reverses
the famous opening of Kyd's *Spanish
Tragedy*, wherein the 'sommer joyes'
of love are aborted by 'Deaths winter'
(1.1.12–13). By 1601 Shakespeare's
lines were famous enough to be quoted
in mockery (*Parnassus*, 343).

2 son Edward IV, Richard's brother, son
of the Duke of York killed in *3H6*, but
possibly a punning reference to the sun
that Edward assumed as his emblem
after three suns appeared during his
victorious battle with the Lancastrians
(*3H6* 2.1.21–40; cf. C. Ross, *Wars*, 53);
cf. 1.3.265–6. GWW suggests that
son refers to the infant prince (later
Edward V) introduced in *3H6* as the
future hope of his father and kissed by
Richard, who informs the audience of
his evil intentions toward this child who
stands between him and the throne.

1.1] *F (Actus Primus. Scæna Prima.); not in Qq, which lack act and scene divisions throughout*
0.1 Gloucester, *alone] F, Qq (Gloster, solus subst.)*   **1 SP]** *Capell (Ric.); not in Qq, F*   of our] *F, Q1–2;*
of *Q3–6*   **2 son]** *F (Son); sonne Qq*

133

And all the clouds that loured upon our house
In the deep bosom of the ocean buried.
Now are our brows bound with victorious wreaths,   5
Our bruised arms hung up for monuments,
Our stern alarums changed to merry meetings,
Our dreadful marches to delightful measures.
Grim-visaged War hath smoothed his wrinkled front;
And now, instead of mounting barbed steeds   10
To fright the souls of fearful adversaries,
He capers nimbly in a lady's chamber
To the lascivious pleasing of a lute.

3   **loured** frowned
    house the York family
6   **bruised** bruisèd
    bruised arms . . . monuments war-
    battered weapons displayed as memo-
    rials; cf. *Luc* 110.
7   **alarums** calls summoning to arms
    (*OED sb.* 4a) made with drums (4.4.149)
    or trumpets (*2H6* 5.2.3); or sudden or
    unexpected attacks (*OED sb.* 11)
    meetings encounters, possibly play-
    ing on encountering in arms, battles
    (*OED sb.* 2a)
8–13 Lyly's *Campaspe* opposes dancing
    'measurs' to a military 'march' (4.3.32–
    4). Cf. Venus' boasts to have converted
    Mars from 'drum and ensign red'
    and taught him to 'sport and dance,
    / To toy, to wanton, dally, smile, and
    jest' (*VA* 97–108). Edward III rejects
    the drum for the amorous lute (*E3*
    2.2.56). Opposition of weaponry to
    music and dance is conventional in
    soldierly admonition (cf. de Somogyi,
    44). Richard was successful militarily,
    especially against the Scots in 1481–2
    (Mancini, 65).
8   **measures** tunes or melodies (*OED
    sb.* 17); with possible senses of grave
    or stately dances (*OED sb.* 20a) or the

boundaries of a fencer's reach (*OED
sb.* 2e)
9   **Grim-visaged War** Cf. 'Warre . . .
    With visage grym' (*Mirror*, 'Induction',
    386–7).
    wrinkled front frowning brow
10–13 Cf. 'Is the warlike sou[n]d of
    drumme and trumpe turned to the soft
    noyse of lire and lute? the neighing of
    barbed steeds . . . to dilicate tunes and
    amorous glaunces?' (Lyly, *Campaspe*,
    2.2.35–9).
10 **barbed** barbèd; prepared for combat
    with an armoured covering for the
    breast and flanks
11 **fearful** either dreadful, terrifying,
    or frightened, timorous (*OED a.* 1a,
    3a)
12–13 **capers . . . lute** Cf. 'they are too
    dainty for the wars. / Their fingers
    made to quaver on a Lute, / Their
    armes to hang about a Ladies necke:
    / Their legs to dance and caper in the
    aire' (Marlowe, *Works*, *2 Tamburlaine*,
    1.3.28–31); also 'Ignoto' in Davies
    and Marlowe (see p. 82). Near *mount-
    ing*, *lascivious*, *sportive*, *tricks* and
    amorous, capering 'in a lady's chamber'
    carries clear sexual connotations.
13 **pleasing** pleasure

7 alarums] *F, Q2–6; Q1 (*alarmes*)   8 measures] *F, Q1–3;* pleasures *Q4–6*   10 instead] *F, Q2–6 subst.;*
in steed *Q1*   13 lute] *F;* loue *Qq*

But I, that am not shaped for sportive tricks,
Nor made to court an amorous looking-glass;   15
I, that am rudely stamped, and want love's majesty
To strut before a wanton ambling nymph;
I, that am curtailed of this fair proportion,
Cheated of feature by dissembling Nature,
Deformed, unfinished, sent before my time   20
Into this breathing world, scarce half made up,
And that so lamely and unfashionable
That dogs bark at me as I halt by them –
Why, I, in this weak piping time of peace,

14 **But I** Since Irving, it has been custom-
ary to mark this transition to personal
assessment. Irving's production halted
its festive bells (Hankey, 89); Sher
lurched forward spectacularly (Colley,
239).
   sportive amorous or wanton
   tricks games, ways
15 **amorous** pertaining to paraphernalia
   commonly associated with lovers
16 **rudely stamped** roughly fashioned,
   as in a crudely pressed coin
   want lack
17 **wanton ambling nymph** woman
   who walks in a sexually provocative
   manner; Hamlet calls Ophelia 'nymph'
   and claims 'you jig and amble and you
   lisp' (*Ham* 3.1.88, 143).
18–23 **I . . . halt** Richard's claim to
   have been born unfinished parallels the self-characterization of the
   lame Emperor Claudius in *Mirror,
   Additions*, 'Claudius', 11–12. See
   p. 66 and Jones, *Origins*, 217–18.
18 **curtailed . . . proportion** shortened,
   cut off in respect of proper dimensions
   curtailed cùrtailed
19 **feature** outward appearance
   dissembling Nature another
   personification, here oddly depicting

Nature as being – as Richard proclaims
himself to be – a dissembler, a cheating
hypocrite. Richard earlier claims that
Love bribed 'frail' Nature to deform
him (*3H6* 3.2.153–5; cf. *VA* 729–44).
Sixteenth-century interpreters typically treated birth abnormalities as
witnessing divine power and wrath
(Cressy, *Travesties*, 39).
20 In *3H6* Richard is called 'an undigested
   and deformed lump' (5.6.51); stories
   about his birth and body go back to
   Rous, who claims he was 'retained
   within his mother's womb for two
   years' (Hanham, 120; cf. p. 52n.).
   Sources suggest that his mother's
   difficult labour was lengthy (cf.
   4.4.163–4).
21 **breathing** i.e. mortal (cf. *Son* 81)
22 **lamely and unfashionable** gram-
   matically, a double adverb with single
   adverbial termination; Richard represents himself as only partially finished,
   lamely created by nature, as well as
   unfashionable – i.e. not stylish – in the
   new time of love and peace.
23 **halt** limp
24 **piping** musical, or specifically referring
   to music of the pastoral pipe (as distinguished from the martial fife or trumpet)
   (*OED ppl. a.* 1b); cf. *MA* 2.3.13–15.

14 shaped for] *F* (shap'd for*)*, *Q1–3* (shapte for*)*; sharpe for *Q4–5;* sharpe of *Q6*   15 Nor] *F, Q1,
3–6;* Not *Q2*   21 scarce] *F, Q1–2;* om. *Q3–6*

Have no delight to pass away the time,   25
Unless to see my shadow in the sun
And descant on mine own deformity.
And therefore, since I cannot prove a lover
To entertain these fair well-spoken days,
I am determined to prove a villain   30
And hate the idle pleasures of these days.
Plots have I laid, inductions dangerous,
By drunken prophecies, libels and dreams,
To set my brother Clarence and the King
In deadly hate, the one against the other;   35
And if King Edward be as true and just
As I am subtle, false and treacherous,
This day should Clarence closely be mewed up
About a prophecy, which says that 'G'
Of Edward's heirs the murderer shall be.   40

27 **descant on** comment upon or, in musical terms, sing or play a melodious accompaniment to a theme
28 **prove** become, turn out to be
29 **entertain** occupy, while away (cf. *Son* 39); used with two other senses in this act: to employ (1.2.259) and to permit oneself (1.3.4).
30 **determined** determinèd; Richard may mean that he is personally resolved or that his role has been determined by birth, a sense supported by his self-designation as 'ordained' to kill Henry VI (*3H6* 5.6.58); cf. *3H6* 2.2.137 and 5.7.23 on his physical features as destined and ordained.
32 **inductions** initial steps (*1H4* 3.1.2), suggesting literary or theatrical prefaces or preambles (*OED* 3c, 3b) as at 4.4.5–7, which connects inductions with the generically 'tragical'; *Plots* reinforces theatrical association.

Richard provides an 'induction' to *Richard III* as a Prologue figure might (cf. *2H4*).
33 **libels** accusatory or defamatory bills or pamphlets, publicly posted or circulated; libels were frequent in the 1580s and 1590s, with prominent figures often accused of being their hidden instigators; cf. pp. 36–7.
38 **closely** securely
mewed up caged, often referring to hawks or poultry (*OED v.*[2]); cf. 132 and 1.3.138.
40 **Edward's heirs** King Edward's children; sources record this prediction, but not that Richard originated it. Holinshed reports that this 'foolish prophesie, which was, that, after K. Edward one should reigne, whose first letter of his name should be a G', was later taken to refer to Richard (Holinshed, 3.703); see pp. 36–7.

26 see] *F;* spie *Qq*   32 inductions] *F, Q3–6;* inductious *Q1–2;* inductious, *Oxf*[1]   39 a prophecy] *F, Q1–3, 6;* adrohesie *Q4–5*   40 murderer] *F, Q3–6 (*murtherer*);* murtherers *Q1–2*

Dive, thoughts, down to my soul; here Clarence comes.

Enter CLARENCE, *guarded, and* BRAKENBURY

Brother, good day. What means this armed guard
That waits upon your grace?

CLARENCE   His majesty,
Tendering my person's safety, hath appointed
This conduct to convey me to the Tower.   45

RICHARD

Upon what cause?

CLARENCE   Because my name is George.

RICHARD

Alack, my lord, that fault is none of yours;
He should for that commit your godfathers.
O, belike his majesty hath some intent
That you should be new christened in the Tower.   50
But what's the matter, Clarence, may I know?

41 **Dive, thoughts** Honigmann notes
this unusual admission that a soliloquy
is spoken aloud; cf. 1.3.338n.
41.1 *guarded* surrounded by guards
BRAKENBURY Other accounts do not give
Sir Robert Brakenbury a role in impris-
oning Clarence, since he only became
Constable of the Tower five years after
Clarence's death; cf. 1.4.75.1n.
42 **armed** armèd
43 **waits upon** attends; ironic, given
Clarence's constraint by armed guards
44 **Tendering** caring for; cf. 2.4.73.
safety Clarence plays upon the meaning 'confinement or close custody'
(*OED* 2; cf. *KJ* 4.2.158).
45 **conduct** escort

the **Tower** the Tower of London; the
first of some 25 references
48 **commit your godfathers** i.e. because
Clarence was given his name in the
baptismal ceremony; *commit* = consign
to imprisonment (also at 61)
49 **belike** probably
50 **new christened** Cf. 1.4. In *The
Mirror for Magistrates* Clarence
describes his murder by drowning in
a wine barrel as a baptism (*Mirror*,
'Clarence', 370–1). New christening
would award him a new name and
thus enable him to evade the accusations against him.
51 **the matter** i.e. the real cause at issue
(between King Edward and himself)

41] *F; Qq line* soule, / comes, / 41.1] *F; opp. 41 Qq (lined with / men. /) guarded, and* BRAK-
ENBURY] *Rowe³; and Brakenbury, guarded F; with / a gard of men Qq subst.* 42 day] *F; dayes Qq
subst.* 43–5] *Pope (43 one line Steevens); F lines* Grace? / safety, / Tower / ; *Qq line* grace? / ap- /
pointed *(ap- / p* nted *Q1 BL, Hn)* / tower. / 44 Tendering] *F (*tendring*), Qq* 45 the Tower]
Qq; th'Tower *F* 46+ SP] *F (Rich.); Glo. Qq* 46] *Steevens; F, Qq line* cause? / George. / 48 god-
fathers] *F, Q1–3; good fathers Q4–6* 50 should be] *F; shalbe Q1; shall be Q2–6* christened] *F,
Q2–5 (*Christned*), Q1, 6* 51 what's] *F, Q1–2 subst.;* what is *Q3–6*

CLARENCE

Yea, Richard, when I know; but I protest
As yet I do not. But, as I can learn,
He hearkens after prophecies and dreams,
And from the crossrow plucks the letter G;   55
And says a wizard told him that by 'G'
His issue disinherited should be.
And for my name of George begins with G,
It follows in his thought that I am he.
These, as I learn, and such like toys as these,   60
Hath moved his highness to commit me now.

RICHARD

Why, this it is, when men are ruled by women:
'Tis not the King that sends you to the Tower;
My Lady Grey his wife, Clarence, 'tis she

---

52 **but** Some editors prefer Qq's 'for',
presuming compositorial or scribal
anticipation; however, F's repeated
'but' could suggest Clarence's excited
emotional state.
54 **hearkens after** pays attention to
55 **crossrow** the alphabet, called the
Christ-crossrow for the cross printed
with it in the hornbook from which
children learned their letters
58 **for** because
60 **toys** trifles
61 **Hath** singular form used with a plural subject, frequent in Shakespeare
(Abbott, 334)
62–116 This sequence replays a passage in *3H6* that begins with Richard
prompting Clarence's animosity
against Queen Elizabeth by glancing
at her humble origins and then referring to Edward's uncontrollable lust
before being warned by a third party
to 'forbear this talk' (*3H6* 4.1.1–6).
62 Cf. Richard's insult wishing that
Queen Margaret 'might still have

worn the petticoat / And ne'er have
stol'n the breech from Lancaster'
(*3H6* 5.5.23–4).
63–5 Although the charge that the
Queen sends Clarence to prison
appears clearly fabricated, Dominic
Mancini (unlike others) maintains
that the Queen 'concluded that her
offspring by the king would never
come to the throne, unless the duke
of Clarence were removed; and of
this she easily persuaded the king.'
Mancini reports that Richard swore
vengeance for Clarence's death
(Mancini, 63).
64 **My Lady Grey** Richard demeans
the Queen by invoking the name of
her deceased first husband, Sir John
Grey; in part, Richard's hostility
arises from her lower social rank.
In *3H6* she rightly says she is 'not
ignoble of descent' (*3H6* 4.1.70). Hall
calls her marriage to Edward 'ioyous
to the quene & profitable to her
bloud, which were so highly exalted,

---

52 I know] *F, Q1–5;* I doe know *Q6*   but] *F;* for *Qq*   59 follows] *F, Q1–4, 6;* fellowes *Q5*   61 Hath]
F; Haue *Qq*

That tempers him to this extremity. 65
Was it not she and that good man of worship,
Anthony Woodeville, her brother there,
That made him send Lord Hastings to the Tower,
From whence this present day he is delivered?
We are not safe, Clarence; we are not safe. 70

CLARENCE

By heaven, I think there is no man secure
But the Queen's kindred and night-walking heralds

yea, & so sodainly promoted, that all the nobilitie more maruayled then allowed this sodayne risyng and swift eleuacion' (*Edward IV*, fol. cxcv[r]).

65 **tempers** governs, overrules, often with a sense of moulding or shaping (cf. *2H4* 4.3.127–8); Q2's 'tempts' could have prompted F's addition of 'harsh' for metrical reasons; but cf. *TxC*, 232–3. 'Tempts' appears frequently in association with Richard's interactions with others (1.4.12; 4.2.35, 39; 4.4.418, 419); *tempers* continues a theme from *Mirror for Magistrates*: 'This made [Richard] plye the while the waxe was soft' ('Clarence', 341).

66 **good . . . worship** sarcastic, since 'goodman' was for persons under the rank of gentlemen and could be used ironically (*OED* 3b; cf. 'goodman Dull', *LLL* 4.2.36); a 'man of worship' was a person of good reputation, but the phrase could imply non-noble standing. Stow (1.327) differentiates between persons of 'worship' and those of 'honour' (i.e. belonging to the nobility). See also 3.7.137n. Richard shows lack of respect in employing Woodeville's family name rather than his new title, Earl Rivers. Social prejudices against

the Woodevilles as upstart nobility are widely reported, but Mancini (67–9) records that his moral goodness won Earl Rivers exemption from 'hatred' and 'jealousy' (cf. More, *CW2*, 14).

67 ***Woodeville** F's '*Woodeulle*' allows trisyllabic pronunciation; Steevens claims that it was so pronounced by a contemporary of his. In *1H6* the name is disyllabic, and F spells it 'Wooduile' (*1H6* 1.3.22).
there probably conveying denigration (*OED adv.* 3b), but taken in some productions to indicate presence within sight of the speaker

72 **Queen's kindred** The association of the Queen's family members with the nocturnal go-betweens employed by King Edward suggests participation in sexual debauchery. The Queen's sons, Dorset and Grey, and her brother, Edward Woodeville, were reputed 'promoters and companions of [Edward's] vices' (Mancini, 67–9). Richard twice proclaimed such charges against Elizabeth's male kin (Mancini, 113n; *Paston Letters*, 6.81).
night-walking heralds i.e. secret messengers between the King and his mistress; 'night-walker' could suggest criminal intent.

65 tempers] *Q1;* tempts *F, Q2, 4–6;* temps *Q3* extremity] *Qg;* harsh Extremity *F* 67 Woodeville] *Capell; Woodeulle F;* Wooduile *Qq* 71 secure] *F;* is securde *Q1–3;* securde *Q4–6 subst.*

That trudge betwixt the King and Mistress Shore.
Heard you not what an humble suppliant
Lord Hastings was ^Qto her^Q for his delivery?   75

RICHARD

Humbly complaining to her deity
Got my Lord Chamberlain his liberty.
I'll tell you what: I think it is our way,
If we will keep in favour with the King,
To be her men and wear her livery.   80
The jealous o'erworn widow and herself,
Since that our brother dubbed them gentlewomen,
Are mighty gossips in our monarchy.

---

73 **trudge** Clarence's term carries ironic connotations; 'trudging' meant walking laboriously, wearily or without spirit, or was 'an undignified equivalent' for walking (*OED v.*[1] 1).
  Mistress Shore Jane (historically Elizabeth) Shore, notorious mistress of Edward IV and later of Hastings (see pp. 55–6 and 3.1.185). 'Mistress' was a title of respect for a female ruler and a title for a woman, married or unmarried (as 'Ms': *OED sb.* 5a, 14a–b), so here it conveys superficial, minimal respect, ironic hyperbole (see 76) and awareness of Shore's illicit relations with Edward (*OED sb.* 11).

75 *****was . . . his** Qq's wording makes more sense than F's 'was, for her'. GWW suggests that Qq's line might have an unaccented 11th syllable elided as 'de-liv- | -ry'.

76 **her deity** mock title attributing god-like status to Mistress Shore

77 **Lord Chamberlain** Hastings; the Lord Chamberlain was a chief officer with shared oversight of all officers of the Royal Household.

78 **way** i.e. most advisable course of action, best hope of success (*OED sb.*[1] III 12b)

80 **her men . . . livery** the uniformed servants or badged retainers of Mistress Shore; in fact she has neither livery nor retainers.

81 **o'erworn widow** i.e. Queen Elizabeth (see 64n.); *o'erworn* conveys advanced age (see *Son* 63), but coupling it with *widow* insinuates being worn out from much use by men (cf. *AC* 1.2.166–75). *o'erworn* also continues the clothing metaphor from *livery* (80), contrasting the two women in King Edward's life (Jowett).

82 **Since that** since
  dubbed a parodic usage, in that only knights were dubbed
  gentlewomen sarcastically inaccurate: Queen Elizabeth was born to gentle status and had claim to noble standing when her father was made Baron (later Earl) Rivers, before she met Edward IV. Jane Shore was neither gentle nor noble, and never would be. Typically, Richard elides differences to evoke a grouping that his interlocutor would find socially distasteful.

83 **gossips** either female friends, insinuating their light or trifling character, or godparents, perhaps covertly alluding to the impending

---

74 you] *F;* ye *Qq*   75 was . . . his] *Qq;* was, for her *F;* was, for his *F2*   76 Humbly] *F, Q1–4;* Humble *Q5–6*   83 our] *F;* this *Qq*

BRAKENBURY

  I beseech your graces both to pardon me.

  His majesty hath straitly given in charge   85

  That no man shall have private conference,

  Of what degree soever, with your brother.

RICHARD

  Even so; an't please your worship, Brakenbury,

  You may partake of any thing we say.

  We speak no treason, man; we say the King   90

  Is wise and virtuous, and his noble Queen

  Well struck in years, fair and not jealous.

  We say that Shore's wife hath a pretty foot,

  A cherry lip, a bonny eye, a passing pleasing tongue,

  And that the Queen's kindred are made gentlefolks.   95

  How say you, sir? Can you deny all this?

'christening' of Clarence in 1.4. Gossips could be men or women. Richard's joke about dubbing foregrounds gender as well as social baseness; hence his oxymoronic assessment of them as *mighty gossips* threatening the patriarchal order. Given the importance of the play's female voices, the sense of gossips as women who delight in 'idle talk' (*OED sb.* 3) carries unintended irony. No evidence supports Richard's assertions concerning alliance between Elizabeth and Jane Shore (cf. 3.4.69–71).

85 **straitly . . . charge** strictly ordered

87 **Of . . . soever** no matter how high in rank (referring to *man* in 86)

88 **an't please** if it please; 'and' in such constructions is generally regularized to conditional 'an' (*OED* an' 2; cf. *LLL* 5.2.575).

92 **Well struck** perhaps euphemistic,

suggesting 'well preserved' (Jowett); the basic meaning is 'advanced in age' (*OED* struck *ppl. a.*).

*jealous F's 'iealious' may record tri-syllabic pronunciation. Perhaps a typical Compositor B spelling even where metre requires a disyllable (*TxC*, 233), but at 81, where a disyllable is required, the spelling is 'iealous' (Lull). Cf. 'iealious' in F's *Oth* 3.4.157–61.

93–4 **foot . . . tongue** More concentrates on Jane Shore's discursive skills: she 'delited not men so much in her bewty, as in her plesant behauiour' (*CW2*, 56).

94 *Editors since Pope have abbreviated or modified this extra-syllabic line. Thompson suggests that it might be a snatch from an old song in 'fourteen' metre (cf. *MND* 5.1.324–6: 'Must cover thy sweet eyes. / These lily lips, / This cherry nose').

passing exceptionally

84+ SP] *F (Bra.); Bro. Qq*   87 your] *F;* his *Qq*   88 an't] *F, Qq* (and*), Pope*   88, 105 Brakenbury] *F;* Brokenbury *Qq*   92 jealous] *F (*iealious*), Qq (*iealous*)

BRAKENBURY

With this, my lord, myself have nought to do.

RICHARD

Naught to do with Mistress Shore? I tell thee, fellow,
He that doth naught with her, excepting one,
Were best to do it secretly, alone.   100

BRAKENBURY

What one, my lord?

RICHARD

Her husband, knave. Wouldst thou betray me?

BRAKENBURY

I do beseech your grace to pardon me, and withal
Forbear your conference with the noble Duke.

CLARENCE

We know thy charge, Brakenbury, and will obey.   105

RICHARD

We are the Queen's abjects, and must obey.

97–8 *nought . . . Naught F's spelling
suggests a pun which distinguishes
between 'nought' (nothing) and
'naught' (mischief, evil: *OED sb.* A
2, citing this line). Jane Shore was
'naught of her body' (Hall, *Edward
V*, fol. xvi'); to 'be naught with' had
sexual connotation (*OED* naught *sb.*
B 2c)
98–104 *These frequently unmetrical lines
have prompted emendation. Richard
may approach prose as he becomes
sexually suggestive (Hammond).
98 thee, fellow Richard descends from
mock formality (*your worship* and *you,
sir*) to nearly contemptuous intimacy
(*OED* fellow *sb.* 10a; Abbott, 231); see
1.2.263n., 3.2.104.
101–2 *These two lines first appear in
Q2, which is otherwise merely derivative from Q1, and are reprinted in

all subsequent early editions, including F. They may be a stop-press
correction, a change introduced into
some copies of a text (in this case
Q1) in the course of printing. For
a change in Q2 that appears to be
such a correction, see 1.3.120. See
pp. 433–4.
102 betray me i.e. prompt me to reveal
what I think concerning this delicate
and potentially dangerous subject of
royal infidelity
103 withal in addition, besides, likewise
104 conference conversation
106 Queen's abjects (abjècts) i.e.
instead of being the King's subjects;
Richard combines two meanings of
'abject' – one who is rejected and
one who is degraded – to suggest
that they have been not only rejected
by the Queen but degraded by

---

97 nought] *F, Q1, 6;* naught *Q2–5* 98–100] *Qq; F lines* Shore? */ her / alone. /* 100 to] *F;* he
Qq 101–2] *F, Q2–6; not in Q1* 103–4] *Capell; F lines* Grace / forbeare / Duke. / *; Qq line* forbeare
/ Duke. / 103 do] *F; not in Qq*

Brother, farewell. I will unto the King,
And whatsoe'er you will employ me in,
, Were it to call King Edward's widow 'sister',
I will perform it to enfranchise you.   110
Meantime, this deep disgrace in brotherhood
Touches me deeper than you can imagine.

CLARENCE
I know it pleaseth neither of us well.

RICHARD
Well, your imprisonment shall not be long;
I will deliver you, or else lie for you.   115
Meantime, have patience.

CLARENCE   I must perforce. Farewell.

        Exeunt Clarence [*, Brakenbury and guard*].

RICHARD
Go, tread the path that thou shalt ne'er return;

---

their submission. 'Abject' is used theologically for the reprobate cast out of God's favour (*OED ppl. a.*, *sb.*). Lyly suggests difference between proper subjection and objectionable abjection: 'I accompt all those abiects, that be not hir [Elizabeth's] subiectes' (2.208).

109 **widow** i.e. the widow whom King Edward has made his wife
110 **enfranchise** release from confinement (*OED v.* 2)
112 Some editors (following Marshall) direct that Richard tearfully embraces Clarence. This seems clumsy (cf. 1.4.243–4). Simon Russell Beale's Richard did embrace Clarence, burying his head in his brother's chest, but this unexpected intimacy awakened obvious amazement in Clarence (Day, 167).

113 **I know** The misplaced assurance of Richard's first victim–associate concerning Richard's thoughts and feelings anticipates the presumption of the second victim, Hastings, also present in this scene; see 3.2.70, 3.4.14.
114 equivocal, since Richard does not expect Clarence to live long in any case
115 **lie for you** take your place; Richard equivocates, reminding the audience of his self-announced capacity for lying and deceiving. For a similar play on 'lie', see *Oth* 3.4.1–13. In *Othello* the jokes on 'lie' belong to a Clown, suggesting Richard's genealogy in such stock theatrical figures (cf. 3.1.82 and pp. 6–8).
116 **patience . . . perforce** proverbial (Dent, P111); see *RJ* 1.5.89, Kyd, *Spanish Tragedy*, 3.9.12–13.
    perforce of necessity

108 whatsoe'er] *F; Qq* (whatsoeuer)   112 deeper] *F, Qq;* dearer *Oxf;* nearer *Cam¹*   115 else] *F; not in Qq*   116] *Steevens; F, Qq line* patience. / Farewell. /   SD] *Capell; Exit Clar. F, Qq; Ex.* Brak. Clar. *Rowe*   117 ne'er] *F, Q1, 3–6 subst.;* neare *Q2*

Simple, plain Clarence, I do love thee so
That I will shortly send thy soul to heaven,
If heaven will take the present at our hands.   120
But who comes here? The new-delivered Hastings?

Enter Lord HASTINGS.

HASTINGS
Good time of day unto my gracious lord.
RICHARD
As much unto my good Lord Chamberlain.
Well are you welcome to this open air.
How hath your lordship brooked imprisonment?   125
HASTINGS
With patience, noble lord, as prisoners must;
But I shall live, my lord, to give them thanks
That were the cause of my imprisonment.
RICHARD
No doubt, no doubt; and so shall Clarence too,
For they that were your enemies are his   130
And have prevailed as much on him as you.
HASTINGS
More pity that the eagles should be mewed,

---

118 **thee** Richard uses 'you' to Clarence while he is present; cf. Cassius' contemptuous shift in pronominal usage (*JC* 1.2.307; cf. Abbott, 233).
120 Richard parodies the idea of sacrifice in which the supplicants render a tribute that they hope will be acceptable to God. Richard's plural *our* follows the communal language in the communion service of the *Book of Common Prayer* (Jowett). Richard's parodic invocations of religious language and sentiment in early soliloquies (cf. 151) allow the audience to appreciate the irony

attending his expressions of piety to onstage characters.
122 **Good . . . day** conventional salutation (*OED* good *a*. III 10c); cf. 2.1.48.
125 **brooked** endured
127 **give them thanks** pay them back, vengefully; another perversion of religious idiom, but, as with Hastings's wordplay (135n.), the irony is less pointedly deployed by characters other than Richard.
132–3 **eagles . . . buzzards** In many Renaissance accounts, the proper order of nature resembled a hierarchi-

121 new-delivered] *F, Qq* (new deliuered), hyphen *Pope*   124 this] *F, Q3–6;* the *Q1–2*   132 eagles] *F;* Eagle *Qq*

Whiles kites and buzzards play at liberty.

RICHARD

What news abroad?

HASTINGS

No news so bad abroad as this at home: 135
The King is sickly, weak and melancholy,
And his physicians fear him mightily.

RICHARD

Now by Saint John, that news is bad indeed.
O, he hath kept an evil diet long,

cal human society: eagles, as the most royal of birds, would stand in freedom and dignity above the lower ranks, amongst which kites and buzzards, as scavengers, would be inferior (cf. 1.3.69–70 and *Cym* 1.2.70–1).

134 An odd question to ask a man just released from prison (Jowett). Richard prompts others to reveal what they feel and think – the strategy imputed to Brakenbury at 102. However, Richard's reactions at 145 suggest that he has genuinely learned an important fact about King Edward's illness.

   news This word occurs more frequently in *Richard III* than in any other of Shakespeare's works except *2H4*; characters repeatedly discuss the *news*, often asking versions of Richard's question: the citizens (2.3.3), the Archbishop (2.4.38), the Duchess of York (2.4.42), Hastings (3.2.36) and, above all, Richard (4.2.46; 4.3.24, 45; 4.4.432, 456, 462).

   abroad at large, circulating generally

135 **abroad . . . home** Hastings's response superficially mimics one of Richard's characteristic verbal modes, taking a term from his interlocutor and twisting its sense: so, instead of taking *abroad* to mean 'at large', Hastings playfully turns it to mean 'in foreign

regions' by opposing it to *at home* (i.e. domestically). Hastings's witticism is pointless, suggesting clumsy jocularity and ease in Richard's presence, while Richard's playing on the words of others (as at 98 or 1.2.123–4) is almost invariably pointed, even sinister.

137 **fear him** fear for him (cf. *1H4* 4.1.24 and Abbott, 200)

138–42 Richard here first plays the deceptively pious moralist; this effect is heightened by his oath, his exclamatory *O* as he disapproves of Edward's *evil* diet, and his pained references to the *grievous* torments he has suffered at his brother's sinful behaviour. For the most egregious instance of such posturing, see 3.7.103–246. This element does not characterize Richard in *2H6* and *3H6*.

138 *Saint John Qq give Richard his typical oath, 'by Saint Paul' (cf. 1.2.36n.).

139 **evil** unwholesome (*OED a.* 7b) and morally wicked (*OED a.* 1)
   diet way of life (*OED sb.*[1] 1); from More (*CW*2, 8), used to refer to sexual overindulgence (cf. *surfeit*, 1.3.196), but also with a play on overeating (cf. *consumed*, 140). Mancini (67) reports that Edward grew fat from overeating and taking emetics.

133 Whiles] *F*; While *Qq*   play] *F*; prey *Qq*   138 Saint John] *F* (S. Iohn*)*; Saint Paul *Qq*   that] *F*; this *Qq*

And over-much consumed his royal person. 140
'Tis very grievous to be thought upon.
Where is he, in his bed?

HASTINGS   He is.

RICHARD

Go you before, and I will follow you.   *Exit Hastings.*
He cannot live, I hope, and must not die   145
Till George be packed with post-horse up to heaven.
I'll in to urge his hatred more to Clarence
With lies well steeled with weighty arguments,
And if I fail not in my deep intent,
Clarence hath not another day to live;   150
Which done, God take King Edward to His mercy,
And leave the world for me to bustle in.
For then, I'll marry Warwick's youngest daughter.

---

141 **grievous** painful
142 ***Where** Qq's 'What' renders the line an (unpunctuated) exclamation, i.e. 'What! is he in his bed?' This sense is supported by a comma in Q4–6 ('What, is he . . . ?'). On F arising from 'incorrect conjectural emendation' of Q3 copy, see Walton, *Copy*, 83–4. However, Richard's prosaic question about the royal bed may rhetorically reiterate his disgust at the inevitability of finding the King, yet again, *in his bed* – now in illness as earlier in the lust that Richard implies to have been the cause of that illness.
146 **with post-horse** i.e. by the swiftest means possible; a post-horse was kept at a post-house or inn for post-riders or travellers (*OED*). Richard's echo of 2 Kings, 2.11, describing Elijah borne into heaven by horses of fire, is 'characteristic . . . blasphemy' (Wilson).

147 **his** i.e. King Edward's
148 **steeled** hardened, as a warrior armed or protected with steel (*OED ppl. a.* 2, *a.* 5)
149 **deep** profound in craft and subtlety (*OED a.* 17); cf. 2.1.38; the word is used variously throughout the play, occurring more often than in any other work by Shakespeare.
151 **God . . . mercy** Cf. 120n.
152 **bustle** bestir oneself or display activity with noise or agitation, usually implying excessive or obtrusive show of energy (*OED v.* 2a); or scuffle, contend, and elbow one's way (*v.* 3)
153 **Warwick's youngest daughter** Lady Anne Neville, daughter of the Earl of Warwick (the 'King-maker'; cf. *3H6* 2.3.37), widow of Prince Edward, son of Henry VI. Anne is erroneously taken to be Warwick's elder daughter in *3H6* (3.3.242, 4.1.118).

142 Where] *F*; What *Qq*   144 ²you] *F, Q1–2, 4–6*; yon *Q3*

What though I killed her husband and her father?
The readiest way to make the wench amends   155
Is to become her husband and her father;
The which will I, not all so much for love
As for another secret close intent
By marrying her which I must reach unto.
But yet I run before my horse to market: 160
Clarence still breathes; Edward still lives and reigns.
When they are gone, then must I count my gains.   *Exit.*

154 **What though** i.e. what if? what does it matter that?
  husband . . . father husband and her father-in-law; Shakespeare's earlier plays follow Hall and Holinshed in making Richard the accomplice of his brothers Edward and Clarence in the killing of Prince Edward (*3H6* 5.5). See 1.4.200–6.
155 **wench** insulting for an aristocrat, but in keeping with Richard's general social reduction of women (cf. *gossips*, 83)
156 **husband . . . father** Richard proposes to marry Anne and care for her in a fatherly way, replacing the men he has taken from her, but this confusion of kinship relations and marital relations has wider historical resonance. Richard was denounced vehemently by Hall and Holinshed for attempting to wed his niece Elizabeth, and tyrants are traditionally associated with unnatural crimes such as incest (McCabe, 156–9).
157–8 Richard's intention is left unstated, though the historical figures wed and had a son (nowhere mentioned in this play). In *3H6* the marriages of Anne to Prince Edward and her sister Isabel to Clarence signify alliance with their father, the Earl of Warwick (3.3.240–50, 4.1.120–2). Hall describes hopes for alliance between Warwick and Margaret's forces in the conjunction

of Anne and Prince Edward in 1470, suggesting that power politics motivated the 'straunge' marriages of one daughter to the Yorkist Clarence and the other to the princely descendant of the Lancastrian Henry VI (*Edward IV*, fols ccvi[v]–ccvii[r]). By contrast, Shakespeare represents Richard's marital plans as obscure of motive, manifest in villainy and prompting witty self-congratulation – a combination recalling the dramatic tradition of the Vice (see pp. 6–8). Anne's substantial property and standing in the northern region suggest compelling historical explanations for Richard's desire. Richard, the youngest son, was largely dependent on the favour of his royal brother; the 16-year-old Anne and her elder sister Isabel, married to Clarence, were joint heiresses of the substantial Warwick inheritance. Although the historical Anne and Richard appear to have been acquainted in childhood, there is no evidence of an extended relationship before their marriage. Cibber (*Richard III*, 2.1.24–35) invents a prehistory for Richard's encounter with Anne.
160 **run . . . market** proverbial for over-hasty behaviour (Dent, M649). Although Richard often invokes familiar proverbs, this tendency is more pronounced in *3H6*, where he is compared to Aesop (5.5.25).

1.2   *Enter the corse of Henry the Sixth with Halberds to*
guard it, Lady ANNE *being the mourner [, attended by*
TRESSEL, BERKELEY *and other* Gentlemen].

ANNE

Set down, set down your honourable load,
If honour may be shrouded in a hearse,
Whilst I awhile obsequiously lament
Th'untimely fall of virtuous Lancaster.
Poor key-cold figure of a holy king,   5
Pale ashes of the house of Lancaster,
Thou bloodless remnant of that royal blood,
Be it lawful that I invocate thy ghost

1.2 location: '*a Street*' (Theobald)
0.1–3 This is not a vast stately procession (as it has often been staged) but
an act of personal and familial grief.
Henry VI's funeral took place in May
1471, and Anne was not part of it.
Holinshed records that Henry's corpse
bled before spectators. The body was
subsequently taken to Chertsey by
boat, 'without priest or clerke, torch
or taper, singing or saieng', for burial
(Holinshed, 3.690–1; see 243).
0.1 *corse* corpse (*OED sb.* 2b)
   Halberds men armed with halberds,
weapons with points like spears and
blades like battle-axes on handles five
to seven feet long; Henry's corpse was
'conveied with billes and glaues pomp-
ouslie (if you will call that a funerall
pompe)' (Holinshed, 3.690–1), suggesting that glaives – halberds – were
hardly pompous.
0.2 **mourner** It is likely that Anne is
dressed in black (cf. Dessen &
Thomson, 145).
1 **Set down, set down** Cf. 'Set downe,
set downe the load not worth your
pain' (*TRKJ*, Pt 2, xiii.1, sig. D2ᵛ);

see 5.3.177–206n. To 'set down' the
corpse was a ritual feature of funeral
processions (*Lancaster, 1590*, 5–6).
*load Folger and Huntington Q1 have
'l', but Bodleian and British Library
Huth have 'lo:' and 'lo', possible abbreviations for 'lord', the word found in
subsequent quartos (including Q7–8);
cf. *holy load* (29).
2 **hearse** either a wooden framework
supporting a funeral pall, the cloth
itself covering the body, or a coffin
(*OED sb.* 3, 4, 5)
3 **obsequiously** mournfully, as in performance of funeral obsequies; cf. *Tit*
5.3.151.
4 **virtuous Lancaster** Henry VI,
depicted in *3H6* and elsewhere as
especially pious, here addressed by his
family name, embodying the family
displaced by the *son of York* (1.1.2)
5 **key-cold** very cold, as a key; cf. *Luc*
1774 and Tilley, K23.
   figure image, likeness (*OED sb.* 9)
6 **Pale ashes** mortal remains (Dent,
A339; cf. *RJ* 3.2.55)
8 **Be it** i.e. let it be (Abbott, 365)
   lawful Anne unhistorically alludes to

1.2] *F (Scena Secunda.); not in Qq   0.1–3] *Enter the Coarse of Henrie the sixt with Halberds to guard it,*
/ *Lady Anne being the Mourner.* F; *Enter Lady Anne with the hearse of Harry the 6.* Qq   **0.2–3** *attended*
... *Gentlemen] Ard²*   **1 SP]** F; *Lady An[.]ne* Qq   Set . . . set] *F, Q1, 3–6;* Sit . . . sit *Q2*   load,] *F;*
l *(Fo, Hn),* lo *(BL),* lo: *(Bod) Q1;* lord *Q2;* Lord, *Q3–6*   **4** Th'untimely] *F;* The vntimely *Qq*

To hear the lamentations of poor Anne,
Wife to thy Edward, to thy slaughtered son,   10
Stabbed by the selfsame hand that made these wounds.
Lo, in these windows that let forth thy life
I pour the helpless balm of my poor eyes.
O, cursed be the hand that made these holes;
Cursed the heart that had the heart to do it;   15
Cursed the blood that let this blood from hence.
More direful hap betide that hated wretch
That makes us wretched by the death of thee
Than I can wish to wolves, to spiders, toads
Or any creeping venomed thing that lives.   20

Protestant objections to the invocation of saints in prayer (Whitaker, 80; Goodland, 144); see *Homilies*, 115–17; cf. 4.4.75, 5.3.241. Henry VI was widely venerated into the reign of Henry VIII (Knox, 3–7).
invocate invoke, as in prayer (*OED v.* 1), but suggesting 'conjure' (*OED* invoke *v.* 2a); cf. *H5* 1.2.103–5, where Henry V is urged to 'invoke' the spirits of his ancestors, with no nervousness about the lawfulness of such prayer.
10 **Wife** Anne was betrothed and then married to Henry's son, Prince Edward, in 1470.
11 *hand** F's sense of a single murderer (see 14), is contradicted by *3H6* 5.5.38–40, where all three York brothers stab Prince Edward.
12 **windows** i.e. wounds
13 **helpless** useless, unavailing (*OED a.* 3)
   balm figuratively, a healing or restorative agency (*OED sb.* 6); literally an aromatic ointment for soothing pain or healing wounds (*OED sb.* 5)

14 **cursed** cursèd; F's dissyllabic pronunciation is suggested by Qq's use of 'fatall' to complete the line opening with monosyllabic 'Curst'.
15, 16 **Cursed** cursèd
16 *Alice Walker (32) suggests that this line 'possibly' belongs before the previous one, connecting *blood* to *holes*; Walton agrees (*Quarto*, 143); as does Wilson. Hammond judges insufficient warrant for changing F's order.
17 **direful hap betide** terrible consequence befall
19 **wolves, spiders, toads** Richard's connection with these animals (see 1.3.241–5, 4.4.23) goes back to Rous (Hanham, 118, 120) and recurs in *Mirror* ('Richard, Duke of Gloucester', 124, 'Rivers', 480). Richard's father denounces Margaret as a 'she-wolf' with a poisonous tongue (*3H6* 1.4.111–12). The repeated preposition *to* appears to cut the connection between wolves and creeping things; Richard's anti-Lancastrian violence has been a wolflike open attack rather than secret treachery.

11 hand . . . wounds] *F;* hands . . . holes *Qq*   12 these] *F;* those *Qq*   14 O, cursed . . . these] *F;* Curst . . . these fatall *Q1–2;* Curst . . . the fatall *Q3–6*   15 Cursed] *F;* Curst be *Qq*   16] *F (Cnrsed); not in Qq*   19 wolves, to spiders] *F;* adders, spiders *Qq*

If ever he have child, abortive be it,
Prodigious, and untimely brought to light,
Whose ugly and unnatural aspect
May fright the hopeful mother at the view,
And that be heir to his unhappiness.   25
If ever he have wife, let her be made
More miserable by the death of him
Than I am made by my young lord and thee.
– Come now towards Chertsey with your holy load,
Taken from Paul's to be interred there;   30
And still, as you are weary of this weight,
Rest you, whiles I lament King Henry's corse.

Enter RICHARD, Duke of Gloucester.

RICHARD
Stay, you that bear the corse, and set it down.
ANNE
What black magician conjures up this fiend

21–8 Anne echoes and outdoes Margaret's
  curses upon Richard and his brothers
  for murdering her son (*3H6* 5.5.65–7).
21 **abortive** born prematurely; also useless, unsuccessful (*OED a.* A 1a, 2)
22 **Prodigious** monstrous in appearance
  (cf. *KJ* 2.2.46); unnatural and ominous
  (*OED a.* 1, 2, 3)
  untimely prematurely
23 **aspect** aspèct (on shifting accents generally, see Abbott, 490); appearance,
  countenance
25 **that** i.e. the child
  unhappiness evil, misfortune; with
  an active quality: the 'unhappy' person
  can work evil, an association missing
  in the current sense of 'unhappiness'
  as an emotional state.

27–8 *F is clear enough (Anne prays that
  Richard's hypothetical wife may feel
  even sorrier when Richard dies than
  she does now), cf. Walton, *Quarto*,
  143–4. Cibber simplifies to 'More miserable by the Life of him, / Than I
  am now by *Edward's* death and thine'
  (*Richard III*, 2.1.78–9); cf. 4.1.74–6.
28 **by . . . thee** i.e. by the deaths of Prince
  Edward and his father, Henry VI
29 **Chertsey** monastery in Surrey, west
  of London, south of the River Thames
  near Staines
30 **Paul's** St Paul's Cathedral in London
  interred interrèd
31 **still** ever, whenever
34 **black magician** a specifically malevo-
  lent agent who *conjures* for evil intent

25] *F; not in Qq*   26 made] *F, Q1–5;* mad: *Q6*   27 More] *F;* As *Qq*   28 Than . . . young] *F;* As
. . . poore *Qq*   31 weary] *F, Q1–2;* awearie *Q3–6 subst.*   this] *F;* the *Qq*   32.1] *F; Enter Glocester.*
Qq   33+ SP] *F (Rich.); Glo. Qq*   34+ SP] *F (An[ne].); La[d[y]]. Qq*

To stop devoted charitable deeds?   35

RICHARD

Villains, set down the corse, or by Saint Paul,
I'll make a corse of him that disobeys.

GENTLEMAN

My lord, stand back and let the coffin pass.

RICHARD

Unmannered dog, stand thou when I command!
Advance thy halberd higher than my breast,   40
Or by Saint Paul, I'll strike thee to my foot
And spurn upon thee, beggar, for thy boldness.

ANNE

What, do you tremble? Are you all afraid?

---

35 **devoted** vowed, dedicated, consecrated

36 ***Villains** F/Qq frequently disagree when a noun is followed by a word beginning with *s*; see 'lip'/'lips' (174) and 'eagles'/'eagle' (1.1.132) (cf. Var, 50).
by Saint Paul Richard's favourite oath (see 41, 1.1.138n., 3.4.75–6n., 5.3.216) derives from a single instance in More. Here the oath may reflect Richard's assertion of dominance, since Saint Paul was associated with demands for deference to authority (cf. p. 15). The Hand D portion of *Sir Thomas More* has More warn that 'th'apostle' urges 'obedience to authority' (*STM* 2.3.99–101). This refers to Romans, 13.1–2: 'Let euerie soule be subiect vnto the higher powers: for there is no power but of God: & the powers that be, are ordeined of God . . . and they that resist, shal receiue them selues iudgement' (Geneva). The reference to conjuring in 34 may allude to Paul's struggles with the exorcists of Ephesus (Acts, 19.17–19) (Jowett).

38 **coffin** either a coffin or the bier on which the body rests (*OED sb.* 3b)

39–40 *There is debate about Richard's addressee(s). A gentleman could be a halberdier (Davison). If 36–7 address the attendants generally or the corpse-bearers as *Villains*, then 39 may respond to the Gentleman who speaks 38. At 40 Richard could command another individual, an eager halberdier, to cease threatening him.

39 **Unmannered** unmannerly
stand halt; F's 'Stand'st' could be a demand in the form of a question: i.e. are you going to stand still or not when I issue the order?
thou Richard's pronoun, depending on its addressee, could either be an unmarked form of address to a social inferior or a strong signal of anger or contempt to a gentle stranger (Abbott, 233); cf. 46.

40 i.e. return your halberd to an upright, non-aggressive position.

42 **spurn** trample contemptuously (*OED v.*[1] II 5)

43 **What** interjection expressing surprise or indignation

---

36 Villains] *F;* Villaine *Qq*   38 SP] *F, Q3–6 (Gen.), Q1–2 (Gent.); Halberdier Ard*[2]   My lord] *F, Q1–5 (My L. Q3); om. Q6*   39] *Qq; F lines* Dogge, / commaund: /   stand] *Qq;* Stand'st *F*

Alas, I blame you not, for you are mortal,
And mortal eyes cannot endure the devil.   45
– Avaunt, thou dreadful minister of hell!
Thou hadst but power over his mortal body;
His soul thou canst not have. Therefore begone.

RICHARD

Sweet saint, for charity, be not so curst.

ANNE

Foul devil, for God's sake hence, and trouble us not,   50
For thou hast made the happy earth thy hell,
Filled it with cursing cries and deep exclaims.
If thou delight to view thy heinous deeds,
Behold this pattern of thy butcheries.
– O gentlemen, see, see dead Henry's wounds   55
Open their congealed mouths, and bleed afresh.

---

46 **Avaunt** begone; Shaheen relates to Jesus's rejection of the devil: 'Auoyde Sathan' (Matthew, 4.10). Cf. 4.4.418–19n. and *2H6* 1.4.40.

thou Anne's pronoun signals contempt for a social equal for whom she feels no affection (Abbott, 233; cf. Buckingham at 3.2.120–1). Use of *thou* might mark her speech as directed to a supernatural being, here to a 'minister of hell'; cf. Horatio and Hamlet to the Ghost from heaven or hell (*Ham* 1.1.45–50, 1.4.40–56).

minister agent (*OED sb.* 2a); cf. 1.4.219 and *2H6* 5.2.33–4.

47–8 Anne draws on familiar Christian distinctions (Matthew, 10.28: 'And feare ye not them, which kyll the body, but are not able to kyll the soule. But rather feare hym, which is able to destroy both soule and body in hell').

49 **saint, charity** Adopting Anne's language concerning *charitable deeds* (35), Richard hypocritically recalls Gospel demands for the 'charitie' that

is a 'fulfyllyng of the lawe' (Romans, 12.10). Richard invokes Christian charity to taunt Young Clifford (*2H6* 5.1.213).

curst ill-tempered (*OED ppl. a.* 4a)

50–2 **Foul devil . . . cursing** Anne continues Richard's form and vocabulary: *Sweet saint* is countered with *Foul devil*; admonition about *curst* behaviour is echoed in references to the *cursing* that his deeds have occasioned.

50 **hence** go hence, depart

51 **made . . . hell** Cf. the Duchess of York on Richard's making 'the earth my hell' (4.4.167).

52 **exclaims** exclamations; cf. 4.4.135.

54 **pattern** prime example, epitome (*OED sb.* 1a, 6)

56 **bleed afresh** referring to the belief that a victim's body would bleed in the presence of the murderer (cf. *Arden*, 16.4–6). Holinshed (but not Hall) mentions that King Henry's body bled (3.691), but does not connect this legend to Richard.

---

46 dreadful] *F, Q1–5;* fearefull *Q6* 50] *Qq; F lines* Diuell, / not, /

– Blush, blush, thou lump of foul deformity,
For 'tis thy presence that exhales this blood
From cold and empty veins where no blood dwells.
Thy deeds, inhuman and unnatural,   60
Provokes this deluge most unnatural.
– O God! which this blood mad'st, revenge his death.
O earth! which this blood drink'st, revenge his death.
Either heaven with lightning strike the murderer dead,
Or earth gape open wide and eat him quick,   65
As thou dost swallow up this good king's blood,
Which his hell-governed arm hath butchered.

RICHARD

Lady, you know no rules of charity,
Which renders good for bad, blessings for curses.

ANNE

Villain, thou knowst nor law of God nor man.   70

---

57 **lump . . . deformity** King Henry calls Richard 'an undigested and deformed lump' (*3H6* 5.6.51).

58 **exhales** causes to flow, draws forth (*OED v.*² 1b, citing this line)

60–1 **deeds . . . Provokes** Plural subjects (perhaps singular in thought) paired with verbs ending in *-s* are 'extremely common' in F (Abbott, 333); cf. 2.3.35.

60 **inhuman** 'human' and 'humane' were interchangeable (*OED* inhuman).

62 **F's exclamation marks (also at 63, 73) are unusual for this play.

63 The image of the earth drinking blood is derived from the story of Cain and Abel: 'the voyce of thy brothers blood crieth vnto me out of the grounde' (Genesis, 4.10–11; cf. *1H4* 1.1.5–6, *R2* 1.1.104–5). While Richard's crime is not fratricide, Henry was Richard's

cousin. See also 4.4.29–30.

65 Noble (131) notes biblical parallels, including Numbers, 16.30, which describes the destruction of the men of Korah: God makes 'the earth open her mouth, and swallowe them vp . . . and they go downe quicke into the pit'. There is a possible classical intersection with Seneca's *topos* '*Dehisce tellus*' ('Yawn, *or* Gape, earth': *Hippolytus*, 1238–9; cf. *Oedipus*, 868, *Troades*, 519). See also 4.4.75 and *3H6* 1.1.161.
quick alive

67 **butchered** butcherèd

68–9 A favourite Christian precept: 'loue your enemies, blesse them that curse you, do good to them that hate you, pray for the[m] which hurt you and persecute you' (Matthew, 5.43–4); cf. Romans, 12.14.

70 **nor . . . nor** i.e. neither . . . nor

---

60 deeds] *F*; deed *Qq* inhuman] *F, Q1–5* (inhumane), *Rowe*; inhumaine *Q6* 62 mad'st] *F; Qq* (madest) 64 heaven] *F* (Heau'n), *Qq* murderer] *F* (murth'rer), *Qq* (murtherer) 66 dost] *F;* doest *Q1–5;* didst *Q6* 70 knowst nor] *F;* knowest (knowst *Q3–6*) no *Qq*

No beast so fierce but knows some touch of pity.
RICHARD

But I know none, and therefore am no beast.
ANNE

O wonderful, when devils tell the truth!
RICHARD

More wonderful, when angels are so angry.
Vouchsafe, divine perfection of a woman,   75
Of these supposed crimes, to give me leave
By circumstance, but to acquit myself.
ANNE

Vouchsafe, diffused infection of ^Qa^Q man,
Of these known evils, but to give me leave
By circumstance, to curse thy cursèd self.   80
RICHARD

Fairer than tongue can name thee, let me have
Some patient leisure to excuse myself.

71–3 A notoriously lame non-argument:
Anne implies that Richard is not only
inhuman but less than a beast since
even beasts feel pity. Richard replies
that since he feels none, he is not a
beast. Anne deduces Richard to be a
devil.

71 **but knows** i.e. but it knows (Abbott,
123)
touch feeling, sensation (*OED sb.* III
13b; as *TGV* 2.7.18: 'the inly touch of
love') or slight amount or trace (*OED
sb.* 19a; as 4.4.158)

73 **devils . . . truth** Cf. Dent, D266: 'The
Devil sometimes speaks the truth.'

75 **Vouchsafe** grant

76 **supposed** supposèd

77 **circumstance** fact which makes an
action more or less criminal, or an

accusation more or less probable (*OED
sb.* I 3)

78 **diffused** confused, disordered,
obscure or spread abroad, dispersed
(*OED ppl. a.* I 1, II 2); F, Qq spell
'defus[e]d'. Richard appears either
compounded of a diseased disorder or
the source of spreading pestilence. The
sense of 'disordered' appears in *H5*
5.2.61. Given its close echo of 75, the
formula *diffused . . . man* may be 'more
for sound than sense' (Holland).

80 **cursed** cursèd

81 Cibber's Richard offers rapturous
praises: 'But see, my Love appears:
Look where she shines, / Darting pale
Lustre, like the Silver Moon' (*Richard
III*, 2.1.54–5).

82 **leisure** opportunity (*OED sb.* 1b)

73 truth] *F, Q2–6;* troth *Q1*   75 Vouchsafe] *F, Q3–6; Q1 (*Voutsafe*), Q2 (*Vouchafe*)   76 crimes]
F; euils *Qq*   78 diffused] *F, Qq (*defused *subst.*)   79 Of] *F;* For *Qq*   80 curse] *F, Qq;* accuse *Cam¹
(Spedding)*

ANNE

Fouler than heart can think thee, thou canst make
No excuse current but to hang thyself.

RICHARD

By such despair I should accuse myself.   85

ANNE

And by despairing shalt thou stand excused
For doing worthy vengeance on thyself
That didst unworthy slaughter upon others.

RICHARD

Say that I slew them not.

ANNE

Then say they were not slain.   90
But dead they are, and, devilish slave, by thee.

RICHARD

I did not kill your husband.

ANNE

Why then he is alive.

RICHARD

Nay, he is dead, and slain by Edward's hands.

ANNE

In thy foul throat thou liest; Queen Margaret saw   95
Thy murderous falchion smoking in his blood,

---

84 **current** with the quality of current
coin; sterling, genuine: opposed to
counterfeit (*OED a.* 5)
85–7 **despair . . . vengeance**   Anne
recommends that Richard kill himself in despair to avenge those he
has killed; neither despair nor taking
vengeance on a malefactor, in this case
himself, could palliate eternal judgement. Richard echoes this exchange at
5.3.185–6; see also 5.3.200n.
89–90, 92–3 For other trimeter couplets

in dialogue exchange, see 195–205 and
Abbott, 500.
94 **by Edward's hands** a partial truth:
Edward, Richard and Clarence stab
Prince Edward in turn (*3H6* 5.5.38–40);
cf. 1.1.154n. on *husband . . . father*.
95 **In . . . liest** 'to lie in one's throat'
meant lying outrageously (Dent, T268;
cf. *LLL* 4.3.10–11).
96 **falchion** curved broad sword
smoking giving off a vapour, steam-
ing

83–4] *Qq; F lines* thee, / currant, / selfe. /   86 shalt] *F;* shouldst *Qq*   88 That] *F;* Which *Qq*
89 not.] *F, Q1, 3–6;* not? *Q2*   90] *F;* Why then they are not dead, *Qq*   94 hands] *F;* hand *Qq*
95–6] *Qq; F lines* Ly'st, / saw / blood: /   95 Margaret] *F, Qq (*Margret *Q3–6)*   96 murderous]
*F (*murd'rous*);* bloudy *Q1–2;* bloodly *Q3–6*

155

The which thou once didst bend against her breast,
But that thy brothers beat aside the point.

RICHARD

I was provoked by her slanderous tongue,
That laid their guilt upon my guiltless shoulders.   100

ANNE

Thou wast provoked by thy bloody mind,
That never dream'st on aught but butcheries.
Didst thou not kill this king?

RICHARD   I grant ye.

ANNE

Dost grant me, hedgehog? Then God grant me too
Thou mayst be damned for that wicked deed.   105
O, he was gentle, mild and virtuous.

RICHARD

The better for the King of Heaven that hath him.

ANNE

He is in heaven, where thou shalt never come.

RICHARD

Let him thank me that holp to send him thither,
For he was fitter for that place than earth.   110

ANNE

And thou unfit for any place but hell.

---

97 **bend** aim or direct
99, 101 **provoked** provokèd
102 **aught** anything
103 Richard 'slewe with his owne handes
    king Henry the sixt', More writes
    (*CW*2, 8), surrounding the claim with
    typical hedging (see pp. 59–60); cf.
    3H6 5.6.
    *ye Q1–2's 'yea' is one spelling of
    'ye' (*TxC*, 233); on 'ye' in F, see
    Honigmann, 'Variants', 193–4.

104 **hedgehog** referring to the hump-
    backed animal, bristled like the boar,
    Richard's heraldic emblem (see
    1.3.227, 3.2.10, 5.2.7–10).
105 **damned** damnèd
107–8 Cf. *Leir* ('You are fitter for the
    King of heauen', sig. F3ʳ, 1604; 'to
    send vs both to heauen / Where, as I
    thinke, you neuer mean to come', sig.
    I4ʳ, 2596–7).
109 **holp** helped

98 brothers] *F, Q1–2;* brother *Q3–6* 99 slanderous] *F* (sland'rous*), Qq* (slaunderous*) 100 That]
F; Which *Qq* guilt] *F, Q1–5;* guift *Q6* 102 That . . . dream'st] *F;* Which . . . dreamt *Qq* 103]
Qq; F lines King? / ye. / ye] *F;* yea *Q1–2;* yee *Q3–6* 104] *Qq; F lines* Hedge-hogge, / too / 105
mayst] *F;* maiest *Qq* damned] *F, Q3–6;* damnd *Q1–2* 107 better] *F;* fitter *Qq*

RICHARD

Yes, one place else, if you will hear me name it.

ANNE Some dungeon.

RICHARD Your bedchamber.

ANNE

Ill rest betide the chamber where thou liest.   115

RICHARD

So will it, madam, till I lie with you.

ANNE

I hope so.

RICHARD I know so. But, gentle Lady Anne,

To leave this keen encounter of our wits

And fall something into a slower method:

Is not the causer of the timeless deaths   120

Of these Plantagenets, Henry and Edward,

As blameful as the executioner?

ANNE

Thou wast the cause, and most accurst effect.

---

114 McKellen's film renders this as an aside, whispered in confidence to the camera; thus Anne (Kristin Scott Thomas) is shocked by Richard's subsequent direct approaches and surprised into spitting at him (McKellen, 76).

115 **betide** befall

115–16 **chamber . . . lie** recalling double meanings at 1.1.12, 15

117 **I hope so** Anne presumes that she will never lie with him.

119 **something** somewhat
method In the context of lines concerning cause and effect, the term carries associations with logical investigation, and may suggest the ordered procedure specific to rhetorical exposition and literary com-

position (*OED sb.* II 4, 6a).

120 **timeless** out of its proper time, premature (*OED a.* 1a), but suggesting the unparalleled nature of the crime and the loss it has occasioned

122 **executioner** the agent who enacts a design or perpetrates an evil deed (*OED* 1) and the one who puts another to death (*OED* 4, citing 188)

123 **accurst** execrable, damnable (*OED ppl. a.* 2)
effect perhaps meaning 'effecter', i.e. agent; alternatively, Anne may say that everything is entirely Richard's fault since he begins and ends (as cause and effect) the entire murderous sequence. In 124 Richard reduces *effect* to mean 'result'.

---

112 you] *F, Q1–2, 6;* ye *Q3–5*   113–14] *F; one line Qq*   117] *Steevens; F, Qq line* so. / *Anne, /*   118 keen] *F, Q1;* kinde *Q2–6*   119 something] *F;* somewhat *Qq*   120 timeless] *F, Q1–3, 5–6;* teem-lesse *Q4*   123 wast] *F (*was't*);* art *Qq*   and most] *F, Qq;* of that *Cam¹(Walker);* of most *Oxf¹*

157

RICHARD

> Your beauty was the cause of that effect:
> Your beauty, that did haunt me in my sleep 125
> To undertake the death of all the world,
> So I might live one hour in your sweet bosom.

ANNE

> If I thought that, I tell thee, homicide,
> These nails should rend that beauty from my cheeks.

RICHARD

> These eyes could not endure that beauty's wrack; 130
> You should not blemish it, if I stood by.
> As all the world is cheered by the sun,
> So I by that. It is my day, my life.

ANNE

> Black night o'ershade thy day, and death thy life.

RICHARD

> Curse not thyself, fair creature; thou art both. 135

ANNE

> I would I were, to be revenged on thee.

RICHARD

> It is a quarrel most unnatural,
> To be revenged on him that loveth thee.

ANNE

> It is a quarrel just and reasonable,
> To be revenged on him that killed my husband. 140

RICHARD

> He that bereft thee, lady, of thy husband,

---

128 **homicide** murderer
129 **nails . . . beauty** Cf. *2H6* 1.3.141–3, *Luc* 1472.
130 **wrack** destruction (*OED sb.*[1] 2)

132–3 Hammond points to sonneteers' clichés (with examples from Sidney).
132 **cheered** cheerèd

125 that] *F;* which *Qq*   127 live one] *F;* rest one *Q1–4;* rest that *Q5–6*   129 rend] *Qq;* rent *F*   my] *F, Q1–5;* their *Q6*   130 not endure that] *F;* neuer indure sweet *Qq*   131 it] *F;* them *Qq*   132 sun] *F, Q3–6 (*Sunne*);* sonne *Q1–2*   134 o'ershade] *F (*ore-shade*);* ouershade *Qq*   135] *Qq; F lines* Creature, / both. /   136 were,] *F;* were *Qq*   138 thee] *F;* you *Qq*   140 killed] *F;* slew *Qq*   141 thee] *F (*the*), Qq*

Did it to help thee to a better husband.

ANNE

His better doth not breathe upon the earth.

RICHARD

He lives that loves thee better than he could.

ANNE

Name him.

RICHARD   Plantagenet.

ANNE   Why, that was he.   145

RICHARD

The selfsame name, but one of better nature.

ANNE

Where is he?

RICHARD   Here.   ^Q*She*^Q *spits at him.*
                         Why dost thou spit at me?

ANNE

Would it were mortal poison, for thy sake.

RICHARD

Never came poison from so sweet a place.

ANNE

Never hung poison on a fouler toad.   150
Out of my sight! Thou dost infect mine eyes.

---

145 **Plantagenet** family name dating back to the nickname of Geoffrey of Anjou, father of Henry II of England. Although technically belonging to both sides in the Wars of the Roses (as Anne notes), the name was apparently first affirmed by the Duke of York, Richard's father, for himself, in hopes of strengthening his royal claim (see *1H6* 2.4). Richard will be the last monarch to claim the name, his demise bringing in the Tudor dynasty.

146 **nature** inherent disposition, character

147–8 **spit . . . poison** Cf. Dent, V28: 'He has spit his venom.'

150 **toad** thought to be poisonous (cf. 1.3.245 and *3H6* 2.2.138)

151–2 That the eyes of the beloved could infect the lover with love was a poetic commonplace (cf. *LLL* 5.2.421); proverbially, a person with an eye disease could impart it to a sound person by looking at him or her (Dent, E246).

151 *****mine** For the use of 'mine' instead of 'my' before a vowel, see 1.4.22–3, 3.7.20, 4.1.80, 81.

---

144 He] *F;* Go to, he *Qq*   145] *Steevens; F lines* him. / *Plantagenet.* / he. / ; *Qq line* Plantagenet. / hee. /   that was he] *F, Q1–2;* what was he? *Q3–6*   147] *Steevens; F, Qq line* he? / Heere: / me. / SD] *F, Q2–5; after* he *Q1*   spits] *F;* spitteth *Qq*   151 mine] *F;* my *Qq*

RICHARD

Thine eyes, sweet lady, have infected mine.

ANNE

Would they were basilisks, to strike thee dead.

RICHARD

I would they were, that I might die at once;
For now they kill me with a living death.   155
Those eyes of thine from mine have drawn salt tears,
Shamed their aspects with store of childish drops;
These eyes, which never shed remorseful tear –
No, when my father York and Edward wept
To hear the piteous moan that Rutland made   160
When black-faced Clifford shook his sword at him;

---

153 **basilisks** mythical serpentlike creatures (sometimes identified with cockatrices), named for a spot resembling a crown on their heads (*OED* 1) and supposed to kill by gazing; cf. 1.3.224 and 4.1.54–5 and Richard's threat to 'slay more gazers than the basilisk' (*3H6* 3.2.187).

155 **living death** sonnet usage; cf. Thomas Watson's 'Loue is a sowr delight; a sugred greefe, / A liuinge death' (*Hekatompathia*, Sonnet xviii) and *VA* 413.

156–7 Richard refused to weep at his father's murder, choosing revenge instead (*3H6* 2.1.79–88). His readiness to appear to weep in this play is noteworthy: he claims he will shed *repentant tears* (1.2.218) and *beweep* the fate of Clarence (1.3.327); Clarence claims Richard parted weeping from him (1.4.243–5); Richard protests readiness to weep for the loss of Hastings's loyalty (3.5.24). Of course, he mocks tears as the recourse of *fools* (1.3.352) and asserts that 'Tear-falling pity dwells not in this eye' (4.2.65). Richard does not weep in More, but he employs grossly hypocritical tears in *Mirror*

('Rivers', 400–2).

157 **aspects** aspècts; looks, glances (*OED sb.* 1b)
store abundance (*OED sb.* 4a)

158–69 *This passage appears only in F. It has been argued that it was cut to accelerate the scene (Patrick, 124–5), or to remove historical inaccuracies (Smidt, *King Richard*, 123–4) or obscure references (Hammond, 333). Conversely, Grace Ioppolo (130) argues that it was 'added by the author' to provide 'dramatic and theatrical unity and continuity' in the first tetralogy; against this claim, see 160–1n. Speed seems the most likely motivation for omission.

158 **remorseful** compassionate, full of pity (*OED* 2)

159 **Edward** Richard's eldest brother, now Edward IV

160–1 **Rutland . . . Clifford** For the death of Rutland, second son of Richard, Duke of York, at Clifford's hands, see *3H6* 1.3. Neither York nor Edward was present, a fact which perhaps tells against the notion that the tetralogy was conceived as a unified construction. Cf. 162.

161 **black-faced** ominous looking

---

155 they] *F, Q1–4, 6;* thy *Q5*   157 aspects] *F;* aspect *Qq*   158–69] *F; not in Qq*

Nor when thy warlike father, like a child,
Told the sad story of my father's death
And twenty times made pause to sob and weep,
That all the standers-by had wet their cheeks   165
Like trees bedashed with rain – in that sad time
My manly eyes did scorn an humble tear;
And what these sorrows could not thence exhale,
Thy beauty hath, and made them blind with weeping.
I never sued to friend, nor enemy;   170
My tongue could never learn sweet smoothing word.
But now thy beauty is proposed my fee,
My proud heart sues, and prompts my tongue to speak.
    She looks scornfully at him.
Teach not thy lip such scorn, for it was made
For kissing, lady, not for such contempt.   175
If thy revengeful heart cannot forgive,
Lo, here I lend thee this sharp-pointed sword,

---

162 **thy warlike father** the Earl of Warwick; a messenger, not Warwick, announces the death of Richard's father (*3H6* 2.1).

165 **That** i.e. so that (Abbott, 283)

166 **bedashed** injured or spoiled as the wind dashes flowers (*OED* dash *sb.*[1] 1a)

168 **exhale** See 58.

170 **sued to** petitioned

171 **smoothing** flattering (*OED* smooth *a.* 7b). Qq's 'soothing' has a similar sense; cf. 1.3.297.

172 **proposed my fee** offered to me as a reward; legal vocabulary (as *sues* in 173)

177–81 Cf. Seneca, *Hercules Oetaeus*, 1000–1, 1015. John Studley's translation for Newton's volume reads, 'My breast lies bare unto thy hand.

Stryke, I thy gylt forgeve . . . Th' offence I did was ment in loue' (2.228). Cf. Phaedra to Hippolytus: 'I would not hesitate to offer my breast to naked swords' (*Hippolytus*, 616), and her offer in the presence of his corpse: 'in my wicked heart will I thrust the sword' (*Hippolytus*, 1176–7). Shakespeare quotes elsewhere from *Hippolytus* (*Tit* 4.1.81–2). Legge's Richard similarly attempts to woo young Elizabeth in a passage laced with physical threats (*Richardus Tertius*, 4190–204). The offer to *lay . . . naked* his *breast* if she may be *please[d] to hide* the blade in it constitutes a remarkable verbal regendering of the sexual dynamic (cf. 4.4.229n.). For staging, see Hankey; for Olivier's film, see Hassel, 13–14.

---

170 friend] *F, Q1–5;* friends *Q6*   171 smoothing word] *F;* soothing words *Qq*   173 SD] *F; not in Qq*   174 lip . . . it was] *F;* lips . . . they were *Qq*

Which if thou please to hide in this true breast
And let the soul forth that adoreth thee,
I lay it naked to the deadly stroke   180
And humbly beg the death upon my knee.

*He [kneels and] lays his breast open, she offers at [it]
with his sword.*

Nay, do not pause; for I did kill King Henry,
But 'twas thy beauty that provoked me.
Nay, now dispatch; 'twas I that stabbed young Edward,
But 'twas thy heavenly face that set me on.   185

She falls the sword.

Take up the sword again, or take up me.

ANNE

Arise, dissembler; though I wish thy death,

---

178 *this true The curious inversion of Q3
('true this') is the first of several striking
F/Qq reversals (194, 198, 202). F shows
careful correction (e.g. 194, where F corrects 'thou shalt' from Q2–6), but also
remarkable oversights (e.g. omission of
205) and discrepancies (228).
180 lay it naked bare my breast
181 the death death, execution in a judi-
cial context
181 SD The dialogue directs that Richard
be kneeling here. Capell plausibly had
him kneel at 176. He might rise when
ordered in 187 (since he would presumably, but not certainly, be upright
when offering to kill himself in 189).
The sequence probably derives from
Phaedra's confession of her passion
while 'grovel[ing]' before Hippolytus
with his drawn sword (Whitaker, 66;
Seneca, *Hippolytus*, 710–14).
offers at makes an attempt or show of
intention towards

182–4 *Qq preserve the chronological
sequence of Richard's crimes, but F
gains rhetorical force by naming last
the loss that nearest concerns Anne.
Arguments about order and correction based on chronology also enter
into editorial considerations of discrepancies between Q1–2 and Q3–F at
5.3.145.1–158.
183 provoked provokèd
185 SD *falls* lets fall (cf. 5.3.163)
186 These are hardly the only alternatives, but the arch manipulator drives
Anne into a corner, knowing her incapable of using the sword. For phrasing, cf. *The First Part of Hieronimo*
(1591?, printed 1605): 'Take up
thy pen, or I'll take up thee' (Kyd,
Hieronimo, 6.28).
187 *Arise Richard may rise during or
immediately after this line; but he
might remain kneeling until the offer
of the ring in 204.

---

178 this true] *F, Q1–2, 4–6;* true this *Q3*   breast] *F;* bosome *Qq*   180 the] *F, Q1–5;* thy *Q6*   181
SD] *F; not in Qq*   kneels and] *Capell after 176*   it] *Rowe*   182 for . . . Henry] *F;* 'twas I that kild
your husband *Qq*   184 stabbed young Edward] *F;* kild King Henry *Qq*   185 SD] *F; Here she lets
fall / the sword. Qq opp. 185–6*

I will not be thy executioner.

RICHARD

Then bid me kill myself, and I will do it.

ANNE

I have already.

RICHARD   That was in thy rage.   190

Speak it again and, even with the word,

This hand, which for thy love did kill thy love,

Shall for thy love kill a far truer love;

To both their deaths shalt thou be accessary.

ANNE

I would I knew thy heart.   195

RICHARD

'Tis figured in my tongue.

ANNE

I fear me both are false.

RICHARD

Then never man was true.

ANNE

Well, well, put up your sword.

188 Cf. Phoebe's remark to Silvius (*AYL* 3.5.8).

194 *shalt thou Cf. 178.
accessary trisyllabic (àc-cess-ry); participating in a crime (*OED a.* 1)

195–205 Such clear stichomythia is unusual in Shakespeare, but see Edward's wooing of Lady Grey (*3H6* 3.2). Abbott uses this passage to illustrate trimeter couplets in brief dialogue exchanges (Abbott, 500). Jowett's sense that Anne has the initiative is complicated by the fact that the sequence starts with the highly compromised lovers' diction of 195; the dynamic changes at 200 when Richard takes the lead, posing demands to which Anne must respond or offer resistance.

195 familiar lovers' discourse (cf. 'I would I knew his mind', *TGV* 1.2.33), marking a development in the interaction

196 figured displayed

197 fear me fear

198 *man was F agrees with Q3, but offers a more metrical (and more unusual) word-order than Q1–2 (*TxC*, 234); cf. 178, 194.

199 your Anne's respectful 'you' may register surrender (Davison, 154; cf. Abbott, 231).

188 thy] *F;* the *Qq* 190] *Steevens; F, Qq line* already. / rage: / That] *F;* Tush that *Qq* thy] *F, Q1–2;* the *Q3–6* 192 This] *F;* That *Qq* 194 shalt thou] *F, Q1;* thou shalt *Q2–6* be] *F, Q1–5;* by *Q6* 198 man was] *F, Q3–6;* was man *Q1–2*

RICHARD

    Say then my peace is made.   200

ANNE

    That shalt thou know hereafter.

RICHARD

    But shall I live in hope?

ANNE

    All men I hope live so.

ᵠRICHARDᵠ

    Vouchsafe to wear this ring.

ᵠANNE

    To take is not to give.ᵠ   205

RICHARD

    Look how my ring encompasseth thy finger;

    Even so thy breast encloseth my poor heart.

    Wear both of them, for both of them are thine.

    And if thy poor devoted servant may

    But beg one favour at thy gracious hand,   210

    Thou dost confirm his happiness forever.

ANNE   What is it?

RICHARD

    That it may please you leave these sad designs

---

203 Anne's Christian commonplace – all humanity hopes for heaven – characteristically evades responsibility for its implied assent to Richard's specific erotic request, which is that he may *hope* for her assent (cf. Siemon, 'Power').

204–5 *F omits 204 SP and all of 205, indenting 204 and setting it at the same distance from the edge of the page as SPs elsewhere.

204 **Vouchsafe** grant

205 Wilson detects parody of the marriage service: a pledge of troth is given and a ring is taken. Qq's line neatly encapsulates Anne's complicity while seeming to deny her own agency (and guilt); cf. 203 and pp. 15–17.

206 **Look how** just as (*OED* look *v.* 4b)

207 **breast . . . heart** a familiar conceit: 'My true love hath my hart and I have his' (Sidney, 75), 'My heart is in thy breast' (*LLL* 5.2.810); cf. *Son* 22 and Dent, L565.

213 **leave** i.e. to leave; 'to' omitted in infinitive (Abbott, 349)

201 shalt thou] *F;* shall you *Qq*   202 shall I] *F, Q1;* I shall *Q2–6*   204 SP] *Qq (Glo.)*   Vouchsafe] *F, Q2–6; Q1 (*Voutsafe*)*   205 SP] *Qq (La.)*   206 my] *F;* this *Qq*   207 my] *F, Q1–4;* me *Q5–6*   208 Wear] *F, Q1–3;* Were *Q4–6*   209 devoted] *F, Q1; om. Q2–6*   servant] *F;* suppliant *Qq*   213 may please you] *F;* would please thee *Qq*

To him that hath most cause to be a mourner,
And presently repair to Crosby House,   215
Where, after I have solemnly interred
At Chertsey Monastery this noble king
And wet his grave with my repentant tears,
I will with all expedient duty see you.
For diverse unknown reasons, I beseech you,   220
Grant me this boon.

ANNE

With all my heart, and much it joys me too
To see you are become so penitent.
– Tressel and Berkeley, go along with me.

RICHARD

Bid me farewell.

ANNE   'Tis more than you deserve;   225
But since you teach me how to flatter you,
Imagine I have said farewell already.

Exeunt two with Anne.

GENTLEMAN   Towards Chertsey, noble lord?

---

215 **presently** at once, immediately (*OED adv.* 3)
repair go, proceed (*OED v.*[1] 1)
Crosby House one of Richard's London residences, also called Crosby Place (cf. 1.3.344, 3.1.190)

219 **expedient** quick, expeditious

220 **diverse unknown** i.e. various secret, such as must not be told; although what requires secrecy remains unclear, the point may be Richard's demonstration of dominance in making such a demand. In any case, how remarkable to direct a single gentlewoman to go and wait at the house of an unmarried man (GWW), abandoning the body of a relative to the disposing of his slayer.

227 SD The '*two*' are Tressel and Berkeley (see 224).

228 *Qq include Richard's command – 'Sirs take vp the corse' – and 228 is spoken by a servant. F's sequence also makes sense, since F's '*Gent.*' would be merely doing what other characters routinely do in anticipating – sometimes mistakenly – Richard's wishes.

---

214 most] *F;* more *Qq*   215 House] *F;* place *Qq*   217 Monastery] *F (*Monast'ry*), Qq*   224
Berkeley] *F, Q1–2 (*Barkley*);* Bartley *Q3–6*   225] *Steevens; F, Qq line* farwell. / deserue: /   227 SD]
F (Exit . . . Anne), Rowe; Exit. Qq   228] *F; Glo.* Sirs take vp the corse. / *Ser.* Towards . . . Lord. /
Qq subst.   SP] *F (Gent.)*

RICHARD

No, to Whitefriars; there attend my coming.

Exeunt [the rest with the] corse.

Was ever woman in this humour wooed?   230
Was ever woman in this humour won?
I'll have her, but I will not keep her long.
What? I that killed her husband and his father,
To take her in her heart's extremest hate,
With curses in her mouth, tears in her eyes,   235
The bleeding witness of my hatred by,
Having God, her conscience and these bars against me,
And I, no friends to back my suit withal
But the plain devil and dissembling looks?
And yet to win her? All the world to nothing!   240
Ha!
Hath she forgot already that brave prince,

229 **Whitefriars** Carmelite priory in London; Holinshed follows More in saying that the body went to Blackfriars (Hall does not specify) and thence by water to Chertsey (Holinshed, 3.690–1). Specifics may be less significant than the peremptoriness of Richard's redirection of the cortège, behaviour repeated throughout the play.

230–40 Cf. Berowne's surprise and consternation at the absurdity of his falling in love (*LLL* 3.1.169–200).

230, 231 **humour** temporary mood (*OED sb.* II 5), as in 4.1.64; the meaning should be contrasted with the more settled disposition implied at 4.4.269. Cf. *JC* 2.2.56.

230–1 **wooed . . . won** Cf. 'All women may be won' (Dent, W681), 'She is a woman, therefore may be wooed; / She is a woman, therefore may be won'

(*Tit* 2.1.83–4).

236 **by** near

237 **Having** Abbott suggests an elided or softened *v* rendering the word monosyllabic (Abbott, 466); cf. *VA* 828, *1H4* 3.1.33.
bars impediments

238 **friends . . . suit** relatives (*OED sb.* 3) to support my wooing; *friends* were important to the corporate process of wedding (cf. *MND* 1.1.139). A possible legal connotation to *suit* could continue the metaphor begun with *bars* (237).
withal *Although *withal* first appears here in Q3 for Q1–2's 'at all', it is frequent in this play (e.g. 3.7.56, 3.7.196, 5.3.315, 5.5.6). Here it means 'in addition' or 'besides' (cf. *R2* 4.1.18 and Abbott, 196).

240 **All . . . nothing** against enormous odds; cf. *RJ* 3.5.213.

229 SD] *Capell; Exit Coarse. F; Exeunt. manet Gl. Qq opp. 230* 233 his] *F, Q1–2;* her *Q3–6* 234 hate] *F, Q1;* heate *Q2–6* 236 my] *F;* her *Qq* 238 no friends] *F;* nothing *Qq* withal] *F, Q3–6 subst.;* at all *Q1–2* 240–1] *F; one line Qq*

Edward, her lord, whom I, some three months since,
Stabbed in my angry mood at Tewkesbury?
A sweeter and a lovelier gentleman, 245
Framed in the prodigality of Nature,
Young, valiant, wise and, no doubt, right royal,
The spacious world cannot again afford;
And will she yet abase her eyes on me,
That cropped the golden prime of this sweet prince 250
And made her widow to a woeful bed?
On me, whose all not equals Edward's moiety?
On me, that halts and am misshapen thus?
My dukedom to a beggarly denier,
I do mistake my person all this while! 255

243 **her lord** i.e. her husband
　three months since This marks the
date as August 1471 (Malone), while
Act 2 dramatizes King Edward's death
(April 1483). Richard's dating is off
in any case: the battle of Tewkesbury
was fought on 4 May 1471, and King
Henry's body was taken to Chertsey
that same month.
244 **Tewkesbury** site of Henry VI's
defeat by Edward IV
245–8 Syntax becomes confused as the
comparative opening shifts to a claim
that the world cannot *again* produce a
sweeter gentleman.
246 **Framed ... Nature** gifted, fashioned from Nature's most generous
creative force. Cf. Boyet's praise of the
Princess of France as endowed with
graces by 'Nature ... When she did
starve the general world beside / And
prodigally gave them all to you' (*LLL*
2.1.9–12).
247 **no doubt** apparently an ironic quali-
fier, since there were no doubts about
Edward's royal descent or princely
character; Fabyan dismisses slanders
concerning his paternity (2.456).
　royal noble, majestic, generous, munificent (*OED sb.* 9a, citing this line); but
OED observes that the term's force
is 'not always clear' in Shakespeare.
Here there is a possible joke (a likelihood heightened by *no doubt*) based on
the simple meaning 'of kingly blood',
whereby Richard enjoys a laugh at
the expense of hereditary royalty: this
prince never got a chance to prove
royal. The financial terms in subsequent lines reinforce an economic
sense ('generous, munificent').
249 **abase** lower, with a possible economic sense of depreciating or debas-
ing (cf. Qq 'debase') coinage (*OED
v.* 1, 3)
250 **cropped ... prime** cut short the
springtime of early manhood (*OED*
crop *v.* 4)
　golden flourishing (*OED a.* 7), also
playing on a metallurgical sense conveyed by *abase* in 249
252 **not equals** i.e. does not equal
(Abbott, 305; cf. *2H4* 4.1.98)
　moiety half
253 **halts** limps
254 **denier** the twelfth of the sou; a cop-
per coin used as the type of a very
small sum

249 abase] *F;* debase *Qq* 253 halts] *F;* halt *Qq* misshapen] *F;* vnshapen *Qq* 254 to] *F, Q1–4;* to
be *Q5–6*

Upon my life, she finds, although I cannot,
Myself to be a marvellous proper man.
I'll be at charges for a looking-glass
And entertain a score or two of tailors
To study fashions to adorn my body;   260
Since I am crept in favour with myself,
I will maintain it with some little cost.
But first I'll turn yon fellow in his grave
And then return lamenting to my love.
Shine out, fair sun, till I have bought a glass,   265
That I may see my shadow as I pass.   *Exit.*

1.3   *Enter* QUEEN ELIZABETH, Lord RIVERS,
         [*the* Marquess of DORSET] *and* Lord GREY.

257 **proper** well-made, handsome
258 **be . . . for** i.e. pay for
259 As Ian McKellen says, 'Forty tailors
  indeed!' (McKellen, 88).
  entertain employ
261–5 The immediate sense of 261 is
  'since I have crept into my own good
  graces', but Abbott suggests: 'since I
  have crept into (Lady Anne's) favour
  with the aid of my personal appearance,
  I will pay some attention to my person'
  (Abbott, 193). The self-reflexivity (and
  the vocabulary of sun, shadow and
  love) recalls Richard's earlier medita-
  tions on his own image (1.1.14–27) and
  anticipates his later division of self and
  conscience (5.3.179–206); *crept* echoes
  creeping things (20).
262 **some little** i.e. considerable? But
  contrast 2.2.120.
263 **fellow** The term is insulting when
  used for a king, but it appears in
  other ways that implicate social difference. Lords may properly address
  a messenger, a pursuivant or a sher-

iff as *fellow* (3.2.18, 104; 5.1.10), but
Richard abruptly terminates his display of mock respect to Brakenbury
by calling him *fellow* (1.1.98), the
term Brakenbury uses for a murderer
(1.4.85). Richard calls Richmond *a
paltry fellow* (5.3.323).
  in into (Abbott, 159)
265–6 Cf. 1.1.24–7.
265 **Shine . . . sun** The elation and
  newly-won self-confidence of David
  Troughton's Richard took visible
  form, as the lighting responded to his
  cue (Troughton, 90).
  glass mirror
1.3 location: '*the Palace*' (Theobald)
0.1 QUEEN ELIZABETH F prematurely calls
  Elizabeth '*Queene Mother*' (as Qq 4.1.0.1).
  In 4.1 she is queen mother to young
  King Edward, but here she is '*Queene*',
  i.e. Edward IV's queen consort.
0.2 DORSET Dorset does not speak until
  185, but the entry often given him
  (41.1) brings him on with his enemy,
  Richard.

257 marvellous] *F* (maru'llous*), Qq* (*merueilous subst.*)   258 looking-glass] *F; Qq* (looking glass*)
259 a] *F*; some *Qq*   260 adorn] *F, Q1–2*; adore *Q3–6*   262 some] *F, Q1–2*; a *Q3–6*   263 yon]
F, Q1–3; you *Q4–6*   265 out] *F, Q1–5*; our *Q6*   1.3] *F (Scena Tertia.*); not in *Qq*   0.1–2] *F*;
Enter Queene, Lord Riuers, Gray. Qq subst.   0.1 ELIZABETH] *Malone*; the *Queene Mother F*   0.2 *the
. . .* DORSET] *Hanmer subst.*

RIVERS

Have patience, madam. There's no doubt his majesty
Will soon recover his accustomed health.

GREY

In that you brook it ill, it makes him worse;
Therefore for God's sake entertain good comfort
And cheer his grace with quick and merry eyes.   5

QUEEN ELIZABETH

If he were dead, what would betide on me?

GREY

No other harm but loss of such a lord.

QUEEN ELIZABETH

The loss of such a lord includes all harms.

GREY

The heavens have blessed you with a goodly son
To be your comforter when he is gone.   10

QUEEN ELIZABETH

Ah, he is young, and his minority
Is put unto the trust of Richard Gloucester,
A man that loves not me, nor none of you.

RIVERS

Is it concluded he shall be Protector?

---

3 **brook it ill** endure or tolerate it badly (*OED* brook *v.* 3)
4 **entertain good comfort** accept cheer or consolation
5 ***with** Q2 corrects Q1's omission.
quick lively, alert, vigorous (*OED a.* III 20a)
quick . . . eyes Qq's 'quick . . . words' is attractive, but 'quick eyes' are vital for courtiers; cf. 47–9 and 'let thine eye look like a friend on Denmark' (*Ham* 1.2.69).
6 ***Repeated in F perhaps as the result of its position at the foot of one page and the head of the next. The F catch-

word '*Gray*.' indicates that he has the first line of the next page (sig. r1ʳ). If the repetition were intended, Queen Elizabeth would be more distraught than her subsequent speeches suggest.
betide on become of (*OED v.* 2)
11 **minority** condition of being under-age, too young to rule
14 **Protector** regent, in charge of the kingdom during the minority, absence or incapacity of the sovereign (*OED sb.* 2a); Edward IV's will 'commyttyd [his sons] to the tuytion of Rycherd his brother' (Vergil, 171). For issues and dates, see Hanham, 5–6.

---

3 it ill,] *F, Q2–6;* it, ill *Q1*   5 with quick] *F, Q2–6;* quick *Q1*   eyes] *F;* words *Qq*   6+ SP] *F, Qq (Qu.), Malone subst.*   6 on] *F;* of *Qq*   *F repeats last line from sig. q6ᵛ on sig. r1ʳ; F sig. q6ᵛ c.w. Gray.*
7 SP] *F (Gray.); Ry. Q1; Ri. Q2–6*   8 harms] *F;* harme *Qq*   11 Ah] *F;* Oh *Qq*   12 Richard] *F;* Rich. *Qq*   14 Is it] *F, Q1–5;* It is *Q6*

QUEEN ELIZABETH

It is determined, not concluded yet;   15

But so it must be, if the King miscarry.

Enter BUCKINGHAM *and* [STANLEY, Earl of] Derby.

GREY

Here come the lords of Buckingham and Derby.

BUCKINGHAM

Good time of day unto your royal grace.

STANLEY

God make your majesty joyful, as you have been.

QUEEN ELIZABETH

The Countess Richmond, good my lord of Derby,   20

To your good prayer will scarcely say amen.

Yet Derby, not withstanding she's your wife

And loves not me, be you, good lord, assured

I hate not you for her proud arrogance.

STANLEY

I do beseech you, either not believe   25

---

15 **determined, not concluded** resolved, but not yet officially instituted

16 **miscarry** die (*OED v.* 1); given the frequent references to abortive or malformed birth, associations with premature or unviable foetuses (*OED v.* 4; cf. *2H4* 5.4.10) are perhaps relevant.

16.1 ***Derby** Thomas, Lord Stanley, only became Earl of Derby in 1485. Qq, F call him 'Derby' (or 'Darby') in this scene's SDs, SPs and dialogue, but use 'Stanley' in dialogue after this scene. Names in later SDs and SPs vary (see pp. 450–1).

17 ***come the lords** Q3 changes 'come' to 'comes', but F has 'Lord', thereby either making two lords appear one person ('Lord of Buckingham & Derby')

or reducing Derby to an afterthought; 'comes' could be plural (Abbott, 333).

20 **Countess Richmond** Stanley's wife, Margaret Beaufort, whose first marriage (1455) had been to Edmund Tudor, Earl of Richmond and half-brother to Henry VI. By her first marriage she is mother of the play's Richmond. Stanley was her third husband. Historically, she formed a 'conspiracie' against Richard with Queen Elizabeth in an 'enterprise betweene the two mothers' to wed Richmond to Queen Elizabeth's daughter, Elizabeth of York (Holinshed, 3.742).

21 **say amen** i.e. concur with, ratify (a wish or prayer) (*OED sb.* 2a); cf. 3.7.240, 5.5.41.

16.1] *F; Enter Buck. Darby Qq opp. 16* STANLEY, Earl of] *Theobald subst.* 17 come the lords] *Q1–2;* comes the Lord *F;* comes the Lords *Q3–6* 19+ SP] *Theobald; Der. F; Dar. Qq* 21 prayer] *F;* praiers *Qq* 24 arrogance] *F, Q1–2;* arrogancie *Q3–6* 25 do] *F, Q1–2; om. Q3–6*

The envious slanders of her false accusers,
Or, if she be accused on true report,
Bear with her weakness, which I think proceeds
From wayward sickness, and no grounded malice.

QUEEN ELIZABETH
Saw you the King today, my lord of Derby?   30
STANLEY
But now the Duke of Buckingham and I
Are come from visiting his majesty.
QUEEN ELIZABETH
What likelihood of his amendment, lords?
BUCKINGHAM
Madam, good hope. His grace speaks cheerfully.
QUEEN ELIZABETH
God grant him health. Did you confer with him?   35
BUCKINGHAM
Ay, madam; he desires to make atonement
Between the Duke of Gloucester and your brothers,

---

26 **envious** malicious, spiteful, emulous (*OED a.* 2, 3); her descent from Edward III might have occasioned envy. This lineal distinction will provide one source of Richmond's claim and perhaps explains remarks about her *proud arrogance* (24).

28–9 **weakness . . . sickness** The sources suggest concern for the Countess's health (Holinshed, 3.741; Vergil, 195), but Stanley's exculpations – either she is innocent or she is impaired, perhaps sick, perhaps wilful (see 29n.) – employ (rhetorically useful) misogynist stereotypes to excuse her as a weak or *wayward* woman rather than fear her as the political force that Margaret Beaufort was historically, if not in this play (see p. 18).

29 **wayward** not yielding readily to treatment, obstinate (*OED* 1e); suggesting

'erratic' or 'perverse' in judgement (*OED a.* 1c, 2a) as opposed to *grounded*
grounded immovable, firmly fixed (*OED ppl. a.*[1] 1)

30 SP *Qq give this line to Rivers.

31 **But** just

33 **amendment** recovery from illness (*OED* 4)

36 **atonement** reconciliation

37 **brothers** Only one of Queen Elizabeth's historical brothers (Lord Rivers) appears in the play, but the F, Qq plural here (also 67, F only) is echoed at 4.4.92 (F, Qq), 4.4.380 (F only) and 3.1.6, 12 (F, Qq). Shakespeare may mistake Elizabeth's son by a previous marriage, Lord Grey, for one of her brothers (Furness). F mistakes Anthony Woodeville's name and two titles (Earl Rivers and Lord Scales) as referring to three individuals (cf. Hall,

---

26 false] *F, Q1–2; om. Q3–6*   27 on] *F; in Qq*   30 SP] *F; Ry. Qq subst.*   of] *F, Q1–5; om. Q6*   32 Are come] *F; Came Qq; Came forth Oxf*[1]   33 What] *F, Q3–6; With Q1–2*   34 speaks] *F, Q1–2, 4–6; speaketh Q3*   36 Ay, madam] *F; Madame we did Qq*   to make] *F, Q1–3, 5–6; make Q4*   37 Between] *F; Betwixt Qq*

And between them and my Lord Chamberlain,
And sent to warn them to his royal presence.

QUEEN ELIZABETH

Would all were well, but that will never be;   40
I fear our happiness is at the height.

Enter RICHARD [*and* HASTINGS].

RICHARD

They do me wrong, and I will not endure it!
Who is it that complains unto the King
That I, forsooth, am stern and love them not?
By holy Paul, they love his grace but lightly   45
That fill his ears with such dissentious rumours.
Because I cannot flatter, and look fair,
Smile in men's faces, smooth, deceive and cog,
Duck with French nods and apish courtesy,
I must be held a rancorous enemy.   50
Cannot a plain man live and think no harm

Edward V, fol. v^r: 'lord Antony Wooduile erle Ryuers and lorde Scales, brother to the quene'). Qq avoid confusion: see 67, 2.1.0.2, 2.1.67–8 and pp. 458–9.

38 **Lord Chamberlain** i.e. Hastings
39 **warn** summon
41 **at the height** i.e. as elevated as it will ever be
41.1 Although Richard's theatrical repertoire includes unaccompanied entry (1.2.32.1, 3.4.20.1), Hastings has no entry elsewhere in F or Qq, so he may enter here. He seems to be absent at 38; at 182 he takes the lead, perhaps significantly, given the conjectural entry with Richard, in supporting Richard's Yorkist perception of past events.
44 **forsooth** a mild oath ('in truth'), often laughable (cf. Jonson, *Poetaster*, 4.1.33–4). Pious Henry VI used no oath but

'forsooth' (Holinshed, 3.691).
45 **holy Paul** Saint Paul
46 **dissentious** quarrelsome
47 **cannot . . . fair** Cf. Richard's looks at 3.4.48–53.
48 **smooth** flatter (cf. 1.2.171)
   cog employ feigned flattery, fawn, wheedle (*OED v.* 5); senses include cheating and sleight of hand (*OED v.* 3).
49 **Duck** bow or stoop quickly, often connoting cringing servility (*OED v.* 2a); cf. Marlowe, *Jew of Malta*, 3.3.53.
   French . . . courtesy affected gestures of foolish or imitative courtliness; see *RJ* 2.4.28–45, and Thomas Dekker's denunciation of '*Apishnesse*' (58).
50 **held** considered, taken for
51–2 **plain . . . simple** terms typical of authorial personae in contemporary

38 between] *F;* betwixt *Qq*   41 height] *F;* highest *Qq*   41.1 RICHARD] *F; Glocester Qq   and* HASTINGS] *Hanmer*   43 is it] *F;* are they *Qq*   44 That] *Qq;* Thar *F*   and] *F, Q1–5;* om. *Q6*   47 look] *F;* speake *Qq*

But thus his simple truth must be abused
With silken, sly, insinuating jacks?

GREY

To who in all this presence speaks your grace?

RICHARD

To thee, that hast nor honesty nor grace.   55
When have I injured thee? When done thee wrong?
– Or thee? – Or thee? – Or any of your faction?
A plague upon you all! His royal grace,
Whom God preserve better than you would wish,
Cannot be quiet scarce a breathing while   60
But you must trouble him with lewd complaints.

QUEEN ELIZABETH

Brother of Gloucester, you mistake the matter:
The King, on his own royal disposition
And not provoked by any suitor else,
Aiming, belike, at your interior hatred,   65

complaint and satire; Richard uses these adjectives pejoratively to characterize Clarence (1.1.118).

52 **truth** veracity, sincerity

53 **With** by
silken elegant; ingratiating, flattering (*OED* II 7b)
jacks contemptuous term for commoners (*OED sb.*[1] 2a; cf. *TS* 2.1.285); Shakespeare elsewhere uses the term (mistakenly) for the keys on virginals (*OED sb.*[1] 14), suggesting flattery and courtly insinuation (*Son* 128); cf. 71–2. Such an association would continue Richard's musical vocabulary (e.g. 1.1.8–13, 27). For 'jack' as a mechanical figure on a clock, see 4.2.112.

54, 55 **grace** Richard evokes the theological and courteous senses of the honorific title, maintaining that Grey lacks divine favour and courtly gracefulness

(cf. 320, 2.1.120–33, 2.4.20–4). As a duke, Richard may be addressed as *your grace*; Grey, as son of a knight, is not so entitled. Richard reminds Grey of their differences in birth. Cf. *True Tragedy*, 809–10.

55 **thee** an insulting pronoun; cf. 1.2.46. Richard's *your* at 57 is plural.
nor . . . nor neither . . . nor (cf. 1.2.70)

60 **breathing while** short time, the time of a breath

61 **lewd** foolish, ill-mannered, suggesting social denigration, as *jacks* (53) (*OED* 3, 4)

62 **Brother** i.e. her brother-in-law

63–8 **King . . . send** i.e. the fact that the King guesses your hatred makes him send (Abbott, 376)

63 **disposition** inclination

65 **Aiming, belike** guessing, perhaps

52 his] *F, Q1–4;* in *Q5–6*   53 With] *F;* By *Qq*   54 SP] *F; Ry. Qq subst.*   who] *F;* whom *Q1–5;* home *Q6*   all] *F, Q1–5; om. Q6*   55 ²nor] *F, Q1–3, 5–6;* not *Q4*   58 grace] *F;* person *Qq*   63 on] *F;* of *Qq*

That in your outward action shows itself
Against my children, brothers and myself,
Makes him to send, that he may learn the ground.

RICHARD

I cannot tell; the world is grown so bad
That wrens make prey where eagles dare not perch.   70
Since every Jack became a gentleman,
There's many a gentle person made a jack.

QUEEN ELIZABETH

Come, come, we know your meaning, brother
    Gloucester.
You envy my advancement, and my friends'.
God grant we never may have need of you.   75

RICHARD

Meantime, God grants that I have need of you.
Our brother is imprisoned by your means,
Myself disgraced, and the nobility
Held in contempt, while great promotions

---

67 **children, brothers** See 37n.
68 *F, Qq appear difficult or garbled. Many editors follow Pope ('Makes him to send, that he may learn the ground / Of your ill will, and thereby to remove it').
    Makes causes
    ground i.e. the basis (of your ill will)
69 **I cannot tell** I have no idea.
70 Cf. 1.1.132–3. For tiny wrens to dominate mighty eagles, one familiar early modern hierarchical order would have to be inverted; however, Richard's insults go further: the lowly insectivorous wren appears as an audacious bird of prey, daring to hunt where eagles fear to perch. Cf. *Mac* 2.4.12–13.
71, 72 **Jack, jack** Cf. 53n.
71 **Jack . . . gentleman** proverbial for social climbing: 'Jack would be a

gentleman' (Dent, J3).
72 **gentle** well-born, belonging to a family of position; originally synonymous with 'noble', but afterwards distinguished, either as a wider term, or as designating a lower degree. Also heraldic: having the rank or status of 'gentleman', distinguished by the right to bear arms (*OED a.* 1a).
74 **advancement** social elevation; cf. 4.4.242.
    friends' kinsmens' (*OED* 3)
76 **you** Richard appears to switch from 'thou' to 'you' forms (see 55), but his *you* may be a plural directed toward the Queen and her *friends* (74); his *you* to Queen Elizabeth (89) certainly employs the respectful form.
77 See 1.1.63–5.

66 That] *F;* Which *Qq*   action] *F;* actions *Qq*   67 children, brothers] *F;* kindred, brother *Qq*   68] *F;* Makes him to send that thereby he may gather / The ground *(*grounds *Q6)* of your ill will and to remoue it. / *Qq*   70 make prey] *F, Q2;* make pray *Q1;* may prey *Q3–6*   71 Jack] *Qq (*Iacke*);* Iaeke *F*   74 my advancement] *F, Q1;* mine aduancement *Q2–6*   76 grants] *F, Q1–2;* grant *Q3–6*   I] *F;* we *Qq*   79 while great] *F;* whilst many faire *Qq*

Are daily given to ennoble those   80
That scarce some two days since were worth a noble.

QUEEN ELIZABETH

By Him that raised me to this careful height
From that contented hap which I enjoyed,
I never did incense his majesty
Against the Duke of Clarence, but have been   85
An earnest advocate to plead for him.
My lord, you do me shameful injury
Falsely to draw me in these vile suspects.

RICHARD

You may deny that you were not the mean
Of my Lord Hastings' late imprisonment.   90

RIVERS

She may, my lord, for –

RICHARD

She may, Lord Rivers; why, who knows not so?
She may do more, sir, than denying that:
She may help you to many fair preferments,
And then deny her aiding hand therein   95
And lay those honours on your high desert.
What may she not? She may, ay, marry, may she.

---

81 **noble** gold coin worth one third of a pound in the mid-16th century
82 **careful height** elevated position full of cares
83 **hap** condition, fortune (*OED sb.*[1] 1)
86 **advocate to plead** attorney to argue his case
88 **in** into
   suspects suspicions
89 **deny . . . not** double negative used as an intensifier (Abbott, 406)
   mean means, cause (*OED sb.*[2] II 10a)
91 **for –** This truncated utterance (not in Qq) makes Richard's verbal dominance especially apparent.
92 On Richard's play with *may* as 'vir-

tuoso performance', see McDonald.
94 **preferments** advancements or promotions
96 **lay . . . on** attribute those honours to
   high desert great merit
97 *****ay** F, Qq differ frequently (including 120, 125, 135, 262) over 'ay' (meaning 'yes' and written as 'I') and 'yea'; on F's preference as authorial, and Q1's 'yea' as attributable to Valentine Simmes, see *TxC*, 234. However, two variants occur in the portion of Q1 printed by Short (4.4.249, 282). On F's prejudice against 'yea', see Honigmann, 'Variants', 192–3. **marry** indeed, to be sure; derived from invocation of the Virgin Mary

89 mean] *F;* cause *Qq*   91 lord, for –] *F;* Lord. *Qq*   96 desert] *F;* deserts *Qq*   97 ay] *F (I);* yea *Qq*

RIVERS
> What, marry, may she?

RICHARD
> What, marry, may she? Marry with a king,
> A bachelor, and a handsome stripling too;   100
> Iwis your grandam had a worser match.

QUEEN ELIZABETH
> My lord of Gloucester, I have too long borne
> Your blunt upbraidings and your bitter scoffs.
> By heaven, I will acquaint his majesty
> Of those gross taunts that oft I have endured.   105
> I had rather be a country servant maid
> Than a great queen with this condition,
> To be so baited, scorned and stormed at.

Enter old QUEEN MARGARET.

> Small joy have I in being England's queen.

QUEEN MARGARET [*aside*]
> And lessened be that small, God I beseech Him.   110

---

100 **stripling** youth, just passing from boyhood to manhood (*OED* 1)

101 **Iwis** certainly; 'I wis' (F, Q4–5, 7–8) suggests confusion of the adverb (resembling German *gewiß*) with the subject–verb form, 'I know'.
  grandam Richard's insult attacking the grandmother of Rivers and Queen Elizabeth instead of their mother, who had notoriously married beneath her (Hall, *Henry VI*, fol. cxxxiv^r), has been much discussed (see Var). Jowett suggests the play's uncertainty about Elizabeth's male relatives ('Pre-editorial', 129–30).
  worser worse, a double comparative (Abbott, 11)

106–7 Similar contrasts between queen

and maid appear in Elizabeth I's 1576 parliament speech and in anecdotes about her (Shannon, 151n.).

107 **condition** stipulation, limitation

108 **baited** persecuted or harassed (*OED v.* 4)
  stormed stormèd

108.1 *old* QUEEN MARGARET Margaret (born 1429), widow of Henry VI; following the battle of Tewkesbury (1471) she was imprisoned until exiled to France (1476), where she died (1482) at the age of 53. This scene occurs in 1483, and F flaunts its fictionalized chronology at 166–7.

110 SP *For Qq's SPs, see Walton, *Copy*, 74–6.

100 and a] *F*; a *Qq*   101 Iwis] *Q1–3, 6*; I wis *F, Q4–5*   a worser] *F, Q1–4, 6 subst.*; worser *Q5*   105 Of] *F*; With *Qq*   that oft I] *F*; I often *Qq*   108 so . . . stormed] *F* (scorn'd*)*; thus taunted, scorned, and baited *Qq*   108.1] *F after 109; Qq opp. 108–9*   old] *F; not in Qq*   110+ SP] *Qq (Q[u]. M[ar]. except 279); Mar., Margaret., Q.M. F*   110, 117, 125, 133, 136, 142, 154 SD] *Marshall*   110 lessened] *F, Qq (*lesned*), Bevington⁴*   Him] *F*; thee *Qq*

Thy honour, state and seat is due to me.

RICHARD

    What? Threat you me with telling of the King?

    ^QTell him and spare not. Look what I have said^Q

    I will avouch't in presence of the King.

    I dare adventure to be sent to th' Tower.   115

    'Tis time to speak; my pains are quite forgot.

QUEEN MARGARET [*aside*]

    Out, devil! I do remember them too well:

    Thou killed'st my husband Henry in the Tower,

    And Edward, my poor son, at Tewkesbury.

RICHARD

    Ere you were queen, ay, or your husband king,   120

    I was a packhorse in his great affairs,

    A weeder-out of his proud adversaries,

    A liberal rewarder of his friends.

    To royalize his blood, I spent mine own.

QUEEN MARGARET [*aside*]

    Ay, and much better blood than his, or thine.   125

RICHARD

    In all which time, you and your husband Grey

---

111 **Thy** Margaret uses 'thee/thou' forms to everyone.
    state condition, prosperity (*OED sb.* 1)
    seat throne

112 **Threat** threaten
    with telling of i.e. with the act of telling (Abbott, 178)

113 *Absent from F for no clear reason. It would not be absolutely necessary for sense, given F's 'avouch't' in 114 instead of Qq's 'auouch'.
    Look what whatever

114 **avouch't** acknowledge it as one's own

115 **adventure** risk

116 **pains** efforts (on King Edward's behalf)

117 **Out** exclamation expressing abhorrence or indignant reproach
    them Margaret twists Richard's *pains* to mean both his 'efforts' and the sufferings that he inflicted on her family.

121 **packhorse** beast of burden; possibly referring to Richard's shape (see 148n.)

---

112 of] *F, Q1, 3–5;* or *Q2; om. Q6*   113 have] *Q1–2; om. Q3–6*   114 avouch't] *F;* auouch *Qq*   115] *F; not in Qq*   116] *Qq; F lines* speake, / forgot. /   my] *F, Q1–5;* when *Q6*   117] *Qq; F lines* Diuell, / well: /   do] *F; not in Qq*   118 killed'st] *F (*killd'st*);* slewest *Qq*   120] *Qq; F lines* Queene, / King: / ay] *F (*1*);* yea *Qq*   or] *F, Qq;* of *Q2 Tn*   122 weeder-out] *F, Qq (*weeder out*),* hyphen *Capell*   124 spent] *F;* spilt *Qq*   125] *Qq; F lines* blood / thine. / Ay] *F;* Yea *Qq*

Were factious for the house of Lancaster.
– And Rivers, so were you. – Was not your husband
In Margaret's battle at Saint Albans slain?
– Let me put in your minds, if you forget,   130
What you have been ere this, and what you are;
Withal, what I have been, and what I am.

QUEEN MARGARET [*aside*]

A murderous villain, and so still thou art.

RICHARD

Poor Clarence did forsake his father Warwick,
Ay, and forswore himself – which Jesu pardon –   135

QUEEN MARGARET [*aside*]   Which God revenge.

RICHARD

To fight on Edward's party for the crown,
And for his meed, poor lord, he is mewed up.
I would to God my heart were flint, like Edward's,
Or Edward's soft and pitiful, like mine.   140
I am too childish-foolish for this world.

QUEEN MARGARET [*aside*]

Hie thee to hell for shame, and leave this world,
Thou cacodemon. There thy kingdom is.

---

127 **factious for** i.e. promoting dissension in the special interest of
128 **your husband** Sir John Grey, Queen
Elizabeth's first husband, was slain fighting for the Lancastrians at St Albans
(1461), although Holinshed leaves his
allegiance doubtful (Holinshed, 3.668).
This passage corrects *3H6* 3.2.1–7,
where 'Richard Grey' is a Yorkist.
129 **Margaret's battle** 'Battle' may
mean a body of troops (*OED sb.* II
8a), so Richard says Grey died among
Margaret's supporters. Alternatively,
Margaret's battle may be so-called to
distinguish the second battle of St
Albans from an earlier conflict in 1455.

132 **Withal** besides
134–7 Clarence first deserted his brothers to marry Isabel Neville, Warwick's
elder daughter and Lady Anne's sister.
Subsequently he betrayed his oath
to Warwick to fight on Edward's side
(*3H6* 4.1, 5.1; Hall, *Edward IV*, fols
cc^r, ccvii^r, ccxvi^r); cf. 1.4.49–51.
134 **father** father-in-law
138 **meed** reward
mewed up caged (cf. 1.1.38)
139 **heart were flint** Cf. Dent, H311.
142 **Hie** hasten
leave this world Margaret ironically
echoes Richard's words at 1.1.152 (RP).
143 **cacodemon** evil spirit

---

130 minds] *F, Q1–4 subst.;* minde *Q5;* mind *Q6*   you] *F;* yours *Qq*   131 this] *F;* now *Qq*   133
murderous] *F (*murth'rous*), Qq (*murtherous)*   135 Ay] *F;* Yea *Qq*   141 childish-foolish] *F, Q3–6
(*childish foolish*), hyphen Theobald;* childish, foolish *Q1–2*   142 this] *F;* the *Qq*

RIVERS

My lord of Gloucester, in those busy days
Which here you urge to prove us enemies,   145
We followed then our lord, our sovereign king.
So should we you, if you should be our king.

RICHARD

If I should be? I had rather be a pedlar.
Far be it from my heart, the thought thereof.

QUEEN ELIZABETH

As little joy, my lord, as you suppose   150
You should enjoy, were you this country's king,
As little joy you may suppose in me
That I enjoy, being the queen thereof.

QUEEN MARGARET [*aside*]

As little joy enjoys the queen thereof,
For I am she, and altogether joyless.   155
I can no longer hold me patient.   [*Comes forward.*]
Hear me, you wrangling pirates, that fall out
In sharing that which you have pilled from me:
Which of you trembles not, that looks on me?
If not, that I am queen, you bow like subjects,   160
Yet that, by you deposed, you quake like rebels.

---

145 **urge** refer to
148 **pedlar** Honigmann suggests reference to Richard's back, which makes him resemble a pedlar bearing a sack.
154 ***As** F, Qq agree on 'A', but Margaret would be saying she has 'a little joy' before calling herself 'altogether joyless' (*TxC*, 234). 'As' echoes 152. Alternatives are: 'Ah' (Bevington, Wells & Taylor, Jowett), 'Ay' (Hammond), 'As' (Dyce following Heath, 292), Wilson, Mowat

& Werstine), 'And' (White). 'Ah' is spelled 'A' at Qq 3.7.23, but F, Qq print 'Ah' as 'Ah' in 4.4.9.
157–8 ironically echoing the Duke of York (*2H6* 1.1.219–28); now a Lancastrian watches Yorkists squabble over spoils (Tillyard, *History Plays*, 200).
158 **pilled** plundered (*OED v.*[1] 1a)
160–1 i.e. if you do not bow to your queen, you nevertheless quake like rebels before me, the monarch you have deposed (cf. Abbott, 378).

---

146 sovereign] *F;* lawfull *Qq*   147 you, if] *F, Q1–5 subst.;* now, if *Q6*   148 If I] *F, Q1–5;* If *Q6*   149 thereof] *F;* of it *Qq*   150 SP] *F, Q1–2 (Qu.), Q3–4 (Q.M.), Q5–6 (Qu. Mar. subst.)*   152 you may] *F;* may you *Qq*   154 As] *Dyce (Heath);* A *F, Qq;* And *White;* Ay, *Ard²;* Ah, *Oxf*   156 SD] *Capell (advancing.)*   158 sharing] *F, Q1;* sharing out *Q2–6*   159 of] *F (off), Qq*   looks] *F, Q1–4;* looke *Q5–6*   160 am] *F;* being *Qq*   161 by you] *F, Q1–2, 5–6;* byou *Q3;* by on *Q4*

   – Ah, gentle villain, do not turn away.

RICHARD

   Foul wrinkled witch, what mak'st thou in my sight?

QUEEN MARGARET

   But repetition of what thou hast marred;

   That will I make before I let thee go.   165

RICHARD

   Wert thou not banished on pain of death?

QUEEN MARGARET

   I was, but I do find more pain in banishment

   Than death can yield me here by my abode.

   A husband and a son thou ow'st to me;

   – And thou a kingdom; – all of you, allegiance.   170

   This sorrow that I have, by right is yours,

   And all the pleasures you usurp are mine.

RICHARD

   The curse my noble father laid on thee

   When thou didst crown his warlike brows with paper,

   And with thy scorns drew'st rivers from his eyes,   175

   And then to dry them, gav'st the Duke a clout

   Steeped in the faultless blood of pretty Rutland –

---

162 **gentle** well-born; combining *gentle*
with *villain* invokes the social and
moral senses of *villain*.

163 **what ... sight?** What are you doing
here?

164 Margaret first takes Richard's question literally before playing upon a
commonplace – 'to make and/or mar'
– meaning 'to do and undo' (Dent,
M48; cf. *LLL* 4.3.187–8).
   repetition recital (*OED* 1 3)

166–8 *Patrick (108) ascribes absence
from Qq to actorial omission, but
Malone and Smidt (*Impostors*, 107)
note the odd question of *banishment*

with Margaret apparently remaining
free. Hammond observes her non-
naturalistic treatment including her
mysteriously untrammelled movement.

166 **banished** banishèd

168 **here ... abode** by my living here

169 **thou** i.e. Richard

170 **thou** i.e. Queen Elizabeth

171 **by right** rightfully

173 **curse** See *3H6* 1.4.

175 **scorns** scoffs

176 **clout** cloth

177–93 For Rutland's death, see 1.2.160–
1n.

---

162 Ah] *F;* O *Qq*   166–8] *F; not in Qq*   169 ow'st] *F; Qq (owest)*   to] *F, Q1–5;* vnto *Q6*   171
This] *F;* The *Qq*   172 are] *F, Q1–2;* is *Q3–6*   173 my] *F, Q1–5;* me *Q6*   175 scorns] *F;* scorne *Qq*
177 faultless] *F, Q1–2; om. Q3–6*

His curses then, from bitterness of soul
Denounced against thee, are all fall'n upon thee;
And God, not we, hath plagued thy bloody deed.   180

QUEEN ELIZABETH

So just is God, to right the innocent.

HASTINGS

O, 'twas the foulest deed to slay that babe,
And the most merciless, that e'er was heard of.

RIVERS

Tyrants themselves wept when it was reported.

DORSET

No man but prophesied revenge for it.   185

BUCKINGHAM

Northumberland, then present, wept to see it.

QUEEN MARGARET

What? Were you snarling all before I came,
Ready to catch each other by the throat,
And turn you all your hatred now on me?
Did York's dread curse prevail so much with heaven   190
That Henry's death, my lovely Edward's death,
Their kingdom's loss, my woeful banishment,
Should all but answer for that peevish brat?

178 **bitterness of soul** See Job, 10.1, 21.25.

180–2 The phrasing creates a strong impression that *thy bloody deed* is the murder of Rutland by Margaret herself, a sense supported by Hastings's lines about the *deed*, but contrary to fact (Adelman, 240–1).

181 a familiar sentiment; cf. *Thomas Lord Cromwell* (1602): 'How iust is God to right the innocent' (2.3.63).

182 **babe** Hall says Edmund, Earl of Rutland, was 12 when he died (*Henry VI*, fol. clxxxiii^r). The two princes, also

in early adolescence, are called *babes* (4.3.9; cf. 2.2.84). If *babe* is intended to exaggerate Rutland's youth, this usage would anticipate Queen Margaret's rhetorical advice to Queen Elizabeth to 'Think that thy babes were sweeter than they were' (4.4.120).

185 **No . . . prophesied** i.e. there was no one who did not prophesy

186 Cf. *3H6* 1.4.150–1.

187–9 For the canine pack dynamic, see Dent, C917.1.

193 **but** merely
peevish foolish, silly (*OED* 1)

179 all] *F, Q1–2; om. Q3–6*   fall'n] *F* (falne*), Qq* (fallen*)*   183 e'er] *F; Qq* (euer*)*   189 all . . . now] *F, Q1;* now . . . all *Q2–6*   193 Should] *F;* Could *Qq*

Can curses pierce the clouds and enter heaven?
Why then give way, dull clouds, to my quick curses.   195
Though not by war, by surfeit die your king,
As ours by murder, to make him a king.
– Edward thy son, that now is Prince of Wales,
For Edward our son, that was Prince of Wales,
Die in his youth, by like untimely violence.   200
Thyself a queen, for me that was a queen,
Outlive thy glory, like my wretched self.
Long mayst thou live to wail thy children's death
And see another, as I see thee now,
Decked in thy rights, as thou art stalled in mine.   205
Long die thy happy days before thy death,
And, after many lengthened hours of grief,
Die neither mother, wife, nor England's queen.
– Rivers and Dorset, you were standers-by,
And so wast thou, Lord Hastings, when my son   210
Was stabbed with bloody daggers. God, I pray Him,
That none of you may live his natural age,

194 **pierce the clouds** Shaheen detects an echo of the Homilies: 'For the prayer of them that humble them-selues, shall pearce through the clouds' (*Homilies*, 142). Cf. Marlowe, *Jew of Malta*, 3.2.33.

195 **dull** gloomy, overcast (*OED* 7), but antithesis with *quick* suggests 'insen-sible, obtuse, senseless' (*OED* 2).
quick keen, strongly felt (*OED a.* A II 17)

196 **surfeit** overindulgence; cf. King Edward's *diet* (1.1.139); also *Mirror*, 'Clarence', 337–8.

197 **as our king was murdered to make yours king**

203–8 Most of Margaret's curses come to pass, but this one is not entirely fulfilled, as any Elizabethan would

have known (see p. 21; cf. Brooks, 727).

205 **stalled** installed, enthroned

206 **Long . . . days** i.e. long may your happy days be dead (Abbott, 365).

209–10 **Rivers . . . Dorset . . . Hastings** Richard, Clarence and King Edward were present at Tewkesbury when Prince Edward was slain before Margaret's eyes (*3H6* 5.5). Hall blames those who 'stode about' – Richard, Clarence, Dorset and Hastings – for the killing: 'The bitternesse of which murder, some of the actors, after in their latter dayes tasted and assayed by the very rod of Iustice and pun-ishment of God' (*Edward IV*, fol. ccxxiᵛ). See also 3.3.14–16n.

211 **God . . . Him** I pray God

196 Though] *F;* If *Qq*   197 ours] *F, Q1–2;* our *Q3, 5–6;* out *Q4*   198 that] *F;* which *Qq*   199 our son, that] *F;* my sonne which *Qq*   200 violence] *F, Q1–5;* violences *Q6*   203 death] *F;* losse *Qq*   205 rights] *F, Q1;* glorie *Q2–6*   210 wast] *F, Q1–2;* was *Q3–6*   212 his] *F;* your *Qq*

But by some unlooked accident cut off.

RICHARD

Have done thy charm, thou hateful withered hag.

QUEEN MARGARET

And leave out thee? Stay, dog, for thou shalt hear me.   215
If heaven have any grievous plague in store
Exceeding those that I can wish upon thee,
O, let them keep it till thy sins be ripe,
And then hurl down their indignation
On thee, the troubler of the poor world's peace.   220
The worm of conscience still begnaw thy soul;
Thy friends suspect for traitors while thou liv'st,
And take deep traitors for thy dearest friends;
No sleep close up that deadly eye of thine,
Unless it be while some tormenting dream   225
Affrights thee with a hell of ugly devils.
Thou elvish-marked, abortive, rooting hog,

213 **But ... unlooked** but be by an unanticipated

214 **charm** curse, associating Margaret's prayer with demonic magic as Anne associates Richard's appearance with *conjur[ing]* (1.2.34)

hag evil spirit or demon in female form (*OED sb.*[1] 1a), or a woman supposed to have dealings with infernal powers, a witch (*OED sb.*[1] 2); cf. *1H6* 3.2.51.

215 **Stay** Margaret's command that Richard stop speaking and/or stand still repeats Richard's command at 1.2.33.

218 **them** i.e. the heavens (for a similar plural, see 5.5.21).

221–3 **worm ... begnaw ... deep traitors** biblical vocabulary (see 221n.); Henry Smith describes the 'gnawing conscience' that will afflict the sinner unable to resist Satan, 'this wretched traytor. His subtilties are wel called the depth of Sathan: for he is so deepe, that few can sou[n]d him' (*Sermons*, 901).

221 **worm of conscience** a pain of hell (*OED* 6); cf. the Geneva Bible gloss for 'their worm shall not die': 'a continuall torment of conscience, whiche shall euer gnawe them and neuer suffer them to be at rest' (Isaiah, 66.24).

still ever

224 **deadly eye** alluding to the power of the mythical basilisk (see 1.2.153)

227 **elvish-marked** birth-marked by elves, who were thought to be spiteful **abortive** prematurely born, but also useless (see 1.2.21)

rooting hog alluding to Richard's heraldic emblem, the white boar (see 1.2.104n.); *rooting* connects with the metaphors of lineage and vegetation (see 2.2.41–2): Richard attacks lineal succession as a hog uproots plants. Cf. the title-page of Hall's *Union* (1550), depicting Yorkist and Lancastrian branches (Fig. 1), and pp. 69–72.

215 thee?] *F, Q3–6;* the *Q1–2* 222 while] *F, Q1–5;* whilst *Q6* liv'st] *F;* liuest *Qq* 223 for thy] *F, Q1–3, 5–6;* forth *Q4* 225 while] *F;* whilest *Q1–5;* whilst *Q6* 227 elvish-marked] *F, Qq (*eluish mark'd *subst.), hyphen Rowe*

Thou that wast sealed in thy nativity
The slave of nature and the son of hell;
Thou slander of thy heavy mother's womb,   230
Thou loathed issue of thy father's loins,
Thou rag of honour, thou detested –

RICHARD   Margaret.

QUEEN MARGARET   Richard!

RICHARD
Ha?

QUEEN MARGARET   I call thee not.

RICHARD
I cry thee mercy then, for I did think

---

228 **sealed** stamped
229 **slave of nature** i.e. nature has
   marked Richard for its own through
   birthmarks. In a theological sense he
   remains enslaved to sinful nature rather than being in a state of redemption;
   cf. *Thirty-Nine Articles*, Article 9, concerning Original Sin, the 'corruption
   of the nature of euery man'.
   son of hell i.e. demon
230 **slander** source of discredit, disgrace
   (*OED sb.* 3d)
   *****heavy mother's womb** *heavy* may
   be a displaced modifier of *womb* (as
   Qq), meaning 'heavy with child', or it
   might mean 'sorrowful' and so modify
   mother.
231 **loathed** loathèd
232 **rag** small, worthless fragment or
   shred (*OED sb.*[1] I 1a)
   *****detested** – Qq's 'detested, &c.' might
   indicate actors should ad lib (Davison,
   21), but the dramatic point is Richard's
   rapid verbal intervention, which turns
   Margaret's curse upon herself and is
   not an opportunity for further discussion.
   Margaret Richard's interjection resembles Barabas's comic deflection of an

accusation – 'Thou hast committed' –
when he interjects, 'Fornication? / But
that was in another country: / And
besides, the wench is dead' (Marlowe,
Jew of Malta, 4.1.40–2). Stage Vices
were sometimes empowered to impro-
vise verbal counter-turns, as *All for
Money* has it: 'Here the vyce shal turne
the proclamation to some contrarie sence
everie time all for money hath read it' (S.
Thomas, 32). In *True Tragedy* Richard
finishes Buckingham's 'God saue the
King' by interjecting 'Richard' (785–6).
In *3H6* Richard breaks into Henry VI's
line with 'I'll hear no more! Die, prophet, in thy speech' and a dagger thrust
(5.6.56–7; cf. *R2* 2.1.115).
232–3 *****QUEEN MARGARET . . . Ha?** F follows Qq in printing this exchange
   as a single shared line. This unusual
   typographical practice argues for the
   reliance of F printers on annotated Q
   copy (Walker, 14).
233–5 **call . . . called** a play on 'call'
   as summoning by name (to which
   Richard's *Ha?* responds) and as calling
   someone insulting names
234 **I . . . mercy** I beg your pardon (cf.
   4.4.513, 5.3.224).

---

230 heavy mother's] *F;* mothers heauy *Qq*   232–3] *this edn (RP); F, Qq line* detested – / Margaret. /
Ha. / not. / *subst.*   232 detested –] *F;* detested, &c. *Qq*   233 Ha?] *Q8;* Ha. *F, Q1–7*   thee] *F, Q1–5;*
the *Q6*   234] *F;* Then I crie thee mercy, for I had thought *Qq*

That thou hadst called me all these bitter names. 235

QUEEN MARGARET

Why, so I did, but looked for no reply.

O, let me make the period to my curse.

RICHARD

'Tis done by me and ends in 'Margaret'.

QUEEN ELIZABETH [*to Queen Margaret*]

Thus have you breathed your curse against yourself.

QUEEN MARGARET

Poor painted queen, vain flourish of my fortune, 240

Why strew'st thou sugar on that bottled spider,

Whose deadly web ensnareth thee about?

Fool, fool, thou whet'st a knife to kill thyself.

The day will come that thou shalt wish for me

To help thee curse this poisonous bunch-backed toad. 245

HASTINGS

False-boding woman, end thy frantic curse,

Lest to thy harm thou move our patience.

QUEEN MARGARET

Foul shame upon you, you have all moved mine.

RIVERS

Were you well served, you would be taught your duty.

---

237 **period** conclusion, but also with the
sense of completing a rhetorically constructed sentence of several clauses
240 **painted** artificial, feigned, unreal
vain . . . fortune worthless and ostentatious embellishment of my own substance – i.e. the throne and office. The
first of F's 12 mentions of *fortune*.
241 **strew'st thou sugar** do you flatter, attempt to ingratiate; cf. *Ham*
3.1.47–8.
bottled swollen, protuberant
243 **whet'st . . . thyself** Cf. Dent,

K157.2: 'To whet a knife for one's
own throat'.
245 ***poisonous** 'poisoned' (Q2–8) may
represent metrical adjustment and
meant 'venomous' (*OED ppl. a.* 3).
bunch-backed hump-backed (*OED*
bunch *sb.*[1] 1a)
246 **False-boding** falsely prophesying
frantic lunatic, insane
247 **move** disturb
249 **Were . . . served** i.e. if you were
treated as you deserve
duty deference, obedience

235 That] *F, Q1; om. Q2–6* 236 looked] *F (look'd), Q1–5 (lookt);* looke *Q6* 238 in] *F, Q1–5;* by
Q6 239 SD] *Oxf subst.* 244 day] *F;* time *Qq* that] *F, Q1;* when *Q2–6* 245 this] *F;* that *Qq* poi-
sonous] *F, Q1;* poisoned *Q2–6* 246 False-boding] *F, Qq (False boding), hyphen Theobald*

QUEEN MARGARET

> To serve me well, you all should do me duty: 250
> Teach me to be your queen, and you my subjects.
> O, serve me well, and teach yourselves that duty.

DORSET

> Dispute not with her; she is lunatic.

QUEEN MARGARET

> Peace, master Marquess, you are malapert.
> Your fire-new stamp of honour is scarce current.   255
> O, that your young nobility could judge
> What 'twere to lose it and be miserable.
> They that stand high have many blasts to shake them,
> And if they fall, they dash themselves to pieces.

RICHARD

> Good counsel, marry. Learn it, learn it, Marquess.   260

DORSET

> It touches you, my lord, as much as me.

RICHARD

> Ay, and much more; but I was born so high.
> Our aerie buildeth in the cedar's top,

250–2 Margaret again appropriates the discourse of others for her own ends, adapting Rivers's vocabulary to demand the service and homage appropriate to one who ought to be queen.

254 **master Marquess** Margaret couples the exalted title *Marquess* (a degree between Duke and Earl) with the reductive *master*, a (minimal) title of respect for ordinary learned or gentle folk or for holders of minor office (e.g. 'Master Parson', *MW* 3.1.42). King Edward properly refers to Dorset as *Lord Marquess* (2.1.25).

malapert impudent, presumptuous

255 **fire-new stamp ... current** Margaret employs terminology derived from coinage (as does Richard

at 81), telling Dorset that his title is so recent (he became Marquess in 1475; Holinshed, 3.702) that it is now just barely accepted (cf. Dent, M985: 'New out of the mint', *TN* 3.2.21).

current having the quality of current coin; genuine

258–9, 262–5 The equation of physical elevation and social standing is frequent in admonitions against the desire to be raised above the station allotted by birth (cf. Dent, T509, W450).

259 Cf. Dent, S823: 'The higher standing (up), the lower (greater) fall.'

263 **aerie ... cedar** An aerie is the nest of a bird of prey, often the eagle (cf. *KJ* 5.2.149), and also, figuratively, the brood in the nest (*OED* 1, 2). The eagle

251 you] *F, Q1, 3–6;* yon *Q2*   258 blasts] *F, Q2–6;* blast *Q1*   261 touches] *F;* toucheth *Qq*   262 Ay] *F (I);* Yea *Qq*

And dallies with the wind, and scorns the sun.

QUEEN MARGARET

And turns the sun to shade. Alas, alas,   265

Witness my son, now in the shade of death,

Whose bright out-shining beams thy cloudy wrath

Hath in eternal darkness folded up.

Your aerie buildeth in our aerie's nest.

O God, that seest it, do not suffer it;   270

As it is won with blood, lost be it so.

BUCKINGHAM

Peace, peace, for shame, if not for charity.

QUEEN MARGARET

Urge neither charity nor shame to me.

[*to the others*] Uncharitably with me have you dealt,

And shamefully my hopes by you are butchered.   275

My charity is outrage, life my shame,

was thought the monarch of birds and the cedar the highest-ranking among evergreen trees (cf. Ezekiel, 17.3).

264 **scorns the sun** Eagles were thought uniquely able to gaze directly into the sun (cf. *LLL* 4.3.222–4, Dent, E3).

265 **turns** converts, transforms. 'Turning' occurs with various senses: in Richard's clouds changed to sunshine and war to love; in his 'turn[ing]' King Henry's corpse into the earth and 'return[ing]' to his love (1.2.263–4); in Margaret's complaint about those who have 'turn[ed]' their hatred toward her (1.3.189); in Buckingham's protestations that he will not *turn* against King Edward (2.1.32) and his recognition that his prayers and sword have 'turn[ed]' against himself (5.1.21, 24); in Herbert's speculations that allies will *turn* from Richard (5.2.19); and in Richmond's mercy to soldiers who will *return* to accept him as king (5.5.17).

265–6 **sun . . . son** Cf. 1.1.2.

270 **suffer** permit

271 **is** i.e. was, is and will be; in the context of her prayer for the future, occasioned by memory of past sufferings and by knowledge of present trends, Margaret's pan-temporal verbal construction makes sense.

272 **charity** Once again, the principal Gospel command occurs in an admonition that could be construed to be, as at 1.2.68, self-interested. Buckingham's twisted usage suggests the alliance that becomes overt at 1.3.295.

274 SD *Mowat and Werstine's SD answers objections concerning F, Qq attribution of 272 to Buckingham; *you* in 274 is plural (contrast *thee* in 280).

276 **My . . . outrage** i.e. the only charity I have received is the outrage you have done me; or, the nearest thing to charity I feel is my outraged anger.
life my shame i.e. my whole life is a shame; or, continuing to live is shameful for me.

266 son] *F, Q1–4 (*sonne *F, Q2–4); *sunne *Q5–6   271 is] *F;* was *Qq*   272 SP] *F, Qq; Gloucester Cam¹ (Walker)*   Peace, peace] *F;* Haue done *Qq*   274 SD] *Folg*   275 my . . . you] *F (*my hopes (by you)*);* by you my hopes *Qq*

And in that shame, still live my sorrow's rage.

BUCKINGHAM

Have done, have done.

QUEEN MARGARET

O princely Buckingham, I'll kiss thy hand
In sign of league and amity with thee.   280
Now fair befall thee and thy noble house.
Thy garments are not spotted with our blood,
Nor thou within the compass of my curse.

BUCKINGHAM

Nor no one here, for curses never pass
The lips of those that breathe them in the air.   285

QUEEN MARGARET

I will not think but they ascend the sky,
And there awake God's gentle sleeping peace.
O Buckingham, take heed of yonder dog.
Look when he fawns, he bites; and when he bites,
His venom tooth will rankle to the death.   290

---

277 **in . . . rage** i.e. while I continue to
   live in shame may the rage born of my
   treatment live too.
279 **princely** This epithet appears 15
   times in F (13 in Q1); Buckingham's
   royal blood came by direct descent
   from Thomas of Woodstock, next-to-
   youngest son of Edward III, and by
   Beaufort descent from John of Gaunt,
   an ancestry he shared with Henry
   Tudor (Hanham, 4).
   thy Margaret appears to single out
   Buckingham as worthy of intimacy
   in this, for her, rare non-vituperative
   speech (Jowett); cf. Edward to *princely
   Buckingham* (2.1.29–30).
280 **league** alliance
281 **fair befall** may good fortune come
   to; cf. 3.5.47.

283 **compass** scope
284–5 **curses . . . air** i.e. curses never
   affect anyone but the one who curses;
   ironically recalling Margaret's warning to Suffolk (*2H6* 3.2.330–2).
286 **think but** think otherwise than that
287 **awake . . . peace** For the image of
   God awakened from sleep, see Psalms,
   44.23.
288 **yonder** Richard is now evidently
   some distance from Margaret (cf.
   294).
289 Cf. 'We Jews can fawn like span-
   iels when we please; / And when we
   grin we bite' (Marlowe, *Jew of Malta*,
   2.3.20–1); also Tilley, D445.
   Look when whenever
290 **venom** venomous (*OED a.*)
   rankle fester

277 that] *F;* my *Qq*   still] *F, Q1–5;* shall *Q6*   278] *F;* Haue done. *Qq*   279 SP] *F, Q1–4; Q. Mary*
Q5–6   princely] *F, Q1–3, 5–6;* pricely *Q4*   I'll] *F;* I will *Qq*   281 noble] *F;* Princely *Qq*   285 those]
F, Q1–5; them *Q6*   286 I . . . think] *F;* Ile not beleeue *Qq*   288 take heed] *F;* beware *Qq*   290 rankle]
F, Q2–6; rackle *Q1*   to the] *F;* thee to *Qq*

Have not to do with him, beware of him;
Sin, death and hell have set their marks on him,
And all their ministers attend on him.

RICHARD
What doth she say, my lord of Buckingham?

BUCKINGHAM
Nothing that I respect, my gracious lord.   295

QUEEN MARGARET
What, dost thou scorn me for my gentle counsel,
And soothe the devil that I warn thee from?
O, but remember this another day,
When he shall split thy very heart with sorrow,
And say poor Margaret was a prophetess.   300
– Live each of you, the subjects to his hate,
And he to yours, and all of you to God's.   *Exit.*

BUCKINGHAM
My hair doth stand on end to hear her curses.

RIVERS
And so doth mine. I muse why she's at liberty.

RICHARD
I cannot blame her; by God's Holy Mother,   305
She hath had too much wrong, and I repent
My part thereof that I have done to her.

QUEEN ELIZABETH
I never did her any to my knowledge.

---

292 **marks** Cf. 227.
293 **attend on** wait upon, serve
295 **respect** heed, pay attention to
297 **soothe** support, humour, flatter
  (*OED v.* 3, 5)
303 SP *Either Buckingham's hair stood
  on end (F) or Hastings's did (Qq).
  Buckingham has claimed not to *respect*
  Margaret's utterances (295), but his
  speeches may be rhetorical, seeking
  to downplay the effect of Margaret's

speeches in the earlier remark and
to associate himself with Richard's
expressions of shock and horror at her
freedom in the later (Hammond).
303 **on** F, Qq spellings are interchangeable (*OED* on).
304 **muse** wonder
308 SP *Walton explains F's confusion
  concerning the speaker by the hypothesis that F was set throughout from Q3
  (*Copy*, 74–7).

296] *Qq; F lines* me / counsell? /   297 soothe] *F, Q1–5 subst.;* soothd *Q6*   301 to] *F;* of *Qq*   302
yours] *F;* your *Q1–2;* you *Q3–6*   303 SP] *F; Hast. Qq*   on] *F (*an*), Qq*   304 muse why] *F;* wonder
Qq   307 to her] *F; not in Qq*   308 SP] *Q1–5 (Qu.); Mar. F; Hast. Q6*

RICHARD

Yet you have all the vantage of her wrong.
I was too hot to do somebody good   310
That is too cold in thinking of it now.
Marry, as for Clarence, he is well repaid:
He is franked up to fatting for his pains.
God pardon them that are the cause thereof.

RIVERS

A virtuous and a Christian-like conclusion,   315
To pray for them that have done scathe to us.

RICHARD

So do I ever – (*Speaks to himself.*) being well advised,
For had I cursed now, I had cursed myself.

Enter CATESBY.

CATESBY

Madam, his majesty doth call for you,
– And for your grace, – and yours, my gracious lord.   320

QUEEN ELIZABETH

Catesby, I come. – Lords, will you go with me?

309 **vantage** advantage
310 **hot** eager, zealous
   somebody i.e. King Edward
313 **franked . . . fatting** penned up as an animal in a sty to be fattened
   pains efforts
315–16 These lines convey Jesus's commands – 'loue your enemies, blesse them that curse you, do good to them that hate you, pray for the[m] which hurt you, and persecute you' (Matthew, 5.44) – but typically turn Christian sentiments to aggressive uses as Rivers derides Richard for hypocrisy.
316 **scathe** injury (*OED sb.* 2)
317 **well advised** judicious

320 *The final word has provoked debate as to whether it should be singular or plural, although the sense of F and Q1–2 is not especially obscure. After summoning the Queen in 319, Catesby addresses the two onstage dukes – Richard and Buckingham – in turn as 'your grace, and yours' ('your grace', once exclusively used to kings and queens, came to be used for dukes and archbishops, *OED sb.* II 16b). Subsequently, Rivers speaks for the attending lords beneath ducal rank, reminding everyone that his faction has a *grace* – Queen Elizabeth – on its side (Paul Werstine, private communication).
321 *F avoids the royal plurals of Qq (Davison).

309 Yet . . . her] *F*; But . . . this *Qq*   314 thereof] *F*; of it *Qq*   317 SD] *F after* aduis'd*; not in Qq*   318.1] *F; not in Qq*   320 grace] *F, Q1–2*; noble Grace *Q3–6*   yours] *F*; you *Qq*   gracious lord.] *F*; noble Lo: *Q1–2*; noble Lord. *Q3–6*; noble lords. *Capell*; gracious lords. *Alexander*   321 I . . . me] *F*; we . . . vs *Qq*

RIVERS

    We wait upon your grace.

            Exeunt all but ^Q*Richard*^Q [, *Duke of*] *Gloucester.*

RICHARD

    I do the wrong, and first begin to brawl.

    The secret mischiefs that I set abroach

    I lay unto the grievous charge of others.   325

    Clarence, who I indeed have cast in darkness,

    I do beweep to many simple gulls,

    Namely to Derby, Hastings, Buckingham,

    And tell them 'tis the Queen and her allies

    That stir the King against the Duke my brother.   330

    Now they believe it, and withal whet me

    To be revenged on Rivers, Dorset, Grey.

    But then I sigh, and, with a piece of scripture,

    Tell them that God bids us do good for evil;

    And thus I clothe my naked villainy   335

    With odd old ends, stol'n forth of Holy Writ,

---

323 Cf. Dent, C579 and *CE* 4.1.50–1.
  brawl raise a clamour, make a distur-
  bance (*OED v.* 2)

324 **abroach** afoot

325 **lay . . . others** blame others

326 **cast in darkness** biblical diction,
  as in Matthew, 8.12 ('the chyldren
  of the kyngdome shalbe caste out,
  into vtter darcknesse'); *cast in darkness* could mean 'put in prison', but
  shade of death and *eternal darkness*
  (266, 268) provide ominous reson-
  ances.

327 **beweep** weep for
  gulls simpletons, credulous dupes

328 **Derby, Hastings, Buckingham**
  Richard's list of *simple gulls* should
  be remembered as we discover their
  reservations and resistance. Given the

familiarity of stories about Richard,
audiences might register his over-
confidence.

329 **allies** allies

331 **withal** furthermore
  whet urge, incite

332 *****Dorset** Vaughan, not Dorset, is
  executed in 3.3; however, Dorset is
  more prominent in the play and more
  important as Richard's enemy.

333–7 On Richard as Shakespeare's 'fullest portrayal of explicitly religious
  hypocrisy', see Frye, 185.

334 **do . . . evil** a biblical commonplace:
  see 315–16n.

335–7 Cf. Dent, D230: 'The devil can cite
  scripture for his own purpose.'

336 **odd old ends** variation on 'odds
  and ends'

---

322 We wait upon] *F;* Madame we will attend *Qq subst.* SD] *F (Gloster); Exeunt man. Ri. (Clo. Q3, 5,*
6; Glo. Q4) Qq   Duke of] *Eccles*   323 the] *F, Q1–3;* thee *Q4–6*   begin] *F;* began *Qq*   324 mischiefs]
F, Q1–2; mischiefe *Q3–6*   326 who . . . cast] *F;* whom . . . laid *Qq*   328 Derby, Hastings] *F;* Hastings,
Darby *Qq*   329 tell them 'tis] *F;* say it is *Qq*   331 it] *F;* me *Qq*   332 Dorset] *F;* Vaughan *Qq*   333 I sigh]
F, Q1–2, 4; sigh *Q3, 5–6*   334 do] *F, Q1–4;* to do *Q5–6*   336 odd old . . . forth] *F;* old odde . . . out *Qq*

And seem a saint when most I play the devil.

Enter two Murderers.

But soft, here come my executioners.
– How now, my hardy, stout, resolved mates;
Are you now going to dispatch this thing?   340

1 MURDERER
We are, my lord, and come to have the warrant,
That we may be admitted where he is.

RICHARD
Well thought upon. I have it here about me.
When you have done, repair to Crosby Place;
But sirs, be sudden in the execution,   345
Withal obdurate; do not hear him plead,
For Clarence is well-spoken and perhaps
May move your hearts to pity, if you mark him.

1 MURDERER
Tut, tut, my lord, we will not stand to prate.
Talkers are no good doers; be assured   350

---

337 **play** A strikingly theatrical verb, given Richard's resolution to 'prove a villain' (1.1.30). Since the proverb is 'To seem a saint but be a devil' (Tilley, S30), in what sense could Richard mean to *play* rather than to 'be' satanic?

338 **soft** an imperative exclamation, enjoining silence or urging restraint (*OED* soft *adv.* 8a; cf. *Ham* 3.1.87); thus, Richard either acknowledges that a soliloquy has been spoken aloud (as 1.1.41) or anticipates his next tricky move.

339 **hardy, stout, resolved** This triple adjectival sequence without a conjunction is unusual for Shakespeare (Var). The point may be the exaggerated nature of the attributes projected upon the killers.

Richard and his helpers have difficulty maintaining resolution (see 1.4.104–277, 5.3.177–206); the Murderers will have to reassure themselves about their own stoutness (1.4.148–9).
resolved resolvèd; determined, firm of purpose

341 SP *Neither F nor Qq differentiates the assassins here (although they do in 1.4), awarding 341–2 and 349–51 to '*Vil.*' (F) or to '*Execu.*' and '*Exec.*' (Q1).

344 **repair** go (*OED v.* 1)

348 **mark** pay attention to

349 **prate** chatter, talk idly

350 **Talkers . . . doers** Cf. *H8* 2.2.77–8 and Dent, T64: 'Greatest talkers are the least doers.'

337.1] *F (murtherers); Enter Executioners. Qq opp. 338*   338 come] *F, Q1;* comes *Q2–6*   340 you] *F, Q1–2;* ye *Q3–6*   now] *F, Q1–5;* not *Q6*   thing] *F;* deede *Qq*   341+ SP] *Capell subst.; Vil. F; Execu. Qq*   343 Well] *F;* It was well *Qq*   347 well-spoken] *F, Qq (well spoken), hyphen F3*   349 Tut, tut] *F;* Tush feare not *Qq*   350 doers; be assured] *F4 (doers; be assur'd,);* doers, be assured: *Q2, F;* doers be assured: *Q1, 3–6*

We go to use our hands and not our tongues.

RICHARD

Your eyes drop millstones when fools' eyes fall tears.

I like you lads. About your business straight.

Go, go, dispatch.

1 MURDERER   We will, my noble lord.   ^Q*Exeunt.*^Q

1.4   *Enter* CLARENCE *and* Keeper.

KEEPER

Why looks your grace so heavily today?

CLARENCE

O, I have passed a miserable night,

So full of fearful dreams, of ugly sights,

That, as I am a Christian faithful man,

I would not spend another such a night   5

Though 'twere to buy a world of happy days,

So full of dismal terror was the time.

KEEPER

What was your dream, my lord? I pray you tell me.

CLARENCE

Methoughts that I had broken from the Tower,

---

352 **eyes drop millstones** Cf. Dent, M967: 'He weeps millstones'; the cliché connotes hard-heartedness.
fall drop, shed (*OED v.* IX 49a)
353 **straight** immediately (*OED adv.* 2)
354 SD Given the conspiratorial enterprise, Richard probably departs separately.
1.4 location: the Tower of London
0.1 **Keeper Qq have Brakenbury ('Brokenbury') for *Keeper*.
Keeper jailer
1 **heavily** with sorrow, grief or displeasure (*OED* 3)
4 **as . . . man** an expression attesting to a statement (*OED* as *adv.* 14), here

on the basis of Christian faith; use of *faithful* in this religious sense appears to be unique in Shakespeare (Var). It might mean 'true to one's word' – which would be ironic when employed by a character prominently accused of breaking his word (see 1.3.134–5, 1.4.50, 55, 200–7).
5 **a** used redundantly (Abbott, 85)
6 **world** age or (long) period of time (*OED* I 5a)
9, 24, 58 **Methoughts, methought** it seemed to me; cf. *MV* 1.3.67, *WT* 1.2.154.
9 **had . . . Tower See 13n. on **There.*

---

351 go] *F;* come *Qq*   352 fall] *F;* drop *Qq*   353 straight] *F; not in Qq*   354] *F; not in Qq*   *Steevens; F lines* dispatch. / Lord. /   SP] *Capell subst.; Vil. F; Both. Ard²*   SD] *Qq opp. 353*   1.4] *F (Scena Quarta.); not in Qq*   0.1] *F; Enter Clarence, Brokenbury Qq*   1+ SP] *F (Keep.); Brok. Qq subst.*   3 fearful . . . sights] *F;* vgly sights, of gastly dreames *Qq*   8 my . . . me] *F;* I long to heare you tell it *Qq*   9–10] *F;* Me thoughts I was imbarkt for Burgundy, *Qq subst.*   9 Methoughts] *F, Q1–3 (*Me thoughts*);* Me thought *Q4–6*

And was embarked to cross to Burgundy;   10
And in my company my brother Gloucester,
Who from my cabin tempted me to walk
Upon the hatches. There we looked toward England,
And cited up a thousand heavy times,
During the wars of York and Lancaster,   15
That had befall'n us. As we paced along
Upon the giddy footing of the hatches,
Methought that Gloucester stumbled, and in falling
Struck me (that thought to stay him) overboard
Into the tumbling billows of the main.   20
O Lord, methought what pain it was to drown,
What dreadful noise of water in mine ears,
What sights of ugly death within mine eyes.
Methoughts I saw a thousand fearful wracks,

10 **embarked . . . Burgundy** Clarence
and Richard had made the voy-
age before when, in danger from
Margaret's troops, they were sent in
1461 to Utrecht to the care of Duke
Philip the Good of Burgundy (C.
Ross, *Richard*, 5), their sister's husband (see 5.3.324n.).

13 **hatches** deck (*OED* 3)
***There** As elsewhere in this scene,
F sometimes sides with Q6 or other
derivative Qq against Q1, sometimes
agrees with earlier Qq against Q6 or
agrees with Q1 against Q3–6, and
sometimes offers alternatives varying
slightly from readings in all Qq. Q1–5's
'thence' is more precise in meaning
'from that place' (*OED* 1) than Q6, F's
'There', so F hardly constitutes considered 'correction', but the effect is
relatively inconsequential. By contrast,
at 9, Qq lack the irony of Clarence's
failure to connect Richard with his

imprisonment; cf. 36–7, where Qq lack
Clarence's suicidal wishes.

14 **cited up** called to mind, referred to
(*OED* 5)

17 **giddy** causing or apt to produce dizzi-
ness

19 **thought to stay** intended to support
(*OED* stay *v.*² 1)

20 **main** open ocean

22 ***water** The many nearby plurals make
it easy to imagine Q1–5's 'waters' as
a mistake by a compositor, copyist or
corrector (Walton, *Copy*, 25).

22, 23 ***mine** This first person possessive pronoun (Q2–6, F) is more typically used in Shakespeare than Q1's
'my' before vowels when the possessive
form is unemphatic (Abbott, 237); cf.
1.2.151, 3.7.20, 4.1.80, 81.

24–33 The *thousand heavy times* during the 'wars of York and Lancaster'
(14–15) produce a vision of *a thousand
fearful wracks* and *a thousand men*, their

13 There] *F, Q6;* thence *Q1–5* toward] *F, Q1–5;* towards *Q6* 14 heavy] *F;* fearefull *Qq* 16
befall'n] *F (*befalne*), Qq (*befallen*) paced] *F (*pac't*), Q1 (*pact*);* past *Q2–6* 18 falling] *F;*
stumbling *Qq* 21 O Lord] *F;* Lord, Lord *Qq* 22 water] *F, Q6;* waters *Q1–5* mine] *F, Q2–6;*
my *Q1* 23 sights of ugly] *F;* vgly sights of *Qq* mine] *F, Q2–6;* my *Q1* 24 Methoughts] *F (*Me
thoughts*);* Me thought *Qq*

A thousand men that fishes gnawed upon,   25
Wedges of gold, great anchors, heaps of pearl,
Inestimable stones, unvalued jewels,
All scattered in the bottom of the sea.
Some lay in dead men's skulls, and in the holes
Where eyes did once inhabit, there were crept –   30
As 'twere in scorn of eyes – reflecting gems,
That wooed the slimy bottom of the deep
And mocked the dead bones that lay scattered by.

KEEPER

Had you such leisure in the time of death
To gaze upon these secrets of the deep?   35

CLARENCE

Methought I had, and often did I strive
To yield the ghost, but still the envious flood
Stopped in my soul and would not let it forth
To find the empty, vast and wandering air,

lifeless *skulls* anticipating the Bishop
of Carlisle's prophecy (*R2* 4.1.144–5).
Cf. *H5* 1.2.164–5 for the 'bottom of
the sea / With sunken wrack and sum-
less treasuries'; and Spenser's Cave of
Mammon for 'heapes of Gold' including 'great Ingowes and . . . wedges
square' where 'all the grownd with
sculs was scattered / And dead mens
bones' (*Faerie Queene*, 2.7.5, 7; Brooks,
'Antecedents', 149).

24 **wracks** wrecked ships (*OED sb.* 2)
27 **Inestimable, unvalued** too valuable
  to be measured (*OED* unvalued 1), but
  also 'unvalued' in being lost beyond
  recovery (*OED* 2)
  jewels Cf. *Son* 21: 'sea's rich gems'.
28 *Many editors since Pope follow Qq in
  omitting this line (cf. Smidt, *Impostors*,
  70).
30–3 **crept . . . scorn . . . reflecting
  . . . wooed . . . mocked** These terms

link the death's head with Richard;
cf. creeping (1.2.20, 1.2.261, 4.4.47),
scorn (1.2.167, 1.3.108), reflection
in a mirror (1.1.15, 1.2.258), wooing
(1.2.230, 4.3.43) and abundant mockery of others throughout.
30–1 Cf. the pearls that replace the eyes
  of the drowned in *Tem* 1.2.399.
31 **scorn** mockery, derision
36–7 *and . . . ghost See 13n. on
  *There.
37 **yield the ghost** give up, release the
  spirit or soul; cf. Matthew, 27.50:
  'Jesus . . . yeelded up yᵉ ghost'.
  envious . . . malicious, spiteful (*OED* 2)
38 **Stopped in** closed in, shut up in a vessel with a cover, plug or other stopper
  (*OED* stop *v.* 7a)
39 **wandering** The air's freedom to wander is biblical. See John, 3.8, likening it
  to the motions of the spirit; also *AYL*
  2.7.47–9.

25 A] *F;* Ten *Qq*   28] *F; not in Qq*   29 lay in] *F, Q1–3, 5–6;* lay *Q4*   dead men's] *F* (dead-mens),
Q1–3, 5–6; Q4 (deadmens)   the] *F;* those *Qq*   32 That] *F;* Which *Qq*   wooed] *F, Q1–4;* wade
Q5–6   35 these] *F;* the *Qq*   36–7 and . . . ghost,] *F; not in Qq*   37 but] *F;* for *Qq*   38 Stopped] *F;*
Kept *Qq*   39 find] *F;* seeke *Q1–2;* keepe *Q3–6*   wandering] *F, Q3–6* (wand'ring), *Q1–2*

But smothered it within my panting bulk,   40
Who almost burst to belch it in the sea.

KEEPER
Awaked you not in this sore agony?

CLARENCE
No, no, my dream was lengthened after life.
O, then began the tempest to my soul.
I passed, methought, the melancholy flood,   45
With that sour ferryman which poets write of,
Unto the kingdom of perpetual night.
The first that there did greet my stranger-soul
Was my great father-in-law, renowned Warwick,
Who spake aloud: 'What scourge for perjury   50
Can this dark monarchy afford false Clarence?'
And so he vanished. Then came wandering by
A shadow like an angel, with bright hair
Dabbled in blood, and he shrieked out aloud:

40 **bulk** physical body; the belly or trunk (*OED sb.*[1] 2a)
41 **Who** which
   belch vent with vehemence or violence; sometimes compared to the action of a volcano or cannon (*OED v.* 2)
42 **agony** intense distress, also specifically the throes or pangs of death
44 **tempest . . . soul** Cf. Marlowe, *Works, 1 Tamburlaine*, 3.2.86: 'tempest to my daunted thoughts'.
45 **melancholy flood** the river Styx, over which the souls of the dead were ferried by the boatman Charon to the classical underworld
46 **sour ferryman . . . of** For Charon's foreboding appearance, see Seneca, *Hercules Furens*, 764–71.
47 **perpetual night** Cf. Marlowe, *Works, Faustus* [2.1.]445, where Lucifer is 'Chiefe Lord and Regent of perpetuall night'; Seneca, *Hippolytus*, 221 ('*nocte*

perpetua' (perpetual night)); see also 2.2.46n.
49 **renowned** renownèd
49–50 **Warwick . . . perjury** See 1.3.134–7. Hall describes Clarence's 'condigne punishment, for violatyng and brekyng hys othe . . . to the erle of Warwycke, for God not many yeres after, suffered hym lyke a periured person to dye a cruell & a stra[n]ge death' (*Edward IV*, fol. ccxvi[r]).
50 **scourge** punishment (literally a whip or lash)
53 **shadow** ghost (of Prince Edward, Henry VI's murdered son); 'shadow like an angel' combines classical and Christian elements (Clemen, 72).
54 **Dabbled** spattered, sprinkled
   shrieked Ghosts were often said to have shrill, squeaking or shrieking voices (*Ham* 1.1.115; *JC* 2.2.24); Qq's 'squeakt' (or 'squakt') is possible.

41 Who] *F*; Which *Qq* 42 in] *F*; with *Qq* 43 No, no] *F*; O no *Qq* 44 to] *F, Q1–5*; of *Q6*
45 I] *F*; Who *Qq* 46 sour] *F*; grim *Qq* 50 spake] *F*; cried *Qq* 52 wandering] *F, Qq* (wand'ring)
53 with] *F*; in *Qq* 54 shrieked] *F*; squakt *Q1*; squeakt *Q2–6 subst.*

'Clarence is come, false, fleeting, perjured Clarence,   55
That stabbed me in the field by Tewkesbury.
Seize on him, furies! Take him unto torment!'
With that, methought, a legion of foul fiends
Environed me, and howled in mine ears
Such hideous cries, that with the very noise   60
I, trembling, waked, and for a season after
Could not believe but that I was in hell,
Such terrible impression made my dream.

KEEPER
No marvel, lord, though it affrighted you;
I am afraid, methinks, to hear you tell it.   65
CLARENCE
Ah keeper, keeper, I have done these things,
That now give evidence against my soul,
For Edward's sake; and see how he requites me.
– O God! If my deep prayers cannot appease Thee,

---

55 **fleeting** fickle, inconstant, vacillating (*OED ppl. a.* 2)
57 Famously, *The Spanish Tragedy* evokes hell's regions and the threat of the 'deepest hell, / Where bloudie furies shakes their whips of steele' (Kyd, 1.1.64–5). The furies were classical deities with snakes twined in their hair, sent from the underworld to avenge wrong and punish crime.
58 **legion** vast multitude, frequently referring to spirits or angels (*OED* 3a); cf. *Mac* 4.3.55–6 and Mark, 5.9.
59 **Environed** surrounded with hostile intention (*OED v.* 2b)
   howled howlèd
61 **for a season** for some time
64 **No marvel . . . though** i.e. it is not strange that (cf. *VA* 390)
   affrighted frightened
68 **Edward's** i.e. Edward IV's

requites repays
69 **deep** solemn, weighty, important (*OED* II 7a, b)
69–72 *Hammond (333) conjectures that incompatibility between Christian terminology and the classical imagery of Clarence's dream led to Qq omission, but Clarence's self-assessment as a *Christian faithful man* (4) remains. Smidt suggests that historical inaccuracy is the issue, since Clarence's wife had died before the time of the scene (*Impostors*, 124), but this presumes unduly stringent standards. Divine vengeance 'in the thirde and fourth generations' is biblical (Numbers, 14.18), and Richard's reign provides examples of condign punishment for the 'offence of the parentes' (Hall, *Edward IV*, fol. ccxv'); but Clarence's children were actually executed under Henry VII

---

57 unto torment] *F;* to your torments *Qq*   58 methought] *F, Q2–6 (*me thought*);* me thoughts *Q1*
59 me] *F;* me about *Qq*   63 my] *F;* the *Qq*   64 lord] *F;* my Lo: *Qq subst.*   65 am afraid, methinks,]
F; promise you, I am afraid *Qq*   66 Ah keeper, keeper . . . these] *F;* O Brokenbury . . . those *Qq*
67 That . . . give] *F;* Which . . . beare *Qq*   69–72] *F; not in Qq*   69 prayers] *F (*prayres*)*

But Thou wilt be avenged on my misdeeds,   70
Yet execute Thy wrath in me alone;
O, spare my guiltless wife and my poor children.
– Keeper, I prithee sit by me awhile;
My soul is heavy, and I fain would sleep.

KEEPER

I will, my lord. God give your grace good rest.   75

Enter BRAKENBURY, *the Lieutenant.*

BRAKENBURY

Sorrow breaks seasons and reposing hours,

(the play's Richmond) and Henry VIII, not under Richard, so Campbell (314) cites awareness of this Tudor violence as a possible explanation for Qq omission. Clarence's daughter is absent from Qq 4.1.1–2. For Clarence's speech in relation to arguments about divine providence, see Kelly, 278–9 and Prior, 52.

70 **But** except, unless, on the other hand (Abbott, 121)

72 **wife** Historically, Clarence's wife Isabel was dead in 1476, before the time in which this scene is set.

73, 82 ***prithee, between** Honigmann argues that F's 'prithee' (cf. 117, 2.1.97, 2.4.26, 31) represents a general F 'prejudice' ('Variants', 194). Jackson suggests that it goes against Shakespeare's own pre-1600 preference for 'pray thee' but reflects his post-1600 orthography ('Copy', 354). Jackson also maintains that Qq's 'atypical' preference for 'betwixt' over 'between' suggests their 'lesser authority' ('Two', 189).

74 **My . . . heavy** Shaheen compares Jesus's pronouncement – 'My soule is heauy' – as he watches and prays, aware that betrayal and death are at hand, and rebukes his disciples for falling asleep (Matthew, 26.38, 40–6).

heavy sorrowful, grieved, despondent
fain gladly

75.1 BRAKENBURY On the play's ahistorical association of Brakenbury with Clarence's death, see 1.1.41n. Brakenbury does appear (with his keys) as a figure whose resistance must be overcome in the murder of the princes as depicted by More, Hall, Holinshed, *Mirror* and *True Tragedy*.

76–83 *Hammond finds it 'odd' that Brakenbury should speak this monologue with the Keeper present. Marshall suggests Brakenbury pauses at some distance from Clarence to contemplate his plight. Perhaps the Keeper has already moved to *sit by* Clarence as he has been asked to do (73). Brakenbury's meditation on princes and outward ceremony echoes Henry VI's laments about the oppressive life and troubled sleep of monarchs (*3H6* 2.5.41–54) and anticipates Henry V's similar utterance (*H5* 4.1.234–82); all three stand at odds with the perspective of the ordinary sentinel of *1H6* 2.1.5–7. On the monologue's disconnection from its dramatic occasion, see Clemen (78); on its eight-line *strambotto* form and its subject shared with Wyatt's 'Stand whoso list upon the slipper toppe', see

73] *F;* I pray thee gentle keeper stay by me *Qq*   75.1] *F; not in Qq*   76 SP] *F; not in Qq*   breaks] *F, Q2–6;* breake *Q1*

Makes the night morning, and the noontide night.
Princes have but their titles for their glories,
An outward honour for an inward toil;
And for unfelt imaginations   80
They often feel a world of restless cares,
So that between their titles and low name
There's nothing differs but the outward fame.

Enter two Murderers.

1 MURDERER   Ho, who's here?

Jones (*Origins*, 194). Clarence evokes the 'careful crowne' in *Mirror*. This speech furnishes two of the play's five entries in *Englands Parnassus* (Allott, 1401, 1551).

76–7 See Job, 17.11–12: 'My dayes are past, and my counsailes and thoughtes of my heart are vanished away, Chaunging the night into day, and the light approching into darkenesse.'

76 **breaks** interrupts
   seasons right, proper, due or appointed times (*OED sb.* II 14)
   reposing hours proper time for resting

78 **but** only

79 an external reward that is the only consolation for mental labour and care

80 **unfelt imaginations** i.e. non-existent pleasures that others (wrongly) imagine princes to enjoy

82–3 Cf. 1.3.82–3, 106–9.

82 **low name** the undistinguished reputation of the common person

84–end *There is more difference between Qq and F from here to the end of 1.4 than in most of the rest of the text. Aside from possible revision of F to avoid prosecution for profanity under the Statute of 1606 (e.g. the deletion of 'In God's name' from 85 or 'Zounds' from 125, and the omissions at 188–9;

see p. 457), the reasons for divergence are unclear; nor are such excisions consistent, since 'In God's name' appears in Qq and F at 162. Clemen (79–80) argues that the contrast between the Murderers as 'clownish ruffians' (in their prose dialogue) and as 'eloquent accusers . . . using language and scriptural references quite out of character' suggests that the two parts were not conceived as a unit. However, the gravity of their undertaking – signalled by reference to *thunder* (166) and the claim, 'My voice is now the King's' (167) – renders their role awful in its seriousness for early modern political theology. The dramatic rhythm of this extended delay, in which the audience knows what is going to happen, or thinks that it knows, but must endure a protracted verbal exchange, is typical of the play (cf. Richard and Anne in 1.2, Richard and Queen Elizabeth in 4.4).

84+ SP MURDERER The designations 'murderers' (F) and 'executioners' (Qq) are discussed in *3H6* when Richard comes to slay Henry VI. To Richard's question – 'Think'st thou I am an executioner?' – King Henry replies: 'If murdering innocents be executing, / Why then, thou art an executioner' (5.6.30–3).

80 imaginations] *F;* imagination *Qq*   82 between] *F;* betwixt *Qq*   their] *F, Q1–2;* your *Q3–6*   name] *F;* names *Qq*   83.1] *F; The murtherers enter. Qq*   84] *F; not in Qq*   85 SP] *F; not in Qq*   What . . . fellow?] *F;* In Gods name what are you, *Qq*   cam'st thou] *F;* came you *Qq*

BRAKENBURY

> What wouldst thou, fellow? And how cam'st thou
>   hither?   85

2 MURDERER   I would speak with Clarence, and I came
hither on my legs.

BRAKENBURY   What, so brief?

1 MURDERER   'Tis better, sir, than to be tedious. – Let
him see our commission, and talk no more.   90

> [*Brakenbury*] *reads.*

BRAKENBURY

> I am in this commanded to deliver
> The noble Duke of Clarence to your hands.
> I will not reason what is meant hereby
> Because I will be guiltless from the meaning.
> There lies the Duke asleep, and there the keys.   95

85–7 Cf. Dent, L191.
85 *Qq anticipate Qq, F 162 (Greg, *Problem*, 83). Cf. *R2* 5.5.69, where the imprisoned King Richard quizzes the groom: 'What art thou, and how comest thou hither . . . ?'
  how i.e. by whose permission
86 SP *Many editors since Malone allocate this speech to 1 Murderer and 89 to 2 Murderer. This might make sense, since the speaker of 84 is 1 Murderer. However, the passage could be choric, and its speakers interchangeable (Hammond); alternatively, the entrance sequence may be either physically confusing, with the Second Murderer actually first to approach Brakenbury, and/or vocally clamorous. Some claim the First Murderer's greater ferocity (Clarke, *Characters*, 464; Smidt, *Impostors*, 49; Lull), but the Second Murderer assumes an active, leading role at 145–51.
93–5 Cf. 'The keyes he rendered, but partaker would not be / Of that flagi-

tious facte' (*Mirror*, 'Richard, Duke of Gloucester', 85–6).
93 **reason** question, discuss, consider (*OED v.* 4a)
94 **will be** desire to be (Abbott, 319)
  guiltless from innocent of; attempting to remain *guiltless* by refusing to interpret would be futile, for 'not only he is a murtherer & a Homicide before God who slayeth or killeth, a Man with materiall sword, but he also who may preuent the same, and will not. And not onely, he is guiltie of haynous transgression that committeth any euill really, but also he who consenteth to it as he doth, who holdeth his peace, or he who by any means might auoid it, and either for negligence wil not, or for feare of the world dare not' (Stubbes, sig. ¶3ʳ).
95 **there the keys** The keys are possibly left lying or now tossed at the feet of the intruders. Such a transfer, which removes Brakenbury even further

---

86 SP] *F (2. Mur.); Execu. Qq*   88 What] *F;* Yea, are you *(ye Q3–6) Qq*   89 SP] *F (1.);* 2 Exe. *Qq*   'Tis better, sir] *F;* O sir, it is better *Qq*   than to be] *F;* to be briefe then *Q1–2;* be briefe then *Q3–6*   89–90 Let him see] *F;* Shew him *Qq*   90 and] *F; not in Qq*   SD] *F (Reads);* He readeth it. *Qq*   93 hereby] *F, Q1–2;* thereby *Q3–6*   94 from] *F;* of *Qq*   95] *F;* Here are the keies, there sits the Duke a sleepe *Qq*

I'll to the King, and signify to him
That thus I have resigned to you my charge.

1 MURDERER   You may, sir; 'tis a point of wisdom. Fare
you well.   *Exeunt [Brakenbury and Keeper]*.

2 MURDERER   What, shall we stab him as he sleeps?   100

1 MURDERER   No. He'll say 'twas done cowardly, when
he wakes.

2 MURDERER   Why, he shall never wake until the great
Judgement Day.

1 MURDERER   Why, then he'll say we stabbed him   105
sleeping.

2 MURDERER   The urging of that word 'Judgement' hath
bred a kind of remorse in me.

1 MURDERER   What? Art thou afraid?

2 MURDERER   Not to kill him, having a warrant, but to be   110
damned for killing him, from the which no warrant can
defend me.

1 MURDERER   I thought thou hadst been resolute.

---

from appearance of agency, would be
in keeping with the general displacement of guilt that characters strive
for (see 2.1.57n. and pp. 17, 63). Qq's
'here' implies handing over the keys;
cf. 'here with teares I deliuer you the
keyes, and so farewell maister Terrell'
(*True Tragedy*, 1204).
100 *we Many editors follow Q1–2 and
make this line a personal expression
of individual misgiving; however, F,
Q3–6's 'we' plausibly expresses hesitation about a collective enterprise.
103–4 great Judgement Day referring to the Christian belief in a
final reckoning when all souls will

be judged by God; see Jude, 6 ('the
iudgement of the great Day') and
cf. 3.1.78, 5.1.12. The exchange that
follows may be a comic version of
contemporary theological dialogue
(Rozett, 255); cf. Perkins, *Treatise*,
fols 107ʳ–114ᵛ.
107 **urging** prompting, strong incite-
ment
108 **remorse** either pity for the victim or
a more precise theological term meaning deep regret and repentance for a
sinful undertaking (*OED* 2a, 3a)
113–14 *Smidt believes Qq omission is
deliberate, and 114 out of 'character'
(*Impostors*, 108). For similar wavering

96] F; Ile to his Maiesty, and certifie his Grace Qq   97 to . . . charge] F; my charge (place Q3–6) to
you Qq   98–159] prose Pope; Qq line as verse; F lines 98–9, 110–12, 117–19, 133–6 as verse, otherwise
prose   98+ SP] F (1 until 278); Exe. Qq   98–9] F lines wisedome: / well. /   98 You . . . 'tis] F;
Doe so, it is Qq   98–9 Fare you well.] F; not in Qq   99 SD] Evans (subst.); Exit. after 97 F; not
in Qq   100+ SP] F (2 until 275), Qq (2)   100 we] F, Q3–6; I Q1–2   101 He'll] F; then he will
Qq   103 Why] F; When he wakes, / Why foole Qq   until the great] F; till the Qq   105 he'll] F; he
will Qq   110–12] prose Pope; F lines Warrant, / which / me. / ; Qq line dānd / vs. /   110 warrant]
F; warrant for it Qq   111–12 the which . . . me] F; which . . . vs Qq   113–14] F; not in Qq

2 MURDERER	So I am, to let him live.	
1 MURDERER	I'll back to the Duke of Gloucester and tell him so.	115
2 MURDERER	Nay, I prithee stay a little. I hope this passionate humour of mine will change. It was wont to hold me but while one tells twenty.	
1 MURDERER	How dost thou feel thyself now?	120
2 MURDERER	^QFaith,^Q some certain dregs of conscience are yet within me.	
1 MURDERER	Remember our reward when the deed's done.	
2 MURDERER	Zounds, he dies! I had forgot the reward.	125
1 MURDERER	Where's thy conscience now?	
2 MURDERER	O, in the Duke of Gloucester's purse.	
1 MURDERER	When he opens his purse to give us our reward, thy conscience flies out.	
2 MURDERER	'Tis no matter; let it go. There's few or none will entertain it.	130

and invocation of 'resolution', see *True Tragedy*, 1294–1301; cf. 1211. For resolution see also 1.3.339n.

118 **passionate humour** compassionate (*OED* 5b, citing this line) mood
  wont accustomed

119 **tells** counts (*OED v.* B II 21a); Wells and Taylor, Davison and Jowett add indications that the Murderers pause. However, one can imagine effects that involve virtually no pause at all. It might seem unlikely that the two would actually observe Wells and Taylor's '*He counts to twenty*', but Terry Hands's 1970 production had the count run to twenty and resume with 'twenty-one, twenty-two, twenty-three' after 122 (Hankey, 126).

121 **Faith* 'Faith' may have been excised from F along with 'Zounds' (125, 143), but 'Faith' was a much milder oath.

Bishop Cooper claims '*by my faith* signifieth no more, but *in very trueth, bona fide, in trueth, assuredly*' (Cooper, 62). 'In faith' occurs throughout More's account (e.g. *CW*2, 19, 30, 35). F leaves variants of 'faith' or 'in/by/on my faith' or 'good faith' intact elsewhere (e.g. 2.4.16, 23; 3.2.114; 4.4.176), but correction for oaths is uneven (see 84–end n.), and other offensive phrasing in 1.4 may have prompted cuts here.
  dregs small remnant, residue

125, 143 **Zounds** contraction of 'God's wounds!', referring to Christ's bodily sufferings during the crucifixion; a strong oath, definitely covered by the prohibition of 1606 (see 84–end n.).

131 **entertain** receive, show hospitality to, as a guest (*OED v.* 13); or employ (cf. 1.2.259)

115 I'll] *F; not in Qq* and] *F; not in Qq* 117–19] *prose Pope; F lines* little: / change, / twenty. / ; *Qq line* will / xx. / 117 Nay, I prithee . . . little] *F;* I pray thee . . . while *Qq* 117–18 this . . . mine] *F;* my holy humor *Qq* 118–19 It was . . . tells twenty] *F;* twas . . . would tel xx *Qq* 123 deed's] *F;* deede is *Qq* 125 Zounds] *Qq;* Come *F* 126 Where's] *F;* Where is *Qq* 127 O,] *F; not in Qq* 128 When] *F;* So when *Qq* 130 'Tis no matter] *F; not in Qq* let it] *F, Q1, 3–6;* Let vs *Q2*

1 MURDERER   What if it come to thee again?

2 MURDERER   I'll not meddle with it; it makes a man a
coward: a man cannot steal but it accuseth him; a man
cannot swear but it checks him; a man cannot lie with   135
his neighbour's wife but it detects him. 'Tis a blushing,
shamefaced spirit that mutinies in a man's bosom. It
fills a man full of obstacles. It made me once restore
a purse of gold that by chance I found. It beggars any
man that keeps it. It is turned out of towns and cities   140
for a dangerous thing, and every man that means to live
well endeavours to trust to himself, and live without it.

1 MURDERER   �QZounds,Q 'tis even now at my elbow,
persuading me not to kill the Duke.

2 MURDERER   Take the devil in thy mind, and believe   145

133–4 it   makes ... coward Cf.
Richard's lonely panic at his affliction
by *coward conscience* (5.3.179) and his
hollow boast, 'Conscience is but a
word that cowards use' (5.3.309).

134–6 Relevant Commandments forbid
stealing, taking the name of the Lord
in vain and adultery; see Exodus,
20.3–17.

135–6 lie ... wife Possibly derived from
the *BCP* Commination: 'Cursed is he
that lieth with his neighbour's wife'
(Noble, 133); cf. 196n.

137 *shamefaced F's word arose as
an 'etymological misinterpretation'
of Qq's term 'shamefast', meaning 'restrained by shame', abashed
or ashamed (*OED* shamefast). Henry
VI is called 'shamefac'd' in F's *3H6*
(4.8.52; cf. 'shamefast' in its octavo
form, *The Tragedy of Richard, Duke
of York*). The obvious facial reference
in *blushing* prompts Jowett's Q-based
edition to accept F's term.

139 beggars reduces to beggary

140 keeps either retains for employment
(*OED* v. 20; cf. *MW* 1.2.256), a sense
which continues the personification
of *entertain* (131); or cares for, regards
(*OED* v. 9c). Langland writes of conscience as a counsellor to be kept,
i.e. regarded (*Piers Plowman: The
A Version*, ed. George Kane (1988),
Passus iv, 156).

140–1 turned   out ... for thrown
out ... as

143 at my elbow i.e. close by (*OED*
elbow *sb.* 4a); cf. Dent, D243.1: 'The
devil is at one's elbow.'

145–6 Take ... not A difficult phrase:
either, apprehend (*OED* take v. B II
2a) or attack (see 152) the devil (who
appears diabolical from the Murderer's
inverted perspective because he counsels mercy) and do not credit his
advice; or, conversely, mentally accept
the devil (who is, because diabolical, against mercy) and, following the

---

132 What] *F;* How *Qq*   133–6 I'll ... him;] *prose Pope; F lines* Coward: / cannot / his / ; *Qq line*
thing, / steale, / him: / detects /   133 it; it] *F;* it, it is a dangerous thing, / It *Qq*   134–5 a man
cannot swear] *F;* he cannot sweare *Q1–2;* he cannot steale *Q3–6*   135 a man cannot lie] *F;* He cannot lie *Qq*   136 'Tis] *F;* It is *Qq*   137 shamefaced] *F* (shamefac'd), *Q1, 3, 6* (shamefast), *Q2, 4–5*
(shamfast)   138 a man] *F;* one *Qq*   139 purse] *F, Q1–2;* piece *Q3–6*   by chance] *F; not in Qq*   140
of] *F;* of all *Qq*   142 trust to] *F, Q2–6;* trust to / To *Q1*   live] *F;* to liue *Qq*   143 'tis] *F;* it is *Qq*

him not. He would insinuate with thee but to make
thee sigh.

1 MURDERER   I am strong-framed; he cannot prevail with
me.

2 MURDERER   Spoke like a tall man that respects thy   150
reputation. Come, shall we fall to work?

1 MURDERER   Take him on the costard with the hilts of
thy sword, and then throw him into the malmsey butt
in the next room.

2 MURDERER   O excellent device! And make a sop of   155
him.

1 MURDERER   Soft, he wakes.

---

devil, reject the advice of *conscience*
(i.e. *him*) which pleads for mercy. For
a case resembling the confusion of values in the first reading, cf. Launcelot
Gobbo's internal debate (*MV* 2.2).

146 **insinuate** ingratiate himself
146–7 **make thee sigh** i.e. with unhappiness
148 **strong-framed** Qq's 'strong in
fraud' sounds like a perversion of biblical 'strong in fayth' (Romans, 4.20).
Although both versions suggest misplaced confidence, they carry different implications. F's speaker suggests
misplaced faith in physical resources
when spiritual resources are required;
Qq's speaker presumes that he is experienced enough in cunning practices
to outwit the devil. F's speaker seems
marginally less intelligent, since no
material strength can claim superiority
in its own right to demonic powers, let
alone to those of the prince of demons,
but stories about outwitting the devil
are many.
150 **tall** brave, stout (*OED* I 3); 'like a

tall man' carries unsophisticated, possibly oafish or rustic overtones (cf. *RJ*
2.4.31).
152 **Take** strike (*OED v.* B II 5a)
costard head (applied humorously:
OED sb. 2a); literally, a large apple
hilts hilt
153–4 ***throw . . . room** Cf. *3H6* 5.6.92,
where Richard contemptuously
addresses the murdered Henry VI:
'I'll throw thy body in another room'.
Qq's 'chop' (also at 269) meaning 'to
thrust with sudden force' (*OED v.*[1] 7a)
occurs nowhere else in Shakespeare
with this sense.
153 **malmsey butt** barrel of strong,
sweet wine; More has Clarence
'attainted . . . by parliament and iudged
to the death, and therupon hastely
drouned in a Butte of Malmesey'
(*CW2*, 7). Similar details appear in
Mancini (63, 111n.) and others.
155 **device** project, scheme (*OED* 6)
sop cake or bread soaked in wine
(*OED sb.*[1] 1; see 2d, citing this line)
157 **Soft** Cf. 1.3.338n.

---

146 but] *F; not in Qq*   148 I am strong-framed] *F* (strong fram'd), *hyphen Capell;* Tut, I am strong in
fraud *Qq*   149 me.] *F;* me, / I warrant thee. *Qq*   150 Spoke] *F, Q1–3;* Soode *Q4;* Stood *Q5–6*   man
. . . thy] *F;* fellow . . . his *Qq*   151 fall to work?] *F;* to this geere. *Qq*   152 on] *F;* ouer *Qq*   153
thy] *F, Q1–2;* my *Q3–6*   throw him into] *F;* we wil chop him in *Qq*   malmsey butt] *F* (Malmsey-
Butte), *Q1–2* (malmsey But), *Q3–6* (Malmsey-but); Malmsey, but *Q7–8*   155 And make] *F;* make
Qq   sop] *F, Q1–2; Q4–6* (soppe); scoope *Q3*   157] *F;* Harke he stirs, shall I strike. *Qq*

2 MURDERER   Strike!

1 MURDERER   No, we'll reason with him.

CLARENCE

    Where art thou, keeper? Give me a cup of wine.   160

2 MURDERER

    You shall have wine enough, my lord, anon.

CLARENCE

    In God's name, what art thou?

1 MURDERER   A man, as you are.

CLARENCE   But not as I am, royal.

1 MURDERER   Nor you as we are, loyal.   165

CLARENCE

    Thy voice is thunder, but thy looks are humble.

1 MURDERER

    My voice is now the King's, my looks mine own.

CLARENCE

    How darkly, and how deadly dost thou speak!

    Your eyes do menace me. Why look you pale?

    Who sent you hither? Wherefore do you come?   170

2 MURDERER   To, to, to –

CLARENCE   To murder me?

---

159 Contrast the Murderer's thrice-iterated rejection of talking at 1.3.349–51.

160, 161 **thou, You** As a social superior, Clarence consistently employs 'thou' to inferiors. His *you* (169) is a plural. As the scene continues, the Murderers change from the respectful 'you' to forms of 'thou' expressing condemnation (see 200). At 231 they shift back to 'you' forms (Abbott, 232); cf. 196, 231.

161 **anon** soon

166–9 *humble* looks and *pale* complex-ion seem at odds with menacing eyes (169), since *pale* often denotes feebleness, fearfulness (*OED a.* 3; cf. *H5* 2.0.14), as in *LLL* 1.2.97: 'fears by pale white shown'. But *humble* could mean low in status, and the Murderers might exhibit bold authority, by virtue of their regal commission, along with a socially appropriate timorousness that sits uneasily with that authority.

168 **darkly** in a gloomy, frowning, ominous manner

170 **Wherefore** why

158] *F; not in Qq*   159 SP] *F; 2 Qq*   we'll] *F; first lets Qq*   him.] *F, Q1–2;* him. *Cla. awaketh. Q3–6*   161 SP] *F; 1 Qq*   163 SP] *F; 2 Qq*   165 SP] *F, Q5–6; 2 Q1–4*   167 SP] *F; 2 Qq*   168 speak] *F, Q1–2, 5–6;* spake *Q3–4*   169] *F; not in Qq*   170] *F;* Tell me who are you, wherefore come you hither? *Qq*   171 SP] *F; Am. Qq*

BOTH   Ay, ay.

CLARENCE

> You scarcely have the hearts to tell me so,
> And therefore cannot have the hearts to do it.   175
> Wherein, my friends, have I offended you?

1 MURDERER

> Offended us you have not, but the King.

CLARENCE

> I shall be reconciled to him again.

2 MURDERER

> Never, my lord; therefore prepare to die.

CLARENCE

> Are you drawn forth among a world of men   180
> To slay the innocent? What is my offence?
> Where is the evidence that doth accuse me?
> What lawful quest have given their verdict up
> Unto the frowning judge? Or who pronounced
> The bitter sentence of poor Clarence' death?   185
> Before I be convict by course of law,
> To threaten me with death is most unlawful.
> I charge you, as you hope to have redemption,
> ^QBy Christ's dear blood, shed for our grievous sins,^Q

180–7 This passage shares a general point with *Mirror*'s Clarence, who claims to have been 'Imprisoned first, accused without cause, / And doen to death, no proces had by lawes' ('Clarence', 167–8). *Mirror* also shares many legal terms: offence, accuse, quest, verdict and pronounced ('Clarence', 350–6).

180 **drawn forth** singled out, chosen **world** vast quantity (*OED sb.* IV 19a); cf. *LLL* 5.2.353.

183 **quest** inquiry, body of jurors (*OED sb.*[1] 1, 2); *Mirror*'s Clarence is subject-

ed to a covert 'quest' just before being murdered ('Clarence', 351–7).

186 **convict** convicted; cf. Abbott, 342.

188 **charge** order

188–9 ***to ... sins** Qq's references to Christ might fall under the 1606 statute (see 84–end n. and p. 457). A similar reference to Christian redemption is left untouched in *MM* 2.2.78–82, but censorship was inconsistent. The generally ironic treatment of religion in *Richard III* may have occasioned particularly close scrutiny (Birch, 199–200).

---

173 SP] *F, Qq (Am.)*   Ay, ay.] *F;* I. *Qq*   174 hearts] *F, Q1–5;* heart *Q6*   180 drawn ... among] *F;* cald ... from out *Qq*   182 is ... that doth] *F;* are ... that doe *Q1–2;* are ... to *Q3–6*   185–6 death? ... law,] *F2;* death, ... law? *F, Qq*   188 to have redemption] *Qq;* for any goodnesse *F*

That you depart and lay no hands on me. 190
The deed you undertake is damnable.

1 MURDERER

What we will do, we do upon command.

2 MURDERER

And he that hath commanded is our king.

CLARENCE

Erroneous vassals, the great King of kings
Hath in the table of His law commanded 195
That thou shalt do no murder. Will you then
Spurn at His edict, and fulfil a man's?
Take heed, for He holds vengeance in His hand,
To hurl upon their heads that break His law.

2 MURDERER

And that same vengeance doth He hurl on thee 200
For false forswearing and for murder too.
Thou didst receive the sacrament to fight
In quarrel of the house of Lancaster.

194–9 The *Sermon on Obedience* maintains that 'we may not obey kings, Magistrates, or any other (though they bee our owne fathers) if they would commande vs to doe any thing contrary to Gods commandements' (*Homilies*, 74).

194 **vassals** underlings, servants, but with an insulting sense, as abject persons or slaves (*OED sb.* 2b, 3); the Murderers err in considering themselves primarily as subjects to King Edward (rather than to God).
King of kings God or Christ; the phrasing is biblical (Revelation, 17.14); see Noble, 133–4.

195 **table . . . law** the Ten Commandments, divinely engraved upon tables

or tablets of stone (Exodus, 20.3–17, 32.15–16)

196 **thou . . . you** Clarence shifts from the biblical diction of the Commandments ('Thou shalt not . . . ') to the plural *you* in directly addressing the Murderers. Qq do not register the shift from allusion to direct address. The phrase *do no murder* (for the biblical 'kill' of the Commandment) follows *BCP*: 'Thou shalt do no murder' (Noble, 133).

197 **Spurn at** reject with contempt or disdain (*OED v.*[1] II 6)

201 **false forswearing** perjury, breaking of a sworn promise

202–3 **receive . . . Lancaster** i.e. take an oath upon partaking of the holy Eucharist to fight for the cause of Henry VI; cf. 5.5.18.

---

193 our] *F;* the *Qq* 194 vassals] *F;* Vassaile *Qq* 195 the] *F, Q1–2;* his *Q3–6* table] *F;* tables *Qq* 196 murder] *F, Q3–6 (*murther*), Q1–2* Will you] *F;* and wilt thou *Qq* 198 hand] *F;* hands *Qq* 200 hurl] *F;* throw *Qq* 201 murder] *F, Q6 (*murther*), Q1–5* 202–3 sacrament . . . In] *F;* holy sacrament, / To fight in *Qq*

1 MURDERER

And like a traitor to the name of God
Didst break that vow, and with thy treacherous blade   205
Unrip'st the bowels of thy sovereign's son.

2 MURDERER

Whom thou wast sworn to cherish and defend.

1 MURDERER

How canst thou urge God's dreadful law to us
When thou hast broke it in such dear degree?

CLARENCE

Alas! For whose sake did I that ill deed?   210
For Edward, for my brother, for his sake.
He sends you not to murder me for this,
For in that sin he is as deep as I.
If God will be avenged for the deed,
O, know you yet, He doth it publicly;   215
Take not the quarrel from His powerful arm.
He needs no indirect or lawless course

---

206 **son** Prince Edward, son of Henry VI
208–9 Cf. Romans, 2.23: 'Thou that makest thy boast of the lawe, through breakyng the lawe dishonorest God' (Noble). This verse, together with Romans, 2.21, strongly denounces the hypocrisy (prominent throughout this play) of lecturing others about their wrongs while remaining guilty oneself.
209 **in . . . degree** to such dire extent
214–18 This passage recounts the Christian objection to personal vengeance. For God's exclusive right of vengeance, see Deuteronomy, 32.15–43 and Romans, 12.19: 'auenge not your selues, but rather geue place vnto Wrath: for it is written, Vengeaunce is myne, I wyll repay sayth the Lorde.' Calvin explains: 'it belongs not to

us to revenge, except we would assume to ourselves the office of God' (*Commentaries*, 475; cf. *Homilies*, 69–71). Campbell (310–12) calls this 'Shakespeare's most detailed statement of the whole Elizabethan philosophy of vengeance', with its three related concerns: God's vengeance for sin, public vengeance, executed by the ruler or his representatives as agents of God's justice and punishment, and private vengeance, which usurps divine authority and is therefore forbidden.
216 **quarrel** i.e. settlement of the issue, punishment of the deed
His powerful arm For God's actions characterized in terms of strength of hand and arm, see Jeremiah, 21.5; Ezekiel, 20.33.
217 **indirect** devious, underhanded

---

207 wast] *F;* wert *Qq*   209 such] *F;* so *Qq*   212 He] *F;* Why sirs, he *Qq*   you] *F;* ye *Qq*   murder] *F (*murther*), Qq*   213 that] *F;* this *Qq*   214 avenged for the] *F;* reuenged for this *Qq*   215] *F; not in Qq*   217 or] *F;* nor *Qq*   lawless] *F, Q1;* lawfull *Q2–6*

To cut off those that have offended Him.

1 MURDERER

Who made thee then a bloody minister,
When gallant-springing, brave Plantagenet,   220
That princely novice, was struck dead by thee?

CLARENCE

My brother's love, the devil and my rage.

1 MURDERER

Thy brother's love, our duty and thy faults
Provoke us hither now to slaughter thee.

CLARENCE

If you do love my brother, hate not me.   225
I am his brother, and I love him well.
If you are hired for meed, go back again,
And I will send you to my brother Gloucester,
Who shall reward you better for my life
Than Edward will for tidings of my death.   230

---

218 **cut off** bring to an end or put to death (suddenly or prematurely) (*OED* cut *v.* 56c, d)

219 **minister** agent (*OED sb.* 2a); cf. 1.2.46 and 5.3.113, which cast Richard and Richmond as, respectively, 'ministers' of hell and heaven. Shaheen (83) maintains a contrast between a self-appointed *bloody minister* and a duly appointed 'minister' of God. The Murderers may be now, as Clarence was in the past, agents of providential justice (Prior, 47). In a well-known passage concerning subjection to earthly authorities, Saint Paul characterizes the ruler as a minister for aid and a scourge for punishment: 'For he is the minister of God for thy wealth. But yf thou do euyll, feare; for he beareth not the

sworde in vayne, for he is the minister of God, reuenger of wrath on hym that doth euyll' (Romans, 13.4).

220 **gallant-springing** filled with admirable youthful vigour like a new seedling; cf. youthful Rutland as a tender branch that did 'sweetly spring' (*3H6* 2.6.46–50).
Plantagenet Prince Edward

221 **novice** beginner; Prince Edward is knighted by Henry VI in *3H6* 2.2.58–66.

223 ***our duty** F continues the Murderers' strain of self-righteousness. If Qq's 'the diuell' is not merely taken over by a compositor from the previous line, it could constitute a sarcastic echo.

227 **meed** profit, reward (*OED sb.* 1) or specifically corrupt gain or bribe (*OED sb.* 2)

---

220 gallant-springing] *F, Q1* (gallant springing), *hyphen Pope;* gallant spring *Q2–6* 221 That] *F, Q1–5;* The *Q6* struck] *F;* stroke *Q1;* strooke *Q2–6* 223 our duty . . . faults] *F;* the diuell . . . fault *Qq* 224 Provoke . . . slaughter] *F;* Haue brought . . . murder (murther *Q3–6*) *Qq* 225 If . . . my] *F;* Oh if you loue *Q1–3;* Oh, if you loue *Q4–6* 227 are] *F;* be *Qq* meed] *F, Q1;* neede *Q2–6 subst.* 229 shall] *F;* will *Qq*

2 MURDERER

You are deceived; your brother Gloucester hates you.

CLARENCE

O no, he loves me, and he holds me dear.

Go you to him from me.

1 MURDERER   Ay, so we will.

CLARENCE

Tell him, when that our princely father York

Blessed his three sons with his victorious arm,   235

^QAnd charged us from his soul to love each other,^Q

He little thought of this divided friendship.

Bid Gloucester think on this, and he will weep.

1 MURDERER

Ay, millstones, as he lessoned us to weep.

CLARENCE

O, do not slander him, for he is kind.   240

1 MURDERER

Right, as snow in harvest. Come, you deceive yourself.

'Tis he that sends us to destroy you here.

CLARENCE

It cannot be, for he bewept my fortune,

231–69 *you F's Murderers shift their pronouns for the balance of these exchanges, again employing 'you' as in 161–77. Qq's Murderers continue to use 'thee' forms consistently to Clarence.

236 *Most editors include this Qq line as essential to the meaning of the line which follows in F. The stress on love accords with the extended argument (222–52) concerning brotherly love and kindness. The likely explanation for absence from F would be compositorial omission. The fatherly blessing does not appear in *3H6*.

239 **millstones** See 1.3.352n.
  lessoned instructed
240 **kind** kindly, good-natured; the First Murderer takes the word to mean 'natural'.
241 **as ... harvest** i.e. as unnatural (and destructive) as snow at harvest season (cf. Dent, S590)
241, 242 **you** On the pronominal shift here, see 231–69n.
243–4 **bewept ... hugged** Hammond, following Marshall, takes these lines to direct the staging of 1.1.112, but Furness suggests Clarence seeks

---

231] *Qq; F lines* deceiu'd / you. /   233] *Steevens; F, Qq line* me. / will. /   SP] *F; Am. Qq*   238 on] *F, Q6; of Q1–5*   239 SP] *F; Am. Qq*   241] *Qq; F lines* Haruest: / selfe, /   Right,] *F, Q3–6;* Right *Q1–2*   Come ... yourself] *F;* thou deceiu'st thy selfe *Qq*   242 that sends] *F;* hath sent *Q1;* that sent *Q2–6*   to ... here] *F;* hither now to slaughter thee *Q1;* hither now to murder (murther *Q6)* thee *Q2–6*   243 he ... fortune] *F;* when I parted with him *Qq*

And hugged me in his arms, and swore with sobs
That he would labour my delivery. 245

1 MURDERER

Why so he doth, when he delivers you
From this earth's thraldom to the joys of heaven.

2 MURDERER

Make peace with God, for you must die, my lord.

CLARENCE

Have you that holy feeling in your souls
To counsel me to make my peace with God, 250
And are you yet to your own souls so blind
That you will war with God by murdering me?
O sirs, consider: they that set you on
To do this deed will hate you for the deed.

2 MURDERER

What shall we do?

CLARENCE   Relent, and save your souls. 255

through desperate overstatement to convince the Murderers of a bond between his brother and himself.

245 **labour my delivery** The same phrase appears in *The Spanish Tragedy* (Kyd, 3.7.33).

246–7 Cf. Richard's joking intention to benefit Clarence by sending him to heaven in the first scene (1.1.118–19) and that scene's various uses of 'deliver'.

247 **thraldom** bondage, servitude

249–55 **Have . . . do?** This is Clarence's first clear-cut appeal to conscience, and though it appears to have an effect, it ironically eventuates in a death blow (Wiggins, 119).

253 *****O** For another variation between Qq's 'Ah' and F's 'O', see 4.4.31, but cf. 66, 1.3.11, 2.1.134, 2.2.27 for a few of the

many changes in the opposite direction; Honigmann notes the play's reversal of general F usage ('Variants', 197).

253–4 **they . . . deed** Cf. Dent, K64: 'A King (prince) loves the treason but hates the traitor,' and *R2* 5.6.38.

255–61 *****The discrepancy between F and Qq, along with F's apparent digressiveness, has elicited editorial comment since Johnson's edition and Thomas Tyrwhitt's suggested re-arrangement in *Observations and Conjectures upon Some Passages of Shakespeare* (1766) (Var; Walton, *Quarto*, 147; Wilson). This edition retains Clarence's extended plea for sympathy in F's seemingly awkward position – i.e. between his injunction ('Relent, and save your souls') and First Murderer's response ('Relent? No. 'Tis cowardly and womanish.').

244 And] *F;* He *Qq*   246 SP] *F;* 2 *Qq*   when . . . you] *F;* now . . . thee *Qq*   247 earth's] *F;* worlds *Qq*   248 SP] *F;* 1 *Qq*   Make] *F, Q2–6;* Makes *Q1*   249 Have you . . . your souls] *F;* Hast thou . . . thy soule *Qq*   251 are you . . . your own souls] *F;* art thou . . . thy owne soule *Qq*   252 you will] *F;* thou wilt *Qq*   by] *F, Q1–2;* for *Q3–6*   murdering] *F, Q1* (murd'ring), *Q2–5* (murdering), *Q6* (murthering)   253 O] *F;* Ah *Qq*   they] *F;* he *Qq*   254 the] *F;* this *Qq*   255] *Steevens; F, Qq line* do? / soules: /

Which of you, if you were a prince's son,
Being pent from liberty, as I am now,
If two such murderers as yourselves came to you,
Would not entreat for life? Ay, you would beg,
Were you in my distress.   260

1 MURDERER

Relent? No. 'Tis cowardly and womanish.

CLARENCE

Not to relent is beastly, savage, devilish.
[*to 2 Murderer*] My friend, I spy some pity in thy looks.
O, if thine eye be not a flatterer,
Come thou on my side, and entreat for me;   265
A begging prince, what beggar pities not.

2 MURDERER   Look behind you, my lord.

1 MURDERER

Take that, and that!   (*Stabs him.*)
                        If all this will not do,

Marshall has argued for F's sequence: Clarence's 'rapid and passionate appeal' prevents immediate reply and awakens the Murderers' further reflections, so that the First Murderer's response is a hesitant question ('Relent?') followed by a negative decision ('No.'), while the Second Murderer shows – at least to Clarence's eye – outward signs of relenting (Marshall, 108). Thus, Clarence directs 263–6 to the Second Murderer, hoping to build on his display of pity.

255 **Relent** Perhaps a weak substitute for the Christian formula, 'Repent and save your souls' (Rozett, 257).

259 *****Ay** Many editors have thought that F's line requires emendation for grammatical reasons. Theobald offered 'ah!' for 'as'; Wells and Taylor retain 'As', leaving Clarence's sentence incomplete ('As you would beg / Were you in my distress – ').

261 **womanish** For a similar conjunction of *relent*[*ing*] with a gendered (mis)conception, see 4.4.431; cf. Dent, W724.1: 'To fear is womanish.'

264 **flatterer** i.e. one who encourages hope on false or insufficient grounds (*OED* flatter *v.*[1] 7a)

265 **Come . . . side** Clarence may be asking the Second Murderer to stand next to him in beseeching mercy from the First Murderer, or perhaps simply requesting that he plead on Clarence's behalf.

267 *****This highly dramatic line, in which the Second Murderer attempts to warn Clarence, is not in Qq. The last line on Q1's D3[r] is 266, and the catchword is '1 I' (i.e. 1 MURDERER Ay), which begins the first line on Q1's D3[v].

268 *****Although 'thus' is an all-purpose marker for staged action (see 4.3.9–10), Qq's 'I thus, and thus' repeats the line which accompanies the murder of

---

256–60] *F; not in Qq*   259 Ay] *Ard*[2]*; as F; ah! Theobald*   261 No] *F; not in Qq*   262 devilish] *F, Q1;* and diuelish *Q2–6*   263 SD] *Sisson*   thy] *F, Q1–5;* your *Q6*   264 thine] *F;* thy *Qq*   267] *F; not in Qq*   268] *F;* I thus, and thus: if this wil not serue *Qq*   SD] *F after do; He stabs him. Qq opp.* serue

I'll drown you in the malmsey butt within.   *Exit [with body]*.

2 MURDERER

A bloody deed, and desperately dispatched.   270
How fain, like Pilate, would I wash my hands
Of this most grievous murder.

Enter First Murderer.

1 MURDERER

How now? What mean'st thou that thou help'st me not?
By heaven, the Duke shall know how slack you have been.

2 MURDERER

I would he knew that I had saved his brother.   275
Take thou the fee, and tell him what I say,
For I repent me that the Duke is slain.   *Exit.*

1 MURDERER

So do not I. Go, coward as thou art.
Well, I'll go hide the body in some hole
Till that the Duke give order for his burial.   280
And when I have my meed, I will away,
For this will out, and then I must not stay.   *Exit.*

Horatio in *The Spanish Tragedy* (Kyd, 2.4.56).

If . . . do i.e. if these wounds have not been sufficient to cause death

269 *Q's line is a nearly exact repetition of 153–4.

270 **desperately** recklessly, with utter disregard of risks or consequences (*OED* 4); possibly referring to despair, the spiritual state accompanying rejection of God and usually associated with suicide or a death-wish (see 1.2.84–7, 2.2.36–7, 5.3.120)

271 **fain** gladly

like Pilate see Matthew, 27.24 and Dent, H122; Pontius Pilate's public washing to cleanse himself symbolically of guilt at the sentencing of Jesus was a notorious example of hypocrisy (cf. *R2* 3.1.5–6).

274, 277, 280 **the Duke** As this title shifts its reference from Richard to Clarence and back to Richard, the play anticipates the confusion that accompanies rapid interchanges among proper names elsewhere (see e.g. 4.4.40–6).

275 **would** wish

282 **this will out** This will be discovered (Dent, M1315: 'Murder will out').

---

269 drown you . . . within] *F*; chop thee . . . in the next roome *Qq*   malmsey butt] *F* (Malmesey-But), *Qq* (malmesey But)   SD] *Malone subst.; Exit. F; not in Qq*   270 dispatched] *F*; performd *Qq*   271 hands] *F*; hand *Qq*   272 murder!] *F*; guilty murder done *Qq*   272.1] *F; not in Qq*   273–4] *verse Rowe; prose F*; Why doest thou not helpe me, / By heauens the Duke shall know how slacke thou art *Qq subst.*   274 heauen] *F, Q6*; heauens *Q1–5*   279 Well . . . the] *F*; Now must I hide his *Qq*   280 Till that . . . give] *F*; Vntill . . . take *Qq*   281 will] *F*; must *Qq*   282 then] *F*; here *Qq*   SD] *F; Exeunt. Qq*

2.1   *Flourish. Enter* KING [EDWARD] *sick,*
QUEEN [ELIZABETH], Lord Marquess DORSET, RIVERS,
HASTINGS, CATESBY, BUCKINGHAM.

KING EDWARD

Why, so. Now have I done a good day's work.
You peers, continue this united league.
I every day expect an embassage
From my Redeemer to redeem me hence,
And more in peace my soul shall part to heaven,   5
Since I have made my friends at peace on earth.
– Hastings and Rivers, take each other's hand;
Dissemble not your hatred. Swear your love.

2.1 location: '*The* COURT' (Pope)

0.1 *Flourish* fanfare of horns announcing a person of distinction
sick to '*Enter sick*' frequently entails being led onto the stage (Dessen & Thomson, 198); Edward leaves with 'help' (134).

0.2 *The play names the Queen's brother Anthony Woodeville (1.1.67), but F here creates a second character who is called by his title, Lord Rivers (1.3.37n.), and later a third (2.1.67); see pp. 458–9.

0.3 CATESBY Catesby remains silent in this scene; F includes him here, perhaps as the messenger who has summoned the others to King Edward's presence (1.3.319–20).

3 embassage ambassador, messenger, or the message itself

4 redeem deliver, liberate from sin and its consequences

5 *more in F's 'more to peace' does

not sound right, especially with King Edward's promised departure *to heaven*; Qq's 'now in peace' is possible, but editors often follow Rowe's 'more in' or Capell's 'more at'.
*to Q1–2's 'from' is clearly wrong; corrected copies of Q1 substitute 'to'.

7 *Hastings and Rivers Qq correctly name Edward's addressees, given that Dorset makes no reply in the following exchanges and has no evident quarrel with his uncle Rivers. More names Dorset and Hastings as representing the groups needing reconciliation (*CW2*, 10–11).
take . . . hand Edward's gesture ironically recalls Henry VI's similarly futile attempt to unite the factious Warwick and Clarence (*3H6* 4.6.38–9).

8 Dissemble not Do not disguise (your hatred) by feigned appearance (of affection).

2.1] F *(Actus Secundus. Scæna Prima.); not in Qq*   0.1–3] F *(Flourish. / Enter the King sicke, the Queene, Lord Marquesse Dorset, Riuers, Hastings, Catesby, Buckingham, Wooduill.); Enter King, Queene, Hastings, Ryuers, Dorcet, &c. Q1–2; Enter King, Queene, Hastings, Riuers, &c. Q3–6*   0.1 EDWARD] *Rowe*   0.2 ELIZABETH] *Malone*   1+ SP] *King. F, Q3–6; Kin. Q1–2*   1 Why . . . I] *F;* So, now I haue *Qq*   5 more in] *Rowe;* now in *Qq;* more to *F;* more at *Capell*   to] *F, Q1c (Fo, Bod, Y), Q3–6;* from *Q1u (BL (Huth), Hn), Q2*   6 made] *F;* set *Qq*   friends] *F, Q1–5;* friend *Q6*   7 Hastings and Rivers] *Rowe;* Riuers and Hastings *Qq;* Dorset and *Riuers F*

RIVERS

By heaven, my soul is purged from grudging hate,
And with my hand I seal my true heart's love.   10

HASTINGS

So thrive I, as I truly swear the like.

KING EDWARD

Take heed you dally not before your king,
Lest He that is the supreme King of kings
Confound your hidden falsehood, and award
Either of you to be the other's end.   15

HASTINGS

So prosper I, as I swear perfect love.

RIVERS

And I, as I love Hastings with my heart.

KING EDWARD

Madam, yourself is not exempt from this;
– Nor you, son Dorset; – Buckingham, nor you.
You have been factious one against the other.   20
– Wife, love Lord Hastings. Let him kiss your hand,
And what you do, do it unfeignedly.

QUEEN ELIZABETH

There, Hastings, I will never more remember
Our former hatred, so thrive I and mine.
    [*Hastings kisses her hand.*]

---

10 **seal** ratify an agreement by a ceremonial act (*OED v.*[1] I 1c)
11, 16, 24 **So, so** 'on condition of my speaking the truth' (Abbott, 133)
12 **dally** trifle under the guise of serious action; play with mockingly (*OED* 3)
13 **King of kings** See 1.4.194n.
14 **Confound** defeat utterly, destroy, rout (*OED* 1)
14–15 **award . . . end** destine you to destroy one another; 'Euen so doth

God punish the wicked one by another' (Mornay, 209), cf. *Ham* 3.4.171–3.
19 *****you, son** Since Dorset is present, and since King Edward speaks by turns to the various nobles, F's 'you, son' appears more likely than Qq's 'your son'.
son i.e. stepson
20 **factious** inclined to form parties, or act for party purposes; seditious (cf. 1.3.127)

---

9 soul] *F;* heart *Qq*   10 heart's] *F, Q1–5;* hears *Q6*   11 truly] *F, Q1–2; om. Q3–6*   13 Lest] *F;* Least *Qq*   18 is] *F;* are *Qq*   from] *F;* in *Qq*   19 you, son] *F subst.;* your son *Qq*   23 There] *F;* Here *Qq*   24 SD] *Bevington³; Capell (after* There *23)*

KING EDWARD

> Dorset, embrace him. – Hastings, love Lord Marquess.   25

DORSET

> This interchange of love, I here protest,
> Upon my part shall be inviolable.

HASTINGS

> And so swear I.   [*They embrace.*]

KING EDWARD

> Now, princely Buckingham, seal thou this league
> With thy embracements to my wife's allies,   30
> And make me happy in your unity.

BUCKINGHAM

> Whenever Buckingham doth turn his hate
> Upon your grace, but with all duteous love
> Doth cherish you and yours, God punish me
> With hate in those where I expect most love.   35
> When I have most need to employ a friend,
> And most assured that he is a friend,
> Deep, hollow, treacherous and full of guile
> Be he unto me. This do I beg of God,
> When I am cold in love to you or yours.   40
>   [*They*] *embrace.*

KING EDWARD

> A pleasing cordial, princely Buckingham,

25 **Lord Marquess** i.e. Dorset
29, 41 **princely Buckingham** Cf. 1.3.279n.
30 **to** of
32–5 *Lines constituting one of Wilson's 'tangles' (see also 1.3.68, 2.2.7, 3.7.132–5). The difficulty may arise from combining two strong, but opposed, asseverations in one sentence (Thompson).
33–4 **but . . . Doth cherish** i.e. instead of . . . cherishing (Abbott, 125)

36 **employ** i.e. use for some purpose
37 **most** i.e. I am most
    assured assurèd
38 **Deep** skilled in craft or subtlety (*OED a.* II 17)
39 *God F's 'heauen' possibly reflects the Statute of 1606; cf. 1.4.84–end n. For inconsistency of F's changes, see 34.
41 **cordial** medicine, food or beverage which invigorates the heart (*OED sb.* 2)

25] *Rowe³; F lines* him: / Marquesse. / ; *not in Qq*   26 This] *F, Q1;* Thus *Q2–6*   27 inviolable] *F;* vnuiolable *Qq*   28 I] *F;* I my Lord *Qq*   SD] *Capell*   30 embracements] *F, Q1–5;* embracement *Q6*   33 Upon your grace] *F;* On you or yours *Qq*   39 God] *Qq;* heauen *F*   40 love] *F;* zeale *Qq*   SD] *F; not in Qq   They*] *Capell*

Is this thy vow unto my sickly heart.
There wanteth now our brother Gloucester here
To make the blessed period of this peace.

Enter RATCLIFFE *and* [RICHARD, Duke of] Gloucester.

BUCKINGHAM

And in good time,   45
Here comes Sir Richard Ratcliffe and the Duke.

RICHARD

Good morrow to my sovereign King and Queen,
And princely peers, a happy time of day.

KING EDWARD

Happy indeed, as we have spent the day.
Gloucester, we have done deeds of charity,   50
Made peace of enmity, fair love of hate,
Between these swelling, wrong-incensed peers.

RICHARD

A blessed labour, my most sovereign lord.

---

43 **wanteth** is needed (Abbott, 293)
44 **blessed** blessèd
   period conclusion (*OED* II 5b); cf.
   Richard's surprise *period* (1.3.237–8).
44.1 *RATCLIFFE Ratcliffe has not been
   introduced, has no lines here and will
   not figure in the action until 3.3, so Qq
   omission here makes sense. However,
   his prominence among Richard's
   bloodsuckers (3.3.5) makes it difficult
   to ignore F's inclusion here. More
   describes him as one of Richard's
   closest associates: in 'counsel and in
   theexecucion of such lawles enterprises
   [i.e. the beheading of Rivers and other
   lords], as a man yᵗ had ben long secret
   wᵗ him, hauing experience of yᵉ world
   & a shrewde wit, short & rude in

speche, rough & boustiouse of behauiour, bold in mischief, as far from pite
as from al fere of god' (*CW*2, 57).
45 'And just at the right moment';
this stagey entry is appropriate for
Richard, but Hastings, young York
and Brakenbury all enter *in good time*
(3.1.24, 95, 4.1.12). The formula is
characteristic of Latin New Comedy
(RP).
48 **happy . . . day** a simple greeting, like
'Good time of day' (1.1.122)
52 **swelling** inflated with anger (*R2*
1.1.201), pride (*Oth* 2.3.52) or hatred
(see 2.2.117)
   wrong-incensed incensed by wrongs;
mistakenly incensed; incensèd
53 **blessed** blessèd

44 blessed] *F;* perfect *Qq* 44.1] *F (Gloster) after 46; Enter Glocest. Qq opp. 44* 45–6] *F;* And in
good time here comes the noble Duke. *Qq* 50 Gloucester] *F;* Brother *Qq* 52 wrong-incensed] *F, Qq
(wrong incensed subst.), hyphen Rowe³* 53 my] *F, Q1–2; om. Q3–6* lord] *F;* liege *Qq*

217

Among this princely heap, if any here
By false intelligence or wrong surmise   55
Hold me a foe;
If I unwittingly, or in my rage,
Have aught committed that is hardly borne,
By any in this presence, I desire
To reconcile me to his friendly peace.   60
'Tis death to me to be at enmity;
I hate it, and desire all good men's love.
– First, madam, I entreat true peace of you,
Which I will purchase with my duteous service;
– Of you, my noble cousin Buckingham,   65
If ever any grudge were lodged between us;
– Of you and you, Lord Rivers and of Dorset,
That all without desert have frowned on me;
– Dukes, earls, lords, gentlemen; indeed, of all.
I do not know that Englishman alive   70

---

54 **heap** multitude (*OED sb.* 3); possibly oxymoronic when modified by *princely*. Simon Russell Beale delivered Richard's line 'with a split second of hesitation before choosing the appropriate collective noun and then hitting its final plosive with just sufficient excess force to draw attention to the brilliant precision of the epithet's implications for Woodville pretensions to royalty' (Smallwood, 359).
55 **false intelligence** misinformation
57 *****unwittingly** Qq give a more easily comprehended sense; however, characters throughout the play (and this scene) shirk blame for decisions and actions, so 'unwillingly' is possible.
58 **hardly borne** i.e. taken amiss, resented (*OED* bear *v.*[1] II 16)
59 **presence** company; cf. 79, 85.
60 **me** myself

64 **purchase** obtain
66 **lodged** harboured, entertained (feelings, thoughts); figuratively, as in the reception of a guest (*OED v.* 2c)
67 *****In the light of the confusion about historical identities (see 0.2n.), Qq's phrasing looks like correction; it might also serve Qq's reduction of parts. Qq's 'Gray' is not specifically mentioned in an entry direction. Jowett argues that alternative designations (the title *Dorset* and the family name *Grey*) are used for the same figure in 2.1 and 1.3.
68 **all without desert** altogether without my deserving it
70–3 Citing these lines, Milton's *Eikonoklastes* accuses Charles I of modelling himself on Richard's hypocrisy in affection and religion (Milton, 361).

---

54 Among] *F*; Amongst *Qq*   56–7] *Malone; one line F, Qq*   57 unwittingly] *Qq*; vnwillingly *F*   59 By] *Qq*; To *F*   60 his] *F, Q1, 3–6*; this *Q2*   63 true] *F, Q1–2; om. Q3–6*   64 will] *F, Q1–5; om. Q6*   67] *F;* Of you Lo: Riuers, and Lord Gray of you, *Q1–4;* Of you my Lord Riuers, and Lord Gray of you *Q5–6*   68 me;] *Qq subst.;* me: / Of you Lord *Wooduill*, and Lord *Scales* of you, *F*

With whom my soul is any jot at odds
More than the infant that is born tonight.
I thank my God for my humility.

QUEEN ELIZABETH

A holy day shall this be kept hereafter.
I would to God all strifes were well compounded.   75
My sovereign lord, I do beseech your highness
To take our brother Clarence to your grace.

RICHARD

Why, madam, have I offered love for this,
To be so flouted in this royal presence?
Who knows not that the gentle Duke is dead?   80
    They all start.
You do him injury to scorn his corse.

KING EDWARD

Who knows not he is dead? Who knows he is?

QUEEN ELIZABETH

All-seeing heaven, what a world is this?

BUCKINGHAM

Look I so pale, Lord Dorset, as the rest?

DORSET

Ay, my good lord, and no man in the presence   85
But his red colour hath forsook his cheeks.

70–2 For ironies in Richard's protestations, see R. Watson, 22.
71 **jot** least bit
75 **compounded** settled (*OED v.* II 6a);
cf. *TS* 1.2.26.
77 **to your grace** i.e. into your favour
79 **flouted** mocked, insulted (*OED* flout
v. 1)
81 **scorn his corse** show disrespect to his
corpse
82 *Hammond follows Qq, opposing
F's attribution to King Edward on

the grounds that the line is inconsistent with his being the speaker of
87, but the initial shock expressed
here could be consistent with
Edward's later, more subdued recognition of his own complicity in
the death.
83 **what . . . this?** Cf. *AYL* 2.3.14 and
Dent, W899.1.
84 **pale** Cf. 136–7.
85 **the presence** i.e. the King's presence
(*OED* 1)

76 lord] *F*; liege *Qq*   your] *F, Q1–5*; you *Q6*   highness] *F*; Maiesty *Qq*   79 so flouted] *F*; thus
scorned *Qq*   80 gentle] *F*; noble *Qq*   SD] *F*; *not in Qq*   82 SP] *F (King.)*; *Ryu. Q1*; *Riu. Q2*; *Ri.
Q3–6*   82] *Qq*; *F lines* dead? / is? /   85 man] *F*; one *Qq*   the] *F*; this *Qq*

KING EDWARD

Is Clarence dead? The order was reversed.

RICHARD

But he, poor man, by your first order died,
And that a winged Mercury did bear;
Some tardy cripple bare the countermand,   90
That came too lag to see him buried.
God grant that some, less noble and less loyal,
Nearer in bloody thoughts, and not in blood,
Deserve not worse than wretched Clarence did,
And yet go current from suspicion.   95

Enter [STANLEY,] Earl of Derby.

STANLEY

[*Kneels.*] A boon, my sovereign, for my service done.

---

87 **order** More's Edward 'bewailed and
sorowfully repented' the death of
Clarence (after Parliamentary judgement and at his own command), but
did not attempt to rescind the order
(*CW*2, 7). The close conjunction of
Clarence's death and Edward's (given
by Holinshed as 1477 and 1483 respectively), is Shakespeare's invention.

89 **winged Mercury** wingèd; messenger
of the gods, often depicted with wings
on helmet and feet (cf. 4.3.55)

90 **tardy cripple** perhaps brazenly referring to Richard himself

91 **lag** belatedly (*OED a.* B 1a, citing this
line)
buried burièd

92 **some** i.e. the Queen and her relatives

93 i.e. more 'near', more intimate, with
violent intentions, and less near than
Clarence in blood relationship to King
Edward. There is ambiguity about
who has *bloody thoughts* here, since
Richard could be both accusing the

Queen's family of such thoughts and
also admitting to his own violent
thoughts; they are 'near' to him as a
focus of his antagonism and 'near' to
him physically at this moment. Cf.
Mac 2.3.140–1: 'the near in blood, /
The nearer bloody'.

95 **go . . . suspicion** are received as genuine (*OED a.* 8), passing as current
coin, not counterfeit (*OED a.* 5)
from free from

96–134 When asked for clemency, Hall's
King Edward exclaims, 'O infortunate
brother, for whose lyfe not one creature woulde make intercession, openly
spekyng, and apparauntly meanyng
that by the meanes of some of the
nobilitie, he was circumuented, and
brought to hys confusion' (*Edward IV*,
fols l^v–li^r).

96 **boon** favour
service Stanley's request for a *quid
pro quo* – a *boon* for *service* rendered
– evokes feudal relationships: a tenant

---

88 man] *F*; soule *Qq*   89 winged] *F, Q2–6*; wingled *Q1*   90 bare] *F*; bore *Qq*   93 and] *F*; but
Qq   95.1] *F; Enter Darby. Qq subst.*   STANLEY] *Theobald subst.*   96+ SP] *Theobald subst.; Der. F;
Dar. Qq*   96 SD] *Oxf subst.*

KING EDWARD

I prithee, peace. My soul is full of sorrow.

STANLEY

I will not rise, unless your highness hear me.

KING EDWARD

Then say at once what is it thou requests.

STANLEY

The forfeit, sovereign, of my servant's life, 100

Who slew today a riotous gentleman

Lately attendant on the Duke of Norfolk.

KING EDWARD

Have I a tongue to doom my brother's death,

And shall that tongue give pardon to a slave?

My brother killed no man; his fault was thought, 105

And yet his punishment was bitter death.

Who sued to me for him? Who, in my wrath,

Kneeled at my feet and bid me be advised?

Who spoke of brotherhood? Who spoke of love?

Who told me how the poor soul did forsake 110

---

or knight would render 'service' in exchange for his lord's favour.

96, 126 SD *Kneels . . . rises* Stanley's lines and the royal responses require that he kneel between his entry and 98. He may rise at 126 when the King appears to grant his demand (*OED* hear *v.* 7a: 'accede to, grant [a request or prayer]').

100 i.e. the cancellation of the death penalty upon my servant

101 **riotous** given to wantonness, revelry or dissolute life (*OED a.* 2)

102 **Lately attendant on** recently in the service of

103 **doom . . . death** condemn my brother to death

104 **slave** servant, but here used contemptuously

105 **killed no man** Clarence did kill, and on King Edward's behalf (1.4.199–204). King Edward here (as at 122–3) overstates his innocence; cf. Margaret on the exaggerations necessary for effective curses (4.4.119–23).

fault was thought i.e. he may have thought about wrongs but did not commit them.

107 **sued . . . him** pleaded his case with me

108 ***at . . . bid** Qq's 'at' is certainly correct, and *bid* may serve as a past tense.

be advised i.e. consider, be judicious

110–11 Cf. 1.3.134–7.

---

97 prithee] *F* (prethee), *Qq* (pray thee)   98 hear me] *F;* grant *Qq*   99 say] *F;* speake *Qq*   requests] *F;* demaundst *Qq*   100 SP] *F, Q1–2, 4–6; om. Q3*   104 that tongue] *F;* the same *Qq*   105 killed] *F;* slew *Qq*   106 bitter] *F;* cruell *Qq*   107 wrath] *F;* rage *Qq*   108 at] *Qq; and F*   bid] *F;* bad *Qq*   109 spoke of . . . spoke of] *F;* spake of . . . of *Qq*

The mighty Warwick and did fight for me?
Who told me in the field at Tewkesbury,
When Oxford had me down, he rescued me
And said, 'Dear brother, live, and be a king'?
Who told me, when we both lay in the field,   115
Frozen almost to death, how he did lap me
Even in his garments, and did give himself,
All thin and naked, to the numb-cold night?
All this from my remembrance brutish wrath
Sinfully plucked, and not a man of you   120
Had so much grace to put it in my mind.
But when your carters or your waiting vassals
Have done a drunken slaughter and defaced
The precious image of our dear Redeemer,
You straight are on your knees for pardon, pardon;   125

---

113 The historical sources do not place Oxford at Tewkesbury; however, Shakespeare includes him among the forces that war with King Edward at Tewkesbury in *3H6* 5.4 and 5.5.
116 **lap** enfold in a wrap or wraps, swathe (*OED v.*[2] 3)
118 **thin** i.e. thinly clad (*OED adv.* C 1a)
120–33 This passage is particularly dense with religious vocabulary and allusion. God's grace has been freely offered to pardon sinful mankind. King Edward measures his own *ungracious* failure to pardon Clarence and the failure of his followers to beg for that pardon against the supreme sacrifice by the *dear Redeemer*. Having failed to grant or seek *pardon* for Clarence, he fears that he and his court will be judged undeserving of mercy and suffer divine *justice* rather than attain mercy by means of divine *grace*. 'Like many of Richard's victims, [Shakespeare's] Edward finally accepts his guilt but

soothes his conscience with the perverse consolation that he will not suffer alone' (E. Berry, 87).
122 **carters** literally, drivers of carts, but also stock figures of rough demeanour and low birth; in reference to Stanley's *servant* (100) this constitutes rhetorical exaggeration (cf. *slave*, 104).
waiting vassals servants acting as attendants (*OED* waiting *ppl. a.* 1)
123 **drunken slaughter** Stanley refers to a 'riotous gentleman', saying nothing about the sobriety of his slayer; King Edward again denigrates the figure for whom Stanley pleads and, hence, the merit of his plea.
123–4 **defaced . . . Redeemer** referring to the idea that humanity is made in the image and likeness of God (Genesis, 1.26–7); cf. Calvin, 2.8.40: 'If we do not wish to violate the image of God, we ought to hold our neighbour sacred.'
125 **straight** immediately

---

112 at] *F;* by *Qq*   117 garments] *F;* owne garments *Q1–5;* owne armes *Q6*   did give] *F;* gaue *Qq*   118 numb-cold] *F, Q3–6 (*numbe cold*), Q1–2 (*numbcold*), hyphen Capell*   120 plucked] *F, Q2–6;* puckt *Q1*

And I, unjustly too, must grant it you.   *[Stanley rises.]*
But for my brother, not a man would speak,
Nor I, ungracious, speak unto myself
For him, poor soul. The proudest of you all
Have been beholding to him in his life,   130
Yet none of you would once beg for his life.
O God! I fear Thy justice will take hold
On me, and you, and mine and yours for this.
– Come, Hastings, help me to my closet. – Ah, poor
    Clarence.   *Exeunt some with King and Queen. [Richard,*
                         Buckingham, Stanley and Ratcliffe remain.]

RICHARD

This is the fruits of rashness: marked you not   135
How that the guilty kindred of the Queen
Looked pale when they did hear of Clarence' death?
O! They did urge it still unto the King.
God will revenge it. Come, lords, will you go
To comfort Edward with our company?   140

BUCKINGHAM

We wait upon your grace.   *Exeunt.*

---

127 Cf. 96–134n.
130 **beholding** obliged, indebted
  in his life while he lived
134 **Hastings** As Lord Chamberlain,
Hastings's duties included attendance
on the sovereign in private chambers.
closet private room, inner chamber
134 SD Minimally, King Edward, Queen
Elizabeth and Hastings leave while
Buckingham and Richard remain, but
Richard invites *lords* to depart (139)
in F. Richard's accusations against the
Queen's *kindred* (136) dictate that Dorset
and Rivers be no longer onstage. This
leaves Stanley and Ratcliffe probably
present. Although Catesby is at some

point *sworn* to Richard's faction (3.1.158–
60), the fact that his alliance needs
explicit mention may argue against his
remaining here; so he probably departs
among '*some*' (134 SD).
135 **This . . . rashness** Cf. Iago's self-
righteous rhetoric: 'This is the fruits
of whoring' (*Oth* 5.1.116).
136–7 There are two obvious problems with
Richard's imputation of guilt: first, everyone looks *pale* at the news of Clarence's
death (84–6); secondly, paleness could be
caused by other strong emotions, especially fear (*LLL* 1.2.97); cf. 3.5.1n.
138 **still** continually
139 **God . . . it** Cf. 1.4.214–18, 2.2.14.

---

126 SD] *Cam¹ (Furnivall)*   127 man] *F, Q1–2, 6;* mast *Q3–5*   130 beholding] *F, Q1–3;* beholden
Q4–6   131 beg] *F;* pleade *Qq*   133 yours] *F, Q1–5;* your *Q6*   134] *Qq; F lines* Closset. / Clarence. /
Ah] *F;* oh *Qq*   SD *Exeunt . . . Queen.*] *F; Exit. Qq   Richard . . . remain.] Oxf¹*   135 fruits] *F;* fruit
Qq   rashness] *F, Q1–2;* rawnes *Q3–6*   139 Come . . . go] *F;* But come lets in *Qq*   141] *F; not in
Qq*   SD] *F; opp.* 140 *Qq*

2.2   *Enter the old* DUCHESS *of* York, *with the two*
              Children *of Clarence.*

BOY

Good grandam, tell us, is our father dead?

DUCHESS   No, boy.

DAUGHTER

Why do ᵠyouᵠ weep so oft, and beat your breast?

And cry, 'O Clarence, my unhappy son'?

BOY

Why do you look on us, and shake your head,   5

And call us orphans, wretches, castaways,

If that our noble father were alive?

DUCHESS

My pretty cousins, you mistake me both;

I do lament the sickness of the King,

As loath to lose him, not your father's death.   10

2.2 location: '*a Room in the Palace*' (Capell)

0.2 **Children** Margaret (b. 1473) and Edward (b. 1475) Plantagenet. Clarence's children are more directly in the line of succession than Richard (see *3H6* 4.6.57 and Hall, *Edward IV*, fol. ccxᵛ). The play does not invoke their dynastic claims, but Richard takes steps against them (4.2.53–5, 4.3.36–7). Historically, Edward was attainted for treason and executed by Henry VII in 1499, and Margaret, later Countess of Salisbury, was attainted and executed by Henry VIII in 1541 (Holinshed, 3.703, 787). Holinshed notes their 'like misfortune' within the same precincts of the Tower where their father's murder took place; with Margaret 'died the verie surname of Plantagenet' (3.703).

1 SP *F names Edward only here. The F annotator may have intended the name to be used throughout the scene (*TxC*, 236), but with so many Edwards inhabiting and haunting the play, retaining '*Boy*' might assist the reader.

1 *grandam grandmother; Qq's 'grannam' may be a colloquial form.

4 **unhappy** unfortunate (*OED a.* 2)

6 **castaways** literally, ones who are cast away or rejected, but also conveying a theological sense of being numbered among the reprobate, rejected by God (*OED sb.* B, citing this line); cf. *Homilies*, 128.

7 **If that . . . were** For the conditional form and 'that' as a conjunctional affix, see Abbott, 287, 371. One of Wilson's linguistic 'tangles'.

8 **cousins** relatives (*OED sb.* 1)

2.2] *F (Scena Secunda.); not in Qq*   0.1–2] *F;* Enter Dutches of Yorke, with Clarence Children. *Qq*   1 SP] *Qq; Edw. F*   Good . . . us] *F;* Tell me good Granam *Qq*   3 SP] *F (Daugh.); Boy. Qq*   weep so oft] *F;* wring your hands *Qq*   5 SP] *F; Gerl. Qq*   6 orphans, wretches] *F;* wretches, Orphanes *Qq*   7 were] *F;* be *Qq*   8 both] *F;* much *Qq*   10 not . . . death] *F, Q1–5;* now . . . dead *Q6*

It were lost sorrow to wail one that's lost.

BOY

Then you conclude, my grandam, he is dead.

The King mine uncle is to blame for it.

God will revenge it, whom I will importune

With earnest prayers, all to that effect.   15

DAUGHTER

And so will I.

DUCHESS

Peace, children, peace. The King doth love you well.

Incapable and shallow innocents,

You cannot guess who caused your father's death.

BOY

Grandam, we can, for my good uncle Gloucester   20

Told me the King, provoked to it by the Queen,

Devised impeachments to imprison him;

And when my uncle told me so, he wept,

And pitied me, and kindly kissed my cheek,

11 A remarkable objection, given the copious wailing for the lost in this play; cf. Dent, T127: 'For a lost thing care not.'

12 **conclude** reach the conclusion, demonstrate, prove (*OED v.* 9)

13 *****to blame** F, Qq have 'too', perhaps meaning 'too blameworthy, culpable'; see *OED* blame *v.* 6, citing this line, and Abbott, 73 (cf. *1H4* 3.1.173; *Oth* 3.3.214).

14 **God . . . it** Cf. 2.1.139 and also Clarence's more tentative, but self-serving, invocation of divine vengeance (1.4.214–18).
importune beg (*OED v.* 4)

15 **all** entirely

18 **Incapable and shallow** unable to take in (*OED a.* I 2) and deficient in ordinary capacity (*OED a.* I 5);

for *shallow* referring to inadequacy, see 3.2.24, 4.4.361, 4.4.431, 5.3.219. Contrast the many uses of *deep* (e.g. 2.1.38, 4.2.42).

20 **good** Richard will be called *good* by allies and those seeking favour, but this is the first time that he has been so called since Henry VI rejected the epithet as 'preposterous' (*3H6* 5.6.2–5).

22 **impeachments** charges

23 **wept** On Richard's tears and the theatrical Vice, see Spivack, 399.

24 **kindly** affectionately, lovingly, with sympathy (*OED adv.* 2), but, given subsequent references to family relationships, with a sense of that which is natural, especially among kin (*OED a.* 1, 2); cf. 1.4.233–41 and More's ironic reference to Richard as a 'kindly king' (*CW2*, 83).

11 sorrow to wail] *F;* labour to weepe for *Qq*   12 you . . . grandam] *F;* Granam you conclude that *Qq*   13 mine . . . it] *F;* my . . . this *Qq*   to] *F, Qq (too), F2*   15 earnest] *F;* daily *Qq*   16] *F; not in Qq*   21 to it] *F; not in Qq*   23 my uncle] *F;* he *Qq*   24 pitied me] *F;* hugd me in his arme *Qq*   cheek] *F, Q2–5;* checke *Q1;* cheekes *Q6*

Bade me rely on him as on my father,   25
And he would love me dearly as a child.

DUCHESS

Ah! That deceit should steal such gentle shape,
And with a virtuous visor hide deep vice.
He is my son, ay, and therein my shame,
Yet from my dugs he drew not this deceit.   30

BOY

Think you my uncle did dissemble, grandam?

DUCHESS   Ay, boy.

BOY

I cannot think it. Hark, what noise is this?

Enter QUEEN [ELIZABETH] *with her hair about her ears,*
RIVERS *and* DORSET *after her.*

QUEEN ELIZABETH

Ah! Who shall hinder me to wail and weep,
To chide my fortune, and torment myself?   35
I'll join with black despair against my soul
And to myself become an enemy.

26 *a Qq's 'his' is attractive, given the
   blandness of 'love me dearly as a
   child'.
27 *Ah! F frequently follows introductory exclamations with exclamation
   marks (e.g. 34, 62, 80, 86). Q1 has no
   such exclamatory punctuation in this
   scene.
   shape guise, disguise (*OED sb.*[1] 7); by
   1604 the term occurs with a theatrically
   specific sense, meaning make-up and
   costume suited to a part (*OED sb.*[1] 8).
28 **visor** mask to conceal the face (*OED
   sb.* 2), used figuratively for an outward
   appearance concealing something

(*OED sb.* 3a)
30 **dugs** breasts; cf. Dent, E198: 'He
   sucked evil from the dug.'
33.1 **with . . . ears** Dishevelled hair signalled emotional extremity, especially
   grief (cf. *TC* 2.2.96 SD; Dessen &
   Thomson, 107).
33.2 *On Qq absence of Rivers and
   Dorset here and abbreviation elsewhere, see pp. 451–4.
37 The divided self is an image for
   despair, desperation (cf. 5.3.185–90)
   or civil dissension (2.4.63–4); warring
   upon oneself is a metaphor for self-
   destructiveness (cf. 1.2.83–8).

25 Bade] *F (*Bad*);* And bad *Qq*   [2]on] *F, Q2–6;* in *Q1*   26 a] *F;* his *Qq*   27 Ah!] *F;* Oh *Qq*   shape]
F; shapes *Qq*   28 visor . . . vice] *F;* visard hide foule guile *Qq*   29 ay,] *F (*I,*);* yea, *Q1–3;* yea
Q5–6; om. Q4   33.1–2] *F (the Queene); Enter the / Quee. Qq (subst. opp. 33–4)*   33.1 ELIZABETH]
Malone   34 Ah! Who] *F;* Oh who *Q1–2, 4;* Wh who *Q3;* Whoy *Q5 (Edin., Hn, Fo 1);* Who
Q5–6   36 soul] *F, Q1–4;* selfe *Q5–6*

DUCHESS

What means this scene of rude impatience?

QUEEN ELIZABETH

To make an act of tragic violence.

Edward, my lord, thy son, our king, is dead. 40

Why grow the branches, when the root is gone?

Why wither not the leaves that want their sap?

If you will live, lament; if die, be brief,

That our swift-winged souls may catch the King's,

Or like obedient subjects follow him 45

To his new kingdom of ne'er-changing night.

DUCHESS

Ah, so much interest have ^QI^Q in thy sorrow

38–9 **scene . . . act . . . tragic** As else-where (3.5.1–11), the play employs common theatrical discourse, building on *shape* and *visor* (27, 28); see p. 6.

38 **rude** violent, harsh (*OED a.* A I 5)
impatience failure to bear suffering with equanimity (*OED* 1), conveying emotional distress; cf. *JC* 4.3.150.

39 i.e. to enact a violent action and emotion proper to tragic narrative; *make* may mean 'make up' or 'complete', as in *Cym* 1.4.9 (Thompson).

40 **Edward** King Edward actually died in 1483; Clarence had been dead since 1478.
lord i.e. husband

41–2 probably proverbial, roughly paralleled in *E3* 2.1.419–20. Shaheen detects an echo of John, 15.4–6: 'As the braunche can not beare fruite of it self, except it byde in the vine . . . he is cast foorth as a braunch, and withereth.' Given another nearby echo possibly from Kyd's *Spanish Tragedy* (see 46n.), the invocation of vegetative nature might recall Isabella's laments for her murdered son, pro-

claiming, 'I will not leave a root, a stalke, a tree, / A bowe, a branch, a blossome, nor a leaf' (Kyd, *Spanish Tragedy*, 4.2.10–11).

41 *gone Hammond, following Patrick, argues that Qq's 'witherd' confuses what is clear and apt in F, which has King Edward, the root, gone and not merely withered.

42 **want** lack

43 **brief** expeditious or hasty (*OED a.* 1b)

44 **swift-winged** swift-wingèd

46 *ne'er-changing night This phrase and its Qq alternative ('perpetuall rest') have occasioned debate about relative merits, especially since Qq approximate 1.4.47 ('the kingdom of perpetual night'). F recalls *The Spanish Tragedy* ('Through dreadfull shades of ever glooming night', Kyd, 1.1.56); Qq resemble *Doctor Faustus* (see 1.4.47n.).

47–8 **interest . . . title** legal metaphors: to have 'interest' is to possess a right to a share in something (*OED sb.* I 1c); 'title' is the right to the possession of property (*OED sb.* 7a).

---

39 make] *F, Qq;* mark *Cam¹ (Maxwell)*   40 thy] *F;* your *Qq*   41 when . . . gone] *F;* now . . . witherd *Qq*   42 that . . . sap] *F;* the sap being gone *Qq*   46 ne'er-changing night] *F;* perpetuall rest *Qq*

As I had title in thy noble husband.
I have bewept a worthy husband's death
And lived with looking on his images;   50
But now two mirrors of his princely semblance
Are cracked in pieces by malignant death,
And I, for comfort, have but one false glass
That grieves me when I see my shame in him.
Thou art a widow, yet thou art a mother,   55
And hast the comfort of thy children left;
But death hath snatched my husband from mine arms
And plucked two crutches from my feeble hands,
Clarence and Edward. O, what cause have I,
Thine being but a moiety of my moan,   60
To overgo thy woes and drown thy cries!

BOY

Ah, aunt! You wept not for our father's death.
How can we aid you with our kindred tears?

DAUGHTER

Our fatherless distress was left unmoaned;
Your widow-dolour likewise be unwept.   65

---

50 **with** i.e. by
50–1 **images . . . mirrors** i.e. children;
oddly, given the Yorkists' repeated rec-
ollections of Rutland's death (1.2.160–
1, 1.3.177–93), the Duchess fails to
invoke his memory, thinking only of
King Edward and Clarence as her
husband's *images*.
51–3 **mirrors . . . semblance . . . glass**
Cf. Lucretius' lament for his dead
daughter: 'Poor broken glass, I often
did behold / In thy sweet semblance
my old age new born; / But now that
fair fresh mirror dim and old, / Shows
me a bare-boned death by time out-

worn' (*Luc* 1758–61).
51 **semblance** the likeness of someone or
something (*OED* 2)
60 **moiety** half (see 1.2.252)
61 **overgo thy woes** surpass your lamentations
62–5 The children address Queen
Elizabeth.
63 **kindred** showing resemblance (*OED*
A 1b); belonging to family, relatives
(*OED* B 1b); allied in nature (*OED* B
2); cf. 24n.
65 i.e. may (or let) your grief as a widow
similarly be unbewept (Abbott, 365; cf.
1.3.206).

---

50 with] *F;* by *Qq*   54 That] *F;* Which *Qq*   56 left] *F;* left thee *Qq*   57 husband] *F;* children
Qq   58 hands] *F;* limmes *Qq*   59 Clarence and Edward] *F;* Edward and Clarence *Qq*   60 Thine . . .
a moiety] *F;* Then, . . . moity *Qq subst.*   moan] *F;* griefe *Q1–5;* selfe *Q6*   61 woes] *F;* plaints *Qq*
(plants *Q2*)   ²thy] *F, Q1–4;* the *Q5–6*   62 Ah] *F;* Good *Qq*   63 kindred] *F;* kindreds *Qq*   64 SP]
F; Gerl. Qq   65 widow-dolour] *F;* widdowes dolours *Qq*

QUEEN ELIZABETH

> Give me no help in lamentation,
> I am not barren to bring forth complaints:
> All springs reduce their currents to mine eyes,
> That I, being governed by the watery moon,
> May send forth plenteous tears to drown the world.   70
> Ah, for my husband, for my dear lord Edward!

CHILDREN

> Ah, for our father, for our dear lord Clarence!

DUCHESS

> Alas for both, both mine, Edward and Clarence!

QUEEN ELIZABETH

> What stay had I but Edward? And he's gone.

CHILDREN

> What stay had we but Clarence? And he's gone.   75

DUCHESS

> What stays had I but they? And they are gone.

QUEEN ELIZABETH

> Was never widow had so dear a loss.

---

66 **Give me** i.e. even if you give me (though possibly a command)

67 **barren ... forth** i.e. unable to give birth to

68–70 apocalyptic rhetoric demonstrating Queen Elizabeth's capacity for lamentation; she asks that the earth's sources of water all return their liquid to her eyes so that her tears may drown the world.

68 **reduce** i.e. be brought back (*OED* I 3); cf. 5.5.36 and Abbott, 365.

69 **governed ... moon** The moon's connection to tides is familiar in Shakespeare: Falstaff refers to his fortune's 'being governed, as the sea is, by ... the moon' (*1H4* 1.2.27–8); thus the moon is the 'watery moon' (*MND* 2.1.162).

71 ***dear** Qq's 'eire' or 'heire' would be

possible if the second half of Queen Elizabeth's line were taken to refer to the anticipated plight of her son Edward rather than to the death of her husband King Edward (but *both* in 73 makes this unlikely, DSK).

74–9 *Variants in phrasing subsequent to Q1 incline progressively towards rhetorical questions rather than exclamations (as in Q1 and F).

74 **stay** support (*OED sb.*² 1b)

77–9 **Was never ... Were never** i.e. there was/were never (Abbott, 414). Wilson detects 'Spenserism' ('Was neuer Prince so faithfull and so faire, / Was neuer Prince so meeke and debonair', Spenser, *Faerie Queene*, 1.2.23, ll. 4–5).

77 **dear** grievous, severe (*OED a.*² 2)

---

67 complaints] *F;* laments *Qq*   69 watery moon] *F;* watry moane *Qq*   71 Ah, for] *F;* Oh for *Qq*   dear] *F;* eire *Q1–2;* heire *Q3–6*   72, 75, 78 SP] *F (Chil.);* Am[bo][.] *Qq*   72 Ah] *F;* Oh *Qq*   74, 75 he's] *F;* he is *Q1–5;* is he *Q6*   76 stays] *F, Q1–5;* stay *Q6*   77 never] *F, Q1–3, 5–6;* euer *Q4*

CHILDREN

    Were never orphans had so dear a loss.

DUCHESS

    Was never mother had so dear a loss.

    Alas! I am the mother of these griefs.   80

    Their woes are parcelled; mine is general.

    She for an Edward weeps, and so do I.

    I for a Clarence weep, so doth not she.

    These babes for Clarence weep, ᵠand so do I;

    I for an Edward weep,ᵠ so do not they.   85

    Alas! You three, on me, threefold distressed,

    Pour all your tears. I am your sorrow's nurse,

    And I will pamper it with lamentation.

DORSET [*to Queen Elizabeth*]

    Comfort, dear mother. God is much displeased

    That you take with unthankfulness His doing.   90

    In common worldly things, 'tis called ungrateful

    With dull unwillingness to repay a debt

    Which with a bounteous hand was kindly lent;

    Much more to be thus opposite with heaven,

    For it requires the royal debt it lent you.   95

RIVERS

    Madam, bethink you, like a careful mother,

80–1 Cf. Hecuba's claim to all 'woes' (Seneca, *Troades*, 1060–2); see p. 76.

80 **mother** i.e. as the eldest authority figure of the house of York

81 **parcelled** divided up into small portions (*OED ppl. a.*)

84–5 *Hammond suggests compositor 'eye-skip' to explain F's abbreviation. Confusions here may result in part from a position spanning a page-break in F at sig. r4ʳ⁻ᵛ.

87 **nurse** one who suckles or cares for an infant (*OED sb.*¹ 1a)

89–100 *Absence of these lines from Qq, combined with other omissions, eliminates Rivers and Dorset from the scene.

92 **dull** insensible, obtuse (*OED a.* 1, 2)

94 **opposite** hostile, antagonistic, adverse (*OED a.* A 4a); cf. *TN* 2.5.144.

95 **For** because
   royal debt cf. Dent, G237: 'I owe God a death.' For the debt/death pun see *1H4* 5.1.126.

96 **bethink you** i.e. think

---

78 Were] *F;* Was *Qq*   78, 79 never] *F, Q1;* euer *Q2–6*   78, 79 so dear a] *F;* a dearer *Qq*   80 griefs] *F;* mones *Qq*   81 is] *F;* are *Qq*   82 an] *F; not in Qq*   83 weep] *Qq;* weepes *F*   84–5] *Qq; one line F*   85 weep] *Q1–3, 5–6; om. Q4*   so do not] *F, Q1;* and so do *Q2–6*   87 Pour] *F (Power), Q1 (Poure), Q3–6 (Powre);* Proue *Q2*   88 lamentation] *F;* lamentations *Qq*   89–100] *F; not in Qq*   89 SD] *Bevington*⁷

Of the young prince your son: send straight for him;
Let him be crowned. In him your comfort lives.
Drown desperate sorrow in dead Edward's grave
And plant your joys in living Edward's throne. 100

Enter RICHARD, BUCKINGHAM, [STANLEY, Earl of]
Derby, HASTINGS *and* RATCLIFFE.

RICHARD

Sister, have comfort. All of us have cause
To wail the dimming of our shining star,
But none can help our harms by wailing them.
– Madam my mother, I do cry you mercy;
I did not see your grace. Humbly on my knee 105
I crave your blessing. [*Kneels.*]

DUCHESS

God bless thee and put meekness in thy breast,
Love, charity, obedience and true duty.

RICHARD

Amen, [*rising; aside*] and make me die a good old man.

100 **plant** Lull suggests a play on the royal family name, Plantagenet; cf. 3.7.215.

100.1 *Enter* RICHARD Cibber entered weeping and commenting on his own performance in an aside; Kean took out a white handkerchief before coming forward (Hankey, 141). On the group that enters with Richard here, see 2.1.134 SDn.

100.2 RATCLIFFE For the second time F has Ratcliffe enter with Richard (see 2.1.44.1) only to remain silent; in Qq he does not appear until 3.3.

101 *Sister F (unlike Qq) has Richard here fulfil his sarcastic promise to address the Queen by a title he finds distasteful (1.1.109); cf. 2.2.143.

104 **I . . . mercy** i.e. I beg your pardon.

105–6 **on . . . blessing** For children asking a blessing upon greeting their parents and often kneeling while doing so, see *Tit* 1.1.164–6, *KL* 4.7.57–9 and *Cor* 2.1.169–73; for the historical practice, see Young. This is the second time Richard begs a female figure *humbly* – and hypocritically – upon his knee (see 1.2.181).

109–11 The solemn blessing often constituted an opportunity for early modern stage clowning; cf. *MV* 2.2.72–94; for Tarleton's blessing joke, see Peacham, 102–5 and Siemon, 'Power'.

109 SD *rising* Richard's rise here differentiates his *Amen* from his subsequent words, which are clearly not directed

100.1–2] *F; Enter Glocest. / with others. / Qq opp. 88, 101* 100.1 STANLEY, Earl of] *Theobald subst.* 101+ SP] *F (Rich.); Gl[o]. Qq* Sister] *F;* Madame *Qq* 103 help our] *F;* cure their *Qq* 106 your] *F, Q1–5;* you *Q6* SD] *Cam¹ after* grace *105* 107 breast] *F;* minde *Qq* 109 SD *rising*] *Ard² subst.* aside] *Collier; after 111 Hanmer* and] *F, Q1–5; om. Q6*

That is the butt-end of a mother's blessing;   110
I marvel that her grace did leave it out.
BUCKINGHAM
You cloudy princes and heart-sorrowing peers
That bear this heavy mutual load of moan,
Now cheer each other in each other's love.
Though we have spent our harvest of this king,   115
We are to reap the harvest of his son.
The broken rancour of your high-swoll'n hates,
But lately splintered, knit and joined together,
Must gently be preserved, cherished and kept.
Meeseemeth good that with some little train   120
Forthwith from Ludlow the young Prince be fet
Hither to London, to be crowned our king.
RIVERS
Why with some little train, my lord of Buckingham?

to at least some onstage audience members.
aside Most recent editors follow Collier in taking *Amen* as spoken aloud, with subsequent lines uttered aside.
110 **butt-end** mere concluding part (*OED sb.* 1b, citing this line); Jowett suggests *butt* as in cask (*OED sb.²*), a sardonic pun given the copious lamentation for Clarence's death in this scene.
112 **cloudy** gloomy, sullen, troubled (*OED a.* 6b); cf. *Luc* 1084.
113 **moan** grief; cf. 'mass of moan' (*TC* 2.2.107).
117–19 Buckingham's images urge that limbs, previously broken by factional division and still swollen, be gently handled to permit continuation of a healing process that was recently begun when they were splinted by King Edward's attempts at reconcilia-

tion. Cf. 'To show the rancour of their high-swoll'n hearts' (*E3* 3.1.131).
118 **splintered** splinted (*OED v.* 2, citing this line); cf. *Oth* 2.3.317–18.
120 **Meeseemeth** it seems to me
train retinue, body of attendants (*OED sb.¹* III 9a); Buckingham also suggests removing the Prince from his allies in *True Tragedy* (409–13), but More's Richard persuades the Queen to this action without Buckingham's input (*CW2*, 16–17).
121 **Ludlow** castle in Shropshire near the Welsh border, 150 miles from London
fet fetched (an obsolete form: *OED* fet)
123–40 *On the possible theatrical economy that might explain Qq omission, see 89–100n. The lines explain the strategic decision to greet the Prince with a reduced train. The decision is described as treachery in *Mirror* ('Rivers', 365–92,

110 That is] *F*; Thats *Qq*   a] *F, Q1*; my *Q2–6*   111 that] *F*; why *Qq*   113 heavy mutual] *F*; mutuall heauy *Qq*   115 of] *F, Q1*; for *Q2–6*   116 son] *F, Q1–5* (sonne); soone *Q6*   117 high-swoll'n] *F* (high-swolne), *Qq* (high swolne)   hates] *F*; hearts *Qq*   118 splintered] *F, Q1* (splinter'd); splinted *Q2–6*   119 gently] *F, Q1*; greatly *Q2–6*   121 fet] *F*; fetcht *Qq*   123–40] *F; not in Qq*   123] *Pope; F lines* Traine, / Buckingham? /

BUCKINGHAM

    Marry, my lord, lest by a multitude

    The new-healed wound of malice should break out,   125

    Which would be so much the more dangerous

    By how much the estate is green and yet ungoverned.

    Where every horse bears his commanding rein

    And may direct his course as please himself,

    As well the fear of harm as harm apparent,   130

    In my opinion, ought to be prevented.

RICHARD

    I hope the King made peace with all of us,

    And the compact is firm and true in me.

RIVERS

    And so in me, and so, I think, in all.

    Yet since it is but green, it should be put   135

    To no apparent likelihood of breach,

    Which haply by much company might be urged;

    Therefore I say with noble Buckingham

    That it is meet so few should fetch the Prince.

HASTINGS

    And so say I.   140

RICHARD

    Then be it so, and go we to determine

519–53). More represents the logic here articulated by Buckingham as Richard's own. The parts have sometimes been editorially redistributed, often by exchanging the attribution of the speeches of Richard and Rivers at 132 and 134, but Richard may appear strategically lukewarm to allow Rivers the opportunity to talk himself into the proposed arrangement (Hammond).

124 **Marry** indeed

127 **By . . . green** to the extent that the condition of the state is immature; *green* refers to the newness of the peace brokered by King Edward.

128 **bears . . . rein** commands himself according to his own will (rather than submitting to a master)

129 **as please himself** i.e. as it should please him (the horse)

132 **with** i.e. among

134 The agreement of Rivers with Buckingham's devious recommendation is remarkable, but perhaps the play here represents the helpless confusion or deluded shortsightedness of the characters who surround Richard. Lull suggests intimidation by Buckingham at 123–4.

135 **green** See 127n.

137 **haply** perhaps

    urged incited, impelled (*OED* urge *v.* II 3)

139 **meet** appropriate

Who they shall be that straight shall post to Ludlow.
– Madam, and you my sister, will you go
To give your censures in this business?

^QQUEEN ELIZABETH, DUCHESS
With all our hearts.^Q   145

Exeunt all but Buckingham and Richard.

BUCKINGHAM

My lord, whoever journeys to the Prince,
For God's sake let not us two stay at home;
For by the way I'll sort occasion,
As index to the story we late talked of,
To part the Queen's proud kindred from the Prince.   150

RICHARD

My other self, my counsel's consistory,

---

142 **post** hasten, as on post-horses (*OED sb.*² III 8i)

143 **sister** Cf. 101n.; Thompson favours Qq's wording, which puts the queen-dowager first, since Richard would appropriately address the ranking person before addressing his mother. Dyce argues that F's version, which has Richard first addressing his mother, allows him a subtle insult to Elizabeth; however, Marshall counters that first addressing his own mother, who is after all Elizabeth's elder, implies no disrespect for the Queen, who is not herself a queen regnant (see Var).

144 **censures** judgements, opinions (*OED sb.* 3)

145 *Most recent editors include this Qq line. It provides an opportunity for actors to register degrees of compliance and/or reluctance on the part of Queen Elizabeth and the Duchess of York in this matter. Qq's SP '*Ans.*' may be a corruption of '*Amb*' for '*Ambo*' ('both') (Marshall; cf. 2.2.72, 75, 78); '*Ans.*' might stand for 'Answer'

(Jowett; cf. Perkins, 1.162). Line 144 occupies the last line of the first column of F sig. r4^v; that position and the SDs which surround it – '*Exeunt.*' at the end of column a and, at the top of column b, '*Manet Buckingham, and Richard*' – may have resulted in confusion and F's omission of 145.

148 **sort occasion** i.e. choose an opportunity

149 **index** preface, introduction (*OED sb.* 5a); cf. 4.4.85. Buckingham will take the first step in the plot to separate Queen Elizabeth's family and followers from Prince Edward.

150 **Prince** Qq title Edward 'King', but he was never crowned and is referred to throughout the play as 'Prince'. Hall and Holinshed give '*Kyng Edwarde the fyft*' a chapter, but Hall's 1550 frontispiece shows the crown hovering above Edward's head. See Fig. 1.

151 **My other self** i.e. my close confidant (see Dent, F696: 'A friend is one's second self'); the idea appears in Aristotle, and Erasmus invokes it (31.31).

---

142 Ludlow] *Qq;* London *F*   143 sister] *F;* mother *Qq*   144 business] *F;* waighty busines *Qq*
145 SP] *Qq (Ans.)*   SD] *F (Exeunt. Manet Buckingham, and Richard.); Exeunt man. Glo. Buck.*
Qq   146 whoever] *F, Q1–3, 5–6;* who *Q4*   147 God's] *Qq;* God *F*   stay] *F, Q1;* be *Q2–6*   at home]
F; behinde *Qq*   149 late] *F, Q1;* lately *Q2–6*   of] *F, Q1–2;* off *Q3–6*   150 Prince] *F;* King *Qq*

My oracle, my prophet, my dear cousin,
I, as a child, will go by thy direction:
Toward Ludlow then, for we'll not stay behind.   *Exeunt.*

2.3   *Enter one* Citizen *at one door, and* Another *at the other.*

1 CITIZEN

Good morrow, neighbour; whither away so fast?

2 CITIZEN

I promise you, I scarcely know myself.
Hear you the news abroad?

1 CITIZEN   Yes, that the King is dead.

2 CITIZEN

Ill news, by'r Lady. Seldom comes the better.

---

consistory council chamber; thus Buckingham would be figuratively the meeting room in which Richard's counsels may be articulated to himself. The notion of Buckingham as an echo-chamber is apt, at least at this point in the play. Richard's own secret 'counsels' with himself and his yes-man also stand in punning place of the learned 'councils' demanded by humanist notions of right rule. Of course we, as audience members, also share Richard's confidences.

152 **oracle** person of great wisdom or knowledge; cf. *H8* 3.2.104.

prophet given the importance of prophecy and curse in the play, a striking term to make light of here.

153 **as a child** Compare this sinister remark from the notorious child-slayer with other invocations of childish vulnerability at 26, 1.2.162 and 4.3.8.

2.3 location: '*a Street near the* Court' (Theobald). This scene was usually cut, from Cibber until the mid-20th century, but it has been important to later productions (Hankey, 144). More

mentions 'muttering amonge the people, as though al should not long be wel' (*CW2*, 44) in response to the several councils of June 1483 (see 3.1.179).

0.1 **Citizen** inhabitant of a city or town, especially one possessing civic rights and privileges, as a burgess or freeman (*OED* 1)

1 **neighbour** anyone who lives nearby, but, with *masters* (9) and *friends* (18), suggesting the idiom of an urban middling sort; cf. Menenius to Rome's 'Citizens' as 'masters, my good friends, mine honest neighbours' (*Cor* 1.1.61).

3 **abroad** i.e. currently circulating

4 **by'r Lady** by Our Lady (an oath by the Virgin Mary)

Seldom . . . better See Dent, B332; accepting what one has rather than hoping for something better. Cf. the political ballad (appending a picture of Elizabeth I) 'Seldome comes the better: Or, An admonition to all sorts of people . . . to auoid mutability, and to fix their minds on what they possesse' (pr. 1629; STC 22179).

---

153 as] *F;* like *Qq*   154 Toward] *F;* Towards *Qq*   Ludlow] *Qq;* London *F*   we'll] *F;* we will *Qq*   SD] *F; Exit. Q3–6; not in Q1–2*   **2.3**] *F (Scena Tertia.); not in Qq*   0.1] *F; Enter two Cittizens. Qq subst.*   1, 2, 6 SP] *F, Qq (1. Cit., 2. Cit., 3. subst.;* I, 2, 3 *throughout)*   1 Good morrow, neighbour] *F;* Neighbour well met *Qq*   whither] *F (whether), Qq*   3] *Steevens; F, Qq line* abroad? / dead. /   Hear] *F;* I *(SP)* Heare *Qq*   SP] *F (1.);* 2 *Qq*   Yes] *F;* I *Qq*   4 SP] *F (2.);* I *Qq*   Ill] *F;* Bad *Qq*

I fear, I fear, 'twill prove a giddy world.   5

Enter another Citizen.

3 CITIZEN

Neighbours, God speed.

1 CITIZEN   Give you good morrow, sir.

3 CITIZEN

Doth the news hold of good King Edward's death?

2 CITIZEN

Ay sir, it is too true, God help the while.

3 CITIZEN

Then, masters, look to see a troublous world.

1 CITIZEN

No, no, by God's good grace, his son shall reign.   10

3 CITIZEN

Woe to that land that's governed by a child.

2 CITIZEN

In him there is a hope of government,

Which in his nonage, council under him,

---

5   **giddy** mad, insane, foolish (*OED a.* 1)

6   **God speed** i.e. may God cause you to prosper.

7   **Doth . . . hold** i.e. is the news confirmed?

8   **God . . . while** i.e. may God help us in the meanwhile; an expression of grief.

9   **masters** title of compliment, used vocatively like 'sirs' (*OED sb.*[1] 20); here an address appropriate to male heads of household (*OED sb.*[1] 5a) or guild members (*OED sb.*[1] 15a); see 1n.
    troublous causing trouble or grief; troubled, disordered

11   From Ecclesiastes, 10.15–16; cf. More (*CW2*, 74); Hall ('woo to that realme whose king is a child', *Edward V*, fol.

xxii[r]'); and Dent, W600. In *1H6* anxieties about infant rulers and dangerous *emulation* (25) are accompanied by the claim that even a 'simple man' can predict ill events in a 'factious' court (4.1.187–91).

12–15   i.e. he shows promise that he may govern well, first with a good *council* governing in his name, and then in his own right when he comes of age; this difficult passage prompted Johnson and Malone to conjecture a missing line. The emphasis on proper counsel for the child contrasts with the inside joke about *counsel* made by the factiously childlike Richard (2.2.151–3).

13   **nonage** condition of being under age; the period of legal infancy (*OED* 1)

---

5 giddy] *F;* troublous *Q1;* troublesome *Q2–6*   5.1] *F; Ent. ano-* / *ther Citt. Qq opp. 5–6*   6] *Steevens; F lines* speed. / sir. / ; *Qq differ*   Neighbours, God speed.] *F;* Good morrow neighbours. *Qq* 1 CITIZEN . . . sir.] *F; not in Qq*   7 the] *F;* this *Qq*   King] *F, Q1–2, 4, 6;* Kings *Q3, 5*   8 2 CITIZEN Ay . . . while.] *F;* 1 *(SP)* It doth. *Qq*   10 good] *F, Q1;* om. *Q2–6*   13 Which] *F;* That *Qq*

And in his full and ripened years, himself,
No doubt shall then, and till then, govern well. 15

1 CITIZEN

So stood the state when Henry the Sixth
Was crowned in Paris but at nine months old.

3 CITIZEN

Stood the state so? No, no, good friends, God wot,
For then this land was famously enriched
With politic grave counsel; then the King 20
Had virtuous uncles to protect his grace.

1 CITIZEN

Why, so hath this, both by his father and mother.

3 CITIZEN

Better it were they all came by his father,
Or by his father there were none at all,
For emulation who shall now be nearest 25
Will touch us all too near, if God prevent not.
O, full of danger is the Duke of Gloucester,
And the Queen's sons and brothers haught and proud;
And were they to be ruled, and not to rule,

---

16 **Henry the Sixth** Henry became king at nine months of age in 1422; see *2H6* 4.9.4. During his minority, England was governed by royal council under the direction of the Bishop of Winchester and the dukes of Bedford and Gloucester.

18 **wot** knows

19 **famously** probably conveying a sense of 'excellently' (cf. *Cor* 1.1.35)

20 **politic** judicious, expedient (*OED a.* A 2a)
grave respected, dignified (*OED a.* 1, 3a)

21 **virtuous uncles** the Bishop of Winchester (actually a great-uncle) and the dukes of Bedford and Gloucester,

elsewhere called 'wurthy' (*Mirror*, 'Salisbury', 104–5), though *1H6* and *2H6* depict their violent, often selfish contentions

25 **emulation** ambitious rivalry for power or honours; contention between rivals
nearest i.e. to the Prince in trust

26 **touch . . . near** i.e. concern us all too seriously

27 More reports popular opinion that Gloucester would be likely to take the throne on Edward's death (*CW2*, 9).

28 **haught** haughty, high in their own estimation; cf. *3H6* 2.1.168.

29 **And . . . ruled** i.e. if indeed they were to be ruled by others

---

16 Henry] *F;* Harry *Qq* 17 in] *F;* at *Qq* nine] *F, Q1, 3–6 subst.;* xi. *Q2* 18 No . . . wot] *F;* no good my friend not so *Qq* 22 SP] *F; 2 Qq* Why, so . . . his] *F;* So . . . the *Qq* 23, 24 his] *F;* the *Qq* 25 who shall now] *F;* now, who shall *Qq* 26 Will] *F, Q1;* Which *Q2–6* 28 sons . . . haught] *F;* kindred hauty *Qq* 29 ²to] *F, Q1–5; om. Q6*

This sickly land might solace as before.   30

1 CITIZEN

Come, come, we fear the worst; all will be well.

3 CITIZEN

When clouds are seen, wise men put on their cloaks;
When great leaves fall, then winter is at hand;
When the sun sets, who doth not look for night?
Untimely storms makes men expect a dearth.   35
All may be well; but if God sort it so,
'Tis more than we deserve, or I expect.

2 CITIZEN

Truly, the hearts of men are full of fear.
You cannot reason almost with a man
That looks not heavily and full of dread.   40

3 CITIZEN

Before the days of change, still is it so.
By a divine instinct, men's minds mistrust
Ensuing danger, as by proof we see
The water swell before a boisterous storm.
But leave it all to God. Whither away?   45

---

30 **solace** take comfort or consolation; cf.
RJ 4.5.47.
31 Cf. Dent, W912: 'It is good to fear the
worst.'
35 **Untimely** unseasonal
36 **sort** dispose, ordain (*OED v.*[1] I 1b); cf.
MV 5.1.132.
39 **cannot . . . with** can scarcely talk
with (*OED* reason *v.* 2; cf. 1.4.93, 159);
on 'almost' in negative sentences, see
Abbott, 29.
40 **heavily** with sorrow, grief, displeasure
(*OED adv.* 2)
41–4 More writes: 'before such great
thinges, mens hartes of a secret

instinct of nature misgiueth them. As
yᵉ sea wᵗout wind swelleth of himself
somtime before a tempest' (*CW2*, 44);
rendered almost verbatim in Hall and
Holinshed. For the Senecan original,
see *Thyestes*, 961–4.
41 **still** always
42 **instinct** instinct (Abbott, 490)
mistrust suspect the existence of or
anticipate the occurrence of (something evil) (*OED v.* 3)
43 ***Ensuing** F prints 'Pursuing', but
the catchword on the previous page is
'Ensuing'.
proof experience (*OED sb.* II 5)

---

31 SP] *F;* 2 *Qq*   will be] *F;* shalbe *Qq*   32 are seen] *F;* appeare *Qq*   33 then] *F;* the *Qq*   35
makes] *F;* make *Qq*   36 may] *F, Q1–5;* men *Q6*   38 SP] *F;* I *Qq*   hearts] *F;* soules *Qq*   fear] *F;*
bread *Q1–2;* dread *Q3–6*   39 You] *F;* Yee *Qq*   reason almost] *F (*reason (almost)*);* almost reason
Qq   40 dread] *F;* feare *Qq*   41 days] *F;* times *Qq*   43 Ensuing] *F (sig. r4ᵛ c.w.), Qq;* Pursuing *F (sig.
r5ᵛ)*   danger] *F;* dangers *Qq*   see] *F;* see. *Q1–2;* see, *Q3–6*   44 water] *F;* waters *Qq*   boisterous] *F
(*boyst'rous), Q1–2 (*boistrous), *Q3–6 (*boystrous)*

2 CITIZEN

Marry, we were sent for to the justices.

3 CITIZEN

And so was I. I'll bear you company.   *Exeunt.*

2.4   *Enter* ARCHBISHOP [of York], *young* [Duke of]
YORK, QUEEN [ELIZABETH] *and the*
DUCHESS ᵠof Yorkᵠ.

ARCHBISHOP

Last night, I hear, they lay at Stony Stratford,
And at Northampton they do rest tonight.
Tomorrow, or next day, they will be here.

46 **justices** It is unclear why and to whom the citizens have been summoned; perhaps to a sessions of the Justices of Assize to give evidence or serve on a jury (Wilson). Honigmann notes apparent contradiction with line 2.

2.4 location: '*the* Court' (Theobald); '*A Room in the Palace*' (Capell)

0.1 ARCHBISHOP Qq call the Archbishop 'Cardinall', the title of the Archbishop of Canterbury, Thomas Bourchier, who appears in 3.1 (where Qq call him 'Cardinall' and F closely follows Q3). There he urges delivering the young Duke of York from sanctuary. The prelate in the present scene who supports the flight to sanctuary is Thomas Rotherham, Archbishop of York. Rotherham was Lord Chancellor, his office providing him the Great Seal he promises (71–2); however, evidence suggests confusion about whether Rotherham or Bourchier actually held the Seal at this point (Mancini, 119n., 121n.). More's English version (followed by Holinshed, 3.716–17) con-

fuses the two figures, making York the priest of 3.1 (*CW*2, 27); Hall distinguishes them, having Rotherham advocate sanctuary in the events of 2.4 (*Edward V*, fols viiʳ, ixʳ). Cf. 3.1.0.

1 *hear** Many editors since Capell have favoured Q1–2 to prevent the ambiguity concerning the time they lay at Stony Stratford that is created by the past tense in Q3–6, F.

1, 2, 3 **they** the Prince and those thought to accompany him (see 43–4, 2.2.120–54)

1–2 **Stony Stratford . . . Northampton** F follows sources which have Prince Edward's travel from Ludlow towards London interrupted by Richard at Stony Stratford, where the Prince spent one night. After the arrest of Rivers, Grey and Vaughan, the Prince was taken away from London to Northampton, where he spent the next night (Hall, *Edward V*, fol. viʳ⁻ᵛ). Qq reverse the names of Northampton and Stony Stratford, showing geographical insight but not historical knowledge.

46 Marry, we were] *F;* We are *Qq*   justices] *F;* Iustice *Qq*   **2.4**] *F (Scena Quarta.); not in Qq*   0.1–3] *F (the Queene); Enter Cardinall, Dutches of Yorke, Quee. young Yorke. Qq subst.*   0.1 of York] *Rowe*   Duke of] *Rowe*   0.2 ELIZABETH] *Malone*   1+ SP] *F (Arch.); Car. Qq*   1 hear] *Q1–2;* heard *F, Q3–6*   Stony Stratford] *F;* Northhampton *Qq*   2 And . . . rest] *F;* At Stonistratford will they be *Qq*

DUCHESS

    I long with all my heart to see the Prince.

    I hope he is much grown since last I saw him.   5

QUEEN ELIZABETH

    But I hear no. They say my son of York

    Has almost overta'en him in his growth.

YORK

    Ay, mother, but I would not have it so.

DUCHESS

    Why, my good cousin, it is good to grow.

YORK

    Grandam, one night as we did sit at supper,   10

    My uncle Rivers talked how I did grow

    More than my brother. 'Ay,' quoth my uncle
        Gloucester,

    'Small herbs have grace; great weeds do grow apace.'

    And since, methinks I would not grow so fast

    Because sweet flowers are slow and weeds make haste.   15

DUCHESS

    Good faith, good faith, the saying did not hold

    In him that did object the same to thee.

    He was the wretched'st thing when he was young,

    So long a-growing, and so leisurely,

    That if his rule were true, he should be gracious.   20

---

9 **cousin** kinsman, relative (see 2.2.8n.)

12 ***uncle** Q1's 'Nnckle' is possibly an attempt to render 'nuncle' (cf. *KL* 1.4.170).

13 **grace** virtue or efficacy (*OED sb.* 13); cf. *RJ* 2.3.11–14.
    great . . . apace proverbial: 'An ill weed grows apace' (Dent, W238); cf. 3.1.103.
    apace rapidly

14 **since** i.e. since then (Abbott, 62)

16 **Good faith** i.e. in fact, truth to say (*OED sb.* 12b); cf. 23, 1.4.121n.
    hold prove true (*OED v.* II 23c, citing this line)

17 **object** apply, adduce

18 **wretched'st** most lacking in ability, capacity or character (*OED* wretched 5)

20, 21 **gracious** echoing the titular address ('your grace') appropriate to dukes, duchesses and archbishops and playing on the discussion of actual *grace*

ARCHBISHOP

And so no doubt he is, my gracious madam.

DUCHESS

I hope he is, but yet let mothers doubt.

YORK

Now by my troth, if I had been remembered,

I could have given my uncle's grace a flout

To touch his growth nearer than he touched mine.   25

DUCHESS

How, my young York? I prithee let me hear it.

YORK

Marry, they say my uncle grew so fast

That he could gnaw a crust at two hours old;

'Twas full two years ere I could get a tooth.

Grandam, this would have been a biting jest.   30

DUCHESS

I prithee, pretty York, who told thee this?

YORK

Grandam, his nurse.

DUCHESS

His nurse? Why, she was dead ere thou wast born.

---

21 SP *Most editors assign this line to the Archbishop, despite F's '*Yor.*' Little York does not address his *grandam* as *gracious madam*. Since the Archbishop is Archbishop of York, the three onstage Yorks create ample opportunity for confusion. Qq assign to '*Car.*'; cf. 37.

23 by my troth by my faith (a mild oath); see 1.4.121n.
   been remembered remembered (Abbott, 295)

24 uncle's grace York puns on the title *grace* and the attribute of *grace*. See also 13, 20, 21; cf. 2.1.120–33, 1.3.320.

flout mocking speech, jeer

25 i.e. to tease him about his size more tellingly than he mocked mine

27–8 Following Rous, More writes: 'It is for trouth reported, that the Duches his mother had so muche a doe in her trauaile, that shee coulde not bee deliuered of hym vncutte: and that hee came into the world with the feete forwarde . . . and (as the fame runneth) also not vntothed' (*CW2*, 8, 167n.) Cf. 4.4.49.

30 *biting Q2 misses the pun on *biting* as 'sharp', and later Qq follow.

---

21 SP] *Capell; Car. Qq; Yor. F* And] *F;* Why Madame, *Qq*   is . . . madam] *F;* is *Qq*   22 he is] *F;* so too *Qq*   25] *F;* That should haue neerer toucht his growth then he did mine. *Qq*   26] *Qq; F*   *lines* Yorke, / it. /   young] *F;* prety *Qq*   26, 31 prithee] *F; Qq (*pray thee*)*   27 say] *F, Q1;* say that *Q2–6*   28 old] *F, Q1–2, 4, 6;* hold *Q3, 5*   30, 32 Grandam] *F;* Granam *Qq*   30 biting] *F, Q1;* pretie *Q2–6*   31 this] *F;* so *Qq*   33 His nurse] *F, Q1; om. Q2–6*   wast] *F;* wert *Qq*

YORK

If 'twere not she, I cannot tell who told me.

QUEEN ELIZABETH

A parlous boy; go to, you are too shrewd.   35

DUCHESS

Good madam, be not angry with the child.

QUEEN ELIZABETH   Pitchers have ears.

Enter a Messenger.

ARCHBISHOP

Here comes a messenger. – What news?

MESSENGER

Such news, my lord, as grieves me to report.

QUEEN ELIZABETH

How doth the Prince?   40

MESSENGER

Well, madam, and in health.

DUCHESS

What is thy news?

MESSENGER

Lord Rivers and Lord Grey are sent to Pomfret,
And with them Sir Thomas Vaughan, prisoners.

DUCHESS

Who hath committed them?

---

35 **parlous** dangerously cunning, clever, mischievous (*OED a.* 2, citing this line); cf. 3.1.154–6.
   shrewd naughty (*OED* 1a), but also cunning, artful (*OED* 13)
36 SP *Qq assign to '*Car.*' (cf. 21).
37 **Pitchers . . . ears** proverbial: 'Small pitchers have wide ears' (Dent, P363); cf. *TS* 4.4.52.
37.1 *Messenger Patrick (21) argued that

Qq's '*Dorset*' here makes little dramatic sense because the Queen would greet her son; Urkowitz (450–2) suggests 'coldness between mother and son'. Variants suggest Qq revision to accommodate the replacement of 'Messenger' by Dorset. See 49n. and pp. 454–6.
43–4 See 1–2n.
43 **Pomfret** the castle at Pontefract, in Yorkshire; see 3.3.9n.

35 parlous] *F;* perilous *Qq*   36 SP] *F; Car. Qq*   37.1] *F; Enter Dorset. Qq (after 38 Q2)*   38] *F;* Here comes your sonne, Lo: M. Dorset. / What newes Lo: Marques? / *Qq subst.*   39+ SP] *F (Mes.);* Dor. *Qq*   39 report] *F;* vnfolde *Qq*   40 doth] *F;* fares *Qq*   42 thy] *F, Q1;* the *Q2–6*   news] *F;* newes then *Qq*   43–4] *Qq; F lines* Grey, / them, / Prisoners. /   44 And with] *F;* With *Qq*

MESSENGER   The mighty Dukes,   45
  Gloucester and Buckingham.
ARCHBISHOP   For what offence?
MESSENGER
  The sum of all I can, I have disclosed.
  Why, or for what, the nobles were committed
  Is all unknown to me, my gracious lord.
QUEEN ELIZABETH
  Ay me! I see the ruin of my house: 50
  The tiger now hath seized the gentle hind;
  Insulting tyranny begins to jut
  Upon the innocent and aweless throne.
  Welcome destruction, blood and massacre.
  I see, as in a map, the end of all.   55
DUCHESS
  Accursed and unquiet wrangling days,
  How many of you have mine eyes beheld?
  My husband lost his life to get the crown,

---

45 **committed** imprisoned
47 **can** i.e. have knowledge of (Abbott, 307); the Messenger says he has disclosed all that he knows.
48 **Why . . . what** *Why* may perhaps refer to the past cause for which they were imprisoned and *what* to the future object of that imprisonment (Abbott, 75); cf. *CE* 2.2.43–4: 'they say every why hath a wherefore'.
49 **lord** Qq's 'Lady' suggests an adaptation of this speech to the character of Dorset, who could be addressing his mother rather than his questioner (Var; cf. Davison, 168).
50 **my** F's 'my' is more appropriate for Queen Elizabeth speaking to an anonymous messenger; Qq's 'our' better fits mother speaking to son (Delius in Var; cf. *TxC*, 237).

51 **hind** female deer
52 **Insulting** scornfully triumphant (*OED ppl. a.*); cf. Death's 'insulting tyranny' (*1H6* 4.7.19).
  jut encroach; the same word as Qq's 'iet' (*OED* jet *v.²* I 1b); cf. *Tit* 1.2.64. Given Richard's lameness, there may be an association with the sense of 'jet' meaning to walk or move in an ostentatious manner, to strut or swagger (*OED v.¹* 1a); thus 'Insulting tyranny' would be deporting itself offensively while seizing the throne.
53 **aweless** inspiring no awe (*OED* 3, citing this line)
55 **map** metaphorically, an outline or projection of the future
  end outcome; destruction
56 **Accursed** accursèd

45–6 The . . . Buckingham] *Steevens; one line F, Qq* 48 or for] *F, Q1, Q3–6; or Q2* the] *F;* these *Qq* 49 lord] *F;* Lady *Qq* 50 ruin of my] *F;* downfall of our *Qq* 52 jut] *F;* iet *Qq* 53 aweless] *F;* lawlesse *Qq* 54 blood] *F;* death *Qq*

And often up and down my sons were tossed
For me to joy and weep their gain and loss.   60
And being seated, and domestic broils
Clean overblown, themselves the conquerors
Make war upon themselves, brother to brother,
Blood to blood, self against self. O preposterous
And frantic outrage, end thy damned spleen,   65
Or let me die, to look on earth no more.

QUEEN ELIZABETH
Come, come my boy, we will to sanctuary.
Madam, farewell.

DUCHESS   Stay, I will go with you.

QUEEN ELIZABETH
You have no cause.

ARCHBISHOP [*to Queen Elizabeth*]   My gracious lady, go,
And thither bear your treasure and your goods.   70
For my part, I'll resign unto your grace

---

61 **seated** i.e. on the throne
  broils conflicts (cf. *1H4* 1.1.3)
62 **Clean overblown** completely finished; cf. *TS* 5.2.3.
63–4 **Make . . . self** Cf. representations of civil contention elsewhere
  in Shakespeare ('this house against
  this house', *R2* 4.1.146; 'rebellious
  arm 'gainst arm', *Mac* 1.2.57) and at
  5.5.23–4. Cf. images of self-division at
  2.2.37, 5.3.186.
64 **preposterous** monstrous, contrary to
  natural order, to reason or to common
  sense (*OED* 2). King Henry claims
  'Good Gloucester' or 'good devil'
  would be 'preposterous' (*3H6* 5.6.4–5).
  On preposterousness in wider senses,
  see Parker.
65 **frantic** lunatic, insane; also used of
  diseases, attended with delirium (*OED*
  a. 1, 3a)

damned damnèd
  spleen violent ill-nature or ill-humour
  (*OED sb.* 6a)
66 *****earth** Qq's 'death' has in its favour
  the fact that the Duchess has just been
  talking about the violence of civil conflict.
67 **sanctuary** a church or other place
  in which a fugitive from justice, or
  a debtor, was entitled to immunity
  from arrest (*OED sb.*[1] II 5a). Here
  the reference is to the precinct of
  Westminster Abbey, a legal refuge
  for criminals and persons in danger
  until the dissolution of the monastery,
  and for debtors until 1602. Queen
  Elizabeth took 'her yonger sonne and
  her doughters oute of the Palyce of
  westminster in whiche shee then laye,
  into the Sainctuarye' (More, *CW2*,
  20–1).

63 brother to brother] *F; not in Qq*   64 Blood to blood] *F;* bloud against bloud *Qq after* themselues
63   66 earth] *F;* death *Qq*   68] *Steevens; F lines* farwell. / you. / ; *one line Qq*   Madam, farewell]
F; not in Qq   Stay . . . go] *F;* Ile go along *Qq*   69] *Steevens; F, Qq line* cause. / go, /   SD] *Malone
subst.*

244

The seal I keep; and so betide to me
As well I tender you and all of yours.
Go, I'll conduct you to the sanctuary.   *Exeunt.*

3.1   *The Trumpets sound. Enter young* PRINCE [Edward],
         the Dukes of Gloucester *and* BUCKINGHAM,
         [F]Lord[F] CARDINAL, [CATESBY,] *with others.*

BUCKINGHAM
Welcome, sweet Prince, to London, to your chamber.
RICHARD
Welcome, dear cousin, my thoughts' sovereign.

72 **seal** the Great Seal of England; for
the Archbishop's gift of the Seal to
Elizabeth, his second thoughts and
subsequent secret recovery of it,
fearing charges of 'ouermuch light-
nesse' and departure from precedent,
see Holinshed, 3.716; see also Hall,
Edward V, fol. vii[r].

72–3 **so . . . yours** So may my fortune
turn out as well as I take care of you
and your family.
*Note: The basic text for 3.1.1–166 is
Q1. Thus the order of texts collated is
different in this portion of the textual
apparatus. See p. 435.*

3.1 **location**: '*A Street*' (Capell)
0.1 *young* PRINCE Until Cibber, the
Prince and his brother were played by
boys (Tommy Kent and 'a little boy' in
1689–90). Cibber's 1700 cast includes
Mrs Allison and Miss Chock in these
parts; young women played them into
the 20th century (Hankey, 150).

0.3 **Lord** CARDINAL Thomas Bourchier,
Cardinal Archbishop of Canterbury;
the identity of this figure suggests
indebtedness to Hall (contrast 195–6,
where Holinshed is the source; cf.
164n., 165n.). Holinshed follows
More's English version (*History*),
which has, through a mistake not in

the Latin, the Archbishop of York,
Thomas Rotherham (*CW2*, 27, 28,
194n.). If Shakespeare had followed
Holinshed, the same figure who aids
the Queen in 2.4 (called 'Cardinal' in
Qq) would now be coming round to
work for Richard; he would also have
re-entered immediately after speaking at the close of the previous scene,
an unusual violation of early modern
theatrical norms. For another interpretation of the Cardinal's apparent co-
operation with Richard, see 57n. The
churchmen may be, like the nobility,
divided. Historically, the Archbishop
of 2.4, Thomas Rotherham, was a
member of the Woodeville party, and
the Cardinal of 3.1, Thomas Bourchier,
among 'neutral councillors' (Hanham,
4–5). In *True Tragedy* a 'Cardinal'
persuades the Queen to abandon sanctuary (840–90).

1 **chamber** capital or metropolis (*OED
sb.* I 6); Hall and Holinshed repeat
More's terms for London – 'the kings
especiall chamber' (Holinshed, 3.729;
Hall, *Edward V*, fol. xx[r]).

2 **my thoughts' sovereign** The Prince
is Richard's actual sovereign, but
Richard turns regal address toward
sonneting usage; see *Son* 57.

74 Go] *F;* Come *Qq*   3.1] *F (Actus Tertius. Scæna Prima.); not in Qq*   0.1–166] *text is that of
Q1*   0.2 Dukes] *Q1–5, F; Duke Q6*   0.3 CATESBY] *Capell   with others] F; &c. Qq*   1] *Qq; F lines
London, / Chamber. /*   2, 7, 17, 181, 188, 190, 193, 198 SP] *F (Rich.); Glo. Qq*

The weary way hath made you melancholy.

PRINCE

No, uncle, but our crosses on the way
Have made it tedious, wearisome and heavy.   5
I want more uncles here to welcome me.

RICHARD

Sweet Prince, the untainted virtue of your years
Hath not yet dived into the world's deceit,
Nor more can you distinguish of a man
Than of his outward show, which, God He knows,   10
Seldom or never jumpeth with the heart.
Those uncles which you want were dangerous;
Your grace attended to their sugared words
But looked not on the poison of their hearts.
God keep you from them, and from such false friends.   15

PRINCE

God keep me from false friends, but they were none.

RICHARD

My lord, the Mayor of London comes to greet you.

Enter Lord MAYOR [*with others*].

MAYOR

God bless your grace with health and happy days.

---

4 **crosses** troubles, adversities (*OED* cross *sb*. B I 10b), i.e. the arrests of the Queen's relatives, referred to obliquely in 6; cf. 126 for a possible biblical echo.

5 **heavy** hard to perform or accomplish; laborious (*OED a*. VI 24a)

6, 12 **want** desire or lack (*OED v*. 2)
uncles Earl Rivers was the Prince's uncle, but Grey was his half-brother – continuing the apparent confusion about Grey (cf. 1.3.37n.).

9–11 i.e. you can tell no more about someone than you can glean from out-ward appearances, which, God knows, seldom or never coincide with inner reality (Abbott, 174); cf. 1 Samuel, 16.7: 'man loketh on the outward appearaunce, but the Lorde beholdeth the heart'; also Luke, 16.15.

10 **God He knows** i.e. God knows; see Abbott, 243.

11 **jumpeth** agrees completely, coincides (*OED* jump *v*. I 5)

17.1 **with others** The Prince's thanks to *you all* (19) reveal that the Mayor is accompanied.

8 Hath] *Q1–5, F;* Haue *Q6*   9 Nor] *Qq;* No *F*   16] *Qq; F lines* Friends, / none. /   from] *Q1–3, 5–6, F;* frõ such *Q4*   17.1 *with others*] *Folg; and his train. / Capell*   18 SP] *Qq (Lo: M.), F (Lo. Maior.)*

PRINCE

I thank you, good my lord, and thank you all.
I thought my mother and my brother York   20
Would long ere this have met us on the way.
Fie, what a slug is Hastings, that he comes not
To tell us whether they will come or no.

Enter Lord HASTINGS.

BUCKINGHAM

And in good time, here comes the sweating lord.

PRINCE

Welcome, my lord. What, will our mother come?   25

HASTINGS

On what occasion God He knows, not I,
The Queen your mother and your brother York
Have taken sanctuary. The tender Prince
Would fain have come with me to meet your grace,
But by his mother was perforce withheld.   30

BUCKINGHAM

Fie, what an indirect and peevish course
Is this of hers! – Lord Cardinal, will your grace
Persuade the Queen to send the Duke of York
Unto his princely brother presently?
– If she deny, Lord Hastings, go with him,   35

22 **slug** slow, lazy fellow, sluggard
24 **in good time** See 2.1.45n.
25 **What** interjection introducing an expression of surprise, exclamation or question (*OED adv.* 21, *int.* 1–2)
26 **On what occasion** for what reason
God . . . I See Dent, G189.1; cf. *Oth* 3.3.302, where 'Heaven knows, not I' may imply that Emilia does not *want* to know the reasons for what is happening.

29 **fain** gladly
30 **perforce** forcibly (*OED adv.* 1); see 36.
31 **indirect** devious
peevish foolish (cf. 1.3.193), but also perverse, headstrong, obstinate, capricious (*OED* 4)
course way of action, manner of proceeding
34 **presently** at once

23.1] *F; opp.* 23 *Qq (Enter L. Ha[st].)*   29 have come] *Q1–2, 4, F;* come *Q3, 5–6*   33 to send] *Q1–2, 4, 6, F;* thesend *Q3;* they send *Q5*   35 him] *Q1–4, F;* them *Q5–6*

247

And from her jealous arms pluck him perforce.

CARDINAL

My lord of Buckingham, if my weak oratory
Can from his mother win the Duke of York,
Anon expect him here; but if she be obdurate
To mild entreaties, God in heaven forbid   40
We should infringe the holy privilege
Of blessed sanctuary. Not for all this land,
Would I be guilty of so deep a sin.

BUCKINGHAM

You are too senseless-obstinate, my lord,
Too ceremonious and traditional.   45
Weigh it but with the grossness of this age,
You break not sanctuary in seizing him.

36 **jealous** suspicious, apprehensive of evil (*OED* 5)
   perforce Implications of moral or physical force (30) here become distinctly physical and violent.
39 **Anon** shortly, instantly
40–2 **God . . . sanctuary** Cf. the Cardinal's scruples: 'God forbyd that any manne shoulde, for any yeartely, enterprise to breake the immunyte and libertie of that sacred sanctuary' (Hall, *Edward V*, fols viii[v]–ix[r]).
42 **blessed** blessèd
44 **senseless-obstinate** unreasonably obstinate (*OED* senseless 3b), one of a number of unusual verbal compounds in the play (cf. 4.2.42, 4.4.55)
45 **ceremonious** punctilious in observing formalities (*OED* 5), but when coupled with accusations of being too *traditional*, a powerful charge to levy in the 1590s against a prelate. The *Book of Common Prayer* (1559) proclaims the long-standing Protestant rejection of 'ceremonial' emphases in worship (*BCP*, 19). Such strictures were balanced by fears of 'innovations and

newfangleness' and an emphasis on retaining those ceremonies that were in keeping with 'order' and 'quiet discipline in the Church' (*BCP*, 20).
46–7 *Frequently emended: how can the 'grossness of this age' – a phrase often taken to mean the 'lack of refinement' in habits, ideas or morality of the times – justify an argument asserting legal technicalities rather than indicting current mores? It has been argued that 46 should refer to the previous remarks about being too ceremonious and traditional. Dr Johnson suggested that the sense of the lines is that if one compare the act of seizure with the gross practices of these times it will not be considered wrong, for the act may be defended with the kind of coarse reasons men have grown accustomed to accepting (Var). Buckingham's self-serving pronouncements are frequently sophistic and may not sustain scrutiny for logical coherence.
47–56 A concise excerpt from an extended argument (*CW2*, 28–33, repeated

38 the] *Q1–2, 4–6, F;* to *Q3*   40 in heaven] *Q1–2; om. Q3–6, F*   43 deep] *Q1–2; great Q3–6, F*   44 senseless-obstinate] *Qq, F (sencelesse obstinate), hyphen Theobald*   46 grossness] *Q1–5, F; greatnesse Q6*

The benefit thereof is always granted
To those whose dealings have deserved the place
And those who have the wit to claim the place.   50
This prince hath neither claimed it nor deserved it
And therefore, in mine opinion, cannot have it.
Then taking him from thence that is not there
You break no privilege nor charter there.
Oft have I heard of sanctuary men,   55
But sanctuary children, never till now.

CARDINAL

My lord, you shall o'errule my mind for once.
– Come on, Lord Hastings, will you go with me?

HASTINGS

I go, my lord.

PRINCE

Good lords, make all the speedy haste you may.   60
                                        Exeunt Cardinal and Hastings.
Say, uncle Gloucester, if our brother come,
Where shall we sojourn till our coronation?

---

in Hall, and Holinshed, 3.718). Cf.
Richard's similarly specious reasoning
concerning an oath to Henry VI (*3H6*
1.2.22–7).
50 **wit** intelligence
54 **charter** privilege, immunity (*OED sb.*[1]
3)
   there in that respect
55–6 **sanctuary men ... children** This
claim from More (Holinshed, 3.718) is
not necessarily true for Shakespeare's
day (Machyn, 121).
56 ***never** Qq's 'neuer' is closer
to Holinshed than is F's 'ne're'
(Honigmann, 'Text', 50).
57 Motivation for the Cardinal's co-
operation is unclear. Mancini (89)
claims, 'the cardinal was suspecting

no guile, and had persuaded the queen
to do this, seeking as much to prevent a violation of the sanctuary as to
mitigate by his good services the fierce
resolve of the duke'.
60 **speedy haste** Does this redundancy
pun on Hastings's name? *Leicester's
Commonwealth* (1584) plays on the
Hastings family name of the Earl of
Huntingdon, calling him 'the Hastie
Earle' (*Copy*, 106); cf. 'Hastynges I
am, whose hastned death, whoe knewe'
(*Mirror*, 'Hastings', 1).
61–2 **our ... we** i.e. my ... I; the
Prince's first unambiguous royal
plural (cf. 4, 21, 23). He is now King
Edward V although not yet crowned.
See 96.

53 taking] *Q1–5, F;* take *Q6*   56 never] *Qq;* ne're *F*   57 o'errule] *F (*o're-rule*), Qq (*ouerrule*)   60
SD] *Q3–6, F opp. 59; not in Q1–2   Exeunt] Rowe; Exit Q3–6, F*

RICHARD

    Where it seems best unto your royal self.

    If I may counsel you, some day or two

    Your highness shall repose you at the Tower;   65

    Then where you please and shall be thought most fit

    For your best health and recreation.

PRINCE

    I do not like the Tower, of any place.

    – Did Julius Caesar build that place, my lord?

BUCKINGHAM

    He did, my gracious lord, begin that place,   70

    Which since succeeding ages have re-edified.

PRINCE

    Is it upon record, or else reported

    Successively from age to age, he built it?

BUCKINGHAM

    Upon record, my gracious lord.

PRINCE

    But say, my lord, it were not registered,   75

    Methinks the truth should live from age to age,

63–7 Beginning with an apparent offer of self-determination to the Prince, Richard's show of deference and tentative advice becomes insistence with his *shall*, only to morph again in his final ambiguous offer. The 'Machiavel who delights in manipulating others to do his bidding revealingly qualifies the ascription of choice to the prince in a line that could refer to himself but elides subject and agency: "shall be thought most fit"' (Dubrow, 357).

64 **some** On 'some' used with numeral adjectives qualifying nouns of time, see Abbott, 21.

65 **the Tower** The Tower had been used as a royal residence, even by Edward IV. According to Vergil 'this [lodging] causyd no suspytion' (178); but by Shakespeare's time it had acquired a sinister reputation, in part through the events depicted in this play. The murders of Henry VI and Clarence (cf. 144–5) would account for the Prince's reluctance.

68 **of any place** i.e. of all places; cf. Abbott, 409.

69–74 Buckingham affirms a legend; the oldest parts of the Tower, built close inside the city's Roman walls, date only to the 11th century (see Stow, 1.48).

71 **re-edified** rebuilt; cf. *Tit* 1.1.356.

72 **upon record** i.e. written down

75 **registered** set down in writing

63–154 SP] *Capell (Ric.)*; *Glo. Qg, F*   63 seems] *Q1–2*; thinkst *Q3–6, F*

As 'twere retailed to all posterity,
Even to the general all-ending day.

RICHARD [*aside*]

So wise so young, they say, do never live long.

PRINCE

What say you, uncle?   80

RICHARD

I say, without characters fame lives long.
[*aside*] Thus, like the formal Vice, Iniquity,
I moralize two meanings in one word.

PRINCE

That Julius Caesar was a famous man,
With what his valour did enrich his wit,   85

77 **retailed** recounted, repeated to others (*OED v.* 2); cf. 4.4.335. See also 86.

78 **the . . . day** Judgement Day, the biblical end of the world (see 1.4.103–4). On its 'general trumpet' summoning all humanity, see *2H6* 5.2.40–3.

79 See Dent, L384: 'Too soon wise to live long'; but also presumed medical fact (see Bright, 54). Mancini, who knew the Prince's physician, John Argentine, writes that 'he gave . . . many proofs of his liberal education, of polite, nay rather scholarly, attainments far beyond his age' (93; cf. C. Ross, *Richard*, 71).

81 **characters** charàcters; writing (cf. *Son* 59), literally, written letters of the alphabet. Contrast written 'characters' as a defence against time in *MM* 5.1.10–13.

82 **formal Vice, Iniquity** the 'unmistakable' or 'precise' (*OED* formal 3, 6) stage figure of the Vice named Iniquity; cf. *1H4* 2.4.441. Vices often equivocate and invite audience appreciation for 'dexterity in deceit' (Spivack, 394–5). See pp. 6–8.

83 **moralize** interpret morally or symbolically (*OED* 1, citing this line); cf. *AYL* 2.1.44.

one word a single sentence, utterance (*OED* 1) or, perhaps, a single word. Cf. Speed's punning observation: 'your old vice still: mistake the word' (*TGV* 3.1.278). In *3H6* Richard uses 'word' to mean utterance (*3H6* 5.5.27). It is difficult to single out a word from Richard's lines for special notice; suggestions include *characters, say* or *lives long.*

84–8 A notoriously difficult speech, despite the apparent clarity of 87–8. For similarly idealistic (and ill-fated) pronouncements, see *LLL* 1.1.1–7; cf. *Son* 55, 63–5. For a counter-perspective on Caesar as an ambitious, bloody monster difficult to reconcile with his writings, see *Fennes Frutes* (1590; STC 10763), fol. 9ʳ⁻ᵛ. In *True Tragedy* Richard's simple formula – 'Valour brings fame, and fame conquers death' (397–8) – leaves 'wit' out of the equation.

85 **what** i.e. that with which (Abbott, 252)

78 all-ending] *Q1;* ending *Q2–6, F*   79 SD] *Johnson*   82 SD] *F2*   Thus] *Q1–5, F;* That *Q6*

His wit set down to make his valure live.
Death makes no conquest of this conqueror,
For now he lives in fame, though not in life.
I'll tell you what, my cousin Buckingham.

BUCKINGHAM

What, my gracious lord?   90

PRINCE

An if I live until I be a man,
I'll win our ancient right in France again
Or die a soldier as I lived a king.

RICHARD [*aside*]

Short summers lightly have a forward spring.

Enter young [Duke of] YORK, HASTINGS ^F*and*^F CARDINAL.

BUCKINGHAM

Now in good time here comes the Duke of York.   95

---

86 **set down** put into writing (*OED* set *v.*¹ 143a; cf. *Ham* 1.5.107), but given the proximity of *valure* and *conqueror*, possibly hinting at 'set down' meaning to besiege, to encamp an army (*OED* 143b), as *Cor* 5.3.1–2. 'Set down' also signified establishing a price for something (*OED* 143e), a meaning apparently irrelevant here except for the proximity of *enrich* and *valure* and the troublesome obscurity of the phrasing.

***valure** This term (Q1–2) has the same triple meaning as 'valour' (Q3–6, F), but *valure* reminds one of its polysemousness. Both terms could mean worthiness, courage and monetary or material value (*OED* valour 1a, 1c, 2, 3). The material sense is reinforced by reference to enrichment and by *retailed* in 77. *The Mirror of Friendship* (1584; STC 17979.7) uses 'valure' in all three senses (sigs Aiii^r, B6^v–B7^r, C1^r).

88 **lives in fame** Cf. *Tit* 1.1.161.
91 **An if** i.e. if
92 **ancient . . . France** the claim dating at least to Edward II's marriage in 1308 to Isabella, daughter of Philip IV of France, repeatedly asserted by English invasions during the Hundred Years' War (1337–1453). Henry V was named 'King of England and Heir of France' in 1420, but by 1453 his son, Henry VI, had lost what Henry V had gained in battle (see *1H6*, *2H6*). For Elizabethan invocation of Caesar's conquests and the English 'right' in France, see the *Preface* to *The Eight Books of Caius Julius Caesar* (1590; STC 4336).
94 proverbial (Tilley, F774: 'Sharp frosts bite forward springs'); Dent excludes.
    lightly probably, commonly (*OED* 6)
    forward early (*OED a.* 5b; cf. *TGV* 1.1.45), playing on 'forward' as presumptuous, pert (*OED a.* 8); see 155.
95 **in good time** i.e. just at the right moment

---

86 valure] *Q1–2;* valour *Q3–6, F*   87 this] *Q1;* his *Q2–6, F*   91 An] *Qq, F* (And), *Theobald*
94 SD] *Johnson*   94.1 Duke of] *Ard*²

PRINCE

    Richard of York, how fares our loving brother?

YORK

    Well, my dread lord – so must I call you now.

PRINCE

    Ay, brother, to our grief, as it is yours.

    Too late he died that might have kept that title,

    Which by his death hath lost much majesty.   100

RICHARD

    How fares our cousin, noble lord of York?

YORK

    I thank you, gentle uncle. O my lord,

    You said that idle weeds are fast in growth.

    The Prince my brother hath outgrown me far.

RICHARD

    He hath, my lord.

YORK   And therefore is he idle?   105

RICHARD

    O my fair cousin, I must not say so.

YORK

    Then he is more beholding to you than I.

RICHARD

    He may command me as my sovereign,

    But you have power in me as in a kinsman.

---

96 **our** The Prince's royal plurals signal his difference in rank from his brother (see 61–2n.).

97 **dread** held in awe, revered (*OED ppl. a.* 2); appropriate to his now kingly brother, but probably with playful exaggeration as in York's subsequent lines.

99 **late** lately, recently
  he Edward IV, their father
  that might i.e. who we wish would (Abbott, 313)

101 **cousin** kinsman

103 **idle** useless (*OED* 3); cf. 2.4.13n.

106 **must** Richard denies that the Prince is idle, but his utterance leaves open the possibility that he might say such a thing if it were not forbidden by deference.

107 **beholding** obliged (see 2.1.130)

109 **power . . . kinsman** For the range of interpersonal claims that could be empowered by early modern kinship relations, see Cressy, 'Kinship'.
  in . . . in over me in that I am

96 Richard] *Q6, F; Rich. Q1–5* loving] *Q1–2;* noble *Q3–6, F*   97 dread] *Q1–2;* deare *Q3–6, F*   105] *Steevens; Qq, F line* Lo: / idle? /

YORK

    I pray you, uncle, give me this dagger.   110

RICHARD

    My dagger, little cousin? With all my heart.

PRINCE

    A beggar, brother?

YORK

    Of my kind uncle, that I know will give,

    And being but a toy, which is no grief to give.

RICHARD

    A greater gift than that I'll give my cousin.   115

YORK

    A greater gift? O, that's the sword to it.

RICHARD

    Ay, gentle cousin, were it light enough.

YORK

    O, then I see you will part but with light gifts;

    In weightier things you'll say a beggar nay.

RICHARD

    It is too heavy for your grace to wear.   120

110–31 The 1970 Terry Hands prompt-book registers the tensions generated by young York's insults and petulance and Richard's barely concealed resentment and menace: Richard offered a toy, which York threw down, demanding the dagger, only to throw it down at *greater gift* (116). At *light gifts* (118) he stamped on the toy; the Prince cried out York's name ('Richard!') and picked up the toy, while York went for Richard's sword. When his uncle bent down for the dagger, York jumped on his back at 'bear me on your shoulders' (131), to be shaken off and fall to the floor (Hankey, 155).

110–11 **dagger** The prominence of Richard's dagger in the sources and, possibly, in early performances is suggested only here. See p. 84; cf. 4.1.84n.

111 **With … heart** Richard's superficially eager generosity suggests that he would give the Prince his dagger by stabbing him with it.

112 **A beggar** Are you now a beggar?

114 **toy** trifle (*OED sb.* II 5)
    grief trouble

116 **to it** that goes along with it (i.e. the dagger)

117–18 **light … light** light in weight … trivial, inconsequential

119 **weightier** more valuable or consequential
    say … nay deny one who begs

111 With all] *Q3–6, F;* withall *Q1–2*   114 grief] *Q1–5, F;* gift *Q6*   120 heavy] *Q1;* waightie *Q2–6, F*   your] *Q1–5, F;* you *Q6*

YORK

I weigh it lightly, were it heavier.

RICHARD

What, would you have my weapon, little lord?

YORK

I would, that I might thank you as you call me.

RICHARD   How?

YORK   Little.   125

PRINCE

My lord of York will still be cross in talk.

Uncle, your grace knows how to bear with him.

YORK

You mean to bear me, not to bear with me.

– Uncle, my brother mocks both you and me.

Because that I am little, like an ape,   130

He thinks that you should bear me on your shoulders.

---

121 Literally, 'I consider it light even if it were heavier'; figuratively, 'I consider it merely a trivial gift even if it were of more value or consequence'. On the inappropriateness of such a statement from someone who has just requested the dagger and on the oddity of Richard's response, see *TxC*, 239. Richard's *What* may signal surprise or incomprehension, and his line might mean 'What, do you want it or not?' Richard may resent the challenge to his verbal dominance.

122 **weapon** i.e. Richard's sword

123 ***as*** F's retention of Q3's mistaken 'as as' constitutes crucial evidence for Q3 as the basic text for F 3.1. See p. 435.

125 **Little** i.e. York would give him small thanks, just as Richard gives him little respect by terming him paltry, contemptible (*OED* little *a*. I 9).

126 **still** always

cross perverse, inclined to quarrel

(*OED a.* 5a); possibly introducing a play in 127 on Jesus's reference to one who does not 'beare his crosse' (Luke, 14.27); cf. 4.

130–1 **ape . . . shoulders** In popular entertainments a bear might carry a monkey on its shoulders, so York's insults suggest Richard's ungainliness and his shape recalling the burdened bear. Fools, too, carried apes (as does Will Somers in the anonymous Hampton Court painting of Henry VIII's family, *c*. 1545). For late Elizabethan association of ape-bearing and hunchbacks, see p. 33. As a little ape on Richard's shoulders, York recalls the image of the scolding jackanapes (*Almond*, sig. E4^r). York's triple play on *bear* – to endure, to carry and the animal – outpuns Touchstone (*AYL* 2.4.10–12). Richard's failure to respond verbally may suggest 'vulnerability' to 'contempt that he neither initiates nor directs' (Anderson, 115),

---

123 would,] *Q1;* would *Q2–6, F* as] *Q1–2, 4–6;* as as *Q3;* as, as, *F*   124–5] *F; one line Qq*   130 ape,] *Q1–4, F;* Ape. *Q5–6*

BUCKINGHAM [*aside*]

    With what a sharp-provided wit he reasons:

    To mitigate the scorn he gives his uncle,

    He prettily and aptly taunts himself.

    So cunning and so young is wonderful.   135

RICHARD [*to the Prince*]

    My lord, will't please you pass along?

    Myself and my good cousin Buckingham

    Will to your mother to entreat of her

    To meet you at the Tower and welcome you.

YORK [*to the Prince*]

    What, will you go unto the Tower, my lord?   140

PRINCE

    My Lord Protector needs will have it so.

YORK

    I shall not sleep in quiet at the Tower.

RICHARD   Why, what should you fear?

YORK

    Marry, my uncle Clarence' angry ghost.

    My grandam told me he was murdered there.   145

PRINCE

    I fear no uncles dead.

but strong stage reactions date back to Irving's 1896 production, which gave Richard a 'look of concentrated rage and hatred'. A related stage tradition (see e.g. Olivier's film and Sam Mendes's 1992 production) has York leap upon Richard's shoulders (see p. 115 and Fig. 9).

132 SD *aside* Capell suggested direction to Hastings, but perhaps an observation shared with the audience.

132 **sharp-provided** agile, pointed, ready for any occasion (here, with witticisms) (*OED* provided *ppl. a.* 2);

Richard's own *sharp* wit goes back to Vergil (227).

133 **scorn** taunt; cf. *1H4* 3.2.64.

134 **prettily** cleverly, skilfully (*OED* 1, citing this line)

135 **cunning** clever, skilful and/or crafty, guileful (*OED a.* 2, 5)

136 **pass along** continue on your way

140 **What,** The comma might be omitted, making the line less exclamatory (Jowett) and taking *What* as 'Why' (Abbott, 253; cf. *Tit* 1.1.192).

141 **needs** Q1 provides the syllable missing from Q2–6, F (Thompson).

132 SD] *Capell (to* Hastings.)   sharp-provided] *Qq, F (*sharpe prouided), *hyphen Theobald*   133 gives] *Q1–2, 4, F;* giue *Q3, 5–6*   136, 140 SD] *Folg, Bevington⁴*   141 needs] *Q1; om. Q2–6,* F 145 grandam] *F;* Granam *Qq*   murdered] *Qq (*murdred), *F (*murther'd)

RICHARD

Nor none that live, I hope.

PRINCE

An if they live, I hope I need not fear.

But come, my lord. With a heavy heart,   149

Thinking on them, go I unto the Tower.   ^F*A sennet.*^F

  Exeunt [all but] Richard, Buckingham ^F*and Catesby*^F.

BUCKINGHAM

Think you, my lord, this little prating York

Was not incensed by his subtle mother

To taunt and scorn you thus opprobriously?

RICHARD

No doubt, no doubt. O, 'tis a perilous boy,

Bold, quick, ingenious, forward, capable.   155

He is all the mother's, from the top to toe.

BUCKINGHAM

Well, let them rest. – Come hither, Catesby.

---

148 **An if** if; the Prince does not directly answer Richard's question, but suggests concern about his recently arrested relatives (see 2.4.43–6).

148–50 **they . . . them** referring to Rivers and Grey; Grey was the Prince's half-brother (see 6n., 1.3.37n.).

150 SD 1 *sennet* set of notes on a trumpet or cornet, signalling a ceremonial entrance or exit

152 **incensed** incensèd; incited to action (*OED v.*² 4)

153 **opprobriously** abusively (*OED* 1)

154 **perilous* Qq and F agree on 'perilous', but F employs the alternative 'parlous' at 2.4.35 (set by Compositor B). Both forms could convey danger as well as cunning. Q7–8 have 'perlous'.

155 **quick** full of vigour, energy or activity (*OED a.* III 19a)

 forward precocious, pert (*OED a.* 7, 8);

when Richard and his brothers coerce him into entailing the crown upon the Yorkist line, Henry VI calls them York's 'forward sons' (*3H6* 1.1.203).

 capable intelligent, competent; contrast the Duchess's *Incapable* grandchildren (2.2.18).

156 **mother's** In *3H6* Richard makes a similar claim about young Prince Edward of Lancaster: 'Whoever got thee, there thy mother stands, / For well I wot thou hast thy mother's tongue' (*3H6* 2.2.133–4).

 from . . . toe proverbial (Dent, T436).

157 Once again, as in 31–56 and 2.2.120–50, Buckingham appears to take charge. His prominence at such moments prompted 18th- and 19th-century cuts to effect a 'neutralization' of his part (Hankey, 151, 158).

 let them rest i.e. let them be

---

148 An] *Qq*, F (*And*), *Theobald* 149 With] *Qq;* and with F 150 SD2 *Exeunt . . . Buckingham*] *Qq*, F *subst.* (*Exeunt Prin. Yor. Hast. (Hast. Hast. Q3) Dors. manet, Rich. Buc[k]. Q1–4; Exeunt Prin. Yor. Hast. Dors manet. Bich. Buc. Q5; Exeunt Prin. Yor. Hast. Dors manet. Bish. Buc. Q6; Exeunt Prince, Yorke, Hastings, and Dorset. / Manet Richard, Buckingham, F*)

257

Thou art sworn as deeply to effect what we intend
As closely to conceal what we impart.
Thou knowst our reasons, urged upon the way.   160
What think'st thou? Is it not an easy matter
To make William, Lord Hastings, of our mind
For the instalment of this noble Duke
In the seat royal of this famous isle?

CATESBY

He for his father's sake so loves the Prince   165
That he will not be won to aught against him.

BUCKINGHAM

What think'st thou then of Stanley? Will not he?

CATESBY

He will do all in all as Hastings doth.

BUCKINGHAM

Well then, no more but this: go, gentle Catesby,
And as it were far off, sound thou Lord Hastings   170
How he doth stand affected to our purpose

160 **urged . . . way** discussed on the journey (from Ludlow to London)
163 **instalment** installation (*OED* 1, citing this line)
164 **seat royal** Richard 'sate in the seate roial' after being proclaimed king (Hall, *Richard III*, fol. xxv^r; Hardyng, *Richard III*, fol. lxxvii^v); More and Holinshed do not use the phrase. See evidence for Hall as source at 0.3n.; for Holinshed as source, see 195–6n.
165 **for . . . sake** i.e. for the sake of King Edward, the Prince's father; Hastings is Edward's 'chiefest friend' (*3H6* 4.3.11). Queen Elizabeth disliked Hastings 'for the great fauour the king bare him: and also for that she thought him secretlie familiar with the king in wanton companie' (Holinshed, 3.713).

167 *At this point F resumes full textual authority, no longer reprinting Q3 verbatim. This line is the last on sig. F2^r in Q3, 6.
170–7 Catesby's actions in 3.2 differ from his orders in 172–3 (Smidt, *Impostors*, 112), thus providing a possible explanation for absence of these lines from Qq. More characterizes Buckingham as speaking 'wyth some words cast out a farre of' (*CW2*, 46; cf. Holinshed, 3.722). Cf. 'It is better to sound a person with whom one deals, afar off, than to fall upon the point at first' (Bacon, *Works*, 6.493).
170 **far off** i.e. elliptically (cf. 3.5.93) **sound** discover by conversational means; cf. 3.4.16n.
171 **doth stand affected** i.e. is disposed

160 knowst] *F* (know'st), *Qq* (knowest) 161 think'st] *F; Qq* (thinkest) 167] *F resumes as text until 5.3.49* think'st] *F; Qq* (thinkest) Will not] *F;* what will *Qq* 169–71] *Pope; F lines* this: / off, / Hastings, / purpose, / ; *Qq line* this: / off, / affected / willing, / 170 far] *F;* a farre *Qq* thou] *F, Q1–2; om. Q3–6* 171 doth stand . . . to] *F;* stands . . . Vnto *Qq* our] *F, Q1–3, 5–6;* your *Q4*

And summon him tomorrow to the Tower
To sit about the coronation.
If thou dost find him tractable to us,
Encourage him, and tell him all our reasons.   175
If he be leaden, icy, cold, unwilling,
Be thou so too, and so break off the talk,
And give us notice of his inclination;
For we tomorrow hold divided councils,
Wherein thyself shalt highly be employed.   180

RICHARD

Commend me to Lord William. Tell him, Catesby,
His ancient knot of dangerous adversaries
Tomorrow are let blood at Pomfret Castle,
And bid my lord, for joy of this good news,
Give Mistress Shore one gentle kiss the more.   185

BUCKINGHAM

Good Catesby, go effect this business soundly.

CATESBY

My good lords both, with all the heed I can.

---

173 **sit about** discuss in council
179 **divided councils** separate meetings – one concerning the coronation, one in private consultation with Richard (at Crosby House according to Hall) about making him king. More says Richard and Buckingham 'set the lord Cardinall, the Archebishoppe of Yorke than lorde Chauncellor, the Bishoppe of Ely, the lord Stanley & the lord Hastinges than lord chamberleine, w^t many other noble men to commune & deuise about the coronacion in one place: as fast were they in an other place contryuyng the contrary, & to make the protectour kyng'. These proceedings occasioned 'muttering amonge the people' (*CW*2, 44).

181 SP *With this line the SPs for Richard in Qq and F, '*Glo.*' and '*Rich.*', stabilize until 3.7.245.
181 **Lord William** i.e. Hastings
182 **ancient knot** long-standing group (*OED* knot *sb.*[1] III 18); cf. *JC* 3.1.117.
183 **are let blood** i.e. will bleed; surgical bleeding here used euphemistically for execution
185 **Mistress Shore** More says Jane Shore became Hastings's mistress after King Edward's death (*CW*2, 53).
186 **soundly** thoroughly (*OED* 3)
187 **heed** care, attention (*OED sb.* 1a)

172–3] *F; not in Qq*   174] *F; if he be willing, Qq*   175 tell] *F; shew Qq*   177 the] *F; your Qq*   181+ SP] *F (Rich.); Glo. Qq*   184 lord] *F; friend Q1–5; friends Q2 (Hn 69352), Q6*   185 Mistress] *F, Q1–2; gentle Mistresse Q3–6*   186 go] *F; not in Qq*   187 can] *F; may Qq*

RICHARD

Shall we hear from you, Catesby, ere we sleep?

CATESBY

You shall, my lord.   189

RICHARD

At Crosby House, there shall you find us both. *Exit Catesby.*

BUCKINGHAM

Now, my lord, what shall we do if we perceive

Lord Hastings will not yield to our complots?

RICHARD

Chop off his head; something we will determine.

And look when I am king, claim thou of me

The earldom of Hereford and all the moveables   195

188–9 *A version of these lines occurs again at Qq 4.2.81. Catesby does not carry out this commission until the next morning; therefore Daniel (xix) reasons that the lines were transposed in revision of F to a place in Qq where they better fit the situation but were never struck out here. Jowett (381) argues that Qq's repetition is 'purposefully echoic, drawing attention to the compulsively repetitive nature of Richard's crimes'.

192 yield . . . complots assent to our conspiracies
    complots complòts (còmplots in 200)

193 *Hammond argues for Qq, with its familiar 'man' expressing Richard's 'hail-fellow-well-met tone'; White (290) appreciates F's pun on *determine* as 'bring to an end'. F's sequence has a characteristic feel: immediate decision ('Chop off his head') followed by teasing reference to *something* later to be *determine[d]* to justify the precipitous execution (cf. Richard's unspecified *secret intent* at 1.1.56–8 and vague com-

plots at 3.1.200).

194 look when as soon as

195–6 Holinshed, closely following More (*CW*2, 44), records that Richard agreed to Buckingham's 'quiet possession of the earldome of Hereford', and 'of his owne mind promised [Buckingham] a great quantitie of the kings treasure, and of his household stuffe' (3.721). Buckingham could claim the earldom of Hereford by descent from Thomas of Woodstock, who had been married to Eleanor, daughter and co-heiress of Humphrey de Bohun, Earl of Hereford, Essex and Northampton. Buckingham's claim to the Earldom of Hereford was a claim to the moiety of the Bohun possessions which, by the marriage of a younger co-heiress, had passed to an elder branch of the royal family (Thompson; cf. Horrox, 133; More, *CW*2, 267n.; Vergil, 192–3). See also 4.2.87–120. Hall does not include this material.

195 moveables moveable personal property (as opposed to real estate) (*OED* B *sb.* 2)

---

190 House] *F;* place *Qq*   SD] *F; opp. 189 Q3–6; not in Q1–2*   191] *Qq; F lines* Lord, / perceiue /
192 Lord] *F;* William Lo: *Qq*   193] *Qq; F lines* Head: / determine: / head; something . . . determine] *F;* head man, somewhat . . . doe *Qq*   195 Hereford] *F, Q1–2;* Herford *Q3–5;* Hertford *Q6*   all] *F; not in Qq*

Whereof the King my brother was possessed.

BUCKINGHAM

I'll claim that promise at your grace's hand.

RICHARD

And look to have it yielded with all kindness.

Come, let us sup betimes, that afterwards   199

We may digest our complots in some form.   *Exeunt.*

3.2   *Enter a* Messenger *to the door of Hastings.*

MESSENGER   My lord, my lord. [*Knocks.*]

HASTINGS [*within*]   Who knocks?

MESSENGER   One from the Lord Stanley.

HASTINGS [*within*]

What is't o'clock?

MESSENGER   Upon the stroke of four.

Enter Lord HASTINGS.

HASTINGS

Cannot my Lord Stanley sleep these tedious nights?   5

199 **betimes** soon

200 **digest** ponder, settle and arrange
methodically (*OED v.* 3), but, given *sup*
(199), also playing on physical digestion
complots See 192n.

3.2 location: '*before Lord* Hastings's
House' (Theobald)

0.1 *door* Elizabethan staging dictates the
Messenger's entry at one rear door to
knock at the other, with subsequent
entries and exits through the first door.
Mirror mentions Jane Shore in Hastings's
arms at this moment ('Hastings', 393–4);
many productions bring her on with him

(Hankey, 160). The knock at his door
ironically connects Hastings's guilty past
and doomed future: in *3H6* he knocks at
the city door of York for King Edward,
who falsely swears his innocence of any
plot against Henry VI (*3H6* 4.7.16).
Hall excoriates this perjury as meriting
punishments extending into the reign
of Richard III (*Edward IV*, fols ccxiv^v–
ccxv^r).

1–4 *Qq dialogue conveys that the speaker is a 'messenger' who knocks 'at the
door'. F's SDs typically specify such
details (Greg, *Problem*, 172).

196 was] *F; stood Qq*   197 hand] *F; hands Qq*   198 all kindness] *F; all willingnes Q1; willingnesse
Q2–6*   **3.2**] *F (Scena Secunda.); not in Qq*   0.1 *the door of*] *F; Lo: Qq*   1] *F;* What ho my Lord.
Qq SD] *Capell subst.*   2 SD] *Theobald* knocks?] *F;* Who knockes at the dore. *(dore? Q2–5;* coore?
Q6) Qq   3 One] *F;* A messenger *Qq*   4] *Steevens; F, Qq line* Clocke? / foure. /   SD] *Steevens; not in
F, Qq*   What is't o'clock] *F (*a Clocke*);* Whats a clocke *Qq*   4.1] *F; opp. 3 Qq*   5 my Lord Stanley]
F; thy Master *Qq*   these] *F, Q1;* the *Q2–6*   tedious] *F, Q1–2, 4, 6;* teditous *Q3, 5*

MESSENGER

So it appears by that I have to say.

First, he commends him to your noble self.

HASTINGS What then?

MESSENGER

Then certifies your lordship that this night

He dreamt the boar had razed off his helm.   10

Besides, he says there are two councils kept,

And that may be determined at the one

Which may make you and him to rue at th'other.

Therefore he sends to know your lordship's pleasure,

If you will presently take horse with him   15

And with all speed post with him toward the north,

To shun the danger that his soul divines.

HASTINGS

Go, fellow, go. Return unto thy lord.

Bid him not fear the separated council:

His honour and myself are at the one,   20

9 **certifies** informs
10 **boar** Richard's heraldic animal (1.3.227); Q1's 'beare' persists until Q6 changes to 'Boare', a remarkable persistence since Hastings's next Qq speech has 'boare' four times.
razed . . . helm slashed, torn off his helmet, suggesting erasing (razing) the heraldic family crest (see *Son* 25 for 'rased/razed' as erasure). More's Stanley dreamed 'that a bore with his tuskes so raced [Hastings and himself] bi the heddes, that the blood ranne aboute both their shoulders' (*CW2*, 50; cf. Hall, *Edward V*, fol. xiv'; Holinshed, 3.722).
11 **two councils** See 3.1.179.
*kept held (*OED v.* 34); since to 'keep counsel' means to keep something

secret (*OED v.* 31; cf. *RJ* 2.4.195), F's 'kept' may carry more sinister associations than Qq's 'held'.
12 **that** i.e. something
13 **rue** repent, regret
15 **presently** immediately
16 **post** ride quickly, see 1.1.146.
north perhaps towards Stanley's holdings in Lancashire or Hastings's in Leicestershire and Northampton (Hall, *Edward V*, fol. xiii'). Holinshed has Stanley advising escape 'so farre the same night, that they should be out of danger' by day (Holinshed, 3.723); *Mirror* has him suggest riding 'strayght homewarde' ('Hastings', 389).
17 **divines** predicts or prophesies (*OED v.* I 3, citing this line)
20 **His honour** i.e. Stanley

6 appears] *F;* should seeme *Qq* 7 self] *F;* Lordship *Qq* 8–9] *F; one line Qq* 8 What] *F;* And *Qq* 9] *F;* And then he sends you word. *Qq* 10 dreamt] *F;* dreamt to night *Qq* boar] *F, Q6;* beare *Q1–5* razed off] *F (rased off);* raste *Q1–4;* caste *Q5;* cast *Q6* 11 kept] *F;* held *Qq* 13 th'other] *F;* the other *Qq* 15 you will presently] *F;* presently you will *Qq* 16 with him toward] *F;* into *Qq* 18 Go, fellow] *F, Q1–2;* Good fellow *Q3–6* 19 council] *F (Councell);* counsels *Qq subst.*

And at the other is my good friend Catesby,
Where nothing can proceed that toucheth us
Whereof I shall not have intelligence.
Tell him his fears are shallow, without instance;
And for his dreams, I wonder he's so simple   25
To trust the mockery of unquiet slumbers.
To fly the boar before the boar pursues
Were to incense the boar to follow us
And make pursuit where he did mean no chase.
Go, bid thy master rise and come to me,   30
And we will both together to the Tower,
Where he shall see the boar will use us kindly.

MESSENGER
I'll go, my lord, and tell him what you say.   *Exit.*

Enter CATESBY.

CATESBY
Many good morrows to my noble lord.

HASTINGS
Good morrow, Catesby. You are early stirring.   35
What news, what news, in this our tottering state?

21 *good friend F follows More, Hall and Holinshed in having Hastings designate Catesby a trusted associate (Holinshed, 3.722); *Mirror*'s Hastings calls him 'the apple of myne eye' ('Hastings', 319–28). Qq's 'seruant' need not imply a menial position (see *OED sb.* 2e, 4a; cf. 1.2.209, Qq 3.7.57).
22 **toucheth** concerns
24 **instance** cause, motive (*OED sb.* I 2); sign, token or mark (*OED sb.* III 7; cf. *Luc* 1511)
26 **mockery** unreal appearance (*OED* 2); cf.

Mac 3.4.106: 'Unreal mock'ry, hence!'
32 **kindly** Hastings means that Richard will treat them with kindness, but 16th-century audiences would have been aware that Hastings will be notoriously dealt with in a manner that is in kind with Richard's violent, boarish nature; cf. 2.2.24n. and Hamlet's pun on 'kind' (*Ham* 1.2.65).
33 *Cf. Qq here and at 3.7.69 ('Ile tell him what you say my Lord.'); cf. 3.1.188–9n. for similar Qq repetition. For F repetition, see 110n.

21 good friend] *F;* seruant *Qq* 24 without] *F;* wanting *Qq* instance] *F, Q1;* instancie *Q2–6* 25 he's] *F;* he is *Qq* so simple] *F;* so fond *Q1–3, 5–6;* fond *Q4* 26 mockery] *F* (mock'ry), *Qq* 27 pursues] *F;* pursues vs *Q1–2;* pursue vs *Q3–6* 29 no chase] *F, Q1–3, 5–6;* to chase *Q4* 33 I'll . . . and] *F;* My gratious Lo: Ile *Qq* SD] *F, Q3–6; not in Q1–2* 33.1] *F; Enter / (Cates. Q1–2 opp. 33–4; Enter Catesby to L. Hastings. Q3–6* 36 tottering] *F* (tott'ring), *Qq*

CATESBY

It is a reeling world indeed, my lord,
And I believe will never stand upright
Till Richard wear the garland of the realm.

HASTINGS

How? Wear the garland? Dost thou mean the crown?   40

CATESBY   Ay, my good lord.

HASTINGS

I'll have this crown of mine cut from my shoulders
Before I'll see the crown so foul misplaced.
But canst thou guess that he doth aim at it?

CATESBY

Ay, on my life, and hopes to find you forward   45
Upon his party for the gain thereof;
And thereupon he sends you this good news,
That this same very day your enemies,
The kindred of the Queen, must die at Pomfret.

HASTINGS

Indeed, I am no mourner for that news,   50
Because they have been still my adversaries.
But that I'll give my voice on Richard's side
To bar my master's heirs in true descent,
God knows I will not do it, to the death.

CATESBY

God keep your lordship in that gracious mind.   55

---

39 **garland** The term appears in More, Hall (*Edward V*, fol. xxiᵣ) and *Mirror* ('Richard', 262).
42 **crown** i.e. head; cf. Stanley's dream (10) and Hastings's later beheading.
44 **canst thou guess** i.e. do you imagine
45 **forward** ready, eager (*OED a.* 6a)
46 **Upon his party** on his side (cf.

1.3.137)
51 **still** always
53, 57 **my master's** Edward IV's; cf. Richard's mocking use of *master's* at 3.4.39.
53 i.e. to prevent King Edward's heirs from inheriting the throne
54 **to the death** i.e. even though it cost my life (which it will)

38 will] *F;* it will *Q1–2;* twill *Q3–6*   40] *Qq; F lines* Garland? / Crowne? / How] *F, Q1–2;* Who *Q3–6*   43 Before I'll] *F;* Ere I will *Qq*   45 Ay . . . life] *F;* Vpon my life my Lo: *Qq*   50 that] *F, Q1–3, 5;* this *Q4, 6*   51 my adversaries] *F;* mine enemies *Qq*

HASTINGS

But I shall laugh at this a twelve-month hence,
That they which brought me in my master's hate,
I live to look upon their tragedy.
Well, Catesby, ere a fortnight make me older,
I'll send some packing that yet think not on't.   60

CATESBY

'Tis a vile thing to die, my gracious lord,
When men are unprepared and look not for it.

HASTINGS

O monstrous, monstrous! And so falls it out
With Rivers, Vaughan, Grey; and so 'twill do
With some men else that think themselves as safe   65
As thou and I, who, as thou knowst, are dear
To princely Richard and to Buckingham.

CATESBY

The princes both make high account of you –
[*aside*] For they account his head upon the Bridge.

HASTINGS

I know they do, and I have well deserved it.   70

Enter Lord STANLEY.

Come on, come on. Where is your boar-spear, man?
Fear you the boar and go so unprovided?

57–8 i.e. that I will see those who brought me into King Edward's disfavour suffer downfall and death

59 *Qq's line with Catesby breaking into Hastings's speech resembles similar interruptions in Qq's 3.4.30–1 (Davison).

60 **packing** Cf. 1.1.146.

68 **make . . . of** i.e. have high regard for; *high* is ironic in such contexts,

where advancing, rising or mounting are routinely associated with ascending to the gallows (cf. 4.4.242–3; Kyd, *Spanish Tragedy*, 3.2.98; *1H4* 1.2.37).

69 **account** expect, reckon or count on (*OED v.* I 2a)

upon the Bridge on London Bridge, where traitors' heads were displayed on poles

56 twelve-month] *F; Q1–5* (tweluemonth*), Q6* (twelmonth*)   57 which] *F; who Qq*   59 Well, Catesby] *F;* I tell thee Catesby. *Cat.* What my Lord? *Qq*   older] *F;* elder *Qq*   60 on't] *F;* on it *Qq*   65 that] *F; who Qq*   66 knowst] *F, Q3–6; Q1–2* (knowest*)   69 SD] *F4*   70 deserved it.] *F, Q1–2, 4, 6;* deserued i. *Q3, 5*   71 Come on, come on] *F;* What my Lo: *Qq*   72 go] *F, Q1–5;* goe you *Q6*

STANLEY

My lord, good morrow. – Good morrow, Catesby.
– You may jest on, but, by the Holy Rood,
I do not like these several councils, I.   75

HASTINGS

My lord, I hold my life as dear as ^Qyou do^Q yours,
And never in my days, I do protest,
Was it so precious to me as 'tis now.
Think you, but that I know our state secure,
I would be so triumphant as I am?   80

STANLEY

The lords at Pomfret, when they rode from London,
Were jocund, and supposed their states were sure,
And they indeed had no cause to mistrust;
But yet you see how soon the day o'ercast.
This sudden stab of rancour I misdoubt.   85
Pray God, I say, I prove a needless coward.
What, shall we toward the Tower? The day is spent.

HASTINGS

Come, come, have with you. Wot you what, my lord?

74 **Holy Rood** the cross of Christ
75 For emphatic repetition of 'I', see
  TGV 5.4.130: 'I care not for her, I.'
  several separate
76 *The meaning of Qq and F appears
  clear – Hastings values his own life as
  dearly as Stanley values his – but the
  lines have frequently prompted editorial intervention.
79 **but that I** i.e. if I did not
  state condition
80 **triumphant** exultant (*OED* 4)
84 **o'ercast** became overcast
85 **stab of rancour** unclear, probably

referring to Richard's move against the
Queen's faction
  misdoubt suspect (*OED* v. 3); cf.
  LLL 4.3.191.
86 **needless coward** i.e. fearful for no
  reason
87 *spent F's statement that day is 'spent'
  appears to contradict line 4. However,
  Marshall claims that Adonis' 'The
  night is spent' (*VA* 717) means that
  night has arrived and is well under way.
88 **have with you** i.e. I will accompany
  you.
  Wot know

75 councils, I] *F (*Councels, I*)*; councels I *Qq* 77 days] *F*; 78 so . . . as 'tis] *F*; more . . .
then it is *Qq* 81 at] *F, Q1–5*; of *Q6* 82 were] *F*; was *Qq* 83 they] *F, Q1–2*; *om. Q3–6* 84 o'ercast]
*F (*o're-cast*), Q3–6 (*orecast*)*; ouercast *Q1–2* 85 stab] *F*; scab *Qq* 86 I say] *F, Q1–3, 5–6*; *om.*
Q4 87] *F*; But come my Lo: shall we to the tower? *Qq* 88] *Pope; F lines* you: / Lord, / ; I go: but
stay, heare you not the newes, *Qq*

Today the lords you talked of are beheaded.

STANLEY

They, for their truth, might better wear their heads   90
Than some that have accused them wear their hats.
But come, my lord, let's away.

Enter a Pursuivant.

HASTINGS

Go on before. I'll talk with this good fellow.
Exeunt Lord Stanley and Catesby.
How now, sirrah? How goes the world with thee?

PURSUIVANT

The better that your lordship please to ask.   95

HASTINGS

I tell thee, man, 'tis better with me now
Than when thou met'st me last where now we meet.
Then was I going prisoner to the Tower
By the suggestion of the Queen's allies;
But now I tell thee – keep it to thyself –   100

---

90 **truth** honesty
91 **wear their hats** Fran Teague (private communication) agrees with Evans (1959) that this probably refers to Richard and Buckingham, who might wear the ducal cap in the presence of the monarch, no hat-like head-covering being allowed to any below the rank of duke.
92.1 *Qq follow More, Hall and Holinshed in naming this pursuivant 'Hastings'; see p. 457.
   Pursuivant royal or state messenger empowered to execute warrants; a junior heraldic officer attendant on the

heralds (*OED* 1, 2)
94 **sirrah** address used to men or boys, usually expressing contempt, reprimand or assumption of authority by the speaker
97 ***when . . . last** Qq's 'when I met thee' repeats Holinshed (3.723) and Hall (*Edward V*, fol. xvʳ) (Honigmann, 'Text', 49).
99 **suggestion** instigation
   allies kindred, relatives (*OED* II 3); Rivers was a chief instigator of Hastings's fall into disgrace with King Edward (More, *CW*2, 51); cf. 1.1.66–8.

---

89 Today the lords] *F;* This day those men *Qq*   talked] *Q1–2* (talkt*); talke *F, Q3–6*   91 hats] *F, Q1, 6;* hat *Q2–5*   92 let's] *F;* let vs *Qq*   92.1] *F; Enter Hastin. / (a Purssuant. / opp. 92–3 Q1–2, after 93 Q3–6*   93 on] *F;* you *Qq*   talk . . . fellow] *F;* follow presently *Qq*   SD] *F; opp. 92 Q3–6; not in Q1–2 Exeunt] Rowe; Exit F, Q3–6*   94 How now, sirrah] *F; Hast.* Well met Hastings *Qq*   95 your lordship please] *F;* it please your Lo: *Q1–2;* it please your good Lordship *Q3–6*   96 man] *F;* fellow *Qq*   97 thou met'st me] *F;* I met thee *Qq*

This day those enemies are put to death,
And I in better state than e'er I was.

PURSUIVANT

God hold it to your honour's good content.

HASTINGS

Gramercy, fellow. There, drink that for me.
Throws him his purse.

PURSUIVANT   I thank your honour.   *Exit.*

Enter a Priest.

PRIEST

Well met, my lord. I am glad to see your honour.   106

HASTINGS

I thank thee, good Sir John, with all my heart.
I am in your debt for your last exercise.
Come the next sabbath, and I will content you.
    ᑫ*He whispers in his ear.*ᑫ

PRIEST

I'll wait upon your lordship.   110

---

103 **hold it** i.e. preserve your condition
as it is
104 **Gramercy** thank you
drink that i.e. enjoy this
106, 110 *Qq omissions eliminate a
speaking part, but references to the
priest remain (Smidt, *Impostors*, 112).
David Troughton's Richard doubled
as this priest (Day, 210).
107 **Sir** title of respect given to a priest
(*OED sb.* II 11); cf. Sir Christopher
Urswick in 4.5. 'Sir John' was itself
a generic name for a priest (*OED*
John 3).
108 **exercise** i.e. religious observance
(*OED sb.* 10a; cf. *Oth* 3.4.41), probably

the rite of confession, *shriving work*
(113), which was remunerated by the
penitent in pre-Reformation England
(Lea, 1.404–11). Sermon, preaching or
prophesying (*OED sb.* 10c, citing this
line) are possible meanings; however,
a stage Puritan refers to 'exercise of
prayer' as apparently differing from
sermonizing or 'godly exhortation on
Sunday' (*Knack*, 1650–60).
109 **content** compensate to your satisfac-
tion (*OED v.* 4)
110 *i.e. I am at your service. F repeats
the phrase at 121, perhaps reinforcing
the sense in which Hastings occupies a structurally similar position

---

102 e'er] *F (ere);* euer *Qq*   104 fellow] *F;* Hastings *Qq*   There . . . me] *F;* hold spend thou that
Qq   SD] *F; He giues / (him his purse. Qq opp. 104–5*   105] *F;* God saue your Lordship *Qq*   SD]
F, Q3–6 (Exit Pursuiuaunt. (Pur. Q3–6)); not in Q1–2   105.1] *F; opp.* What Sir Iohn, you are wel
met, *which follows 105 Q1–2; opp. 105 Q3–6*   106] *F; not in Qq*   107] *F;* What Sir Iohn, you are wel
met, *Qq*   108 in your debt] *F;* beholding to you *Qq*   exercise] *F;* daies exercise *Qq*   109 SD] *opp.*
109–110.1 Qq   110] *F; not in Qq*

268

Enter BUCKINGHAM.

BUCKINGHAM

What, talking with a priest, Lord Chamberlain?
Your friends at Pomfret, they do need the priest;
Your honour hath no shriving work in hand.

HASTINGS

Good faith, and when I met this holy man
The men you talk of came into my mind.   115
What, go you toward the Tower?

BUCKINGHAM

I do, my lord, but long I cannot stay there.
I shall return before your lordship thence.

HASTINGS

Nay, like enough, for I stay dinner there.

BUCKINGHAM [*aside*]

And supper too, although thou knowst it not.   120
– Come, will you go?

HASTINGS   I'll wait upon your lordship.   *Exeunt.*

---

vis-à-vis Buckingham to that which
the priest occupies in his attendant
relation to Hastings. F, Qq provide
the priest no exit direction; *this holy*
man (114) suggests his presence (but
see 5.5.0.2–3n.). He may withdraw
from Hastings's immediate proximity upon Buckingham's appearance
(*TxC*, 240).
111 SP Holinshed, following More, has
Sir Thomas Howard 'merilie' ask
Hastings about his 'need of a priest'
(3.723; *CW2*, 51; cf. p. 56).
113 **shriving work** confession and abso-
lution; rites appropriate for those

about to die (cf. *Ham* 5.2.47, 'shriving
time').
in hand in process (*OED sb.* 29f)
114 **and** used emphatically in statements
after ejaculations (Abbott, 98)
119 **like** i.e. likely
stay i.e. stay for
120 **supper** Shaheen suggests the heavenly supper promised in Revelation,
19.9. Cf. Richard's threat: 'you shall
sup with Jesu Christ tonight' (*2H6*
5.1.214).
thou perhaps signifying secret contempt (Abbott, 233)
121 See 110.

111] *F;* How now Lo: Chamberlaine, what talking with a priest, *Qq*   115 The] *F;* Those *Qq*   116
toward] *F;* to *Qq*   Tower] *F;* tower my Lord *Qq*   117 do, my lord . . . cannot stay there] *F;* doe, . . .
shall not stay *Qq*   119 Nay] *F;* Tis *Qq*   120 SD] *Rowe*   knowst] *F, Q3–5; Q1–2 (*knowest*);* knowh
Q6   121] *Steevens; F lines* goe? / Lordship. / ; Come . . . along? *Qq*   will you go] *F;* shall we go
along *Qq*   I'll . . . lordship] *F; not in Qq*

3.3   *Enter* Sir Richard RATCLIFFE, *with Halberds,*
          carrying the nobles ^Q^RIVERS, GREY *and*
          VAUGHAN^Q^ *to death at Pomfret.*

RIVERS

Sir Richard Ratcliffe, let me tell thee this:
Today shalt thou behold a subject die
For truth, for duty and for loyalty.

GREY

God bless the Prince from all the pack of you.
A knot you are of damned bloodsuckers.   5

VAUGHAN

You live, that shall cry woe for this hereafter.

RATCLIFFE

Dispatch. The limit of your lives is out.

RIVERS

O Pomfret, Pomfret! O thou bloody prison,

3.3 location: 'Pomfret-*Castle*' (Theobald), i.e. Pontefract Castle in West Yorkshire. This is the only scene in the first four acts set outside London and Westminster.

0.1 *Halberds* guards bearing halberds; see 1.2.0.1n.

0.2 *carrying* leading as prisoners (Dessen & Thompson, 43)

2 **Today** More has this scene's events occurring as Hastings is beheaded in the Tower (*CW*2, 57); the play sandwiches 3.3 between Buckingham's ominous remark concerning Hastings (3.2.120) and his arrest and condemnation to immediate death (3.4.75).

4 **bless** protect, guard (*OED v.* I 3; cf. *KL* 3.4.56)
  pack set of persons, implying low

character, evil purpose, or the speaker's contempt (*OED sb.*[1] 3a); here and in *Tim* 5.1.112, 115 suggesting dogs in violent pursuit (Bate, *Ovid*, 147n.).

5 **knot** small group; cf. 3.1.182.
  damned damnèd

6 *Qq's omission of 6 appears deliberate, since 7 is virtually transferred to 23 (Thompson). This might save a speaking part here, but Vaughan remains in Qq's entry SD, is addressed in 24 and retains lines as a ghost (5.3.142–3). Cf. the Priest (Qq 3.2.106, 110).
  cry woe Cf. 'Woe, woe for England' (3.4.79).

7 **Dispatch** hurry
  The limit . . . out i.e. your lives have run their course.

3.3] *F (Scena Tertia.); not in Qq*   0.1 Richard RATCLIFFE] *F; Rickard Ratliffe Q1; Richard Ratliffe Q2–5; Richad Ratliffe Q6*   0.1–2 Halberds, carrying the nobles] *F; the Lo: Q1; the Lord Q2–6*   0.3 to . . . Pomfret] *F; prisoners Qq*   1] *F; Ratl. (Rat. Q3–6)* Come bring foorth the prisoners. / *Ryu.* Sir . . . this: *Qq*   4 bless] *F;* keepe *Qq*   6] *F; not in Qq*   7 Dispatch . . . lives] *F;* Come come dispatch, . . . linea *(*lines *Q2;* liues *Q3–6) Qq after 22*

Fatal and ominous to noble peers!
Within the guilty closure of thy walls,   10
Richard the Second here was hacked to death;
And for more slander to thy dismal seat,
We give to thee our guiltless blood to drink.

GREY

Now Margaret's curse is fall'n upon our heads,
When she exclaimed on Hastings, you and I,   15
For standing by when Richard stabbed her son.

RIVERS

Then cursed she Richard; then cursed she Buckingham;
Then cursed she Hastings. O, remember, God,
To hear her prayer for them, as now for us.
And for my sister and her princely sons,   20
Be satisfied, dear God, with our true blood,

9 **Fatal and ominous** Before the time
of the play's action, Pontefract Castle
saw the execution of Thomas, Earl of
Lancaster, for rebelling against Edward
II (1322), the murder of Richard II
(1400), the pre-execution imprisonment of Archbishop Scrope (1405)
and the murder of Richard Neville,
Earl of Salisbury (1460).

10 **closure** bound or limit

11 **Richard the Second** See *R2* 5.5.

12 **slander** discredit, disgrace, shame
(*OED sb.* 3)
dismal boding or bringing misfortune; unlucky, sinister (*OED a.* 2)
seat residence, abode

14–16 *Margaret does not curse
Grey but exclaims against Dorset
(1.3.209–13). Daniel suggests that
absence of 15 from Qq may represent
an attempt to avoid the discrepancy;
but Buckingham is not cursed by
Margaret, as is said in Qq 17 (Daniel,
xviii). Buckingham regards himself

as falling under Margaret's prophecies (5.1.25–7). Historically, Rivers,
Grey and Vaughan had no connection with the killing of Margaret's
son (More, *CW2*, 57–8). The play's
modifications emphasize a 'sym-
metrical pattern of retribution' (E.
Berry, 90–1).

14 **Margaret's curse** Cf. 3.4.91, 4.1.45,
5.1.25; this scene marks the first recollection and partial fulfilment of curses
from 1.3. The listing of those cursed
and of further potential victims (17–
20) prepares for Richard's subsequent
crimes and downfall (Clemen, 137).

18–22 **O . . . spilt** Hall's Vaughan
appeals to God, recalls the prophecy
about Edward's heirs, identifies 'G'
as Richard and proclaims his own
innocence (*Edward V*, fol. xvii^r–v); cf.
Mirror ('Rivers', 562–3). Holinshed
has Ratcliffe prevent the men from
speaking (3.725).

20–2 Cf. 1.4.69–72.

9 ominous] *F, Q1, 6;* dominious *Q2–3;* ominious *Q4–5*   12 seat] *F;* soule *Qq*   13 to thee] *F;* thee vp
Qq   blood] *F;* blouds *Qq*   14 Margaret's] *F, Q1–5;* Margarts *Q6*   is] *F, Q1–5;* if *Q6*   15] *F; not in
Qq*   17] *Qq; F lines Richard, / Buckingham, /*   17–18 Richard . . . Hastings] *F;* Hastings . . . Richard
Qq   19 prayer] *F;* praiers *Qq*   20 sons] *F;* sonne *Qq*   21 blood] *F;* blouds *Qq*

Which, as thou knowst, unjustly must be spilt.

RATCLIFFE

Make haste. The hour of death is expiate.

RIVERS

Come, Grey, come, Vaughan. Let us here embrace.   24
Farewell, until we meet again in heaven.   *Exeunt.*

3.4   *Enter* BUCKINGHAM, [STANLEY, Earl of] Derby,
HASTINGS, Bishop of ELY, NORFOLK,
RATCLIFFE, LOVELL, *with others, at a table.*

HASTINGS

Now, noble peers, the cause why we are met
Is to determine of the coronation.
In God's name speak: when is the royal day?

BUCKINGHAM

Is all things ready for the royal time?

---

23 **expiate** fully come (*OED ppl. a.*, citing this line); 'expiate' could mean 'end' (cf. *Son* 22). Here it may play on the idea of propitiation, echoing Rivers's prayer that God might be *satisfied* with their blood.

24–5 The embrace and anticipation of heavenly reunion ironically recall Warwick, Edward and Richard at the battle of Towton (*3H6* 2.3.42–5).

3.4 location: '*The Tower*' (Pope)

0.1–3 Qq's cast is abbreviated: Lovell is not here (nor anywhere in Qq); Norfolk (mute in F's 3.4) is not named; Qq do not mention F's '*others*'. Catesby replaces F's Ratcliffe (as in Qq 3.5), possibly because 3.3 depicts Ratcliffe in Yorkshire on the same day (but see 6 SPn.). This obvious contradiction in F is compounded by F's deviation

from early modern theatrical practice, which normally precluded re-entry in subsequent scenes (see p. 459 and Qq 'Cardinal' in 2.4, 3.1).

0.2 **Bishop of** ELY John Morton, later Archbishop of Canterbury (1486), Chancellor (1487) and Cardinal (1493); he was Thomas More's patron and perhaps his informant.

0.3 *at a table* '*to Councell*' (Qq) probably implies F's '*at a table*' (Dessen & Thomson, 58).

1–3 Hastings assumes control as Lord Chamberlain; cf. 1.1.77.

2 **determine of** decide about
coronation i.e. of Prince Edward as King Edward V

4 **Is* F's verb form is consistent with Stanley's response (*It is*); cf. 'Is all things well?' (*2H6* 3.2.11).

---

22 knowst] *F*; *Qq* (knowest*)*   23] *F*; *see above at 7 Qq*   24 here] *F*; all *Qq*   25 Farewell] *F*; And take our leaue *(*leaues *Q6) Qq*   again] *F*; *not in Qq*   **3.4**] *F (Scæna Quarta); not in Qq*   0.1–3] *F*; *Enter the Lords to Councell. Qq*   0.1 STANLEY, Earl of] *Theobald subst.*   1 Now, noble peers] *F*; My Lords at once *Qq*   3 speak] *F*; say *Qq*   the] *F*; this *Qq*   4 Is . . . ready for the] *F*; Are . . . fitting for that *Qq*

STANLEY

It is, and wants but nomination. 5

ELY

Tomorrow, then, I judge a happy day.

BUCKINGHAM

Who knows the Lord Protector's mind herein?

Who is most inward with the noble Duke?

ELY

Your grace, we think, should soonest know his mind.

BUCKINGHAM

We know each other's faces; for our hearts, 10

He knows no more of mine than I of yours,

Or I of his, my lord, than you of mine.

– Lord Hastings, you and he are near in love.

HASTINGS

I thank his grace, I know he loves me well;

But for his purpose in the coronation, 15

I have not sounded him, nor he delivered

His gracious pleasure any way therein.

But you, my honourable lords, may name the time,

And in the Duke's behalf I'll give my voice,

---

5 **wants but nomination** lacks only the naming of a date

6 SP *Q1's '*Ryu.*' (Rivers) is corrected by Q3 to '*Bish.*' Rivers has just been led to execution in 3.3. Perhaps Q1's compositor misread '*By.*' (Bishop) as '*Ry.*' (Hammond).

6 **happy** fortunate, favourable (*OED a.* 3)

8 **inward** intimate (*OED* A *a.* I 3)

10–12 Discussion of Richard's 'heart' recalls Anne's 'I would I knew thy heart' (1.2.195) and Richard's lec-

ture to the Prince about discrepancy between *outward show* and *the heart* (3.1.9–11), and anticipates 53–5. (Cf. Dent, F1.)

10 **for** as for

15 **purpose in** intention concerning

16 **sounded him** i.e. examined him in conversation; cf. 3.1.170n. on *sound*.

19 **give my voice** As Lord Chamberlain, Hastings would serve as the monarch's official mouthpiece (Chambers, *Stage*, 1.38).

5+ SP] *Theobald; Darb. F; Dar. Qq* 5 wants] *F, Q1–2;* let *Q3, 5–6;* lack *Q4* 6 SP] *F; Ryu. Q1; Riu. Q2; Bish. Q3–6* judge . . . day] *F;* guesse . . . time *Qq* 9+ SP] *F; Bi./By./Bish. Qq* 9 Your . . . think,] *F;* Why you my Lo: me thinks you *Qq* 10–12] *F;* Who I my Lo? we know each others faces: / But for our harts, he knowes no more of mine, / Then I of yours: nor I no more of his, then you of mine: / *Qq* 17 gracious] *F;* Graces *Qq* 18 honourable lords] *F;* noble Lo: *Q1–2;* L. *Q3–6*

Which I presume he'll take in gentle part.   20

Enter [RICHARD, Duke of] Gloucester.

ELY

In happy time, here comes the Duke himself.

RICHARD

My noble lords and cousins all, good morrow.
I have been long a sleeper, but I trust
My absence doth neglect no great design
Which by my presence might have been concluded.   25

BUCKINGHAM

Had you not come upon your cue, my lord,
William, Lord Hastings, had pronounced your part –
I mean your voice for crowning of the King.

RICHARD

Than my Lord Hastings, no man might be bolder;
His lordship knows me well, and loves me well.   30
– My Lord of Ely, when I was last in Holborn
I saw good strawberries in your garden there;

---

20 **in gentle part** graciously (as 'in good part': *OED* part *sb.* 26b)
22 **lords and cousins** Richard speaks to Buckingham and other relations; Qq's 'L.' could be singular or plural, so in Qq he might be singling out one addressee before turning to the others. 'Cousin' was also 'used by a sovereign in addressing or formally naming another sovereign, or a nobleman of the same country' (*OED sb.* 5a).
23 **been . . . sleeper** Richard attempts to appear uninterested in the proceedings; the claim is found in More. Cf. *True Tragedy* (925–6).

24 **neglect** cause to be neglected (*OED v.* 5)
26–7 **cue . . . part** Buckingham employs theatrical discourse (cf. 3.5.5–11).
28 **voice** i.e. opinion or vote; cf. 19.
32 **strawberries** This bizarre episode appears in More with no explanation for its motivation. Perhaps More records an anecdote (maybe from Morton himself) with no larger purpose; however, strawberries have emblematic connections to unseen treachery (cf. L.J. Ross). The episode conveys Richard's 'careless ease, in the midst of all his crimes' (Griffith,

---

20 he'll] *F;* he will *Qq* gentle] *F, Q1–5;* good *Q6* 20.1] *F;* Ent. Glo. *Q1–2 turned down below 21; Enter Gloster. Q3–6 after 21* RICHARD, Duke of] *Evans 1959* 21 In happy] *F;* Now in good *Qq* 22 lords] *F;* L. *Qq* 23 a sleeper] *F, Q1–5;* a sleepe *Q6* but] *F, Q1;* but now *Q2–6* trust] *F;* hope *Qq* 24 design] *F;* designes *Qq* 26 you not] *F;* not you *Qq* cue] *F (Q), Qq (*kew*), Rowe* 27 had] *F;* had now *Qq* your] *F, Q1–5;* you *Q6* 30 well.] *F;* well. / *Hast.* I thanke your Grace. / *Qq* 31 Ely, when] *F;* Elie, *Bish.* My Lo: / *Glo.* When *Qq*

I do beseech you, send for some of them.

ELY

Marry and will, my lord, with all my heart.

Exit Bishop [of Ely].

RICHARD

Cousin of Buckingham, a word with you.   35

[*They talk apart.*] Catesby hath sounded Hastings in
    our business,

And finds the testy gentleman so hot

That he will lose his head ere give consent

His master's child, as worshipfully he terms it,

Shall lose the royalty of England's throne.   40

BUCKINGHAM

Withdraw yourself awhile. I'll go with you.

Exeunt [Richard and Buckingham].

STANLEY

We have not yet set down this day of triumph.

Tomorrow, in my judgement, is too sudden,

For I myself am not so well provided

As else I would be, were the day prolonged.   45

Enter the Bishop of ELY.

---

317). Relaxed improvisation amid
otherwise tense circumstances is
characteristic of Richard until he gets
the crown.

34 **Marry and will** i.e. indeed I will (cf.
'Marry, and shall', *3H6* 5.5.42).

37 **testy** Jowett detects sardonic allusion
to the (early modern) French *teste*,
'head'.

39 **worshipfully . . . it** with due honour
he puts it

41 *****go with** Qq omit Buckingham from
the exit SD here and the re-entry at
57.1 (see p. 427).

42 **set down** established
triumph public festivity (*OED sb.* 4)

44 **provided** prepared

45 **prolonged** postponed (*OED v.* 3)

33 do] *F, Q1–3, 5–6;* now *Q4* 34] *F;* I go my Lord. *Qq* SD] *F; not in Qq of Ely*] *Rowe subst.*
35 of] *F; not in Qq* 36 SD] *Capell subst.* 37 testy] *F, Q1–3, 5–6;* resty *Q4* 38 That] *F;* As *Qq* ere]
*F, Q2–4, 6; Q1, 2 (BL, Hn 69352) (*eare*);* are *Q5* 39 child] *F;* sonne *Qq* worshipfully] *F;* wor-
shipfull *Qq* 41 yourself awhile] *F;* you hence my Lo: *Qq* go with] *F;* follow *Qq* SD *Exeunt*] *F;*
Ex. Gl. Qq subst. Richard and Buckingham] *Pope* 43 my judgement] *F;* mine opinion *Qq* sudden]
F, Q1; soone *Q2–6* 45.1] *F, Q3–6; Enter B. / of Ely. Q1–2 opp. 44–5*

ELY

> Where is my lord the Duke of Gloucester?
> I have sent for these strawberries.

HASTINGS

> His grace looks cheerfully and smooth this morning.
> There's some conceit or other likes him well
> When that he bids good morrow with such spirit.   50
> I think there's never a man in Christendom
> Can lesser hide his love or hate than he,
> For by his face straight shall you know his heart.

STANLEY

> What of his heart perceive you in his face
> By any livelihood he showed today?   55

HASTINGS

> Marry, that with no man here he is offended,
> For were he, he had shown it in his looks.

Enter RICHARD *and* BUCKINGHAM.

RICHARD

> I pray you all, tell me what they deserve

---

48 **smooth** i.e. smoothly, pleasantly (adverbial ellipsis; cf. 'lamely and unfashionable', 1.1.22); *looks* = directs the eyes (*OED v.* 1)
49 **conceit** idea, conception (*OED sb.* I 1)
likes him well pleases him (cf. *Ham* 5.2.242)
53 **straight** immediately
55 **livelihood** i.e. liveliness, animation (cf. *AW* 1.1.49–50); Qq's 'likelihood'

is possible, meaning 'a ground of probable inference' (*OED* likelihood 3).
57 *Qq follow with an unmetrical line for Stanley.
57.1 *Enter* RICHARD More's Richard returns 'al changed with a wonderful soure angrye countenaunce, knitting the browes, frowning and froting and knawing on hys lippes' (*CW2*, 47).

46–7] *F; one line Qq*   46 lord . . . Gloucester] *F;* L. protector *Qq*   48 this morning] *F;* to day *Qq*   49 well] *F, Q1–3, 5–6 (*well,*)*; well. *Q4*   50 that he bids] *F;* he doth bid *Qq*   such] *F;* such a *Qq*   spirit.] *F, Q1–4;* spirit, *Q5–6*   51 there's] *F;* there is *Qq*   52 Can] *F;* That can *Qq*   55 livelihood] *F;* likelihood *Qq*   57 were he] *F;* if he were *Qq*   had shown] *F (*had shewne*);* would haue shewen *(*shewne *Q6) Qq*   looks.] *F;* lookes. *(*face. *Q2–6) / Dar.* I pray God he be not, I say. / *Qq*   57.1] *F; Enter Glocester. Qq*   58 tell me what] *F;* what doe *Qq*

That do conspire my death with devilish plots
Of damned witchcraft, and that have prevailed   60
Upon my body with their hellish charms?

HASTINGS

The tender love I bear your grace, my lord,
Makes me most forward in this princely presence
To doom th'offenders, whosoe'er they be.
I say, my lord, they have deserved death.   65

RICHARD

Then be your eyes the witness of their evil.
Look how I am bewitched! Behold, mine arm
Is like a blasted sapling withered up;
And this is Edward's wife, that monstrous witch,
Consorted with that harlot, strumpet Shore,   70
That by their witchcraft thus have marked me.

HASTINGS

If they have done this deed, my noble lord –

---

59 **conspire** conspire for
59–65 **devilish . . . hellish . . . death**
  Charges of 'sorcery & witchcraft'
  come from More (*CW2*, 48), but not
  the stress on demonic association.
  Sixteenth-century English religious,
  legal and popular understandings of
  witchcraft did not stress devil worship or make supposed non-lethal
  bodily injury a capital offence (K.
  Thomas, 442). More's Richard advocates the special appropriateness of
  the death penalty on the basis of his
  royal blood (*CW2*, 48). For parallels in attitude and vocabulary see
  Newes. Peter Hall's 1963–4 production directs 'they all clap' at 65
  (Hankey, 170).
60 **damned** damnèd
63 **forward** ready, prompt, eager in a cause

presence company
64 **doom** condemn
65 **deserved** deservèd
67–71 Sources agree that 'no man
  was there present, but wel knew
  that his harme [i.e. arm] was euer
  such since his birth' (*CW2*, 48; cf.
  Mirror, 'Hastings', 574–6). More
  originates the charge of collabora-
  tion with Mistress Shore (Hanham,
  169; contrast Vergil, 180–1), noting its preposterousness, since the
  Queen would hardly collaborate with
  her late husband's lover, 'whom of
  all women she most hated' (*CW2*,
  48).
68 **blasted** blighted; stricken by supernatural agency (*OED ppl. a.* 1)
70 **Consorted** associated (*OED v.* 4)
71 **marked** markèd

63 princely] *F;* noble *Qq*   64 th'offenders] *F; Qq* (the offenders*)*   whosoe'er] *F;* whatsoeuer *Qq*   66
their evil] *F;* this ill *Qq*   67 Look] *F;* See *Qq*   69 And this is] *F;* This is that *Qq*   71 witchcraft]
F, Q1; witchcrafts *Q2–6*   72 deed . . . lord –] *Rowe;* deed . . . Lord. *F;* thing my gratious Lo: *Qq*

RICHARD

If? Thou protector of this damned strumpet,
Talk'st thou to me of ifs? Thou art a traitor.
– Off with his head! Now by Saint Paul I swear   75
I will not dine until I see the same.
– Lovell and Ratcliffe, look that it be done.
– The rest that love me, rise and follow me.
       Exeunt. Lovell and Ratcliffe remain with the Lord Hastings.
HASTINGS

Woe, woe for England, not a whit for me,
For I, too fond, might have prevented this.   80
Stanley did dream the boar did raze his helm,

---

73 **protector** wonderfully ironic, given the recent reiteration of Richard's official title as 'Lord Protector' (7) **damned** damnèd

74 **ifs** More's Richard berates Hastings for using 'iffes' and 'andes' (*CW2*, 48; cf. Hall, *Edward V*, fol. xiv^{r–v}; Holinshed, 3.722); see also Dent, I16. The *ifs* have elicited stage business: Charles Macready in 1821 struck a table for emphasis; Edwin Booth in the 1870s stamped his foot on the word to accompany his blows upon the table (Colley, 84, 110). In More, Richard's blow to the table signals entry of his armed men (cf. *Mirror*, 'Hastings', 583–4). Armed entry has been staged here since Phelps and Irving in the 1840s and 1870s (Hankey, 170).

75–6 **Saint Paul . . . same** Execution before dinner is familiar in Tudor drama (cf. *Jack Straw*, 933–4), but this line comes from More ('by saynt Poule (quod he) I wil not to dinner til I se thy hed of', *CW2*, 49) and appears in Hall, Holinshed and *True Tragedy*. More's 'by saynt Poule' constitutes the sole warrant for the habitual oath of Shakespeare's Richard (see 1.2.36n.).

There is possibly an allusion to Acts, 23.12–14 in which 'certayne of the Iews' vow 'we wyll eate nothyng untyll we haue slayne Paul'.

77 *Ratcliffe F's glaring inconsistency (see 0.1–3n.) is probably preferable to Qq's awkward and inconsistent substitutions of Catesby for Ratcliffe and Lovell; see pp. 452–3.

78 Cf. Clarence's exit demanding, 'You that love me and Warwick, follow me,' leaving Richard and Hastings behind among King Edward's allies (*3H6* 4.1.123). Consistent loyalty to Edward IV and his line results in Hastings's victimization here. By omitting Richard's troops from Hastings's downfall, Shakespeare portrays Richard (once again) exercising his performative power to force others – Stanley and Ely, as before Anne – into demonstrating 'love' for him.

80 **fond** foolish

81–90 More originates these omens (*dream, horse, priest, pursuivant*), but laces them with scepticism (Hanham, 172–3); see 83n. on *stumble* and p. 56.

81 *raze Qq 'race' is a form of 'raze'; cf. 3.2.10.

---

74 Talk'st thou to] *F;* Telst thou *Qq*   75 I swear] *F; not in Qq*   76–7] *F;* I will not dine to day I sweare, / Vntill I see the same, some see it done, / *Qq*   78 rise] *F;* come *Qq*   SD Exeunt.] *Qq, opp.* 77 F   Lovell . . . Hastings.] *F (Manet Louell and Ratcliffe, with the / Lord Hastings.); manet / Cat. with Ha. Qq opp.* 78–9   81 raze his helm] *Qq (race); rowse our Helmes F*

And I did scorn it and disdain to fly.
Three times today my foot-cloth horse did stumble,
And started when he looked upon the Tower,
As loath to bear me to the slaughterhouse.   85
O, now I need the priest that spake to me.
I now repent I told the pursuivant,
As too triumphing, how mine enemies
Today at Pomfret bloodily were butchered,
And I myself secure in grace and favour.   90
O Margaret, Margaret, now thy heavy curse
Is lighted on poor Hastings' wretched head.

RATCLIFFE

Come, come, dispatch. The Duke would be at dinner.
Make a short shrift. He longs to see your head.

HASTINGS

O momentary grace of mortal men,   95
Which we more hunt for than the grace of God!

---

83 **foot-cloth** large, richly ornamented
cloth laid over the back of a horse; a
mark of dignity and state (*OED*); cf.
2H6 4.1.54, 4.7.43.
stumble Horses stumble naturally,
More notes, 'yet hath it ben of an olde
rite & custome, obserued as a token
often times notably foregoing some
great misfortune' (*CW2*, 50).
84 **started** moved suddenly, involuntar-
ily
85 **As** as if
86–7 **priest . . . pursuivant**   Cf.
3.2.92.1–122.
88 **too triumphing** i.e. too much exult-
ing
90 **secure** often conveying culpable
carelessness (*OED* security 3); cf.
Mac 3.5.32–3. A 17th-century reader

records: 'hastings securest confidence
. . . of constant / successe when he wes
going to put his head in his / ennemies
hand to be cut off' (Yamada, 157). On
the perils of spiritual 'security', see
Perkins, 488–9.
93–4 **dispatch . . . head** Cf. *The Wounds
of Civil War* (1594): 'Dispatch . . . For
sore I long to see the traitor's head'
(Lodge, 2050–5).
94 **short shrift** hasty confession (from
More, *CW2*, 49)
95–6 ***grace . . . grace** F   opposes
worldly to divine 'grace'; Qq miss
this point.
96 ***God** F and Qq reverse their normal
terms for the Deity (see 1.4.84n. and
p. 457). Cf. 2.1.39: 'heauen' (F) and
'God' (Qq).

82 And . . . disdain] *F;* But I disdaind it, and *(*disdained, and *Q4)* did scorne *Qq*   83 foot-cloth horse]
*F (*Foot-Cloth-Horse*), Qq (*footecloth horse*)*   84 started] *F;* startled *Qq*   86 need] *F;* want *Qq*   88
too triumphing, how] *F;* twere triumphing at *Qq*   89 Today] *F;* How they *Qq*   92 lighted] *F, Q1–5;*
lightened *Q6*   93 SP] *F (Ra.); Cat. Qq*   Come, come, dispatch] *F;* Dispatch my Lo: *Qq*   95 grace
of mortal] *F;* state of worldly *Qq*   96 than] *F, Q1–2 (*then*);* then for *Q3–6*   God!] *F;* heauen: *Qq*

Who builds his hope in air of your good looks
Lives like a drunken sailor on a mast,
Ready with every nod to tumble down
Into the fatal bowels of the deep.   100

LOVELL

Come, come, dispatch. 'Tis bootless to exclaim.

HASTINGS

O bloody Richard! Miserable England,
I prophesy the fearfull'st time to thee
That ever wretched age hath looked upon.
– Come, lead me to the block; bear him my head.   105
They smile at me who shortly shall be dead.   *Exeunt.*

[3.5]   *Enter* RICHARD *and* BUCKINGHAM *in rotten
armour, marvellous ill-favoured.*

RICHARD

Come, cousin, canst thou quake and change thy colour,

---

97 **air** manner, outward appearance (*OED sb.*[1] III 13); cf. 'the air of the court' (*WT* 4.4.734). 'Building in air' means trusting in the unsubstantial or conjectural (*OED* air *sb.*[1] 3).
your good looks approving glances granted by the imaginary figure who personifies the 'grace of mortal men'
97–100 The fall into the sea recalls Clarence's dream (1.4); cf. Proverbs, 23.31–4 on drunkenness as resembling sleep 'vppon the top of the maste of a ship' (also *Homilies*, 99). *Mirror* reflects on the 'slyppery state wherein aloft we swymme' ('Hastings', 634).
101 **bootless** pointless, unprofitable
exclaim cry out
106 **They** Hastings's enemies in general, but perhaps specifically referring to the present (smirking?) insolence of Lovell and Ratcliffe

3.5 location: '*the* Tower-*walls*' (Theobald). Cibber, all 19th-century and many later productions cut this scene, often inserting 72ff. into 3.1 (Hankey, 172).
0.1–2 More describes Richard and Buckingham wearing 'old il faring briginders' as if 'some sodaine necessitie had constrained them' (*CW*2, 52; 'briginders' or 'briganders' are body-armour for foot-soldiers) to 'set some color vpon' the execution of Hastings. Cf. 'In rousty armure as in extreame shyft, / They cladd them selues, to cloake theyr diuelysh dryft' (*Mirror*, 'Hastings', 689–90).
0.1 **rotten** unsound, in decay and disorder (*OED* 2b, 8a)
0.2 *marvellous ill-favoured* i.e. remarkably ugly-looking
1–11 On this passage and acting, see pp. 10–12.
1 **change thy colour** i.e. change your

---

97 hope] *F;* hopes *Qq*   good] *F;* faire *Qq*   looks] *F, Q1–3, 5–6;* looke *Q4*   98 a drunken sailor] *F, Q1–3, 5–6;* drunken Saylers *Q4*   100 the fatal] *F, Q1–5;* fatall *Q6*   101–4] *F; not in Qq*   106 who] *F;* that *Qq*   3.5] *Capell*   0.1–2] *F; Enter Duke of Glocester and Buckingham in armour. Qq*   1+ SP] *F; Glo. Qq*   1] *Qq; F lines* Cousin, / colour, /

Murder thy breath in middle of a word,
And then again begin, and stop again,
As if thou were distraught and mad with terror?

BUCKINGHAM

Tut, I can counterfeit the deep tragedian,   5
Speak, and look back, and pry on every side,
Tremble and start at wagging of a straw,
Intending deep suspicion. Ghastly looks
Are at my service, like enforced smiles,
And both are ready in their offices,   10
At any time to grace my stratagems.
But what, is Catesby gone?

RICHARD

He is, and see, he brings the Mayor along.

Enter the [Lord] MAYOR *and* CATESBY.

appearance; flush with emotion or grow pale with fear are possible. For pallor related to shock or guilt, see 2.1.84–6, 136–8.

2 **Murder** i.e. choke off, extinguish, possibly suggesting 'to spoil by bad execution or pronunciation' (*OED v.* 2); cf. 34n.

4 **were** *thou were* is subjunctive (*OED* be A III 7), but Shakespeare nowhere else employs F's form (Wilson).
   distraught driven to madness; cf. Juliet's images of living entombment (*RJ* 4.3.49) for melodramatic connotations.

5 **counterfeit** imitate, frequently used for playing a role (e.g. *1H4* 5.4.113–18; *AYL* 4.3.165–81; *KL* 3.6.60).
   deep tragedian tragic actor of grave, serious aspect (*OED* deep II 7b)

6 **look . . . side** i.e. glance over one's shoulder and peer around apprehensively; cf. 19.

7 **wagging** slight movement; cf. Dent, W5.

8 **Intending** asserting, pretending (*OED* 22, citing this line); cf. 3.7.44.

9 **like** i.e. as well as
   enforced enforcèd

10 **offices** functions, uses

11 **grace** embellish (*OED v.* 4a), but in proximity with *offices* playing on the meaning 'countenance' (*OED v.* 2a) as an official might 'grace' a subordinate; cf. 3.4.95–6.

12 *Qq omit because Catesby is the executioner of Hastings in the previous scene in Qq, and in Qq enters with Hastings's head at 20.1; for the problem with 17 in Qq, see p. 453 and 20.1n.

13 **Mayor** More describes enlisting the Lord Mayor, Edmund Shaa (Shaw), that he 'vpon trust of his own aduauncement, whereof he was of a proud hart highly desirouse, shold frame the cite [i.e. city] to their appetite' (*CW2*, 58).

2 Murder] *F, Qq* (Murther), *Q8*   3 again begin] *F;* beginne againe *Qq*   4 were] *F;* wert *Qq*   5 Tut, I] *F;* Tut feare not me. / I *Qq*   7] *F; not in Qq*   7–8 straw, . . . suspicion.] *Pope* (straw, . . . suspicion:)*; Straw: . . . suspition, *F*   8 deep] *F, Q1–3, 5–6;* deere *Q4*   11 At any time] *F; not in Qq*   12] *F; not in Qq*   13] *F;* Here comes the Maior. *Qq*   13.1] *F; Enter Maior. Qq opp. 11*   Lord] *Rowe*

BUCKINGHAM

Lord Mayor –

RICHARD

Look to the draw-bridge there!   15

BUCKINGHAM   Hark, a drum!

RICHARD

Catesby, o'erlook the walls!   [*Exit Catesby.*]

BUCKINGHAM

Lord Mayor, the reason we have sent –

RICHARD

Look back! Defend thee! Here are enemies.

BUCKINGHAM

God and our innocency defend and guard us.   20

Enter LOVELL *and* RATCLIFFE, *with Hastings's head.*

RICHARD

Be patient. They are friends: Ratcliffe and Lovell.

LOVELL

Here is the head of that ignoble traitor,
The dangerous and unsuspected Hastings.

16, 18 *Qq reverse. Qq's order might allow Buckingham to go on pretending to converse with the Mayor before shouting with Richard (Smidt, *Impostors*, 45).

16 **drum** probably imaginary, which would suit an exchange exhorting the Mayor to *imagine* a non-existent plot (35–9)

17 **o'erlook** look over the top of

19 **Look back** i.e. look behind you (cf. 6).

20 **innocency** innocence (as *KJ* 4.3.110)

20.1 *Qq have Catesby enter here with Hastings's head, but this leaves Qq 17

without an onstage addressee. Perhaps 'Catesby' in Qq 17 is 'as imaginary as the unnamed figure [Richard] calls to "Looke to the drawbridge"' (*TxC*, 241).

head Hastings's head has occasioned grotesque stage business: Donald Wolfit's Richard ate strawberries while gloating over the head in a bag; José Ferrer's Richard waved his bloody sack at the Mayor, driving him from the stage; Terry Hands's 1970 promptbook calls for tossing the head to the Mayor, who faints (Hankey, 173).

14] *F;* Let me alone to entertaine him. Lo: Maior, *Qq*   16] *F;* The reason we haue sent for you. *Qq*   17 o'erlook] *F* (o're-looke), *Qq* (ouerlooke)   SD] *Ard²*   18] *F;* Harke, I heare a drumme. *Qq*   20 innocency] *F, Q2–6* (Innocencie); innocence *Q1*   and guard] *F; not in Qq*   20.1] *F; Enter Catesby / with Hast. head. Qq* (opp. 20-1 *Q1–2; after 21 Q3–6*)   21] *F;* O, O, be quiet, it is Catesby. *Qq*   22 SP] *F; Cat. Qq*

RICHARD

So dear I loved the man that I must weep.
I took him for the plainest harmless creature   25
That breathed upon the earth a Christian;
Made him my book, wherein my soul recorded
The history of all her secret thoughts.
So smooth he daubed his vice with show of virtue
That, his apparent open guilt omitted –   30
I mean his conversation with Shore's wife –
He lived from all attainder of suspects.

BUCKINGHAM

Well, well, he was the covert'st sheltered traitor
That ever lived.
Would you imagine, or almost believe,   35

24 **weep** Cf. 1.2.156–7n.
25 **plainest harmless** i.e. plainest,
(most) harmless; or perhaps a compound word, 'plainest-harmless'
(Abbott, 398)
27 **book** i.e. commonplace book, or diary
where Richard recorded his thoughts
29 A 'typical act of cunning displacement' (Maus, 52), but also ascribing
to Hastings a term that permeates
Richard's verbal environment: *smooth*
has been repeatedly employed to characterize others from whom Richard
differentiates himself as *plain* (cf. 25)
– War's *smoothed* front (1.1.9), the
smoothing words of others (1.2.171),
his flattering enemies' ability to *smooth*
(1.3.48) – and it occurs ominously
in Hastings's misapprehension of
Richard's *smooth* appearance (3.4.48).
daubed covered with a specious exte-
rior; whitewashed (*OED v.* 7)
30 **apparent** manifest, obvious
31 **conversation** sexual intimacy
(*OED* 3)

32 **from** free from
attainder stain of dishonour (*OED*
2b, citing this line); cf. *LLL* 1.1.155.
suspects suspicion
33 **Well, well** Cf. Dent, W269 ('Well,
well is a word of malice') and *R2*
3.3.170.
covert'st sheltered most deceitful
(*OED* covert *a.* 1, 3), protected from
punishment (*OED* shelter *v.* 1c); perhaps retorting to *plainest harmless* (25).
34 *Qq attach this half-line to a version
of the next line. Some editors omit it;
others add a half-line from Qq's 26,
'Look ye, my Lord Mayor'. This edition joins Mowat and Werstine, Lull
and Jowett in retaining F's half-line.
Could this short line possibly represent Buckingham following Richard's
suggestions about histrionic pauses
and hesitations (2–4)?
35 **almost** hardly, nearly; 'Would you
suppose without evidence, or (I may
almost say) believe upon evidence?'
(Abbott, 29).

25 creature] *F;* man *Qq* 26 the] *F, Q4;* this *Q1–3, 5–6* Christian;] *F (*Christian.*);* christian, /
Looke ye my Lo: Maior. / *Qq* 27 Made] *F, Q1–4;* I made *Q5–6* 32 lived . . . suspects] *F;* laid . . .
suspect *Qq* 34–6] *F; Qq line* imagined, / preseuration / 34] *F; om. Pope;* That ever liv'd. – Look
you, my lord mayor, *Capell* 35 imagine] *F;* haue imagined *Qq*

Were't not that by great preservation
We live to tell it, that the subtle traitor
This day had plotted in the council house
To murder me and my good lord of Gloucester?

MAYOR

Had he done so?   40

RICHARD

What? Think you we are Turks or infidels?
Or that we would, against the form of law,
Proceed thus rashly in the villain's death,
But that the extreme peril of the case,
The peace of England, and our persons' safety,   45
Enforced us to this execution?

MAYOR

Now fair befall you! He deserved his death,
And your good graces both have well proceeded
To warn false traitors from the like attempts.

BUCKINGHAM

I never looked for better at his hands   50
After he once fell in with Mistress Shore.

36 **great preservation** protection by Providence; Richard has been protected by divine intervention.
41 **Turks or infidels** The third collect for Good Friday prays: 'Have mercy upon all Jews, Turks, infidels, and heretics' (*BCP*, 144).
43 **rashly** speedily
44 **But** except
47 **fair befall you** i.e. may it be well with you (Abbott, 297); cf. 1.3.281.
49 **the like** similar
50–2 *Q1–2 assign 50–1 to the Mayor and give a SP at 52 ('*Dut.*') that

apparently misreads Buckingham ('*Buc.*'). Q3 assigns it to someone who is at least onstage, but misspells the prefix ('*Clo.*'); Q4 corrects to '*Glo.*' Thompson suggests that Buckingham attempts to work on the Mayor's prejudices by underlining the charge mentioned at 31. Wells and Taylor note that the chief problem with F's attribution to Buckingham is the shift in first-person pronouns to what look like regal plurals (except in 56), but see 56n.
50 **at his hands** i.e. from him

36 Were't] *F, Q1–5 (*Wert*);* were *Q6* that] *F; not in Qq* 37 it, that the] *F;* it you? The *Qq* 38 This day had] *F;* Had this day *Qq* 39 murder] *F (*murther*), Qq* 40] *F;* What, had he so? *Qq* 41 you] *F, Q1–2;* ye *Q3–6* 42 form] *F, Q1–2;* course *Q3–6* 43 in] *F;* to *Qq* 44 extreme] *F, Q1–3, 5–6;* very extreame *Q4* 46 this] *F, Q1–3, 5–6;* that *Q4* 48 your good graces] *F;* you my good Lords *Qq* 50 SP] *F; not in Qq*

Yet had we not determined he should die
Until your lordship came to see his end –
Which now the loving haste of these our friends,
Something against our meanings, have prevented –   55
Because, my lord, I would have had you heard
The traitor speak and timorously confess
The manner and the purpose of his treasons,
That you might well have signified the same
Unto the citizens, who haply may   60
Misconster us in him and wail his death.

MAYOR

But, my good lord, your graces' words shall serve
As well as I had seen and heard him speak;
And do not doubt, right noble princes both,
But I'll acquaint our duteous citizens   65
With all your just proceedings in this case.

---

52 **had . . . die** ambiguous: either 'we
had not determined he should die' or
'we would not have determined that he
should die'
54 **friends** Lovell and Ratcliffe; Qq retain
this plural, despite Catesby's replacement of Lovell and Ratcliffe in Qq.
See p. 453.
55 **Something . . . meanings** somewhat
contrary to our intentions
have prevented has anticipated (*OED*
prevent *v.* I 1); *have* may be a plural
due to *friends* in 54.
56 **I** Buckingham possibly changes back
to first person singular (as in 50) to
express his individual reasoning.
had you heard i.e. have wished you to
have heard (cf. Abbott, 491)
58 ***treasons** Hall and Holinshed three
times use the singular (as do Qq) in

this context (Smidt, *Memorial*, 40).
59 **signified** communicated
60 **haply** perhaps
61 **Misconster . . . him** i.e. misconstrue
our treatment of him; the Elizabethan
written forms 'conster' and 'construe'
were both pronounced 'cònster' (*OED*
construe *v.*).
62 ***graces'** Hammond argues for the
plural possessive, referring to the
words of both Buckingham and
Richard, but 'my good lord' prompts
many editors to adopt the singular
form ('grace's').
63 **as** as if (Abbott, 107)
65 **But** i.e. but that
66 ***case** F's 'case' may arise from a Q6
misprint ('ease'), but 'case' and 'cause'
could carry the same meaning (*OED*
case *sb.*[1] 6; cause *sb.* II 8).

52 Yet] *F; Dut.* Yet *Q1–2; Clo.* Yet *Q3, 5; Glo.* Yet *Q4, 6*   we not] *F;* not we *Qq*   53 end] *F;* death
Qq   54 loving] *F;* longing *Qq*   55 Something . . . meanings] *F;* Somewhat . . . meaning *Qq*   56 I] *F;*
we *Qq*   58 treasons] *F;* treason *Qq*   60 haply] *F;* happily *Qq*   61 Misconster] *F, Q1–5;* Misconstrue
Q6   62 But, my] *F, Q1–2 subst.;* My *Q3–6*   words] *F;* word *Qq*   63 and] *F;* or *Qq*   64 do not doubt]
F; doubt you not *Qq*   65 our] *F;* your *Qq*   66 case] *F;* cause *Q1–5;* ease *Q6*

285

RICHARD

And to that end we wished your lordship here,
T'avoid the censures of the carping world.

BUCKINGHAM

Which, since you come too late of our intent,
Yet witness what you hear we did intend.   70
And so, my good Lord Mayor, we bid farewell.

Exit [Lord] Mayor.

RICHARD

Go after, after, cousin Buckingham.
The Mayor towards Guildhall hies him in all post.
There, at your meetest vantage of the time,
Infer the bastardy of Edward's children.   75
Tell them how Edward put to death a citizen
Only for saying he would make his son
Heir to the crown, meaning indeed his house,
Which, by the sign thereof, was termed so.

68 **carping** censorious
69 **Which** i.e. as to which (Abbott, 272)
  of our intent i.e. to help our plan
70 **witness** i.e. bear witness to
71 *F's farewell is less abrupt than Qq's.
73 **Guildhall** meeting hall of the
  Corporation of the City of London
  hies . . . post i.e. goes with great
  haste
74 *meetest vantage** i.e. most appropriate moment; Qq/F variants have been
  important to debates about the roles of
  Q3 and Q6 in constituting F's text. See
  p. 440.
75 **Infer** allege; cf. 3.7.12.
  bastardy See 3.7.4–6n. for the complicated basis of this charge.
76 **put . . . citizen** Probably the notori-

ous story of Walker, a citizen from
Cheapside, whom Hall calls Burdet:
this merchant, who dwelled at the
sign of the Crown, told his son that
he would inherit the Crown 'meaning his awne house: but these wordes
kyng Edward made to be myscon-
strued, & interpreted that Burdet
meante the croune of the realme:
wherfore within lesse space then iiii.
houres, he was apprehended, iudged,
drawen and quartered' (*Edward V*,
fol xxiʳ). Holinshed tells an analogous
story concerning Thomas Burdet of
Warwickshire (3.703). Richard's *citizen*
suggests indebtedness to Hall.
78 **house** tavern
79 **termed** termèd

67 wished] *F, Q1–5 subst.;* wish *Q6*   68 T'avoid] *F; Qq (*To auoyde*) subst.*   censures . . . world]
F; carping censures of the world *(word Q3) Qq*   69 Which] *F;* But *Qq*   come] *F, Q1–2;* came
Q3–6   intent] *F;* intents *Qq*   70 you hear] *F; not in Qq*   intend.] *F;* intend, and so my Lord adue.
Qq   71] *F; not in Qq*   SD] *F; opp. 72 Qq*   72 Go] *F; not in Qq*   74 meetest vantage] *F;* meetst
*(*meetest *Q6)* aduantage *Qq*

Moreover, urge his hateful luxury 80
And bestial appetite in change of lust,
Which stretched unto their servants, daughters, wives,
Even where his raging eye or savage heart,
Without control, lusted to make a prey.
Nay, for a need, thus far come near my person: 85
Tell them, when that my mother went with child
Of that insatiate Edward, noble York
My princely father then had wars in France,
And by true computation of the time
Found that the issue was not his begot, 90
Which well appeared in his lineaments,
Being nothing like the noble duke, my father.
Yet touch this sparingly, as 'twere far off,
Because, my lord, you know my mother lives.

BUCKINGHAM
Doubt not, my lord; I'll play the orator 95

80–4 Accusations concerning Edward's promiscuous desires are prominent in the speeches More gives Buckingham (*CW*2, 71–2; Holinshed, 3.729); they also appear in Mancini (67); cf. 3.7.8.

80 **urge** assert, present forcefully
luxury lechery; cf. *Ham* 1.5.83.

81 **change of lust** i.e. pursuit of sexual variety

83 **Even where** wherever
raging violent, passionate with sexual desire (*OED* rage *sb.* 6a, b); cf. 'His rage of lust' (*Luc* 424).

85 **for a need** i.e. if necessary

86–90 Hall's and Holinshed's Dr Shaw asserts the bastardy of Edward IV and Clarence based on their dissimilarity to the Duke of York and their physical resemblance to other men (Hall, *Edward V*, fol. xxʳ; Holinshed, 3.727). Mancini (95) writes that Richard 'so

corrupted preachers of the divine word' that they preached that Edward 'was conceived in adultery and in every way was unlike the late duke of York, whose son he was falsely said to be, but Richard, duke of Gloucester, who altogether resembled his father, come to the throne as the legitimate successor'; cf. 3.7.9–14.

86–7 **went . . . Edward** i.e. was pregnant with the child that would become the insatiable Edward

90 **issue . . . begot** i.e. child was not fathered by him

93 **as . . . off** i.e. elliptically, by hints; cf. 3.1.170 and *H5* 1.2.240.

95 **Doubt** i.e. fear
play the orator i.e. assume the role of an accomplished rhetorician; cf. Dent, O74.1. Richard boasts, 'I'll play the orator as well as Nestor' (*3H6* 3.2.188),

---

81 bestial] *F, Q6 (*beastiall*), Q1–5* 82 unto] *F;* to *Qq* 83 raging] *F;* lustfull *Qq* 84 lusted . . . a] *F;* listed . . . his *Qq* 85 come] *F, Q1–3, 5–6;* comes *Q4* 87 insatiate] *F;* vnsatiate *Qq* 89 true] *F;* iust *Qq* 93 Yet . . . 'twere] *F;* But . . . it were *Qq* far] *F, Q1–3, 5–6;* a farre *Q4* 94 my . . . know] *F;* you know, my Lord *Qq* my mother] *F, Q1–4;* my *(*me *Q6) brother *Q5–6* 95 Doubt] *F;* Feare *Qq*

As if the golden fee for which I plead
Were for myself. And so, my lord, adieu.

RICHARD

If you thrive well, bring them to Baynard's Castle,
Where you shall find me well accompanied
With reverend fathers and well-learned bishops.   100

BUCKINGHAM

I go, and towards three or four o'clock
Look for the news that the Guildhall affords.

Exit Buckingham.

RICHARD

Go, Lovell, with all speed to Doctor Shaw.
[*to Ratcliffe*] Go thou to Friar Penker. Bid them both

so Buckingham might be modelling himself on Richard, but elsewhere Edward also claims to 'play the orator' (*3H6* 1.2.2), and Henry VI similarly describes Clifford's rhetoric (*3H6* 2.2.43). Even King Henry is mocked for attempting to 'play the orator' (*1H6* 4.1.175).

96 **golden fee** i.e. the crown; 'fee' could refer to a prize or a monetary reward, or to goods or a heritable estate (*OED sb.*[1], *sb.*[2]).

98 **Baynard's Castle** Richard's London residence on the north bank of the Thames, between London Bridge and Blackfriars. After belonging to Henry VI it became a possession of the York family until Richard's death. In 1483 it was the residence of the Duchess of York. In Shakespeare's day it was in the possession of William Herbert, Earl of Pembroke.

103–5 *These lines are not in Qq, presumably because of Lovell's absence from Qq. Smidt claims on the basis of 98–100 that Richard has already had the idea of appearing with

the clerics at Baynard's Castle, so that Qq's omission of 103–5 may represent an (incompletely executed) authorial decision to let Buckingham later claim Richard's appearance with the clerics as his own idea (*Impostors*, 165–6). But Richard may be vaguely suggesting an idea and subsequently arranging its implementation before allowing Buckingham the (mistaken) illusion of his own originality in 3.7.

103–4 **Doctor Shaw . . . Friar Penker** both notorious for preaching in support of Richard's claim. More discusses Shaw's sermon (see 86–90n.) and characterizes both as having 'no scrupilouse conscience' (*CW2*, 58).

104 SD *Addressing this line to Catesby (following Capell) leaves Ratcliffe idle; if Catesby exits at 17, however, then Ratcliffe is the only choice for Richard's errand here. This makes F's stage direction at 105 ('*Exit.*') a false singular and 109 a false plural, but they may have been transposed in transcription.

97 And . . . adieu] *F; not in Qq, but see 102*   101–2] *F; About three or foure a clocke look to heare / What news Guildhall affordeth, and so my Lord farewell. / Qq*   102 SD] *F; Exit Buc. Qq opp. 106*   103–5] *F; not in Qq*   104 SD] *Rowe*   Penker] *Capell; Peuker F*

288

Meet me within this hour at Baynard's Castle.   105

> *Exeunt [Ratcliffe and Lovell]*.

Now will I go to take some privy order
To draw the brats of Clarence out of sight,
And to give order that no manner person
Have any time recourse unto the princes.   *Exit*.

[3.6]   *Enter a* Scrivener ^Q*with a paper in his hand*^Q.

SCRIVENER

Here is the indictment of the good Lord Hastings,
Which in a set hand fairly is engrossed,
That it may be today read o'er in Paul's.
And mark how well the sequel hangs together:
Eleven hours I have spent to write it over,   5
For yesternight by Catesby was it sent me;

---

106 **take ... order** i.e. make secret arrangements
107 **brats of Clarence** On Clarence's children, see 2.2.0.2n.
108 ***manner person** An elliptical form (abbreviating 'manner of person') shared by F, Q3–4 and not by Q1–2, 5–6 and thus supporting the argument that Q3 furnished copy for F throughout the play (see p. 439).
109 **recourse** access
3.6 location: '*A Street*' (Capell); omitted by Cibber
0.1 **Scrivener** professional copyist, notary. Any child might have perceived problems with the proclamation against Hastings, More writes, and bystanders joked about its being written by 'prophesie' (Holinshed, 3.724–5; More, *CW*2, 54; Hall, *Edward V*, fol. xvi^r); Mancini (91) says 'the

real truth was on the lips of many'. Here, an ordinary person pursuing his occupation realizes that he aids Richard's injustice. For an Elizabethan case in which time factors involved in prosecution were interpreted as implicating higher, even royal, involvement, see Sir John Perrot's treason trial of April 1592 (Howell, 1.1329).
2 **set hand** formal, ceremonious handwriting (*OED* set *ppl. a.* I 5a)
engrossed written out large
3 **read ... Paul's** read aloud in St Paul's churchyard at Paul's Cross where there were 'sermons ... euery Sundaye in the forenoone' (Stow, 1.331).
4 **sequel** sequence (of events)
4–11 **hangs together ... palpable** terminology (*res cohaerens, manifestaque est*) derived from classical rhetorical *confirmatio* (Baldwin, 2.326–8)

---

105 SD] *Rowe subst.; Exit. F; not in Qq*   106 go] *F; in Qq*   108 order] *F; notice Qq*   manner] *F, Q3–4; maner of Q1–2, 5–6*   109 Have any time] *F; At any tyme haue Qq*   SD] *Qq; Exeunt. F*   3.6] *Capell*   1 SP] *F (Scr.); not in Qq*   Here] *F; This Qq*   3 today] *F; this day Qq*   o'er] *F; Qq (ouer)*   5 have] *F; not in Qq*   6 sent] *F; brought Qq*

The precedent was full as long a-doing;
And yet within these five hours Hastings lived,
Untainted, unexamined, free, at liberty.
Here's a good world the while. Who is so gross   10
That cannot see this palpable device?
Yet who so bold but says he sees it not?
Bad is the world, and all will come to nought
When such ill dealing must be seen in thought.   *Exit.*

[**3.7**] *Enter* RICHARD *and* BUCKINGHAM *at several doors.*

RICHARD
How now, how now, what say the citizens?
BUCKINGHAM
Now by the Holy Mother of our Lord,
The citizens are mum, say not a word.

7 **precedent** the original document from which a copy is made
a-doing i.e. in writing out
8 **within . . . hours** i.e. five hours ago
9 **Untainted** not accused (see 3.5.32)
10 **Here's . . . while** Cf. *KJ* 4.2.100: 'bad world the while'.
gross lacking discernment, stupid (*OED a.* A IV 13a)
11 **palpable device** obvious trick
13 **nought** nothing (*OED sb.*1); used interchangeably with Q1–2's 'naught' = evil (*OED* A *sb.* 2) (cf. 1.1.97–8).
14 **seen in thought** i.e. perceived but not spoken about (cf. *TGV* 4.4.170); 'thought' could mean anxiety, distress of mind (*OED* 5a).
3.7 location: 'Baynard's *Castle*' (Theobald); cf. 3.5.98–105.
0.1 *several* separate
1 Richard Simpson (436–7) suggests that Richard's quest for acclama-

tion from the *citizens* represents a new historical understanding of a power-base more important to future politics than the barons of the earlier plays. The role of the commons here resembles that implied by the attempt of Richard's father to use the Cade rebellion to 'perceive the commons' mind, / How they affect the house and claim of York' (*2H6* 3.1.373–4).
How now i.e. how is it now? (*OED* how *adv.* 4)
citizens inhabitants of a city or town, often specifically those possessing rights and privileges as freemen (*OED* 1); see 200.
3 **mum** silent, possibly suggesting an inarticulate sound signifying inability or unwillingness to speak (*OED sb.*[1] 1); cf. *KL* 1.4.185–7 and Dent, W767: 'No word but mum'.

8 Hastings lived] *F;* liued Lord Hastings *Qq*   10–11] *Qq; F lines* while. / deuice? /   10 Who is] *F;* Why whoes *Qq*   11 cannot see] *F;* sees not *Qq*   12 who] *F, Q3–6;* whoes *Q1–2*   bold] *F;* blinde *Qq*   13 nought] *F, Q3–6;* naught *Q1–2*   14 ill] *F;* bad *Qq*   dealing] *F, Q1–3, 5–6;* dealings *Q4*   3.7] *Pope*   0.1] *F; Enter Glocester at one doore, Buckingham at another. Qq*   1 How . . . [2]now] *F;* How now my Lord *Qq*   3 say] *F;* and speake *Qq*

RICHARD

Touched you the bastardy of Edward's children?

BUCKINGHAM

I did, with his contract with Lady Lucy   5
And his contract by deputy in France;
Th'unsatiate greediness of his desire
And his enforcement of the city wives;
His tyranny for trifles; his own bastardy,
As being got your father then in France,   10
And his resemblance being not like the Duke.
Withal, I did infer your lineaments,
Being the right idea of your father,
Both in your form and nobleness of mind;

---

4 **Touched you** i.e. did you bring up
4–6 **bastardy . . . France** According
to More, Edward IV had a child by
Elizabeth Lucy, without formally con-
tracting marriage; this relationship
was publicly brought against him by
his mother, the Duchess of York, when
he sought to wed Elizabeth Grey. His
marriage to Elizabeth Grey alienated
the Earl of Warwick, who had been in
France as Edward's deputy contract-
ing a dynastic union with the Lady
Bona of Savoy (*CW2*, 64–5; cf. *3H6*
3.3.49–265). More says the 'pretext'
supporting the charge of bastardy
against Edward's children rests on the
claim that his earlier commitments
made his relationship with Lady Grey
bigamous (*CW2*, 59).
5–6, 8, 11 *Absence from Qq has been
explained as motivated by a desire to
avoid offending Elizabeth I, since some
of the charges roughly resemble those
brought against her father, Henry VIII
(Marshall). Smidt suggests Q1 cut to
avoid repetitiveness (of 3.5.75–92 and
178–90) (*Impostors*, 114–15).
5 **contract** betrothal

7 **unsatiate** insatiable; F and Qq reverse
their former usage (see 3.5.87).
8 **enforcement** sexual compulsion
9 **tyranny for trifles** i.e. excessive punishment for minor infractions. More's
Buckingham says that Edward IV
inflated all charges 'aboue the mesure'
(*CW2*, 70).
9–14 **bastardy . . . form** Cf. 3.5.86–92.
10 **got** begotten, conceived
11 **resemblance** appearance, characteristic features; see 3.5.86–90n.
Duke the Duke of York, Richard's and
Edward's father
12 **Withal** in addition
13 **idea** image, likeness, figure (*OED sb.* II
7a); the *right idea* suggests the closest
approximation to an original. How egregious is Buckingham's flattery supposed
to be when he likens Richard 'in form' to
the Duke of York despite his limp, arm
and back (cf. *TxC*, 242)? The flattering
portrait of Richard by More's Dr Shaw
(*CW2*, 67–8) emphasizes facial likeness
(cf. Hall, *Edward V*, fol. xxʳ; Holinshed,
3.727). Vergil's Shaw claims discrepancy
in body and face between the Duke of
York and King Edward (184).

5–6 his . . . France] *F; not in Qq*   7 Th'unsatiate] *F; the insatiate Qq*   desire] *F; desires Qq*   8] *F; not in Qq*   11] *F; not in Qq*   14 your] *F, Q1–2;* one *Q3–6*

Laid open all your victories in Scotland,   15
Your discipline in war, wisdom in peace,
Your bounty, virtue, fair humility;
Indeed, left nothing fitting for your purpose
Untouched or slightly handled in discourse.
And when mine oratory drew toward end,   20
I bid them that did love their country's good
Cry, 'God save Richard, England's royal King!'

RICHARD

And did they so?

BUCKINGHAM

No, so God help me, they spake not a word,
But like dumb statues or breathing stones   25
Stared each on other and looked deadly pale;
Which when I saw, I reprehended them

---

15 **Laid open** i.e. brought up
victories in Scotland Richard
commanded the English invasion of
Scotland in 1482, captured Berwick
and advanced as far as Edinburgh; his
warlike prowess is prominent in *3H6*.
16 **discipline** training or skill in military
affairs (*OED sb.* 3b)
17 **bounty** generosity
fair spotless, unblemished (*OED a.*
III 9); or possibly, plainly to be seen
(*OED a.* IV 17). The second meaning
would underline the outrageousness of
Richard's inherently self-contradictory
claims to *humility*, which Buckingham
here echoes (cf. 2.1.73).
19 **slightly handled** i.e. passed lightly
over
20–41 closely following Hall (*Edward V*,
fol. xxii') and Holinshed (3.730–1),
though they have Buckingham twice
attempting to move the assembly;
contrast Fabyan's emphasis (2.515)

on Buckingham's eloquence, which
moves even 'wise men' with his 'sugred wordes' and their 'good ordering'.
20 *mine ... toward** F agrees with
Q3–6, preferring 'my' to Q1–2's
'mine'; however, F's 'drew toward'
may allow for the same syllable count
as Q1–2, 4 ('grew to an') and thus both
may differ from 'grew to' in Q3, 5–6.
Abbott (237) claims 'mine' and 'my' to
be generally interchangeable, but when
Shakespeare uses 'my' as the possessive before a noun beginning with a
vowel, as in F, usually the effect is
emphatic. Thus F's 'my' might stress
Buckingham's claim to his own oratory while Q1–2's 'mine' would be
unemphasized, with the stress falling
on *oratory*; cf. 1.4.22, 23n., 4.1.81n.
23 *Qq's 'A' might represent 'Ah!' (cf.
1.3.154n.).
25 **statues** trisyllabic, as *JC* 2.2.76
26 **each on other** i.e. at one another

15 open] *F, Q1–5;* vpon *Q6*   victories] *F, Q1–3, 5–6;* victorie *Q4*   18 your] *F;* the *Qq*   20 mine]
Q1–2; my *F, Q3–6*   drew toward] *F;* grew to an *Q1–2, 4;* grew to *Q3, 5–6*   21 bid] *F, Q1–4;* bad
Q5–6   did love] *F, Q1–2;* loues *Q3–6*   23 And] *F;* A and *Q1;* A, and *Q2–6;* Ah! and *Cam*   24 they .
. . word] *F; not in Qq*   25 statues] *F, Qq;* statuas *Steevens*   breathing] *F, Q1–2;* breathlesse *Q3–6*   26
Stared] *F;* Gazde *Qq*

And asked the Mayor what meant this wilful silence?
His answer was, the people were not used
To be spoke to but by the Recorder.   30
Then he was urged to tell my tale again:
'Thus saith the Duke; thus hath the Duke inferred' –
But nothing spoke in warrant from himself.
When he had done, some followers of mine own
At lower end of the hall hurled up their caps,   35
And some ten voices cried, 'God save King Richard!'
And thus I took the vantage of those few:
'Thanks, gentle citizens and friends,' quoth I;
'This general applause and cheerful shout
Argues your wisdom and your love to Richard:'   40
And even here brake off and came away.

RICHARD

What tongueless blocks were they! Would they not
    speak?
Will not the Mayor then, and his brethren, come?

---

30 **Recorder** rècorder; legal official appointed to 'record' the proceedings of the courts and the customs of the city. Holinshed terms him 'the mouth of the citie' (3.730).

32 **inferred** asserted, alleged (*OED v.* 2)

33 **in . . . himself** on his own authority

35 **lower end** the end of the hall opposite the raised upper end, with its dais
   hall Guildhall's great hall, approximately 150 by 50 feet (45 by 15 metres), capable of holding a large assembly and central to city government

37 **vantage of** i.e. the opportunity provided by (cf. 3.5.74)

38–40 ***gentle . . . cheerful . . . love** F's progression from 'gentle', flattering the common (i.e. not gentle) citizens, to 'cheerful', with its interpretation of

their approbation, to the culminating claim of 'love' suggests a developing argument (Hammond). Qq's 'louing', 'louing' and 'loue' show no rhetorical development.

40 **Argues** proves, indicates (*OED* I 1)

41 **brake** broke

43 **brethren** i.e. fellow-citizens, perhaps carrying civic or religious connotations, since guild or corporation members (*OED* brother *sb.* 4) or co-religionists among Elizabethan Puritans (*OED sb.* 3) could be so called. The religious sense is, of course, inappropriate to the time of the play, but religious divisions were hotly discussed, debated and satirized by the 1590s. See pp. 31–6. In *3H6* 'brethren' are identified with aldermen (*3H6* 4.7.16.1–2, 34.1).

---

28 meant] *F, Q1–5;* meanes *Q6*   29 used] *F;* wont *Qq*   33 spoke] *F;* spake *Q1–5;* speake *Q6*
35 lower] *F;* the lower *Qq*   37] *F; not in Qq*   38 gentle] *F;* louing *Qq*   39 cheerful] *F;* louing *Qq*
40 wisdom] *F, Q3–6;* wisedomes *Q1–2*   love] *F, Q1–2;* loues *Q3–6*   41 even here] *F;* so *Qq*   42] *Qq;*
F lines they, / speake? /   speak?] *F;* speake? / *Buc.* No by my troth my Lo: / *Qq*

BUCKINGHAM

The Mayor is here at hand. Intend some fear.
Be not you spoke with but by mighty suit;   45
And look you get a prayer book in your hand,
And stand between two churchmen, good my lord,
For on that ground I'll make a holy descant.
And be not easily won to our requests;
Play the maid's part: still answer nay, and take it.   50

RICHARD

I go, and if you plead as well for them
As I can say nay to thee for myself,
No doubt we bring it to a happy issue.

BUCKINGHAM

Go, go up to the leads, the Lord Mayor knocks.
                                    ᵠ*Exit*ᵠ [*Richard*].

Enter the [Lord] MAYOR *and* Citizens.

---

44 **Intend** pretend (*OED* 22) (cf. 3.5.8)
45 **but . . . suit** i.e. unless they entreat you urgently
48 **ground** melody upon which the descant or melodious variation is raised (cf. 1.1.27); Richard perhaps anticipates Buckingham's scenario (cf. 3.5.98–100). ***make** Qq's 'build' plays on the musical and architectural senses of *ground*.
49 ***And** Buckingham's speech in F appears as an additive series of recommendations, as if each were occurring to him at the moment; in contrast to F's four uses of *and* in this speech, Qq have only two instances of the word.
50 i.e. say no, but do it anyway (see Dent, M 34); cf. *TGV* 1.2.55–6. Richard exploits a 'feminine' position. **still** always
51–2 **you . . . thee** Explaining F's pro-

nouns, Abbott asserts that 'thou' may be used in statements and requests while 'you' is employed in conditional and other sentences in which there is no direct appeal to the person addressed (Abbott, 234; contrast *TxC*, 242).
51 **for them** i.e. to me on their behalf
52 i.e. as I am able to pretend plausibly, in my own person, to refuse your offers
53 *This line begins the portion of Q1 printed by Peter Short (see Hammond, 21–4; cf. pp. 425–31). **it** i.e. the entire transaction **issue** conclusion
54 **leads** the roof, covered with sheets or strips of lead (*OED sb.*[1] I 7a)
54.1 MAYOR Since the 18th century the Mayor has frequently been played as a buffoon (see Hankey, 179–80 for horseplay).

44 SP] *F, Q3–6 subst.; Glo. Q1–2* at hand] *F, Q1–2; om. Q3–6* Intend] *F; and intend Qq* 45 you spoke with] *F; spoken withall Qq* by] *F; with Qq* 47 between] *F; betwixt Qq* 48 make] *F; build Qq* 49 And] *F; not in Qq* easily] *F, Q1; easie Q2–6* requests] *F; request Qq* 50 still . . . and] *F; say no, but Qq* 51 I . . . you] *F; Feare not me, if thou canst Qq* 53 we] *F; weele Qq* 54] *F; You shal see what I can do, get you vp to the leads. Qq* 54.1] *F; not in Qq* Lord] *Rowe*

294

Welcome, my lord; I dance attendance here.   55
I think the Duke will not be spoke withal.

Enter CATESBY.

BUCKINGHAM

Now, Catesby, what says your lord to my request?

CATESBY

He doth entreat your grace, my noble lord,
To visit him tomorrow, or next day.
He is within, with two right reverend fathers,   60
Divinely bent to meditation;
And in no worldly suits would he be moved
To draw him from his holy exercise.

BUCKINGHAM

Return, good Catesby, to the gracious Duke;
Tell him myself, the Mayor and aldermen,   65
In deep designs, in matter of great moment,
No less importing than our general good,

---

55 **dance attendance** wait upon a person with assiduous attention (*OED* dance *v.* 5). Cf. *2H6* 1.3.172, *H8* 5.2.30; also Dent, A392.

56 **withal** with

57 *Cf. Qq's announcement of Catesby's entrance with 81 F; Qq again employ the term 'seruant' for Catesby (cf. 3.2.21).

60–3 Shakespeare develops Richard's 'pious exercises' from a single phrase in Hall describing his appearance between two bishops (see 93.1n.); otherwise, the sources have him acting as if anxious about the uncertain purposes of such a large assembly (Hall, *Edward V*, fol. xxiii'; Holinshed, 3.731).

60 **right reverend** title properly belong-

ing to bishops (*OED* reverend 2)

61 **bent** mentally inclined, disposed (*OED v.* 16), here perhaps implying a physical sense

62 **worldly suits** i.e. secular concerns

63 **exercise** act of devotion, religious observation; cf. 3.2.108.

65 **aldermen** originally, officials or wardens of guilds, but later, magistrates next in dignity to the mayor (*OED* 2, 3). Qq's 'Cittizens' might spare the expense of aldermen's robes (Patrick, 27).

66 **deep** serious, weighty (*OED a.* II 7b), but when coupled with *designs* also conveying a sense of being profound in craft or subtlety, as at 2.1.38

67 **No less importing** i.e. concerned with nothing less

---

55 Welcome, my lord] *F;* Now my L. Maior *Qq* 56 spoke] *F, Q1–2;* spoken *Q3–6* 57] *F;* Here coms his seruant: how now *Catesby* what saies he. *Qq* 58 He . . . grace, my noble lord] *F;* My Lord, he . . . grace *Qq* 60 right] *F, Q1–2; om. Q3–6* 62 suits] *F;* suite *Qq* 64 the gracious Duke] *F;* thy Lord againe *Qq* 65 aldermen] *F;* Cittizens *Qq* 66 in matter] *F;* and matters *Qq* 67 than] *F, Q1–5 (then);* them then *Q6*

Are come to have some conference with his grace.

CATESBY

I'll signify so much unto him straight.   *Exit.*

BUCKINGHAM

Ah ha, my lord, this prince is not an Edward.   70
He is not lulling on a lewd love-bed,
But on his knees at meditation;
Not dallying with a brace of courtesans,
But meditating with two deep divines;
Not sleeping, to engross his idle body,   75
But praying, to enrich his watchful soul.
Happy were England, would this virtuous prince
Take on his grace the sovereignty thereof.
But sure I fear we shall not win him to it.

MAYOR

Marry, God defend his grace should say us nay.   80

BUCKINGHAM

I fear he will. Here Catesby comes again.

Enter CATESBY.

Now, Catesby, what says his grace?

CATESBY

He wonders to what end you have assembled

---

71 **lulling** leaning idly, reclining in a relaxed attitude (*OED* loll *v.* 1 4)
love-bed perhaps a Shakespearean coinage (*OED* love *sb.*[1] 15a, citing this line) carrying, like Qq's 'day-bed' (*OED* day-bed, citing this line), sexual associations (*TN* 2.5.46–7)
73 **brace** pair, originally of dogs, also of game (*OED sb.*[2] III 15a); cf. *3H6* 2.5.129.
74 **deep** learned

75 **engross** fatten, make gross (*OED v.* III 9); associations with sexuality occur in *RJ* 2.4.165, *Ham* 1.2.136 and *Oth* 1.1.132.
76 **watchful** wakeful, accustomed to keeping awake; cf. 5.3.115. Jesus repeatedly admonishes his followers to 'watch' or to 'watch and pray' (Mark, 13.33–8, Matthew, 26.38–44).
80 **God defend** God forbid

69] *F;* Ile tell him *(*Ile him *Q6)* what you say my Lord *Qq*   71 love-bed] *F;* day bed *Qq*   77 virtuous] *F;* gracious *Qq*   78 his grace . . . thereof] *F;* himselfe . . . thereon *Qq*   79 not] *F;* neuer *Qq*   80 defend] *F;* forbid *Qq*   81 Here . . . again] *F;* how now Catesby *Qq*   81.1] *F, Q1–2; after* 80 *Q3–6*   82] *F;* What saies your Lord? *Qq*   83 He] *F;* My Lo. he *Qq*

Such troops of citizens to come to him,
His grace not being warned thereof before.   85
He fears, my lord, you mean no good to him.

BUCKINGHAM

Sorry I am my noble cousin should
Suspect me that I mean no good to him.
By heaven, we come to him in perfect love;   89
And so once more return and tell his grace.   *Exit* ᵠ*Catesby* ᵠ.
When holy and devout religious men
Are at their beads, 'tis much to draw them thence,
So sweet is zealous contemplation.

Enter RICHARD *aloft, between two Bishops.*
[*Enter* CATESBY.]

84 **troops** This potentially inflated claim for the number of citizens has often been played for laughs (Hankey, 180).

92 **beads** prayers, by Shakespeare's time usually implying reference to the rosary (*OED sb.* 1a, b)
much a great matter, difficult

93 **zealous** intensely earnest (*OED* 1d); by the early 1590s a potentially divisive term when employed to characterize religious attitudes, practices and factions. In attacking Puritanism, Richard Hooker refers to 'this present age, wherein zeal hath drowned charity, and skill meekness' (*Laws*, 170). By contrast, Henry Smith laments that religious 'zeale is counted no vertue' and the zealous 'are counted curious, factious, precise, phantasticall', adding 'some giddy spirites thinke now, that they which are zelouser than the[m] selues know not what they say nor doe' (*Sermons*, 935–6, 921).

93.1 **aloft . . . Bishops** More describes Richard's appearance 'aboue in a galarye' (*CW2*, 77); '*alofi*' is the usual Shakespearean term for the playing space above the main stage platform (Dessen & Thomson, 4). Richard plays the rest of the scene from this elevated location. No clerics appear here in More (*CW2*, 77) or Holinshed (3.731); in Grafton's edition of Hardyng and in Hall, Richard appears 'with a bishop on euery hande of hym' (Hall, *Edward V*, fol. xxiiiᵛ; Hardyng, *Edward V*, fol. lxxvʳ). Two clerics flank the royal person in coronation pageantry (Lyons, 23); cf. Richard's historical coronation between two bishops (Sutton & Hammond, 216).

93.2 CATESBY Since Catesby left at 90 to fetch Richard and has lines at 202ff., this seems like a good time for his re-entry; F and Qq provide no indications. He enters to the main playing stage rather than above.

84 **come to**] *F;* speake with *Qq*   86 He . . . lord] *F;* My Lord, he feares *Qq*   89 we . . . love] *F (*perfit*);* I come in perfect loue to him *Qq*   92 **much**] *F;* hard *Qq*   thence] *F, Q1–4;* hence *Q5–6*   93.1] *F; Enter Rich. with (and Q3–6) two bishops a loste (aloft Q2–6). Qq*   93.2] *Theobald (*Catesby returns.*)*

MAYOR

    See where his grace stands, 'tween two clergymen.

BUCKINGHAM

    Two props of virtue for a Christian prince,   95

    To stay him from the fall of vanity;

    And see a book of prayer in his hand,

    True ornaments to know a holy man.

    – Famous Plantagenet, most gracious prince,

    Lend favourable ear to our requests,   100

    And pardon us the interruption

    Of thy devotion and right Christian zeal.

RICHARD

    My lord, there needs no such apology.

    I do beseech your grace to pardon me,

    Who, earnest in the service of my God,   105

    Deferred the visitation of my friends.

    But leaving this, what is your grace's pleasure?

BUCKINGHAM

    Even that, I hope, which pleaseth God above

    And all good men of this ungoverned isle.

95–8 **props, ornaments** Richard's public exploitation of bishops in his tyrannical usurpation suggests contentious issues for the early 1590s (see pp. 31–6). The word *props* means 'supports'; the sense of stage requisites is not recorded before the 19th century (*OED* property *sb.* 3), though Quince speaks of a 'bill of properties' (*MND* 1.2.98–9; cf. *MW* 4.4.77).

96 **stay** prevent, restrain (*OED v.*[1] III 23) **fall of vanity** i.e. succumbing to worthless worldly temptations and falling into sin

97 **book of prayer** Qq lack 97–8, but the prayer-book seems made for the moment. A similar devotional book is employed hypocritically in *Ham* 3.1.43–5. Henry VI's piety is registered by his entry 'with a prayer book' (*3H6* 3.1.12.1), and by his reading of a devotional 'book' just before his murder by Richard (*3H6* 5.6.1). For 'book' as *Book of Common Prayer*, see *OED* book *sb.* 5b.

98 **ornaments** the bishops and the prayer-book (cf. 95–8n.) **to know** i.e. by which to recognize

102 **right** true, proper (*OED a.* II 7a) **zeal** see 93n.

109 **ungoverned** i.e. lacking a supreme ruler

---

94 his grace . . . 'tween] *F;* he . . . between *Qq* 97–8] *F; not in Qq* 100 ear] *F;* eares *Qq* our] *F, Q1;* my *Q2–6* requests] *F;* request *Qq* 104 I . . . to] *F;* I rather do beseech you *Qq* 106 Deferred] *F;* Neglect *Qq*

RICHARD

> I do suspect I have done some offence 110
> That seems disgracious in the City's eye,
> And that you come to reprehend my ignorance.

BUCKINGHAM

> You have, my lord. Would it might please your grace,
> On our entreaties, to amend your fault.

RICHARD

> Else wherefore breathe I in a Christian land? 115

BUCKINGHAM

> Know then, it is your fault that you resign
> The supreme seat, the throne majestical,
> The sceptered office of your ancestors,
> Your state of fortune, and your due of birth,
> The lineal glory of your royal house, 120
> To the corruption of a blemished stock;
> Whiles in the mildness of your sleepy thoughts,
> Which here we waken to our country's good,

---

111 **disgracious** displeasing, out of favour (*OED* 2); cf. 4.4.178.

112 **ignorance** offence or sin caused by ignorance (*OED* 2); cf. the Litany: 'That it may please thee to give us true repentance, to forgive us all our sins, negligences, and ignorances' (*BCP*, 71).

115 **Else wherefore** i.e. otherwise why **breathe** live; cf. 1.1.21.

116 **resign** relinquish, surrender (*OED* v.¹ 1); cf. *VA* 1039–40.

119, 126 *Absence from Qq may represent an effort at tightening up this speech (Jowett), but reference to Richard's *state of fortune* (119) contributes an element of *realpolitik* in urging him to make good on the opportunity that fortune has provided, and reference to

grafting (126) recalls plant imagery in other early plays by Shakespeare (see 126n.). Richard later expounds upon Buckingham's themes (166–7, 171).

119 **state of fortune** i.e. the status and power that fortune has granted you

120 **house** i.e. family, house of York

121 **corruption . . . stock** The metaphor is horticultural: Edward is a bastard; the York family is corrupted by his effect upon their lineal stem. See 126, 166, 215 for development of the metaphor. Cf. the text of Dr Shaw's Paul's Cross sermon: 'Bastard slippes shall neuer take deepe root' (Holinshed, 3.727). For visual embodiments of the metaphor, see pp. 69–72 and the frontispiece to Hall's 1550 edition (Fig. 1).

---

111 seems] *F, Q1–4;* seeme *Q5–6* eye] *F;* eies *Qq* 113] *Qq; F lines* Lord: / Grace, / might] *F; not in Qq* 114 On . . . your] *F;* At . . . that *Qq* 116 Know then] *F;* Then know *Qq* 119] *F; not in Qq* 122 Whiles] *F;* Whilst *Q1;* Whilest *Q2–6* your] *F, Q1, 3–6;* you *Q2* 123 our] *F, Q1–4;* your *Q5–6*

The noble isle doth want her proper limbs;
Her face defaced with scars of infamy,   125
Her royal stock graft with ignoble plants,
And almost shouldered in the swallowing gulf
Of dark forgetfulness and deep oblivion;
Which to recure, we heartily solicit
Your gracious self to take on you the charge   130
And kingly government of this your land,
Not as protector, steward, substitute,
Or lowly factor for another's gain,
But as successively from blood to blood,
Your right of birth, your empery, your own.   135

---

124 **want** lack

124, 125, 126 **her, Her** For England personified as female in a passage that echoes *Richard III* 1.4.24–33, see *H5* 1.2.155–73. Thompson argues that the F repetition of 'his' and its occurrence in a line peculiar to F (126) suggest that it is not an error (cf. Smidt, *Memorial*, 53). The alternative argument is that 'his' first appeared in 124 as a Q3 error, went uncorrected in F and influenced F's 'His' in 125, so that F's added 126, although derived from FMS, was altered in print to agree with the mistaken pronouns in 124–5 (Hammond). This edition somewhat uneasily accepts this argument. The gendering here is interesting in a play where one crippled male character 'want[s] his proper limbs' and another promiscuous male figure is said to have had his 'stock graft with ignoble plants'.

124 **proper** rightful, own (*OED a.* I 1), but also, given Richard's limbs, ironically implying 'well-made, handsome' (*OED a.* II 9)

126 **graft** engrafted; cf. *2H6* 3.2.212–14.

127 **shouldered in** pushed roughly into with the shoulder, jostled (*OED v.* 1); cf. *1H6* 4.1.189–90, where 'factious' nobles engage in 'shouldering' each other.

swallowing gulf A *gulf* might be an abyss or chasm, but *swallowing* determines the sense as 'whirlpool' (*OED sb.* 3; cf. *H5* 2.4.10). For destruction and death associated with falling into water, see 1.4.18–62, 3.4.97–100. Cf. Henry VI to Richard for having murdered his son: 'thyself, the sea / Whose envious gulf did swallow up his life' (*3H6* 5.6.24–5).

129 **recure** remedy, redress (*OED v.* 2b)

130 **charge** responsibility of taking care of (*OED sb.* 13)

132–5 another of Wilson's linguistic 'tangles'

133 **factor** one who acts for another as agent (*OED sb.* 3); cf. 4.4.72.

134 **successively ... to blood** i.e. by succession of descent from generation to generation

135 **empery** absolute dominion or territory of an absolute ruler

---

124 The] *F;* This *Qq*   her] *Q1–2;* his *F, Q3–6* 125 Her] *Qq;* His *F*   scars] *F, Q1, 5–6;* stars *Q2–4*   126] *F; not in Qq*   Her] *Pope;* His *F*   127 the] *F, Q1–2;* this *Q3–6*   128 dark ... deep] *F;* blind ... darke *Qq*   129 recure] *F, Q1–5;* recouer *Q6*   130–1 charge ... land] *F;* soueraingtie thereof *Qq*   133 Or] *F, Q1–2;* Nor *Q3–6*

For this, consorted with the citizens,
Your very worshipful and loving friends,
And by their vehement instigation,
In this just cause come I to move your grace.

RICHARD

I cannot tell if to depart in silence   140
Or bitterly to speak in your reproof
Best fitteth my degree or your condition.
If not to answer, you might haply think
Tongue-tied ambition, not replying, yielded
To bear the golden yoke of sovereignty,   145
Which fondly you would here impose on me.
If to reprove you for this suit of yours,
So seasoned with your faithful love to me,
Then on the other side I checked my friends.
Therefore, to speak, and to avoid the first,   150

136 **consorted** associated (*OED v.* 4); cf. 3.4.70.
137 **worshipful** honourable; while the term could mean distinguished in rank or importance (see 3.4.39), it had begun to evolve in Shakespeare's day towards more restricted application to members of livery companies (*OED* 2, 3); see also 1.1.66–7. In passages from Hall that Shakespeare drew upon for *3H6*, Edward addresses the aldermen of York as 'worshipfull' (*Edward IV*, fol. ccxiv^v).
142 **degree** position in the scale of dignity or rank (*OED* 4)
condition state in regard to wealth or circumstances (*OED sb.* 10); or character, moral disposition (*OED sb.* 11). Condition and degree appear nearly synonymous in *2H4* 4.3.1–8, but here Richard differentiates them, asking whether it better befits his exalted degree and the citizens' lower

social or moral condition to leave without responding or to reprove them for their inappropriate solicitations.
143–52 *Absence of these lines from Qq abbreviates Richard's lengthy remarks, but results in omission of the carefully crafted development they give to 140–2; Patrick (127) suggests inexact parallelism between 140–2 and 153.
143–5 Cf. Dent, S446: 'Silence is (gives) consent.'
143 **haply** perhaps
144 **yielded** i.e. yielded to your entreaties
146 **fondly** foolishly
148 **seasoned** qualified by a beneficial admixture (*OED v.* 1d)
149 **on . . . side** i.e. going to the other extreme
checked rebuked, reprimanded; 'you might haply think' is implied from 143.

137 very] *F, Q1–2; om. Q3–6* loving] *F, Q1–2; very louing Q3–6* 139 cause] *F; suite Qq*
140 cannot tell if] *F; know not whether (whither Q5–6) Qq* 143–52] *F; not in Qq*

And then, in speaking, not to incur the last,
Definitively thus I answer you:
Your love deserves my thanks, but my desert
Unmeritable shuns your high request.
First, if all obstacles were cut away, 155
And that my path were even to the crown
As the ripe revenue and due of birth,
Yet so much is my poverty of spirit,
So mighty and so many my defects,
That I would rather hide me from my greatness, 160
Being a bark to brook no mighty sea,
Than in my greatness covet to be hid
And in the vapour of my glory smothered.
But, God be thanked, there is no need of me,
And much I need to help you, were there need. 165
The royal tree hath left us royal fruit,
Which, mellowed by the stealing hours of time,
Will well become the seat of majesty,
And make, no doubt, us happy by his reign.

153–4 **desert / Unmeritable** i.e. unworthiness, undeserving merit
155–6 **cut . . . crown** Cf. Richard's image of hewing through thorny woods to the crown (*3H6* 3.2.174–81); see also 121n., 126n.
156 **that** if
   even smooth, unimpeded
157 **ripe revenue** rèvenue (as *R2* 2.1.226); benefit or return that is ready to be inherited (*OED* revenue 3); there may be an anticipated (but implicit) contrast between Richard's ripeness in age and the immaturity of the Prince, the *fruit* that needs further mellowing (166–7).
158 **poverty of spirit** biblical (Matthew, 5.3: 'Blessed are the poore in spirite: for theirs is the kyngdome of heauen.')

160 **my greatness** i.e. my royal title
161 **bark** small ship
   brook endure
162 **covet** i.e. desire
163 **vapour** exhalation of the nature of steam, here denoting something unsubstantial or worthless (*OED sb.* 2a, 2c)
165 **much I need** i.e. I am lacking in the quality necessary (to help you, if help were needed).
167 **stealing** i.e. slipping away imperceptibly; cf. 5.3.85.
168 **well become** i.e. be well suited to
169 **no doubt** Denying doubt rhetorically raises the possibility of doubt; cf. Mark Antony's damning asseveration: 'And sure he is an honourable man' (*JC* 3.2.100).

157 the ripe] *F*; my ripe *Q1*; my right *Q2–6*   of] *F*; by *Qq*   160 That I would] *F*; As I had *Qq*   164 thanked, there is] *F* (thank'd, there is); thanked there's *Qq*   of] *F, Q1–2*; for *Q3–6*   165 were there need] *F*; if need were *Qq*

On him I lay that you would lay on me: 170
The right and fortune of his happy stars,
Which God defend that I should wring from him.
BUCKINGHAM
My lord, this argues conscience in your grace,
But the respects thereof are nice and trivial,
All circumstances well considered.   175
You say that Edward is your brother's son;
So say we too, but not by Edward's wife.
For first was he contract to Lady Lucy –
Your mother lives a witness to his vow –
And afterward by substitute betrothed   180
To Bona, sister to the King of France.
These both put off, a poor petitioner,
A care-crazed mother to a many sons,

---

171 **happy stars** i.e. fortunate destiny; cf. 119n.
172 **defend** forbid
    wring wrest or wrench, acquire by exaction or extortion (*OED v.* 7); cf. *3H6* 2.1.153, *JC* 4.3.73.
173 **this argues conscience** i.e. this speech evidences scrupulous conscience.
174 **respects thereof** considerations (*OED sb.* 14) that support your argument
    nice unimportant (*OED* 10b), suggesting overly subtle (*OED* 7); cf. *3H6* 4.7.58, where Richard urges Edward to seize the crown, 'Why, brother, wherefore stand you on nice points?' Richard's blunt demand that his brother take forceful action in spite of (Edward's own) principled objections provides an ironic contrast to Buckingham's tortuously constructed rhetorical justifications for usurpation.

175 **considered** considerèd
176 **Edward** i.e. Prince Edward
177–81 See 4–6.
178 **contract** contràct; i.e. contracted (Abbott, 342); cf. 5.
181 **sister** sister-in-law; Lady Bona's eldest sister was King Louis's second wife; cf. *3H6* 3.3.0.1.
182 **put off** i.e. thrust aside
    a poor petitioner For Elizabeth Grey's petitions to Edward IV and his lustful response, see *3H6* 3.2.
183 **care-crazed** shattered by care; cf. woe-wearied (4.4.18).
    a many 'a' is frequently inserted before 'many' to indicate that the objects enumerated are thought of collectively as one (Abbott, 87).
    sons Before marrying Edward IV, Elizabeth had three children, a daughter and two sons, by her first husband, Sir John Grey; the two sons in this play are the Marquess of Dorset and Lord Grey.

---

170 that] *F;* what *Qq*   178 was he] *F;* he was *Qq*   contract] *F, Q1–5;* contracted *Q6*   179 his] *F;* that *Qq*   180 afterward] *F, Q1–5;* afterwards *Q6*   182 off] *F;* by *Qq*   183 to a . . . sons] *F;* of a . . . children *Q1;* of . . . children *Q2–6*

A beauty-waning and distressed widow,
Even in the afternoon of her best days,   185
Made prize and purchase of his wanton eye,
Seduced the pitch and height of his degree
To base declension and loathed bigamy.
By her, in his unlawful bed, he got
This Edward, whom our manners call the Prince.   190
More bitterly could I expostulate,
Save that, for reverence to some alive,
I give a sparing limit to my tongue.
Then, good my lord, take to your royal self
This proffered benefit of dignity,   195
If not to bless us and the land withal,
Yet to draw forth your noble ancestry
From the corruption of abusing times
Unto a lineal, true-derived course.

186 **prize and purchase** gains, winnings; especially that which is taken in the hunt, in pillage, robbery or in war (*OED* purchase *sb.* 8)
187 **pitch** height to which a falcon or other bird of prey soars before swooping down on its prey (*OED sb.*² 18a); cf. *1H6* 2.4.11. The line continues the play's social commentary by means of references to birds (see e.g. 1.1.132–3).
188 **declension** decline from a standard, here the standard of Edward's royal rank (*OED* 2); cf. *Ham* 2.2.146.
   bigamy Not only was Edward IV bound by previous 'contract' to Lady Lucy (see 4–6n.), but according to ecclesiastical law remarriage after death of a first wife or husband and marriage of, or with, a widow or widower also constituted bigamy (*OED* 2,

citing this line). Edward's own mother raised the accusation of adultery against him to dissuade him from his marriage (Holinshed, 3.726). The charge is remarkable, given Richard's own marriage to Anne, the widow of Prince Edward (Furness).
190 **our manners** i.e. our sense of politeness
191 **expostulate** expound the matter
192 **some alive** i.e. the Duchess of York, Richard and Edward IV's mother (see 3.5.93–4)
193 **give . . . to** i.e. restrain
195 **benefit of dignity** benefaction, gift (*OED sb.* 2c) of high estate
197 **draw forth** rescue
198 **of abusing times** arising from the abuses of Edward IV's reign
199 **true-derived** true-derivèd; lawfully descended

186 wanton] *F;* lustfull *Qq*   187 Seduced] *F, Q1–5 subst.;* Seduce *Q6*   his degree] *F;* al his thoughts *Qq*   189 his] *F, Q1–5;* this *Q6*   190 call] *F;* terme *Qq*   191 I] *F, Q1–5; om. Q6*   197 forth . . . ancestry] *F;* out your royall stocke *Qq*   198 times] *F;* time *Qq*   199 true-derived] *F, Qq (*true deri-ued*), hyphen Theobald*

MAYOR

    Do, good my lord. Your citizens entreat you.   200

BUCKINGHAM

    Refuse not, mighty lord, this proffered love.

CATESBY

    O, make them joyful. Grant their lawful suit.

RICHARD

    Alas, why would you heap this care on me?

    I am unfit for state and majesty.

    I do beseech you, take it not amiss;   205

    I cannot, nor I will not, yield to you.

BUCKINGHAM

    If you refuse it, as in love and zeal

    Loath to depose the child, your brother's son –

    As well we know your tenderness of heart

    And gentle, kind, effeminate remorse,   210

    Which we have noted in you to your kindred,

    And equally indeed to all estates –

    Yet know, whe'er you accept our suit or no,

    Your brother's son shall never reign our king,

    But we will plant some other in the throne   215

    To the disgrace and downfall of your house.

---

200 **Your citizens** Perhaps strategically ambiguous: in a loose sense the phrase suggests popular partisanship (i.e. the citizens that are on your side), but its strict sense was reserved for the sovereign (i.e. the citizens that belong to you by virtue of your sovereignty); cf. 1n.

207 **as** being

210 **effeminate** gentle, tender, compassionate (*OED a.* 1c, citing this line); Tawney notes this as the only non-pejorative use in Shakespeare (Var). Cf.

womanish compassion (1.4.261). Hall speaks positively of Prince Edward, son of Henry VI, as 'a goodly femenine & a well feautered yonge gentelman' (*Edward IV*, fol. ccxxi^r).

remorse pity, compassion (*OED sb.* 3); cf. 1.2.158 and *Mac* 1.5.43.

211 **to** toward

212 **estates** orders, ranks, sorts of people (*OED sb.* 5)

213 **whe'er** whether (see also 228)

215 Cf. 2.2.100.

200 Do,] *F4;* Do *F, Qq*   201] *F; not in Qq*   203 this care] *F;* those *(*these *Q1)* cares *Qq*   204 majesty] *F;* dignitie *Qq*   211 kindred] *F;* kin *Qq*   212 equally] *F, Q3–6 (*egally*), Q1–2 (*egallie*)*   213 know, whe'er] *Theobald;* know, where *F;* whether *Qq*   accept] *F, Q1–5;* except *Q6*

And in this resolution here we leave you.
– Come, citizens. Zounds, I'll entreat no more.

^QRICHARD

 O, do not swear, my lord of Buckingham!^Q

     Exeunt [Buckingham and some others].

CATESBY

 Call him again, sweet prince; accept their suit.   220
 If you deny them, all the land will rue it.

RICHARD

 Will you enforce me to a world of cares?
 Call them again.   *[Exit Catesby.]*
     I am not made of stones,
 But penetrable to your kind entreaties,
 Albeit against my conscience and my soul.   225

    Enter BUCKINGHAM *and the rest.*

 Cousin of Buckingham, and sage, grave men,

218–19 *F's omission of Richard's memorable line would be difficult to understand if not for the need to excise Buckingham's 'Zounds' – i.e. by His (Christ's) wounds – in keeping with the Statute of 1606 (see 1.4.84–end n.). Richard's pious admonition contributes a puritanical emphasis to his hypocrisy; the deceitful priest in *Knack* proclaims, 'Fie, not an oath we sweare', taking this principle as definitive for those who would be 'tearmed pure Precisians' (338–44).

219 SD *Since Catesby in F speaks of calling 'him back' (220) but also refers to 'them' (221), and since F also has a re-entry for '*Buckingham, and the rest*' (225), F's '*Exeunt*' includes Buckingham and others. Not everyone exits, since 223–5 are addressed

to someone as Catesby goes to summon Buckingham and the others. Richard's reference in both F and Qq to 'Buckingham, and [you Qq] sage graue men' (226) suggests that the leaders – the Mayor and certain aldermen – depart with Buckingham.

221 *Qq have an anonymous speaker ('*Ano.*'), which potentially makes the sentiments of the crowd seem less obviously the product of manipulation.

222 **enforce me to** i.e. force upon me

223 SD There is not much time for Catesby to exit and summon the group that re-enters two lines later, which makes an incomplete exit by Buckingham and the others and a summoning gesture from Catesby staging possibilities (Hammond).

218 Zounds, I'll] *Qq;* we will *F* 219 SD *Exeunt*] *F;* not in *Qq* *Buckingham . . . others*] *Oxf* 220 him . . . prince;] *F;* them again, my lord, and *Qq* 221] *F; Ano.* Doe, good my lord, least all the land do rew it. *Qq* 222 Will . . . cares] *F;* Would . . . care *Qq* 223 Call] *F;* Well, call *Qq* SD] *Theobald subst.* 224 entreaties] *F;* intreates *Qq subst.* 225.1] *F;* not in *Qq* 226 sage] *F;* you sage *Qq*

Since you will buckle fortune on my back,
To bear her burden, whe'er I will or no,
I must have patience to endure the load;
But if black scandal or foul-faced reproach   230
Attend the sequel of your imposition,
Your mere enforcement shall acquittance me
From all the impure blots and stains thereof,
For God doth know, and you may partly see,
How far I am from the desire of this.   235

MAYOR

God bless your grace; we see it and will say it.

RICHARD

In saying so, you shall but say the truth.

BUCKINGHAM

Then I salute you with this royal title:
Long live King Richard, England's worthy king!

---

227 **buckle . . . back** An odd image, calling attention to Richard's spinal configuration; Lyons (23) suggests emblems representing Hope as a man walking doubled over, burdened by Fortune's wheel strapped to his back; cf. *bent* (61).

231 **Attend** follow, accompany
sequel . . . imposition i.e. the aftermath of the duty you impose on me

232 **mere** unassisted, sole (*OED a.* 2)
acquittance acquit

239 Cf. the proclamation of Richard's father, the Duke of York, as king: 'Long live our sovereign Richard, England's king!' (*2H6* 2.2.63). In the 2001 Michael Boyd–Aiden McArdle RSC production, Buckingham (Richard Cordery) encouraged the audience (who had been introduced to Richard as 'these good friends' in

a modified 3.7.65 and included in the action by raised house lights) to join in acclaiming 'King Richard the Third'; he then responded to the silence (or laughter) of the house by quickly turning to question Richard about the date of the coronation (Day, 184).

***King Richard** Many editors drop Richard's title, recognizing the Q3 origin of *King* and perhaps prompted by a sense of redundancy. However, Buckingham's lines frequently indulge in repetitiveness and rhetorical overkill. Furthermore, 238 is clearly intended to introduce a 'salute' to Richard with 'this royal (F)/kingly (Qq) title' – i.e. with the exact phrase that names his new pre-eminence, 'King Richard', at this juncture in More. In sum, it seems inadvisable to alter F here when the hard-sell tactics employed in peddling

---

227 you] *F, Q1–2, 4–6;* your *Q3*   228 her] *F, Q1–2;* the *Q3–6*   whe'er] *Rann;* where *F;* whether *Qq*   230 foul-faced] *F;* soule-fac't *Q1–2;* so foule fac't *Q3–5;* so foulefac't *Q6*   234 doth know] *F;* he knowes *Qq*   235 of this] *F;* thereof *Qq*   238 this royal] *F;* this kingly *Q1–3, 5–6;* the kingly *Q4*   239 King Richard] *F, Q3–6;* Richard *Q1–2*   worthy] *F;* royall *Qq*

ALL   Amen.   240
BUCKINGHAM
  Tomorrow may it please you to be crowned?
RICHARD
  Even when you please, for you will have it so.
BUCKINGHAM
  Tomorrow, then, we will attend your grace,
  And so most joyfully we take our leave.
RICHARD
  Come, let us to our holy work again.   245
  – Farewell, my cousin, farewell gentle friends.   *Exeunt.*

4.1   *Enter* QUEEN [ELIZABETH], *the* DUCHESS of York
     and Marquess [of] DORSET ^Q*at one door*^Q; ANNE, Duchess
         of Gloucester [, *with Clarence's* Daughter,]
                   ^Q*at another door*^Q.

Richard's kingship are so evident and when the speaker has already demonstrated linguistic limitations. Peele's *Edward I* (1593) has a line resembling Q3, F's phrasing: 'God saue king *Baliol* the Scottish king' (742; sig. C4ʳ).	Hall to assume rule.
	246 ***cousin** F has Richard address everyone familiarly as 'Cousins', a plural form he elsewhere uses to a group that includes non-relatives (3.4.22), but then Richard speaks with nobles and peers as well as family. It seems improbable that he would be so familiar with mere citizens, since he has expressly distinguished his own *degree* from their *condition* (142).
240 SP *Qq have the Mayor speak for everyone.	
242 Richard's denial of his own agency echoes, yet again, his rhetorical stance throughout the scene.	
243 **Tomorrow** According to Shakespeare's sources, the interview with the Mayor and citizens took place on 25 June 1483; Richard was crowned on 6 July (More, *CW*2, 82), but his accession was dated from 26 June, when he went publicly to Westminster	246 SD Cibber has Richard send everyone off while he gloats in soliloquy. Garrick added a touch that has had a long theatrical afterlife by flinging away his prayer-book (Hankey, 187).
	4.1 location: '*before the* Tower' (Theobald). Cibber sets in the Tower.

240 SP] *F; M yor. Q1; Mai. Q2–4; May. Q5–6*   241 may] *F; will Qq*   242 please, for] *F; will, since Qq*   244] *F; not in Qq*   245 work] *F; taske Qq*   246 my] *F; good Qq*   cousin] *Qq; Cousins F*   SD] *F, Q1, 3–6; om. Q2*   4.1] *F (Actus Quartus. Scena Prima.); not in Qq*   0.1–4] *Enter the Queene, Anne Duchesse of Gloucester, the / Duchesse of Yorke, and Marquesse Dorset. F; Enter Quee. mother, Duchesse of Yorke, Marques Dorset, at / one doore, Duchesse of Glocest. at another doore. Qq*   0.3 *with Clarence's* Daughter] *Eccles; leading Clarence's young Daughter. / Theobald*

DUCHESS

Who meets us here? My niece Plantagenet,
Led in the hand of her kind aunt of Gloucester?
Now, for my life, she's wandering to the Tower,
On pure heart's love, to greet the tender Prince.
– Daughter, well met.

ANNE   God give your graces both   5
A happy and a joyful time of day.

QUEEN ELIZABETH

As much to you, good sister. Whither away?

ANNE

No farther than the Tower, and, as I guess,
Upon the like devotion as yourselves,
To gratulate the gentle Princes there.   10

QUEEN ELIZABETH

Kind sister, thanks. We'll enter all together.

Enter [BRAKENBURY,] *the Lieutenant.*

1   **My niece Plantagenet** Theobald
recognized that this referred to
Clarence's daughter, the Duchess's
granddaughter (*OED* niece 1a). Qq
lack the second line, so Qq's Duchess
may refer to Anne, her 'niece' ('female
relative' *OED*) by marriage, losing the
touching detail of Anne's caring for
Clarence's daughter, a demonstration
of humanity remarkable for this play.

2   **in** by (cf. *Tit* 5.3.138)
      aunt of Gloucester i.e. Lady Anne

3   **for my life** i.e. upon my life (Abbott,
150); a mild oath
      wandering Since the Duchess (cor-
rectly) guesses that Anne and Clarence's

daughter travel to the Tower, perhaps
they proceed 'by uncertain and devious routes' (*OED* wandering *ppl. a*).

4   **On** i.e. out of; cf. Abbott, 180 and *AC*
3.6.58: 'On my free will'.
      tender having the delicacy of youth,
immature (*OED a.* 4) and perhaps also
the object of tender feeling, precious
(*OED a.* 8b); cf. 98.
      Prince See 14–16n.

5   **Daughter** i.e. daughter-in-law

7   **sister** i.e. sister-in-law

9   **Upon . . . devotion** i.e. with the same
devoted purpose (*OED sb.* II 7)

10 **gratulate** greet, salute (*OED v.* 1); cf.
Tit 1.1.225.

1+ SP] *Rowe subst.; Duch. Yorke. F; Du[ch].[yor.] Qq subst.* 1] *Qq; F lines* heere? / Plantagenet, /
2–4] *F; not in Qq* 3 wandering] *F (*wandring*)* 5 Daughter, well met.] *F; Qu. Sister well met,*
Qq 5–6 ANNE . . . day.] *F (lines* happie / day. / *)*, *Pope; not in Qq* 7 As . . . sister] *F; not in*
Qq Whither away] *F; whether awaie so fast Qq subst.* 8 SP] *F; Duch. Q1; Du. Q2; Dut. Glo.*
Q3–6 10 gentle] *F; tender Qq* 11.1] *F; Enter / Lieutenant. Q1–2 opp. 11–12; Enter the Lieutenant*
of the Tower. Q3–6 BRAKENBURY] *Capell*

And in good time, here the Lieutenant comes.
Master Lieutenant, pray you, by your leave,
How doth the Prince and my young son of York?

BRAKENBURY

Right well, dear madam. By your patience,   15
I may not suffer you to visit them.
The King hath strictly charged the contrary.

QUEEN ELIZABETH

The King? Who's that?

BRAKENBURY   I mean the Lord Protector.

QUEEN ELIZABETH

The Lord protect him from that kingly title.
Hath he set bounds between their love and me?   20
I am their mother. Who shall bar me from them?

DUCHESS

I am their father's mother. I will see them.

ANNE

Their aunt I am in law, in love their mother.
Then bring me to their sights. I'll bear thy blame

14–16 ***Prince . . . them** In F the object
of the visitors first appears to be singular (4) and then ultimately to be plural
(10). Qq initially refer to 'Princes' (10)
but later to 'the Prince' (14) and to
'him' (16).

15 **By your patience** with your permission, indulgence (*OED* patience *sb.* 3);
cf. *Tem* 3.3.3.

16 **suffer** allow

17–18 **King . . . Lord Protector** His
clumsy self-correction (*I mean*)
makes it clear that Brakenbury's
slip is designed to be noticed; yet its
significance for a non-aligned speaker

is uncertain. Without the Vice's wit or
deceptive purpose, Brakenbury's verbal
substitution suggests self-betraying
utterance (see e.g. King Edward's
verbal slip in *E3*, 2.2.34–42). In Hall
and Holinshed the Prince learns that
Richard has taken the title of King
and deduces his danger from this
(Hall, *Richard III*, fol. xxvii^v). In *True
Tragedy* the Prince hears Myles Forest
refer to Richard as King (1271).

20 **bounds** limits, boundaries

23 **in law** by marriage

24 **their sights** i.e. the sight of them; cf.
Tim 1.1.250.

14] *F;* How fares *(feares Q6)* the Prince? *Qq*   15, 18, 26 SP] *Capell; Lieu. F, Qq*   15] *F;* Wel
Madam, and in health, but by your leaue, *Qq*   16 them] *F;* him *Qq*   17 strictly] *F;* straightlie
Qq   18] *Steevens; F, Qq line* that? / Protector. /   Who's] *F;* whie, whose *(who's Q3–6) Qq*   I mean]
F; I crie you mercie, I meane *Qq*   20 between] *F;* betwixt *Qq*   21 shall bar] *F;* should keepe *Qq*
22 SP] *F, Q1; om. Q2–6*   their . . . I] *F (*Fathers*);* their Fathers, Mother, I *Q1;* their father, Mother,
and *Q2–3, 5–6;* theirs father mother, and *Q4*   23+ SP] *F; Duch.[glo]. Qq*   24 bring . . . sights] *F;*
feare not thou *Qq*

And take thy office from thee, on my peril.   25

BRAKENBURY

No, madam, no. I may not leave it so.

I am bound by oath, and therefore pardon me.   *Exit.*

Enter STANLEY.

STANLEY

Let me but meet you ladies one hour hence,

And I'll salute your grace of York as mother

And reverend looker-on of two fair queens.   30

[*to Anne*] Come, madam, you must straight to
    Westminster,

There to be crowned Richard's royal queen.

QUEEN ELIZABETH

Ah, cut my lace asunder

That my pent heart may have some scope to beat,

Or else I swoon with this dead-killing news.   35

ANNE

Despiteful tidings. O, unpleasing news.

25 **office** duty, assigned charge
26 *Hammond (5–6) adduces the similarity between Brakenbury's Q1 26, Q1, F 1.1.84 ('I beseech your Graces both to pardon me') and Q1, F 1.1.103 ('I do beseech your Grace / To pardon me' (F); 'I beseech your Grace to pardon me' (Q1)) to argue for memorial construction of Q1.

leave it i.e. abdicate my obligation
29–30 **mother . . . queens** mother-in-law of Elizabeth, widow of King Edward, and of Anne, wife of King Richard
31 **straight** go immediately
Westminster i.e. Westminster Abbey
32 **crowned** crownèd
33 **lace** cord or string drawing together the opposite edges of a bodice
34 **scope** room (*OED sb.*[2] 8)
35 **dead-killing** deadly; cf. Tarquin's 'dead-killing eye' (*Luc* 540).
36 **Despiteful** cruel, malignant (*OED* 2)

26] *F;* I doe beseech your graces all to pardon me: *Qq* 27 and . . . me] *F;* I may not doe it. *Qq* SD] *F (Exit Lieutenant.); not in Qq* 27.1 STANLEY] *F;* L. Stanlie *Q1–2;* Lord Standly (Stanley *Q4) Q3–6* 28 you ladies one] *F;* you Ladies an *Q1–4;* you Ladies at an *Q5;* your Ladies at an *Q6* 30 reverend] *F;* reuerente *Qq* 31 SD] *Johnson subst.* straight] *F;* go with me *Qq* 33–5] *F; Qq line* heart, / sound, / newes. / 33 Ah] *F;* O *Qq* asunder] *F;* in sunder *Qq* 35 else I] *F, Q1, Q3 (all but Hn), Q5–6;* else *Q2, Q3 (Hn), Q4* swoon] *F;* sound *Qq* dead-killing] *F; Q1–4 (dead killing);* dead liking *Q5–6* 36] *F; not in Qq*

DORSET

Be of good cheer, mother. How fares your grace?

QUEEN ELIZABETH

O Dorset, speak not to me. Get thee gone.
Death and destruction dogs thee at thy heels.
Thy mother's name is ominous to children.   40
If thou wilt outstrip death, go, cross the seas
And live with Richmond, from the reach of hell.
Go hie thee, hie thee from this slaughterhouse,
Lest thou increase the number of the dead
And make me die the thrall of Margaret's curse,   45
Nor mother, wife, nor England's counted queen.

STANLEY

Full of wise care is this your counsel, madam.
[*to Dorset*] Take all the swift advantage of the hours.
You shall have letters from me to my son
In your behalf, to meet you on the way.   50
Be not ta'en tardy by unwise delay.

DUCHESS

O ill-dispersing wind of misery.

---

39 **dogs** Death and destruction are taken
as a collective singular.
41 **outstrip** outrun (*OED v.*¹ 1), continuing the image of *dogs* (39)
42 **with Richmond** i.e. with Henry Tudor,
Earl of Richmond, and later Henry VII,
who had taken refuge in Brittany after
the battle of Tewkesbury in 1471 (*3H6*
4.6.89–102). Since Shakespeare's early
history plays often spell out historical
details, this brief reference, the play's
first mention of Richmond, presumes
audience familiarity. Richmond's name
will be spoken another 16 times before
he finally appears in 5.2.0.1.

from beyond
43 **hie** hasten (*OED v.* 2)
45 **thrall** subject, slave, captive (*OED sb.*¹
1)
45–6 **Margaret's curse ... queen** See
1.3.208.
46 **Nor ... nor** neither ... nor
counted accepted
49 **son** Richmond, Stanley's stepson (see
5.3.82) by marriage to Richmond's
mother, Lady Margaret Beaufort, *c.*
1482
51 **ta'en** taken, caught
52 **ill-dispersing** i.e. scattering evil
abroad

37 Be . . . mother.] *F* (Be of good cheare: Mother,); Madam, haue comfort, *Qq*   38 gone] *F*; hence
Qq   39 dogs . . . thy] *F*; dogge . . . the *Qq*   40 ominous] *F*, *Q1–4, 6*; ominious *Q5*   41 outstrip] *F*,
Q1–5; ouerstrip *Q6*   42 reach] *F*, *Q1–5*; race *Q6*   48 SD] *Marshall*   hours] *F*; time *Qq*   49 my] *F*,
Q1–5; me *Q6*   50] *F*; To meete you on the way, and welcome you, *Qq*   51 ta'en] *F*, *Q1 subst.*; taken
Q2–6   52 ill-dispersing] *F*, *Qq* (ill dispersing), *hyphen Theobald*

O my accursed womb, the bed of death.
A cockatrice hast thou hatched to the world,
Whose unavoided eye is murderous.   55

STANLEY

Come, madam, come. I in all haste was sent.

ANNE

And I with all unwillingness will go.
O, would to God that the inclusive verge
Of golden metal that must round my brow
Were red-hot steel to sear me to the brains.   60
Anointed let me be with deadly venom,
And die ere men can say 'God save the Queen'.

QUEEN ELIZABETH

Go, go, poor soul; I envy not thy glory.
To feed my humour wish thyself no harm.

ANNE

No? Why? When he that is my husband now   65
Came to me as I followed Henry's corse,
When scarce the blood was well washed from his hands

---

53 **accursed** accursèd
    bed i.e. place of procreation and of birth
54 **cockatrice** serpent, identified with the basilisk (*OED* 1) (see 35n., 1.2.153n., 1.3.224); for hatching a cockatrice's egg as bringing evil into the world, see Dent, C496.1.
55 **unavoided** not avoided or escaped (*OED* 1); contrast 4.4.218, where the word means 'unavoidable'.
58 **inclusive** enclosing (*OED a.* 1)
    verge circle or rim (*OED sb.*[1] 13); i.e. the crown (cf. *R2* 2.1.102). 'Verge' also meant the bounds or limits of a jurisdiction (*OED sb.*[1] 11, 12), and the 12-mile radius surrounding the king's court.

59 **round** encircle (*OED v.* 11a); cf. *R2* 3.2.160–1: 'the hollow crown / That rounds the mortal temples of a king'.
60–1 possibly alluding to the murder of Creusa by Medea (Seneca, *Medea*, 573–4, 817–39), or possibly suggesting punishment by placing a heated crown upon the criminal or regicide
61 a grotesque parody of the use of holy oil in the coronation ceremony
64 **feed my humour** please my mood (cf. 1.2.230, 1.4.118)
66 **corse** corpse (cf. 1.2.0); Qq's 'course' could also mean route or progress in a path (*OED sb.* 11, 2).
67 **scarce** scarcely

54 hatched] *F, Q2–6 (*hatcht*); hatch *Q1* 56 madam, come] *F;* Madam, *Qq* sent] *F, Q1–2;* sent for *Q3–6* 57 with] *F;* in *Qq* 58 O] *F;* I *Qq* 60 red-hot] *F, Qq (*red hot*), hyphen Pope* brains] *F;* braine *Qq* 61 me be] *F, Q1–2, 4, 6;* me *Q3, 5* venom] *F;* poyson *Qq* 63 Go, go] *F;* Alas *Qq* thy] *F, Q1, 3–6;* the *Q2* 65 Why?] *F; not in Qq* 66 as I] *F, Q1–5;* I *Q6* corse] *F;* course *Qq*

Which issued from my other angel husband
And that dear saint which then I weeping followed;
O when, I say, I looked on Richard's face,   70
This was my wish: 'Be thou', quoth I, 'accursed
For making me, so young, so old a widow;
And when thou wed'st, let sorrow haunt thy bed;
And be thy wife, if any be so mad,
More miserable by the life of thee   75
Than thou hast made me by my dear lord's death.'
Lo, ere I can repeat this curse again,
Within so small a time, my woman's heart
Grossly grew captive to his honey words
And proved the subject of mine own soul's curse,   80
Which hitherto hath held mine eyes from rest;
For never yet one hour in his bed

68–9 angel husband . . . dear saint i.e. the deceased Prince Edward and his father, Henry VI; cf. Edward as an angel (1.4.53).

72 so young, so old i.e. so young in age but made so old by suffering and sorrow, or perhaps so young but doomed to so long a life of widowhood

74–6 *F recalls but alters 1.2.26–8, changing a curse asking that any wife of Richard's be *made* more miserable by his *death* into a wish that anyone so 'mad' as to marry him may be made even more miserable by continued 'life'. The Qq 1.2, 4.1 passages are closer to one another, both wishing Richard's 'death' might cause misery in anyone who might marry him. Hammond accepts F, presuming Anne's 'growth': by 4.1 it is clear that life with Richard would mean more suffering to a wife than his death (cf. Lull). Jowett accepts

F's 'Life', presuming Anne lacked 'foreknowledge' in 1.2.

79 Grossly stupidly (*OED* 6; see 3.6.10); Q2–8's 'Crosselie' could mean 'adversely', perhaps suggesting 'perversely' (*OED* 3, 4). Either would suggest historically available misogynist discourse. For sexual insinuations, see 3.7.75n.

honey i.e. honied; cf. *venom tooth* (1.3.290).

81 hitherto until now
*mine Although F's possessive form may have originated with Q6, or from a compositor's eye-skip, or from the compositors' preference for 'mine' over 'my' before vowels (Walker, 25), Abbott's point concerning the unemphatic nature of 'mine' (Abbott, 237) argues for retaining the Q6, F reading here (Walton, *Copy*, 26); cf. 1.4.22–3n., 3.7.20n.

69 dear] *F;* dead *Qq*   74 mad] *F; Q1–2 (*madde*);* badde *Q3–6*   75 More] *F;* As *Qq*   life] *F;* death *Qq*   76 Than] *F (*Then*);* As *Qq*   77 ere] *F; Q1 (*eare*);* euen *Q2–6*   78 Within . . . time] *F;* Euen in so short a space *Qq*   79 Grossly] *F, Q1;* Crosselie *Q2;* Crosly *Q3–6*   80 subject] *F, Q1;* subiectes *Q2, 4–6 subst.;* subsects *Q3*   mine] *F;* my *Qq*   81 hitherto . . . held mine] *F;* euer since . . . kept my *(*mine *Q6) Qq*   rest] *F;* sleepe *Qq*

Did I enjoy the golden dew of sleep,
But with his timorous dreams was still awaked.
Besides, he hates me for my father Warwick,   85
And will, no doubt, shortly be rid of me.

QUEEN ELIZABETH
Poor heart, adieu. I pity thy complaining.

ANNE
No more than with my soul I mourn for yours.

DORSET
Farewell, thou woeful welcomer of glory.

ANNE
Adieu, poor soul, that tak'st thy leave of it.   90

DUCHESS [*to Dorset*]
Go thou to Richmond, and good fortune guide thee,

---

83 **golden . . . sleep** For Richard's brief
overconfidence as 'golden sleepe', see
Holinshed, 3.752 and Hall, *Richard
III*, fol. xlix'; cf. the 'golden sleep' that
Hotspur has lost through care (*1H4*
2.3.40) and the 'honey-heavy dew
of slumber' that Brutus forgoes (*JC*
2.1.229). Although *gold* and *golden*
appear frequently in the play, this line,
1.2.250 and 5.3.19, where the associations are respectively with sleep, youth
and the sun, are the only places in which
the words appear outside a context of
contention, ambition and greed.
84 **timorous** fearful; Richard's (offstage)
wakefulness and nightmares are here
treated as characteristic rather than
specifically occasioned by the murder
of the princes, as in the sources. Hall,
closely following More, writes: 'after
this abhominable deed done, [Richard]
neuer was quiet in his mynde, he neuer
thought himselfe sure where he wente
abroade, his body priuely feinted, his
eyen wherled aboute, his hande euer

on his dagger, his countenaunce and
maner lyke alwaies to stricke againe,
he toke euill reste on nightes, laye long
wakyng and musying, forweried with
care and watche, rather slombred then
slept, troubled with fearefull dreames'
(*Richard III*, fol. xxviii'; cf. Holinshed,
3.735).
still continually
85 Warwick changed allegiances, invaded
England on behalf of Lancastrian
interests and forced Richard to flee to
the continent with Edward IV; Richard
led the opposing forces when Warwick
fell at Barnet (see *3H6*).
87 **complaining** lamentation
89 SP *Q2's '*Qu.*' (for F, Q1's Dorset)
appears thoughtful given the ongoing
exchange between the two women and
Anne's response at 90, contrasting her
interlocutor as taking leave of glory
to herself as its *welcomer*. Q2 offers
another correction at 1.1.101–2.
89 **welcomer of glory** so-called because
she is about to be crowned

---

83 Did I enjoy] *F;* Haue I enioyed *Qq*   84] *F;* But haue bene waked by his timerous dreames,
Qq   86 no doubt] *F, Q1; om. Q2–6*   87 Poor heart, adieu] *F;* Alas poore soule *Qq*   complaining]
F; complaints *Qq*   88 with] *F;* from *Qq*   89 SP] *F, Q1; Qu. Q2–6*   90 that] *F;* thou *Qq*   91, 92,
93 SD] *F2 subst.*

[_to Anne_] Go thou to Richard, and good angels tend
    thee.
[_to Queen Elizabeth_] Go thou to sanctuary, and good
    thoughts possess thee.
I to my grave, where peace and rest lie with me.
Eighty-odd years of sorrow have I seen,   95
And each hour's joy wracked with a week of teen.

QUEEN ELIZABETH
Stay, yet look back with me unto the Tower.
– Pity, you ancient stones, those tender babes
Whom envy hath immured within your walls,
Rough cradle for such little pretty ones;   100
Rude ragged nurse, old sullen playfellow
For tender princes, use my babies well.
So foolish sorrows bids your stones farewell.   _Exeunt._

---

93 **sanctuary** perhaps disyllabic (cf. 3.1.42)
95 **Eighty-odd** The Duchess was actually 68 at Richard's accession in 1483.
96 **wracked** destroyed (_OED ppl. a._), or tortured, racked (_OED_ racked _erron. ppl. a._ 3)
    teen misery, grief (_OED sb._[1] 3); cf. _LLL_ 4.3.161.
97–103 *F's 'sentimental apostrophe' follows an apparent exit couplet (Patrick, 127); however, Margaret has a similar couplet at 4.4.114–15, but stays onstage. Here the Duchess is called upon to _Stay_. Queen Elizabeth's reference to her _foolish sorrows_ (103) suggests self-awareness at her extreme personification of the Tower as a nurse or playmate;

compare Titus' address to the stones of Rome (_Tit_ 3.1.35–47). Qq's 4.4.385 echoes this passage (Hammond, Appendix 1).
99 **immured** imprisoned, shut up within walls (_OED v._ 2)
100 **little pretty** Cf. Dent, T188: 'Little things are pretty'; cf. Jonson, _Volpone_, 3.3.10 and _LLL_ 1.2.21–2.
101 **ragged** rough, irregular, having a jagged outline (_OED a._[1] 2); cf. _2H4_ Ind.35.
103 SD With their goals defined by the Duchess (91–6), characters may leave by both doors as they entered. Wells and Taylor give characters individual exits during her lines; such departure makes more sense in Qq, which omit Queen Elizabeth's final speech.

92 tend] _F_; garde _Qq_   93 and] _F_; _not in Qq_   95 Eighty-odd] _F, Q1–4_ (Eightie odde), _hyphen_ _Bevington_[4]; Eightie olde _Q5–6 subst._   96 of teen] _F_; ofteene _Qq_   97–103] _F_; _not in Qq_   103 SD] _F; not in Qq_

4.2   ^Q*The trumpets^Q sound a sennet. Enter* RICHARD *in*
pomp, BUCKINGHAM, CATESBY, RATCLIFFE,
LOVELL ^Q*with other Nobles^Q* [*and a* **Page**].

KING RICHARD
Stand all apart. – Cousin of Buckingham.
BUCKINGHAM
My gracious sovereign.
KING RICHARD
Give me thy hand.
        ^Q*Here he ascendeth the throne.^Q Sound* [*trumpets*].
        Thus high, by thy advice
And thy assistance is King Richard seated.
But shall we wear these glories for a day?   5

4.2 location: '*The Court*' (Pope); '*A Room of State*' (Capell)

0.1 *sennet* set of notes on the trumpet to signal ceremonial entrance or exit (*OED* 1)

0.1–2 *in pomp* in splendour, perhaps in formal procession (*OED sb.*[1] 1, 2); Qq's '*crownd*' and SP '*King*' or '*King Ri.*' (see 1 SPn.) register regality. On public wearing of the crown by Richard and by Edward IV, see C.A.J. Armstrong.

0.2–3 *RATCLIFFE, LOVELL* not included in Qq's scene

1 SP *Although Qq refer to '*Rich.*' or '*Glocester*' in SDs, until this scene Richard's speeches are headed '*Glo.*' (once '*Gl.*'). Here the designation changes to '*King*', and with occasional exceptions (e.g. '*King Ri.*' at 8) remains so to the end of the play. Up to this point, F generally has '*Rich.*' (or variations) for SPs, except for a portion of that part of 3.1 (63–180) set directly from Q3, where Richard is '*Glo.*' After 4.2, F sometimes agrees with Qq in SDs,

sporadically calling him '*King Richard*', and F, Qq SPs also sometimes agree on '*King*'. This form becomes dominant in the final portion of the play set directly from Q3 (5.3.49–end of play), with exceptions, such as 5.3.53–78 and all of 5.4, where F employs '*Rich.*' as SP.

1 **apart** aside

3 SD *ascendeth* perhaps onto a raised platform (Dessen & Thomson, 15).

3–4 **Thus . . . seated** The use of *Thus* (with accompanying trumpets in F) indicates Richard's movement to the throne, as Qq's SD demands, assisted by Buckingham's hand. The metaphor of being seated *high* in fortune is commonplace (see 5n.). The hypocritical ruler seating himself in glory before lesser figures who seek reward recalls the Chester *Coming of Antichrist* (Lumiansky & Mills, 1.408–38).

5–17 This exchange, in which a usurper attempts to commission assassination by indirect insinuation, resembles – until Richard's direct statement at 18

4.2] *F (Scena Secunda.); not in Qq*   0.1 *a sennet*] *F; not in Qq*   0.1–2 *in pomp*] *F; crownd Qq*   0.2–3 RATCLIFFE, LOVELL.] *F; not in Qq*   0.3 *and a* Page] *Capell*   1+ SP] *Qq (King[.] [Ri.]); Rich. F*   2] *F; not in Qq*   3–4] *Rowe; F lines* hand. / assistance; / seated: / ; *Qq line* hand: / aduice / seated: /   3 SD *Here . . . throne.*] *Qq (Here he ascendeth / the (his Q4–6, om. Q3) throne. opp.* hand: *and* aduice*)   Sound*] *F; not in Qq*   trumpets] *after 2 White*   5 glories] *F; honours Qq*

Or shall they last, and we rejoice in them?

BUCKINGHAM

Still live they, and forever let them last.

KING RICHARD

Ah, Buckingham, now do I play the touch
To try if thou be current gold indeed:
Young Edward lives; think now what I would speak.   10

BUCKINGHAM

Say on, my loving lord.

KING RICHARD

Why, Buckingham, I say I would be king.

BUCKINGHAM

Why so you are, my thrice-renowned lord.

KING RICHARD

Ha! Am I king? 'Tis so – but Edward lives.

BUCKINGHAM

True, noble prince.

KING RICHARD   O bitter consequence   15
That Edward still should live 'true noble prince'!

– the reported conversation between the newly-crowned Henry IV and Sir Piers Exton (*R2* 5.4). King John's attempt to enlist Hubert in murdering young Arthur (*KJ* 3.2) similarly progresses from insinuation to direct statement.

5 The question is rhetorical, but from this moment on, Richard's difficulties recall a passage in Hall: 'from thence forth not onely all his counsailles, doynges and procedynges, sodainlye decayed and sorted to none effecte: But also fortune beganne to froune and turne her whele douneward from him' (*Richard III*, fol. xxxʳ; cf. Churchill, 334).

7 **Still live they** i.e. may they long continue

8 **play the touch** i.e. test (Buckingham's) genuineness, as a touchstone rubbed against a metal allowed differentiation of true gold

9 **current gold** genuine coin, as opposed to counterfeit (*OED* current *a.* 5)

13 **thrice-renowned** thrice-renownèd
*lord Many editors since Pope have accepted 'liege' from Qq, though 'Q is generally unreliable with respect to such formulae' (*TxC*, 243).

15 **consequence** i.e. conclusion from what has been said

16 **true noble prince** Richard again moralizes two meanings in one word, turning Buckingham's designation of him as a *noble prince* (i.e. king) into a bitter rejoinder that young Edward remains the *true* 'noble prince'; cf. 4.4.471–2n.

7 forever] *Q7;* for euer *F, Q1, 3–6;* for for euer *Q2*   let them] *F;* may they *Qq*   8 Ah] *F;* O *Qq*   do I] *F, Q1–2;* I do *Q3–6*   10 speak] *F;* say *Qq*   11 loving lord] *F;* gracious soueraigne *Qq*   13 lord] *F;* liege *Qq*   15] *Steevens; F, Qq line* Prince. / consequence! /

Cousin, thou wast not wont to be so dull.
Shall I be plain? I wish the bastards dead,
And I would have it suddenly performed.
What sayst thou now? Speak suddenly. Be brief.   20

BUCKINGHAM
Your grace may do your pleasure.

KING RICHARD
Tut, tut, thou art all ice; thy kindness freezes.
Say, have I thy consent that they shall die?

BUCKINGHAM
Give me some little breath, some pause, dear lord,
Before I positively speak in this.   25
I will resolve you herein presently.   *Exit.*

CATESBY [*aside to others*]
The King is angry. See, he gnaws his lip.

KING RICHARD [*aside*]
I will converse with iron-witted fools

---

17 **wont** accustomed
  dull obtuse, wanting intelligence or, possibly, hard of hearing (*OED a.* 1, 2a)
19, 20 **suddenly** immediately (*OED* 2)
23–31 Shakespeare invents this falling out over Buckingham's refusal to murder the princes, although Hall's Buckingham tells Morton he 'neuer agreed nor condiscended' to their deaths (*Richard III*, fol. xxxiv'). The figure who refuses Richard's commission is Sir Robert Brakenbury, who 'plainly answered' Richard's emissary 'that he woulde neuer put them to deathe' (fol. xxvii').
24 **breath** i.e. breathing space (*OED* 8); cf. *H5* 2.4.145.
25 **positively** definitely
26 **resolve you** i.e. give you an answer to your question; cf. *3H6* 3.2.19.
  herein i.e. in this matter
27 It is not clear to whom Catesby speaks.

gnaws his lip Vergil (227) and More (*CW2*, 47) mention Richard's lip-gnawing as, respectively, habitual or feigned; cf. 3.4.57.1n. Here it appears to be one of the first signs of his genuine anger, fear and uncertainty; More's Richard only becomes subject to anxious fears, torments of conscience and uncertainty *after* the murder of the princes (Ornstein, 72; More *CW2*, 87). Cf. 4.1.84 and p. 11. Nineteenth-century Richards emphasized nervous tics: Cooke resorted to 'fiddling with his sword, the quivering of his lip and under jaw, the convulsive starting of his muscles, the clawing with his fingers' (Colley, 56)
28–9 **iron-witted ... boys** Contrast the ideal royal counsellor: an adult between the ages of 30 and 60 with 'a quicke and liuely wytte', never 'dull

17 wast] *F;* wert *Qq* 20 sayst thou now] *F;* saist *(*saiest *Q6)* thou *Qq* 22 freezes] *F;* freezeth *Qq* 24 little . . . dear] *F;* breath, some little pause my *Qq* 25 in this] *F;* herein *Qq* 26 you herein presently] *F;* your grace immediatlie *Qq* 26 SD] *F (Exit Buck.); Exit. Q1; om. Q2–6* 27 SD] *after Capell (to a Stander-by.; after Hanmer [Aside.])* gnaws his] *F;* bites the *Qq* 28 SD] *Ard²*

And unrespective boys. None are for me
That look into me with considerate eyes.   30
High-reaching Buckingham grows circumspect.
– Boy!

PAGE   My lord?

KING RICHARD

Knowst thou not any whom corrupting gold
Will tempt unto a close exploit of death?   35

PAGE

I know a discontented gentleman
Whose humble means match not his haughty spirit.
Gold were as good as twenty orators,
And will, no doubt, tempt him to anything.

KING RICHARD

What is his name?

PAGE   His name, my lord, is Tyrrel.   40

KING RICHARD

I partly know the man. Go, call him hither, boy.   *Exit [Page]*.
[*aside*] The deep-revolving, witty Buckingham

and gross wytted' (Blundeville, sigs L2ᵛ–L3ʳ, E1ʳ–E2ʳ).

28 **iron-witted** dull-witted, stupid (*OED* iron *a*. 3d, 4)

29 **unrespective** inattentive, heedless (*OED* 1); contrast *considerate* (30) and 'respective' (*RJ* 3.1.126).
   for me i.e. appropriate to be among my associates (cf. 'these are not men for me', Marlowe, *Works*, *Edward II*, 1.1.50); on my side

30 **considerate** thoughtful, careful (*OED* 1, 2)

31 **High-reaching** aspiring, ambitious (*OED*); as a possible rival
   circumspect attentive, cautious (*OED a*. 2)

34–41 More's Richard converses with a 'secrete page' (*CW*2, 83–4; Holinshed, 3.734); cf. *True Tragedy*, 973–1017.

35 **close** secret
   exploit explòit; an act or deed, a feat (*OED sb.* 3)

38 Cf. Dent, G285a: 'Gold speaks.'

41 **partly** partially, imperfectly (cf. *TC* 3.1.17)

42 **deep-revolving** profoundly meditating, seriously turning things over (*OED* revolve *v*. 4b); cf. *Cym* 3.3.14. Given Buckingham's earlier inclusion among *simple gulls* (1.3.327), Richard may be sneering at his pretensions to cunning (cf. 4.4.332). Following More, Hall reports both Buckingham

31 High-reaching] *F*; Boy, high reaching *Q1–5*; *Boy*, high reaching *Q6*   32] *F*; *not in Qq*   33+ SP] *F*; *Boy. Qq*   33 My lord] *F*, *Q1–2*; Lord *Q3–6*   34 Knowst] *F*, *Q1*, *3–6*; *Q2 (*Knowest*)*   35 Will] *F*; Would *Qq*   36 I] *F*; My lord, I *Qq*   37 spirit] *F*; mind *Qq*   40] *Steevens*; *F*, *Qq line* Name. / Tirrell. /   41 I . . . man] *F*; *not in Qq*   hither, boy] *F (*hither, / Boy.*)*; hither presentlie *Qq*   SD] *Pope subst.*; *Exit. F*; *not in Qq*   42 SD] *Ard²*   deep-revolving] *F*, *Qq (*deep reuoluing*), hyphen Pope*

No more shall be the neighbour to my counsels.
Hath he so long held out with me, untired,
And stops he now for breath? Well, be it so.   45

Enter STANLEY.

How now, Lord Stanley, what's the news?

STANLEY

Know my loving lord,
The Marquess Dorset, as I hear, is fled
To Richmond, in the parts where he abides.

KING RICHARD

Come hither, Catesby. Rumour it abroad   50
That Anne my wife is very grievous sick.
I will take order for her keeping close.

and Richard as having a 'deepe dis-
symulyng nature' (*Richard III*, fol.
xxx^v).

witty cunning, crafty (*OED* 2b); cf.
MA 4.2.25.

43 **neighbour to** i.e. close associate of
(*OED sb.* 2b)

44 **held out** continued, endured

47–9 *These lines have been frequently
emended in attempts to regularize
them metrically. Pope deletes both
Know and *loving*. Rann (here followed)
retains F with minimal relineation.

48–9 Dorset did not flee to Richmond
until after Buckingham's ill-fated
expedition, in which he played a leading role (Hall, *Richard III*, fol. xxxix^v);
cf. 4.4.311–14.

50–65 Although Richard's change of
subjects makes it seem that he fails
to register Stanley's news, his later
remark (84) reveals that he has heard

what he has been told; his plans for
Anne and the children of Clarence
provide the first of his panic reactions
(Honigmann, 229n.).

51, 57 **sick, die** Anne's illness is treated
here as if it were merely a false
rumour to be spread about. The
sources speculate about whether
Richard effected Anne's death by
aggravated mental stress or by poison (Hall, *Richard III*, fol. xlviii^v;
Holinshed, 3.751). Sixteenth-century
polemic invokes Richard's rumours
'secretlie . . . giuen abroode that his
own wyfe was dead' in accusing the
Earl of Leicester of murdering his
wife (*Copy*, 105). Qq print Richard's
'That Anne my wife is sicke and like
to die' at both 51 and 57.

52 **take order** i.e. make secret arrangements; cf. 3.5.106.

keeping close secluded confinement

43 counsels] *F;* counsell *Qq*   45 Well . . . so] *F; not in Qq*   45.1 STANLEY] *F; Darby Qq*   46 Lord
. . . news] *F;* what neewes vvith you *(yon Q3) Qq*   47+ SP] *F; Darby. Qq subst.*   47–9] *Rann; F
lines Dorset / Richmond,* / abides. / ; My Lord, I heare the Marques Dorset / Is fled to Richmond, in
those partes beyond the seas where he / abides. / *Qq subst.*   50 Come hither] *F; not in Qq*   Catesby.]
F (Catesby,); Catesby. *Cat.* My Lord. *Qq*   Rumour] *F; King.* Rumor *Qq*   51 very grievous sick] *F;*
sicke and like to die *Qq*

Inquire me out some mean poor gentleman,
Whom I will marry straight to Clarence' daughter.
The boy is foolish, and I fear not him.   55
Look how thou dream'st! I say again, give out
That Anne my queen is sick and like to die.
About it, for it stands me much upon
To stop all hopes whose growth may damage me.

                                              [*Exit Catesby.*]

I must be married to my brother's daughter,   60
Or else my kingdom stands on brittle glass.
Murder her brothers, and then marry her –
Uncertain way of gain. But I am in
So far in blood that sin will pluck on sin.

---

53 **Inquire me out** find for me
mean inferior in rank or quality (*OED a.*[1] 2), thus *mean poor* is not redundant. In fact, she will marry Sir Richard Pole and give birth to the famous Cardinal Pole. Holinshed relates Richard's plan to marry off Lady Cecily Plantagent (with whom Shakespeare confuses Clarence's daughter) to 'a man ... of an vnknowne linage and familie' (3.752).
54 **straight** immediately
55 **boy** Clarence's son Edward
foolish Clarence's son is not depicted as particularly *foolish* unless belief in Richard's sincerity (2.2.20–33) signifies lack of intelligence. Holinshed and Hall (following Vergil) do describe him later in life at the time of his execution by Henry VII (1499) as a dazed victim of prolonged imprisonment who 'coulde not decerne a Goose from a Capon' (Hall, *Henry VII*, fol. I[r]).
56 **dream'st ... again** For the second time in this scene, Richard, formerly master of effective communication, appears unable to get his message across. Perhaps Catesby is 'taken aback by Richard's murderous intentions' (Lull).

give out let it be known
58 **About** i.e. set about
stands ... upon is imperative upon me (Abbott, 204). Cf. *Ham* 5.2.62.
59 **hopes** i.e. the possible claimants to the throne as well as the feelings that they might elicit in those subjects who look to them for the future
60 **brother's daughter** i.e. Elizabeth of York (1465–1503), daughter of Edward IV and Queen Elizabeth, later wife of Henry Tudor (this play's Richmond and Henry VII) and grandmother of Elizabeth I (see pp. 71–8).
61 **brittle glass** common image for the fragility of power and office; e.g. *Mirror*, 'Wolsey', 466–7; *R2* 4.1.287–8; Dent, G134
63 **of gain** i.e. to prosper
63–4 **But ... sin** While suggesting the notorious Senecan code of Elizabethan stage revengers: '*per scelera semper sceleribus tutum est iter*' ('through crime ever is the safe way for crime', Seneca, *Agamemnon*, 115; cf. Kyd, *Spanish Tragedy*, 3.13.6), this line remarks the *Uncertain way* that Richard must pursue, anticipating Macbeth's realization that he is self-

53 poor] *F*; borne *Qq*   57 queen] *F*; wife *Qq*   59 SD] *Johnson*   64 will pluck] *F, Q1*; plucke *Q2–5*; plucks *Q6*

Tear-falling pity dwells not in this eye.   65

Enter TYRREL.

Is thy name Tyrrel?
TYRREL
James Tyrrel, and your most obedient subject.
KING RICHARD
Art thou indeed?
TYRREL   Prove me, my gracious lord.
KING RICHARD
Dar'st thou resolve to kill a friend of mine?
TYRREL
Please you. But I had rather kill two enemies.   70
KING RICHARD
Why then thou hast it. Two deep enemies,
Foes to my rest, and my sweet sleep's disturbers,
Are they that I would have thee deal upon.
Tyrrel, I mean those bastards in the Tower.

entrapped 'in blood' (3.4.137–9). 'So far in blood' recalls Buckingham's 'So diepe in blud' (*Mirror*, 'Buckingham', 348), rhetorically heightening the entrapment that More suggests (*CW*2, 43).

64 **pluck on** drag, pull along (*OED* pluck *v.* 2a); cf. *MM* 2.4.146.

65 **Tear-falling pity** i.e. pity that prompts tears to fall (cf. 1.3.352)

68 **Prove** test

70 *Q2 appears to anticipate the next line in its 'two deepe enemies'; Q3–8 follow.
Please you i.e. if it please you

71 **deep** great, profound (*OED a.* 18); strikingly hyperbolic in imputing threatening agency to the victimized

children – a rhetorical trend continued when Richard blames them for his disturbed sleep (72). The word *deep* appears elsewhere in the play with other senses – 'cunning' (2.1.38) and 'profoundly learned' (3.7.74); cf. Drakakis, 32.

72 *disturbers** Thompson compares Qq's substantive – 'disturbs' – to Qq 'intreates' (3.7.224).

73 **deal upon** set to work upon (*OED v.* 2. 18)

74 Richard's self-explication appears remarkably unmotivated given Tyrrel's anticipations and compliance in 70. Why would he feel the need to be so specific to someone who clearly knows the score?

65 Tear-falling] *F; Q1–5* (Teare falling*); Teares falling Q6* 65.1 TYRREL] *F; Tirrel Qq* 68] *Steevens; F lines* indeed? / Lord. / ; *Qq line* indeed? / soueraigne, / lord] *F; soueraigne Qq* 70] *Qq; F lines* you: / enemies. / Please you] *F; I my Lord Qq* enemies] *F, Q1;* deepe enemies *Q2–6* 71 then] *F;* there *Qq* 72 disturbers] *F;* disturbs *Qq*

TYRREL

Let me have open means to come to them,   75
And soon I'll rid you from the fear of them.

KING RICHARD

Thou sing'st sweet music. Hark, come hither, Tyrrel.
Go by this token. Rise, and lend thine ear,
        �935*He*ᵠ *whispers* ᵠ*in his ear*ᵠ.
There is no more but so. Say it is done,
And I will love thee and prefer thee for it.   80

TYRREL

I will dispatch it straight.   *Exit.*

Enter BUCKINGHAM.

BUCKINGHAM

My lord, I have considered in my mind
The late request that you did sound me in.

KING RICHARD

Well, let that rest. Dorset is fled to Richmond.

BUCKINGHAM

I hear the news, my lord.   85

KING RICHARD

Stanley, he is your wife's son. Well, look unto it.

75 **open . . . come** i.e. unimpeded access
78 **by this token** Richard apparently hands Tyrrel some symbol, perhaps a ring, that will allow access to the prisoners on Richard's authority.
79 **There . . . so** i.e. there's nothing more to say (than what Richard has whispered); cf. 'No more but so?' (*Ham* 1.3.10). Cf. Abbott, 411; Dent,

M1158.1.
   ***it is** The interrogative word order ('is it') of Q1–2, 6–8 is obviously wrong; Q3–5 agree with F.
80 **prefer** promote, advance
81 ***Qq's exchange between Richard and Tyrrel recalls F at 3.1.188–9.
83 **sound me in** ask me about
86 **he** i.e. Richmond (see 1.3.20)

77] *Qq; F lines* Musique: / Tyrrel, / Hark] *F; not in Qq*   78 this] *F;* that *Qq*   79 There is] *F;* 'Tis *Qq* it is] *F, Q3–5;* is it *Q1–2, 6*   80 for it] *F;* too *Qq*   81] *F;* 'Tis done my gracious lord. / *King* Shal we heare from thee *Tirrel* ere we sleep? Enter Buc. / *Tir.* Ye shall my lord, *(Tir.* Yea my good Lord. *Q6) Qq* SD] *F; not in Qq*   83 request] *F;* demand *Qq*   84 rest] *F;* passe *Qq*   85 the] *F;* that *Qq*   86 wife's] *F, Q2–6 (*Wiues*), Q1 (*wifes*) son] *F, Q4–6;* sonnes *Q1–3* unto] *F;* to *Qq*

BUCKINGHAM

My lord, I claim the gift, my due by promise,
For which your honour and your faith is pawned:
Th'earldom of Hereford and the moveables
Which you have promised I shall possess.   90

KING RICHARD

Stanley, look to your wife; if she convey
Letters to Richmond, you shall answer it.

BUCKINGHAM

What says your highness to my just request?

KING RICHARD

I do remember me, Henry the Sixth
Did prophesy that Richmond should be king,   95
When Richmond was a little peevish boy.
A king perhaps –

87–90 Richard's refusal to grant the earldom of Hereford has political contexts. More calls the title 'enterlaced
with the title to the crowne', and
says Richard's 'spiteful' rejection of
Buckingham's claim aroused hatred,
mistrust and fear in him (*CW2*, 89;
cf. Holinshed, 3.736). Vergil's Richard
compares Buckingham to the usurper
Henry IV and accuses him of trying
to open a way to the crown for himself
(193). On Buckingham's claim to the
throne and Richard's promises, see
More, *CW2*, 267; for the Hereford
inheritance, cf. 3.1.194–8.
88 **pawned** pledged
89 **moveables** goods belonging to the
earldom but not attached to the soil
(see 3.1.195). Lands would be entailed
and go with the title; portable possessions required specific mention.
91 The accounts of Richard's concern
about Margaret Beaufort's corre-
spondence with Richmond comment

on gender politics. Holinshed writes:
'forsomuch as the enterprise of a
woman was of [Richard] reputed of
no regard or estimation; and that the
lord Thomas hir husband had purged
himselfe sufficientlie to be innocent
of all dooings and attempts by hir
perpetrated and committed: it was
giuen [Stanley] in charge to keepe hir
in some secret place at home, without
hauing anie seruaunt or companie'
(3.746).
92 **answer** i.e. answer for
94 **remember me** i.e. recollect
94–6 See *3H6* 4.6.68–76.
96 **peevish** foolish or fretful (cf. 1.3.193)
97–114 *The longest passage exclusive
to Qq in the play; most commenta-
tors agree that it is Shakespearean.
Explanations for its Qq presence and
F absence differ widely. Hammond
surveys the critical positions laid out in
Var, 300–1. The main alternative lines
of argument are that the passage was:

---

87 the] *F*; your *Qq*   89 Th'earldom] *F*; The Earledome *Qq*   Hereford] *Q1–3, 5–6 (*Herford*)*;
Hertford *F*; Herfort *Q4*   90 Which] *F*; The which *Qq*   you have] *F*; you *Q1, 3–6*; your *Q2*   shall]
F; should *Qq*   93 request] *F*; demand *Qq*   94 I . . . me] *F*; As I remember *Qq*   97 perhaps –] *Pope*;
perhaps. *F*; perhaps, perhaps. *Q1–3, 5–6*; perhaps, *Q4*

^QBUCKINGHAM   My lord.

KING RICHARD

How chance the prophet could not at that time
Have told me, I being by, that I should kill him?

BUCKINGHAM

My lord, your promise for the earldom –   100

KING RICHARD

Richmond! When last I was at Exeter,
The Mayor in courtesy showed me the castle
And called it Rougemont, at which name I started,
Because a bard of Ireland told me once
I should not live long after I saw Richmond.   105

BUCKINGHAM

My lord –

KING RICHARD

Ay, what's o'clock?

BUCKINGHAM

I am thus bold to put your grace in mind
Of what you promised me.

---

originally part of the play, but subsequently cut by Shakespeare (Spedding in *Var*); omitted by a corrector when printing F for its metrical irregularities (Pickersgill, 94); originally part of the play but lost due to a defective manuscript (Patrick); a playhouse addition for the benefit of the actor playing Richard, later 'deliberately struck out' of Q copy by the printers of F (Daniel, ix); a revision added to the first version of the play by the author (Hammond). One line of argument proposes that F cut to avoid offending the Jacobean Duke of Buckingham and his patron, James I, who had a palace at Richmond (Griffin). For an argument concerning Jacobean political implications attending the abbreviation of the role of the Duke of Buckingham in F's *2H6*, see Hodgdon, *End*, 62. Both Hall (*Richard III*, fol. xxxiv^{r–v}) and Holinshed (3.739) have Buckingham describe a prolonged

ordeal rather than F's tyrannically curt exchange.

98 **How chance** i.e. how was it that (*OED v.* 5)
    prophet Henry VI; Richard murders Henry with the taunt, 'Die, prophet' (*3H6* 5.6.57).

99 **by** nearby; Richard was not onstage when Henry VI uttered his prophecy in *3H6* 4.6.

101–5 This incident during Richard's 1483 visit to Exeter appears only in the second edition of Holinshed: Richard 'came to the castell; and when he vnderstood that it was called Rugemont, suddenlie he fell into a dumpe, and (as one astonied) said; Well, I see my daies be not long. He spake this of a prophesie told him, that when he came once to Richmond, he should not long liue after' (3.746).

103 **Rougemont** pronounced like 'Richmond'

KING RICHARD   Well, but what's o'clock?

BUCKINGHAM
Upon the stroke of ten.

KING RICHARD   Well, let it strike.   110

BUCKINGHAM
Why let it strike?

KING RICHARD

Because that, like a jack, thou keep'st the stroke
Betwixt thy begging and my meditation.
I am not in the giving vein today.^Q

BUCKINGHAM
May it please you to resolve me in my suit?   115

KING RICHARD
Thou troublest me; I am not in the vein.

Exit [followed by all but Buckingham].

BUCKINGHAM

And is it thus? Repays he my deep service
With such contempt? Made I him king for this?
O, let me think on Hastings and be gone   119
To Brecknock while my fearful head is on.   *Exit.*

---

112 **jack** the figure who struck the hours on clocks (*OED sb.*[1] I 6, citing this line), but also meaning a commoner or an ill-mannered person (*OED sb.*[1] I 2), as at 1.3.53. The deposed Richard II expresses his own futile inconsequence by comparing himself to a 'jack o' the clock' (*R2* 5.5.60).

keep'st the stroke continue to strike

114 **vein** mood (*OED sb.* 14)

115 **F reiterates a question that has repeatedly been raised, despite the insults in the immediately previous passage as it appears in Qqs; contrast Qq's forceful alternative – 'Whie then resolue me whether you wil or no?'

(*TxC*, 244). F's line could be inflected many different ways, expressing frustration, despair, incredulity or any combination of these emotions mixed with a desire not to offend.

116 Edmund Kean expressed 'sarcastic petulance', but Hazlitt claimed the line should have conveyed 'stifled hatred, and cold contempt' (5.183). J.B. Booth portrayed 'fretful anger' rather than a 'cool and kingly slight' (Gould, 44).

117 **deep** serious, weighty

120 **Brecknock** Buckingham's family estate of Brecon in south-east Wales

109] *Cam*[1]; *Qq line* me. / clocke? /   110] *Cam*[1]; *Qq line* ten. / strike. /   112 keep'st] *Q1, 3, 5–6*; keepest *Q2, 4*   115] *F*; Whie then resolue me whether you wil or no? *Qq*   116 Thou] *F*; Tut, tut, thou *Qq*   SD *followed . . . Buckingham*] *Cam subst.*   117] *F*; Is it euen so, rewardst *(rewards Q2–6)* he my true seruice *Qq*   118 contempt] *F*; deepe contempt *Qq*

[4.3]   *Enter* TYRREL.

TYRREL

The tyrannous and bloody act is done,
The most arch deed of piteous massacre
That ever yet this land was guilty of.
Dighton and Forrest, who I did suborn
To do this piece of ruthful butchery,   5
Albeit they were fleshed villains, bloody dogs,
Melted with tenderness and mild compassion,
Wept like to children in their deaths' sad story.

4.3 location: '*The same*' (Capell). F lacks a new scene here, but the stage has been cleared with Buckingham's exit, and time has advanced from 10 a.m. (4.2.110) to evening (4.3.31).

1–22 Holinshed, following More, says Tyrrel 'shewed [Richard] all the manner of the murther; who gaue him great thanks' (3.735; cf. Hall, *Richard III*, fol. xxvii'). Charles Lamb found it difficult to reconcile Shakespeare's pathos-laden speech with its speaker; however, the royal infanticide evoked strong emotional reaction (More, *CW2*, 85–7; Hall, *Richard III*, fol. xxxii'). Cf. Heywood's melodramatic rendering in *2Ed4*, 3.5 and Mancini's claim (93) that 'many men burst forth into tears and lamentations' after Edward's disappearance. This soliloquy changes audience relation to Richard by describing his most heinous act without allowing him to shape our responses as he had in previous soliloquies (Van Laan, 142).

2 **arch** pre-eminent (*OED a*. 1)

3 *With this line, which begins a new page in F, Compositor B begins setting F until deep into 4.4. On the

large number of Qq/F variants in this scene, see Hammond.

4 **Dighton, Forrest** More names Miles Forest, 'a felowe fleshed in murther', and Iohn Dighton, Tyrrel's 'horsekeper, a big brode square strong knaue', as the murderers and recounts their fittingly horrible futures (*CW2*, 85–7).

suborn bribe or procure by underhand means to commit a misdeed (*OED* 1)

5 *ruthful Most editors since Pope have preferred F's word-order while also preferring Qq's term 'ruthles' to F's 'ruthfull' (compassionate: see *OED* 1), which first appears in Q3. However, 'ruthful' could mean 'lamentable' (*OED* 2), as in 'villainies / Ruthful to hear' (*Tit* 5.1.65–6).

6 **fleshed** inured to bloodshed, hardened (*OED* fleshed *ppl*. 2); appropriate to the subsequent image of *bloody dogs* since a hawk or hound might be rewarded with flesh of the game in order to whet its appetite for hunting (*OED* flesh *v*. 1); cf. 4n. for More's use.

8 *to Qq's 'two' has been preferred by many editors since Pope, but weeping

---

4.3] *Pope*   0.1] *F; Enter Sir Francis Tirrell. Qq*   1 act] *F; deed Qq*   2 arch deed] *F; arch-act (arch act Q4) Qq*   4 who] *F; whom Qq*   5 piece of ruthful] *F; ruthles peece of Q1–2; ruthfull peece of Q3–6; piece of ruthless Pope*   6 Albeit] *F; Although Qq*   7 Melted] *F; Melting Qq*   mild] *F; kind Q1–5; om. Q6*   8 to] *F; two Qq*   deaths'] *F, Q1–3, 5–6 (deaths); death Q4*   story] *F; stories Qq*

'O thus', quoth Dighton, 'lay the gentle babes'.
'Thus, thus', quoth Forrest, 'girdling one another   10
Within their alabaster innocent arms.
Their lips were four red roses on a stalk,
And in their summer beauty kissed each other.
A book of prayers on their pillow lay,
Which once', quoth Forrest, 'almost changed my mind.   15
But, O, the Devil – ' There the villain stopped;
When Dighton thus told on: 'We smothered
The most replenished sweet work of nature,
That from the prime creation e'er she framed.'
Hence both are gone with conscience and remorse;   20
They could not speak, and so I left them both
To bear this tidings to the bloody King.

like to children makes sense; for two/ too/to spelling variants, see 4.4.385n.

in . . . story i.e. in the telling of the sad story of their deaths

9–10 **thus** implying action; in this case, a mimicry of the postures of the princes

11 **alabaster** Shakespeare often likens the skin of sleeping victims to alabaster (cf. *Luc* 419), which, as Othello's simile 'smooth as monumental alabaster' (*Oth* 5.2.5) suggests, was frequently employed in statuary figures recumbent upon tombs. 'Alablaster' is an alternative spelling.

14 **book of prayers** Mancini (93) records Edward's attending physician's report that 'the young king, like a victim prepared for sacrifice, sought remission of his sins by daily

confession and penance, because he believed that death was facing him'. Contrast the treatment of a *book of prayer* at 3.7.97.

17 **smothered** smothered

18–19 Contrast Richard as 'Cheated of feature by dissembling Nature' (1.1.19).

18 **replenished** replenishèd; full, perfect (*OED*), here modifying *sweet*

19 **prime** first
*she F, Qq disagree on gender again; cf. England's personification (3.7.124–6).
framed created, fashioned

20 **gone with** overcome by; cf. 'too far gone with grief' (*R2* 2.1.184).

22 **To** in order to
tidings construed as singular (cf. *KJ* 4.2.115)

9 O] *F; Lo Qq   the gentle] *F;* those *(these Q6)* tender *Qq*   10 one] *F, Q3–6;* on *Q1–2*   11 alabaster innocent] *F (Alablaster);* innocent alablaster *Qq*   12 were] *F, Q1;* like *Q3–6;* om. *Q2*   13 And] *F;* Which *Q1–5;* When *Q6*   15 once] *Qq;* one *F*   16 But . . . There] *Theobald (after Rowe);* But oh the Diuell, there *F;* But ô the Diuell their *Q1;* But ô the diuel: their *Q2;* But O the diuel: there *Q3–4;* But O the diuel! there *Q5–6*   17 When] *F;* Whilst *Qq*   19 e'er she] *F;* euer he *Qq*   20] *F, Q1–2;* om. *Q3–6*   Hence] *F;* Thus *Q1–2*   22 bear] *F;* bring *Qq*   this] *F, Q1–5;* these *Q6*

Enter ^QKING^QRICHARD.

And here he comes. All health, my sovereign lord.

KING RICHARD

Kind Tyrrel, am I happy in thy news?

TYRREL

If to have done the thing you gave in charge   25
Beget your happiness, be happy then,
For it is done.

KING RICHARD   But didst thou see them dead?

TYRREL

I did, my lord.

KING RICHARD   And buried, gentle Tyrrel?

TYRREL

The chaplain of the Tower hath buried them,
But where, to say the truth, I do not know.   30

KING RICHARD

Come to me, Tyrrel, soon at after-supper,
When thou shalt tell the process of their death.
Meantime, but think how I may do thee good,
And be inheritor of thy desire.
Farewell till then.

TYRREL   I humbly take my leave.   ^Q*Exit.*^Q

---

25 **gave in charge** i.e. ordered
29–30 Combining two stages of More's account: Tyrell had the bodies buried 'at the stayre foote . . . vnder a great heape of stones'; subsequently Richard had 'a prieste of syr Robert Brakenbury' rebury them 'secretely' (*CW2*, 86).

31 **after-supper** dessert; cf. *MND* 5.1.33–4 concerning the three hours 'Between our after-supper and bed-time'. F's Richard requests to be spoken to after he has eaten.
32 **process** narration (*OED sb.* 4a)
34 **inheritor** possessor; cf. 'inherit', *R2* 1.1.85.

22.1 KING] *Qq (Ki[.][ng])*   23 comes] *F, Q1–5;* come *Q6*   health . . . lord] *F;* haile . . . leige *Qq*   24+ SP] *F (Ric[h].), Qq (King.)*   24 am] *F, Q1–5;* and *Q6*   25 gave] *F, Q3–6;* giue *Q1–2*   27] *Steevens; F lines* done. / dead. / ; *Qq line* Lord. / dead? / done] *F;* done my Lord *Qq*   28] *Steevens; F, Qq line* Lord. / Tirrell. /   30 where . . . truth] *F;* how or in what place *Qq*   31 SP] *F (Rich.), Q3–6 (King.); Tir. Q1–2*   at] *Qq;* and *F*   32 When] *F;* And *Qq*   33 thee] *F (the), Qq*   35] *Steevens; F lines* then / leaue. / ; *Qq different*   then] *F;* soone *Qq*   TYRREL I . . . leave.] *F; not in Qq*   SD] *Qq (Exit Tirrel.) opp. 34*

KING RICHARD

The son of Clarence have I pent up close,   36
His daughter meanly have I matched in marriage,
The sons of Edward sleep in Abraham's bosom,
And Anne my wife hath bid this world good night.
Now, for I know the Breton Richmond aims   40
At young Elizabeth, my brother's daughter,
And by that knot looks proudly on the crown,
To her go I, a jolly thriving wooer.

Enter RATCLIFFE.

RATCLIFFE   My lord.
KING RICHARD
Good or bad news, that thou com'st in so bluntly?   45

36–43 Even without the culminating bravado of 43, Cibber's triumphant speech furnished Macready an opportunity to elicit a sustained ovation in his first performance as Richard (Macready, 141).

36–9 References to the accomplishment of plots only just articulated, as if in panic, in the previous scene emphasize Richard's speed and efficiency. Actions here occurring within a day transpired over three years, from the murder of the princes after Richard's coronation (1483) to Anne's death (1485), 'either by inwarde thought and pensyuenes of hearte, or by intoxicacion of poyson' (Hall, *Richard III*, fol. xlix[r]; cf. Vergil, 211). The temporal compression here resembles that in *Richard II* (2.1) when news of Bolingbroke's armed expedition comes in the same scene that depicts the action precipitating it. For the historical accounts and the play's depiction of Richard's actions against Clarence's children, see 4.2.53n., 55n.

38 **sleep . . . bosom** Cf. Luke, 16.22; also *R2* 4.1.104–5 and Dent, A8.
40 **for** because (Abbott, 151)
   Breton Richmond had been in Brittany, and Richard elsewhere uses the term as abuse (cf. 5.3.333); Jowett suggests denigration of Richmond's Welsh identity (cf. 4.4.476) since 'Briton' could mean 'Welshman' (*OED* Briton *sb*. 1b). For spellings, see *OED* Britain *sb*[2] and *a*.
42 **knot** i.e. marriage
   looks . . . crown i.e. arrogantly expects to possess the crown
43 **jolly** lively, gallant (*OED a*. 1, 5), suggesting showy (*OED* 8a) or handsome (*OED* 10) appearance
   thriving flourishing, prosperous
43.1 *RATCLIFFE There have been problems with Ratcliffe and Catesby since 3.4 and 3.5, where the roles are interchanged in Qq. See pp. 452–4.

39 this] *F;* the *Qq*   good night] *F; Q1–2 (*godnight*), Q3–6 (*goodnight*)   40 Breton] *F (*Britaine*), Qq (*Brittaine*), *Capell*   41 At] *F, F, Q1–5;* And *Q6*   42 on] *F;* ore *Qq*   43 go I] *F;* I go *Qq*   43.1 RATCLIFFE] *F; Catesby Qq*   44+ SP] *F (Rat.); Cat[es]. Qq*   45 or bad news] *F;* newes or bad *Qq*   com'st] *F, Q1; Q2–6 (*comest*)

RATCLIFFE

Bad news, my lord. Morton is fled to Richmond,
And Buckingham, backed with the hardy Welshmen,
Is in the field, and still his power increaseth.

KING RICHARD

Ely with Richmond troubles me more near
Than Buckingham and his rash-levied strength.　　　　50
Come, I have learned that fearful commenting
Is leaden servitor to dull delay.
Delay leads impotent and snail-paced beggary;
Then fiery expedition be my wing,
Jove's Mercury, and herald for a king.　　　　55
Go muster men. My counsel is my shield.
We must be brief when traitors brave the field.　　　*Exeunt.*

---

46 **Morton** John Morton, Bishop of
Ely (see 3.4.0.2n.); More reports
him imprisoned for plotting against
Richard, and later drawing on his
'depe insighte in politike worldli
driftes' to encourage Buckingham to
revolt (*CW*2, 90–3). Morton fled to
Flanders 'secretlie disguysed' (Hall,
Richard III, fol. xxxvi'); cf. 4.4.467n.
Qq have 'Ely' for F's 'Morton' at
4.4.467.

47–8 Time is again foreshortened: the
disillusioned Buckingham (4.2) has
already fielded an army.

48 **in the field** i.e. on the march

49 **near** closely, directly

50 **rash-levied** hastily raised; but perhaps suggesting instability. Holinshed
describes the 'wild Welshmen' as
'falshearted' (3.743). Cf. *R2* 2.4.

51 **fearful commenting** anxious discussion

52 **leaden servitor** slow servant

53 **leads** leads to
snail-paced beggary Cf. Dent, S579:
'As slow as a snail'.

54 **expedition** haste, speed (*OED* 5)
wing i.e. figuratively, power or means
of flight, or of action figured as flight
(*OED sb.* 3b); *fiery expedition* may also
be invoked here as a prosthetic substitute for Richard's impaired arm.
'Wing' could refer to either of the two
divisions (right and left) on each side
of the main body of an army in battle
array (*OED sb.* 7a).

55 **Jove's Mercury** Mercury was the
speedy messenger of the king of the
gods, Jove; Richard invokes the haste
(*expedition*) of Mercury to serve as his
own royal herald and messenger in his
undertaking.

56 **My counsel … shield** i.e. my only
concerns will be deeds of arms rather
than deliberations with councillors (cf.
51–2).

57 **brief** expeditious, hasty (*OED a.* A
1b)
brave challenge; cf. *KJ* 4.2.243.

57 SD 'Go' in F 56 suggests departure
'severally'; Qq's 'Come' suggests leaving together.

---

46 Morton] *F; Ely Qq*　50 rash-levied] *F, Qq* (rash leuied*), hyphen Pope*　strength] *F;* armie *Qq*　51
learned] *F;* heard *Qq*　54 wing] *F, Q1–2;* wings *Q3–6*　55 Jove's] *F, Q1–2* (Ioues*);* Ioue, *Q3, 5–6;*
Loue, *Q4*　56 Go] *F;* Come *Qq*

[4.4]   *Enter old* QUEEN MARGARET.

QUEEN MARGARET
So now prosperity begins to mellow
And drop into the rotten mouth of death.
Here in these confines slyly have I lurked
To watch the waning of mine enemies.
A dire induction am I witness to,   5
And will to France, hoping the consequence
Will prove as bitter, black and tragical.
Withdraw thee, wretched Margaret. Who comes
        here?   [*Stands aside.*]

Enter DUCHESS ᑫof Yorkᑫ *and* QUEEN [ELIZABETH].

QUEEN ELIZABETH
Ah, my poor princes! Ah, my tender babes,

4.4 location: '*Before the Palace*' (Capell)

1–2 Contrast *glorious summer* (1.1.2); cf. the prophetic 'fall like mellowed fruit with shakes of death' (Marlowe, *Works*, *1 Tamburlaine*, 2.1.47). As Richard begins the play with a soliloquy, so Margaret's *induction* (5) launches its final action, Richard's downfall – and then she leaves (6, 125); cf. Furor's opening of Actio 3 of Legge's *Richardus Tertius* and subsequent departure, with the declaration: 'I, Madness, shall spare England here-after, and seek for myself a new home' (2772–4).

1 **mellow** ripen (*OED v.* 1b)

3 **confines** region, territory (*OED* confine *sb.*[2] 2)

5 **induction** introductory part of a work; cf. 1.1.32n.; *tragical* (7) continues the literary vocabulary.

6 **will to France** Historically, Margaret had been in France since 1476, nine years before the time of this scene, and dead since 1482. While most of the

play's characters suffer confinement, Margaret moves unimpeded through space and time, lurking *slyly* (3), commenting or cursing, exiting when she pleases, provoking wonder at her *liberty* (1.3.304).

consequence outcome, result

7 **black and tragical** Black trappings were associated with Elizabethan stage tragedy; see *1H6* 1.1.1, *Luc* 766 and Marston's *Insatiate Countess* (4.5.4–5).

8 **Withdraw thee** i.e. step aside (implicit SD); since she declares her intention to withdraw before questioning who *comes here*, Margaret may hear the approaching characters before seeing them. The women may wear mourning veils (Jowett), which might explain Richard's apparent failure to recognize his mother (136).

9, 10 **my, My** In the Sher–Alexander production, Frances Tomelty's Elizabeth emphasized self-reference by accenting these possessive pronouns (Day, 201).

4.4] Pope; Scena Tertia. F; not in Qq   0.1] F; Enter Queene Margaret sola. Qq   1+ SP] Qq (Q[u]. Mar.); Mar. F   4 enemies] F; aduersaries Qq   8 SD] Collier (Retiring.)   8.1] F (Enter Dutchesse and Queene.); Enter the Qu. and the Dutchesse of Yorke. Qq   ELIZABETH] Malone   9 poor] F; young Qq

My unblowed flowers, new-appearing sweets!   10
If yet your gentle souls fly in the air
And be not fixed in doom perpetual,
Hover about me with your airy wings
And hear your mother's lamentation.

QUEEN MARGARET [*aside*]

Hover about her; say that right for right   15
Hath dimmed your infant morn to aged night.

DUCHESS

So many miseries have crazed my voice
That my woe-wearied tongue is still and mute.
Edward Plantagenet, why art thou dead?

QUEEN MARGARET [*aside*]

Plantagenet doth quit Plantagenet;   20
Edward for Edward pays a dying debt.

QUEEN ELIZABETH

Wilt thou, O God, fly from such gentle lambs

---

10 **unblowed** unopened, still in the bud; form of Qq's 'unblown' (*OED ppl. a.* 2) **sweets** fragrant flowers or herbs (*OED sb.* 7); cf. *Ham* 5.1.232.

12 **doom** judgement, not necessarily negative (*OED sb.* 2)

13 **airy** ethereal (*OED a.* 3)

15 **right for right** 'justice answering to the claims of justice' (Johnson)

15–16 **right . . . night** These rhymes may signal an aside (Abbott, 515), but rhymes elsewhere (e.g. 166–71) do not necessarily indicate asides.

16 **aged** agèd

17 **crazed** cracked (*OED ppl. a.* 1)

19 **Edward Plantagenet** her grandson Edward V or her son Edward IV (though Clarence's son is also Edward Plantagenet)

20 **Plantagenet** the name they all, whether York or Lancaster, share; see 1.2.145n.

quit balance, be an equivalent for (*OED v.* 11c); cf. Dent, M800: 'Measure for measure'.

21 **Edward for Edward** probably Edward V, Elizabeth's son, for Edward, Prince of Wales, son of Margaret and Henry VI

dying debt i.e. a debt paid by a death; with proverbial echoes (Dent, D148: 'Death pays all debts') frequent in Shakespeare (e.g. *Tem* 3.2.131; *Cym* 5.4.157). Here the specific reference is to the *debt* of reciprocated vengeance; cf. *royal debt* (2.2.95) and Hal to Falstaff: 'Thou owest God a death' (*1H4* 5.1.126).

22–3 The lines echo John, 10.12–13, in which Christ, the good shepherd who gives his life for the sheep, is contrasted with the hireling who 'seeth the wolf commyng, and leaueth the sheepe, and fleeth, and the

---

10 unblowed] *F*; vnblowne *Qq* flowers] *F, Q1–5*; flower *Q6* new-appearing] *F, Qq* (new appearing), *hyphen* Pope 13 about] *F, Q1–5*; aboue *Q6* 15, 20, 25 SD] Collier *subst.* 17–19] *F; after 34 Qq* 18 still and mute] *F*; mute and dumbe *Qq* 20–1] *F; not in Qq*

And throw them in the entrails of the wolf?
When didst thou sleep when such a deed was done?

QUEEN MARGARET [*aside*]

When holy Harry died, and my sweet son.   25

DUCHESS

Dead life, blind sight, poor mortal living ghost,
Woe's scene, world's shame, grave's due by life usurped,
Brief abstract and record of tedious days,
Rest thy unrest on England's lawful earth,   [*She sits.*]
Unlawfully made drunk with innocent blood.   30

QUEEN ELIZABETH

Ah, that thou wouldst as soon afford a grave,

---

wolfe catcheth them, & scattereth the sheepe'. Cf. 229, Rous's *Historia* (Churchill, 47) and *3H6* 5.6.7. More characterizes Prince Edward as 'the lamb . . . betaken to the wolfe to kepe' (*CW*2, 24–5).

22 **fly from** abandon

23 **throw** probably to twist about, wreathe (*OED v*[1] 1); or perhaps to cast abruptly into some relation (32a)
entrails *OED* cites as meaning 'intestines' (entrail *sb.*[1] II 1b) as *Tit* 1.1.147, but *throw* suggests 'coils' (*OED sb.*[2]) as in 'folds . . . stretcht now forth at length without entraile' (Spenser, *Faerie Queene*, 1.1.16).

24 **sleep** Cf. 1.3.287n.; this image begins a series of echoes of Kyd's *Spanish Tragedy*, which has Revenge asleep onstage while evil proceeds apparently unchecked.

25 **holy Harry** Henry VI (called 'holy' by Hall) is associated with exceptional piety throughout the Henry VI plays (cf. *2H6* 1.1.244).

26 These extreme oxymorons, used to convey emotional intensity, suggest other Shakespearean passages which treat oxymoronic rhetoric ironically (e.g. *RJ* 1.1.176–81).

27 **grave's due** i.e. that which rightfully belongs to death

28 **abstract** epitome, summary (*OED sb.* 2)
record recòrd; account preserved in writing or otherwise, here in a person (*OED sb.* 5, citing this line)

29 **Rest thy unrest** also found in *Tit* 4.2.31, but here perhaps recalling Kyd's grieving Viceroy (Kyd, *Spanish Tragedy*, 1.3.5; cf. 3.13.29). The Duchess may seat herself to be joined subsequently by Queen Elizabeth; grief is frequently associated with sitting or lying on the ground (cf. *R2* 3.2.155, 178). In *The Three Lords and Three Ladies of London* (1590) three female figures sit and bemoan their miseries; each is then, as Queen Elizabeth will be, wooed by a Vice-like character (Wilson, *Three Lords*, sigs D1[v]–E1[r]); cf. pp. 7–8. Margaret earlier laments that mischance has 'laid me on the ground, / Where I must take like seat unto my fortune' (*3H6* 3.3.9–10).
lawful i.e. law-abiding

29–30 **earth . . . drunk** Cf. the image of civil conflict in *1H4* 1.1.5–6.

31 **thou** i.e. the earth
soon readily (*OED* soon 8)
afford grant, yield

25 Harry] *F, Q1–2; Mary Q3–6*   26 Dead . . . sight] *F;* Blind sight, dead life *Qq*   27 due by] *Qq;* due, by *F*   28] *F; not in Qq*   29 thy] *F, Q1–4;* they *Q5;* their *Q6*   SD] *Capell subst.*   30 Unlawfully] *F, Q1–5;* Vnlawfull *Q6*   innocent] *F;* innocents *Qq*   31 Ah] *F;* O *Qq*   as soon] *F* (*assoone*)*;* aswel *Qq*

As thou canst yield a melancholy seat,
Then would I hide my bones, not rest them here.
Ah, who hath any cause to mourn but we?   [*She sits.*]
QUEEN MARGARET [*Comes forward.*]
If ancient sorrow be most reverend,   35
Give mine the benefit of seniory,
And let my griefs frown on the upper hand.
If sorrow can admit society,
ᵠTell over your woes again by viewing mine.ᵠ
I had an Edward, till a Richard killed him;   40
I had a husband, till a Richard killed him.
Thou hadst an Edward, till a Richard killed him.

32 **melancholy seat** i.e. a place fitting to
the expression of melancholy
34 ***we** Qq's 'I' accords with the play's
pervasive self-centredness, but this
moment is about as close as the speakers come to genuine sympathy (ironically counterpointed by Margaret's
asides). For the female bonding here as
opposed to more constrictive notions
of family and place, see Willis, 102–3
and pp. 19–20.
35–7 Cf. the competing mourners for
Lucrece; Collatine even 'bids Lucretius
give his sorrow place' (*Luc* 1773). This
contestatory element creates a contrast
with the otherwise similar scene in
which Henry VI comments on his distress while empathetically witnessing
the lamentations of feuding partisans
(*3H6* 2.5.55–124); it should also quali-
fy comparisons with the medieval staging of the three Marys who lament the
death of Jesus (Clemen, 186). Contrast
the sympathy uniting the three female
lamenters in R. Wilson (see 29n.).
36 **seniory** seniority (*OED* signeurie, citing this line); possibly seigniory (lord-

ship, domination, sovereignty: *OED
sb.* 1). Given reference to 'frown[ing]
on the upper hand' (37) there may
be a sense of 'authority or supremacy
expressed in looks or bearing' (*OED*
signory 1b).
37–8 *Theobald's punctuation corrects
for F's omission of 39.
37 **on . . . hand** i.e. from a position of
superiority; cf. Dent, H95: 'To get the
upper hand'. Margaret may remain
standing, above the mourners.
38 **admit society** allow fellowship
39 **Tell over** narrate (*OED v.* 2a) or enu-
merate (*OED v.* 22b)
40 **Edward** Prince Edward, son of Henry
VI and Margaret, killed at the battle of
Tewkesbury by Richard and his brothers (*3H6* 5.3)
41 **husband** Henry VI, killed by Richard
in the Tower (*3H6* 5.6); F's 'husband'
interrupts a sequence of proper nouns
(Thompson), but Qq's 'Richard' is
clearly wrong.
42 **Edward** young Edward V, Elizabeth's
son, just murdered in the Tower at
Richard's instigation

34 Ah] *F; O Qq*   we] *F; I Qq*   SD] *Steevens subst.*   35 SD] *Collier subst. after 35*   reverend] *Cam;*
reuerent *F, Qq*   36 seniory] *F (*signeurie*); signorie Q1–5; signiorie Q6; seigneury Rowe; seniority*
Pope   37 griefs] *F;* woes *Qq*   37–8 hand. . . . society,] *Theobald;* hand . . . Society. *F;* hand, . . .
societie, *Qq*   41 husband] *F;* Richard *Qq;* Henry *Rann (Capell)*

336

Thou hadst a Richard, till a Richard killed him.

DUCHESS

I had a Richard too, and thou didst kill him;

I had a Rutland too; thou holp'st to kill him.   45

QUEEN MARGARET

Thou hadst a Clarence too, and Richard killed him.

From forth the kennel of thy womb hath crept

A hell-hound that doth hunt us all to death:

That dog, that had his teeth before his eyes,

To worry lambs and lap their gentle blood;   50

That excellent grand tyrant of the earth,

That reigns in galled eyes of weeping souls;

That foul defacer of God's handiwork

Thy womb let loose to chase us to our graves.

O upright, just, and true-disposing God,   55

---

43 ¹**Richard** Richard, Duke of York, the younger of Elizabeth's sons, also murdered by Richard's assassins

44 **Richard** Richard, the late Duke of York, the Duchess's husband and King Richard's father, killed by Margaret's army at Wakefield in 1460 (*3H6* 1.4)

45 **Rutland** the Duchess's second son, Edmund, Earl of Rutland, killed by Clifford (*3H6* 1.3)
   holp'st helped

47–9 **kennel . . . eyes** Richard's alleged birth with teeth, which 'plainly signified' that he should 'snarl and bite and play the dog' (*3H6* 5.6.77), is elaborated to claim that, also like a dog, he was born unable to see. Milton may have recalled this passage in depicting Sin in *Paradise Lost* (Martin).

50 **worry** seize by the throat, tear or lacerate by biting and shaking, said of dogs or wolves attacking sheep (*OED v.* 3)

51–3 *F apparently reverses 51 and 52: *tyrant* should be the subject of *reigns*, putting 51 before 52. However, 53 could come after 50, as it does in F, Qq, without spoiling the sense.

51 **excellent** pre-eminent, supreme (in a neutral or negative sense) (*OED a.* B 1b); cf. 'a very excellent piece of villainy' (*Tit* 2.2.[2.3.]7).
   grand pre-eminent, chief; resembling uses of 'arch' in transferring the sense of an official title, as in 'Grand Turk' (*OED a.* 3a, citing this line). Cf. 'The grand conspirator' (*R2* 5.6.19). See pp. 29–31.

52 **galled** gallèd; sore from chafing (*OED ppl. a.²* 1b); cf. *Ham* 1.2.155.

53 **defacer** disfigurer, mutilator; cf. 3.7.125.
   God's handiwork i.e. humanity, created in God's image (Genesis, 1.26–7); cf. 2.1.123–4.

55 **true-disposing** i.e. rightly ordering (*OED* dispose *v.* 2)

45 too; thou holp'st] *F2 (*too, thou holp'st*)*; too, thou hop'st *F, Q1–2*; too, and thou holpst *Q3–6*   46] *Qq; F lines* too, / him. /   and] *F, Q1*; till *Q2–6*   50 blood] *F*; blouds *Qq*   51–3] *Ard²; in sequence* 53, 52, 51 *F*; 53, 51, 52 *Capell*   51–2] *F; not in Qq*

King Richard III

How do I thank thee that this carnal cur
Preys on the issue of his mother's body
And makes her pew-fellow with others' moan.

DUCHESS

O Harry's wife, triumph not in my woes!
God witness with me, I have wept for thine.   60

QUEEN MARGARET

Bear with me. I am hungry for revenge,
And now I cloy me with beholding it.
Thy Edward he is dead, that killed my Edward,
Thy other Edward dead, to quit my Edward.
Young York, he is but boot, because both they   65
Matched not the high perfection of my loss.
Thy Clarence he is dead that stabbed my Edward,
And the beholders of this frantic play,
Th'adulterate Hastings, Rivers, Vaughan, Grey,
Untimely smothered in their dusky graves.   70

---

56 **carnal** carnivorous, bloody, murderous (*OED a.* 6, citing this line); possibly suggesting 'related in blood' (*OED a.* 2), with the Duchess as Richard's mother

58 **pew-fellow** one who shares a pew in church, a fellow-worshipper (*OED*)
   moan lamentation

60 **God . . . me** i.e. may God witness my claim

61 **Bear with me** i.e. be patient

62 **cloy** surfeit or satiate (*OED v.* 7); cf. *R2* 1.3.296.

63 **Thy Edward . . . my Edward** Edward IV . . . Prince Edward, Margaret's son

64 *****Thy other Edward** The Duchess's grandson, Edward V. F's 'The' injects further ambiguity into a confusing litany, but might interchangeability have been the playwright's point? Margaret's 'hunger' for revenge expresses itself in

the devaluation of her interlocutor's family: the Duchess's two Edwards fail to even the balance.
   quit Cf. 20.

65 **boot** compensation, thrown in to make up a deficiency of value (*OED sb.*[1] 2)

68–9 This exceptional rhyme renders the victims mere parts of a 'generalized accumulation of death' (Brooke, 51).

68 **this frantic play** i.e. the murder of Prince Edward; earlier Margaret mentions Dorset instead of his brother Grey as a witness (1.3.209–10n.).
   frantic lunatic, violently mad (*OED a.* 1; cf. 1.3.246); Qq's 'tragicke' accords with Margaret's theatrical references.

69 **adulterate** i.e. adulterous (for his relationship with Mistress Shore)

70 **Untimely smothered** i.e. prematurely extinguished in burial; Janet Adelman notes the odd emphasis on

---

59 wife] *F, Q2–6;* wifes *Q1*   60 thine] *F, Q1;* thee *Q2–6*   63 killed] *F;* stabd *Qq*   64 Thy] *Qq;* The *F*   quit] *F, Q1–5 subst.;* quite *Q6*   66 Matched] *F;* Match *Qq*   67 stabbed] *F;* kild *Qq*   68 frantic] *F;* tragicke *Qq*   69 Th'] *F; Qq (*The*)*

Richard yet lives, hell's black intelligencer,
Only reserved their factor to buy souls
And send them thither. But at hand, at hand
Ensues his piteous and unpitied end.
Earth gapes, hell burns, fiends roar, saints pray,   75
To have him suddenly conveyed from hence.

smothering and suggests a change from stabbing in the earlier history plays, citing 1.4.40, 4.3.17, 4.4.134 and Clarence's drowning (Adelman, 241). See also *strangling* in the womb (4.4.138).

71 **intelligencer** agent, one who obtains secret information or conveys intelligence (*OED sb.* a; cf. *2H4* 4.2.20), but perhaps working two ways: while Richard spies for Satan, everything about him also conveys information to humanity about hell's nature and designs (Torrey, 142). For official fears about intelligencers during the late 1580s and 1590s, see Fox, 340–50.

72 **Only reserved** i.e. preserved alive solely in order to be
   their hell's
   factor mercantile agent (*OED sb.* 4a) or someone who works for another (*OED sb.* 3); cf. 3.7.133. 'Satans chiefest drift & maine point . . . is the inlargement of his owne kingdome' by acquiring more damned souls (Mason, 55), but *buy* lends this line a quality of understatement (contrast the melodrama of 75). The mundane commercial sense of *factor* here differs from that in *Mirror* passages concerning disguised fiends who walk the earth as 'factours for all evylls' ('Hastings', 246), but it does connect with Elizabethan religious discourse. Henry Smith acknowledges Satan's title as '*The God of this World*', but, more humbly, he is 'a factor between the Merchant and the Mercer, and

the Gentleman and the tenant' or a master artisan: 'there is a craft of compassing, and Satan is the craftesmaster, and the rest are prentises, or factors vnder him' (*Sermons*, 987, 994–6).

73 **at hand** near in time, rapidly approaching (*OED sb.* II 25b)

74 **piteous and unpitied** A wonderfully expressive formula for this play, in which the most deplorable (*OED* piteous 3) suffering frequently fails to elicit pity from onstage observers.

75 **gapes** i.e. opens wide, like a mouth, with an association of the opening and the mouth of hell (*OED v.* 1b); cf. 1.2.65n.
   fiends . . . saints Both hell and heaven have a stake in Richard's actions and their consequences. The conjunction of otherwise opposing forces accurately suits Richard's complicated role as an unwitting instrument of heavenly purposes, even as he pursues the goals of hell on earth. This is the second reference to the practice – strongly denounced by Protestants – of prayer to or by the saints (see 1.2.8n., 5.3.241n.). Hammond detects 'Faustian overtones' in 71–6, but Richard's roles include that of the tyrannical scourge who, with divine allowance, inflicts punishment upon sinners, while Marlowe's Faustus fulfils no such function.

76 **conveyed** carried away forcibly (*OED v.* 3)

73 thither] *F, Q2–6; Q1* (thether) hand, at hand] *F, Q2–6;* hand at handes *Q1*   75 hell] *F, Q1–5;* hels *Q6*   76 from hence] *F;* away *Qq*

Cancel his bond of life, dear God I pray,
That I may live and say, 'The dog is dead.'

QUEEN ELIZABETH

O, thou didst prophesy the time would come
That I should wish for thee to help me curse   80
That bottled spider, that foul bunch-backed toad.

QUEEN MARGARET

I called thee then vain flourish of my fortune;
I called thee then, poor shadow, painted queen,
The presentation of but what I was,
The flattering index of a direful pageant,   85
One heaved a-high, to be hurled down below,
A mother only mocked with two fair babes,
A dream of what thou wast, a garish flag
To be the aim of every dangerous shot,
A sign of dignity, a breath, a bubble,   90

---

77 **bond of life** covenant or agreement, respecting the term of his life; cf. *Mac* 3.2.49. While Richard's life has been preserved that he might function as hell's spy and agent, God is capable of terminating the bond that sets the terms of his life.
I pray Margaret joins the *saints* who *pray* (75); cf. 1.3.211.
79–80 See 1.3.244–5.
81 **bottled** See 1.3.241–5.
82–115 On the figure of anaphora, or repetition, prominent in this speech, see 153n.
82–3 **flourish . . . painted** See 1.3.240.
83 **shadow** image; elsewhere used to characterize actors (*MND* 5.3.209–10, 417)
84 **presentation of but** representation, likeness only of (*OED* presentation III 5b). See Abbott, 129 on placement of 'but'.
85 **flattering index** prologue, preface (*OED sb.* 5a; cf. 2.2.149), *flattering*

because, although pleasing to the imagination, ultimately unreal (cf. *TS* Ind.1.43: 'a flatt'ring dream')
direful dreadful, terrible (*OED*)
pageant scene acted upon the stage (*OED sb.* 1a)
86 suggesting the rolling of Fortune's wheel
a-high aloft, on high
87 **only mocked with** i.e. merely deceived in thinking that she truly had (the children); cf. 'mock'd . . . with a husband' (*MM* 5.1.415).
88–9 **garish . . . shot** gaudy military standard that attracts the shots of enemy marksmen
90 **sign** badge, emblem (*OED sb.* 5a, b) or vestige (here, of lost *dignity*) (*OED sb.* 8a); either sense emphasizes the insubstantiality of the signifier – *breath, a bubble* – as opposed to the substance signified (cf. 'honour' as 'mere scutcheon', *1H4* 5.1.139–40).
breath Cf. Falstaff's 'What is in that

---

78 and] *F;* to *Qq*   81 bunch-backed] *F, Q1;* hunch-backt *Q2–6*   86 a-high] *F, Qq (*a high*), hyphen Dyce*   87 fair] *F;* sweete *Qq*   88–90] *F;* A dreame of which thou wert a breath, a bubble, / A signe of dignitie, a garish flagge, / To be the aime of euerie dangerous shot, / *Qq subst.*

340

A queen in jest, only to fill the scene.
Where is thy husband now? Where be thy brothers?
Where be thy two sons? Wherein dost thou joy?
Who sues, and kneels, and says, 'God save the Queen'?
Where be the bending peers that flattered thee?   95
Where be the thronging troops that followed thee?
Decline all this, and see what now thou art:
For happy wife, a most distressed widow;
For joyful mother, one that wails the name;
For one being sued to, one that humbly sues;   100
For queen, a very caitiff crowned with care;
For she that scorned at me, now scorned of me;
For she being feared of all, now fearing one;

word "honour"? What is that "honour"? Air' (*1H4* 1.1.134–5).
   bubble Cf. Dent, M246: 'Man is but a
bubble.'
91 **in jest** without serious intention, the
opposite of 'in earnest' (*OED sb.* 6a;
cf. *R2* 5.3.99–100), but also with a
theatrical connotation: *jest*, meaning
pageant or masque (*OED sb.* 8; cf.
Kyd, *Spanish Tragedy*, 1.4.137 or *Ham*
3.2.228, where both meanings appear
present, supported by reference to
filling a *scene*.
92–6 **Where is ... Where be** Cf. the
medieval *ubi sunt* formula, lamenting
the mutability of the world, its people
and goods by demanding where they
may have gone; cf. 144–8.
92 **be** On 'be' used to refer to a number of
persons and for 'euphony and variety',
see Abbott, 300.
94 **sues** petitions
95 **bending** bowing
   peers nobles of the degrees of duke,
marquess, earl, viscount or baron
(*OED sb.* 4a)
96 **troops** retinue, attendants

97 **Decline** say or recite in formal order
(*OED v.* 20b, citing this line), but the
exhaustiveness and formulaic nature
of what follows suggests the grammatical exercise of declining a word
through different cases (*OED v.* 20a).
Cf. Thersites' attempt to 'decline the
whole question' of Patroclus (*TC*
2.3.50–65).
98 **For** instead of (Abbott, 148)
99 **wails the name** bewails, laments at
the very title (of mother)
100–4 *F preserves the sequence of
categories in 92–5 – questions about
spouse, children, suitors and queenly
office (Patrick, 42; Greg, *Problem*, 82)
– more nearly constituting a 'declension' than Qq (Hammond).
100 *to Q2–6, F appear to disagree with
Q1, but see 385n. on *too*.
101 **very caitiff** truly poor wretch, absolutely miserable person (*OED* 2)
102 **scorned at ... scorned of** mocked,
derided ... mocked by
103 **feared ... fearing** playing on *feared*
= respected (by all) and *fearing* = being
afraid of (Richard)

93 be ... sons] *F; are (*be *Q3–6*) thy children *Qq*   94 'and ... says] *F; to thee, and cries *Qq*   100–4]
*F; in sequence 101, 100, 104, 102 *Qq*   100 to] *F, Q2–6 (*too*), Q1*   102 she] *F; one *Qq*   103] *F; not
in *Qq*

For she commanding all, obeyed of none.
Thus hath the course of justice whirled about   105
And left thee but a very prey to time,
Having no more but thought of what thou wast
To torture thee the more, being what thou art.
Thou didst usurp my place, and dost thou not
Usurp the just proportion of my sorrow?   110
Now thy proud neck bears half my burdened yoke,
From which, even here I slip my wearied head
And leave the burden of it all on thee.
Farewell, York's wife, and queen of sad mischance.
These English woes shall make me smile in France.   115

QUEEN ELIZABETH

O thou, well skilled in curses, stay awhile
And teach me how to curse mine enemies.

QUEEN MARGARET

Forbear to sleep the night, and fast the day;
Compare dead happiness with living woe;

---

105 **course** onward path (*OED sb.* 2a) or,
given *prey* (106), the action of pursuing game with dogs (*OED sb.* 7a)
whirled about turned about an axis
like a wheel (Qq 'whe'eld'), possibly
referring to Fortune's wheel (cf. 86);
cf. 'justice always whirls in equal measure' (*LLL* 4.3.358).
106 **very** in the fullest, most emphatic
sense (*OED a.* A 3a)
prey to time Cf. 'cormorant devouring time' (*LLL* 1.1.4), 'Devouring
time' (*Son* 19) and Dent, T326: 'Time
devours all things.'
107 **thought** memory
110 **just proportion** i.e. the amount (of
sorrow) allotted (to me) by right (of
my woes)

111–12 See Dent, N69: 'To slip one's
neck out of the collar'. F's 'wearied
head' emphasizes the mental nature of
the sufferings bequeathed to Elizabeth
as *crowned with care* (101) and permits
a remark on the (false) pride embodied
in her *proud neck.*
117–23 Seneca's Chorus seeks instruc-
tion in grieving from Hecuba, who
complies by detailing how to lament
(Seneca, *Troades*, 79–98); cf. Lucrece's
demand: 'Teach me to curse him that
thou taught'st this ill' (*Luc* 996).
118 ***night ... day** F agrees with Q3–6's
singular forms; cf. *TS* 5.2.151 ('To watch
the night in storms, the day in cold') and
Mirror, 'Buckingham', 675 ('To wayle
the daye, and wepe the weary night').

---

104 she] *F;* one *Qq*   105 whirled] *F;* whe'eld *Q1;* wheel'd *Q2–6*   107–8 wast ... art.] *F4* (wast,
. . . art.); wast. . . . art, *F;* wert, . . . art, *Q1–2;* art, . . . art. *Q3–6*   112 wearied] *F, Q6;* wearie *Q1–2;*
weary *Q3–5*   head] *F;* necke *Qq*   115 woes] *F, Q1–3, 5–6;* wars *Q4*   shall] *F;* will *Qq*   118 night
. . . day] *F, Q3–6;* nights . . . daies *Q1–2*

342

Think that thy babes were sweeter than they were,   120
And he that slew them fouler than he is.
Bettering thy loss makes the bad causer worse.
Revolving this will teach thee how to curse.

QUEEN ELIZABETH

My words are dull. O, quicken them with thine.   124

QUEEN MARGARET

Thy woes will make them sharp and pierce like mine.   *Exit.*

DUCHESS

Why should calamity be full of words?

QUEEN ELIZABETH

Windy attorneys to their clients' woes,
Airy succeeders of intestate joys,
Poor breathing orators of miseries,
Let them have scope, though what they will impart   130
Help nothing else, yet do they ease the heart.

DUCHESS

If so, then be not tongue-tied. Go with me,

120–3 On Margaret's methods of cursing, see p. 21.

120 *sweeter Qq's 'fairer' provides an antithesis with *fouler* (121); cf. 'sweete' (Qq) and 'faire' (F) in 87.

122 **Bettering** exaggerating, amplifying, as in rhetorical hyperbole
causer Cf. 1.2.120.

123 **Revolving** pondering (cf. 4.2.42)

124–5 **dull . . . sharp** Following an antithesis of *dead* and *living* (119), Margaret recasts Elizabeth's opposition of *dull* to *quick[en]* (124) by taking *dull* to mean 'blunt' rather than 'slow', thereby, characteristically, heightening the verbal aggression.

124 **quicken** animate, enliven

125 SD And just like that, Margaret simply goes – for good (see 6).

127–31 In effect, words are insubstantial

representatives for substantial griefs that are their motivating *clients*, or words are fruitless inheritors of joys that have died leaving no inheritance to their successors, or they are merely empty speakers who give speeches about unfelt miseries. Cf. *Luc* 1016–27. See p. 23.

128 *intestate not having made a will (*OED a.* 1); F's 'intestine' would render *airy* succession alimentary (Lull).

130 **scope** liberty, room for exercise (*OED sb.*[2] 7a)

130–3 **impart . . . smother** Cf. Dent, G447: 'Grief is lessened when imparted to others.' The Duchess renders 'imparting' – i.e. sharing with other sufferers – as violence, to *smother* Richard with what they have to impart (communicate) to him (see G. Bloom, 92–3).

120 thy] *F, Q1–3, 5–6; om. Q4*   sweeter] *F;* fairer *Qq*   122 Bettering] *F, Qq* (Bett'ring*)*   causer] *F, Q1–3, 5–6;* causes *Q4*   125] *Qq; F lines* sharpe, / mine. /   SD] *F (Exit Margaret.); Exit. Mar. Qq opp. 126*   127 their] *F;* your *Qq*   clients'] *F, Q4* (Clients*);* Client *Q1–3, 5–6*   128 intestate] *Qq;* intestine *F*   130 will] *F;* do *Qq*   131 nothing else] *F;* not at al *Qq*   132 If so, then] *Qq;* If so then, *F*

And in the breath of bitter words let's smother
My damned son, that thy two sweet sons smothered.

                                              [*Trumpet sounds.*]
The trumpet sounds. Be copious in exclaims.   135

Enter KING RICHARD *and his Train* [*including* CATESBY],
        ^Q*marching with drums and trumpets*^Q.

KING RICHARD
Who intercepts me in my expedition?

DUCHESS
O, she that might have intercepted thee,
By strangling thee in her accursed womb,
From all the slaughters, wretch, that thou hast done.

QUEEN ELIZABETH
Hid'st thou that forehead with a golden crown   140
Where should be branded, if that right were right,
The slaughter of the prince that owed that crown

---

135 **exclaims** exclamations (cf. 1.2.52)
135.1–2 Catesby needs to enter before 442. Richard needs the drums and trumpets (mentioned only in Qq SD) at 149.
136 **Who** Richard's seeming lack of recognition admits at least three interpretations. Socially, Richard's question might rhetorically express the offended dignity of a monarch who finds himself interrupted – even by his mother – in an important undertaking. Physically, entry in military order may insulate him from immediate contact with onlookers; or perhaps the women wear mourning veils (see 8n.).
   expedition warlike enterprise (*OED* 2), possibly conveying 'haste' (*OED* 5) as at 4.3.54.

137–9 **might have . . . From** i.e. could have . . . from committing
138 **accursed** accursèd
140–1 **forehead . . . branded** Shaheen suggests allusion to God's mark upon Cain for his fratricide, but Cain's mark is meant to preserve him from violent retribution (Genesis, 4.15) while Richard's brand should manifest guilt, as in the case of Shore's wife, who protests, 'If thy faults were so written in thy forehead as mine is, it would be as wrong with thee' (*True Tragedy*, 1175–6). Cf. Isaiah, 3.9: '[God] shall finde marke of their impietie in their forehead' (Geneva). Addressing the mark on the forehead of the biblical Whore of Babylon, an Elizabethan sermon invokes a commonplace: 'Wee vse

---

134 that] *F;* which *Qq*   sweet] *F, Q1–2; om. Q3–6*   SD] *Collier subst.*   135 The trumpet sounds] *F; I* heare his drum *Qq*   135.1 *and his Train*] *F; not in Qq   including* CATESBY] *Ard²*   136+ SP] *King[.] Qq; Rich. F*   136 me in] *F; not in Qq*   137 O] *F;* A *Qq*   141 Where] *Qq;* Where't *F*   should] *F, Q1–3, 5–6;* would *Q4*   branded] *F;* grauen *Qq*   right,] *Qq;* right? *F*

And the dire death of my poor sons and brothers?
Tell me, thou villain-slave, where are my children?

DUCHESS

Thou toad, thou toad, where is thy brother Clarence,   145
And little Ned Plantagenet his son?

QUEEN ELIZABETH

Where is the gentle Rivers, Vaughan, Grey?

DUCHESS

Where is kind Hastings?

KING RICHARD

A flourish, trumpets! Strike alarum, drums!
Let not the heavens hear these tell-tale women   150
Rail on the Lord's anointed. Strike, I say! *Flourish. Alarums.*

to say if euerie mans faults were written in their foreheads, some would pull
down their hats very low' (Gifford,
328; cf. Dent, F120).

142 **owed** owned (*OED v.* B 1)

143 **brothers** See 1.3.37n.

144–8 Here the *ubi sunt* formulae (see
92–6n.) are woven into interactive dialogue, as actual demands rather than
as a generalized lyrical lament. See
also p. 25.

147 *Qq's 'kind Hastings' is unlikely from
Queen Elizabeth, given her antagonism towards him.

149–430 On the strange 'temporal loop'
in this scene, the odder for keeping Richard's forces onstage during
the prolonged verbal struggle between
Richard and Queen Elizabeth, see
Jones, *Origins*, 221–6.

149–54 The opposing of drums to voices
resembles *KJ* 5.2.159–80.

149 **flourish** A flourish is a fanfare
announcing the approach of a person of distinction (*OED sb.* 7a), as at
2.1.0.1 and 5.5.0.4, so perhaps ironically Richard has to command his own
flourish – after he has already arrived

on the scene and while he attempts
to assert his legitimacy to his own
mother!

alarum Cf. 1.1.7n.

150 **tell-tale** tale-telling, or in the present
case, those who are 'tell-tales' (*OED a.*
3a, citing this line); a 'tell-tale' idly or
maliciously discloses private or secret
matters (*OED sb.* 1a). Richard typically
condescends to the women as idle gossips who trade in mere tales, but in fact
they threaten his authority by public
accusation (see pp. 23–5).

151 **Rail ... anointed** referring to
the practice of anointing the newly
crowned monarch with oil, based on
biblical precedent: in 1 Samuel, 16
God summons Samuel to render David
'the Lordes annoynted', recognizing
him, the Bishops' Bible explains, as
'appoynted of God to be made king'.
Richard's biblical language shares
terms with official attempts to silence
critics of the Elizabethan ecclesiastical
authorities. Bishop Bancroft quotes
Exodus, 22.28 and 1 Samuel, 24.10:
'Thou shalt not rayle vpon the *Iudges*,
neyther speake euill of the Ruler of

143 poor] *F;* two *Qq*   145] *Qq; F lines* Toade, / *Clarence?* /   146 Plantagenet] *F, Q1–2, 6; Q3–5*
*(*Plantaget*)*   147 the gentle] *F;* kind *Hastings Qq*   148] *F; not in Qq*   151 SD] *F; The trumpets Q1;*
The trumpets sound. (sounds. Q3–6) Q2–6

Either be patient and entreat me fair,
Or with the clamorous report of war
Thus will I drown your exclamations.

DUCHESS

Art thou my son?   155

KING RICHARD

Ay, I thank God, my father and yourself.

DUCHESS

Then patiently hear my impatience.

KING RICHARD

Madam, I have a touch of your condition,
That cannot brook the accent of reproof.

DUCHESS

O, let me speak.

KING RICHARD   Do then, but I'll not hear.   160

DUCHESS

I will be mild and gentle in my words.

KING RICHARD

And brief, good mother, for I am in haste.

---

the people. The Lord keepe me from
laying my hand on him. For he is the
Lordes annointed' (Bancroft, *Positions*,
sig. A3'). See p. 23.
    Rail complain vehemently
151 SD Plutarch's Lepidus, fearful that
    Antony, wearing 'a mourning gowne'
    for Caesar, will win his troops' alle-
    giance from him, commands 'all the
    trompetts to sownd together to stoppe
    the souldiers eares' (Plutarch, 978;
    Honigmann, 232).
152 **patient** composed, calm in suffering
    (*OED a.* 1)
    entreat me fair treat (*OED entreat v.*
    1) or beseech (*OED v.* 9) me politely
    (cf. *3H6* 1.1.271)
153 **report** resounding noise (*OED sb.*
    7a), but possibly conveying a specific

response, especially a musical note
answering to or repeating another
(*OED sb.* 6a). Puttenham (108) uses
'report' for anaphora or 'Repetition
in the first degree', a verbal device
relevant to this highly repetitive
scene and also to the sense in which
Richard's noises answer in the
masculine register of *Grim-visaged
War* (1.1.9) the lamenting accusations
of the female characters.
155 Cf. Lear's weighty reproof, 'Are you
    our daughter?' (*KL* 1.4.209; Pierce,
    123n.) and Leontes to Mamillius, 'Art
    thou my boy?' (*WT* 1.2.120).
158 **condition** temperament, disposition
    (cf. *Oth* 2.1.248)
159 **brook** endure (*OED v.* 3a)
    accent tone (*OED sb.* 5)

---

153 clamorous] *F, Q1–3, 5–6;* clamour *Q4*   159 That] *F;* Which *Qq*   160] *Steevens; F lines* speake. /
heare. / ; *not in Qq*   161 words] *F;* speach *Qq*

DUCHESS

> Art thou so hasty? I have stayed for thee,
> God knows, in torment and in agony.

KING RICHARD

> And came I not at last to comfort you?   165

DUCHESS

> No, by the Holy Rood, thou knowst it well:
> Thou cam'st on earth to make the earth my hell.
> A grievous burden was thy birth to me;
> Tetchy and wayward was thy infancy.
> Thy school days frightful, desperate, wild and furious;   170
> Thy prime of manhood daring, bold and venturous;
> Thy age confirmed proud, subtle, sly and bloody,
> More mild, but yet more harmful, kind in hatred.
> What comfortable hour canst thou name
> That ever graced me with thy company?   175

KING RICHARD

> Faith, none but Humfrey Hower, that called your grace

163 **stayed for** awaited the coming of (*OED v.*[1] 14), here referring to the labour of childbirth

166 **Holy Rood** cross of Christ (see 3.2.74)

169 **Tetchy** peevish, testy (*OED a.* 1; cf. *RJ* 1.3.32)
    wayward refractory, disobedient (*OED a.* 1)

170 **frightful** alarming
    desperate reckless or violent (*OED a.* II 4a); F elides (desp'rate).

171 *This line appears in Q1–2 and F, and is absent from Q3–6, suggesting the close relationship of FMS and QMS. See p. 446.
    prime first age in time, perfection or vigour (*OED sb.*[1] 6, 9); cf. 1.2.250.

172 **age confirmed** i.e. maturity; the historical Richard lived only to 33.

173 **kind in hatred** possibly alluding to Richard's behaviour toward Clarence in 1.1 (Thompson)

174 **comfortable** pleasant (*OED a.* 5a)

176 **Humfrey Hower** never satisfactorily explained (Var); certainly punning on (and an alternative spelling for) *hour* (174). To 'dine with Duke Humphrey' meant to go dinnerless (*OED* dine *v.* 1b), and there was an association with walking in St Paul's church or sitting there in 'the chair of Duke Humphrey' while others were elsewhere eating (Harvey, 1.206; J. Hall, *Satire* III, vii.6–7; Dent, D637). Richard perhaps personifies hunger as Humphrey Hower who summoned his mother to breakfast by 'gracing' her (i.e. calling her *your grace*), leaving Richard alone and thereby providing him a *comfortable* time with her no longer around.

164 torment and in] *F;* anguish, paine and *Qq*   170 desperate] *F* (desp'rate*), Qq*   171] *F, Q1–2; om. Q3–6*   172 sly and bloody] *F;* bloudie, trecherous *Qq*   173] *F; not in Qq*   175 with] *F;* in *Qq*   176] *Qq; F lines* Hower, / Grace /

To breakfast once, forth of my company.
If I be so disgracious in your eye,
Let me march on and not offend you, madam.
Strike up the drum.

DUCHESS   I prithee, hear me speak.   180

KING RICHARD
You speak too bitterly.

DUCHESS   Hear me a word,
For I shall never speak to thee again.

KING RICHARD   So.

DUCHESS

Either thou wilt die by God's just ordinance
Ere from this war thou turn a conqueror,   185
Or I with grief and extreme age shall perish
And nevermore behold thy face again.
Therefore take with thee my most grievous curse,

---

177 **forth of** away from
178 **disgracious** unpleasing
181 David Troughton (88–9) cried out
'desperately' here, deprived of motherly love.
183 **So** George Bernard Shaw observed,
'I would sacrifice anything else in the
play sooner than that monosyllable
"So"; which tells more of Richard than
a dozen stabbings and baby smother-
ings' (Pierce, 123–4n.); Pierce (115)
suggests Richard's 'irony is reduced
to a petulant "So" by her measured
tones'.
184 **ordinance** divine ordering or dis-
pensation (*OED sb.* 5b), possibly punning on 'implements of war' (*OED*
ordnance)
185 **turn** return

188–96 Cf. Richard's mockery of his
mother's blessing at 2.2.107–11 (E.
Berry, 97). On the early modern dread
of the parental curse, see K. Thomas,
505–6. John Barrymore's Richard
nervously crossed himself and cow-
ered (Colley, 156); David Troughton's
Richard, who curled up with his head
in his mother's lap, was shocked by
the betrayal of his desire for maternal
comfort (88).
188 **grievous** burdensome, pressing
heavily (*OED a.* 1a), synonymous with
'heauy' (Qq); appropriate to the curse
of fatigue which follows
curse Willis (102) suggests the (relatively) positive nature of cursing here
and its ultimately beneficial effect in
the ghostly visitations of 5.3.

177 my] *F, Q1–3, 5–6; om. Q4*   178 I] *F, Q1; it Q2–3, 5–6; om. Q4*   disgracious] *F, Q1–2; gratious
Q3–6*   eye] *F; sight Qq*   179 you, madam] *F; your grace Qq*   180] *Steevens; F lines* Drumme. /
speake. / *; not in Qq, but see 181–2 t.n.*   181] *Steevens; F lines* bitterly. / word: /   You . . . bitterly] *F;
not in Qq, but see 183 t.n.*   181–2 Hear . . . again] *F;* O heare me speake for I shal neuer see thee *(the
Q2–4)* more. *Qq*   183] *F;* Come, come, you are *(are Q2–6)* too bitter. *Qq*   187 nevermore behold] *F
(neuer more behold);* neuer looke vpon *Qq*   188 grievous] *F;* heauy *Qq*

Which in the day of battle tire thee more
Than all the complete armour that thou wear'st.   190
My prayers on the adverse party fight,
And there the little souls of Edward's children
Whisper the spirits of thine enemies
And promise them success and victory.
Bloody thou art; bloody will be thy end.   195
Shame serves thy life and doth thy death attend.   *Exit.*

QUEEN ELIZABETH

Though far more cause, yet much less spirit to curse
Abides in me. I say amen to her.

KING RICHARD

Stay, madam, I must talk a word with you.

QUEEN ELIZABETH

I have no more sons of the royal blood   200
For thee to slaughter. For my daughters, Richard,
They shall be praying nuns, not weeping queens,
And therefore level not to hit their lives.

KING RICHARD

You have a daughter called Elizabeth,
Virtuous and fair, royal and gracious.   205

QUEEN ELIZABETH

And must she die for this? O, let her live,
And I'll corrupt her manners, stain her beauty,

---

189 **tire** i.e. let it tire; perhaps a pun on
'attire' continued in 190 (Lull).
190 **complete armour** còmplete
armour; contrasted with the foot-
soldier's partial armour or brigander
(cf. 3.5.0.1–2n.)
192–4 See 5.3.146–53.
193 **Whisper** whisper to (subjunctive)
196 **Shame** is personified as an attendant
who *serves* Richard during his life and
who anticipates (*OED* attend *v.* III 15)

'attending' him in death.
202 **nuns** Elizabeth's third daughter, Bridget, was a nun (Holinshed,
3.711).
203 **level** aim (*OED v.*[1] II 6, 7a), with a
weapon
205 ***gracious.** F's '?' could serve for
either an exclamation mark or a question mark. RP suggests the comic
potential of an interrogatory tone here.
Qq's full stop is more neutral.

---

193 spirits] *F, Q1–3, 5–6;* spirit *Q4*   195 art] *F, Q1–5;* art, and *Q6*   be] *F, Q1–4, 6;* by *Q5*   198 her]
F; all *Qq*   199 talk] *F;* speake *Qq*   200 more] *F, Q2–6;* moe *Q1*   201 slaughter.] *F;* murther *Q1;*
murther, *Q2–6*   205 gracious.] *Qq;* Gracious? *F*

Slander myself as false to Edward's bed,
Throw over her the veil of infamy.
So she may live unscarred of bleeding slaughter, 210
I will confess she was not Edward's daughter.

KING RICHARD
Wrong not her birth. She is a royal princess.

QUEEN ELIZABETH
To save her life, I'll say she is not so.

KING RICHARD
Her life is safest only in her birth.

QUEEN ELIZABETH
And only in that safety died her brothers. 215

KING RICHARD
Lo, at their birth good stars were opposite.

QUEEN ELIZABETH
No, to their lives ill friends were contrary.

KING RICHARD
All unavoided is the doom of destiny.

---

209 **veil of infamy** Queen Elizabeth suggests protecting her daughter by making her 'shame or disgrace' (*OED* infamy) visible and repulsive; such an outward *veil of infamy* reverses the familiar sense of the veil as concealing shame, disgrace or ugliness (e.g. 'Where beauty's veil doth cover every blot', *Son* 95; *MV* 3.2.98–9). A similar reversal occurs in the description of the young Henry V as having 'obscured his contemplation / Under the veil of wildness' (*H5* 1.1.63–4). See also 8n.

210 **So** i.e. provided that (Abbott, 133)
of i.e. by

211 **confess** A nice irony that false confession may protect rather than

destroy one of Richard's victims; contrast the defamation of Hastings (3.5.56–61).

214 **safest only in** i.e. only protected by

215 **only . . . safety** i.e. merely as a result of that protection

216 **Lo** interjection directing attention to what is about to be said (*OED int.*[1])
opposite hostile, opposed; when good stars are opposed, their beneficent effects are neutralized. For astrological 'opposition' among 'evil aspects', see Lilly, 24; cf. 402.

218 Cf. Dent, F83: 'It is impossible to avoid Fate.'
unavoided inevitable (*OED*, citing this line); contrast 4.1.55.

208–9 bed, . . . infamy.] *Pope;* bed: . . . Infamy, *F;* bed . . . infamie, *Q1;* bed, . . . infamie, *Q2–6* 210 of] *F;* from *Qq* 212 a royal princess] *F;* of roiall bloud *Qq* 214 safest only] *F;* onlie safest *Qq* 216 birth] *F;* births *Qq* 217 ill] *F;* bad *Qq*

QUEEN ELIZABETH

    True, when avoided grace makes destiny.

    My babes were destined to a fairer death,   220

    If grace had blessed thee with a fairer life.

KING RICHARD

    You speak as if that I had slain my cousins.

QUEEN ELIZABETH

    Cousins indeed, and by their uncle cozened

    Of comfort, kingdom, kindred, freedom, life.

    Whose hand soever lanched their tender hearts,   225

    Thy head, all indirectly, gave direction.

219–21 Referring to the controversial idea that one might reject God's grace and make one's own damnable destiny, Queen Elizabeth counters both the emphasis on divine predestination in contemporary Calvinism and Richard's assertion of irrefutable destiny by positing the importance of the individual human will in accepting or rejecting God's grace. However, she also reactivates a sense of over-riding divine direction by invoking the lives the princes were denied because God's 'grace' had not 'blessed [Richard] with a fairer life'. These complicated lines suggest the compromises of the Elizabethan Church in these matters.

219 **avoided** probably, given the context of 219–21, with an active sense, as in refuted or made to no effect (*OED* avoid 2), rather than merely evaded (as at 3.5.68)

220 **were** i.e. would have been

222–35 *This F only passage displays more melodramatic emotional intensity than Queen Elizabeth's other exchanges with Richard (Hammond, Appendix I). Otherwise cooler and more controlled, she here employs elaborately vituperative rhetorical figures recalling the *Henry VI* plays (see Hodgdon, *End*, 269n.). However, there

is verbal consistency in her references to *lambs* and *entrails* (229; see 22–3), so perhaps here she erupts with a *wild grief* implied in her earlier lines. The metaphor of 'Lambes' surrendered to 'the rauenous wolfe' is in the sources (Hall, *Richard III*, fol. xlviii^r); the play on *indirectly . . . direction*, the analogy equating desperation with a boat out of control and the idea of whetting a knife on one's heart are Shakespearean (see *2H4* 4.5.106–7, *MV* 4.1.123–4). Absence from Qq may represent abbreviation.

222 **that** used as a conjunctional affix (Abbott, 287)

223 **cozened** cheated (*OED v.* 1b); cf. Dent, C739.

225 **Whose hand soever** i.e. whosoever's hand

    lanched lanced, pierced (*OED* launch 1; lanch); cf. Edmund's 'lancht' arm (*KL* 2.1.51). Lull suggests discrepancy with claims that the princes were smothered (4.3.17, 4.4.134).

226 **all** altogether

    indirectly by suggestion rather than in express terms (*OED* 2b), or wrong-fully (*OED* 1b)

    indirectly . . . direction Cf. 'By indirections find directions out' (*Ham* 2.1.63) and 'Yet indirection thereby grows direct' (*KJ* 3.1.202).

222–35] *F; not in Qq*

No doubt the murderous knife was dull and blunt
Till it was whetted on thy stone-hard heart,
To revel in the entrails of my lambs.
But that still use of grief makes wild grief tame,   230
My tongue should to thy ears not name my boys
Till that my nails were anchored in thine eyes,
And I in such a desperate bay of death,
Like a poor bark of sails and tackling reft,
Rush all to pieces on thy rocky bosom.   235

KING RICHARD
Madam, so thrive I in my enterprise
And dangerous success of bloody wars,
As I intend more good to you and yours
Than ever you and yours by me were harmed.

QUEEN ELIZABETH
What good is covered with the face of heaven,   240

---

227 **murderous** F elides to 'murd'rous'.
227–8 **knife . . . heart** Cf. 'Thou hid'st
a thousand daggers in thy thoughts,
/ Which thou hast whetted on thy
stony heart' (*2H4* 4.5.106–7; cf. *MV*
4.1.123–4) and Dent, H311.
229 **revel** Richard's knife first *dull and*
blunt, then whetted to an edge by his
hard heart to *revel* (i.e. make merry,
OED v.[1] 1) in the entrails of the children renders infanticide grotesquely
sexual. Cf. 1.2.177–81n., male arousal
as a keen edge (*Ham* 3.2.242–3) and
Cym 3.4.93.
230 **still** constant (Abbott, 69)
232 For threats to use finger nails, see
2H6 1.3.141–2, *MND* 3.2.298.
233–5 The ship bereft of tackling and
wildly tossed toward destruction is a
common Petrarchan image for love's
desperation; see Petrarch, *Rime* 189,
Thomas Wyatt's 'My galley charged
with forgetfulness' and the suicidal

Romeo (*RJ* 5.3.117–18).
233 **desperate** F elides ('desp'rate').
bay inlet of water (*OED sb.*[2] 1), as in
the following image of the ship; or
the final extremity of a hunted animal
turned at bay to face the pursuing
hounds (*OED sb.*[4] 3)
234 **bark** boat
reft bereft, robbed (*OED* reave *v.*[1])
236–8 **so thrive I . . . As I intend** i.e.
may I prevail . . . to the extent that I
intend; cf. 397–8.
237 **dangerous success** hazardous result
(*OED* success *sb.* 1a)
239 *****and** Many editors prefer 'or' (Q1–
5); 'and' (Q6, F) maintains parallelism with 238 (*you and yours*) in a play
'where one line is often exactly balanced
against another' (Walton, *Copy*, 25).
Alternatively, compositors of Q6 and of
F may have assimilated 239 to 238 (RP).
240 **covered . . . heaven** i.e. is to be
found anywhere under heaven

227 murderous] *F (*murd'rous*) 233 desperate] *F (*desp'rate*) 236–7] *F;* Madam, so thriue *I* in
my dangerous attempt of hostile armes *Qq* 238 I intend] *F, Q1–5;* Intend *Q6* 239 and] *F, Q6;* or
Q1–5 by . . . harmed] *F;* were by me wrongd *Qq*

To be discovered, that can do me good?

KING RICHARD

Th'advancement of your children, gentle lady.

QUEEN ELIZABETH

Up to some scaffold, there to lose their heads.

KING RICHARD

Unto the dignity and height of fortune,

The high imperial type of this earth's glory.   245

QUEEN ELIZABETH

Flatter my sorrow with report of it:

Tell me what state, what dignity, what honour,

Canst thou demise to any child of mine?

KING RICHARD

Even all I have – ay, and myself and all –

Will I withal endow a child of thine;   250

So in the Lethe of thy angry soul

Thou drown the sad remembrance of those wrongs

Which thou supposest I have done to thee.

---

241 **discovered** i.e. uncovered, revealed

242 **advancement** Richard echoes Queen Elizabeth's attack upon him (1.3.74).

243 reminiscent of Richard's own brand of humour, as in offering to *deliver* Clarence or *lie for* him (1.1.115)

245 **imperial** having the rank or authority of a supreme ruler (*OED a.* 4)

type symbol, emblem (*OED sb.*[1] 1a) and/or summit (*OED* tipe *sb.*[1] 2; literally, cupola or dome: *sb.*[1] 1). Cf. 'high tipe [type, Holinshed] of his honor' (Hall, *Edward IV*, fol. cxcix[r]). The royal position is both emblem and acme of earthly glory.

246 **Flatter** falsely indulge

247 **state** high status, exalted position (*OED sb.* II 16)

248 **demise** convey, transmit (*OED v.* 2, citing this line); perhaps the conveying or transferring of a title, as by the death or abdication of a sovereign (Jones, *Origins*, 223)

250 **withal** On placement of 'withal', see Abbott, 196.

thine Richard shifts pronouns as he begins his earnest appeal (Abbott, 231).

251 **So** provided that

Lethe river of the classical underworld whose waters produced forgetfulness (Virgil, *Aeneid*, 6.713–15)

242 Th'advancement] *F; Qq* (The aduancement) gentle] *F;* mightie *Qq*   244 Unto] *F;* No to *Qq* fortune] *F;* honor *Qq*   245 high] *F, Q1;* height *Q2–6*   246 sorrow] *F;* sorrowes *Qq*   249 ay] *F (I);* yea *Qq*

QUEEN ELIZABETH

Be brief, lest that the process of thy kindness

Last longer telling than thy kindness' date.   255

KING RICHARD

Then know that from my soul I love thy daughter.

QUEEN ELIZABETH

My daughter's mother thinks it with her soul.

KING RICHARD   What do you think?

QUEEN ELIZABETH

That thou dost love my daughter from thy soul;

So from thy soul's love didst thou love her brothers,   260

And from my heart's love I do thank thee for it.

KING RICHARD

Be not so hasty to confound my meaning:

I mean that with my soul I love thy daughter

And do intend to make her queen of England.

QUEEN ELIZABETH

Well then, who dost thou mean shall be her king?   265

KING RICHARD

Even he that makes her queen. Who else should be?

254–5 **process . . . date** *process* may
mean 'narration' (see 4.3.32), but
'the proceedings in any action at law'
(*OED sb.* 7a) seems likely, given surrounding legal discourse, from *demise*
(248) to *date*. Compare 'date', 'term',
'forfeit' and 'suit' together in *RJ*
1.4.108–13.

255 **date** duration (*OED sb.* 4)

258 Richard's need to have a stichomythic
response explained to him should be
related to various changes, including
diminished verbal acuity, that have
come over him since his enthronement

in 4.2; cf. his need to self-explicate
at 263.

259–61 **from . . . from . . . from**
Elizabeth plays on Richard's 'from
my soul I love thy daughter', taking his *from* to mean 'apart from'
(Abbott, 158). Her verbal capacity
matches Richard in aggressiveness, if
not deviousness. On her amphibology,
see Kehler, 118–20.

263 **I mean** For the third time since
his crowning, Richard appears compelled to explain his own utterances;
cf. 4.2.18, 74.

255 date] *F;* doe *Qq*   256] *Qq; F lines* know, / Daughter. /   259 soul;] *F4 subst.;* soule *F;* soule,
Qq   260 soul's love] *F, Q1–5;* soule *Q6*   thou love] *F, Q1, 6;* thou *Q2–5*   264 do intend] *F;* meane
Qq   265 Well] *F;* Saie *Qq*   266] *Qq; F lines* Queene: / bee? /   Who . . . be] *F;* who should be else
Q1; who should else *Q2–4, 6;* how should else *Q5*

QUEEN ELIZABETH
    What, thou?
KING RICHARD   Even so. How think you of it?
QUEEN ELIZABETH
    How canst thou woo her?
KING RICHARD   That would I learn of you,
    As one being best acquainted with her humour.
QUEEN ELIZABETH
    And wilt thou learn of me?
KING RICHARD   Madam, with all my heart.   270
QUEEN ELIZABETH

    Send to her, by the man that slew her brothers,
    A pair of bleeding hearts; thereon engrave
    'Edward' and 'York'. Then haply will she weep.
    Therefore present to her – as sometime Margaret
    Did to thy father, steeped in Rutland's blood –   275
    A handkerchief, which say to her did drain
    The purple sap from her sweet brother's body,
    And bid her wipe her weeping eyes withal.
    If this inducement move her not to love,
    Send her a letter of thy noble deeds: 280
    Tell her thou mad'st away her uncle Clarence,

---

268 *would I Most recent editors prefer
  'would I' (Q1–2) to 'I would' (Q3–6,
  F).
269 humour disposition (*OED sb.* II 5b);
  here with more the sense of a settled
  and characteristic temperament than
  in 1.2.230–1 or 4.1.64
270 And used to suggest emphatic inter-
  rogation; i.e. 'Do you indeed wish to
  learn of me?' (Abbott, 99).

273 haply perhaps
274 sometime once (*OED adv.* 2b);
  'sometime' (Q3–6, F) seems preferable to Q1–2, 7–8's 'sometimes' since
  the remark concerns a single action;
  however, 'sometimes' could have this
  meaning (*OED adv.* 2a).
275–7 *See pp. 446–7.
275 Rutland's blood See 1.3.176–7 and
  3H6 1.4.78–83.

267–8] *Steevens; F lines* thou? / it? / her? / you, / ; *Qq line* thou? / Maddame? / her? / you. /
267 Even so] *F;* I euen I *Qq* How] *F;* what *Qq* it] *F;* it Maddame *Qq* 268 would I] *Q1–2;* I
would *Q3–6, F* 269 being] *F;* that are *Q1–2;* that were *Q3–6* 270] *Steevens; F, Qq line* me? /
heart. / 273 haply will she] *F;* happelie she wil *Qq* 274 sometime] *F, Q3–6;* sometimes *Q1–2,
7–8* 275–7] *F;* Did to thy father, a handkercher steept in Rutlands bloud, *Qq subst.* 278 wipe . . .
withal] *F;* drie . . . therewith *Qq* 279 move] *F;* force *Qq* 280 letter . . . deeds] *F;* storie . . . acts
Qq 281 mad'st] *F, Q3–6; Q1* (madst)*; Q2* (madest)

355

Her uncle Rivers, ay, and for her sake
Mad'st quick conveyance with her good aunt Anne.

KING RICHARD

You mock me, madam. This ᵠisᵠ not the way
To win your daughter.

QUEEN ELIZABETH   There is no other way,   285
Unless thou couldst put on some other shape
And not be Richard, that hath done all this.

KING RICHARD

Say that I did all this for love of her.

QUEEN ELIZABETH

Nay, then indeed she cannot choose but hate thee,
Having bought love with such a bloody spoil.   290

KING RICHARD

Look what is done cannot be now amended.
Men shall deal unadvisedly sometimes,
Which after-hours gives leisure to repent.
If I did take the kingdom from your sons,
To make amends, I'll give it to your daughter.   295
If I have killed the issue of your womb,
To quicken your increase I will beget

---

283 **conveyance** removal (*OED sb.*[1] 3,
 citing this line); often with a sense of
 contrivance and trickery (cf. *1H6* 1.3.2)
288–342 *In this F only passage, Richard
 briefly revisits his verbal strategies
 of 1.2: he offers the excuse of doing
 everything for love, and then rapidly
 returns to wooing.
289–90 These lines cast intense disapproval on Anne's acquiescence in 1.2
 (cf. 4.1.65–9).
289 **cannot choose but** i.e. must, of
 necessity (cf. *MW* 5.3.17)
290 **spoil** damage, plunder (*OED sb.* 7, 3)

291 Cf. Dent, T200 ('Things done cannot
 be undone') and *Mac* 5.1.69.
 Look what i.e. whatever (*OED* look *v.*
 4b), an indefinite relative rather than
 an imperative
292 **Men shall** expressing necessity, i.e.
 men must (Abbott, 315)
 deal unadvisedly act imprudently
 – quite a euphemism, given the mag-
 nitude of the crimes to which it refers
293 **Which** i.e. which dealing
297 **quicken your increase** i.e. bring
 your offspring to life (*OED* increase
 sb. 2b)

---

282 ay] *F (1); yea Qq*   283 Mad'st] *F; Q1 (*Madst*), Q2–6 (*Madest*)*   284 You] *F;* Come, come,
you *(ye Q3–6) Qq*   me, madam] *F;* me *Qq*   285] *Steevens; F, Qq line* daughter. / way, /   288–342]
F; not in Qq

Mine issue of your blood upon your daughter.
A grandam's name is little less in love
Than is the doting title of a mother. 300
They are as children but one step below,
Even of your metal, of your very blood,
Of all one pain, save for a night of groans
Endured of her for whom you bid like sorrow.
Your children were vexation to your youth, 305
But mine shall be a comfort to your age.
The loss you have is but a son being king,
And by that loss your daughter is made queen.
I cannot make you what amends I would;
Therefore accept such kindness as I can. 310
Dorset your son, that with a fearful soul
Leads discontented steps in foreign soil,
This fair alliance quickly shall call home
To high promotions and great dignity.
The king that calls your beauteous daughter wife 315
Familiarly shall call thy Dorset brother.
Again shall you be mother to a king,

301 **one step below** one grade or degree (*OED* step *sb.*[1] 8a) removed genealogically from being your own children

302 **metal** substance, character (*OED sb.* 1f)

303–4 Her grandchildren, Richard claims, will demand the same trouble and efforts from her as they would from their mother, excepting only the night of labour pains their mother will suffer, but Queen Elizabeth herself underwent similar painful labour for her own daughter's birth.

303 **pain** trouble, effort (*OED sb.*[1] 5, 6)

304 **bid** underwent, suffered (past tense of bide, *OED* 9)

307 **son being king** i.e. son's occupation of the office of king

309 **would** i.e. would wish

310 **can** am able to provide

311–14 The promise to advance Dorset appears in Richard's offers (Hall, *Richard III*, fol. xlviii[r]). However, after leaving sanctuary, Dorset did not go directly to Richmond (as in 4.1.38–51, 91; 4.2.48–9), but gathered forces in Yorkshire to help Buckingham (Hall, *Richard III*, fol. xxxviii[v]). After Buckingham's rebellion failed, Dorset fled to Richmond (see 518).

312 **foreign soil** i.e. Brittany (cf. 4.1.42)

316 **Familiarly** i.e. in the manner of an intimate acquaintance, but suggesting pertaining to one's family (*OED* familiar *a.* 1a)

brother Richard eases himself, rhetorically at least, from the generation of Dorset's mother, to that of her son (and daughter) (Lull); cf. his *mother* at 317, 325, 412.

317 **Again** Elizabeth had already been mother to one king, the uncrowned Edward V.

And all the ruins of distressful times
Repaired with double riches of content.
What! We have many goodly days to see.　　　　　320
The liquid drops of tears that you have shed
Shall come again, transformed to orient pearl,
Advantaging their love with interest
Of ten times double gain of happiness.
Go then, my mother; to thy daughter go.　　　　　325
Make bold her bashful years with your experience;
Prepare her ears to hear a wooer's tale;
Put in her tender heart th'aspiring flame
Of golden sovereignty; acquaint the princess
With the sweet silent hours of marriage joys;　　　　　330
And when this arm of mine hath chastised
The petty rebel, dull-brained Buckingham,
Bound with triumphant garlands will I come
And lead thy daughter to a conqueror's bed;
To whom I will retail my conquest won,　　　　　335
And she shall be sole victoress, Caesar's Caesar.

QUEEN ELIZABETH

What were I best to say? Her father's brother

318–22 **ruins . . . times . . . riches
. . . pearl** Perhaps ironically recalling
the *wracks, times, stones* and *heaps of pearl*
from Clarence's dream (1.4.14–26).
320 **What!** interjection introducing an
exclamation or question (*OED* B I 1)
322 **orient** lustrous, shining
323 i.e. increasing the value of the love
that inspired them; the 'advantage' is a
name for the favourable terms received
by a lender (cf. *MV* 1.3.68). Theobald
conjectured that F's 'Loue' should be
'Lone' (i.e. loan).
330 **silent** i.e. either performed in silence
(*OED* 3a), or perhaps not to be spoken of because the *joys* are sexual?
Either way, the insinuation is sexual,
as Richard urges making 'bold her

bashful years' (326) and invokes the
conqueror's bed (334).
331 **chastised** chastisèd
332 **dull-brained Buckingham** Cf.
Buckingham's place among 'simple
gulls' (1.3.327–8); but Richard's
other (sarcastic?) references to 'deep-
revolving, witty Buckingham' are less
securely dismissive (4.2.31, 42).
335 **retail** recount; but for a commercial sense cf. 3.1.77n. and 3.1.86n.
on *valure*
336 **Caesar's Caesar** Cf. 'our great captain's captain' (*Oth* 2.1.74) and 'Our
general's wife is now the general' (*Oth*
2.3.309–10).
337–8 The nomenclatural problem under-
lines the violation of incest taboos; see

324 Of ten times] *Theobald;* Often-times *F*

Would be her lord? Or shall I say her uncle?
Or he that slew her brothers and her uncles?
Under what title shall I woo for thee,   340
That God, the law, my honour and her love
Can make seem pleasing to her tender years?

KING RICHARD

Infer fair England's peace by this alliance.

QUEEN ELIZABETH

Which she shall purchase with still lasting war.

KING RICHARD

Tell her the King, that may command, entreats.   345

QUEEN ELIZABETH

That at her hands, which the King's King forbids.

KING RICHARD

Say she shall be a high and mighty queen.

QUEEN ELIZABETH

To vail the title, as her mother doth.

KING RICHARD

Say I will love her everlastingly.

QUEEN ELIZABETH

But how long shall that title 'ever' last?   350

KING RICHARD

Sweetly in force, unto her fair life's end.

McCabe, 158 (cf. 1.1.156n.). Richard's historical advisers (Catesby and Ratcliffe) were uneasy about public reaction to such a marriage (C. Ross, *Richard*, 145–6).

343 **Infer** adduce (*OED v.* 2); cf. 3.5.75.

344 **still lasting** eternal

345 Cf. 'I entreat where I may command; commaunde thou, where thou should-est entreate' (Lyly, *Sapho*, 4.2.23–5).

346 **King's King forbids** The marriage would be forbidden by God as violating prohibitions on marriage between

uncle and niece (see Leviticus, 18.16–17). The *Book of Common Prayer* prohibited marriage to a 'Brother's Daughter' (Noble, 137). The phrase recalls 1.4.194–9.

348 **vail** abase, lower (*OED v.*[2] 4a); perhaps abandon; *vail* (F) preserves the play on *high* (347), unlike Qq's 'waile'.

349–50 Cf. Orlando's professions of love 'forever and a day' and Rosalind's searching responses (*AYL* 4.2.135–9).

351 **in force** operative

351, 352 **fair, fairly** happy, happily

343 this] *F, Q1–3, 5;* tuis *Q4;* his *Q6*   345 Tell her] *F;* Saie that *Qq*   that] *F;* which *Qq*
346 forbids] *F, Q1;* forbid *Q2–6*   348 vail] *F;* waile *Qq*   350 'ever'] *Dyce, after Theobald (,* ever,*);*
euer *F, Q1–4, 6; om. Q5*

QUEEN ELIZABETH

But how long fairly shall her sweet life last?

KING RICHARD

As long as heaven and nature lengthens it.

QUEEN ELIZABETH

As long as hell and Richard likes of it.

KING RICHARD

Say I, her sovereign, am her subject low.   355

QUEEN ELIZABETH

But she, your subject, loathes such sovereignty.

KING RICHARD

Be eloquent in my behalf to her.

QUEEN ELIZABETH

An honest tale speeds best being plainly told.

KING RICHARD

Then plainly to her tell my loving tale.

QUEEN ELIZABETH

Plain and not honest is too harsh a style.   360

KING RICHARD

Your reasons are too shallow and too quick.

QUEEN ELIZABETH

O no, my reasons are too deep and dead,

Too deep and dead, poor infants, in their graves.

KING RICHARD

Harp not on that string, madam; that is past.

353–4 **lengthens . . . likes** a singular
verb used with a compound subject;
cf. 4.1.39.

354 **likes of** likes; on 'of' after 'like', see
Abbott, 177.

358 Cf. 'Truth's tale is simple' (Dent,
T593).

   speeds succeeds (*OED v.* 2a)

361 **shallow** trivial, superficial; cf. 431n.

361–2 **quick . . . dead** taking Richard's
quick as if it meant 'living' instead of
'hasty'

364 *This line appears after 365 in F and
is omitted from Q2–8. F's misplaced
insertion of a line exclusive to Q1
constitutes strong evidence that F was
set from quarto copy collated against a
manuscript. See pp. 445–6.

352 her sweet life] *F, Q1–2;* that title *Q3–6*   353, 354 As] *F;* So *Qq*   355 low] *F;* loue *Qq*   359
plainly . . . tell] *F;* in plaine termes tell her *Qq*   361 Your] *F;* Madame your *Qq*   363 graves] *F;*
graue *Qq*   364] *Q1; after 365 F; om. Q2–6*   on] *F;* one *Q1*

QUEEN ELIZABETH

Harp on it still shall I, till heart-strings break.   365

KING RICHARD

Now by my George, my Garter and my crown –

QUEEN ELIZABETH

Profaned, dishonoured and the third usurped.

KING RICHARD

I swear –

QUEEN ELIZABETH   By nothing, for this is no oath:

Thy George, profaned, hath lost his lordly honour;

Thy Garter, blemished, pawned his knightly virtue;   370

Thy crown, usurped, disgraced his kingly glory.

If something thou wouldst swear to be believed,

Swear then by something that thou hast not wronged.

KING RICHARD

Then by myself –

QUEEN ELIZABETH   Thyself is self-misused.

KING RICHARD

Now by the world –

Harp ... string proverbial (Dent, S934); used by More (*CW2*, 36; cf. Hall, *Edward V*, fol. xi^{r-v}).

365 **heart-strings** nerves supposed to sustain the heart (*OED sb. pl.* 1); thus figuratively referring to intense feelings, frequently with allusion to stringed instruments (*OED* 2b, 2c).

366–77 Wilson compares *Leir*, in which reiterated offers of 'I sweare' are rebuffed with 'Sweare not by heauen', 'earth', 'hell' etc. (*Leir*, 1625–33; cf. *RJ* 2.2.107–16).

366 **George ... Garter** worn by members of the Order of the Garter: the George was a pendant depicting Saint

George and the dragon, and the Garter was a blue ribbon worn beneath the left knee. The George did not come in until the Tudor era.

369–71 **his** its; on 'his' as the original possessive or genitive neuter and the rise of 'its' in the 16th and 17th centuries, see *OED* its.

374–7 *Steevens's shared lines emphasize Queen Elizabeth's power to interrupt Richard with negations. Hammond asserts the 'rhetorical hierarchy' of Qq's failed oaths (by world, father's death, self, God), but F's oaths by self, world, father's death and heaven enforce a clear progress in the

365 SP] *F, Q1 (Qu.); King Q2; om. Q3–6*   366 crown –] *Rowe;* Crowne. *F, Qq*   368] *Steevens; F lines* sweare. / Oath: /   swear –] *Collier, after Capell (*swear:*);* sweare. *F;* sweare by nothing. *Qq*   369, 370, 371 Thy] *The Qq*   369 lordly] *F;* holie *Qq*   371 glory] *F;* dignitie *Qq*   372 wouldst] *F;* wilt *Qq*   374–7] *in 4 lines as Steevens; F lines* Selfe. / selfe-misvs'd. / World. / wrongs. / death. / dishonor'd. / Heauen. / all: / ; *Qq line* world. / wrongs. / death. / dishonord. / selfe. / misusest. / God. / all, /   374] *F; King.* Then by my selfe. / *Qu.* Thy selfe, thy selfe misusest. *Qq after 376*

QUEEN ELIZABETH   'Tis full of thy foul wrongs.   375
KING RICHARD
  My father's death –
QUEEN ELIZABETH   Thy life hath it dishonoured.
KING RICHARD
  Why then, by God.
QUEEN ELIZABETH   God's wrong is most of all.
  If thou didst fear to break an oath with Him,
  The unity the King my husband made
  Thou hadst not broken, nor my brothers died.   380
  If thou hadst feared to break an oath by Him,
  Th'imperial metal circling now thy head
  Had graced the tender temples of my child,
  And both the princes had been breathing here,
  Which now, too tender bed-fellows for dust,   385
  Thy broken faith hath made the prey for worms.

spiritualization of Richard's references. Richard could conceivably imagine never having wronged himself (as he asserts in F) but not to have left the world unwronged as he claims in Qq (Smidt, *Memorial*, 21).

375 **by the world** a mild oath (see *LLL* 4.3.16)

377 ***God, God's** F prints 'Heaven[s]', according to the directives of 1606; cf. 3.7.218n.

379 **unity** i.e. the reconciliation of contending factions attempted in 2.1

380 **brothers** Earl Rivers is Queen Elizabeth's only brother in this play (cf. 1.3.37n.).

382 **metal** gold (*OED sb.* 1d)

385–6 Cf. Job, 21.26: 'They shal slepe bothe in the dust, & the wormes shal couer them' (Geneva). Cf. Tilley, Dent,

M253. Qq's 'plaie-fellowes' plays on the sound of *prey* (386), but makes little sense in relation to dust; however, it does echo a line omitted from Qq at 4.1.101 describing the Tower as 'old sullen playfellow' (Delius, 150).

385 ***too** Qq, F have 'two'; Roderick (223) suggested *too*. McKerrow (*Prolegomena*, 9) considers 'too'/'two' as possibly variant spellings, adducing 'two much credit' (Nashe, 1.134) and 'two liberall' (Nashe, 3.172). *A most straunge, rare, and horrible murther committed by a Frenchman of the age of too or three and twentie yeares* (1586; STC 11377) repeats 'too' for 'two' on its second page, answering McKerrow's worries about mere typographical errors. See Q1/F variants at 100.

375] *F; after 373 Qq* 376 life] *F, Q1–2; selfe Q3–6* it] *F; that Qq* 377 God] *Qq; Heauen F* God's] *Qq; Heanens F* 378 didst fear] *F; hadst feard Qq* with] *F; by Qq* 379 my husband] *F; my brother Q1–5, 6u (BL C34 k.51; Bod, Tn, Hn copies); thy brother Q6c (other copies)* 380 Thou hadst not] *F; Had not bene Qq* brothers died] *F; brother slaine Qq* 382 Th'imperial] *F; The emperiall Qq* head] *F; brow Qq* 385 too] *F, Qq (two), Capell (Roderick)* bed-fellows] *F; plaie-fellowes Qq* 386 the] *F; a Qq* worms] *F, Q1–5; worme Q6*

What canst thou swear by now?

KING RICHARD   The time to come.

QUEEN ELIZABETH

That thou hast wronged in the time o'erpast;
For I myself have many tears to wash
Hereafter time, for time past wronged by thee.   390
The children live whose fathers thou hast slaughtered,
Ungoverned youth, to wail it in their age;
The parents live whose children thou hast butchered,
Old barren plants, to wail it with their age.
Swear not by time to come, for that thou hast   395
Misused ere used, by times ill-used o'erpast.

KING RICHARD

As I intend to prosper and repent,
So thrive I in my dangerous affairs

---

388 **wronged** wrongèd
    o'erpast i.e. already past
390 **Hereafter time** i.e. in the future
391 *****fathers** Queen Elizabeth's list of
    victims does mention Anne's *convey-
    ance* (283), but since the play makes
    Anne childless, she would not be
    included under Qq's 'parents'; there-
    fore F's 'fathers' makes more sense,
    especially in the light of references to
    Richard's male victims (339).
392 *****in** Since F's 'with' appears in Q5
    and looks half-corrected in Q6 (in
    the incorrect 'with her'), editors since
    Pope have generally accepted Q1's 'in',
    though 'with' would maintain parallels
    between 392 and 394.
394 *****barren** Qq's 'withered' makes
    sense, but F's 'barren' maintains the
    stress on violence to generational con-
    tinuity while suggesting the female
    suffering occluded by *fathers* (391). In

LLL (4.2.28) 'barren plants' refers to a
lack of mental capacity.
395–6 Richard cannot swear by the future
    because he has already compromised it
    by past wrongs that will continue to
    have effects in time to come.
396 *****o'erpast** F's 'repast' may be a mis-
    setting of 'orepast'.
397–9 **As . . . arms** i.e. 'may I succeed in
    my dangerous military ventures only
    insofar as I intend to repent', a parallel
    to 236–7, but here Richard promises to
    repent. In the light of his subsequent
    failure to repent, which assures his
    damnation despite recognition of his
    sins (5.3.177–206), the irony is obvi-
    ous. This is the last appearance of the
    word 'repent'; previously employed
    hypocritically by Richard (1.2.218,
    1.3.306, 4.4.293) and sincerely by
    the Second Murderer (1.4.277) and
    Hastings (3.4.87).

387] *Steevens; F lines* now? / come. /   What . . . now?] *F; not in Qq*   The] *F;* By the *Qq*   388 the]
F; not in Qq   390 past . . . thee] *F;* by the *(*thee *Q5–6)* past wrongd *Qq*   391 fathers] *F;* parents
Qq   392 in their] *Q1–4;* with their *F, Q5;* with her *Q6*   394 barren] *F;* withered *Qq*   plants]
F, Q1–5; plaints *Q6*   396 ere] *F, Q6; Q1–3, 5 (*eare*);* nere *Q4*   times ill-used] *F;* time misused
Qq   o'erpast] *Qq (*orepast*);* repast *F*   398 affairs] *F;* attempt *Qq*

Of hostile arms. Myself myself confound!
Heaven and fortune bar me happy hours.   400
Day, yield me not thy light; nor, night, thy rest.
Be opposite all planets of good luck
To my proceeding, if with dear heart's love,
Immaculate devotion, holy thoughts,
I tender not thy beauteous, princely daughter.   405
In her consists my happiness and thine;
Without her follows to myself and thee,
Herself, the land and many a Christian soul,
Death, desolation, ruin and decay.
It cannot be avoided but by this;   410
It will not be avoided but by this.
Therefore, dear mother – I must call you so –
Be the attorney of my love to her:
Plead what I will be, not what I have been;
Not my deserts, but what I will deserve.   415

399–405 **Myself ... daughter**. Richard details ill-effects that should be visited upon him if he should fail dearly to love Queen Elizabeth's daughter. Once again, a curse will prove accurate. Holland notes that this curse-filled scene gives Richard's self-curse a concluding prominence. Birney (36–42) traces the steps to Richard's self-cursing: Margaret weaves together the women's objections and advises how to curse, and then the Duchess of York echoes Margaret's curses from 1.3 in cursing Richard (184–96); but Queen Elizabeth avoids the cursing mode and traps Richard into cursing himself by depriving him of things to swear by.

399 **Myself myself confound** *confound* = bring to ruin. Cf. 'he himself himself confounds' (*Luc* 160) and Lucrece's curse on Tarquin: 'Himself himself

seek every hour to kill!' (998); cf. 5.3.186–7.

400 **bar** prohibit, prevent (*OED v.* 7)

402 **opposite** opposed, hostile; see 216.

404 Richard's religious language recalls his hypocritical portrayal as *holy and devout*, engaged in *holy exercise* of *meditation* (3.7.91, 61–3).
  Immaculate unsullied, pure

405 **tender** treat with tenderness (*OED v.*[2] 3a)
  princely royal (*OED a.* 1a)

406 **consists** i.e. exists, is comprised (*OED consist v.* 6a)

412 **dear mother** Richard attempts to 're-mother' himself after being cursed (188–96) by his own mother (Hodgdon, *End*, 108).

413 **attorney** i.e. advocate; cf. 5.3.83. *Plead* (414) continues the legal language.

400] *F; not in Qq*   403 proceeding] *F;* proceedings *Qq*   dear] *F;* pure *Qq*   404 Immaculate] *F, Q1;* Immaculatd *Q2;* Immaculated *Q3–6*   405 tender] *F, Q1, 2, 4;* render *Q3, 5–6*   407 myself and thee] *F;* this land and me *Qq*   408 Herself, the land] *F;* To thee her selfe *Qq*   409 Death,] *F;* Sad *Qq*   411 by this] *F, Q2–6;* this *Q1*   412 dear] *F;* good *Qq*   415 my] *F;* by *Qq*

Urge the necessity and state of times,
And be not peevish found in great designs.

QUEEN ELIZABETH

Shall I be tempted of the devil thus?

KING RICHARD

Ay, if the devil tempt you to do good.

QUEEN ELIZABETH

Shall I forget myself to be myself?   420

KING RICHARD

Ay, if your self's remembrance wrong yourself.

QUEEN ELIZABETH

Yet thou didst kill my children.

KING RICHARD

But in your daughter's womb I bury them,
Where, in that nest of spicery, they will breed

---

416 **state of times** present conditions
417 i.e. do not be found to be merely foolish when great plans demand more. Cf. 'have great care / I be not found a talker' (*H8* 2.3.76–7); 'peevish-fond' (Malone) could mean wilfully silly.
   great designs important undertakings
418–19 Citing Christ's temptation in the wilderness (Matthew, 4.1–10, Luke, 4.1–13), Hammond notes that Satan can urge things not necessarily evil, but can only tempt one to 'do good' if, to his limited perception, evil will result. Satan's efforts are, according to Calvin, part of the divine plan (Calvin, *Institutes*, 1.18.1–2, 2.4.2–7). Richard remarkably, if hypothetically, admits his satanic nature (Hammond).
418 **tempted . . . devil** Shaheen refers to Jesus 'tempted of the deuyll' (Matthew, 4.1; cf. Luke, 4.2). For another possible echo of this biblical passage, see 1.2.46n.

420–1 Queen Elizabeth asks if she should forget who she is (by succumbing to Richard's temptations); Richard replies that she should, if remembering her identity causes her harm.
423 Cf. Richard's attack on his brother's marriage to Elizabeth: 'But in your bride you bury brotherhood' (*3H6* 4.1.55).
   *bury Q1–2's past tense ('buried') is an obvious error; Q3 'burie' (F 'bury') uses the present tense for the future (as Q4–8's 'Ile burie'). The unusual agreement of Q3 and F against all other Qq argues for Q3 copy for the whole of F (Walton, *Copy*, 39; but contrast Hammond, 37).
424 **nest of spicery** Steevens suggests allusion to the nest of the phoenix, built of aromatic boughs and from which the new bird arises out of the ashes of the old one (Ovid, *Metamorphoses*, 15.391–407). While the scarcely euphemized anatomical specificity of Richard's words

---

417 peevish found] *F;* pieuish, fond *Q1–2;* peeuish fond *Q3–6*   419 you] *F;* thee *Qq*   422 Yet] *F;* But *Qq*   423 I bury] *F, Q3;* I buried *Q1–2;* Ile burie *Q4–6*   them,] *Qq;* them. *F*   424 they will] *F;* they shall *Q1–2;* there shall *Q3–6*

    Selves of themselves, to your recomforture.   425

QUEEN ELIZABETH

    Shall I go win my daughter to thy will?

KING RICHARD

    And be a happy mother by the deed.

QUEEN ELIZABETH

    I go, write to me very shortly,

    And you shall understand from me her mind.

KING RICHARD

    Bear her my true love's kiss; and so farewell.   430

                             Exit Queen [Elizabeth].

to the girl's mother is grotesque in itself, a further irony is that his dying father predicted Richard himself as a hideous phoenix: 'My ashes, as the phoenix, may bring forth / A bird that will revenge upon you all' (*3H6* 1.4.35–6).

425 **recomforture** consolation, comfort (*OED*, citing this line)

426–31 The reaction of the play's Queen Elizabeth has prompted different interpretations, although the historical sources all have her accept Richard's offers (exchanged by messengers), thereby demonstrating female 'inconstancie', since 'women of the verie bonde of nature will folowe their awne kynde' (Hall, *Richard III*, fol. xlviii[r]; cf. Holinshed, 3.750). A 17th-century Folio reader judges her 'ouercome at last' (Yamada, 159). Tillyard credits Richard's assessment of Elizabeth as a *Relenting fool* (431), assuming that she again changes her mind once offstage (*History Plays*, 214). Thompson adduces '*varium et mutabile semper femina*' ('woman is always various and changeable', Virgil, *Aeneid*, 4.569–70). But Richard rapidly changes his own mind at 456 (Johnson), and Shakespeare may '[displace] those attributes the chronicler ascribes to

the Queen onto Richard' (Hodgdon, *End*, 109–10). Richard also misjudges the Messenger (Sprague, *Histories*, 139; cf. *True Tragedy*, 1425–60). Cibber's Elizabeth explains herself to the audience as only 'seemingly comply[ing]' (*Richard III*, 4.4.114–16). See pp. 62, 89, and 430n.

426–7 **will . . . deed** These lines hinge on 'daughter'/'mother' and 'will'/'deed' oppositions; the *deed* of winning her daughter over to his *will* recalls her opposition of *hand* to *head* (225–6), accusing Richard of planning and fomenting deeds physically perpetrated by others.

429 **you** Despite Richard's repeated, sometimes rapid, alternations between 'you' and 'thee' in addressing Queen Elizabeth (e.g. 316–17, 325–6), this is her first use of the more respectful 'you' form, as if to assure him of her acquiescence (Brown, 113).

430 **kiss** Richard may actually kiss Queen Elizabeth, or he may simply wish her to convey a sentiment. The entire exchange takes place while the army stands waiting for its leader. The Sher–Alexander production made Elizabeth (Frances Tomelty) the physical aggressor and left Richard surprised (Colley, 243; Day, 203). Susan

425 recomforture] *F; Qq (*recomfiture*)*   429] *F; not in Qq*   430 and so] *F; not in Qq*   SD] *Exit Qu. Q3–6; Exit Q. opp.* 429 *F; Exit. Q1–2*

366

Relenting fool, and shallow, changing woman.

Enter RATCLIFFE.

How now, what news?

RATCLIFFE

Most mighty sovereign, on the western coast
Rideth a puissant navy. To our shores
Throng many doubtful hollow-hearted friends,   435
Unarmed and unresolved to beat them back.
'Tis thought that Richmond is their admiral,
And there they hull, expecting but the aid
Of Buckingham to welcome them ashore.

KING RICHARD

Some light-foot friend post to the Duke of Norfolk: 440
Ratcliffe, thyself – or Catesby. Where is he?

CATESBY

Here, my good lord.

KING RICHARD   Catesby, fly to the Duke.

Brown's Elizabeth in the Pimlott production was surprised by Richard's
kiss on her lips rather than upon the
hand she had offered, and once out of
his vision wiped the kiss from her lips
(Brown, 113).

430 SD *F prints Queen Elizabeth's exit
at the end of 429, which might indicate her beginning to leave before
Richard's offer of a kiss, but F's 430
runs nearly to the margin, leaving no
space even for '*Exit Q.*' F's 431 is the
final line on the page, with a catchword immediately below it; thus, the
SD at 429 appears to be a turn-up
from 430.

431 **shallow** cf. 361; used with similar irony when Hastings trivial-

izes Stanley's premonitions (3.2.24)
and Richard dismisses the threat of
Richmond (5.3.219). Elizabeth perhaps performs 'shallowness' as Brutus
enacts a 'shallow habit' of affability
(*Luc* 1814) – an outer show concealing
inner resistance. Simon Russell Beale
hesitated on 'sh-shallow' as if betray-
ing Richard's disbelief in this judgement (Day, 171).

434 **Rideth** lies at anchor (*OED v.* II 7a)
puissant powerful

435 **doubtful** untrustworthy or apprehensive

438 **hull** drift with furled sails (*OED*
v.[2] 1)

440 **light-foot** nimble, light-footed
(*OED* 1)

431.1] *after 432 F; opp. 431 Qq (Enter Rat.)*   432] *F; not in Qq*   433 Most mighty] *F;* My gracious
Qq   434 our shores] *F;* the shore *Qq*   438 they] *F, Q1, 3–6;* thy *Q2*   442] *Steevens; F lines* Lord. /
Duke. / ; *Qq line* Lord. / Salisburie. /   good] *F; not in Qq*   Catesby] *F; not in Qq*

CATESBY

I will, my lord, with all convenient haste.

KING RICHARD

Ratcliffe, come hither. Post to Salisbury.
When thou com'st thither –
[*to Catesby*]   Dull unmindful villain,   445
Why stay'st thou here, and go'st not to the Duke?

CATESBY

First, mighty liege, tell me your highness' pleasure,
What from your grace I shall deliver to him.

KING RICHARD

O true, good Catesby. Bid him levy straight
The greatest strength and power that he can make   450
And meet me suddenly at Salisbury.

CATESBY   I go.   *Exit.*

RATCLIFFE

What, may it please you, shall I do at Salisbury?

KING RICHARD

Why, what wouldst thou do there before I go?

RATCLIFFE

Your highness told me I should post before.   455

KING RICHARD

My mind is changed.

---

443 **convenient** suitable to the conditions (*OED a.* 4b)
449 **levy straight** raise immediately
451 **Salisbury** city south-west of London in Wiltshire; since Richmond is off the south-western coast, Richard hastens to Salisbury to prevent the junction of Richmond with Buckingham's forces from Wales. On the temporal compression in the play, see 531–3n.

456 *Qq's repetition is unusual, especially in close proximity to another instance (466). Editors have often attributed these features to stage practice.

443–4 CATESBY . . . hither.] *F; not in Qq*   444 Ratcliffe] *Rowe; Catesby F*   Post] *F; post thou Qq*   445 com'st thither] *F; comst (comest Q2–6) there Qq*   SD] *Rowe*   villain] *F, Q1–5; villanie Q6*   446 stay'st] *F; standst Q1–3, 5–6; stands Q4*   here] *F; still Qq*   447 liege . . . pleasure] *F; Soueraigne, let me know your minde Qq*   448 to him] *F; them Q1–2; him Q3–6*   450 that] *F; not in Qq*   451 suddenly] *F; presentlie Qq*   452, 452 SD] *F; not in Qq*   453 may . . . I] *F; is it your highnes pleasure, I shall Q1–4; it is your highnes pleasure I shal Q5; is your highnesse pleasure, I shal Q6*   454 wouldst] *F, Q1–3, 5–6; woulds Q4*   456] *Capell; F, Qq line* changd: / you? / changed] *F; changd sir, my minde is changd. Qq*   SD] *F; Enter Darbie. Q1–2 after 456; Enter Darby. Q3–6 opp. 456*   Stanley] *F; How now Qq*

Enter Lord STANLEY.

Stanley, what news with you?

STANLEY

None good, my liege, to please you with the hearing,
Nor none so bad but well may be reported.

KING RICHARD

Hoyday, a riddle! Neither good nor bad.
What need'st thou run so many miles about   460
When thou mayst tell thy tale the nearest way?
Once more, what news?

STANLEY   Richmond is on the seas.

KING RICHARD

There let him sink, and be the seas on him,
White-livered runagate. What doth he there?

STANLEY

I know not, mighty sovereign, but by guess.   465

KING RICHARD

Well, as you guess?

STANLEY

Stirred up by Dorset, Buckingham and Morton,
He makes for England, here to claim the crown.

---

457 *F4's punctuation supplies an anti-
    thesis for *none so bad* in the following
    line.
457–62 This, Stanley's only circumlocu-
    tion, may suggest influence of *True
    Tragedy* (Maguire, 192–3, 374).
459 **Hoyday** hey-day, an exclamation of
    surprise or gaiety (*OED*), but here
    conveying irritated impatience
461 **the nearest way** i.e. directly
464 **White-livered** cowardly; cf. *Mac*
    5.3.15 and Dent, F180.

runagate renegade, vagabond (*OED* 1)
466 *The repetition in Qq's line does not
    appear in F or in Q7–8; cf. 456.
467 After the council meeting (3.4), John
    Morton, Bishop of Ely, was confined
    (see 4.3.46n.) at Buckingham's castle
    at Brecon (4.2.120), where he encour-
    aged Buckingham's rebellion (More,
    CW2, 90–3) before fleeing to Flanders
    to render Richmond 'good seruice'
    (Hall, *Richard III*, fols xxxʳ–xxxviᵛ;
    Holinshed, 3.737–41).

457+ SP] *F (Sta[n].); Dar. Qq*   457 None good,] *F4;* None, good *F;* None good *Qq*   liege] *F;* Lord
Qq   458 well . . . reported] *F;* it may well be told *Qq*   460 What need'st] *F;* Why doest *Qq*   miles]
F; mile *Qq*   461 the nearest] *F;* a neerer *Qq*   462] *Steevens; F, Qq line* newes? / Seas. /   466] *F;*
Well sir, as you guesse, as you guesse. *Q1–6;* Well sir, as you guesse. *Q7–8*   467 Morton] *F;* Elie
Qq   468 here] *F;* there *Qq*

KING RICHARD

　　Is the chair empty? Is the sword unswayed?
　　Is the King dead? The empire unpossessed?　　　　　　470
　　What heir of York is there alive but we?
　　And who is England's king but great York's heir?
　　Then tell me, what makes he upon the seas?

STANLEY

　　Unless for that, my liege, I cannot guess.

KING RICHARD

　　Unless for that he comes to be your liege,　　　　　　475
　　You cannot guess wherefore the Welshman comes.
　　Thou wilt revolt and fly to him, I fear.

STANLEY

　　No, my good lord; therefore mistrust me not.

KING RICHARD

　　Where is thy power, then, to beat him back?
　　Where be thy tenants and thy followers?　　　　　　480

---

469 **chair ... sword** throne and sword
　　of state
　　unswayed unruled
470 **empire** i.e. supreme government of
　　the state (*OED sb.* 1)
471–2 'little Ned Plantagenet' (146) is
　　the male heir of the house of York;
　　other heirs include his sister. Stanley's
　　non-response suggests the importance
　　of self-silencing in the play's depic-
　　tion of tyranny. It might also suggest
　　the fence-sitting and self-preservation
　　attributed to the historical Stanley
　　family (M. Jones, 32–3). Cf. 477n. and
　　pp. 25–7.
472 **great York** the third Duke of York
　　(d. 1460), father of Richard, Clarence
　　and Edward IV
473 **makes he** is he doing
474, 475 **Unless for that** Stanley means
　　that unless Richmond comes for *that*
　　reason – i.e. 'to claim the crown' –

he cannot imagine why he comes.
Richard takes *Unless for that* and turns
it around to mean 'unless Richmond
comes in order to be Stanley's lord';
cf. Richard's echo of Buckingham at
4.2.15–16.
476 **Welshman** Richmond's grandpar-
　　ents were the Welsh Owen Tudor and
　　Katherine of Valois, widow of Henry
　　V. Richard's dismissive treatment of
　　Welsh identity contradicts Tudor affir-
　　mation of this heritage.
477 On Stanley's secret 'intent to be in a
　　perfect readinesse to recieue the earle
　　of Richmond at his first arriuall in
　　England', see Holinshed, 3.751.
478 **therefore** i.e. with respect to that
479 **power** forces
480 **tenants** those who held land by title
　　of a lord (in this case Stanley) (*OED*),
　　and who were obliged to render feudal
　　military service

473 makes] *F;* doeth *Qq*　seas] *F;* sea *Qq*　476 Welshman] *F, Q1–3, 5–6 subst.;* Welchmen *Q4*　478
my good lord] *F;* mightie liege *Qq*　480 be] *F;* are *Qq*

Are they not now upon the western shore,
Safe-conducting the rebels from their ships?

STANLEY

No, my good lord, my friends are in the north.

KING RICHARD

Cold friends to me. What do they in the north
When they should serve their sovereign in the west?   485

STANLEY

They have not been commanded, mighty King.
Pleaseth your majesty to give me leave,
I'll muster up my friends and meet your grace
Where and what time your majesty shall please.

KING RICHARD

Ay, thou wouldst be gone to join with Richmond,   490
But I'll not trust thee.

STANLEY   Most mighty sovereign,
You have no cause to hold my friendship doubtful;
I never was, nor never will be, false.

KING RICHARD

Go then, and muster men, but leave behind
Your son George Stanley. Look your heart be firm,   495

---

483 **in the north** Stanley's lands were in Cheshire and Lancashire, and he had power in North Wales.
484–5 Edmund Kean made this speech a major acting point (Pickersgill, 101).
484 **Cold** i.e. unenthusiastic, but also with a sense of the cold northern climate
487 **Pleaseth** if it please
495 **George Stanley** Thomas Stanley was one whom Richard 'moost mystrusted', and when Stanley pretended to visit his family in order secretly to prepare for Richmond, Richard kept George Stanley 'as an hostage' (Hall, *Richard*

III, fol. xlix[r]; Holinshed, 3.751). George Stanley's prominence (see 4.5.3; 5.3.61, 95, 344–6; 5.5.9–10) may compliment the 5th Earl of Derby, Ferdinando, Lord Strange, who succeeded to the earldom in 1592, and who from 1588 to his death in 1594 was patron of the acting company that may first have performed *Richard III*. George Stanley was the great-great-grandfather of the 5th Earl. Other evidence suggests the play may have been written or adapted for the Earl of Pembroke's Men (see 5.3.28–32n. and p. 51).
Look i.e. take care that

---

484 me] *F;* Richard *Qq*   486 King] *F;* soueraigne *Qq*   487 Pleaseth] *F;* Please it *Qq*   490 Ay] *F* (*1*); I, I *Qq* wouldst] *F, Q2–6; Q1* (wouldest)   491] *Steevens; F lines* thee. / Soueraigne. / ; *Qq line* Sir. / Soueraigne, /   But . . . thee] *F; I* will not trust you Sir *Qq*   494 Go then, and] *F;* Well, go *Qq* but] *F;* but heare you *Qq*   495 heart] *F;* faith *Qq*

Or else his head's assurance is but frail.

STANLEY

So deal with him as I prove true to you.   *Exit Stanley.*

Enter a Messenger.

MESSENGER

My gracious sovereign, now in Devonshire,
As I by friends am well advertised
Sir Edward Courtney and the haughty prelate,   500
Bishop of Exeter, his elder brother,
With many more confederates are in arms.

Enter another Messenger.

2 MESSENGER

In Kent, my liege, the Guilfords are in arms,
And every hour more competitors
Flock to the rebels, and their power grows strong.   505

Enter another Messenger.

3 MESSENGER

My lord, the army of great Buckingham –

---

496 **assurance** security (*OED* 7)
498 **Devonshire** county in the south-west of England
499 **advertised** advertisèd; warned (*OED* 4)
500–1 Hall says, 'Sir Edwarde Courtney and Peter his brother bishop of Exsetter, reised another army in deuonshire and cornewall' (*Richard III*, fol. xxxix^r), but the bishop was actually Edward's cousin. Hall and Holinshed say nothing about either being the *elder* or about

haughtiness, but *haughty prelate* sounds Shakespearean (see *1H6* 1.3.23); cf. 'proud prelate' (*2H6* 1.1.139).
500 **Edward Hall and Holinshed call him both Edward and Edmund (or Edmonde) (Hall, fol. xxxix^{r-v}; Holinshed, 3.743).
503 **Kent** county south-east of London
   Guilfords (or Guildfords) Sir Richard Guilford and his father, Sir John, had long supported Richmond.
504 **competitors** associates, seeking a common goal (*OED* 2, citing this line)

---

497 So] *F, Q1–3, 5–6; om. Q4* SD] *F; Exit Dar. Q3–5; Exit. Q6; not in Q1–2* 500 Edward] *F;* William *Qq* 501 elder brother] *F;* brother there *Qq* 502 more] *F, Q1–6 (mo[e]), Q7* 503 SP] *Capell subst.; Mess. F, Qq* In . . . liege] *F;* My Liege, in Kent *Qq* 505 the . . . strong] *F;* their aide, and still their power increaseth *Qq* 506, 509, 517 SP] *Capell subst.; Mess. F, Qq* 506 My] *F, Q1–3, 5–6; om. Q4* great] *F;* the Duke of *Qq* Buckingham –] *Rowe;* Buckingham. *F, Qq*

KING RICHARD

Out on you, owls! Nothing but songs of death.

He striketh him.

There, take thou that, till thou bring better news.

3 MESSENGER

The news I have to tell your majesty

Is that by sudden floods and fall of waters   510

Buckingham's army is dispersed and scattered,

And he himself wandered away alone,

No man knows whither.

KING RICHARD   I cry thee mercy.

There is my purse to cure that blow of thine.

Hath any well-advised friend proclaimed   515

Reward to him that brings the traitor in?

3 MESSENGER

Such proclamation hath been made, my lord.

Enter another Messenger.

---

507 **Out on you** an expression of impatience

  owls . . . death The owl's cry was supposed to be ominous, accompanying death and disaster; cf. Dent, R33: 'The croaking raven (screeching owl) bodes misfortune.' Henry VI tells Richard, 'The owl shrieked at thy birth' (*3H6* 5.6.44), marking the conjunction in him of birth and death.

510–12 On the terrible weather and floods that thwarted Buckingham's forces and the events that led to his ultimate isolation, see Hall, *Richard III*, fol. xxxix^r and Holinshed, 3.743.

510 **fall of waters** i.e. rainfall

513 **I . . . mercy** I beg your pardon; cf. 1.3.234.

514 **my purse** Davison argues on behalf of Qq that a king would not normally carry a purse, citing *H5* 4.8.58–60.

515 **well-advised** well-advisèd; i.e. prudent, thoughtful (cf. 2.1.108) or provided with satisfactory information (cf. *H5* 2.0.12: 'advised by good intelligence')

507 you] *Q1–5;* ye *F, Q6*   SD] *F; after 506 Qq*   508 There . . . bring] *F;* Take that vntill thou *(you Q6)* bring me *Qq*   509] *F;* Your grace mistakes, the newes *I* bring is good, *Qq*   510 Is] *F;* My newes is *Qq*   floods] *F;* floud *Qq*   waters] *F, Q7–8;* water *Q1–6*   511 Buckingham's] *F;* The Duke of Buckinghams *Qq*   512 wandered away alone] *F;* fled *Qq*   513] *Steevens; F lines* whither. / mercie: / No . . . whither] *F; in 512 Qq (whether Q1)*   I . . . mercy] *F;* O I crie you mercie, I did mistake *Qq*   514] *F;* Ratcliffe reward him, for the blow I gaue him *Qq*   515 proclaimed] *F;* giuen out *Qq*   516 Reward to] *F;* Rewardes for *Qq*   the traitor in] *F;* in Buckingham *Qq*   517 lord] *F;* liege *Qq*

4 MESSENGER

> Sir Thomas Lovell and Lord Marquess Dorset,
> 'Tis said, my liege, in Yorkshire are in arms;
> But this good comfort bring I to your highness: 520
> The Breton navy is dispersed by tempest.
> Richmond in Dorsetshire sent out a boat
> Unto the shore to ask those on the banks
> If they were his assistants, yea or no?
> Who answered him they came from Buckingham,   525
> Upon his party. He, mistrusting them,
> Hoised sail and made his course again for Brittany.

KING RICHARD

> March on, march on, since we are up in arms,
> If not to fight with foreign enemies,
> Yet to beat down these rebels here at home.   530

Enter CATESBY.

CATESBY

> My liege, the Duke of Buckingham is taken.
> That is the best news. That the Earl of Richmond
> Is with a mighty power landed at Milford

518 **Lovell** Sir Thomas Lovell would become Chancellor of the Exchequer under Henry VII and appears prominently in *H8*. He should not be confused with Lord Francis Lovell, who appears in 3.4.
Dorset Cf. 311–14n.
519 **Yorkshire** county in the north-east of England
521 **Breton** Cf. 4.3.40.
522 **in Dorsetshire** i.e. on the south-west coast of England
524 **assistants** supporters

526 **Upon his party** on his behalf, cf. 1.3.137.
527 **Hoised** hoisted (*OED v.* 1)
531 Cibber follows with a famous (and long-lived) flourish: '*Off with his head. So much for* Buckingham.'
531–3 These lines compress Richmond's (failed) attempt to join with Buckingham's forces (October 1483) with the successful expedition here recounted (August 1485).
533 **Milford** Milford Haven, in south-west Wales

518 SP] *Capell; Mess. F, Qq*   519 in Yorkshire are] *F;* are vp *Qq*   520 But] *F;* Yet *Qq*   highness] *F;* grace *Qq*   521–3] *F; Qq line* Dorshire / shore, /   521 Breton] *F, Qq* (Brittaine), *Capell*   by tempest] *F; not in Qq*   522 Dorsetshire] *F, Q6;* Dorshire *Q1–5*   523 Unto the shore] *F; not in Qq*   those ... banks] *F;* them ... shore *Qq*   527 Hoised] *F* (Hoys'd); Hoist *Qq*   his course again] *F;* away *Qq*   Brittany] *F, Qq* (Brittaine), *Cam*   532 That is] *F;* Thats *Qq*

Is colder tidings, yet they must be told.

KING RICHARD

Away towards Salisbury! While we reason here   535
A royal battle might be won and lost.
Someone take order Buckingham be brought
To Salisbury. The rest march on with me.   *Flourish. Exeunt.*

[4.5]   *Enter* [STANLEY, Earl of] Derby *and*
               Sir CHRISTOPHER [Urswick].

STANLEY

Sir Christopher, tell Richmond this from me:
That in the sty of the most deadly boar
My son George Stanley is franked up in hold;
If I revolt, off goes young George's head.
The fear of that holds off my present aid.   5

---

534 **colder** more discouraging (*OED a.*
cold 10a, citing this line)
  *tidings, yet Many editors since Dyce
have favoured Q1–5's phrasing over
F's 'news, but yet'. F suggests an
attempt to pad Q6 to create a metrical
line. See pp. 440–1.

535, 538 ***Salisbury** F's 'Salsbury' differs from 444, 451 and 453 where
it agrees with Qq's 'Salisburie' or
'Salisbury'. The pronunciation
would most likely be the same, but
the contracted form might register
elision.

535 **reason** debate, discuss

536 **royal** in military uses denoting grand
scale, great size or strength (*OED* royal
10a, citing this line)
  won and lost One of many verbal
and thematic links to *Macbeth* (1.1.4);
however, the sense here is clearly

proverbial (Dent, M337: 'No man
loses but another wins') rather than
enigmatic.

537 **take order** i.e. direct that

4.5 location: '*Lord* Stanley's *House*'
(Theobald). Stanley's family residence
is in north-west England.

0.2 **Sir CHRISTOPHER** Christopher
Urswick, chaplain to the Countess of
Richmond, was commissioned to go
to Brittany by her (not by Stanley)
in 1483, but recalled in favour of
a messenger of more consequence
(Holinshed, 3.742). He would later
serve as chaplain to Henry VII. 'Sir'
is a courtesy title for a priest (cf.
3.2.107).

2 **boar** i.e. Richard

3 **franked . . . hold** shut up in a pen (cf.
1.3.313)

5 **present** immediate

---

534 tidings, yet] *Q1–5; newes, yet Q6;* news, but yet *F*   535, 538 Salisbury] *F (*Salsbury*), Qq*
538 SD *Flourish] F; not in Qq   Exeunt] F, Q1; om. Q2–6*   **4.5**] *Capell; Scena Quarta. F; not
in Qq*   0.1] *F; Entee (Enter Q2–6) Darbie, Sir Christopher. Qq*   STANLEY, Earl of] *Pope subst.*
0.2 Urswick] *Theobald*   1+ SP] *Pope subst; Der. F; Dar. Qq*   2 the most deadly] *F; this most bloudie
Qq*   5 holds off] *F; with holdes Qq*

So get thee gone. Commend me to thy lord.
Withal, say that the Queen hath heartily consented
He should espouse Elizabeth her daughter.
But tell me, where is princely Richmond now?

CHRISTOPHER

At Pembroke or at Ha'rfordwest in Wales.   10

STANLEY

What men of name resort to him?

CHRISTOPHER

Sir Walter Herbert, a renowned soldier,
Sir Gilbert Talbot, Sir William Stanley,
Oxford, redoubted Pembroke, Sir James Blunt,
And Rice ap Thomas, with a valiant crew,   15

6-8 *Qq's arrangement may give the most important news 'a more emphatic position' and avoid a 'double dispatch and commendation' (*TxC*, 246), but Marshall's commentary is decisive for F: 'Urswick wants Stanley to declare for Richmond. Stanley answers that he cannot do so openly at present, and then, before sending him off, communicates the important news of Elizabeth's consent to the proposed marriage of her daughter to Richmond. This announcement comes much more properly at the beginning of the scene than thrust in, as a mere afterthought, at the end.'

7 **Withal** in addition

10 **Pembroke** in Wales, near Milford Haven
Ha'rfordwest Haverfordwest, in Pembrokeshire, Wales, north-east of Milford Haven

11 **name** title
resort make their way (*OED v.*[1] 5a)

12-14 **Herbert . . . Pembroke** See 5.3.28-32n.

12 **Herbert** family name of the earls of Pembroke
renowned renownèd

13 **Talbot** ancestor of the Stanley family in Shakespeare's time
Sir William Stanley Stanley's brother

14 **redoubted** feared, respected (*OED ppl. a.*)
Pembroke Jasper Tudor, Earl of Pembroke, a son of Owen Tudor and thus Richmond's uncle
Blunt Blunt's descendants owned land in Stratford-upon-Avon and were related to the Combe family there (Hammond). The Blunts were not knighted until 1588 (Sidney Shanker, 'Shakespeare pays some Compliments', *Modern Language Notes*, 63 (1948), 540-1).

15 **Rice ap Thomas** Rhys ap Thomas, the leader of a Welsh contingent that fought for Richmond, and Sir Walter Herbert 'ruled Wales with egall powre and lyke aucthoritee' (Hall, *Richard III*, fol. lii[v]; Holinshed, 3.754). Hall

---

6 So . . . gone] *F; not in Qq*   6-8 Commend . . . daughter] *F; commend me to him, / Tell him, the Queene hath hartelie consented, / He shall espouse Elizabeth her daughter (after lord in 19) Qq*   10 Pembroke] *Q1-2; F (Penbroke), Q3-6 (Pembrooke subst.)* Ha'rfordwest] *Q1 (Harford-west), Capell; Herford-west Q2, 5; Hertford-west Q3-4; Hertford west Q6; Hertford West F*   12 SP] *F (Chri.); S. Christ. Qq*   14 redoubted] *F, Q1-3, 5-6; doubted Q4*   15 And] *F; not in Qq* ap] *F, Q6; vp Q1-5*

And many other of great name and worth;
And towards London do they bend their power,
If by the way they be not fought withal.

STANLEY

Well, hie thee to thy lord. I kiss his hand.
My letter will resolve him of my mind.   20
Farewell.   *Exeunt.*

5.1   *Enter* BUCKINGHAM *with* [Sheriff *and*] *Halberds,
led to execution.*

BUCKINGHAM

Will not King Richard let me speak with him?

SHERIFF

No, my good lord; therefore be patient.

BUCKINGHAM

Hastings, and Edward's children, Grey and Rivers,
Holy King Henry, and thy fair son Edward,
Vaughan and all that have miscarried   5
By underhand, corrupted, foul injustice,
If that your moody, discontented souls
Do through the clouds behold this present hour,

and Holinshed report that Richard had
'trusted' in their forces.
crew band or company of soldiers
(*OED sb.*[1] 1)
16 **name** reputation
17 **bend their power** i.e. turn their
forces
19 **hie** hasten
20 **resolve . . . mind** inform him of my
thinking
5.1 location: 'SALISBURY' (Pope)
0.1 ***Sheriff** Ratcliffe has the Sheriff's
lines in Qq. See p. 451.

Halberds i.e. halberdiers, armed with
halberds (*OED sb.* 2); cf. 1.2.0.1.
Serving under the Sheriff, they constitute with him the *officers* (28, 29
SD).
1 **speak with him** Elsewhere mention is
made of Buckingham's intended assassination of Richard; see *H8* 1.2.193–9
and Holinshed, 3.864; cf. 3.744.
4 **thy** i.e. Henry VI's
5 **miscarried** miscarrièd; perished,
came to harm
7 **moody** angry, wrathful

16 And] *F;* With *Qq*   other . . . name] *F;* moe of noble fame *Qq*   17 do they] *F;* they doe
Qq   power] *F;* course *Qq*   19 Well . . . to] *F;* Retourne vnto *Qq*   thy] *F, Q1;* my *Q2–6*   1 . . .
hand] *F;* commend me to him *Qq*   20 My letter] *F;* These letters *Qq*   5.1] *F (Actus Quintus. Scena
Prima.); not in Qq*   0.1 Sheriff *and*] *Rowe*   0.1–2 *with Halberds, led*] *F; not in Qq*   2, 11 SP] *F
(Sher.); Rat. Qq*   2 good] *F; not in Qq*   3 Grey and Rivers] *F;* Riuers, Gray *Qq*

Even for revenge mock my destruction.
– This is All Souls' Day, fellow, is it not?   10
SHERIFF   It is.
BUCKINGHAM
Why then, All Souls' Day is my body's doomsday.
This is the day which, in King Edward's time,
I wished might fall on me when I was found
False to his children and his wife's allies.   15
This is the day wherein I wished to fall
By the false faith of him whom most I trusted.
This, this All Souls' Day to my fearful soul
Is the determined respite of my wrongs:
That high All-seer which I dallied with   20
Hath turned my feigned prayer on my head

9   **revenge** Henry VI and his son would have no personal cause to feel vengeful toward Buckingham. 'Revenge' is broadly invoked and sometimes means merely punishment or chastisement (*OED sb.* 5). However, Buckingham's utterance may signify a recognition of guilt for joining with Richard against Henry's descendants and family.
mock It is difficult to imagine 'Holy King Henry' jeering. Does Buckingham project one of Richard's (and the play's) own most prominent verbal modes onto Henry, imagining him responding to the misfortunes of others as does everyone else in the play?
10 **All Souls' Day** 2 November; in the Roman Catholic Church, a day to commemorate those Christians whose souls are believed to be in purgatory. Buckingham was executed in 1483; the Battle of Bosworth occurred in August of 1485. Displacing its closing scenes to November, the play maintains the sense of the seasonal year

that opens the action. References to All Souls' Day and to the hosts of victim/spectators (3–5) prepares for Richard's ghostly visitants in 5.3; on this anticipation and the medieval belief that 'souls in purgatory could appear on this day . . . to persons who had wronged them during their life', see Jones, *Origins*, 226–32.
11 A curt response, omitting Buckingham's title; does the Sheriff take offence at being addressed as *fellow* (Marshall)?
12 **my body's doomsday** The day associated with divine judgement upon departed souls in general (doomsday) is anticipated by the earthly sentence executed upon Buckingham's body (cf. 1.4.103–4).
13–17 See 2.1.32–40.
16 **wherein** on which
19 **determined respite** ordained time to which punishment has been deferred (*OED* respite *sb.* 5)
      wrongs i.e. Buckingham's ill deeds
20 **dallied** trifled
21 **feigned** feignèd; simulated, sham

10 fellow] *F;* fellowes *Qq*   11] *F;* It is my Lord. *Qq*   13 which] *F;* that *Qq*   15 and] *F;* or *Qq*   17 whom . . . trusted] *F;* I trusted most *Qq*   20 That] *F, Q1, 3–6;* What *Q2*   which] *F;* that *Qq*

And given in earnest what I begged in jest.
Thus doth he force the swords of wicked men
To turn their own points in their masters' bosoms.
Thus Margaret's curse falls heavy on my neck: 25
'When he', quoth she, 'shall split thy heart with
    sorrow,
Remember Margaret was a prophetess.'
– Come, lead me, officers, to the block of shame.
Wrong hath but wrong, and blame the due of blame.

Exeunt Buckingham with Officers.

5.2   *Enter* RICHMOND, OXFORD, BLUNT,
        HERBERT *and others, with Drum and Colours.*

RICHMOND
Fellows in arms, and my most loving friends,
Bruised underneath the yoke of tyranny,
Thus far into the bowels of the land
Have we marched on without impediment;
And here receive we from our father Stanley   5

22 **in earnest** in all seriousness
23–4 Psalm 37 promises that 'the meeke
    spirited shall possesse the earth: and
    shalbe delighted in the aboundaunce
    of peace' (11), but that the swords of
    the wicked 'shall go thorow their owne
    heart: & their bow shalbe broken' (15).
25–7 See 1.3.298–300.
26 **he** Richard
29 **blame . . . blame** i.e. censure and
    reproach are the appropriate rewards
    of blameworthiness or culpability
    (*OED* blame *sb.* 1, 3)
29 SD *Officers* the Sheriff and his men
    (see 0.1n.)
5.2 location: '*The Camp*' (Pope), '*near*

Tamworth' (Hanmer), i.e. near
    Bosworth in central England
0.2 *Drum and Colours* drummers and
    standard-bearers
2 **yoke of tyranny** Contrast *yoke of
    sovereignty* (3.7.145).
3–10 **bowels . . . embowelled** 'bow-
    els' means interior (*OED sb.*[1] 4); the
    land of England, being penetrated to
    its heart by Richmond, is related to
    the bodies of individuals, threatened
    with evisceration (embowelment) by
    Richard.
5 **our** Richmond appears to adopt the
    royal plural.
    father stepfather

23 swords] *F, Q1–2;* sword *Q3–6*   24 own points in] *F;* owne pointes, on *Q1–2;* points on
Q3–6   bosoms] *F;* bosome *Qq*   25 Thus] *F;* Now *Qq*   falls . . . neck] *F;* is fallen vpon my head
Qq   28 lead me, officers] *F;* sirs, conuey me *Qq*   29 SD] *F; not in Qq*   **5.2**] *F (Scena Secunda.);*
not in Qq   0.1–2] *F; Enter Richmond with drums and trumpets. Qq*   1, 22 SP] *F (Richm[.]), Qq
(Rich.)*   1 Fellows] *F, Q1–4, 6;* Fellowe *Q5*

Lines of fair comfort and encouragement.
The wretched, bloody and usurping boar,
That spoiled your summer fields and fruitful vines,
Swills your warm blood like wash, and makes his
    trough
In your embowelled bosoms, this foul swine   10
Is now even in the centre of this isle,
Near to the town of Leicester, as we learn.
From Tamworth thither is but one day's march.
In God's name, cheerly on, courageous friends,
To reap the harvest of perpetual peace   15
By this one bloody trial of sharp war.

OXFORD

Every man's conscience is a thousand men
To fight against this guilty homicide.

HERBERT

I doubt not but his friends will turn to us.

---

7   **wretched** reprehensible, hateful (*OED a.* 4)

7–8 See Psalm 80 on the vine: 'The wyld bore out of the wood rooteth it up: and the wyld beast of the fielde deuoureth it' (13). Cf. 15 and 2.2.115–16.

9   **Swills** eats freely or greedily, as a pig (*OED v.* 3)
    wash swill or refuse used as food for swine (*OED sb.* 11a)

10 **embowelled** disembowelled (*OED* 1); cf. *1H4* 5.4.109.

11–12 ***centre ... Near** F's 'centry' is synonymous with 'centre' (*OED* centry 1, citing this line) and hardly evidence of 'uneven correction' (Hammond). Qq/F variation of 'Near' recalls 1.1.117, where a contextually preferable reading (F's 'Ne'er') differs from similar alter-natives. F was here set by Compositor B, who usually spelled 'near' as 'neere'; Walton (*Copy*, 84–5) posits 'incorrect sophistication' in which B misread Q3's 'Neare', but 'Neare' is an alternative spelling of 'Ne'er' (*OED* ne'er).

12, 13 **Leicester, Tamworth** towns in central England

14 **cheerly on** i.e. go forward eagerly

16 **sharp** fierce, keen (*OED a.* 4c)

17 Cf. 5.3.193 and Dent, C601: 'Conscience is a thousand witnesses'; contrast 5.3.309–11.

18 **guilty** Richard's conscience will concur (5.3.199).

19 **doubt not but** i.e. believe (Abbott, 122); cf. 1.3.286.
    friends allies, but Richard will lament that 'no creature loves me' (5.3.200).

8 summer fields] *F; Q1–2* (somer-fieldes*)*; sommer-field *Q3–8* 10 embowelled] *F* (embowel'd*)*; inboweld *Q1–5*; imboweld *Q6* 11 Is] *F*; Lies *Qq* centre] *F* (Centry*)*, *Qq* 12 Near] *Q1–5* (Neare*)*; Neere *Q6*; Ne're *F* 13 thither] *F, Q2–6*; *Q1* (thether*)* 14 cheerly] *F, Q1*; cheere *Q2–6* 17 SP] *F (Oxf.)*; I Lo. *Qq* men] *F*; swordes *Qq* 18 this guilty] *F*; that bloudie *Qq* 19 SP] *F (Her.)*; 2 Lo. *Qq* turn] *F*; flie *Qq*

BLUNT

He hath no friends but what are friends for fear,   20
Which in his dearest need will fly from him.

RICHMOND

All for our vantage. Then in God's name, march.
True hope is swift and flies with swallow's wings;
Kings it makes gods, and meaner creatures kings. *Exeunt all.*

[5.3]   *Enter* KING RICHARD *in arms, with* NORFOLK,
         RATCLIFFE *and the* Earl of SURREY, ^Q*with others*^Q.

KING RICHARD

Here pitch our tent, even here in Bosworth field.
– My lord of Surrey, why look you so sad?

20–1 Some of Richard's forces served 'more for dread than loue' and 'kissed them openlie, whome they inwardlie hated. Other sware outwardlie to take part with such, whose death they secretlie compassed, and inwardlie imagined. Other promised to inuade the kings enimies, which fled and fought with fierce courage against the king. Other stood still and looked on, intending to take part with the victors and ouercommers. So was his people to him vnsure and vnfaithfull at his end, as he was to his nephues vntrue and vnnaturall in his beginning' (Holinshed, 3.757; Hall, *Richard III*, fol. lv^r). Cf. Macbeth's forces (*Mac* 5.2.19–20, 5.4.13–14).

21 **dearest** most urgent

23–4 A remarkable statement, since the desire to be *gods* is the fundamental error of tyrants and the aspiration of *meaner creatures* to be kings motivates countless Elizabethan tragedies. These

lines appear in *Englands Parnassus* (Allott); Cibber's Richmond claims that '*True hope*' actually '*mounts with Eagles wings*' (*Richard III*, 5.1.28). See Siemon, 'Power'.

23 Cf. Dent, S1023: 'As swift as a swallow'.

24 **meaner creatures** i.e. those lesser in rank

5.3 location: 'Bosworth *Field*' (Pope)

0.2 *SURREY Qq have Catesby instead of Surrey throughout 5.3. 5.3.3 is Surrey's only line in the play.

1 *tent Qq have 'tentes'; Richard could refer here to the tents of his forces, and later to his own tent (7, 14). For a similar scene *c*. 1590–1 with a sleeping king (Henry VI) and human and allegorical visitants, see the plot of *2 Seven Deadly Sins* (Greg, *Documents*, 2). *3H6* 4.3 is set outside a king's battlefield tent.

Bosworth The battle of Bosworth Field occurred on 22 August 1485.

2 **sad** serious

---

20 SP] *F; 3 Lo. Qq*   what] *F;* who *Qq*   21 dearest] *F;* greatest *Qq*   fly] *F;* shrinke *Qq*   24 makes] *F, Q6;* make *Q1–5*   SD] *F; Exit. Q1; om. Q2–6   all] F (Omnes)*   5.3] *Pope*   0.1 *in arms, with*] *F; not in Qq*   0.2 *and . . .* SURREY] *F; Catesbie Qq*   1–48 SP] *Qq (King.); Rich. F*   1 tent] *F;* tentes *Qq subst.*   2 My . . . Surrey] *F;* Whie, how now Catesbie *Qq*   look you] *F;* lookst *(*lookest *Q2–6)* thou *Qq*   sad] *F, Q2–6;* bad *Q1*

SURREY

My heart is ten times lighter than my looks.

KING RICHARD

My lord of Norfolk.

NORFOLK   Here, most gracious liege.

KING RICHARD

Norfolk, we must have knocks, ha, must we not?   5

NORFOLK

We must both give and take, my loving lord.

KING RICHARD

Up with my tent. Here will I lie tonight,

    [*Soldiers begin to set up Richard's tent.*]

But where tomorrow? Well, all's one for that.

Who hath descried the number of the traitors?

NORFOLK

Six or seven thousand is their utmost power.   10

KING RICHARD

Why, our battalia trebles that account.

Besides, the King's name is a tower of strength

Which they upon the adverse faction want.

---

5 **knocks** blows (cf. *H5* 3.2.3–8)
6 Cf. 'Give and take' (Dent, G121).
8 possibly an aside (Thompson)
   all's . . . that i.e. be that as it may
9 **descried** discovered by observation, found out (*OED v.*[1] III 7)
10 ***utmost** F's agreement with corrected Q1 argues that Q1 was 'partly set, or set in some partial way, from a sound manuscript . . . linked by unbroken written transmission' with FMS (Smidt, *Memorial*, 36). See pp. 430–1.
10–11 Richmond and 'Standley' discuss the relative strength of the oppos-

ing forces in *True Tragedy*. Richmond encourages himself by saying, 'thou fightest in right, to defende thy countrey from the tyrannie of an vsurping tyrant' (1867–8). The sources do not mention the odds affecting the spirits of the leaders (Churchill, 515).

11 **battalia** large body of men in battle array (*OED* 2); cf. *battle* (88, 134).
12 Cf. Proverbs, 18.10: 'The Name of the Lord *is* a strong towre' (Geneva; 'strong castell' in the Bishops' Bible). Cf. 'Strong as a tower in hope' (*R2* 1.3.102).
13 **adverse** opposing
   want lack

3 SP] *F; Cat, Qq* 4] *Steevens; F lines* Norfolke. / Liege. / My . . . Norfolk] *F;* Norffolke, come hether *(*hither *Q2–6) Qq* Here . . . liege.] *F; not in Qq* 5] *Qq; F lines* knockes: / not? / 6 loving] *F;* gracious *Qq* 7 tent] *F;* tent there *Qq* SD] *after Capell (Tent set up.)* 8 all's] *F;* all is *Qq* 9 traitors] *F;* foe *Qq* 10 utmost] *F, Q1c (BL, Bod, Fo);* greatest *Q1u (Hn), Q2–6* power] *F;* number *Qq* 11 battalia] *F;* battalion *Q1, 4, 6;* battailon *Q2–3, 5* 13 faction] *F;* partie *Qq*

– Up with the tent! – Come, noble gentlemen,
Let us survey the vantage of the ground. 15
Call for some men of sound direction.
Let's lack no discipline, make no delay,
For lords, tomorrow is a busy day. [*Richard's tent is ready.*]
Exeunt.

Enter RICHMOND, *Sir William Brandon,* OXFORD
and DORSET [, *with* BLUNT, HERBERT *and others*
who set up Richmond's tent].

RICHMOND
The weary sun hath made a golden set,
And by the bright track of his fiery car 20
Gives token of a goodly day tomorrow.
– Sir William Brandon, you shall bear my standard.
– Give me some ink and paper in my tent;
I'll draw the form and model of our battle,

---

15 **vantage . . . ground** military opportunity offered by the topography of the land
16 **sound direction** administrative capacity (*OED* direction 2); cf. 302 and 'directions' (*H5* 3.2.71–80).
18.2 DORSET Dorset neither speaks nor is addressed in the scene; sources have him left behind by Richmond in France (Holinshed, 3.752; Hall, *Richard III*, fol. l'). The play earlier has him *in arms* against Richard in England (4.4.518–19).
20 *track F's 'tract' could also mean 'track' (*OED* tract *sb.*³ IV 8).
   car chariot
21 Cf. 'A red sky in the evening is a sign

of a fair day' (Dent, S515); contrast 277–87.
22 **standard** flag
23–6 *Since Pope these lines have been sometimes moved, typically approximating Qq by placement after *Blunt* in 44 or after 44, but F suggests Richmond reacting to evolving plans and events: ordering that supplies be brought (23), issuing preliminary assignments (22, 27–9) and remembering the need for further communications (29–34); cf. York's confusion (*R2* 2.2.87–122). Cf. Richard's camp (49–75) and the demand for *ink and paper* (49).
24 **form and model** i.e. sketch of the plan

14 the . . . noble] *F (*the Tent: Come Noble*)*; my tent there, valiant *Qq*   15 ground] *F;* field *Qq*   17 lack] *F;* want *Qq*   18 SD *Richard's . . . ready.*] *Ard² subst.*   18.1–2 *Sir . . .* DORSET] *F; with the Lordes, &c. Q1–2; with the Lords. Q3–6*   18.2–3 *with . . . tent*] *this edn after Capell*   19 sun] *F, Q2–6 (*Sunne*);* sonne *Q1*   set] *F;* sete *Q1;* seate *Q2–5;* seat *Q6*   20 track] *Qq;* Tract *F*   21 token] *F;* signall *Qq*   22] *F;* Where is Sir William Brandon, he shall beare my standerd, *Qq*   23–6] *F; after Blunt 44 Qq*

383

Limit each leader to his several charge,   25
And part in just proportion our small power.
– My lord of Oxford, you, Sir William Brandon,
And you, Sir Walter Herbert, stay with me.
The Earl of Pembroke keeps his regiment;
– Good Captain Blunt, bear my goodnight to him,   30
And by the second hour in the morning
Desire the Earl to see me in my tent.
Yet one thing more, good captain, do for me:
Where is Lord Stanley quartered, do you know?

BLUNT

Unless I have mista'en his colours much,   35
Which well I am assured I have not done,
His regiment lies half a mile at least
South from the mighty power of the King.

RICHMOND

If without peril it be possible,
Sweet Blunt, make some good means to speak with
     him,   40
And give him from me this most needful note.

BLUNT

Upon my life, my lord, I'll undertake it,
And so God give you quiet rest tonight.

---

25 appoint the leaders to their particular assignments
26 **part** divide
  just exact
28–32 **Herbert . . . Earl** The prominence of Sir Walter Herbert and the Earl of Pembroke here (cf. 4.5.12–14) may compliment their Elizabethan descendant, Henry Herbert, 2nd Earl of Pembroke and patron of Pembroke's Men (Jowett, 5–7). The anticipated interview with Pembroke,

though apparently of extreme importance, is not staged. Gurr argues that Shakespeare was with Pembroke's Men in 1592–3 (*Companies*, 271).
29 **keeps** stays or remains with (*OED v.* 33)
35 **colours** battle flag or ensign (*OED sb.*[1] 7a)
40 *Qq repeat 30.
  make . . . means take the right steps (*OED mean sb.*[2] 10d)
41 **needful** necessary

---

26 power] *F*; strength *Qq*   27–8] *F*; *not in Qq*   28 you] *F2*; your *F*   29 keeps] *F*; keepe *Qq*   33 captain . . . me] *F*; Blunt before thou goest *Qq*   34 do you] *F*; doest thou *Qq*   37 lies] *F, Q1–2*; liet *Q3, 5*; lieth *Q4, 6*   40] *F*; Good captaine Blunt beare my good night to him, *Qq*   41 note] *F*; scrowle *Qq*   43] *F*; *not in Qq*

RICHMOND

Good night, good Captain Blunt.   [*Exit Blunt.*]

Come, gentlemen,

Let us consult upon tomorrow's business.   45

Into my tent; the dew is raw and cold.

[*Richmond, Brandon, Dorset, Herbert and Oxford*]
withdraw into the tent. [*The others exeunt.*]

Enter [*to his tent*] ^QKING^Q RICHARD, RATCLIFFE,
NORFOLK, CATESBY ^Q*and others*^Q.

KING RICHARD

What is't o'clock?

CATESBY

It's supper time, my lord; it's nine o'clock.

KING RICHARD

I will not sup tonight. Give me some ink and paper.

What, is my beaver easier than it was,   50

And all my armour laid into my tent?

46.2 *and others Given the number and kinds of orders issued in the lines that follow (49–75), some, but surely not all, directed to Ratcliffe, Q1–2 appropriately allow for attending figures.

48 **It's . . . it's* ''Tis' was the standard contraction (*OED* it *pron.* A 1a 2–3) employed in the 1590s (Jowett).
  nine Harrison claims, 'the nobility, gentry, and students do ordinarily go to dinner at eleven before noon and to supper at five, or between five and six' (144). Thus 'supper time' ordinarily would more likely be 6 p.m., as Qq; however, the sun sets in 19, suggesting

a later hour for August. Copyists could easily confuse 'nine' and 'six' ('it is six' (Qq) could resemble 'its ix'); *nine* is printed as 'ix.' in Qq 2.3.17.

49–end of play *From 49 on, F evidences very little correction of Q3 copy; thus Q1, the authoritative Quarto, furnishes the basic text for the rest of the play (see p. 419). The order of editions in the text notes is adjusted accordingly (cf. 3.1.1–166).

50 **beaver** lower portion of the face-guard of a helmet, when worn with a visor (*OED sb.*² 1)
  easier looser, better fitting

44] *Capell; F lines Blunt:* / Gentlemen, / Good night] *F;* Farewell *Qq* Captain Blunt] *F;* Blunt *Qq* SD] *Capell* Come, gentlemen] *F; not in Qq* 45 Let] *F;* Come, let *Qq* 46 Into] *F, Q6;* In to *Q1–5* my] *F;* our *Qq* dew] *F;* aire *Qq* 46 SD *Richmond . . . Oxford*] *Ard²; They F; not in Qq withdraw . . . tent*] *F; not in Qq The others exeunt*] *Ard²* 46.1 *to his tent*] *Capell* 46.2 CATESBY *and others*] *Q1–2 (Catesbie, &c.); Catesby. Q3–6; & Catesby. F* 47 is't o'clock] *F (* is't a Clocke*);* is a clocke *Qq* 48] *F (*a clocke*);* It is sixe of clocke *(*the clocke *Q3–6),* full supper time. *Qq* 49–end of play] *Basic text is Q1; order of collated editions adjusted. See p. 419.* 49 SP] *Qq, F (King.)* 49] *Qq; F lines* night, / Paper: /

CATESBY

    It is, my liege, and all things are in readiness.

KING RICHARD

    Good Norfolk, hie thee to thy charge,

    Use careful watch, choose trusty sentinels.

NORFOLK

    I go, my lord.   55

KING RICHARD

    Stir with the lark tomorrow, gentle Norfolk.

NORFOLK

    I warrant you, my lord. ^{F}*Exit.*^{F}

KING RICHARD

    Catesby.

CATESBY

    My lord.

KING RICHARD   Send out a pursuivant-at-arms

    To Stanley's regiment. Bid him bring his power   60

    Before sun-rising, lest his son George fall

    Into the blind cave of eternal night.   [*Exit Catesby.*]

    Fill me a bowl of wine. Give me a watch.

---

53 **hie** hasten (*OED v.*[1] 3)
    charge commission
54 **Use careful watch** guard carefully
    *sentinels F's plural (correcting Qq
    'centinell') makes sense.
56 Cf. 'Go to bed with the lamb and rise
    with the lark' (Dent, B186).
58 *F's 'Ratcliffe' appears to represent an
    attempt to reconcile the inconsistency
    between 58 and 59 in Qq. Richard
    addresses Catesby in Qq 58, but '*Rat.*'
    responds, suggesting confusion of 'C'
    and 'R' in the SP. Surely Richard's
    order to find a pursuivant would be
    immediately acted upon, but Ratcliffe
    has no exit in F or Qq until 78.

59 **pursuivant-at-arms** junior officer
    attendant on the heralds (*OED* pur-
    suivant *sb.* 1)
62 Cf. 1.4.47 and 2.2.46.
    blind dark, obscure (*OED a.* III
    6a)
63–5 On the addressee(s), see 46.2n.; cf.
    72–5.
63 **bowl** drinking vessel (*OED sb.*[1] 1b)
    Give . . . watch Richard may ask that
    a sentinel guard him, or perhaps he
    requests a watch-candle, marked to
    register elapsed time as it melts (*OED*
    watch *sb.* VII 26). Both are plausible
    (see 76 and 180). Jowett suggests a
    time-piece; cf. 276.

53+ SP] *Qq* (Kin*[g][.]*), *exc. 177 (K[ing][.] Ri[c].); Rich. F, exc. 72, 208–347 (K[ing].)* 54
sentinels] *F (*Centinels*); centinell *Qq* 58 Catesby] *Qq*; Ratcliffe *F* 59] *Steevens*; *Qq, F line* lord. /
armes / 59 SP] *Pope*; *Rat. Qq, F* 61 sun-rising] *Q1–5 (*sun rising*), hyphen Q6, F* 62 SD] *Cam*

Saddle white Surrey for the field tomorrow.
Look that my staves be sound and not too heavy.   65
– Ratcliffe.

RATCLIFFE   My lord.

KING RICHARD
Sawst thou the melancholy Lord Northumberland?

RATCLIFFE
Thomas the Earl of Surrey and himself,
Much about cock-shut time, from troop to troop   70
Went through the army, cheering up the soldiers.

KING RICHARD
So, I am satisfied. Give me a bowl of wine.
I have not that alacrity of spirit
Nor cheer of mind that I was wont to have.
[*Wine is brought.*]

64 **white Surrey** Richard rode a 'greate whyte courser' into Leicester (Hall, *Richard III*, fol. lii'; Holinshed, 3.754). His horses apparently included one 'White Surrey' (Kendall, 492). Given other references to Revelation and the ironic reversal of dragon and saint at 349–50, it may be significant that Richard requests a white horse, the Son of God's mount in the final victory over evil in Revelation, 19, the reading appointed for All Saints' Day, 1 November (Shaheen, *History Plays*, 19), i.e. yesterday, according to the play's fictional calendar (see 5.1.10).

65 **staves** shafts of lances (*OED* staff *sb.*[1] 3a); combatants could be armed with several lances (Holinshed, 3.834).

68 **melancholy Lord Northumberland** Northumberland's 'melancholy' has never been clearly explained. Holinshed observes, 'whether it was by the commandement of king Richard, putting diffidence into him; or he did it for the loue and fauour that he bare' for Richmond, Northumberland 'stood still with a great companie, and intermitted not in the battell', which won him 'fauour' of Richmond (3.759). Northumberland's melancholy, like Surrey's *sad* appearance (5.3.2), may suggest reluctance. Richard himself is described as 'Melancolye' at news of Richmond's unopposed approach (Hall, *Richard III*, fol. lii'), and the play elsewhere transfers attributes from one character to another (see 4.4.426–31n.). Kemble relates Richard to Macbeth: 'Each of the tyrants alike, in his concern about the feelings of others, clearly reveals the agitation of his own breast' (116–17).

70 **cock-shut time** i.e. twilight; when poultry are shut up for rest or when woodcocks fly or 'shoot' (*OED*)

72–5 See 46.2n.

73 **alacrity** liveliness (*OED*); Richard 'prognosticated before the doubtfull chance of the battell to come; not vsing the alacritie and mirth of mind and countenance as he was accustomed to doe' (Holinshed, 3.755).

74 **wont** accustomed

65–6] *Rowe*[3]*; one line Qq, F* 66 Ratcliffe] *Q6, F;* Ratliffe *Q1–5* 68 Sawst] *Q1, F; Q2–6* (Sawest) thou] *Qq; om. F* 70 about] *Q1–5, F;* like *Q6* 74 SD] *Capell*

Set it down. Is ink and paper ready?   75

RATCLIFFE

It is, my lord.

KING RICHARD   Bid my guard watch. Leave me.

Ratcliffe, about the mid of night come to my tent

And help to arm me. Leave me, I say.

Exit Ratcliffe [with others].

[*Richard goes into his tent to sleep.*]

Enter [STANLEY, Earl of] Derby *to Richmond*
[*and Lords*] *in his tent.*

STANLEY

Fortune and Victory sit on thy helm.

RICHMOND

All comfort that the dark night can afford   80

Be to thy person, noble father-in-law.

Tell me, how fares our loving mother?

STANLEY

I, by attorney, bless thee from thy mother,

Who prays continually for Richmond's good.

---

76 **watch** stand watch
78 SD2 From 51 and 77 – in which
Richard respectively asks if his armour
has been brought 'into my tent' and
then orders Ratcliffe to 'come to my
tent' – it appears Richard is not yet *in*
his tent at 77. He insists Ratcliffe *Leave*
in 78 and enters the tent where he must
be asleep by 118.
78.1–2 *Richmond . . . tent* Some characters appear to have remained in
Richmond's tent with him; see *lords*
(103) and *lords and gentlemen* (107).
79 ***sit** Q1's 'set' could mean 'sit' (Q2–6,
F), but it risks confusion by con-

veying a directly opposed sense (cf.
351; also 'Fortune her selfe dooth sit
upon our Crests', Marlowe, *Works, 1
Tamburlaine*, 2.2.73). From subsequent
curses employing *Let me sit* (118, 131,
139), Stanley's utterance appears to be
a blessing (i.e. *Let* Fortune and Victory
sit on thy helm); cf. Richard's hollow
declaration that 'Victory sits on our
helms' (351).
81 **father-in-law** i.e. stepfather (*OED* 2)
82–4 Contrast Richard's abuse of family
ties and mockery of his mother's blessing and prayers (2.2.105–11).
83 **by attorney** i.e. by proxy, as a deputy

76] *Steevens; Qq, F line* lord. / me. /   77 Ratcliffe] *Q3, 5–6, F;* Ratliffe *Q1–2, 4*   mid] *Q1–5,
F;* midst *Q6*   78 SD1 *Ratcliffe] Q6, F;* Ratliffe *Q1–5   with others] Cam subst.*   SD2 *Richard . . .
tent] after Malone*   78.1 STANLEY, Earl of] *Pope subst.*   Derby] *F; Qq (Darby)*   78.2 *and Lords*]
Theobald subst.   79+ SP] *Pope; Dar. Qq subst.; Der. F*   79 sit] *Q2–6, F;* set *Q1*   82 loving] *Q1–2;*
noble *Q3–6, F*

So much for that. The silent hours steal on,   85
And flaky darkness breaks within the east.
In brief, for so the season bids us be,
Prepare thy battle early in the morning
And put thy fortune to the arbitrament
Of bloody strokes and mortal-staring war.   90
I, as I may – that which I would, I cannot –
With best advantage will deceive the time
And aid thee in this doubtful shock of arms.
But on thy side I may not be too forward,
Lest, being seen, thy brother, tender George,   95
Be executed in his father's sight.
Farewell. The leisure and the fearful time

85 **So . . . that** i.e. enough about that
steal on go by unobserved (*OED* steal
$v.^1$ II 11a); cf. 'The hour steals on' (*CE*
4.1.52).

86 **flaky darkness breaks** Shakespeare
frequently describes darkness broken
into cloudy fragments with the arrival
of daylight; e.g. 'fleckled darkness'
(*RJ* 2.2.190). Temporal references are
symbolic: in Richmond's camp dawn
approaches, but it is *dead midnight* in
Richard's camp (180).

87 **season** time

88 **battle** body of troops in battle array
(*OED sb.* II 8a)

90 **mortal-staring** both deathly and
glaring; cf. the fatal gaze of the basilisk (1.2.153) and the *wrinkled front* of
Grim-visaged War (1.1.9).

91 **that . . . cannot** perhaps echoing in
a political sense the spiritual dilemma
described in Romans, 7.15: 'for that
which I do I alowe not. For what I
woulde, that do I not: but what I hate,
that do I.' Cf. Dent, M554: 'Men must
do as they may, not as they would.'
Erasmus (32.146) quotes a phrase from
Terence's *Andria* in which a street-

walker modestly confesses her occupation.

92 i.e. [I] will conceal my true intentions in order to take advantage of
the best opportunity that the present
circumstances offer; cf. *Mac* 1.5.63–4.
Holinshed characterizes Stanley as a
'wilie fox' in this deceit (3.754).

93 **doubtful** uncertain
shock encounter of opposing armed
forces in a charge or onset (*OED sb.*[3] 1a)

95 **being seen** i.e. I being seen (Abbott,
378)
brother i.e. half-brother
tender George George Stanley was
an adult by 1485. Hall and Holinshed
describe him as 'the child' (Hall,
Richard III, fol. lviii[v]), but 'child' may
mean 'young nobleman' (Thompson;
cf. *KL* 3.4.178). Richard's very young
victims are called *tender* (4.4.328, 383,
385), and he once berated the 'cruel
child-killer' Clifford for slaying 'tender' Rutland (*3H6* 2.2.112, 115).

97 **leisure** duration of opportunity, time
remaining before it is too late (*OED sb.*
2b); thus, in fact, the lack of leisure (cf.
R2 1.1.5)

85 that.] *F*; that *Q1–2*; that: *Q3, 5–6*; that, *Q4*   89 the arbitrament] *Qq*; *F* (th'Arbitrement*)*
90 mortal-staring] *Qq*, *F* (mortal staring*)*, *hyphen Steevens*   95 brother, tender] *Q1–5*, *F subst.*;
tender brother *Q6*   96 his father's sight] *Q1–3, 5–6*, *F*; thy fathers fight *Q4*

Cuts off the ceremonious vows of love
And ample interchange of sweet discourse,
Which so-long-sundered friends should dwell upon.   100
God give us leisure for these rites of love.
Once more, adieu; be valiant and speed well.

RICHMOND

Good lords, conduct him to his regiment.
I'll strive with troubled thoughts to take a nap,
Lest leaden slumber peise me down tomorrow   105
When I should mount with wings of victory.
Once more, good night, kind lords and gentlemen.

Exeunt ᶠ*all but Richmond*ᶠ.

O Thou, whose captain I account myself,
Look on my forces with a gracious eye;
Put in their hands Thy bruising irons of wrath,   110

---

100 *sundered Q5 offers the modern spelling. 'Sundry' could mean 'separate' or 'apart', but *OED* does not record Q1–2's 'sundried'.

101 *rites F's spelling provides the modern form of the word, which Shakespeare sometimes spells as it appears in Qq (cf. *MND* 4.1.132); see also *OED* right *sb.*².

102 **speed well** i.e. prosper

103 Given Stanley's need for secrecy, perhaps this command responds to the theatrical need to get the attendant lords out of Richmond's tent (Hammond). Lines 103–7 allow the lords to come out of the tent, assemble with Stanley and exit.

104 **with** i.e. against
*thoughts R.G. White argues for F's 'noise', since struggling with troubled *thoughts* lessens Richmond's contrast with Richard (Var). Richmond is addressed as *Quiet, untroubled soul* (157), but he mentions his *watchful soul* (115), and both Holinshed (3.754) and

Hall (*Richard III*, fol. liii') emphasize his initial fears and uncertainties.

105 **leaden** heavy, dull; cf. slumber's 'leaden mace' (*JC* 4.3.266) and Dent, L136.1.
peise burden, oppress (*OED v.* 4a)

107 SD Richard may remain visible, sleeping in his tent as Richmond speaks his prayer in front of his own tent before retiring to sleep in 117.

108 **captain** in serving God as a captain Richmond takes an intermediary role, since the general was the head of a country's forces and normally the monarch (see Burns, 323–5; Cruikshank, 42, 50–5).

110 **bruising irons** i.e. maces; Shakespeare typically uses 'iron' to refer to a sword, but *bruising* contradicts that meaning and suggests the prophecy hailing the Lord's anointed in Psalms, 2.9: 'Thou shalt bruise them with a rod of iron: and breake them in peeces like a potters vessell.' Cf. 112.

---

100 so-long-sundered] *Qg, F (*so long sundried*), hyphens Theobald* sundered] *Q5–6;* sundried *Q1–2;* sundired *Q3–4;* sundred *F* 101 rites] *F;* rights *Qq* 103 lords] *Q1–3, 5–6, F;* Lord *Q4* 104 thoughts] *Qg;* noise *F* 107 SD *all but Richmond*] *F (Manet Richmond.)*

That they may crush down with a heavy fall
The usurping helmets of our adversaries;
Make us Thy ministers of chastisement,
That we may praise Thee in the victory.
To Thee I do commend my watchful soul,   115
Ere I let fall the windows of mine eyes:
Sleeping and waking, O, defend me still!   ^F*Sleeps.*^F

Enter the GHOST *of young* PRINCE EDWARD,
son ^F*to*^F *Harry the Sixth.*

111 **fall** downward stroke (of a sword, etc.) (*OED sb.*¹ 1h); cf. *Oth* 2.3.230.
112 ***The** F's elided form ('Th'') may signal an abbreviation for the sake of rhythm that would be automatic (if difficult to pronounce) (Hammond); *adversaries* is probably trisyllabic.
   usurping helmets an odd metonymy displacing the opprobrium for Richard's individual political usurpation onto the collective military capacity of his forces (Mowat & Werstine). In effect, support for a reigning monarch against an invading army is equated with the original crime(s) of usurpation, a problematic equation since some maintained that continuance in office could render even a violent usurper a 'lawfull prince' (Perkins, 918). Given the echo of Psalms, 2.9 in 110, the crushing of the helmets may recall the Geneva phrasing: 'Thou shalt krush them with a sceptre of yron'.
113 **ministers of chastisement** Richmond appropriates the function of the ruler as defined in Romans, 13.4: 'For he is the minister of God for thy wealth. But yf thou do euyll, feare: for he beareth not the sworde in vayne, for he is the minister of God, reuenger of wrath on hym that doth euyll.' Similar phrasing appears frequently

in the Homilies and elsewhere (cf. *KJ* 2.1.87–8). Hall's Richmond exhorts his troops as 'trew men against traytors, pitifull persones against murtherers, trew inheritors against vsurpers, yᵉ skorges of God against tirau[n]tes' (*Richard III*, fol. lvi).
115 **commend . . . soul** perhaps echoing Jesus's last words: 'Father, into thy handes I commende my spirite' (Luke, 23.46)
   commend entrust for keeping (*OED v.* 1b)
   watchful wakeful
116 ***Ere** Q1's 'Eare' is a variant spelling.
   windows Shakespeare uses *windows* for eyelids (as here and in *RJ* 4.1.100) and for the eyes themselves (*LLL* 5.2.826); cf. *OED sb.* 4a.
117.1 Vergil's account of Richard's demonic visions (not ghosts) is echoed by Grafton, Hall and Holinshed: 'it seemed to him being asleepe, that he did see diuerse images like terrible diuels, which pulled and haled him, not suffering him to take anie quiet or rest' (Holinshed, 3.755; Vergil, 221; Hall, *Richard III*, fol. liii; Hardyng, *Richard III*, fol. civ). However, in *True Tragedy* Richard proclaims that 'nightly dreames' terrorize his 'wounded conscience' as 'their ghoasts comes gaping for reuenge, / Whom I haue

112 The usurping] *Qq; F* (Th'vsurping)   helmets] *Q1–4, F;* helmet *Q5–6*   114 the] *Q1–2, 6;* thy *Q3–5, F*   116 Ere] *Q1* (Eare), *Q2–6, F*   117.1 young] *Q1–2; om. Q3–6, F*   117.2 to] *Q2–6, F; not in Q1*   Harry] *Q1;* Henry *Q2–6, F*   Sixth.] *Q3–6, F* (sixt.); sixt, to Ri. *Q1–2*

GHOST [of PRINCE EDWARD] (*to Richard*)
Let me sit heavy on thy soul tomorrow.
Think how thou stab'st me in my prime of youth
At Tewkesbury. Despair therefore, and die.   120
(*to Richmond*) Be cheerful, Richmond, for the wronged
    souls
Of butchered princes fight in thy behalf.
King Henry's issue, Richmond, comforts thee.   [*Exit.*]

Enter the GHOST *of* HENRY THE SIXTH.

GHOST [of HENRY VI] (*to Richard*)
When I was mortal, my anointed body
By thee was punched full of deadly holes.   125

slaine in reaching for a Crowne . . .
And euery one cries, let the tyrant
die' (1875–85). The ghostly visitants
differ from the 'tormenting dream'
of 'a hell of ugly devils' (1.3.225–6)
that Margaret wishes for Richard
(Greenblatt, 177). Early modern stage
ghosts usually dressed like the characters when alive, but were sometimes
dressed and/or made up in white
(Dessen & Thomson, 100). In 1622
Drayton evokes ghostly victims threatening Richard with their 'pale hands',
a detail possibly derived from early
make-up (*Poly-Olbion*, Song XXII,
1424–5).
118 **sit heavy on** i.e. oppress; for spiritual heaviness wished upon the guilty,
cf. 'Be Mowbray's sins so heavy in his
bosom' (*R2* 1.2.50).
119 **prime of youth** Cf. 1.2.250.
120 **Tewkesbury** Cf. 1.2.244.
    Despair . . . die as Faustus to himself:
'Damned art thou *Faustus*, damned,
despaire and die' (Marlowe, *Works*,
Faustus, [5.1.]1725). The phrase was

bandied back and forth in the Nashe–
Harvey exchanges of 1592 (Nashe,
1.157; Harvey, 1.196).
therefore on that account
121 **wronged** wrongèd
123 **issue** offspring
123–76 SDs **Exit, Exeunt* Nothing
except the limited size of an early
modern acting company demands
that the ghosts exit singly rather than
remaining and vanishing collectively at
176 (as Rowe).
124 **When . . . mortal** echoing the
famous opening of *The Spanish
Tragedy*, 'When this eternall substance
of my soule, / Did live imprisond
in my wanton flesh' (Kyd, *Spanish
Tragedy*, 1.1.1–2).
anointed See 4.4.151.
125 Marshall nominates this as one of the
worst lines in all of Shakespeare.
punched punchèd
*deadly Without Q1's 'deadlie' the
line is a foot short, a fact used to argue
the setting of F from a derivative
Quarto (Var).

118 SP GHOST] *Qq; Gh. F*   SD] *Q1–2, F (to Ri.); to K. Ri[c]. Q3–6*   121] *Qq; F lines* Richmond,
/ Soules /   121 SD] *Qq (To Rich.); Ghost to Richm. F*   123, 130, 138, 145, 153, 158, 166 SD] *Cam¹
subst.*   124 SD] *Q1–2 (to Ri.); to K. Ri. Q3–6; om. F*   125 deadly] *Q1; om. Q2–6, F*

Think on the Tower and me. Despair and die.
Harry the Sixth bids thee despair and die.
(*to Richmond*) Virtuous and holy, be thou conqueror.
Harry, that prophesied thou shouldst be king,
Doth comfort thee in thy sleep. Live and flourish.   [*Exit.*]

Enter the GHOST *of* CLARENCE.

GHOST [of CLARENCE (*to Richard*)]
Let me sit heavy in thy soul tomorrow,   131
I, that was washed to death with fulsome wine,
Poor Clarence, by thy guile betrayed to death.
Tomorrow in the battle think on me,
And fall thy edgeless sword. Despair and die.   135
(*to Richmond*) Thou offspring of the house of
    Lancaster,
The wronged heirs of York do pray for thee.
Good angels guard thy battle. Live and flourish.   [*Exit.*]

Enter the GHOSTS *of* RIVERS, GREY ^F*and*^F VAUGHAN.

[GHOST of RIVERS (*to Richard*)]
Let me sit heavy in thy soul tomorrow,
Rivers that died at Pomfret. Despair and die.   140
[GHOST of] GREY [(*to Richard*)]
Think upon Grey, and let thy soul despair.

---

126 **Tower** the site of Henry VI's death
    at Richard's hand (*3H6* 5.6)
129 See *3H6* 4.6.68–74.
132 **fulsome** cloying, satiating (*OED* 3)
135 **fall** imperative, i.e. drop, let fall (cf.
    1.2.185 SD and Abbott, 291). This line
    is repeated at 163 (cf. 143).
    edgeless blunt
136 Richmond   descended   from   the

Lancastrians by his mother, Margaret
Beaufort, great-granddaughter of John
of Gaunt (although the matter is not as
simple as here presented: see 5.5.30n.).
The support here posthumously offered
by the York family foreshadows the symbolic merger of the two houses (Lull).
137 **wronged** wrongèd
138 **battle** troops (cf. 11, 88)

128, 136 SD] *Qg (To Rich.), F (To Richm.)*   130 thy] *Qg; om. F*   131, 139, 141, 142, 154 SD]
Rowe (To K. Rich.)   131 sit] *Q2–6, F; set Q1*   in] *Q1–4, F; on Q5–6*   138.1 GHOSTS] *Q1–2, 6, F;
Ghoast Q3–5*   139 SP] *Dyce; Riu. Q3–6, F; King Q1–2*   139 in] *Q1–4, F; on Q5–6*   141, 142 SP
GHOST of] *Dyce*

[GHOST of] VAUGHAN [(*to Richard*)]

    Think upon Vaughan, and with guilty fear

    Let fall thy lance. Despair and die.

ALL (*to Richmond*)

    Awake, and think our wrongs in Richard's bosom   144

    Will conquer him. Awake, and win the day.   [*Exeunt.*]

        Enter the GHOSTS *of the two young* PRINCES.

GHOSTS [of PRINCES] (*to Richard*)

    Dream on thy cousins smothered in the Tower.

    Let us be lead within thy bosom, Richard,

    And weigh thee down to ruin, shame and death.

    Thy nephews' souls bid thee despair and die.

    (*to Richmond*) Sleep, Richmond, sleep in peace and

        wake in joy;   150

    Good angels guard thee from the boar's annoy.

    Live, and beget a happy race of kings;

    Edward's unhappy sons do bid thee flourish.   [*Exeunt.*]

---

143 *The Variorum account provides a history of editorial interventions from the adding of an epithet to modify lance – e.g. 'hurtless' (Capell) or 'pointless' (Collier) – to the presumption of physical gesture or verbal repetition (Marshall). The assumed parallelism with 135 also encourages such emendations.

145.1–158 SD *Q3 changes the Q1–2 order, moving the princes to follow Hastings; thus Q3–F follow the sequence of the other ghosts, who appear in order of their deaths. Q3 has no textual authority in this portion of the play (but see 183n.). See also pp. 437–9.

146 **cousins** nephews (cf. 2.2.8)

147 ***lead** Q1's 'lead' better agrees with 148 (and with *heavy* in 139) than does Q2–8, F's 'laid' (Theobald); cf. *leaden slumber* (105).

150 **sleep in peace** Psalms, 4.8 has 'I wil laye me downe, & also slepe in peace' (Geneva), noting that peace comes from the Lord (either God or King David) and that the speaker 'shulde dwel as ioyfully alone as if he had manie about him, because the Lord is with him'.

151 **annoy** that which causes discomfort, annoyance (*OED sb.* 2)

144 SD] *Qq (to Ri[ch].), F (to Richm.)*   144] *Qq; F lines* Awake, / Bosome, /   Richard's] *Q1, F;* Ri. *Q2–5; Ric. Q6*   145 Will] *Q2–6, F;* Wel *Q1*   145.1–153 *Enter . . . flourish.*] *Q1–2; after* 158 *Q3–6, F*   145.1 *the two] Q1–5, F; two Q6*   146 SP GHOSTS] *F; Ghost Q1–2, 6; Gho. Q3–5*   SD] *Q1–2 (to Ri.); to K.R. Q 3–6; om. F*   146] *Qq; F lines* Cousins / Tower: /   147 lead] *Q1;* laid *Q2–6, F*   149 souls bid] *Qq;* soule bids *F*   150] *Qq; F lines* Richmond, / Ioy, /   150 SD] *Qq (To Ri[ch].), F (Ghosts to Richm.)*

Enter the GHOST *of* HASTINGS.

GHOST [of HASTINGS (*to Richard*)]
   Bloody and guilty, guiltily awake,
   And in a bloody battle end thy days.   155
   Think on Lord Hastings. Despair and die.
   (*to Richmond*) Quiet, untroubled soul, awake, awake.
   Arm, fight and conquer for fair England's sake.   [*Exit.*]

Enter the GHOST *of Lady* ANNE, *his wife.*

[F]GHOST [of ANNE] (*to Richard*)[F]
   Richard, thy wife, that wretched Anne, thy wife,
   That never slept a quiet hour with thee,   160
   Now fills thy sleep with perturbations.
   Tomorrow in the battle think on me,
   And fall thy edgeless sword. Despair and die.
   (*to Richmond*) Thou quiet soul, sleep thou a quiet sleep.
   Dream of success and happy victory.   165
   Thy adversary's wife doth pray for thee.   [*Exit.*]

Enter the GHOST *of* BUCKINGHAM.

[F]GHOST [of BUCKINGHAM] (*to Richard*)[F]
   The first was I that helped thee to the crown;
   The last was I that felt thy tyranny.
   O, in the battle think on Buckingham,
   And die in terror of thy guiltiness.   170
   Dream on, dream on, of bloody deeds and death.
   Fainting, despair; despairing, yield thy breath.

---

160 Cf. 4.1.82–4.   172 **Fainting** growing faint of heart
163 See 135.   (*OED*)

153.1 HASTINGS] *Q1–2; L. Hastings Q3–6; Lord Hastings F*   154 SP GHOST] *Q1–2, 6; Gho. Q3–5,
F*   157 SD] *Qq (To Ri[ch].), F (Hast. to Rich.)*   157] *Qq; F lines* soule, / awake: /   158.1 Lady]
Q1–2; Queene Q3–6; om. F   159] *Qq; F lines* Wife, / Wife, /   161 perturbations] *Q2–6, F;* pretur-
bations *Q1*   164] *Qq; F lines* soule, / sleepe: /   164 SD] *Qq (To Rich.), F (Ghost to Richm.)*   167]
Qq; F lines I / Crowne: /

(*to Richmond*) I died for hope ere I could lend thee aid;
But cheer thy heart, and be thou not dismayed.
God and good angels fight on Richmond's side,   175
And Richard fall in height of all his pride.   [*Exit.*]
        Richard starteth up out of a dream.

KING RICHARD

Give me another horse! Bind up my wounds!
Have mercy, Jesu. – Soft, I did but dream.
O coward conscience, how dost thou afflict me!
The lights burn blue. It is now dead midnight.   180

173 *hope Frequently emended, but *hope* makes sense if 'for' means 'for want of' or 'as regards' (cf. *Mac* 1.5.36: 'almost dead for breath'). Thus Buckingham may say: 'I languished for lack of hope before I had opportunity to aid you.' Richard's proposal 'To stop all hopes whose growth may damage me' (4.2.59) is countered by Richmond's affirmation of *True hope* at 5.2.23–4.

176 **Richard fall** i.e. let Richard fall (cf. 163 and Dent, P581: 'Pride will have a fall.')

177–206 Richard's 'strange vision not so suddenlie strake his heart with a sudden feare, but it stuffed his head and troubled his mind with manie busie and dreadfull imaginations' (Holinshed, 3.755). Richard's refusal to repent contrasts with Clarence's response to his dream in 1.4; cf. the Second Murderer's repentance (1.4.270–7) and Dighton and Forrest's *conscience and remorse* (4.3.20). Grafton summarizes Richard's spiritually 'desperate' state: 'I thynke that this was not a dreame, but rather his conscience pricked with the sharpe styng of his mischeuous offences, whiche although they do not pricke alway, yet moost com[m]only they wyll byte

moost towarde the latter daye, representyng vnto vs not onely them selfe, but also the terrible punishement that is ordeyned for the same, as the sight of the deuill tearyng and halyng vs, so that thereby (if we haue grace) we may take an occasyon to be penitent, or else for lacke of the same dye in desperacion' (Hardyng, *Richard III*, fol. civ^r-v). A 17th-century Folio reader annotates: 'Richard affrighted by fearefull visions . . . dispaire of conscience and memorie of abominable cruelties and periuries make Richard madde' (Yamada, 160). This passage shows similarities with a speech from *Troublesome Raigne* already echoed at 1.2.1 (*TRKJ*, Pt 2, xiii.1–13, sigs D2^v–D3^r).

177–8 For Garrick's influential delivery of Cibber's lines, see p. 92.

177 **Give . . . horse** A dream again anticipates the future (see 5.4.13; cf. Toole, 31).

178 **Soft** i.e. wait a moment

179 **coward conscience** Richard blames his conscience for making him cowardly by besieging him with moral accusations and visions of disaster (cf. 193). See also Dent, C606.

180 **lights burn blue** Candles were thought to register the presence of spir-

173 SD] *Qq* (To Ri[ch].), *F* (Ghost to Richm.)   173] *Qq; F* lines hope / Ayde; /   176 fall] *F;* fals *Qq*   176 SD] *Cam^1* (vanishes.); The ghosts vanish. / *Rowe*   176.1 *Richard starteth up] Q1–2; K. Richard starteth Q3–6; Richard starts F*   a] *Qq;* his *F*   177 SP] *Qq* (King Ri[ch].); Rich. *F*   180 now] *Q1;* not *Q2–6, F*

Cold fearful drops stand on my trembling flesh.
What do I fear? Myself? There's none else by.
Richard loves Richard, that is, I am I.
Is there a murderer here? No. Yes, I am.
Then fly! What, from myself? Great reason why?   185
Lest I revenge. What, myself upon myself?
Alack, I love myself. Wherefore? For any good
That I myself have done unto myself?
O, no. Alas, I rather hate myself,
For hateful deeds committed by myself.   190
I am a villain. Yet I lie; I am not.

its by burning low (cf. *JC* 4.3.273) and blue (cf. Lyly's *Galathea*, 2.3.62–5).

*now F's nonsensical 'not', originating with Q2's mistake and continued in all subsequent quartos, argues that this portion of F was set from a derivative quarto with only the most minimal correction (but see changes to *eaves-dropper*, 221).

dead midnight Cf. dawn approaching in 86; time, like the weather (contrast 86 with 277–8), is differently remarked in the two camps.

182–203 **fear . . . love . . . pity** Richard, murdering Henry VI, characterizes himself as 'I that have neither pity, love nor fear' (*3H6* 5.6.68).

183 ***am** Hammond and Jowett prefer 'I and I' (Q1) over 'I am I' (Q2–8, F). Malone wondered if Q1 might be right (Var); Evans has argued that eye-skip involving *I am* (184) could account for 'am' ('Restored', 46). Q2 shows only minimal correction in this scene (e.g. at 2, 147, 180, 282, 320, 321), but 'am' anticipates Richard's self-definition ('I am a villain. Yet I lie; I am not', 191), echoes his claim to singularity ('I am myself alone', *3H6* 5.6.83) and mocks his confident definition of 'what I am' (1.3.132). It parallels the Bastard's

claim to stable self-identity ('I am I, howe'er I was begot', *KJ* 1.1.175). It would also express Richard's resistance to such 'conversion' as represented by Oliver's renunciation of his villainous past (''Twas I, but 'tis not I') to become 'the thing I am' (*AYL* 4.3.134–6). 'I am I' adapts that divine identity statement ('I am that I am') which is deployed strategically by Viola (*TN* 3.1.142), treated cavalierly in *Son* 121 and perverted by Iago's 'I am not what I am' (*Oth* 1.1.64). Cf. Exodus, 3.14: 'God aunswered Moyses, I am that I am. And he said: This shalt thou say vnto the chyldren of Israel, I am, hath sent me'.

186 **myself upon myself** Richard threatens to make good upon his oath at 4.4.399 ('Myself myself confound'); cf. 2.4.64, 4.4.420. Richard's reference to *despair* (200) recalls Queen Elizabeth's threat to join with 'despair . . . And to myself become an enemy' (2.2.36–7).

187 **I love myself** Self-love contradicts the soldier's creed announced by Young Clifford: 'He that is truly dedicate to war / Hath no self-love' (*2H6* 5.2.37–8).

191, 195 **villain** Cf. 1.1.30; Richard has fulfilled his determination 'to prove a villain' (MacDonald & MacDonald, 59).

181 stand] *Q1–4*, 6, *F*; stands *Q5*   182 What . . . Myself?] *Q1*; What do I feare my selfe? *Q2–6*; What? do I feare my Selfe? *F*   183 am] *Q2–6*, *F*; and *Q1*   185 reason why?] *Q1–2*; reason why, *Q3–6*; reason: why? *F*   188 I] *Q1–5*, *F*; om. *Q6*

Fool, of thyself speak well. Fool, do not flatter.
My conscience hath a thousand several tongues,
And every tongue brings in a several tale,
And every tale condemns me for a villain.   195
Perjury, perjury, in the highest degree;
Murder, stern murder, in the direst degree;
All several sins, all used in each degree,
Throng to the bar, crying all, 'Guilty, guilty!'
I shall despair. There is no creature loves me,   200
And if I die, no soul will pity me.

193 Cf. 5.2.17 and Dent, C601; 'Conscience
is a thousand witnesses' (Erasmus,
32.277).
    several individually separate, differ-
ent (*OED a.* 2a)
194 **brings in** adduces as evidence
196–7 **Perjury . . . Murder** The two
lines represent opposed roles in
Richard's imaginary courtroom: the
first voice (196) cries *Perjury*, rejecting
the charge that he is a *villain* which has
been brought by the 'tales' (195); the
second voice responds by reiterating
the charge against him: 'Murder . . .
in the dir'st degree' (197). This internal debate replicates formal features of
Faustus's soliloquies (Marlowe, *Works*,
Faustus, [2.1.]389–402) and recalls the
hybrid morality play; Apius, for example, represents the voices within himself: 'Conscience saith crueltye sure
will detest me: / And Iustice saith,
death in thende will molest me' (*Apius*,
sig. C1ʳ; cf. Spivack, 271).
198 **used . . . degree** i.e. committed in
every stage of intensity or amount
(*OED degree sb.* 6a)
199 **Throng . . . bar** crowd to the barrier
or wooden rail marking the precinct
of the judge's seat, at which prisoners
were stationed for arraignment, trial
or sentence; here evoking the tribunal

of conscience (*OED* bar *sb.*[1] III 22a, b,
citing this line). 'Conscience', Perkins
writes, 'is like to a Iudge that holdeth
an assize and take notice of indite-
ments, and causeth the most notorious
malefactour that is to hold up his hand
at the barre of his iudgement. Nay it
is (as it were) a little god sitting in the
middle of mens hearts arraigning them
in this life as they shall be arraigned
for their offences at the tribunall seate
of the euerliuing god in the day of
iudgement. Wherefore the temporary
iudgement that is giuen by the conscience is nothing els but a beginning
or a fore-runner of the last iudgement'
(*Discourse*, 10). See also Wilks, 97.
200 **shall   despair** Observing   the
iambic stress on *shall*, Troughton
(96) emphasizes the degree to
which Richard commits himself to
despair and its inevitable extension
in self-destruction, ironically recalling
Richard's witty trifling about hanging
himself in 'despair' at 1.2.85.
200–3 **There . . . myself** Objecting
to Henry Irving's 1896 omission of
201–3, George Bernard Shaw imagines Richard should catch the 'sentimental cadence' in his voice in 200 and
awaken 'the mocker' in himself in 201
(Colley, 139).

196 perjury,] *Q1–2; om. Q3–6, F* highest] *Qq; F* (high'st*)* 197 Murder . . . murder] *Q1–5, F*
(*Murther . . . murther), Q6* direst] *Qq; F* (dyr'st*)* 199 Throng] *Q1–2;* Throng all *Q3–6, F* to
the bar] *Qq; F* (to'th'Barre*)* 201 will] *Q1–2;* shall *Q3–6, F*

And wherefore should they, since that I myself
Find in myself no pity to myself?
Methought the souls of all that I had murdered
Came to my tent, and every one did threat   205
Tomorrow's vengeance on the head of Richard.

Enter RATCLIFFE.

RATCLIFFE   My lord.

KING RICHARD   Zounds, who is there?

RATCLIFFE
Ratcliffe, my lord, 'tis I. The early village cock
Hath twice done salutation to the morn;   210
Your friends are up and buckle on their armour.

KING RICHARD
O Ratcliffe, I have dreamed a fearful dream!
What think'st thou, will our friends prove all true?

RATCLIFFE
No doubt, my lord.

KING RICHARD   O Ratcliffe, I fear, I fear.

RATCLIFFE
Nay, good my lord, be not afraid of shadows.   215

---

203 **pity** The last instance of this word in
the play comes appropriately and ironically from Richard, who rejects pity
(4.2.65; see also *3H6* 5.6.68), invokes it
in witty mockery (1.2.71), professes it
hypocritically (1.3.140) and performs
its outward semblance (2.2.24).

204–5 *Walton (*Copy*, 117–18) argues for
F's collation of MS here (and at 202 to
produce 'Nay').

208 William Winter describes Richard
Mansfield mistaking the entering
character 'for yet another apparition'
(Colley, 117).

*Zounds deleted from F in accord
with the Jacobean reform (cf. 1.4.84n.,
1.4.120, 3.7.218).

212–14 *Compositor's eye-skip from *O
Ratcliffe* (212) to Richard's next *O
Ratcliffe* (214) plausibly explains F's
omission. Ratcliffe's *shadows* (215)
refers to the dream mentioned in
the omitted lines (Smidt, *Memorial*,
19–20).

212–13 **fearful . . . true** ironic, given
Richard's admonishment concerning
the futility of *fearful commenting* at
4.3.51–2 (Churchill, 380–1).

202 And] *Qq;* Nay *F*   204 had] *Q1, F;* om. *Q2–6*   murdered] *Qq, F* (murtherd*),* *Johnson*
(*murder'd)*   205 Came] *Q1–2, F;* Came all *Q3–6*   206.1 RATCLIFFE] *Q1–2, 4–6, F;* Ratliffe
Q3   208 Zounds, who is] *Qq;* Who's *F*   there] *Q1–3, 5–6, F;* heare *Q4*   209 Ratcliffe] *Q1–2, 5–6,
F;* Ratliffe *Q3–4*   212–14 KING . . . lord.] *Qq;* om. *F*   214] *Steevens; Qq line* Lord. / feare. /

KING RICHARD

By the Apostle Paul, shadows tonight
Have struck more terror to the soul of Richard
Than can the substance of ten thousand soldiers
Armed in proof, and led by shallow Richmond.
'Tis not yet near day. Come, go with me.   220
Under our tents I'll play the eavesdropper,
To see if any mean to shrink from me.

Exeunt [F] *Richard and Ratcliffe* [F].

Enter the Lords *to Richmond* [F]*sitting in his tent* [F].

LORDS

Good morrow, Richmond.

RICHMOND

Cry mercy, lords and watchful gentlemen,

---

216 **Apostle Paul** Cf. 1.2.36, 41, 3.4.75.

216–18 **shadows . . . substance** Talbot claims that alone he constitutes but 'a shadow of himself', while his true self is corporately embodied in the 'substance' of his soldiers (*1H6* 2.3.61–2). Here, *shadows* of individual conscience appear stronger than armed forces.

218 **ten thousand** Cf. 'six or seven thousand' (10).

219 **Armed** armèd
     proof impenetrable armour, proof armour (*OED sb.* B II 10)
     shallow wanting in depth of mind or character (*OED a.* 6c)

221 **Under** The 'eavesdrop' is the space outside a house overhung by the roof (*OED sb.*); perhaps Richard speaks of standing beneath overhanging portions of tents, as in the tent 'fly'.
     eavesdropper F and Q1 share the same spelling; Q2–6 show remarkable variance: 'ease', 'euse' and 'eaues'

are equivalents (*OED* eaves 1a). The image of a king sneaking about and listening outside tents to ascertain the loyalty of his troops resembles but significantly differs from that of the disguised Henry V engaging his soldiers in discussion (*H5* 4.1). On parallels and contrasts between the two, see Potter. This skulking Richard contrasts with the bold master of circumstances of Act 1 (Ornstein, 73).

222.1 *sitting . . . tent* F makes it clear that Richmond sits in his tent when the lords enter; he will rise to greet them and proceed outside to deliver his oration.

223 SP *F is clearly wrong, and Q1–2 SPs are ambiguous; Q3–6's decisive plural seems preferable (see 226, 235). Richmond could be greeted with a collective *Good morrow* (*TxC*, 248).

224 **Cry mercy** i.e. I'm sorry (omitting pronouns; cf. 1.3.234).
     watchful wakeful (cf. 115)

---

220 day. Come] *F;* day come *Q1;* day, come *Q2–6*   221 eavesdropper] *F4;* ease dropper *Q1;* ewse dropper *Q2;* ewse-dropper *Q3;* eawse-dropper *Q4;* ewese-dropper *Q5–6;* Ease-dropper *F*   222 see] *Q1–2;* heare *Q3–6, F*   mean] *Q1–3, 5–6, F;* means *Q4*   SD *Ratcliffe*] *F (Ratliffe)*   223 SP] *Q1–2 (Lo[r].), 3–6; Richm. F*

That you have ta'en a tardy sluggard here.   225

LORD

How have you slept, my lord?

RICHMOND

The sweetest sleep and fairest-boding dreams
That ever entered in a drowsy head
Have I since your departure had, my lords.
Methought their souls whose bodies Richard murdered   230
Came to my tent and cried on victory.
I promise you my soul is very jocund
In the remembrance of so fair a dream.
How far into the morning is it, lords?

LORD

Upon the stroke of four.   235

RICHMOND

Why, then 'tis time to arm and give direction.

His oration to his soldiers.

More than I have said, loving countrymen,

225 **ta'en ... sluggard** i.e. caught a dila-
tory, lazy person; Richmond's apparent
ease contrasts with Richard's terrors
and with his pretence of nonchalance
at 3.4.23.
226 SP *Unlike the case of 223, Qq
are consistently ambiguous here. Any
lord from the group will do for the
speaker.
227–34 Thompson finds no chronicle
precedents for Richmond's dreams.
227 **fairest-boding** most auspicious
231 **cried on** invoked by outcry (*OED* cry
v. II 17); cf. *Ham* 5.2.348.
235 SP *See 223, 226; Q1–2's '*Lo.*'
remains ambiguous in Q3–6, F's
'*Lor.*' F4 first registers a clearly plural
'*Lords.*'

236 SD Holinshed heads Richmond's
speech with 'The oration of King
Henrie the sea*uenth to his armie*' (3.757)
and also gives a heading to Richard's
battlefield speech (cf. 313 SD). The
play's SDs appear uniquely (for
Shakespeare) aimed at the reader; Legge
similarly follows the sources (*Richardus
Tertius*, 4460, 4526); see p. 450. In
3H6, Margaret and Edward have similarly contrasting battlefield speeches
(5.4.67–82). Hall implies Richmond's
oratorical manner: 'mounted on a lyttel
hyll' before all his troops, 'he pawsed a
while, and after with a lowde voyce and
bolde spirite spake to his compaignions
these or lyke wordes folowyng' (*Richard
III*, fol. lv^r–v).

225 a] *Q1–3, 5–6, F; om. Q4* 226 SP] *Qq (Lo[r].); Lords. F* 227] *Qq; F lines* sleepe, /
Dreames, / fairest-boding] *Qq, F (fairest boding), hyphen Theobald* 229 departure] *Q2–6, F; Q1
(depature)* 230 murdered] *Qq, F (murtherd), Johnson (murder'd)* 232 soul] *Qq; Heart F* 235
SP] *Qq, F (Lo[r].)*

The leisure and enforcement of the time
Forbids to dwell upon. Yet remember this:
God, and our good cause, fight upon our side.   240
The prayers of holy saints and wronged souls,
Like high-reared bulwarks, stand before our faces.
Richard except, those whom we fight against
Had rather have us win than him they follow.
For, what is he they follow? Truly, gentlemen,   245
A bloody tyrant and a homicide;
One raised in blood, and one in blood established;
One that made means to come by what he hath,
And slaughtered those that were the means to help
  him;
A base foul stone, made precious by the foil   250
Of England's chair, where he is falsely set;
One that hath ever been God's enemy.
Then if you fight against God's enemy,
God will, in justice, ward you as His soldiers;
If you do sweat to put a tyrant down,   255

---

238 **leisure** i.e. lack of leisure (cf. 97)

241 **prayers . . . saints** This phrase is not from Hall or Holinshed, and the idea is controversial, since, according to mainstream Protestants, the only saints that could pray would be the living, not the departed (see 1.2.8n. on *lawful*, 4.4.75n. on *fiends . . . saints* and the Second Homily 'concerning Prayer', *Homilies*, 116–17). Shaheen cites Revelation, 5.8, describing the adoration of the Lamb of God, worshipped with 'the prayers of saintes', and 6.9–10, in which the martyrs cry out 'with a loude voyce, saying: howe long taryest thou Lorde, holy and true, to iudge and to auenge our blood'.
 wronged wrongèd

243 **except** excluded

247 **raised** i.e. elevated in status

248 **made means** cf. 40; here the meaning is sinister.

250 **foil** a thin layer of metal placed under a precious stone to increase its brilliancy or under some transparent substance to give it the appearance of a precious stone (*OED sb.*[1] 5a); cf. *R2* 1.3.265–7; *1H4* 1.2.204–5.

251 **chair** throne
 set i.e. as a jewel is set

252, 253 **God's enemy** perhaps suggesting Satan as 'the Enemy' (*OED sb.*1b)

254 **ward** protect

255 **sweat** labour; Hall and Holinshed agree on 'sweat': 'labour for your gayne, and swet for your right' (Hall, *Richard III*, fol. lxvi'); 'sweare' (Q3) misprints Q1–2's 'sweate'.

---

242 high-reared] *Qg, F (*high reard*), hyphen Pope* reared] *Q1–3, 5–6, F; read Q4* 243 Richard except,] *Q3–6; (Richard except) F; Richard, except Q1–2* 249 slaughtered] *Q1–3, 5–6, F; slandered Q4* 250 foil] *Q1–2; soile Q3–5; soyle Q6, F* 255 do sweat] *Q1–2; do sweare Q3–5, F; sweare Q6*

You sleep in peace, the tyrant being slain;
If you do fight against your country's foes,
Your country's fat shall pay your pains the hire.
If you do fight in safeguard of your wives,
Your wives shall welcome home the conquerors.   260
If you do free your children from the sword,
Your children's children quits it in your age.
Then in the name of God and all these rights,
Advance your standards, draw your willing swords.
For me, the ransom of my bold attempt   265
Shall be this cold corpse on the earth's cold face;
But if I thrive, the gain of my attempt
The least of you shall share his part thereof.
Sound drums and trumpets boldly and cheerfully.   269
God, and Saint George, Richmond, and victory!   [*Exeunt.*]

Enter KING RICHARD, RATCLIFFE *and Soldiers.*

258 **fat** wealth, surplus goods (cf. Genesis, 45.18: 'and ye shall eate the fat of the lande'). This biblical language euphemizes Richmond's promises of 'aboundance of riches and copie of profit' (Holinshed, 3.758) and avoids any hint of the greed that tarnished his later reputation as one who 'coveted to accumulate treasure' (Bacon, *Henry VII*, 262; cf. Chrimes, 207–18).
   pay . . . hire pay you the salary for your efforts
262 **quits** requites, repays (*OED v.* II 10; cf. 4.4.20, 64)
264 **Advance** raise, lift up (*OED v.* III 9; cf. 348 and *LLL* 4.3.341)
265–6 i.e. if defeated the only ransom I expect the enemy to be paid is my dead body; cf. Hall's account (with a verbal similarity to 1.1.12): 'you shall fynde me this daye, rather a dead carion vppon the coold grounde, then a fre prisoner on a carpet in a laydes cham-

ber' (*Richard III*, fol. lviᵛ).
265 **ransom** fee paid for release of a prisoner (*OED sb.* 2a), referring to the medieval practice of setting a pre-battle ransom price to be paid for oneself if captured (Mowat & Werstine; see *H5* 4.7.68)
267 Cf. Abbott, 417 for redundant noun clauses.
270 **Saint George** England's patron saint: 'all souldiers, entring into battaile . . . shall haue for their common crie and word, *S. George, S. George*, forward, or vpon them, *S. George*, whereby the souldier is much comforted, and the enemy dismaied' (Garrard, 47); cf. 349–50 and *H5* 3.1.34.
270.1 *F's addition of Catesby perhaps suggests influence (unusual in this portion of the play) of FMS, since Catesby neither speaks nor is spoken or referred to in the remainder of the scene (Walton, *Quarto*, 261).

270 SD] *Capell* 270.1 *and Soldiers*] *Ard²; Attendants, and Forces with them / Capell; &c. Qq; and Catesby F*

KING RICHARD

What said Northumberland, as touching Richmond?

RATCLIFFE

That he was never trained up in arms.

KING RICHARD

He said the truth. And what said Surrey then?

RATCLIFFE

He smiled and said, 'The better for our purpose.'   274

KING RICHARD

He was in the right, and so indeed it is.   *The clock striketh.*

Tell the clock there. Give me a calendar.

Who saw the sun today?

RATCLIFFE   Not I, my lord.

KING RICHARD

Then he disdains to shine, for by the book

He should have braved the east an hour ago.

A black day will it be to somebody.   280

Ratcliffe!

RATCLIFFE

My lord.

KING RICHARD   The sun will not be seen today.

271–5 This passage represents the meagre fruit of Richard's spying (see 220–2).

271 **Northumberland** cf. 68–71; Richard keeps a close eye on Northumberland, despite his going about *cheering up* the soldiers.

as touching concerning

272 **trained** trainèd

276 **Tell the clock** count the strokes of the clock (cf. 1.4.119)

calendar almanac (*OED sb.* 2)

278–87 The sun's absence seems to be Shakespeare's invention (possibly contradicting 86). Richmond 'had

the sonne at his backe and in the faces of his enemies' (Hall, *Richard III*, fol. lvi^v). The dying Richard of *True Tragedy* invokes tragic meteorology: 'you watry heauens rowle on my gloomy day, and darksome cloudes close vp my cheerful sownde, downe is thy sunne Richard, neuer to shine againe' (1989–91; Churchill, 521).

278 **book** i.e. the almanac requested in 276

279 **braved** adorned, made splendid (*OED v.* 5)

280 Cf. Dent, D88: 'To be a black day to somebody'.

---

275 so indeed] *Qq (so in deede Q1c (Hn, Fo), soin deede Q1u (BL)), F   SD] Qq opp. there. 276; Clocke strikes. F opp. there. 276   276] Pope; Qq, F line there. / to day? /   277] Steevens; Qq, F line day? / Lord. /   280–1 A . . . Ratcliffe] Johnson; one line Qq, F   280 somebody.] F; some bodie Qq   281 Ratcliffe!] Rat. Q1–5; Rat. Q6; Ratcliffe. F   282] Steevens; Qq, F line Lord. / day, /   not] Q2–6, F; nor Q1*

The sky doth frown and lour upon our army.
I would these dewy tears were from the ground.
Not shine today? Why, what is that to me   285
More than to Richmond? For the selfsame heaven
That frowns on me looks sadly upon him.

Enter NORFOLK.

NORFOLK

Arm, arm, my lord! The foe vaunts in the field.

KING RICHARD

Come, bustle, bustle. Caparison my horse.
– Call up Lord Stanley; bid him bring his power.   290
– I will lead forth my soldiers to the plain,
And thus my battle shall be ordered:
My foreward shall be drawn out all in length,

---

283 **lour** The 'clouds that loured upon
our house' (1.1.3) have returned.
284 **from** away from (cf. 3.5.32)
286–7 **selfsame . . . him** a perverse echo
of the Sermon on the Mount, where
Jesus spells out God's general providence: 'he maketh his sonne to aryse on
the euyll, and on the good, and sendeth
rayne on the iust, and on the vniust'
(Matthew, 5.45). Contrast Henry IV
concerning an ill-omened sky before
battle: 'with the losers let it sympa-
thize, / For nothing can seem foul to
those that win' (*1H4* 5.1.7–8). Cf. Dent,
S985: 'The sun shines upon all alike.'
288 **vaunts** boasts (*OED v.* 1)
289 **bustle, bustle** Cf. 1.1.152.
   Caparison put trappings on, deck,
harness (*OED v.*); a caparison was a
cloth or covering spread over the saddle or harness of a horse, often gaily
ornamented (*OED sb.*).
291–300 Richard, 'bringing all his men out
of their campe into the plaine, ordered
his fore-ward in a maruellous length,

in which he appointed both horsemen
and footmen . . . and in the fore-front
he placed the archers like a strong
fortristed trench or bulworke. Ouer
this battell was capteine, John duke of
Norfolke, with whome was Thomas
earle of Surrie, his sonne. After this
long vant-gard, followed king Richard
himselfe with a strong companie of
chosen and approued men of warre,
hauing horssemen for wings on both
sides of his battell' (Holinshed, 3.755;
Hall, *Richard III*, fols liii^v–liv^r).
291 **to the plain** i.e. into the field of
battle (*OED* plain *sb.*[1] 2, citing this
line), thus not necessarily describing
the topography of the battle site
292 **ordered** orderèd
293 **foreward** vanguard
   drawn . . . length i.e. stretched out
along a line; Richard attempted to
frighten the enemy by creating the
appearance of a great multitude of
soldiers (Hall, *Richard III*, fols liii^v–
liv^r; Holinshed, 3.755).

287 looks] *Q1–5, F;* looke *Q6*   287.1 NORFOLK.] *Qq (Norffolke. Q1c (Hn, Fo), Norffolke Q1u (BL)),
F*   293 out all] *Q1; om. Q2–6, F*

Consisting equally of horse and foot;
Our archers shall be placed in the midst.   295
John, Duke of Norfolk, Thomas, Earl of Surrey,
Shall have the leading of this foot and horse.
They thus directed, we will follow
In the main battle, whose puissance on either side
Shall be well winged with our chiefest horse.   300
This, and Saint George to boot. What think'st thou,
    Norfolk?

NORFOLK

A good direction, warlike sovereign.
    He sheweth him a paper.
This found I on my tent this morning:
'Jockey of Norfolk, be not so bold,
For Dickon thy master is bought and sold.'   305

---

294 **horse and foot** cavalry and infantry
295 **placed** placèd
298 **we** i.e. Richard
299–300 i.e. the main body of troops will be supported on either side by the best cavalry.
299 **battle** troop formation
    puissance power
300 **winged** wingèd; flanked with forces on the wings (*OED v.* II 9a)
301 **to boot** in addition, besides (*OED sb.* I 1); *OED* also cites this line as meaning 'Saint George to our help' (*OED sb.* II 7c).
302 **direction** battle plan (cf. 16)
304–5 *Since Capell many editors have had Richard read these lines; Wilson reasons that Norfolk would be incapable of reading such an insult aloud to his king. Cibber's Richard does the reading, providing Kemble with an opportunity to demonstrate calm contempt (actually only assumed for his troops) before striking the paper aside

with his sword (Colley, 49). Edmund Kean eyed Norfolk 'suspiciously for a moment, then reads it – strikes it to the ground scornfully with the blade of his sword' (Colley, 75).
304 **Jockey** diminutive of John, Norfolk's Christian name; Hall has 'Iack' (*Richard III*, fol. lvii'); Holinshed has 'Iacke'.
    *so Capell's emendation 'too' (cf. Q6's 'to') follows Hall and Holinshed.
305 **Dickon** diminutive of 'Dick' for Richard
    bought and sold perhaps 'betrayed for a bribe' (*OED* buy II 11b, citing this line), but 'tricked, deceived' is possible (Dent, B787: 'To be bought and sold'); cf. *1H6* 4.4.13 ('bought and sold Lord Talbot') and the insult to Ajax in *TC* 2.1.45–6 ('thou art bought and sold among those of any wit'), which implies being held in contempt. On Henry VII's later reputation and corruption, see 258n.

---

297 this] *Q1–2;* the *Q3–6, F* 299 main] *Q2–6, F;* matne *Q1* 301] *Qg;* F *lines* boote. / Norfolke. / boot] *Q3–6, F;* bootes *Q1–2* think'st] *Q1 (*thinkst*), F; Q2–6 (*thinkest*)* Norfolk?] *Q1, F;* Nor. *Q2–5;* not. *Q6* 302 SD] *Qq (opp. 302–3); om. F* 304] *Qq, F; Ric.* Jockey . . . *bold; [reads. / Capell* so] *Q1–5, F; to Q6*

KING RICHARD

A thing devised by the enemy.

– Go, gentlemen, every man unto his charge.

Let not our babbling dreams affright our souls.

Conscience is but a word that cowards use,

Devised at first to keep the strong in awe.   310

Our strong arms be our conscience, swords our law.

March on, join bravely, let us to it pell-mell,

If not to heaven, then hand in hand to hell.

His oration to his army.

What shall I say more than I have inferred?

---

306 **devised** devisèd

308 **our . . . dreams . . . our souls**
Richard's plurals suggest displacement of his personal dreams and anxieties onto his companions; cf. his plurals when speaking to Clarence (1.1.70). This rhetoric may be meant to appear inauspicious or even desperate, since he offers nothing more on behalf of communal purpose than the amoral precepts of 309–10. These cynical lines could hardly appeal to any but his most compromised followers, and he needs all the *gentlemen* on his side.

309–10 Richard's pronouncements derive from a discourse associated with the Machiavel; cf. Marlowe, *Jew of Malta* (Prol.14–27, 1.1.118–19) and pp. 8–10. This bold amorality contradicts Richard's 'oration' in the sources, which have him admitting his 'abhominable cryme', blaming others for his seduction and proclaiming his tearful penitence (Hall, *Richard III*, fol. liv^{r–v}; Holinshed, 3.756; and p. 63). Trust in the *strong arms* of human forces directly opposes the *powerful arm* of the Lord (1.4.216).

312 **join** meet in conflict (*OED* II 12)
pell-mell without keeping ranks, at

close quarters, hand to hand (*OED* 1c), but suggesting headlong disorder and hurry, recklessly (*OED* 3)

313 Cf. Richard's threat to Young Clifford: 'If not in heaven, you'll surely sup in hell' (*2H6* 5.1.216).

314–41 Wilson notes an abrupt change from Richard's lines urging *pell-mell* combat to the deliberate form of his oration; though *inferred* suggests continuity of utterance. Richmond, by contrast, progresses by orderly degrees from sweet dreams to an oration expanding upon the *prayers* from *wronged souls* heard in those dreams (227–42). If 309–13 are addressed to *gentlemen* (307) and this oration is directed *to his army*, Richard may again be differentiating values assumed to appeal to one audience or another; Richmond's utterances, by contrast, are more generally of a piece (but see 5.2.23–4n.). Richard's oration, like that of Richmond, is sometimes directed to the theatre audience. The SD derives from Hall and Holinshed, but both record the oration as directed '*to the chiefteins of his armie*' (Holinshed, 3.755).

Along with his silence concerning his sins (see 309–10), Shakespeare's

---

306 SP] *Qq, F (King[.])*; *Richard continues, Capell*   307 unto] *Qq;* to *F*   309 Conscience] *Qq;* For conscience *F*   but] *Q1–2; om. Q3–6, F*   310 at] *Q1–4, F;* as *Q5–6*   312 to it] *Q1–2; Q3–6 (*too it*),* *F (*too't*)*   313 SD] *Qq; om. F*

Remember whom you are to cope withal,   315
A sort of vagabonds, rascals and runaways,
A scum of Bretons and base lackey peasants,
Whom their o'ercloyed country vomits forth
To desperate adventures and assured destruction.
You sleeping safe, they bring to you unrest;   320
You having lands and blessed with beauteous wives,
They would restrain the one, distain the other.
And who doth lead them but a paltry fellow?
Long kept in Bretagne at our mother's cost,

Richard also fails to mention his years of good rule, omitting a prominent element in Hall and Holinshed's versions of this speech (cf. Courtenay, 2.114).

314 inferred alleged or reported (*OED* 2), carrying specific associations with oratory (see 3.5.75, 3.7.12, 3.7.32, 4.4.343); cf. *3H6* 2.2.43–4: 'Clifford played the orator, / Inferring arguments of mighty force.'

315 cope encounter, contend, fight (*OED v.²* II 2)

316 sort band, company, group, or set of persons (*OED sb.²* II 17a); given the class-based references to *vagabonds* and *base lackey peasants* (which lack precise equivalents in Hall or Holinshed), also suggesting a group distinguished by social stratum (cf. 'the vulgar sort', *1H6* 3.2.4).

vagabonds vagrants who wander without fixed abodes, but also referring to those lacking regular occupation or obvious means of support and so assumed to be idle loafers (*OED sb.* B 1a); cf. the punishment described in 327–9. Hall and Holinshed have Richard call his enemies 'traytors, thefes, outlawes and ronnegates of our awne nacion' and 'beggerly Britons & faynt harted Frenchmen' (Hall, *Richard III*, fol. liv˅). Richard's assessment may have some historical validity (Chrimes, 40).

317 scum of Bretons Richard's rhetorical xenophobia might appeal to what Ian Archer (30–1) calls 'the most basic element of the political consciousness of Londoners . . . a hatred of "all sorts of strangers"'; such discourse was especially incendiary in the volatile years 1586–93. Hall's Richard characterizes the enemy as 'effeminate & lasciuious' (Hall, *Richard III*, fol. lvʳ; Holinshed, 3.756).

lackey camp follower, hanger-on (*OED sb.* 2), also one who is servilely obsequious (*OED sb.* 1a)

318 o'ercloyed o'ercloyèd; oversatiated (*OED*)

322 restrain withhold, keep back (*OED v.¹* 4a)

distain defile, dishonour (*OED v.* 2)

324 mother's Shakespeare follows Holinshed's 1587 edition which mistakenly prints 'brought up by my moothers meanes' instead of the correct reading – 'my brothers meanes' – which appears in Hall and in Holinshed's first edition and refers to Richmond's support by Charles, Duke of Burgundy, Richard's brother-in-law (see 1.4.10n.). On the felicity of the misprint for Shakespeare's conception of Richard, see Willis, *Nurture*, 204; cf. p. 459.

317 Bretons] *Qq, F* (Brittain/e/s), *Capell*   lackey] *Q1–5, F;* lackey *Q6*   320 to you] *Q1;* you to *Q2–6, F*   321 blessed] *Qq, F* (blest)   wives] *Q2–6, F;* wifes *Q1*   324 Bretagne] *Qq, F* (Brit/t/aine), *Theobald*

A milksop, one that never in his life   325
Felt so much cold as over shoes in snow.
Let's whip these stragglers o'er the seas again,
Lash hence these overweening rags of France,
These famished beggars, weary of their lives,
Who, but for dreaming on this fond exploit,   330
For want of means, poor rats, had hanged themselves.
If we be conquered, let men conquer us,
And not these bastard Bretons, whom our fathers
Have in their own land beaten, bobbed and thumped,
And in record left them the heirs of shame.   335
Shall these enjoy our lands? Lie with our wives?
Ravish our daughters?   *Drum afar off.*[F]
Hark, I hear their drum.
Fight, gentlemen of England! – Fight, bold yeomen!

325 **milksop** from Hall and Holinshed; cf. *1H4* 2.3.31.
326 **over shoes** i.e. the cold felt when snow comes in over one's shoes; proverbial for 'to be deeply immersed in something' (Tilley, Dent, S380), cf. *TGV* 1.1.24. The point is to evoke a minor discomfort.
327–9 The punishment prescribed by the Elizabethan statutes against vagabonds is whipping and return to their place of origin (see Carroll).
328 **overweening rags** Richard's metonymic figure (reminiscent of *usurping helmets* in 112), displaces the self-assertive ambition and financial dependency of Richmond onto tattered garments which stand for the men who allegedly wear them; cf. *rag of honour* (1.3.232).
330 **but . . . on** i.e. if they had not had the consolation of their fantasies about
fond foolish

331 **want of means** lack of the means for survival
333–5 Richard alludes to victories over the French by Edward III, the Black Prince and Henry V during the Hundred Years' War.
333 **bastard** not in Hall or Holinshed's accounts
334 **bobbed** beaten with a fist (*OED v.*[2] 1)
335 **record** recòrd; i.e. historical account (cf. 3.1.72, 4.4.28)
336–7 **Lie with . . . Ravish** This play and *H5* are the only Shakespearean history plays to associate rape with military invasion and to represent marriage as a desired conclusion of the action (Howard & Rackin, 198). *E3* 3.2 (not always attributed to Shakespeare) makes the same association.
338 **yeomen** freeholders under the rank of gentlemen (*OED* II 4a), usually taken to form the bulk of English foot-soldiers (*OED* II 5a)

325 milksop] *Q6, F;* milkesopt *Q1–5* 333 Bretons] *Qq, F* (Brit/t/ain/e/s), *Capell* 335 in] *Q1–2;* on *Q3–6, F* 336 lands?] *F;* lands, *Q1–3, 5–6;* land? *Q4* 337] *Qq; F lines* daughters? / Drumme, / 338 Fight, gentlemen] *Q1–2* (Fight gentlemen); Right Gentlemen *Q3–6, F* bold] *Q1;* boldly *Q2–6, F*

– Draw, archers, draw your arrows to the head!
– Spur your proud horses hard and ride in blood.   340
Amaze the welkin with your broken staves.

^F*Enter a* Messenger.^F

– What says Lord Stanley? Will he bring his power?
MESSENGER
My lord, he doth deny to come.
KING RICHARD   Off with his son George's head!
NORFOLK
My lord, the enemy is past the marsh: 345
After the battle let George Stanley die.
KING RICHARD
A thousand hearts are great within my bosom.
Advance our standards! Set upon our foes!
Our ancient word of courage, fair Saint George,
Inspire us with the spleen of fiery dragons.   350
Upon them! Victory sits on our helms.   *Exeunt.*

---

339 **draw ... head** i.e. pull your bow-
string till the arrow's head touches the
bow (*OED* draw *v.* 9)
340 **in blood** in full vigour of pursuit, as
dogs after game in a hunt (*OED* blood
sb. 7), and literally through the blood
shed on the field of battle
341 perhaps recalling 'shivered Launces
darke the troubled aire' (Kyd, *Spanish
Tragedy*, 1.2.54); cf. *KJ* 5.2.172; *Cor*
4.5.111–12.
welkin sky
staves lance shafts (see 65)
341.1 **Messenger** At 59–60 Richard
orders that a *pursuivant-at-arms* be
sent by Catesby to check on Stanley;
this SD appears only in F, but F, Qq
agree on the SP for 343.
343 **deny** refuse
344 This abrupt order might have sug-

gested Cibber's famous addition after
4.4.531: '*Off with his head. So much for
Buckingham*' (Thompson).
345 **marsh** 'Betweene both armies was a
great marish' (Holinshed, 3.758).
349 **word of courage** phrase, utterance
(*OED sb.* 10) urging courage (cf. 270)
349–50 **Saint   George ... dragons**
Richard asks that his troops be inspired
with the fury of the beast that was
vanquished by the saint; contrast 270
(Clemen, 230). On the apocalyptic
overtones throughout this act, and the
dragon to be overcome in the end of
days, see E. Berry, 101; cf. Revelation,
12, 19.
350 **spleen** courage, resolute mind (*OED
sb.* 5 a); cf. *KJ* 2.1.68: 'fierce dragons'
spleens'.
351 Cf. 79.

351 them! Victory] *Pope;* them victorie *Q1;* them, victorie *Q2–6,* F   helms] *Q1–2, 4;* helpes *Q3, 5–6,*
F   SD] *Q1–2; om. Q3–6,* F

[5.4] *Alarum, excursions. Enter* [NORFOLK *with Soldiers, and*] CATESBY.

CATESBY

Rescue, my lord of Norfolk. Rescue, rescue!

The King enacts more wonders than a man,

Daring an opposite to every danger.

His horse is slain, and all on foot he fights,

Seeking for Richmond in the throat of death.   5

Rescue, fair lord, or else the day is lost.

[*Exeunt Norfolk and Soldiers.*]

^F*Alarums.*^F *Enter* [KING] RICHARD.

KING RICHARD

A horse, a horse, my kingdom for a horse!

CATESBY

Withdraw, my lord. I'll help you to a horse.

KING RICHARD

Slave, I have set my life upon a cast,

And I will stand the hazard of the die.   10

5.4 Location: the action continues at Bosworth Field.

0.1 *Alarum* call to arms (cf. 1.1.7)

excursions sorties (*OED sb.* 3; cf. alarm *sb.* 4)

NORFOLK *with Soldiers* Norfolk is urged to provide rescue, a demand necessitating forces to assist him. Catesby could call to Norfolk and men offstage; however, 2–5 appear to be addressed to someone, unless, as Jowett suggests, they are soliloquy.

2–4 Hall and Holinshed follow Vergil, who describes Richard fighting fiercely and charging directly at Richmond (Vergil, 224; Hall, *Richard III*, fol.

lvii^r), but not as losing his horse; cf. 7n.

2 **than a man** i.e. than are humanly possible

3 i.e. challenging any adversary who presents himself to face every risk of mortal combat

opposite opponent, adversary (*OED sb.* B 3; cf. *TN* 3.4.266)

7 Frequently echoed and parodied (Var) and still an acting 'point' (Hankey, 246n.). For relation to *True Tragedy*, Hall and Holinshed, see p. 77.

9 **cast** throw of the dice (*OED sb.* 3a)

10 **stand . . . die** endure the risk entailed in the roll of the die

---

5.4] *Capell*   0.1–2 NORFOLK . . . *and*] *Capell subst.*   1] *Qq; F lines* Norfolke, / Rescue, Rescue: / 3 an] *Q1–7, F;* and *Q8*   6 SD] *Ard²*   6.1 KING] *Rowe*   7+ SP] *Qq (King[.]);* Rich. *F*   10 die] *Q1–2, 7–8;* dye *Q3, 5–6, F;* day *Q4*

I think there be six Richmonds in the field;
Five have I slain today instead of him.
A horse, a horse, my kingdom for a horse!   [*Exeunt.*]

[**5.5**]   *Alarum, Enter* [KING] RICHARD *and* RICHMOND*;*
            they fight. Richard is slain. Then retreat being
            sounded, [*exit Richmond, and Richard's body is*
            removed.] ᶠ*Flourish.*ᶠ *Enter Richmond,* [STANLEY,
            Earl of] Derby, *bearing the crown, with other*
                              Lords and Soldiers.

RICHMOND

God and your arms be praised, victorious friends:
The day is ours; the bloody dog is dead.

11–12 The sources mention no doubles
and claim that Richard instantly recognized Richmond (Hall, *Richard III*,
fol. lvii^r, following Vergil, 224). The
doubling may come from Henry IV
(Holinshed, 3.523); cf. *1H4* 5.3.1–28.
5.5 Location: the action continues at
Bosworth Field. On scene divisions in
battle sequences involving flourishes,
see G. Williams.
0.2 *Richard is slain* The only onstage
death occurs silently. Vergil reports that
Richard died 'fyghting manfully in the
thickkest presse of his enemyes', and
John Rous claims that he 'defended
himself as a noble knight with great
courage to his last breath' (Vergil, 224;
cf. Michael Jones, 'Richard III as a soldier', in Gillingham, 112). Hall describes
Richard overthrowing Richmond's
standard and slaying its bearer, Sir
William Brandon, overthrowing Sir
John Cheyney, 'a man of great force &
strength', and proceeding 'by dent of
swerde' to Richmond, who 'kept hym at
the swerdes poincte without auantage'
a long time until 'sodainly' Stanley and
his three thousand 'tall men' entered

the fray, causing Richard's men to flee
'and he him selfe manfully fyghtynge
in the mydell of his enemies' to be
slain (*Richard III*, fol. lvii^r–v; Holinshed,
3.759). Cibber's Richard gets a stirring
final speech. Kean's Richard 'fought like
one drunk with wounds . . . as if his will
could not be disarmed' (Hazlitt, 5.182).
Irving's 1896 Richard, by contrast, died
from repeated stabbings by Richmond
while surrounded by Richmond's soldiers. More recent productions have
often emphasized similarities in the two
combatants rather than heroism in either
(Colley, 5).
0.3–4 *exit . . . removed* Since Richmond
re-enters with Stanley, who bears
Richard's crown from the site of his
death, they enter to a different fictional
location than that of the killing (Dyce);
Richard's corpse would therefore have
been removed. The phrase *this bloody
wretch* (5) does not demand presence
(cf. 5.2.10, 18).
2 **bloody . . . dead** Richmond's phrase
fulfils Margaret's and the Duchess of
York's curses (4.4.78, 195); cf. Willis,
Nurture, 202.

13 SD] *Theobald*   **5.5**] *Dyce*   0.1 KING] *Rowe*   0.2–3 *Then . . . sounded*] *Qq; Retreat, and Flourish.* F   0.3–4
exit . . . removed] *Ard²* subst.   0.4–5 STANLEY, Earl of] *Pope subst.*   0.5 Derby] *Qq (Darby), F other*] *Qq;
diuers other* F   0.6 *and Soldiers*] *Ard²; &c. Q1–2; om. Q3–6,* F   1] *Qq;* F *lines* Armes / Friends; /

STANLEY

   Courageous Richmond, well hast thou acquit thee.

   [*Presents the crown.*] Lo, here this long-usurped royalty

   From the dead temples of this bloody wretch   5

   Have I plucked off to grace thy brows withal.

   Wear it, enjoy it and make much of it.

RICHMOND

   Great God of heaven, say amen to all.

   But tell me, is young George Stanley living?

STANLEY

   He is, my lord, and safe in Leicester town,   10

   Whither, if it please you, we may now withdraw us.

RICHMOND

   What men of name are slain on either side?

^FSTANLEY^F

   John, Duke of Norfolk, Walter, Lord Ferrers,

   Sir Robert Brakenbury and Sir William Brandon.

---

3 **acquit** i.e. acquitted (cf. Abbott, 342); discharged the duties of your position (*OED v.* II 13)

4 **SD** Sources have Stanley crown Richmond in response to the cry 'King Henry', 'as though' being 'elected' through acclamation 'by the voyce of the people' (Hall, *Richard III*, fol. lviii^v; Holinshed, 3.760; following Vergil, 226). *True Tragedy* has Stanley tell Richmond 'the Peeres by full consent, in that thou hast freed them from a tyrants yoke, haue by election chosen thee as King' (2087–9). Shakespeare avoids such 'election' by putting Henry to God's approval (8, 41), not that of 'the people' (but see 22). On Stanley as political subject, see Gurr, 'Democratic'.

4 **royalty** the crown (*OED* 5b; cf. *1H4*

4.3.57); Bacon calls it 'a crown of ornament' (*Henry VII*, 70). Carrying the crown into battle was taken by some as signifying leadership (C.A.J. Armstrong, 72), but Vergil interprets it as symbolizing Richard's having staked everything on the battle (Vergil, 225).

6 **withal** with

12 **name** rank or reputation (*OED sb.* 7a, b)

13 **Norfolk** For the irony of Norfolk's death despite his warning, see 5.3.304–5 (cf. Hall, *Richard III*, fol. lvii^v; Holinshed 3.759). Hall and Holinshed praise Norfolk's loyalty as a subject and his faithfulness to his oath of allegiance, but Holinshed reflects on the questionable value of service rendered to a tyrant.

3+ SP] *Pope; Dar. Qq; Der. F* 3–4] *Qq; F lines* Richmond, / Loe, / Royalties, / 4 SD] *Ard²
subst.* this] *Qq;* these *F* royalty] *Q1;* roialties *Q2–6, F* 7 enjoy it] *Q1–2; om. Q3–6, F* 11
Whither] *Q1* (Whether*), Q2–6, F* if . . . you] *Qq;* if you please *F* now] *Qq; om. F* 13–14] *F; Q1
lines* sir / Brandon. / ; *Q2–6 line* Robert / Brandon. / 13 SP] *F* (*Der.*) Walter] *Q1–5* (Water*), Q6,
F* Ferrers] *Qq, F* (Ferris*), Capell* 14 Brakenbury] *Qq, F* (Bro[o]kenbury*), F4*

RICHMOND

Inter their bodies as become their births. 15

Proclaim a pardon to the soldiers fled

That in submission will return to us;

And then, as we have ta'en the sacrament,

We will unite the white rose and the red.

Smile heaven upon this fair conjunction, 20

That long have frowned upon their enmity.

What traitor hears me and says not amen?

England hath long been mad and scarred herself:

The brother blindly shed the brother's blood;

The father rashly slaughtered his own son; 25

The son, compelled, been butcher to the sire.

All this divided York and Lancaster,

Divided in their dire division.

O, now let Richmond and Elizabeth,

---

15 **as . . . births** i.e. according to their ranks

18 **we** unambiguous royal plural
ta'en the sacrament promised upon an oath sealed with the Eucharist (cf. 1.4.202–3 and Hall, *Richard III*, fol. xliᵛ).

19 **white . . . red** the houses of York and Lancaster

20 **Smile heaven** i.e. may heaven smile
conjunction union (with marital and astrological senses)

22 Cf. the coerced *Amen* at 3.7.240; the soldiers may respond. One wonders about early theatre audiences, since failing to say 'Amen' to this announcement of the Tudor regime could mark one as a *traitor* by Richmond's formula.

22, 35, 39 **traitor, traitors, treason** Historically, Richard and a few supporters were convicted and attainted

as traitors for high treason – as of the day of this battle – against the 'rightful king'. This proceeding caused some parliament members to wonder what kind of loyalty this precedent would inspire in future subjects on the day of battle (Chrimes, 63).

23–4 Cf. 2.4.63–4.

25–6 Cf. *3H6* 2.5.

27–8 Much discussed (see Var): Wells and Taylor substitute 'United' for *Divided*; Jowett proposes 'Deformèd'. However, 23–6 evoke the ways that England has been *Divided* (faction against faction, brother against brother, generation against generation) by the two 'divided houses'. All divisions are blamed on the effect and example of the two warring houses. This recalls Hall's Introduction, though the play has largely concentrated on Richard's violence against his own house and faction.

15 Inter] *Q1–4, F;* Enter *Q5–6*   17 to] *Q1–5, F; om. Q6*   21 have] *Q1–5, F;* hath *Q6*

The true succeeders of each royal house,   30
By God's fair ordinance conjoin together;
And let their heirs, God, if Thy will be so,
Enrich the time to come with smooth-faced peace,
With smiling plenty and fair prosperous days.
Abate the edge of traitors, gracious Lord,   35
That would reduce these bloody days again
And make poor England weep in streams of blood.
Let them not live to taste this land's increase

---

30 **true succeeders** rightful heirs; a Tudor commonplace, but hardly self-evident. For all the complex, inter-related claims and claimants, see M. Levine, 15–16. Chrimes (50) argues that 'There is no evidence of much if any overt discussion at the time. It was taken for granted that Henry was the male heir of the house of Lancaster through his mother Margaret Beaufort, whose own claims as heiress were ignored. The God of battles had confirmed such hereditary right as existed, and acclamation on the field itself rounded off the traditional procedure for attainment of the throne'. The genealogical issues remained interesting in Shakespeare's day; cf. Bacon's discussion of the inconveniences resulting from Henry's opportunism and limited foresight in these matters, as well as his determination to 'depress' the line of York (*Henry VII*, 69–71). Even before leaving for London following the battle, Richmond ordered Clarence's son detained in the Tower, where he remained until his execution in 1499 for supposed involvement in the Perkin Warbeck plot. Among those eliminated by Henry as king would also be William Stanley, who some identified as the presenter of the crown at Bosworth (Bacon, *Henry VII*, 70). Henry Peacham (65) reflects how William Stanley 'was shortly after beheaded for treason, albeit he set the

Crowne (found throwne in a haw-thorne bush) upon the kings head in the field'.

31 **ordinance** that which is ordained or decreed by God (*OED sb.* 5b); cf. 4.4.184.

32 *their Q3–F's 'thy', addressing God, emphasizes divine approval. *True Tragedy* and *Richardus Tertius* spe-cify Elizabeth I (granddaughter of Richmond and Elizabeth) as the heir anticipated. By contrast, when James I invokes divine favour in a March 1603 speech to Parliament, both Elizabeths virtually disappear from his patrilin-eal account of England 'first setled and vnited in [Richmond] . . . now reunited and confirmed in me, being iustly and lineally descended, not onely of that happie coniunction, but of both the Branches thereof many times before' (James I, 271; Hodgdon, *End*, 103).

33 **smooth-faced peace** contrast *Grim-visaged War* attempting to [*smooth*] *his wrinkled front* (1.1.9).

35 **Abate . . . edge** literally to turn back or blunt the swords (of traitors) (*OED* abate *v.*[1] III 8), but figuratively to take away the aggressive *edge* of their tongues (*OED* edge *sb.* 2a, citing this line) and dulling their ardour (*OED* edge *sb.* 2b); see 4.4.229n.

36 **reduce** bring back (cf. 2.2.68)

38 **increase** prosperity, especially that which grows from the earth (*OED sb.* II 7a; cf. *Son* 97)

---

32 their] *Q1–2;* thy *Q3–6, F*   Thy] *Q1–4, F;* they *Q5–6*

That would with treason wound this fair land's peace.
Now civil wounds are stopped; peace lives again.   40
That she may long live here, God say amen.   [F]*Exeunt.*[F]

FINIS

---

40 **stopped** stanched, as in preventing the bleeding of a wound (*OED v.* 6)   41 **God say** may God say

41 here] *Q1–3, 5–6 (*heare*), Q4, F*

APPENDIX 1

THE TEXTS OF *RICHARD III*

Richard III exists in two substantive texts: the First Quarto (Q1), printed in 1597, and the First Folio (F), printed in 1623. If either version had survived only by itself, there would be no doubt about its being, as the Second Quarto (Q2, 1598) claims, '*By* William Shake-speare'. Even if Q1 and F were completely independent of one another, there might be questions about which to prefer. However, the two texts are materially and temporally interrelated in complex ways. Q1 was printed from a high-quality manuscript (QMS) of uncertain nature provided by Shakespeare's acting company, the Lord Chamberlain's Men. Twenty-six years later, F was printed from copy that incorporated at least one (Q3, 1602) and probably more than one of the quartos derived from Q1 (Q3, and Q6, 1622), along with accumulated reprinting errors, while also referring to another, different but highly authoritative manuscript (FMS). Furthermore, FMS, employed in the 1623 Folio, appears to represent an earlier state than QMS, the source for 1597 Q1. The hypothetical stemma is:

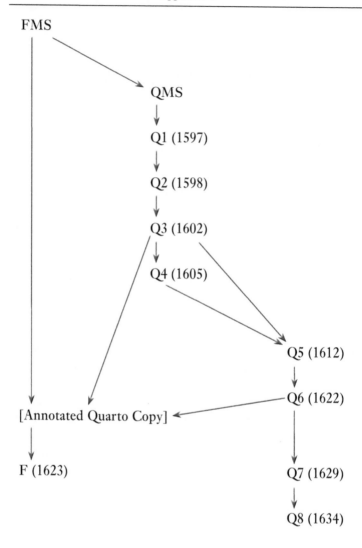

In sum, 'the versions of *Richard III* crisscross: the first printed version, almost all scholars agree, provides a second state of the play, and later printings of this second state, in turn, influenced the printing of the play in the first state' (Mowat &

Werstine, xlvii–xlviii; cf. *TxC*, 230). Neither manuscript (QMS or FMS) has survived, but the two substantive printed texts (Q1 and F) are of very high quality and are, depending on one's angle of vision, either very much alike or strikingly different.[1]

Quarto and Folio *Richard III* are identical for a sixth of the play. From 3.1.1 to 3.1.166 and from 5.3.49 to the end of the play, F simply reprints Q3.[2] For the other five-sixths of the play, the degree of difference varies according to the standard of measurement applied. Statistically, F is about 180 lines longer than Q1, while Q1 contains just under forty lines not in F, including one extended passage of some twenty lines (Smidt, *King Richard*, 7–8). Nevertheless, so much remains roughly the same that E.K. Chambers could claim, with only slight exaggeration, that 'in the main the texts agree in arrangement, speech for speech, and even line for line' (Chambers, *Shakespeare*, 1.297). Theatrically, Peter Davison claims that modern audiences would be unlikely to detect which version had provided the basis for a production (Davison, 5). Nonetheless, differences in word choices, stage directions, lineation, punctuation, spelling and roles are pervasive and serious, so that, for the editor (or the actor), discrepancies run into very high numbers (Hammond, 2).

Since both Q1 and F are by all recent accounts 'Shakespearean' in language, dramatic form and origin, and since they are at times identical word for word while elsewhere closely related but different, several narratives have been constructed to account for the differences. These narratives advance or limit the claims of either text's 'authority'. The vast majority of editions have accepted F; this preference is understandable. F is more regular metrically; many accounts judge Q1's linguistic variants to lack

1 Q1 *Richard III* has never been entirely relegated to 'bad' quarto status, even W.W. Greg finding it 'doubtful' (Kathleen O. Irace, *Reforming the 'Bad' Quartos: Performance and Provenance of Six Shakespearean First Editions* (Newark, Del., 1998), 17, citing Greg, *Problem*, 76–87). Gary Taylor calls it 'far and away the best – that is, the most accurate and most complete – of the bad quartos' (Gary Taylor, 'Copy-text and collation (with special reference to *Richard III*)', *The Library*, series 6, 3 (1981), 33–42, 34n.).
2 R. Koppel first pointed this out in 1877 (Walton, *Copy*, 11).

the precision, force or design of F's alternatives. Almost all agree that Q1 confuses or misallocates roles that F assigns correctly.[1] Q1 has had modern champions: the Cambridge Shakespeare (1864) accepted Q1 as its basis, as did the Eversley (1900) and New Temple (1935) editions. However, the Oxford Shakespeare (1904) and the Arden first series (1907) were based on F, and with the rise of the new bibliography opinion ran against Q1. Building on W.W. Greg, E.K. Chambers and Peter Alexander, D.L. Patrick argued that the manuscript behind Q1 amounted to a 'memorial reconstruction' by the play's first performers. Some designated Q1 a 'bad' quarto, though it was admittedly awfully 'good' to be called 'bad'.[2]

Such assessment of Q1 determined the editorial procedures of the New Cambridge (1954), Riverside (1974), Scott Foresman (1980) and Arden second series (1981) editions. More recently, questions about new bibliographic assumptions and about 'bad quartos' and 'memorial reconstructions' have had positive effects.[3] *Richard III* has appeared in two series of Shakespeare's quartos – Peter Davison's New Cambridge (1996) and John Drakakis's Harvester/Wheatsheaf (1996) editions – and Q1 provides the basic text for the Oxford Shakespeare single-volume *Richard III*, edited by John Jowett (2000). Jowett argues Q1's authority on the basis of its 'theatrical' nature (Jowett, 127), usefully reversing previous denigration of Q1 for 'contamination' by stage practice. However, such arguments also support a traditional critical binary between the 'authorial' (F being closer to Shakespeare's holograph) and the 'theatrical' (Q1 closer to a playbook, exhibiting effects originating with 'the actors').[4] A variant of this narrative claims that Q1 incorporates 'revision',

---

1 On metre, see Hammond, 3; 'loss of force', Davison, 7; 'higher literary quality', Lull, 210–11; 'more compact, more metrical, more meaningful, more crafted', *TxC*, 229; role misallocation, Mowat & Werstine, xlix.

2 See Patrick; Chambers, *Shakespeare*; W.W. Greg, *Two Elizabethan Stage Abridgements* (Oxford, 1922); Peter Alexander, *Shakespeare's Henry VI and Richard III* (Cambridge, 1929).

3 For critique of new bibliographic assumptions, see Maguire.

4 Q1 is 'based on a memorial reconstruction of a lost prompt-book' (Davison, 49); Q1 is based on a 'communal reconstruction' (*TxC*, 229).

and represents Shakespeare's alternative draft (Urkowitz), the work of an 'adapting theatrical scribe, with some contribution from Shakespeare as reviser' (Jowett, 127), or 'revision by a playwright' (Holland, xliii).

Each claim deserves consideration, but given the limits of what we know, no argument for superior 'authority' can be entirely consistent. Too many factors pull in different directions. The five-sixths of F not simply reprinted from Q3 appears to be based on a manuscript that precedes Q1 and from which Q1 is derivative. Q1 is shorter, and certain roles suggest adaptation for performance economy; however, F omits one extended passage and shows cutting elsewhere (Smidt, *Impostors*, 25). Q1 has more non-metrical lines, but F contains verses that are as padded, jumbled and repetitious as some of those in the earlier text (Smidt, *Memorial*, 20; Lull, 212). Sometimes F more closely follows the sources; at other times Q1 can claim closer proximity to them.

In theory, there could be warrant for distinct 'Folio-based' and 'Quarto-based' editions. In practice, recent editions have demonstrated the practical necessity for employing elements from *both* early texts. Even in an age suspicious of 'conflated' editions, the interdependence of Q and F *Richard III* makes its own case. The two New Cambridge editions, based on Q1 (Davison) and F (Lull), include words and entire lines from their alternative texts, as does the Oxford edition based on Q1 (Jowett). Purists may argue that any emendation from an alternative basic text constitutes 'conflation', but instead of textual purity perhaps we need a richer sense of early playtexts in their various manifestations as raw material for acting companies, or even as 'literary' works potentially imagined for readers.

No single theory efficiently accounts for everything about the two early texts or their relationships, nor does any available justification provide sufficient grounds for ignoring the other version when difficulties arise in the basic text. This edition incorporates substantive variants from both Q and F, while joining the overwhelming editorial majority in generally deferring to

421

F as its basic text for portions of the play where F does not simply reprint uncorrected quarto copy. Where F directly reprints Q3 – mistakes and all – then Q1, the only authoritative quarto, becomes the basic text. Furthermore, since F itself appears to be, even when not simply reprinting quarto copy, already a composite text, based on the printer's consultation of manuscript (FMS) and printed copy from Q3 and Q6, and therefore subject to printers' mistakes and interventions in any and all of six quartos, efforts have been made to trace all substantial variants that might have influenced F.[1] This has meant tracking variants in *any* of the six quartos that precede F. Each page records textual variations so readers may evaluate editorial decisions. Superscript markings (^FF and ^QQ) appear whenever a reading is adopted that has no equivalent in the basic text. The goal is a *Richard III* that is both readable and easy to evaluate. You should enjoy Shakespeare, the range of Shakespeare that the various texts provide, but know when you are reading 'Shakespeare' of 1597, 'Shakespeare' of 1623, Pope's 'Shakespeare' of 1725, that of Steevens in 1793 or Siemon in 2009.

THE FIRST QUARTO (Q1), 1597

On 20 October 1597 the Stationers recorded the relevant legal data for what would become the first printed version of *Richard III*: 'Andrewe wise / Entred for his copie vnder th[e h]andes of master BARLOWE, and master warden man. / *The tragedie of kinge RICHARD the THIRD with the death of the Duke of CLARENCE.*' (Arber, 3.25). Andrew Wise, the would-be publisher, fulfilled several legal requirements, each involving a fee. The playtext had been examined by the ecclesiastical authorities (ultimately the Bishop of London or the Archbishop of Canterbury, here represented by Archbishop John Whitgift's Chaplain, William Barlow),

---

1 Turned or dropped letters, fount and case changes, non–syllabic contracted spellings without metric implication and inconsequential spelling variants are uncollated, except in special cases.

who oversaw 'allowance' of any printed book, at least in theory, and probably of any potentially controversial publication, such as works dealing with English history (Blayney, 'Publication', 397). The text was 'licensed' by the Stationers' Company, under its Warden, Thomas Man, giving Wise rights of 'copy'. Thereafter, no one might publish any work – for instance a different version of this or a similar play based on Richard's reign – that might be judged to infringe upon Wise's ability to dispose of his printed copies for sale (Blayney, 'Publication', 399). Licensing also meant that the Stationers did not believe that *Richard III* might negatively affect sales of recently printed similar works, such as *The True Tragedy of Richard III* (entered and licensed on 19 June 1594 and published by Thomas Creede).[1] Finally, the play was 'entered' in Company records, giving the publisher the best protection against infringement and probably indicating optimism about sales prospects (Blayney, 'Publication', 404).

Although, by contrast with verse or devotional works, plays were not particularly hot literary property, *Richard III* and two other Shakespeare history plays – *Richard II* and *1 Henry IV*, also entered for Wise between 29 August 1597 (*R2*) and 25 February 1598 (*1H4*) – proved popular playbooks. The three were among the ten most popular plays of the era, judging by the number of reprints in the twenty-five years following initial publication (they all transferred to Matthew Law in June 1603) (Blayney, 'Publication', 388).[2] By the late seventeenth century, *Richard III* had appeared in eight quartos (Q1–8: 1597, 1598, 1602, 1605, 1612, 1622, 1629 and 1634) and four folios (F–F4: 1623, 1632, 1663 and 1685). Perhaps as remarkably, the reprints of these three plays are the first to carry Shakespeare's name, and they do so in a way unique among dramatic publications of the period.

1   *Henry V* offers a revealing parallel, since the publishers had to get consent from Thomas Creede, who published *The Famous Victories of Henry the Fifth* in 1598 (Blayney, 'Publication', 399).

2   Apart from the three Shakespeare history plays and *Much Ado*, to which he also had rights, Wise published only two sermons before the end of 1600; he disappears from the records after transferring rights in 1603 (Erne, 88).

Before 1598, a few title-pages of printed plays had included the playwright's name; most name only the relevant acting company. Q1 *Richard III* announces itself 'As it hath been lately Acted by the / Right honourable the Lord Chamber- / laine his seruants.'[1] The first reprints of *Richard III* and *Richard II* in 1598 are unusual because they add '*By* William Shake-speare' to their anonymous 1597 title-pages; the anonymous 1598 First Quarto of *1 Henry IV* was similarly reprinted in 1599, with the addition: 'Newly corrected by *W. Shake-speare*'.[2] Not only was it extremely rare to add an author's name to the reprint of a play first published anonymously, but according to Lukas Erne it would remain unrepeated for any other playwright during Shakespeare's lifetime (Erne, 58).

There is one other striking feature of Q1 *Richard III* besides its popularity and the attribution of its reprints – its length. At about 3,480 lines, Q1 *Richard III* is roughly 1,000 lines longer than the period average of 2,400–500 (Hart, 147–9; cf. Smidt, *Impostors*, 26–35).[3] In 1597 it was probably the longest single play ever printed in English.[4] The 1623 Folio text is even longer, running to just under 3,600 lines. This unprecedented length should be remembered when we examine the early printed texts; both Q1 and F show evidence of cutting, though either text would probably have been cut further to be played. Sometime between some version of what Shakespeare wrote and what found its way into print as Q1, someone – perhaps Shakespeare, the acting company, a theatrical scribe, the printers or their

---

1 By the 1590s first editions of some plays name authors – Marlowe's *Massacre at Paris*, *Edward II* and *Dido, Queen of Carthage* (1594); George Peele's *Edward I* (1593) and *David and Bethsabe* (1599); Lyly's *The Woman in the Moon* (1597) – though each playwright had other plays published anonymously (Erne, 63).

2 The claim of authorial 'correction' is supported by no evidence in Q2 *1 Henry 4*, which shows the number and kind of obvious corrections (and new errors) ordinary in reprinting without authorial contribution (Kastan, *1H4*, 111). The 1598 Q1 of *Love's Labour's Lost*, which may be based on a non-extant Q0, also titles itself, 'Newly corrected and augmented / *By W. Shakespere*'.

3 Line numbers differ according to methods of counting, but the proportional relations between Q1 and F and their contemporary plays are generally agreed upon; on Hart's numeration, see Smidt, *Impostors*, 28–35. Erne tabulates from Hart (Erne, 141).

4 It would soon be surpassed by Ben Jonson's *Every Man Out* of 1599 (4,400 lines) (Smidt, *Impostors*, 34) and by *Hamlet* of 1604–5 (3,668) (Erne, 141). These plays were exceptions.

employees – shortened the text. He, they, any or all of them appear to have done other things to it as well.

Sometime after entry into the Stationers' Register, Q1 *Richard III* was printed by Valentine Simmes (see Fig. 13).[1] Simmes shared printing responsibilities for Q1 with the press of Peter Short (*True Tragedy*, v; cf. Jackson, 'Two', 175);[2] such work-sharing was widely practised.[3] Simmes printed the first seven sheets (gatherings A–G, from the opening as far as 3.7.52) of the twelve included in Q1. Short printed the remaining sheets (gatherings H–M, omitting J (a letter then usually undifferentiated from 'I'), from 3.7.53 to the end). The large number of wrong-fount letters in Short's well-produced portion suggests paucity of type. Setting by formes allowed for recycling available type within a single gathering; it suggests working copy legible enough to be precisely cast off and marked up for the compositor before being set (Hammond, 22). Q1 shows little stretching to fill up space, but betrays abundant evidence of compression.

Simmes's pages are far more cramped than Short's, and both printers virtually forgo one common strategy for managing space; neither employs variable numbers of blank lines before and after stage directions (there are exceptions at 1.1.1, sig. A1ʳ, and 5.3.206, sig. M1ʳ). The estimation of space works out so well that there is just room to conclude the final page (sig. M3ᵛ) with '*FINIS*' and a small ornament.[4] Both printers occasionally run together short lines; this space-saving device, like relegation

1 Five copies of Q1 survive: British Library (Huth, 47), Bodleian (Malone 37, Arch. G. d. 44, with missing leaves supplied from Q2), Folger, Huntington and Yale (Elizabethan Club, sheets C and D only). For details, see Smidt, *King Richard*. On Simmes, see W. Craig Ferguson, *Valentine Simmes* (Charlottesville, Va., 1968).

2 The type used by Simmes had been employed for *Richard II*, and Short would re-use his type in printing *1 Henry IV* early in 1598 (Hammond, 21).

3 On shared printing, see Chiaki Hanabusa, 'Shared printing in Robert Wilson's *The Cobbler's Prophecy*', *PBSA*, 97 (2003), 333–49. Blayney includes Short among printers with 'fairly high standards of craftsmanship' (Blayney, 'Publication', 405).

4 The neat fit of M3ᵛ matches that of G4ᵛ, the last page of Simmes's stint (RP). Q1 pages normally run to 38 lines, but 39 lines appear on sigs A2ᵛ, D3ᵛ, E1ᵛ and I2ᵛ; the catchword line contains text at sigs D3ᵛ and E1ᵛ (Smidt, *King Richard*, 16).

THE TRAGEDY OF
King Richard the third.

Containing,
His treacherous Plots againſt his brother Clarence:
the pittiefull murther of his iunocent nephewes:
his tyrannicall vſurpation: with the whole courſe
of his deteſted life, and moſt deſerued death.

As it hath beene lately Acted by the
Right honourable the Lord Chamberlaine his ſeruants.

AT LONDON
Printed by Valentine Sims, for Andrew Wiſe,
dwelling in Paules Chuch-yard, at the
Signe of the Angell.
1597.

13   Title-page of the 1597 First Quarto (Q1) of *Richard III*

of mid-scene entry directions to the right margin and splitting of directions over two lines, is more frequent in Simmes's portion. Spatial considerations had textual effects. Sig. E3^r (2.3.7–8) shows line-sharing that employs every single space and omits final punctuation.[1] Although possibly reflecting authorial lack of specificity, stage directions are frequently abbreviated, sometimes radically: Q1 3.4 opens with '*Enter the Lords to Councell.*' (sig. G1^r); F reads, '*Enter Buckingham, Darby, Hastings, Bishop of Ely, / Norfolke, Ratcliffe, Louell, with others, / at a Table.*' Limits of space may occasionally have determined the representation of action. Richard's exit with Buckingham at 3.4.41 – clearly indicated in F ('Withdraw your selfe a while, Ile goe with you. / *Exeunt.*') – is suggested by Q1's dialogue, but only Richard gets an exit ('*Buc.* Withdraw you hence my Lo: Ile follow you. *Ex. Gl.*' (sig. G1^v)). Q1's line is full measure, and the next line nearly so, precluding further stage direction.[2] The need for compression may have led to a character's absence from an entry direction: despite his substantial speaking part, Buckingham's entries go unspecified at the head of 2.1 (perhaps among '*&c.*', sig. D3^v) and at 2.2.100 (perhaps among '*others*', sig. E2^v).

Throughout Simmes's portion, lines are frequently turned up or down. Short's portion contains only two such resorts (4.4.398–9 (sig. K1^v) and 4.4.453 (sig. K4^r)). It is unclear why there is such difference in the treatment of space. Perhaps Short's printers relaxed, having realized that there was sufficient room to conclude at the bottom of sig. M3^v (Hammond, 23; cf. Jowett, 115). Alternatively, Jackson has suggested a variation in manuscript copy, arguing that placement of stage directions in Simmes's portion reveals that whoever prepared the manuscript copy (QMS) appears 'to have been fully conscious of scene divisions' and to have distinguished between entries which

---

1   This line is repeated unpointed in Q2. For lines shared between speakers, see sigs F2^r (3.1.124–5), G1^v (3.4.31–4), I1^v (4.2.97) and I1^r (4.2.50). For directions split over two lines, see sigs A2^v (1.1.41), E1^v (2.2.33–4), F3^v (3.2.33–4), F4^v (3.2.92–3), G2^r (3.4.78), G3^r (3.5.20–1) and M2^v (5.3.302–3).
2   For other complete-measure lines with abbreviated stage directions in Short's portion of Q1, see sigs H1^r (3.7.54) and I1^v (4.2.81).

head scenes (mostly centred) and entries within scenes (mostly set right). This changes in Short's portion at sig. I3^r with the relaxation of space requirements (Jackson, 'Two', 178).

Q1 printing involved at least two and perhaps three compositors. It appears likely that one compositor worked on Simmes's portion, but Short's portion has occasioned dispute.[1] Given how little is known about Short's compositor(s), it is not clear that compositorial involvement in sheets H–M (3.7.53 to the end of the play) bears editorial implications. However, a good deal has been suggested about changes and errors that Simmes's Compositor A might have contributed. Alan Craven has claimed to identify Compositor A's work in gatherings A–G of Q1 *Richard III* and in Q2 *Richard II* (1598). Comparing Q2 *Richard II* with Q1 *Richard II*, from which it was set, Craven finds A abbreviating names and titles and introducing numerous changes. A's portion of Q2 *Richard II* shows 146 substantive dialogue variants and 9 in the stage directions, about one change in seventeen lines. Only five of these result in obviously unsatisfactory readings (Craven, 'Simmes', 55). Whether or not one accepts this particular compositor for Q1 *Richard III*, these findings suggest interventions that could be virtually impossible to detect. A introduces into *Richard II* 63 substitutions ('what I speake, my' (*R2* Q1) becomes 'what I sayd my' (*R2* Q2)); 30 omissions ('the death or fall of Kings' becomes 'the death of Kings'); 14 interpolations ('our slavish' becomes 'our countries slavish'); 25 literals ('whose taste the' becomes 'whose state the'); 8 transpositions ('But then more why?' becomes 'But more than why?'); 9 sophistications ('to my owne' becomes 'to mine owne'); 6 corrections ('Canst thou' becomes 'Camst thou'). This list includes few additions, omissions or transpositions of letters and many changes and omissions of words, suggesting not misreading of copy-text but 'memorial' errors that 'almost

---

1 See Jackson, 'Two'; Susan Zimmerman, 'The uses of headlines: Peter Short's Shakespearian quartos *1 Henry IV* and *Richard III*', *The Library*, 6.7 (1985), 218–55.

always make tolerably good sense' (Craven, 'Simmes', 56). Thus, so-called 'memorial' errors in Q1 *Richard III* 'may originate with the compositor' (Hammond, 26).[1]

Regarding Short's portion of Q1 *Richard III* (sheets H–M; 3.7.53 to the end of the play), less has been asserted about personnel, but printing by formes requires setting all pages for one side of a sheet and printing them before setting the pages for the other side of the sheet. This meant that 'the two series of pages for the two sides of a sheet were not consecutive but had to interlock with each other' (Gaskell, 41), and do so precisely, without gaps or overrun. The procedure increases the likelihood that compositors will have to adjust copy to demands of space. If the manuscript is confusing or ambiguous, making estimation difficult, then condensation, even omission, becomes likely.[2]

The other process requiring mention is correction. Early modern printers did not discard printed sheets on which errors had been detected but bound them in their uncorrected state. Even the few surviving copies of Q1 differ in minor details. Typically, some obvious flaws like missing and turned letters are corrected. Craven characterizes the correction of sheets A–G in Simmes's shop as 'minimal', none appearing to have demanded consultation of QMS (Craven, 'Proofreading', 363, 369). However, two bits of evidence suggest manuscript consultation in correcting Q1: an addition appears in the otherwise highly accurate Q2 reprint, and a word change occurs in Short's portion of Q1 itself.

Although Q1 has many minor compositorial errors, it corrects some obvious misprints, while leaving other errors – wrong

---

1   Craven has been challenged (see Peter Davison, 'The selection and presentation of bibliographic evidence', *AEB* 1 (1977), 101–36). Paul Werstine (private communication) suggests scepticism about constructed compositors (cf. McKenzie). Charles Forker finds Craven's evidence relevant to A's effects on *Richard II*: 'widespread interpolation, omission and substitution' (Forker, 539).

2   And expansion, 'stretching', is possible, as can be seen in the First Folio (see p. 443n.), which was also set by formes, and left a large blank space after *Richard III* – a luxury perhaps not to be indulged in the much less expensive quarto editions.

letters, turned letters, repeated speech prefixes, misattributed speeches – uncorrected.[1] The missing 'i' in 'appointed' at 1.1.44 in the British Library and Huntington copies (sig. A2^v) appears in the Bodleian and Folger copies; 'soin deede' (at 5.3.275) in the British Library copy (sig. M2^r) is rendered 'so in deede' in the Huntington and Folger copies. A full stop missing after '*Norffolke*' (5.3.287.1) in the British Library copy appears in the Huntington and Folger copies (sig. M2^r). A colon in 1.2.1 of the Bodleian copy reveals the 'l' or 'lo' of other copies as 'lo:' – an abbreviation for 'Lord(s)'. One of the few substantive Q1 press variants corrects 2.1.5 'from heauen' (sig. D3^v; British Library, Huntington) to 'to heauen' (Folger, Bodleian, Elizabethan Club). Such changes do not refute claims that Elizabethan proofreading largely confined itself to correcting superficial blemishes rather than seeking accuracy of copy.[2]

Manuscript copy does appear to have been consulted at 5.3.10, where 'greatest' (Huntington) is corrected to 'vtmost' (Folger, Bodleian, British Library). Unmotivated by grammar, metre or sense, this correction agrees uniquely with F, against all derivative Qq, and thus against any of the printed copies from which scholars have ever claimed F to have been set.[3] This agreement of corrected Q1 with F in a non-essential change argues that F is related to Q1 independently of the derivative quartos. The logical inference is that the copy for F included a manuscript (FMS) closely related to the manuscript behind Q1 (QMS). Ironically, the same line raises questions about the proximity of QMS and FMS.

Corrected Q1 reads 'vtmost number'; F has 'vtmost power'. Since it is difficult to imagine Short's corrector breaking down an otherwise suitable line to adjust a single, perfectly acceptable, word to match manuscript copy without also correcting the word

1 For a partial list, see Davison, 8. Davison notes the rash of errors in 4.1.
2 Against Hinman's dismissal of early modern correction, see McKenzie, 40–9; Gaskell, 110–16.
3 This correction occurs on the same side of sheet L (L2^r) that shows 'lordsc onduct' (L3^v Huntington) corrected to 'lords conduct' (Folger, Bodleian, British Library).

next to it, the Q1/F variance suggests difference in underlying manuscripts. Furthermore, in context, Q1's 'number', which may be inferred to have been present in QMS since it is left uncorrected, seems likely to have been carried over from the preceding line:

> *King.* . . .Who hath discried the number of the foe.
> *Norff.* Sixe or seuen thousand is their vtmost number.
>
> (Q1c, sig. L2^r)

Since two different speakers are involved, any 'memorial' error here seems most likely a simple, and common, compositorial mistake and evidently not present in FMS. 'Memorial' errors bedevil necessary functionaries such as scribes or compositors (or editors!) every bit as much as any hypothetical actor-recounters (Hammond, 29; Maguire, 155; cf. McKerrow, *Bibliography*, 254).[1]

Such differences in early printed texts constitute clues to the nature and relation of QMS and FMS. The many exclusive agreements that may be inferred between them argue for close relationship, but their differences suggest that QMS derived from FMS.[2] Further claims about these absent but conceptually useful entities demand first considering the reprinting of Q1 and the printing of F.

THE DERIVATIVE QUARTOS (Q2–8)

Q1 (1597) begins a remarkable print history with seven subsequent quarto editions, of which five (Q2–6) pre-date the First Folio of 1623 and two (Q7–8) follow it in 1629 and 1634. Although Q3 (1602) announces itself 'Newly augmented, / By *William Shakespeare*', it contains no new dialogue; its minimal adjustments

---

1 According to Joseph Moxon, the compositor 'first reads so much of his *Copy* as he thinks he can retain in his memory till he have *Composed* it, as commonly is five or six words, or sometimes a longer Sentence' (Joseph Moxon, *Mechanick Exercises on the whole art of printing, 1683–4*, ed. Herbert Davis and Harry Carter (1958), 204).

2 Alice Walker numbers some three hundred occasions when a substantive variant exclusive to Q1 is restored to F dialogue (Walker, 24; Hammond, 31).

to stage directions and speaking order do not require authorial intervention. The derivative quartos are widely, but not universally, acknowledged to merely reprint one another, with no generally accepted evidence of consultation of manuscript copy and with plentiful incidental error.[1] The inertia involved in reprinting is evident from the fact that the claim to be 'Newly augmented' is simply passed along by five editions (Q3–7) from 1602 to 1629, before being dropped after thirty-two years in Q8 (1634). One two-line passage first appearing in Q2 is an exceptional case that may arguably support the general rule. Nevertheless, the reprinted quartos deserve attention.

There is no doubt that Q3 provided a sixth of the F text, and it has been long accepted that Q3 and/or Q6 furnished printed copy that Folio collators annotated with reference to a manuscript (FMS) for the other five-sixths. Since Q3 and Q6 incorporate or reject variants from earlier quartos, all six quartos preceding F require scrutiny in a Folio-based edition. That the derivative quartos frequently differ from Q1, sometimes obviously erring, other times usefully 'correcting' it, is not in doubt; nor is it to be doubted that F incorporates readings which agree with the derivative quartos against Q1.[2] Such readings common to F and the derivative quartos may sometimes be coincidence, a matter of quarto printers independently getting something right that happens to differ from Q1 and to agree with FMS, but Mowat and Werstine rightly note that 'no editors . . . have been able to eliminate the possibility that F may have picked up these readings from the derivative quartos' (liii). Thus, attention to Q2–6 variants is crucial to the editorial process, and a process it must be, even when an edition accepts F as its basic text.

Q2 (1598) to Q5 (1612) were printed by Thomas Creede; on 25 June 1603 the profitable title was acquired from Andrew Wise,

---

1 Q5 provides the single deviation from the practice of reprinting each quarto from its immediate predecessor, with sheets C and E–M being printed from Q3 (W.W. Greg, '*Richard III* – Q5 (1612)', *The Library*, 4th series, 17 [1936], 88–97).
2 Smidt finds approximately 80 substantive F agreements with Q3–6 against Q1 in portions of F not directly reproduced from Q3 (Smidt, *Impostors*, 179–90).

along with *Richard II* and *1 Henry IV*, by Matthew Law. Q6 (1622) was printed for Law by Thomas Purfoot. The two quartos that came after F, Q7 (1629) and Q8 (1634), were printed by John Norton. These late reprints testify to the play's continuing popularity in an inexpensive, easily readable format.[1] From this unusually long run, two reprints – Q3 (1602) and Q6 (1622) – are particularly important. F prints Q3 text virtually unaltered from 3.1.1 to 3.1.166 and from 5.3.49 to the end of the play, and many have argued for the role of Q6 in constituting the rest of F's text.

No scholar has asserted such importance for other quartos in determining copy for F, but Q2 (1598) introduces two new lines (1.1.101–2) that are accepted in all subsequent quartos and into F. It is easy to imagine how two lines could be lost in printing; but how could they come to be added to an otherwise careful reprint of Q1? Two opposing theories offer to explain this addition.[2]

In Q1 Richard's joke about Mistress Shore doing 'naught' (with King Edward) (1.1.98–100) elicits only the jailer's reiterated demand that Richard cease conversing with Clarence:

> *Glo.* Naught to do with Mistris Shore, I tell thee fellow,
> He that doth naught with her, excepting one
> Were best he doe it secretly alone.
> *Bro.* I beseech your Grace to pardon me, and withal
>   for- (beare
> Your conference with the noble Duke.

> (Q1, sig. A3ʳ)

Q2 reprints Richard's speech, but adds a query and Richard's response:

> *Bro.* What one my Lord?
> *Glo.* Her husband knaue, wouldst thou betray me?
> (Q2, sig. A3ʳ)

---

1 Q7 and Q8 may sometimes suggest printers' efforts to grapple with textual issues raised by Q6, issues that F's printers might also have had to face (Walton, *Copy*, 27–35).

2 Mowat and Werstine suggest spurious printing-house addition (305).

With minor relineation, F repeats this Q2 exchange.

One argument attributes the new lines to the Q2 printer's use of a press-corrected copy of Q1 for which no exemplar survives. The strongest support for this hypothesis is the absence of conclusive evidence that printers ever consulted manuscript copy in printing any of the derivative quartos. In fact, recognizable patterns of error have enabled scholars to determine exactly which printed quarto served for copy in each case (Hammond, 29; Mowat & Werstine, lii). The convenient hypothesis of a no longer extant Q1 that included this press correction has been countered by claims that in this passage alone the printers working for Thomas Creede, the legal owner of the manuscript copy for Q1, consulted QMS rather than, as elsewhere, following Q1 (Smidt, *Memorial*, 52–3; Jowett, 115–16). This assertion is no more, or less, verifiable than its alternative. The added lines require Q2's printers to modify the preceding page (sig. A2ᵛ) from its form in surviving copies of Q1 by introducing a turn-up and by printing on the catchword line (Jowett, 115). But Q1 and Q2 print elsewhere on a catchword line (sig. E1ᵛ) and begin and end every other page at exactly the same words, so it does not follow that it is less likely that Q1 was press-corrected than that Q2 involved a single instance of manuscript consultation. In sum, Q2 probably reprints a corrected version of Q1 that does not survive among the five extant copies. No instance of 'correction' in subsequent quartos demands the printer's having consulted QMS, though variants introduced by Q2–6 sometimes appear arguably preferable to Q1 alternatives.[1]

The most extensive recent arguments for manuscript consultation concern Q3, printed in 1602 by Andrew Wise, who retained legal rights to QMS. No real change in dialogue justifies Q3's claim to be 'newly augmented', but there is editing of some stage directions and speech prefixes, a correction of fact and

---

1 Q2, for example, changes 5.3.183 'I and I' (Q1) to 'I am I' (Q2–8, F); cf. Wilson, 143–4. See also 1.3.5n. and 5.3.183n. Q2 contributes its share of errors, later corrected (e.g. 1.3.245; 1.4.16; 4.1.35).

an intelligent inversion of two speeches. Some knowledgeable reader in the printing-house closely examined at least portions of Q3. Smidt and Jowett argue for manuscript consultation (Smidt, *Memorial*, 54; Jowett, 116), but intelligent reading – by whom is unclear – could explain Q3's modifications of Q2.

Since Q3 is the direct source for a sixth of F, anything casting light on Q3 may carry considerable textual implications. The play's first two acts exhibit hundreds of substantial verbal differences between Q1 and F. Part-way through the first 166 lines of dialogue in 3.1 such differences decline almost to zero. F even begins to reproduce the distinctive Qq speech prefix for Richard, designating him *Glo.* rather than *Rich.*, which is invariable in F until this point (3.1.63) and to which F returns (3.1.181). These 166 dialogue lines contain only thirteen substantive verbal differences (excluding contractions) between F and Q1. Ten of these are found variously in the derivative quartos (Q2–6) that could theoretically have furnished text for F, but Q3 alone has all ten. At 3.1.123 F repeats a misprint exclusive to Q3. As printed in Q1–2 and substantially repeated in Q4–7, the line reads: 'I would, that I might thanke you as you call me.' Q3 and F print: 'I would that I might thanke you as as you call me.' (Q3) and 'I would that I might thanke you as, as, you / call me.' (F; TLN 1706–7). F repunctuates Q3's dittography to suggest stammering ('as, as,').[1] The fact that Q4 and F2 both correct this Q3/F error indicates its glaring nature. No smoking gun appears elsewhere, but comparable statistical similarities from 5.3.49 to the end of the play again reveal Q3 as the direct basis for F (Mowat & Werstine, liii).

Elsewhere in F *Richard III* the situation is less certain, but scholars have long argued that Q3 and/or Q6 furnished copy that was annotated by F's printers. Neither quarto has been conclusively demonstrated to be *the* one to furnish copy. Since Q3

---

1 Cf. F's apparent attempt at 5.3.199 to compensate for Q3's interpolation of 'all' (found twice in the previous line and once more in the line itself) with elision marks ('to'th'Barre').

literally furnished part of F, and since Q3 and/or Q6 probably influenced what the printers set elsewhere, both are important for their possible effects in determining, supplementing, supporting, clarifying, substituting for or overriding what may have survived to 1623 of FMS. Yet each mostly reprints its preceding reprint, itself already distant from Q1, the only quarto certainly set from manuscript, while introducing new errors (Hammond, 30). What, then, is the evidence that Q3 was printed with consultation of QMS?

Discerning corrections appear scattered throughout Q3 stage directions, but the instances that might be said to be 'newly augmented' merely reveal attention to the previous quarto (Q2). For example, at 1.4.159 Q3 adds '*Cla. awaketh.*' just after dialogue mentions that 'he stirs' in his sleep and just before Clarence speaks.[1] Similarly, at 3.1.59 Q3 adds '*Exit. Car. & Hast.*' after the Cardinal asks Hastings 'will you go with me?' and Hastings replies 'I go my Lord'. Similarly obvious, stage directions are added at 3.2.33.1, 3.2.92, 3.2.105 SD and 4.4.497 SD and in identification of the '*Lieutenant*' at 4.1.11.1 (Q2, sig. H3ʳ) as '*Lieutenant of the Tower*' (Q3–6; not in F).

The same assessment – correct but obvious – applies to Q3's augmentations and changes to other stage directions. The Ghosts explicitly address Richard rather than Richmond at 5.3.118, 124 and 146, because Q3 puts '*to K. Ri.*' or '*to K.R.*' (Q3–6) in place of '*to Ri.*' (Q1–2). '*K.*' (for 'King') may seem useful here, but Q3 inserts titles where there can be no confusion: '*K. Richard starteth out of a dreame.*' (Q3–6) replaces '*Richard starteth vp out of a dreame.*' (Q1–2; 5.3.176 SD2); the ghost of '*Ladie Anne*' (Q2, sig. L4ʳ) becomes that of '*Queene Anne*' (Q3–6; '*Anne*' in F 5.3.158.1); the ghost of '*Hastings*' (Q2, sig. L4ʳ) becomes that of '*L. Hastings*' (Q3–6; '*Lord Hastings*' in F 5.3.153.1). Q3

---

1 Oddly, despite F's close relation to Q3 and Q6, this stage direction is omitted from F. This fact might lend weight to the argument that the direction was *not* in FMS.

stage directions hardly reveal special alertness to 'ambiguity' of address, let alone consultation of QMS (Jowett, 116).

True, certain other Q3 corrections might appear 'authoritative', but, with two possible exceptions, these are roughly equivalent to Q3's additions to stage directions. Obvious mistakes are corrected: a false plural (1.1.40); a mistaken tense (4.4.423); misallocated speeches (3.4.6; 3.5.52; 5.3.139). Elsewhere, Q3 introduces variants that may arguably represent improvements (e.g. 1.3.33; 4.1.35), along with misprints (2.2.34; 2.2.149; 3.1.123; 5.3.250), obvious mistakes (2.1.135; 3.2.83; 3.7.14, 21; 4.4.107–8, 352; 5.3.338, 351), abbreviated entries (5.3.18.2–3, 46.2), and omitted speech headings (2.1.100). Some new corrections, some new mistakes – like *all* the quarto reprints. The exceptions require explanation.

At 2.3.17 Q3 corrects Q2 in historical fact, accurately revising Henry VI's age at coronation from 'xi' (Q2) to 'nine' months (as Q1 'ix'). But this fact is not obscure (see *Mirror*, 'Nicholas Burdet', 78; *2H6* 4.9.4; *3H6* 1.1.112). A much more substantial Q3 variant appears in the altered speaking order of the Ghosts. In Q1–2 all the Ghosts except for Hastings and the princes address Richard according to the chronological sequence of their deaths. Q3 inverts the speaking order of their Q1–2 passages (5.3.146–58) to follow chronological death order. Hammond takes Q1–2's order as arising from misreporting and accepts Q3's reordering as 'inspired correction'. Jowett also invokes theatrical explanations, claiming that the Q1–2 order 'probably reflect[s] actual stage practice' because putting the princes on before Hastings would have allowed for one boy actor to exit and return as Anne (Jowett, 116). Perhaps so, but why would a printer care enough to intervene substantially and uniquely here? Jowett offers multiple hypothetical agents for the change: if the Q3 printers consulted manuscript, they might have seen ambiguous markings; Wise or Shakespeare might have intervened. But without substantial change or manuscript consultation anywhere else and with no obvious reason for Wise or Shakespeare to intervene here and nowhere else with a large-scale change, these alternatives hardly exhaust possible explanations.[1]

Uncertainties might have arisen from Q3's new pagination. To conserve paper, the printer's second most costly expense after labour, Q3 normally prints 39 lines per page, rather than the 38 typical of Q1–2, and often crowds in 40 lines, printing on the catchword line of verso pages, to save one full leaf (ending on sig. M2^v). It could not have been easy to mark up so many repaginations, and since reversing the two speeches provides no obvious spatial advantage, it might be no more than random happenstance. Yet someone examined this portion of Q3 carefully enough to correct an erroneous speech prefix (5.3.139); perhaps this same press reader – who nowhere else betrays independent authority or innovation beyond mere close reading – simply read the final ghostly utterance and drew a conclusion about order from it:

> *Enter the Goast of Buckingham.*
> The first was I that helpt thee to the Crowne,
> The last was I that felt thy tyrannie.
>
> (Q2, sig. L4^v)

One could hardly ask for a clearer suggestion of sequence for the Ghosts; accordingly, Q3's corrector puts them in order of their deaths at Richard's hand.

We do not know why Q3 here differs from Q2, but editions have to make choices. Q3's rearrangement may look like a good one, especially to an editor basing his or her work on the Folio which follows it; nevertheless, the present edition rejects it. What we do know about this portion of 5.3 is that, for the most part, F simply follows Q3, even when Q3 is clearly wrong. It would be ironic, but no surprise, given the unknowns (and unknowables) surrounding the early texts of Shakespeare, to learn that an Elizabethan reader in 1602 correctly deduced a formal aspect

---

1 For 'access to authoritative manuscript which was completely ignored throughout the rest of the text' as the least plausible explanation for Q3's reordering, see *TxC*, 248.

of the play that would otherwise have remained obscure until the Folio printers consulted FMS in 1623. That would be one interesting narrative, and 'coincidental corrections' by quarto printers sometimes hit upon readings eventually proved right by what we can deduce about FMS.[1] However, in this portion of 5.3 there may have been no FMS for Folio printers to consult, since F reproduces Q3 virtually unaltered (but see 5.3.204–5n.). Thus, F might here simply reprint a printer's earlier mistake, a chance error or 'wrong' deduction of 1602 that scholars have since largely accepted as 'By *William Shakespeare*'. I like that story, too. Its ironies implicating authority, purpose, chance, error, individuality, anonymity and scholarship point to issues that surround the Folio itself. Before dealing with F, it is worth briefly considering the remaining derivative quartos, including Q6, the quarto that enjoys with Q3 the most advocates in debates about printed copy for F.

Since P.A. Daniel in 1886, the extent and nature of quarto copy for the five-sixths of F *Richard III* not set from Q3 continues in dispute. The possibility that an annotated copy of Q6 was used for those portions has been rejected by Walton, who judged Daniel's twelve exclusive F/Q6 agreements insufficient to rule out annotated Q3 copy (Walton, *Copy*, 34). Although W.W. Greg, J.D. Wilson and Fredson Bowers also came to agree that Q3 furnished copy throughout, Hammond judges the relative importance of Q3/Q6 impossible to determine beyond the Q3 portions of F (Hammond, 32–41). Bowers changed his mind, admitting possible contributions by Q6 to F (Walton, *Quarto*, 61–2). Taylor has argued that pages from Q6 and Q3 were interleaved with pages from FMS throughout F (*TxC*, 229–30); Jowett concurs.

---

1   For similarly effective correction see 3.2.91, where Q2 introduces a mistake ('hat'), corrected by Q6 ('hats'), which agrees with Q1 and F; 4.4.260, where Q2 reduces Q1's 'thou love' to 'thou' until corrected by Q6, which agrees with Q1 and F; 3.5.26, where Q4 alone agrees with F on 'the' (cf. Hammond, 39).

The principal evidence supporting the use of Q6 in printing F is of two sorts. Firstly, a dozen or so F readings substantively agree with Q6 against all other quartos (Hammond, 35–7). Secondly, two passages suggest F attempting to 'correct' a reading unique to Q6. The first passage occurs at 3.5.74:

Q1–5   There at your meetst aduantage of the time,

Q6   There at your meetest aduantage of the time,

F   There, at your meetest vantage of the time,

Walton argues that Q6 only coincidentally agrees with FMS on 'meetest'. Hammond counters that the F collator could have looked at Q6 copy and emended to make the line metrical (Hammond, 36). But the metre could be easily corrected by eliding 'meetest', the kind of change that appears frequently throughout F (*TxC*, 242). This instance seems inconclusive to me.

A more convincing case for influence of Q6 copy appears at 4.4.534. Q6 replaces Q1–5's 'tidings' with the unmetrical 'news', perhaps because the compositor carries the word over from two lines earlier: 'Thats the best newes, that the *E*arle of Richmond' (Q1–5). F retains Q6's erroneous 'news', but adds a word that renders the line metrical:

Q1–5   *I*s colder tidings, yet they must be told.

Q6   Is colder news, yet they must be told.

F   Is colder Newes, but yet they must be told.
                                    (4.4.534, TLN 3342)

In this case, Q6 might by chance have come up with the very word found in FMS, correctly but accidentally substituting 'news' for 'tidings'. Alternatively, both F and Q6 might share the same mistake, simply and independently, carrying over 'news'. However, both these hypotheses are rendered doubtful by F's addition of 'but', which would not fit metrically with 'tidings'.

This addition suggests F's *post facto* regularization of Q6 rather than consideration of FMS, since attention to FMS might have revealed the mistaken entry of 'news' caught by Q6 from the earlier line and have prompted reinstatement of Q1–5's 'tidings'. This case suggests direct influence of Q6 on F. The force of such evidence has prompted the present edition, in full awareness of its own seeming inconsistency, to follow F in 3.5.74 and Q1 in 4.4.534. Further reasons for such apparent self-contradiction will emerge in considering the strengths and limitations of F itself.

Finally, the later quartos demonstrate that the play, along with two other histories also first published by Wise and later by Law, *Richard II* and *1 Henry IV*, remained popular, outdistancing Shakespeare's comedies and even such popular tragedies as *Hamlet* in reprints (Erne, 50). Their print history suggests that these three plays taken together, as Jowett notes, probably dominated the seventeenth-century perception of Shakespeare's histories before the 1623 Folio, since Law followed Wise's precedent of bringing them out in tandem: Q4 *Richard III* and Q3 *1 Henry IV* (1604–5), Q4 *Richard II* and Q4 *1 Henry IV* (1608), Q5 *Richard III*, Q5 *Richard II* and Q5 *1 Henry IV* (1612–15). In 1619 Thomas Pavier brought out reprints of some other histories – Q3 *2 Henry VI*, Q3 *3 Henry VI* and Q3 *Henry V* – but the Folio put the history plays into their historical order. Q5 *Richard III* (1612) is notable for finally updating the acting company on the title-page, to the King's Majesty's Servants, although Q4 (1605) could have done so seven years earlier. After the Folio, two further quartos (Q7, 1629, and Q8, 1634) appear with little evident awareness of F. Considering the importance of the First Folio for subsequent editions and scholarship, the independent production and marketing of Q7 (with bookseller Matthew Law retaining rights he had held since 1603) and Q8 (printed by John Norton) remind us of the many lives of this play – for readers as well as playgoers.

THE FIRST FOLIO (F)

By any measure, the 1623 Folio edition of *M' William / Shakespeares / Comedies, Histories, & Tragedies. / Published according to the True Originall Copies* constitutes a major historical event in dramatic publication. It must have been conceived and perceived as such. Produced posthumously with the aid of John Heminge and Henry Condell, two of Shakespeare's former colleagues in the King's Men, the Folio is an expensive and carefully printed volume that represented an economic risk. Costing approximately 15s unbound or £1 in plain calf, the Folio was, as Peter Blayney terms it, 'by far the most expensive playbook that had ever been offered to the English public'. It would be followed after a brief nine years by a second edition.[1] The publishers were the relative newcomer Isaac Jaggard and the well-established Edward Blount; the printer was Jaggard's father, William Jaggard (Blayney, 'Intro', xxviii).

Folio *Richard III* is remarkable for changing a play that had been more or less constantly in print for twenty-six years. Intrinsically, there are several new passages, a few substantial cuts and thousands of small changes. Extrinsically, the Folio puts the play within a chronological sequence, making it appear part of a grand 'national' narrative. Beginning with the externally threatened and internally troubled reign of King John (events of 1199–1218), the sequence runs through seven plays depicting troubled rule and disputed dynasty, briefly interrupted by a play that represents Henry V effecting a precarious national unity while waging a successful campaign in France. The whole ends with Henry VIII and the promise-filled birth of Queen Elizabeth (events of 1520–36). This sequence follows neither the order of composition nor that of performance, but has its own logic. The Folio order provides patterns of ideology and

---

1 Blayney, 'Intro', xviii; Ben Jonson's *Workes* (1616) included non-dramatic works, cost less, and would not be reprinted for twenty-four years. Blayney estimates the initial First Folio print-run at something like 750 copies (xxxiii).

outcome that can be paralleled in the primary historical sources; it is unlikely that Shakespeare anticipated anyone encountering these plays in such order, but some early readers did read them in sequence and expected continuity.[1]

Richard III follows *3 Henry VI* and precedes *Henry VIII* in the Folio quires devoted to the histories. 'The Tragedy of Richard the Third: / with the Landing of Earle Richmond, and the / Battell at Bosworth Field' also employs a running title – '*The Life and Death of Richard the Third*' – following a biographical formula also found in *King John* and *Richard II*. F provides numbered acts and scenes, generally conforming, at least through the first four acts, to units adopted by later editions. *Richard III* fills thirty-two double-columned pages (sigs q5^r–t2^v). Like the rest of the Folio, the play was set by formes. Copy was cast-off in advance in units estimated to fill one folio page, with the printing of each twelve-page quire beginning with the middle pages (6 and 7) and working outwards successively through 5 and 8, then 4 and 9 and so on to pages 1 and 12 (Blayney, 'Intro', xxxii). The casting-off of copy for *Richard III* was not always precise. The printers sometimes divide perfectly suitable (and printable) verse lines in two in order to fill up the page.[2] Confused lineation implicates the nature of the copy involved, and argues against passive deference to F lineation.

Richard III was set by compositors known as A and B. Charlton Hinman established their shares of labour (Hinman, 2.113–27; 220–5):

> B set 1.1 through line 1.3.125 (sigs q5^r through r1^r)
> A set 1.3.126 through 1.3.255 (sig. r1^v)
> B set 1.3.256 through 3.1.19 (sigs r2^r through r5^r)

---

1 Marcus, 95; cf. Samuel Schoenbaum, *William Shakespeare: A Documentary Life* (New York, 1975), 144. Contrast Ioppolo's suggestion that Shakespeare may have reworked passages from the history plays to create continuities for a revival (Ioppolo, 130).

2 See 1.2.39, 50, 83–4, 95–6, 104 and 135. This page is the last of the inner forme of gathering q, and Compositor B appears to have stretched copy to prevent a gap at the end of the quire (Hammond, 45). B also expands lines on sig. r1^r at 1.3.116, 117, 120 and 125.

A set 3.1.20 through 4.3.2 (sigs r5^v through s3^v)
B set 4.3.3 through 4.4.431 (sigs s4^r through s5^v)
A set 4.4.432 through 4.4.532 (sig. s6^r)
B set 4.4.533 through end of play (sigs s6^v through t2^v)
(Hinman, 2.113–27; 220–5)

The effects are sometimes obvious: contrast speech prefixes set by B on sig. r1^r (1.3.110–25) and sig. r2^r (1.3.265–96), where Margaret is '*Mar.*' or '*Margaret.*', with those set by A on sig. r1^v (1.3.134–254), where she is '*Q.M.*' Typical spelling preferences are 'heere', 'do', 'go' (B) and 'here', 'doe', 'goe' (A). There was an interruption in setting, with a major break occurring at the end of sig. s6^v (5.3.16) while work was undertaken on the tragedies and on *H8* (Blayney, 'Intro', xxxvi).

Proof corrections are evident in six pages (sigs q6^{r-v}, r2^r, s5^v, s6^v, t1^v), most of them amounting to elimination of technical errors such as inking spaces and letter inversions (Hammond, 44). The few true corrections are: 'and' replaces 'end' (sig. s5^v; 4.4.354); 'off' replaces 'oft' and 'want' replaces 'went' (sig. s6^v; 4.5.4 and 5.3.13). Obvious misprints (for example, 'necke' replaces 'neeke') are corrected on the same page. None of these demands reference to copy, nor do two substantial corrections on sig. r2^r – the obviously mistaken speech prefix '*Riu.*' (Rivers) becomes '*Ric.*' (Richard) at 1.3.343, and the stage direction opening 1.4 ('*Enter Clarence and Keeper.*') is added.[1]

THE FOLIO MANUSCRIPT (FMS)

New dialogue, amounting to over two hundred lines not in Qq and including several extended passages, makes it clear that manuscript (FMS), which has not survived, contributed to F

---

1 For F variants, see Hinman, 1.276–8.

Richard III.[1] We need to consider the nature of that manuscript, its relation to the manuscript that formed the basis for Q1 (QMS), which itself contains just under forty lines not found in F, including one lengthy passage (4.2.97–114), and the means by which FMS was incorporated into F.

Outside the portions of F comprising completely new passages from manuscript and those portions reprinting Q3, evidence suggests that F was set from printed quarto copy annotated with reference to FMS. At 4.4.362–6, for instance, F inserts a line that exists only in Q1 and no other quarto (Greg, *Problem*, 86). This line, which must have come to F from FMS, appears set one line too soon, a dislocation arguing that F's printers inserted lines from FMS into printed quarto copy.

Q1 prints the passage from 4.4 in the following order:

> *Qu.* O no my reasons are to deepe and dead.
> *Too* deepe and dead poore infants in their graue.
> *King* Harpe not one that string Madam that is past.
> *Qu.* Harpe on it still shall I till hartstrings breake.
> *King* Now by my George, my Garter and my crown.
>
> (Q1, sig. K2ᵛ)

Subsequent quartos make a hash of it, omitting Richard's command that Elizabeth drop the subject of her dead children and nonsensically giving Richard himself the rejoinder in which she insists on the right to dwell upon her losses. This confusion is obvious in its initial printed instance because Q2 speech prefixes make Richard answer himself:

> *Qu.* O no my reasons are too deepe and dead.
> Too deepe and dead poore infants in their graue.
> *King.* Harpe on it still shal I, till hartstrings breake.
> *King.* Now by my George, my Garter and my Crowne.
>
> (Q2, sig. K2ᵛ)

---

1 Passages present in F but not (or not entirely) in Qq include 1.2.158–69; 1.4.69–72, 256–60; 2.2.89–100, 123–40; 3.4.101–4; 3.5.103–5; 3.7.143–52; 4.1.2–4, 97–103; 4.4.222–35 and 288–342.

Q3–8 drop the final speech prefix, but retain Q2's misordered form.

F prints this passage with the line missing since 1597 – Richard's 'Harpe not on that string Madam, that is past' – one of approximately three hundred instances in which F dialogue agrees substantively with Q1 against all subsequent quartos. These unique agreements bespeak a close relationship between FMS and QMS. However, F retains Q2's order, putting Richard's newly restored line in the wrong place:

> *Qu.* O no, my Reasons are too deepe and dead,
> Too deepe and dead (poore Infants) in their graues,
> Harpe on it still shall I, till heart-strings breake.
> *Rich.* Harpe not on that string Madam, that is past.
> Now by my George, my Garter, and my Crowne.
> (F 4.4.362–6; TLN 3147–51)

Apparently 'the line was written in the margin of one of the derivative quartos used as Folio copy and . . . either the collator failed to make clear where it was to be inserted or . . . the compositor was careless in incorporating it in the Folio text' (Walker, 15; cf. Hammond, 31; Smidt, *Memorial*, 54). Walker points to other anomalies in F lineation (such as an unusual shared line at 1.3.232–3; disorder at 1.4.255–61) that argue for quarto copy for F (Smidt, *Memorial*, 54). But more can be deduced about FMS and its relation to QMS.

Folio manuscript (FMS) comes first and the manuscript behind Q1 (QMS) is derived from it. The clearest evidence takes two forms. Q1 prints apparently garbled versions of passages that appear competently rendered in F; Q1 portrays characters engaging in actions and delivering speeches that appear inappropriate for them but that are appropriately allocated by F.

D.L. Patrick notes the confusion of Q1's version of 4.4.271–8, with its transposed (and more colloquial) order, its unmetrical line, synonym substitution and missing text (Hammond, 7–8).

Q1's Queen Elizabeth asks Richard to send a handkerchief steeped in Rutland's blood to her daughter Elizabeth; this gesture would make no difference to her, since Richard's murdered brother means nothing to either Elizabeth:

> *Qu.* Send to her by the man that slew her brothers,
> A paire of bleeding harts thereon ingraue,
> Edward and Yorke, then happelie she wil weepe,
> Therefore present to her as sometimes Margaret
> Did to thy father, a handkercher steept in Rutlands bloud,
> And bid her drie her weeping eies therewith

$$\text{(Q1, sig. K2}^r\text{)}$$

By contrast, F makes sense: Queen Elizabeth invites Richard to send her daughter a handkerchief steeped in her brothers' blood, as Margaret had once given a bloody handkerchief soaked in his own son's blood to York, father of Rutland and Richard:

> *Qu.* Send to her by the man that slew her Brothers,
> A paire of bleeding hearts: thereon ingraue
> *Edward* and *Yorke*, then haply will she weepe:
> Therefore present to her, as sometime *Margaret*
> Did to thy Father, steept in Rutlands blood,
> A hand-kercheefe, which say to her did dreyne
> The purple sappe from her sweet Brothers body,
> And bid her wipe her weeping eyes withall.

$$\text{(F 4.4.271–8; TLN 3055–62)}$$

Q1 appears to be a distorted rendering of FMS. For their number and nature, Q1's multiple condensations and confusions seem to derive neither from scribal or compositorial error, nor from specifically authorial revision. This is not to claim that F does not occasionally garble passages that appear coherently rendered in Q1, nor that Q1 does not sometimes get details right where F makes mistakes.

F has its own weak spots: lines necessary to sense are omitted though present in Q1; lines that occur singly in Q1 are simply repeated; lines and passages that Q1 renders clearly are misplaced and confused. For the most part, these weaknesses are readily attributable to composing or printing processes rather than to failings in FMS. For example, by contrast with Q1's confusions about the handkerchief, F's problems at 2.2.83–5 suggest compositorial error rather than bungled derivation. Q1 correctly and clearly reads:

> She for Edward weepes, and so doe I:
> I for a Clarence weep, so doth not she:
> These babes for Clarence weepe, and so do I:
> I for an Edward weep, so do not they.
>
> > (Q1, sig. E2ᵛ)

Q2 mistakenly drops 'not' from the final line, an error repeated by all subsequent quartos. F uniquely agrees with Q1 on 'not', while making the first line metrical, but adds new confusions:

> She for an *Edward* weepes, and so do I:
> I for a *Clarence* weepes, so doth not shee:
> These Babes for *Clarence* weepe, so do not they.
>
> (F, sig. r4ʳ⁻ᵛ; TLN 1356–8; cf. 2.2.82–5)

Here, as in other passages spanning a page or column, F's printers drop the ball (see 1.3.6, 2.2.145). 'I' beginning the second line is the first word on sig. r4ᵛ, and the printer apparently interprets it as an interjection ('Ay') rather than a personal pronoun, and substitutes a third-person verb form ('weepes'), while eyeskip leads directly from the third to fourth lines, neatly and nonsensically excising 'and so do I: / I for an Edward weep'. Such mistakes underline the necessity for editorial vigilance, even if F's text is generally more coherent and based on a manuscript closer to Shakespearean holograph.

MANUSCRIPTS FOR F (FMS) AND Q (QMS)

No manuscript for *Richard III* survives, but both printed versions clearly depend on manuscript copy. The many times when F restores a reading shared exclusively with Q1 testify to the proximity of the two manuscripts and to the thoroughness of F's annotation of its derivative–quarto copy.[1] The evidence of the printed versions strongly supports their basis in manuscripts that were closely related to one another and to Shakespeare's holograph, but that nonetheless differed substantially. Neither manuscript conforms easily to labels like 'foul papers', 'promptbook' or 'playbook' (Jowett, 120).[2] The evidence reveals FMS to be a more originary, 'literary' version of the play's 'raw material' and QMS to be derivative from FMS, possibly registering incomplete adaptation for ostensibly 'theatrical' purposes.[3] The occasion and nature of this partial adaptation is difficult to characterize, and the identity of its agent(s) probably unknowable.[4]

Various stories have been constructed to account for such different yet closely related manuscripts. One narrative maintains that for some reason – loss, damage, exigencies of travel, etc. – Shakespeare's company found themselves compelled to recreate the play from memory and produced QMS from collaborative recall.[5] Such accounts usually rely on instances in which Q1 has been judged to provide a vague, often briefer or less pointed approximation of verbal formulations appearing in F (Davison, 7). Obvious problems haunt such arguments: some Q1 lines are arguably 'better' than F equivalents (e.g. 1.1.133, 2.4.66; cf.

---

1   F restores just under twenty Act 1 readings that agree with Q1 exclusively against all derivative quartos. If one adds instances when F agrees with Q1–2, but with neither quarto (Q3 and Q6) thought to have provided F with copy, the number is larger (see Jowett, 366–8 (Appendix B)).

2   On FMS as prompt copy, see Hammond, 42–3. Inconsistencies weigh against it. As for foul papers: 'F is relatively regular in its speech-prefixes and thorough in its stage directions, far more so than the recognized foul-paper texts' (*TxC*, 230). On 'foul papers' generally, see Paul Werstine, 'Narratives about printed Shakespeare texts: "foul papers" and "bad quartos"', *SQ*, 41 (1990), 65–86.

3   For 'raw material', see Blayney, 'Intro', xxx; Dutton, 174.

4   On FMS as a transcript for a patron, see *TxC*, 230; Jowett offers Henry Herbert, 2nd Earl of Pembroke, patron of Pembroke's Men, and father to dedicatees of the Folio (Jowett, 122). For argument based on the number of supernumeraries mentioned in stage directions that FMS was autograph, see Walton, *Quarto*, 261.

5   For 'memorial transmission' including 'memorial lapses', see Smidt, *Memorial*, 25; for 'not memorial', see Smidt, *Impostors*; concerning the 'memories of individual actors' on 'provincial tour', see *TxC*, 228; or for 'reported text' incorporating cuts 'probably by Shakespeare himself' for 'a smaller or touring company', see Ioppolo, 129. The memorial hypothesis often adduces a decline in F/Q1 similarity in the speeches of Clarence's murderers, anonymous messengers and Buckingham (*TxC*, 228; contrast Smidt, *Impostors*, 140).

Walker, 30; Hammond, 338); Q1 alone contains the clearly Shakespearean jack of the clock passage (4.2.97–114); and Q1 is sometimes closer to historical sources (Smidt, *Memorial*, 42).

Perhaps most difficult to reconcile with oral reconstruction are certain non-dialogue features that Q1 shares with F. For example, Q1 includes notations for two battlefield speeches – '*His oration to his souldiers*' (Q1, sig. M1ᵛ; 5.3.236 SD) and '*His oration to his army*' (Q1, sig. M2ᵛ; 5.3.313 SD) – that closely replicate marginal notations in the sources – 'The oration of King Henrie the sea*uenth to his armie*' and 'The oration of king Richard the third *to the chiefteins of his armie*' (Holinshed, 3.757, 755). It is easy to imagine how F could omit one of these markers, but more difficult to explain how or why an actor or theatre professional would 'remember' such a purely textual feature in recreating QMS from memory. Of course, the 'actor' doing the recollecting could have been Shakespeare, but other non-dialogue elements of Q1 and F show a similarly remarkable consistency that confounds the idea of even authorial 'recollection' as a sufficient, non-textual basis for QMS.

In line with the 'detailed and relatively efficient' correction of quarto copy by F's annotators outside the portions set uncorrected from Q3 (Jowett, 'Derby', 76), F's speech headings are relatively consistent, with one notable exception: the non-dialogue designations for Stanley/Derby/Darby/Darbie are consistent within scenes, but vary among them, and even clash with dialogue. The textual significance of this oddity has been debated. Hammond dismisses it, since 'Derby' – although anachronistic for the action – is Stanley's eventual title. Smidt, by contrast, takes the parallel patterns in Q1 and F non-dialogue names to reveal that 'the manuscript underlying F had an inconsistency similar to that of the manuscript used by Q' (Smidt, *Memorial*, 31; cf. Jowett, 'Derby', 75).

This pattern has been thoroughly examined by Jowett (375). In dialogue, the character begins as Derby/Darby (F/Q1) in 1.3; from 3.1 onwards, he is consistently 'Stanley' or 'Stanlie' in both texts. Non–dialogue identifiers also run parallel in Q1 and F (except for two scenes):

Non–dialogue identifiers Stanley / Derby

F   Derby in 1.3, 2.1 and 2.2
    Stanley in 3.2, 4.1
    Derby in 3.4 (conflicts with dialogue)
    Stanley in 4.2 and 4.4
    Derby in 4.5 to end (conflicts with dialogue)

Q1 Derby in 1.3, 2.1 (not named in Q1 2.2)
    Stanley in 3.2, 4.1
    Derby in 3.4 (conflicts with dialogue)
    Derby in 4.2 and 4.4 (conflicts with dialogue)
    Derby in 4.5 to end (conflicts with dialogue)

This similarity in an unspoken inconsistency appears too extensive, unmotivated and uncorrected to be coincidental, and it argues that QMS and FMS are linked by textual transmission. The handling of dramatic roles in the two texts reveals the direction of that transmission: QMS is derivative from FMS.

Q1 has fewer speaking parts than F, and speeches and actions are often differently attributed: in Q1 Brokenbury absorbs the Keeper's lines (1.4); the Cardinal replaces the Archbishop (2.4); Dorset speaks the Messenger's lines (2.4); Catesby takes over the roles of Lovell and Ratcliffe (3.4, 3.5); Catesby replaces Ratcliffe (4.3); Ratcliffe replaces the Sheriff (5.1); Catesby replaces Surrey (5.3). Dorset and Rivers are absent from 2.2; the Priest loses his speeches in 3.2; Clarence's silent daughter vanishes from 4.1; silent Norfolk disappears from 3.4; silent Brandon, Oxford and Herbert disappear from 5.3. Because such Q1 differences eliminate speaking parts (Keeper, Archbishop, Messenger, Sheriff, Surrey, Priest and Lovell), locally abbreviate others (Ratcliffe in 4.3, Vaughan in 3.3, Dorset and Rivers in 2.2), reduce the number of boy actors required simultaneously in 4.1 and ease doubling in 5.3, they have been taken to reflect – inconsistently realized – attempts at theatrical economy.[1]

Some changes are deft: Richmond's address to Brandon (5.3.22) becomes a reference to an offstage character in Q1 – 'Where is Sir William Brandon, he shall beare my standard' (L2^v).[2] Others are awkward: Catesby, Ratcliffe and Dorset provide useful examples that support the conclusion that Q1 is 'the later version than F' (Mowat & Werstine, xlix).

In Q1 Catesby performs the actions of F's Lovell and Ratcliffe in leading Hastings to execution, while retaining one speech of F's Ratcliffe. This conforms to Q1's omission of Lovell and abbreviation of Ratcliffe's part. In F 3.4 Richard orders Hastings's death, singling out his agents from those who sit '*at a Table*' till Richard bids them 'rise':

> I will not dine, vntill I see the same.
> *Louell* and *Ratcliffe*, looke that it be done: *Exeunt.*
> The rest that loue me, rise, and follow me.
>   *Manet Louell and Ratcliffe, with the Lord Hastings.*
>   (F 3.4.76–8; TLN 2048–52)

No one else aids the designated executioners, and it seems unlikely that anyone but Richard's intimates would risk remaining, given his demand that everyone register affection by leaving. The corresponding Q1 passage reads:

> I will not di[n]e to day I sweare,
> Vntill I see the same, some see it done,
> The rest that loue me, come and follow me   *Exeunt. manet*
>   *Cat. with Ha.*
>   (Q1, sig. G2^r)

Vaguely, 'some' are told to execute the order, but only one stays. Conceivably, Richard's invocation of 'some' to help could be

---

1 And perhaps literal economy; Q1 avoided Archbishop's robes, as Patrick notes.
2 Cf. Clarence's daughter at 4.1.1–5.

rhetorical pressure on the lords: either they stay, aiding contrived murder, or leave, showing their 'loue'. However, this difference between Richard's order and its result resembles other discrepancies where Q1's Catesby stands for F's Lovell and Ratcliffe.

Richard's order to Catesby to overlook the walls appears in 3.5 in both Q1 and F. Two lines later Q1's Catesby – rather than F's '*Louell and Ratcliffe*' – enters bearing the head of Hastings. This entry is preceded by Richard's contrived warning against approaching 'enemies':

> *Glo.* Looke backe, defend thee, here are enemies.
> *Buc.* God and our innocence defend vs.   *Enter Catesby*
> *Glo.* O, O, be quiet, it is Catesby.   *with Hast.head.*
>   (Q1 sig. G3ʳ)

Even if this plural ('enemies') were rhetorical, meant to evoke imaginary offstage forces rather than the single entering character (cf. Urkowitz, 455), similar disagreements vex the following lines. In Q1 and F Buckingham refers to Hastings's executioner(s) as 'these our friends' (3.5.54); 'these' better suits F's Lovell and Ratcliffe than Q1's solitary Catesby.

True, numerical agreement is frequently uncertain in Shakespeare (see 3.5.55n.).[1] 'This' and 'these' may refer to offstage characters (e.g. 1.1.2, 5.5.0.3–4n.). Characters may lack entry directions (e.g. Q1's Catesby at 3.5.13.1 or Ratcliffe at 5.1.0) or exit unremarked (e.g. Q1's Buckingham at 3.4.41). Thus, Richard's 'friends' (3.5.54) might enter with whoever bears Hastings's head and leave similarly without notice. Ultimately, though, a question remains about motivation for the differences, since Q1 elsewhere awkwardly retains Ratcliffe.[2]

Ratcliffe serves as Buckingham's executioner in Q1 5.1, but Buckingham addresses his former ally as if undistinguished

---

1   For 'variants in number' that compromise 'automatic preference' for F, see Honigmann, 'Text', 54.
2   Rivers and Dorset are similarly retained despite local omission from Q1 2.2.

among anonymous 'fellowes' or 'sirs' (Q1), which would be more appropriate for F's Sheriff (whom Buckingham calls 'Fellow') (see 5.1.0.1n.).[1] This impersonality contrasts with the vehemently personal denunciation of Ratcliffe by Rivers and Grey (3.3.1–5), but parallels the surprising lack of emotion Hastings displays towards his own Q1 executioner(s) in 3.4. F's Hastings is led to death by Ratcliffe and Lovell. While they know one another (appearing jointly in 2.1 and 2.2) nothing suggests the intimacy that obtains between Hastings and his Q1 executioner, Catesby. In both texts Hastings earlier shares with Catesby his ill-founded confidences, staking his life on 'my good friend *Catesby*' (F) or 'my seruant Catesby' (Q1) (3.2.21). However, in 3.4.79–106 Hastings and his executioner(s) speak impersonally. In a play filled with ironies of over-confidence and betrayal, it is difficult to explain Hastings's failure to remark Catesby's treachery. Mowat and Werstine judge that this evidence argues Q1 is 'a version derivative from the F version' (li).

Differences concerning Dorset support a similar conclusion. His interaction with his mother in Q1 2.4.40–68 is oddly impersonal, especially when contrasted with their exchanges at 4.1.37–46. At 2.4.39–49 a speaker whom Q1 calls 'Dorset' and F calls 'Messenger' announces the imprisonment of Rivers, Grey and Vaughan, dire news prompting passionate reactions from those onstage, including Queen Elizabeth, Dorset's mother. Dorset reveals Richard's violent onslaught against their family, but mother and son express no concern for one another. However, two tiny variants suggest Q1's 'improvised attempt to make Dorset react to Elizabeth's presence' and vice versa (Hammond, 15–16). Q1 has Dorset address a 'Lady' instead of F's 'Lord' at 2.4.49, and has Queen Elizabeth invoke 'the downfall of our house' instead of

---

1 Buckingham and Ratcliffe are together in 2.1, 2.2, 3.3, 3.4, 3.5 and 4.2, but never directly address one another (Urkowitz, 458).

F's 'ruine of my House' in response. Not much change, and 'Lady' possibly addresses the Duchess. In any case, Queen Elizabeth summons only her youngest son to accompany her in flight, as if no other son were present – true in F but at odds with Q1's inclusion of Dorset.

By contrast, in Q1 4.1 Queen Elizabeth and Dorset express mutual concern at the 'dead killing newes' of Richard's sequestration of Prince Edward. Dorset urges, 'Madam, haue comfort, how fares your grace?' and she responds:

> O Dorset speake not to me, get thee hence,
> Death and destruction dogge thee at the heeles,
> Thy Mothers name is ominous to children,
> If thou wilt outstrip death, go crosse the seas,
> And liue with Richmond, from the reach of hell
> (Q1, sig. H3^v; 4.1.38–42)

These different renderings of the Q1 mother/son relationship support the Cambridge editors: 'The change [from F's Messenger to Q1's Dorset in 2.4] must have been deliberate, and as the Queen does not greet the person who brings the intelligence, and expresses no anxiety for his safety when she herself is going to sanctuary, it seems more proper that the messenger should be one of inferior rank . . . His ignorance of the cause of the arrest of the nobles and the terms in which he speaks of them are in keeping with the character of a messenger' (Cam, 642n.). Some have dissented about details (*TxC*, 237) or attempted refutation.

Steven Urkowitz proposes that Q1 could represent an 'early state' of a work which, in revised form, constitutes the 'later state' of F (Urkowitz, 466). Seconding Kristian Smidt's attacks on faulty arguments for F's priority (cf. Hammond, 16; Maguire, 169), Urkowitz suggests that Shakespeare might have written a draft of QMS and then noticed 'the apparent coldness' of mother and son and revised 'to develop this coldness' while re-assigning Dorset's lines 'to an anonymous messenger' (Urkowitz, 451). Authorial revision is possible, even probable, in both FMS and QMS, but 'coldness' demands more support than the texts provide.[1] On balance, the majority opinion, that FMS precedes QMS, appears credible, but Urkowitz correctly imagines precedence as subject to exceptions and qualifications (cf. Ioppolo, 129). There is no reason to think that a reviser, revisers or an author might not return to a manuscript or manuscripts and change them before one or both reached print. In fact this seems the most likely hypothesis.[2]

VERBAL VARIANTS Q1/F: THEORY AND PRACTICE

If the discrepancies in roles between Q1 and F suggest incomplete attempts at theatrical economy, then the dialogue line totals permit similar inference. The differences add up to over two hundred lines that appear in F but not in Qq, not a great number, but they are sometimes locally purposeful in appearance. Absence from Q1 of two lengthy passages amounting to 69 lines of F 4.4 (4.4.222–35, 288–342) contributes to an approximately 84-line difference between that scene's versions. It is easy to imagine Q1 shortening for theatrical economy but difficult to conceive of F intentionally expanding the scene – at least for the theatre. But Q1 uniquely contains the brilliant jack of the clock passage (4.2.97–114), which is dependent on Holinshed (see 4.2.101–5n.; Churchill, 222) and evidently Shakespearean. This challenging counter-instance may represent the pressures of censorship or self-censorship weighing upon the author, compilers or printers of F, but it remains possible that it was added to QMS rather than subtracted (or omitted) from FMS.[3]

---

1 Taking Dorset's advice in F 2.2 as 'insensitive' ignores early modern admonitions against excessive grieving (see Pigman).
2 For recent views that quartos may provide alternative, abbreviated drafts, incorporating revision and redaction of the longer texts of Shakespeare's plays, see *The First Quarto of King Henry V*, ed. Andrew Gurr (Cambridge, 2000), ix; Halio, 137; Blayney, 'Publication', 394; Erne, 219.
3 For arguments about the passage, see 4.2.97–114n. The missing lines occur very near the end of Compositor A's stint (end of s3ᵛ), and similar locations occasion problems and result in omissions elsewhere (see Forker, 540).

While 'in general, F in its verbal variants is closer than Q to the play's acknowledged sources' (*TxC*, 230), the evidence is not uniform. Historical details constitute some of the strongest evidence for the 'authority' of QMS. Q1 gets some things right that F gets wrong. For example, Q1 follows More, Hall and Holinshed (3.723) in naming the Pursuivant in 3.2 'Hastings', while F vaguely calls him '*a Pursuiuant*' and Hastings calls him 'sirrah' and 'fellow'. Here, one might debate whether Q1 more probably reflects revision of FMS by someone with source in hand or mind, or whether F reflects someone else editing FMS for some other reason. After all, someone edited FMS to remove oaths offensive under an Act of 1606, leaving particularly evident effects of removal in F 1.4 (see notes to 1.4.84–end, 121, 125 and 143, 188–9). The 'Acte to Restrain Abuses of Players' (1606) was aimed not at published texts like Folio *Richard III* but at performers who might 'jestingly or prophanely speake or use the holy Name of God or of Christ Jesus, or of the Holy Ghoste or of the Trinitie . . . in any Stage play, Interlude, Shewe, Maygame, or Pageant' (Chambers, *Stage*, 4.338–9). Thus, F's evident (and imperfect) removal of such materials may represent the efforts of someone interested in constructing a performance text from FMS.[1] Removal of the Pursuivant's name might represent an attempt, possibly but by no means necessarily authoritative, to remove an apparent confusion of identities from Qq.

Ultimately, Q1 is closer than F to the sources here; even in phrasing (Honigmann, 'Text', 49). It is difficult to imagine Q1's printers adding the name or phrasing, so one possible deduction is that QMS contained accurately recorded historical details that FMS lacked.[2] That would make QMS here a revision by a very authoritative reviser. An alternative is that FMS also had these details, but that they were omitted or purposely edited

---

1 On expurgation or substitution of secular for religious oaths in F texts of other plays with quarto editions, see Ioppolo, 79; cf. 1.4.84–end.n., 121n., 188–9n.
2 For Q1 agreements with Holinshed and Hall, see Honigmann, who argues that despite 'memorial corruption, [Q1] is partly based' on a 'very badly damaged' manuscript (Honigmann, 'Text', 52). Smidt offers a similarly complex assessment (Smidt, *Memorial*, 42).

out by someone before or during the production of F. Similarly accurate details occur at Q1 2.2.142 and 154, where the Prince's location is 'Ludlow', rather than F's 'London'. Here, however, F itself is locally inconsistent, because earlier he is said to need fetching 'from Ludlow . . . / Hither to London' (2.2.121–2). This appears to be a production mistake in F rather than a proof of superior authority for QMS. For simple mistakes, Q1's misuse of the 'beare' as a metaphor for Richard at 3.2.10, uncorrected until Q6 despite references to Richard as the boar (3.2.27–32), is strikingly wrong. Q1 gives Tyrrel different names: he is historically 'Iames *Ti*rrell' at 4.2.67, but enters 4.3 as '*Sir Francis Tirrell*'. This discrepancy remains through Q8 but is not present in F. These sorts of errors appear in both texts. Other factual disagreements are more instructive.

F has Richard's party proceed from Stony Stratford to London via Northampton (2.4.1–2); this makes no geographical sense, but follows the sources which describe the Prince being taken to Northampton after the arrest of Rivers, Grey and Vaughan. Q1 corrects this 'mistake' on the basis of geography, an incorrect correction unlikely to originate with the author. F does make a historical error involving Lord Rivers that Q1 avoids. F mistakes 'lord Antony Woouduile erle Ryuers and lorde Scales, brother to the quene' (Hall, *Edward V*, fol. v[r]) for two characters or even three (see 2.1.0.2n.). By contrast, Q1's entry direction names only '*Ryuers*', and its dialogue lacks F's line, 'Of you lord *Woouill*, and Lord *Scales* of you'. This seems to be correction, but determining its agent and authority is complicated, because Q1's choices could merely amount to another of its inconsistent attempts at theatrical economy, while F's proximity to Hall marks FMS as closer to the written sources and hence, perhaps, to authorial draft.

Why, then, does this edition allow F's geography in 2.4 but accept Q1's roles in 2.1? It seems less probable that a printing-house corrector would have to hand the relevant facts of genealogy rather than those of geography (*TxC*, 229). Thus, the case of Q1's Rivers could support a relatively 'authoritative' correction by some knowledgeable person(s) (Jowett, 121). Practically speaking, there seems little to gain in following F's historical error – no matter how 'authoritative' – to add a single appearance by yet another silent character, or even two, in a densely populated play. So the present edition defers to Q1 in this case.

This is not an affirmation of historical 'fact' as determinative in editorial decision-making. Choosing to follow Q1 instead of F regarding Rivers should be balanced against the choice to accept a mistake concerning 'mother's cost' at 5.3.324. Q1 and F both follow a misprint; Holinshed's second edition has 'moothers' instead of the first edition's 'brothers' (as in Hall). Since the line occurs in the portion of F set directly from uncorrected Q3, one cannot argue that F validates Q1. However, Q1's agreement with Holinshed's error argues for the playwright as its likely origin, and this play provides strong thematic relevance for 'mother's' (Willis, *Nurture*, 204). In this case, only a questionable notion of editorial authority might justify setting the author's history straight.

In many cases the decisions are difficult. Q1 follows the historical sources in omitting Ratcliffe from the council scene (3.4). F not only includes him, but has him in Yorkshire executing Rivers, Grey and Vaughan in 3.3 before immediately re-entering in 3.4 for the same day's London meeting. Here Q1 seemingly offers the better choice: historically authoritative, and observant of probability and stage convention; however, choosing is complicated by Q1's other confused and incomplete attempts to remove Ratcliffe. As argued above, Hastings's 3.4 speeches are more appropriate in the presence of Ratcliffe and Lovell (F). Furthermore, even if QMS may have 'corrected' FMS about Ratcliffe's bi-location, it is problematic to invoke concern for theatrical principle or probability, since Q1 has the Cardinal re-enter (3.1.0) and has Rivers in London *after* his Yorkshire execution (see 3.4.6 SPn.).

Small matters, tough editorial decisions, but this edition, following its general tendency, sides with F; you may see it differently. I hope the apparatus will make the editorial choices involved both evident and (appropriately) arguable. This edition attempts to provide as much as it can of the 'raw material' from which actors and readers have constructed and continue to construct *Richard III*.[1] Ultimately, they will make it their own anyway. Shakespeare's plays probably never achieved final form, but existed in multiple, sometimes inconsistent, versions (McKerrow, *Prolegomena*, 6). This multiplicity may have been the case in Shakespeare's lifetime; it has been overwhelmingly so since. 'The' play amounts to the many 'plays' that texts and traditions make of it. Some are probably better than others, but even Cibber's version has its charms; it all depends on how one judges and on who does the judging. I do not think Shakespeare (or 'Shakespeare'), the Lord Chamberlain's Men or the King's Men would mind at all.

---

1   Cf. Blayney, 'Intro', xxx; Dutton, 174.

APPENDIX 2

CASTING

We do not know with certainty how many actors performed *Richard III* in Shakespeare's time, and changing circumstances of performance would obviously have affected casting, doubling and, in all likelihood, cutting. Leaving room for some approximation, T.J. King suggests that 11 adults and 6 boys could have performed the principal parts in the Q1 version of the play as well as in the longer F version (T.J. King, *Casting Shakespeare's Plays: London Actors and their Roles* (Cambridge, 1992), 80); however, David Bradley suggests 12 adults and 8 boys for performing Q1 and 15 to 16 adults and 8 boys for performing F (David Bradley, *From Text to Performance in the Elizabethan Theatre: Preparing the Play for the Stage* (Cambridge, 1992), 52, 233). The difference between such informed estimates conveys the wide range of possibilities. In any case, the play's many minor parts could easily have been covered in various ways by the company's principal adult and child actors. To take one example, in modern productions the actor playing Richard sometimes acts as one of the Citizens in 2.3. The chart which follows offers one suggestion for performing *Richard III* as the play appears in this edition; it does not attempt to distribute the play's many minor and silent parts.

DOUBLING CHART

Actor	Role	1.1	1.2	1.3	1.4	2.1	2.2	2.3	2.4	3.1	3.2	3.3	3.4	3.5	3.6	3.7	4.1	4.2	4.3	4.4	4.5	5.1	5.2	5.3	5.4	5.5	Total
1	Richard	x	x	x		x	x			x			x	x		x		x	x	x				x	x	x	15
2	Buckingham			x		x	x			x	x		x	x		x		x				x		x			11
3	Clarence	x			x																			x			3
4	Hastings	x		x		x	x			x	x		x											x			8
5	Richmond																						x	x		x	3
	King Edward					x																					1
6	Stanley			x		x	x				x		x				x	x		x	x			x		x	11
	Scrivener														x												1
7	1 Murderer			x	x																						2
	Ratcliffe											x	x	x				x	x	x				x	x	x	9
8	2 Murderer			x	x																						2
	Lord Mayor									x				x		x											3
9	Catesby									x	x		x	x		x		x		x				x	x	x	10
	3 Citizen							x																			1
10	Rivers			x		x	x					x												x			5
	Tyrrel																	x	x								2

Actor	Role	1.1	1.2	1.3	1.4	2.1	2.2	2.3	2.4	3.1	3.2	3.3	3.4	3.5	3.6	3.7	4.1	4.2	4.3	4.4	4.5	5.1	5.2	5.3	5.4	5.5	Total
11	Brakenbury	x			x												x										3
	Archbishop								x																		1
12	Dorset			x		x	x										x							x			5
	Messenger										x																1

Boy actor

	Role	1.1	1.2	1.3	1.4	2.1	2.2	2.3	2.4	3.1	3.2	3.3	3.4	3.5	3.6	3.7	4.1	4.2	4.3	4.4	4.5	5.1	5.2	5.3	5.4	5.5	Total
1	Queen Elizabeth			x		x	x		x								x			x							6
2	Queen Margaret			x																x							2
3	Anne		x														x							x			3
4	Duchess of York						x		x								x			x							4
5	Prince Edward									x														x			2
	Daughter of Clarence						x																				1
6	York								x	x														x			3
	Son of Clarence						x										x										2

APPENDIX 3

GENEALOGICAL TABLE

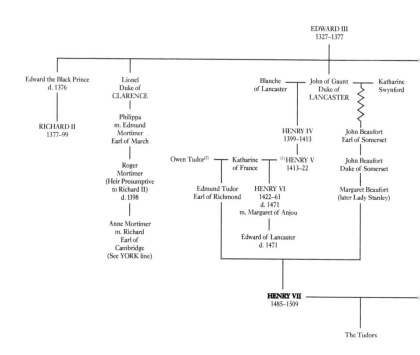

Genealogical table, from *Richard III and the Princes in the Tower*, by A.J. Pollard (New York, 1991), showing the marriages linking families and individuals (by permission of A.J. Pollard and recreated by DC Graphic Design Ltd)

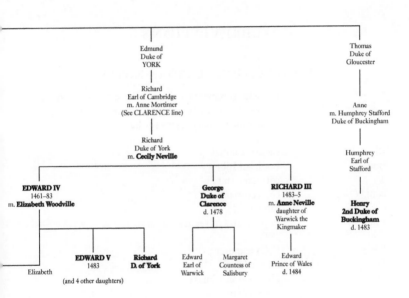

ABBREVIATIONS AND REFERENCES

References to Shakespeare's works are to Arden 3 editions published at the time of writing, and otherwise to Arden 2 editions. Biblical references are taken from the Bishops' Bible (*The holie Bible conteynyg the olde Testament and the newe* (1568; STC 2099)) or from the Geneva Bible (*The Bible and Holy Scriptures conteyned in the Olde and Newe Testament* (Geneva, 1561; STC 2095)); where the source is Geneva, this is indicated in the text. Place of publication is London unless otherwise noted.

ABBREVIATIONS

ABBREVIATIONS USED IN NOTES

*	precedes commentary notes involving textual issues, especially variations and inconsistencies in readings among the primary texts on which this edition is based
BL	British Library
Bod.	Bodleian Library
c.	corrected state
conj.	conjectured by
c.w.	catchword
Edin.	Edinburgh University Library
F	Folio
FMS	Folio manuscript
Fo	Folger Library
Hn	Huntington Library
n.	commentary note
n.d.	no date
O	Octavo
Q	Quarto
QMS	Quarto manuscript
om.	omitted
opp.	opposite
RSC	Royal Shakespeare Company
SD	stage direction
SP	speech prefix

subst.	substantially
this edn	a reading adopted for the first time in this edition
TLN	through line numbering in *The First Folio of Shakespeare, prepared by Charlton Hinman*, Norton Facsimile (New York, 1996)
Tn	Trinity College Library
t.n.	textual note
u.	uncorrected state
Y	Yale University Library

WORKS BY AND PARTLY BY SHAKESPEARE

AC	*Antony and Cleopatra*
AW	*All's Well That Ends Well*
AYL	*As You Like It*
CE	*Comedy of Errors*
Car	*The History of Cardenio*
Cor	*Coriolanus*
Cym	*Cymbeline*
DF	*Double Falsehood*
E3	*King Edward III*
Ham	*Hamlet*
1H4	*King Henry IV, Part 1*
2H4	*King Henry IV, Part 2*
H5	*King Henry V*
1H6	*King Henry VI, Part 1*
2H6	*King Henry VI, Part 2*
3H6	*King Henry VI, Part 3*
H8	*King Henry VIII*
JC	*Julius Caesar*
KJ	*King John*
KL	*King Lear*
LC	*A Lover's Complaint*
LLL	*Love's Labour's Lost*
Luc	*The Rape of Lucrece*
MA	*Much Ado about Nothing*
Mac	*Macbeth*
MM	*Measure for Measure*
MND	*A Midsummer Night's Dream*
MV	*The Merchant of Venice*
MW	*The Merry Wives of Windsor*
Oth	*Othello*
Per	*Pericles*

PP	*The Passionate Pilgrim*
PT	*The Phoenix and Turtle*
R2	*King Richard II*
R3	*King Richard III*
RJ	*Romeo and Juliet*
Son	*Sonnets*
STM	*The Book of Sir Thomas More*
TC	*Troilus and Cressida*
Tem	*The Tempest*
TGV	*The Two Gentlemen of Verona*
Tim	*Timon of Athens*
Tit	*Titus Andronicus*
TN	*Twelfth Night*
TNK	*The Two Noble Kinsmen*
TS	*The Taming of the Shrew*
VA	*Venus and Adonis*
WT	*The Winter's Tale*

REFERENCES

EDITIONS OF SHAKESPEARE COLLATED

Alexander	*William Shakespeare: The Complete Works*, ed. Peter Alexander (1951)
Ard[1]	*The Tragedy of King Richard the Third*, ed. A. Hamilton Thompson, Arden Shakespeare (1909)
Ard[2]	*King Richard III*, ed. Antony Hammond, Arden Shakespeare (1981)
Bevington[3]	See Bevington[4]
Bevington[3]	*The Complete Works of Shakespeare*, ed. David Bevington, 3rd edn (Glenview, Ill., 1980)
Bevington[4]	*The Complete Works of Shakespeare*, ed. David Bevington, 4th edn (New York, 1992)
Cam	*Works*, ed. William George Clark and William Aldis Wright, 9 vols (Cambridge and London, 1863–6)
Cam[1]	*Richard III*, ed. John Dover Wilson (Cambridge, 1954)
Cam[2]	*King Richard III*, ed. Janis Lull (Cambridge, 1999)
Capell	*Mr. William Shakespeare His Comedies, Histories and Tragedies*, ed. Edward Capell, 10 vols (1767–8)
Collier	*The Works of William Shakespeare*, ed. John Payne Collier, 8 vols (1842–4)

Dyce	*The Works of William Shakespeare*, ed. Alexander Dyce, 6 vols (1857)
Eccles	*The Tragedy of Richard the Third*, ed. Marc Eccles (New York, 1964)
Evans	*The Riverside Shakespeare*, ed. G. Blakemore Evans (Boston, 1974)
Evans, 1959	*The Tragedy of Richard the Third*, ed. G. Blakemore Evans (Baltimore, Md, 1959)
F	*Comedies, Histories and Tragedies*, The First Folio (1623)
F2	*Comedies, Histories and Tragedies*, The Second Folio (1632)
F3	*Comedies, Histories and Tragedies*, The Third Folio (1663)
F4	*Comedies, Histories and Tragedies*, The Fourth Folio (1685)
Folger	*The Tragedy of Richard III*, ed. Barbara A. Mowat and Paul Werstine, New Folger Library Shakespeare (New York, 1996)
Furness	See Var
Hammond	See Ard[2]
Hanmer	*The Works of Shakespear*, ed. Thomas Hanmer, 6 vols (1743–4)
Holland	*The Tragedy of King Richard the Third*, ed. Peter Holland (2000)
Honigmann	*King Richard the Third*, ed. E.A.J. Honigmann (Harmondsworth, 1968)
Johnson	*The Plays of William Shakespeare*, ed. Samuel Johnson, 8 vols (1765)
Jowett	See Oxf[1]
Keightley	*The Plays and Poems of William Shakespeare*, ed. Thomas Keightley, 6 vols (1864)
Knight	*The Pictorial Edition of the Works of Shakespere*, ed. Charles Knight, 8 vols (1838–43)
Lull	See Cam[2]
Malone	*The Plays and Poems of William Shakespeare*, ed. Edmond Malone, 10 vols (1790)
Marshall	*The Henry Irving Shakespeare: The Works of William Shakespeare*, ed. Henry Irving and F.A. Marshall, 8 vols (1887–90)
Mowat & Werstine	See Folger
Oxf	*The Complete Works*, ed. Stanley Wells and Gary Taylor (Oxford, 1986)
Oxf[1]	*Richard III*, ed. John Jowett, Oxford Shakespeare (Oxford, 2000)
Pope	*The Works of Shakespear*, ed. Alexander Pope, 6 vols (1723–5)

Q1	*The Tragedy of King Richard the Third* (1597)
Q2	*The Tragedy of King Richard the Third* (1598)
Q3	*The Tragedy of King Richard the Third* (1602)
Q4	*The Tragedy of King Richard the Third* (1605)
Q5	*The Tragedy of King Richard the Third* (1612)
Q6	*The Tragedy of King Richard the Third* (1622)
Q7	*The Tragedy of King Richard the Third* (1629)
Q8	*The Tragedy of King Richard the Third* (1634)

Rann   *The Dramatic Works of Shakespeare*, ed. Joseph Rann, 6 vols (1786–91)

Rowe   *The Works of Mr. William Shakespear*, ed. Nicholas Rowe, 6 vols (1709)

Rowe[2]   *The Works of Mr. William Shakespear*, ed. Nicholas Rowe, 2nd edn, 6 vols (1709)

Rowe[3]   *The Works of Mr. William Shakespear*, ed. Nicholas Rowe, 3rd edn, 8 vols (1714)

Singer   *The Dramatic Works of William Shakespeare*, ed. Samuel Weller Singer, 10 vols (1826)

Sisson   *The Complete Works*, ed. Charles Jasper Sisson (1954)

Steevens   *The Plays of William Shakespeare*, ed. George Steevens and Isaac Reed, 4th edn, 15 vols (1793)

Theobald   *The Works of Shakespeare*, ed. Lewis Theobald, 7 vols (1733)

Thompson   See Ard[1]

Var   *The Tragedy of Richard the Third*, ed. Horace Howard Furness, New Variorum Shakespeare (Philadelphia, 1908)

Warburton   *The Works of Shakespeare*, ed. William Warburton, 8 vols (1747)

Wells & Taylor See Oxf

White   *The Works of William Shakespeare*, ed. Richard Grant White, 12 vols (1857–66)

Wilson   See Cam[1]

OTHER WORKS CITED

Abbott   E.A. Abbott, *A Shakespearian Grammar*, 2nd edn (1870)

Adelman   Janet Adelman, *Suffocating Mothers: Fantasies of Maternal Origin in Shakespeare's Plays* (New York, 1992)

Aduertisement *An Aduertisement Written to a Secretary* (Antwerp, 1592; STC 19885)

Allott   *Englands Parnassus, compiled by Robert Allott, 1600*, ed. Charles Crawford (Oxford, 1913)

470

Almond	*An Almond for a Parrat* (London?, 1589; STC 534)
Anderson	Judith H. Anderson, *Biographical Truth: The Representation of Historical Persons in Tudor–Stuart Writing* (New Haven, Conn., 1984)
Apius	R.B., *A new tragicall comedie of Apius and Virginia* (1575; STC 1059)
Arber	Edward Arber (ed.), *Transcript of the Registers of the Company of Stationers of London*, 5 vols (1874–94)
Archer	Ian W. Archer, 'Popular politics in the sixteenth and early seventeenth centuries', in Paul Griffiths and Mark S.R. Jenner (eds), *Londinopolis: Essays in the Cultural and Social History of Early Modern London* (Manchester, 2000)
Arden	*The Tragedy of Master Arden of Faversham*, ed. M.L. Wine, Revels Plays (1973)
Armstrong, C.A.J.	C.A.J. Armstrong, 'The inauguration ceremonies of the Yorkist kings and their title to the throne', *TRHS*, 4th series, 30 (1948), 51–73
Ascham	Roger Ascham, *English Works*, ed. W.A. Wright (Cambridge, 1904)
Bacon, *Henry VII*	Francis Bacon, *The History of the Reign of King Henry the Seventh*, ed. F.J. Levy (Indianapolis, 1972)
Bacon, *Works*	Francis Bacon, *The Works of Francis Bacon*, ed. James Spedding, Robert Leslie Ellis and Douglas Denon Heath, 14 vols (1861–79)
Baldwin	T.W. Baldwin, *William Shakespere's Small Latine and Lesse Greeke*, 2 vols (Urbana, Ill., 1944)
Bancroft, *Positions*	Richard Bancroft, *Daungerous positions and proceedings* (1593; STC 1344)
Bancroft, *Sermon*	Richard Bancroft, *A Sermon Preached at Paules Crosse, 1588* (1589; STC 1346)
Barton & Hall	John Barton and Peter Hall, *The Wars of the Roses* (1970)
Bate, *Ovid*	Jonathan Bate, *Shakespeare and Ovid* (Oxford, 1993)
Bate, *Romantics*	Jonathan Bate (ed.), *The Romantics on Shakespeare* (1992)
Bate, *Tit*	*Titus Andronicus*, ed. Jonathan Bate, Arden Shakespeare (1995)
BCP	*The Book of Common Prayer 1559*, ed. John E. Booty (Charlottesville, 1976)
Berry, E.	Edward I. Berry, *Patterns of Decay: Shakespeare's Early Histories* (Charlottesville, 1975)
Berry, R.	Ralph Berry, 'Richard III: bonding the audience', in J.C. Gray (ed.), *Mirror up to Shakespeare* (1984), 114–27

Bible	*The holie Bible conteynyg the olde Testament and the newe*, 'The Bishops' Bible' (1568; STC 2099)
Birch	W.J. Birch, *An Inquiry into the Philosophy and Religion of Shakespere* (1848)
Birney	Alice Lotvin Birney, *Satiric Catharsis in Shakespeare: A Theory of Dramatic Structure* (Berkeley, Calif., 1973)
Blayney, 'Intro'	Peter Blayney, 'Introduction to the second edition', *The First Folio of Shakespeare, prepared by Charlton Hinman*, Norton Facsimile (New York, 1996)
Blayney, 'Publication'	Peter Blayney, 'The publication of playbooks', in Cox & Kastan, 383–422
Bloom, G.	Gina Bloom, *Voice in Motion: Staging Gender, Shaping Sound in Early Modern England* (Philadelphia, 2007)
Blundeville	Thomas Blundeville, *A Very Briefe and Profitable Treatise . . . of Counselers* (facsimile reprint, *Of Councils and Counselors*, 1570; STC 11488), ed. Karl-Ludwig Selig (Gainesville, Fla., 1963)
Booth	Edwin Booth, *Edwin Booth's Prompt-book of Richard III*, ed. William Winter (New York, 1878)
Born	Hanspeter Born, 'The date of *2, 3, Henry VI*', *SQ*, 25 (1974), 323–34
Bright	Timothie Bright, *A Treatise of Melancholie* (1586), intro. by Hardin Craig (New York, 1940)
Brooke	Nicholas Brooke, *Shakespeare's Early Tragedies* (1968)
Brooks, 'Antecedents'	Harold F. Brooks, '*Richard III*: antecedents of Clarence's dream', *SS* 32 (1979), 145–50
Brooks, 'Unhistorical'	Harold F. Brooks, '*Richard III*: unhistorical amplifications: the women's scenes and Seneca', *MLR*, 75 (1980), 721–37
Brown	Susan Brown, 'Queen Elizabeth in Richard III', in Robert Smallwood (ed.), *Players of Shakespeare 4* (Cambridge, 1998), 101–13
Buck	Sir George Buck, *The History of King Richard III*, ed. Arthur Noel Kincaid (Gloucester, 1982)
Budra	Paul Budra, *A Mirror for Magistrates and the de casibus Tradition* (Toronto, 2000)
Bullough	Geoffrey Bullough (ed.), *Narrative and Dramatic Sources of Shakespeare*, 8 vols (London and New York, 1957–75)
Burns	*King Henry VI, Part 1*, ed. Edward Burns, Arden Shakespeare (2000)
Calvin, Commentaries	John Calvin, *Commentaries on the Epistle of Paul the Apostle to the Romans*, ed. John Owen, vol. 38 (1948; rpt. Grand Rapids, Mich., 1959)

Calvin, *Institutes*	John Calvin, *Institutes of the Christian Religion*, ed. John T. McNeill, trans. Ford Lewis Battles, 2 vols (Philadelphia, 1960)
Campbell	Lily B. Campbell, *Shakespeare's Histories: Mirrors of Elizabethan Policy* (San Marino, Calif., 1947)
Carroll	William C. Carroll, *Fat King, Lean Beggar: Representations of Poverty in the Age of Shakespeare* (Ithaca, NY, 1996)
Cerasano	S.P. Cerasano, 'Churls just wanna have fun: reviewing *Richard III*', *SQ*, 36 (1985), 618–29
Chambers, *Shakespeare*	E.K. Chambers, *William Shakespeare: A Study of Facts and Problems* (Oxford, 1930)
Chambers, *Stage*	E.K. Chambers, *The Elizabethan Stage*, 4 vols (1923; corrected edn Oxford, 1967)
Charnes	Linda Charnes, *Notorious Identity: Materializing the Subject in Shakespeare* (Cambridge, Mass., 1993)
Chettle	Henry Chettle, *Kind-Harts Dreame* (1593?; STC 5123)
Chrimes	S.B. Chrimes, *Henry VII* (1972; rev. edn New Haven, Conn., 1999)
Churchill	George B. Churchill, *Richard the Third up to Shakespeare* (1900; rpt. Totowa, NJ, 1976)
Cibber, *Richard III*	Colley Cibber, *The Tragical History of King Richard III*, in Christopher Spencer (ed.), *Five Restoration Adaptations of Shakespeare* (Urbana, Ill., 1965)
Clarke, *Characters*	Charles Cowden Clarke, *Shakespeare-Characters* (1863)
Clemen	Wolfgang Clemen, *A Commentary on Shakespeare's Richard III*, trans. Jean Bonheim (1968)
Colley	Scott Colley, *Richard's Himself Again: A Stage History of Richard III* (New York, 1992)
Collinson, *Puritan*	Patrick Collinson, *The Elizabethan Puritan Movement* (Berkeley, Calif., 1967)
Cooper	Thomas Cooper, *An Admonition to the People of London* (1589; STC 5683a)
Copy	*The Copie of a leter, vvryten by a Master of Arte of Cambrige* ([Paris,] 1584; STC 5742.9)
Courtenay	Thomas Peregrine Courtenay, *Commentaries on the Historical Plays of Shakespeare*, 2 vols (1840; rpt. New York, 1972)
Cox & Kastan	John D. Cox and David Scott Kastan (eds), *A New History of Early English Drama* (New York, 1997)
Craven, 'Proofreading'	Alan E. Craven, 'Proofreading in the shop of Valentine Simmes', *PBSA*, 68 (1974), 361–72
Craven, 'Simmes'	Alan E. Craven, 'Simmes' Compositor A and five Shakespeare quartos', *SB*, 26 (1973), 37–60

Cressy, 'Kinship'	David Cressy, 'Kinship and kin interaction in early modern England', *Past and Present*, 113 (1986), 38–69
Cressy, *Travesties*	David Cressy, *Travesties and Transgressions in Tudor and Stuart England: Tales of Discord and Dissension* (Oxford, 2000)
Croft, 'Reputation'	Pauline Croft, 'The reputation of Robert Cecil: libels, political opinion and popular awareness in the early seventeenth century', *TRHS*, 6th series (1991), 43–69
Cruikshank	C.G. Cruikshank, *Elizabeth's Army* (Oxford, 1966)
*CW*2, 3, 15	See More
Daniel	P.A. Daniel, Introduction to William Griggs's facsimile of *Richard the Third, The First Quarto* (1886)
Davies & Marlowe	John Davies and Christopher Marlowe, *Epigrammes and Elegies* (*c.* 1596; STC 6350)
Davison	*The First Quarto of King Richard III*, ed. Peter Davison (Cambridge, 1996)
Day	Gillian Day, *King Richard III* (2002)
Declaration	[Richard Verstegan,] *A Declaration of the true causes of the great troubles* (Antwerp, 1592; STC 10005)
de Jongh	Nicholas de Jongh, *Evening Standard*, 12 August 1992, Shakespeare Centre Clipping Book
de Somogyi	Nick de Somogyi, *Shakespeare's Theatre of War* (Aldershot, 1998)
Dekker	Thomas Dekker, *Seven Deadly Sinnes of London*, in A.B. Grosart (ed.), *The Non-dramatic Works of Thomas Dekker*, 5 vols (1885; rpt. New York, 1963)
Delius	N. Delius, 'Ueber den ursprünglichen Text des *Richard III*', *Shakespeare Jahrbuch*, 7 (1872), 124–69
Dent	R.W. Dent, *Shakespeare's Proverbial Language: An Index* (Berkeley, Calif., 1981)
Dessen & Thomson	Alan C. Dessen and Leslie Thomson, *A Dictionary of Stage Directions in English Drama 1580–1642* (Cambridge, 1999)
Donohue	Joseph Donohue, *Dramatic Character in the English Romantic Age* (Princeton, NJ, 1970)
Downer	Alan S. Downer, *The Eminent Tragedian William Charles Macready* (Cambridge, Mass., 1966)
Drakakis	*King Richard the Third*, ed. John Drakakis, Shakespearean Originals: First Editions (London, 1996)
Draudt	Manfred Draudt, 'Shakespeare's histories at the Vienna Burgtheater', in Hoenselaars, 196–212
Drayton	Michael Drayton, *Works*, ed. J. William Hebel, 5 vols (Oxford, 1933)

DSK	David Scott Kastan, private communication
Dubrow	Heather Dubrow, '"I fear there will a worse come in his place": surrogate parents and Shakespeare's *Richard III*', in Naomi J. Miller and Naomi Yavneh (eds), *Maternal Measures: Figuring Caregiving in the Early Modern Period* (Aldershot, 2000), 348–62
Dutton	Richard Dutton, 'The birth of the author', in Cedric C. Brown and Arthur F. Marotti (eds), *Texts and Cultural Change in Early Modern England* (1997), 153–78
E3	*King Edward III*, ed. Giorgio Melchiori, New Cambridge Shakespeare (Cambridge, 1998)
ELH	*English Literary History*
ELR	*English Literary Renaissance*
Erasmus	Desiderius Erasmus, *Adages*, trans. Margaret Mann Phillips, ann. R.A.B. Mynors, *The Collected Works of Erasmus* (Toronto, 1974–)
Erne	Lukas Erne, *Shakespeare as Literary Dramatist* (Cambridge, 2002)
Evans, 'Restored'	G. Blakemore Evans, '*Shakespeare Restored* – once again!', in Anne Lancashire (ed.), *Editing Renaissance Dramatic Texts* (New York, 1976), 139–56
Fabyan	Robert Fabyan, *The Chronicle of Fabian . . . continued . . . to thende of Queene Mary* (1559; STC 10664)
Fayard	Nicole Fayard, *The Performance of Shakespeare in France since the Second World War* (Lewiston, NY, 2006)
Forker	*King Richard II*, ed. Charles Forker, Arden Shakespeare (2002)
Foulkes	Richard Foulkes, *Performing Shakespeare in the Age of Empire* (Cambridge, 2002)
Fox	Adam Fox, *Oral and Literate Culture in England 1500–1700* (Oxford, 2000)
Freud	Sigmund Freud, 'Some character-types met with in psycho-analytic work', trans. E. Colburn Mayne, in *Collected Papers*, ed. Joan Riviere, 5 vols (1950), vol. 4, 318–44
Frye	Roland Mushat Frye, *Shakespeare and Christian Doctrine* (Princeton, NJ, 1963)
Garber	Marjorie Garber, 'Descanting on deformity: Richard III and the shape of history', in Heather Dubrow and Richard Strier (eds), *The Historical Renaissance* (Chicago, 1988), 79–103
Garrard	William Garrard, *The Arte of Warre* (1591; STC 11623)
Gaskell	Philip Gaskell, *A New Introduction to Bibliography* (Oxford, 1972)

Geneva *The Bible and Holy Scriptures conteyned in the Olde and Newe Testament* (Geneva, 1561; STC 2095)

Gentleman [Francis Gentleman,] *The Dramatic Censor*, 2 vols (1770; rpt. New York, 1972)

George David George, 'Shakespeare and Pembroke's Men', *SQ*, 32 (1981), 305–23

Gifford George Gifford, *Sermons vpon the Whole Booke of the Revelation* (1596; STC 11866)

Gillingham John Gillingham (ed.), *Richard III: A Medieval Kingship*, (New York, 1993)

Goodland Katharine Goodland, *Female Mourning in Medieval and Renaissance English Drama* (Aldershot, 2005)

Gould Thomas R. Gould, *The Tragedian: an Essay on the Histrionic Genius of Junius Brutus Booth* (New York, 1868)

Grafton Richard Grafton, *A Chronicle at Large of the History of the Affairs of England*, 2 vols (1569; rpt. 1809)

Greenblatt Stephen Greenblatt, *Hamlet in Purgatory* (Princeton, NJ, 2001)

Greg, *Documents* W.W. Greg, *Dramatic Documents from the Elizabethan Playhouses* (Oxford, 1931)

Greg, *Problem* W.W. Greg, *The Editorial Problem in Shakespeare* (1942; 2nd edn Oxford, 1951)

Griffin William J. Griffin, 'An omission in the Folio text of *Richard III*', *RES*, 13 (1937), 329–32

Griffith Mrs [Elizabeth] Griffith, *The Morality of Shakespeare's Drama* (1775)

Groatsworth *Greene's Groatsworth of Wit*, ed. D. Allen Carroll (Binghamton, NY, 1994)

Gurr, *Companies* Andrew Gurr, *The Shakespearian Playing Companies* (Oxford, 1996)

Gurr, 'Democratic' Andrew Gurr, '*Richard III* and the democratic process', *Essays in Criticism*, 24 (1974), 39–47

GWW George Walton Williams, private communication

Habicht Werner Habicht, 'Shakespeare and theatre politics in the Third Reich', in Hanna Scolnicov and Peter Holland (eds), *The Play out of Context: Transferring Plays from Culture to Culture* (Cambridge, 1989), 110–20

Halio Jay L. Halio, 'Handy-dandy: Q1/Q2 *Romeo and Juliet*', in Jay L. Halio (ed.), *Shakespeare's Romeo and Juliet': Texts, Contexts, and Interpretation* (Newark, Del., 1995), 123–50

Hall	Edward Hall, *The Union of the Two Noble and Illustre Families of Lancastre & Yorke* (1548, STC 12721)
Hall, J.	Joseph Hall, *The Collected Poems of Joseph Hall*, ed. A. Davenport (Liverpool, 1949)
Hammer	Paul E.J. Hammer, *The Polarisation of Elizabethan Politics: The Political Career of Robert Devereux, 2nd Earl of Essex, 1585–1597* (Cambridge, 1999)
Hanham	Alison Hanham, *Richard III and His Early Historians 1483–1535* (Oxford, 1975)
Hankey	*Richard III*, ed. Julie Hankey (1981)
Hardyng	John Hardyng, *The Chronicle of Ihon Hardyng* (1543; STC 12767), with a *Continuation* by Richard Grafton
Harrison	William Harrison, *The Description of England*, ed. Georges Edelen, Folger Documents of Tudor and Stuart Civilization (Ithaca, 1968)
Hart	Alfred Hart, 'The length of Elizabethan and Jacobean plays', *RES*, 8 (1932), 139–54
Harvey	Gabriel Harvey, *The Works of Gabriel Harvey*, ed. A.B. Grosart, 3 vols (1884; rpt. New York, 1966)
Hassel, 'Context'	R. Chris Hassel, Jr, 'Context and charisma: the Sher–Alexander *Richard III* and its reviewers', *SQ*, 36 (1985), 630–43
Hassel, *Performance*	R. Chris Hassel, Jr, *Songs of Death: Performance, Interpretation, and the Text of Richard III* (Lincoln, Nebr., 1987)
Hattaway, *Companion*	Michael Hattaway (ed.), *Cambridge Companion to Shakespeare's History Plays* (Cambridge, 2002)
Hazlitt	William Hazlitt, *The Complete Works of William Hazlitt*, ed. P.P. Howe, 21 vols (1930)
Heath	Benjamin Heath, *A Revisal of Shakespear's Text* (1765)
Henslowe	*Henslowe's Diary*, ed. R.A. Foakes and R.T. Rickert (Cambridge, 1961)
Heywood, *Apology*	Thomas Heywood, *An Apology for Actors* (1612; STC 13309)
Heywood, *Edward IV*	Thomas Heywood, *The First and Second Partes of King Edward the Fourth* (1600; STC 13342)
Hinman	Charlton Hinman, *The Printing and Proof-Reading of the First Folio of Shakespeare*, 2 vols (Oxford, 1963)
Hodgdon, *End*	Barbara Hodgdon, *The End Crowns All: Closure and Contradiction in Shakespeare's History* (Princeton, NJ, 1991)

Hodgdon, 'Replicating'	Barbara Hodgdon, 'Replicating Richard: body doubles, body politics', *Theatre Journal*, 50 (1998), 207–25
Hoenselaars	Ton Hoenselaars (ed.), *Shakespeare's History Plays: Performance, Translation and Adaptation in Britain and Abroad* (Cambridge, 2004)
Holinshed	Raphael Holinshed, *The Chronicles of England, Scotland and Ireland*, 2nd edn (1587; STC 13569)
Homilies	Mary Ellen Rickey and Thomas B. Stroup (eds), *Certaine Sermons or Homilies (1547–1571)*, facsimile of 1623 edition (Gainesville, Fla., 1968)
Honigmann, *Impact*	E.A.J. Honigmann, *Shakespeare's Impact on His Contemporaries* (1982)
Honigmann, 'Text'	E.A.J. Honigmann, 'The text of Richard III', *Theatre Research*, 7 (1965), 48–55
Honigmann, 'Variants'	E.A.J. Honigmann, 'On the indifferent and one-way variants in Shakespeare', *The Library*, 5th series, 22 (1967), 189–204
Hooker, *Laws*	Richard Hooker, *Of the Lawes of Ecclesiasticall Politie* (1593; STC 13712)
Horrox	Rosemary Horrox, *Richard III: A Study of Service* (Cambridge, 1989)
Hortmann	Wilhelm Hortmann, *Shakespeare on the German Stage: The Twentieth Century* (Cambridge, 1998)
Houlbrooke	R.A. Houlbrooke, 'Women's social life and common action in England from the fifteenth century to the eve of the Civil War', *Continuity and Change*, 1 (1986), 171–89
Howard & Rackin	Jean E. Howard and Phyllis Rackin, *Engendering a Nation: A Feminist Account of Shakespeare's Histories* (1997)
Howell	T.B. Howell (ed.), *A Complete Collection of State Trials*, 21 vols (1816)
Hughes	Alan Hughes, *Henry Irving, Shakespearean* (Cambridge, 1981)
Ioppolo	Grace Ioppolo, *Revising Shakespeare* (Cambridge, Mass., 1991)
Jackson, 'Copy'	MacD.P. Jackson, 'The manuscript copy of the quarto (1598) of Shakespeare's *1 Henry IV*, *N&Q*, ser. 7, 33 (1986), 353–4
Jackson, 'Two'	MacD.P. Jackson, 'Two Shakespeare quartos: *Richard III* (1597) and *1 Henry IV* (1598)', *SB*, 35 (1982), 173–91
Jack Straw	*The Life and Death of Jack Straw* [1594], ed. Kenneth Muir and F.P. Wilson (Oxford, 1957)

James I	King James I, *The Political Works of James I*, ed. Charles Howard McIlwain (Cambridge, Mass., 1918)
Jones, M.	Michael Jones, 'Richard III and the Stanleys', in Rosemary Horrox (ed.), *Richard III and the North*, Studies in Regional and Local History, no. 6 (Hull, 1986), 27–50
Jones, *Origins*	Emrys Jones, *The Origins of Shakespeare* (Oxford, 1977)
Jonson	*Ben Jonson*, ed. C.H. Herford and Percy and Evelyn Simpson, 11 vols (Oxford, 1925–52)
Jowett, 'Derby'	John Jowett, '"Derby", "Stanley", and memorial reconstruction in Quarto *Richard III*', *N&Q*, 245 (2000), 75–9
Jowett, 'Pre-editorial'	John Jowett, 'Pre-editorial criticism and the space for editing: examples from *Richard III* and *Your Five Gallants*', in Christa Jansohn (ed.), *Problems of Editing* (Tübingen, 1999), 127–49
Kastan, *1H4*	*King Henry IV, Part 1*, ed. David Scott Kastan, Arden Shakespeare (2002)
Kehler	Dorothea Kehler, 'Shakespeare's *Richard III*', *Explicator*, 56 (1997–8), 118–20
Kelly	Henry Ansgar Kelly, *Divine Providence in the England of Shakespeare's Histories* (Cambridge, Mass., 1970)
Kemble	John Philip Kemble, *Macbeth and King Richard the Third* (2nd edn, 1817; rpt. 1970)
Kendall	Paul Murray Kendall, *Richard the Third* (1955)
Kennedy	Dennis Kennedy, *Looking at Shakespeare: A Visual History of Twentieth-Century Performance*, 2nd edn (Cambridge, 2001)
Kinney, A.	Arthur F. Kinney (ed.), *Renaissance Drama: An Anthology of Plays and Entertainments* (Oxford, 1999)
Kinney, 'Tyrant'	Daniel Kinney, 'The tyrant being slain: afterlives of More's *History of King Richard III*', in Neil Rhodes (ed.), *English Renaissance Prose* (Tempe, Ariz., 1997), 35–56
Knack	*A Knack to Know a Knave, 1594*, ed. G.R Proudfoot (Oxford, 1964)
Knowles, *2H6*	*King Henry VI, Part 2*, ed. Ronald Knowles, Arden Shakespeare (1999)
Knox	Father Ronald Knox and Shane Leslie, *The Miracles of King Henry VI* (Cambridge, 1923)
Kott	Jan Kott, *Shakespeare Our Contemporary*, trans. Boleslaw Taborski (New York, 1964)
Kyd, *Hieronimo*	Thomas Kyd, *The First Part of Jeronimo*, in *The First Part of Hieronimo and The Spanish Tragedy*, ed. Andrew S. Cairncross (Lincoln, Nebr., 1967)

Kyd,   Thomas Kyd, *The Spanish Tragedy*, ed. T.W. Ross
  Spanish Tragedy   (Berkeley, Calif., 1968)
Lake & Questier   Peter Lake and Michael Questier, *The Antichrist's Lewd
                    Hat: Protestants, Papists and Players in Post-Reformation
                    England* (New Haven, Conn., 2002)
Lambarde   William Lambarde, *Eirenarcha or the Office of Justices of
                    Peace 1581/82*, ed. P.R. Glazebrook (Abingdon, Oxon,
                    1972)
Lancaster, 1590   'A Description . . . of the County of Lancaster, about
                    the Year 1590', ed. F.R. Raines, in *Remains Historical &
                    Literary . . . of Lancaster and Chester*, 96 (1875), 1–48
Lea   Henry Charles Lea, *A History of Auricular Confession
                    and Indulgences in the Latin Church*, 4 vols (Philadelphia,
                    1896)
Leir   *The True Chronicle History of King Leir, 1605*, ed. W.W.
                    Greg, Malone Society Reprints (Oxford, 1907)
Levine, M.   Mortimer Levine, *Tudor Dynastic Problems 1460–1571*
                    (1973)
Lilly   William Lilly, *An Introduction to Astrology* (1647; rpt.
                    1939)
Lodge   Thomas Lodge, *The Wounds of Civil War* (1594), ed. John
                    Dover Wilson, Malone Society Reprints (Oxford, 1910)
Loehlin   James N. Loehlin, '"Top of the world, Ma": *Richard
                    III* and cinematic convention', in Lynda E. Boose and
                    Richard Burt (eds), *Shakespeare the Movie* (London,
                    1997), 67–79
Lumiansky & Mills   *The Chester Mystery Cycle*, ed R.M. Lumiansky and
                    David Mills (1974)
Lyly   *The Complete Works of John Lyly*, ed. R. Warwick Bond,
                    3 vols (1902; rpt. Oxford, 1967)
Lyons   Bridget Gellert Lyons, '"Kings games": stage imagery
                    and political symbolism in *Richard III*', *Criticism*, 20
                    (1978), 17–30
McCabe   Richard A. McCabe, *Incest, Drama and Nature's Law
                    1550–1700* (Cambridge, 1993)
MacDonald &   Andrew and Gina MacDonald, 'The necessity of evil:
  MacDonald   Shakespeare's rhetorical strategy in *Richard III*', *SSt*
                    [Japan], 19 (1980–1), 55–69
McDonald   Russ McDonald, '*Richard III* and the tropes of tragedy',
                    Philological Quarterly, 68 (1989), 465–83
Machyn   Henry Machyn, *The Diary of Henry Machyn*, ed. John
                    Gough Nichols, Camden Society, vol. 42 (1848)

McKellen — Ian McKellen, *William Shakespeare's Richard III: A Screenplay written by Ian McKellen and Richard Loncraine* (Woodstock, NY, 1996)

McKenzie — D.F. McKenzie, 'Printers of the mind: some notes on bibliographical theories and printing-house practices', *SB*, 22 (1969), 1–75

McKerrow, *Bibliography* — R.B. McKerrow, *An Introduction to Bibliography for Literary Students* (Oxford, 1927)

McKerrow, *Prolegomena* — R.B. McKerrow, *Prolegomena for the Oxford Shakespeare* (1939; Oxford, 1969)

Macready — William Macready, *Macready's Reminiscences*, ed. Frederick Pollock (New York, 1875)

Maguire — Laurie E. Maguire, *Shakespearean Suspect Texts: The 'Bad' Quartos and their Contexts* (Cambridge, 1996)

Mancini — Dominic Mancini, *The Usurpation of Richard III*, trans. C.A.J. Armstrong (Oxford, 1969)

Marcus — Leah S. Marcus, *Puzzling Shakespeare: Local Reading and Its Discontents* (Berkeley, Calif., 1988)

Marienstras — Richard Marienstras, 'Of a Monstrous Body', in *French Essays on Shakespeare and His Contemporaries*, ed. Jean-Marie Maguin and Michèle Willems (Newark, Del., 1995), 153–74

Marlowe, *Works* — *The Complete Works of Christopher Marlowe*, ed. Fredson Bowers, 2nd edn, 4 vols (Cambridge, 1981)

Marlowe, *Jew of Malta* — Christopher Marlowe, *The Jew of Malta*, ed. James R. Siemon (1994)

Mar-Martine — *Mar-Martine* (London?, 1589; STC 17461)

Marprelate, *Epistle* — Martin Marprelate, *Oh Read Ouer* ([East Molesey, Surrey], 1588; STC 17453)

Marston — *The Complete Works of John Marston*, ed. A.H. Bullen, 3 vols (1887)

Martin — R.F. Martin, 'Milton's hell-hounds', *N&Q*, 36 (1989), 31–2

Mason — James Mason, *The Anatomie of Sorcerie* (1612; STC 17615)

Matthews & Hutton — Brander Matthews and Laurence Hutton (eds), *Kean and Booth and Their Contemporaries* (New York, 1886)

Maus — Katherine Eisaman Maus, *Inwardness and Theater in the English Renaissance* (Chicago, 1995)

Meres — Francis Meres, *Palladis Tamia* (1598; STC 17834)

Meyer — Edward Meyer, *Machiavelli and the Elizabethan Drama* (1897; rpt. New York, 1969)

481

Migne	J.-P. Migne (ed.), *Patriologia Latina* (Paris, 1844–55), vol. 36
Milton	*The Complete Prose Works of John Milton*, ed. Merritt Y. Hughes, vol. 3 (New Haven, Conn., 1962)
Mirror	William Baldwin, *The Mirror for Magistrates*, ed. Lily B. Campbell (1938; rpt. New York, 1960)
Mirror, Additions	John Higgins and Thomas Blenerhasset, *Parts Added to The Mirror for Magistrates*, ed. Lily B. Campbell (Cambridge, 1946)
MLR	*Modern Language Review*
More, *CW*2	Sir Thomas More, *The History of King Richard III*, ed. Richard Sylvester, in *The Complete Works of St Thomas More*, 21 vols, vol. 2 (New Haven, Conn., 1963)
More, *CW*3	*The Complete Works of St Thomas More*, vol. 3, part 1, ed. Craig R. Thompson (New Haven, Conn., 1974), 25–43
More, *CW*15	Sir Thomas More, *Historia Richardi Tertii: Text and Translation*, ed. Daniel Kinney, in *The Complete Works of St Thomas More*, 21 vols, vol. 15 (New Haven, Conn., 1986), 313–633
Mornay	Philippe de Mornay, *Concerning the Trewnesse of the Christian Religion*, trans. Philip Sidney and Arthur Golding (1587; STC 18149)
Morrison	Michael A. Morrison, *John Barrymore: Shakespearean Actor* (Cambridge, 1997)
N&Q	*Notes and Queries*
Nashe	Thomas Nashe, *The Works of Thomas Nashe*, ed. Ronald B. McKerrow, 5 vols (1958; rpt. New York, 1965, ed. F.P. Wilson)
Neill	Michael Neill, 'Shakespeare's halle of mirrors: play, politics, and psychology in *Richard III*', *SSt*, 8 (1975), 99–129
Nelson	Alan H. Nelson, *Early Cambridge Theatres* (Cambridge, 1994)
Newes	*Newes from Scotland* (1592; STC 10841a)
Noble	Richmond Noble, *Shakespeare's Biblical Knowledge and Use of the Book of Common Prayer* (1935; rpt. Folcroft, Pa., 1969)
ODNB	H.C.G. Matthew and Brian Harrison (eds), *Oxford Dictionary of National Biography* (Oxford, 2004)
OED	*The Oxford English Dictionary*, 2nd edn (Oxford, 1989)
Ornstein	Robert Ornstein, *A Kingdom for a Stage: The Achievement of Shakespeare's History Plays* (Cambridge, Mass., 1972)

Ovid	Publius Ovidius Naso, *Metamorphoses*, trans. Frank Justus Miller, rev. G.P. Goold, 3rd edn, 2 vols (Cambridge, Mass., 1984)
Pappe	*Pappe with an Hatchett* (1589; STC 17463)
Parker	Patricia Parker, 'Preposterous events', *SQ*, 43 (1992), 186–213
Parnassus	*The Three Parnassus Plays*, ed. J.B. Leishman (1949)
Parsons	Robert Parsons, *A Conference about the Next Succession* (1595; STC 19398)
2 Pasquill	*The Returne of the renowned Caualiero Pasquill of England* (1589; STC 19547)
Paston Letters	*The Paston Letters*, ed. James Gairdner, 6 vols (1904)
Patrick	David Lyall Patrick, *The Textual History of Richard III* (Stanford, Calif., 1936)
PBSA	*Papers of the Bibliographical Society of America*
Peacham	Henry Peacham, *The Truth of Our Times* (1638; STC 19517)
Pearlman	E. Pearlman, 'The invention of Richard of Gloucester', *SQ*, 43 (1992), 410–29
Peele, *Edward I*	George Peele, *King Edward I* [1593], ed. W.W. Greg (Oxford, 1911)
Perkins, *Discourse*	William Perkins, *A Discourse of Conscience* (Cambridge, 1596; STC 19696)
Perkins, *Treatise*	*A Treatise tending vnto a Demonstration, whether a man bee in the state of damnation* (1591; STC 19753)
Perkins, *Works*	William Perkins, *Works* (Cambridge, 1603; STC 19647)
Peterson	Richard S. Peterson, 'Laurel crown and ape's tail: new light on Spenser's career from Sir Thomas Tresham', *Spenser Studies*, 12 (1991), 1–31
Pickersgill	Edward H. Pickersgill, 'On the Quarto and Folio of Richard III', *New Shakespere Society's Transactions*, series 1, 3–4 (1875), 77–124
Pierce	Robert B. Pierce, *Shakespeare's History Plays: The Family and the State* (Columbus, Ohio, 1971)
Pigman	G.W. Pigman III, *Grief and English Renaissance Elegy* (Cambridge, 1985)
Plutarch	Plutarch, *The Lives of the Noble Grecians and Romanes*, trans. Thomas North (1579; STC 20065)
Pollard	A.J. Pollard, *Richard III and the Princes in the Tower* (New York, 1991)
Potter	Lois Potter, 'Bad and good authority figures: *Richard III* and *Henry V* since 1945', *Shakespeare Jahrbuch* (1992), 39–54

Prior	Moody Prior, *The Drama of Power: Studies in Shakespeare's History Plays* (Evanston, Ill., 1973)
Puttenham	George Puttenham, *The Arte of English Poesie*, ed. Gladys Doidge Willcock and Alice Walker (1936; rpt. Cambridge, 1970)
Rackin	Phyllis Rackin, 'Women's roles in the Elizabethan history plays', in Hattaway, *Companion*, 71–88
Rainolde	Richard Rainolde, *Foundacion of Rhetorike* (Cambridge, 1563; STC 20925a.5)
Raleigh, *History*	Sir Walter Raleigh, *The History of the World* (1617; STC 20638)
REED	*Records of Early English Drama: Cambridge*, ed. Alan H. Nelson, ongoing series (Toronto, 1989)
RES	*Review of English Studies*
Richardus Tertius	Thomas Legge, *Richardus Tertius*, in *Thomas Legge: The Complete Plays*, ed. and trans. Dana F. Sutton, 2 vols (New York, 1993)
Richmond	Hugh M. Richmond, *King Richard III* (Manchester, 1989)
Righter	Anne Righter (Barton), *Shakespeare and the Idea of the Play* (1964)
Roderick	Richard Roderick, 'Remarks', in Thomas Edwards, *The Canons of Criticism*, 6th edn (1758), 212–38
Rogers, *Sermon*	Thomas Rogers, *A Sermon vpon the 6. 7. and 8. Verses of the 12. Chapter of S. Pauls Epistle vnto the Romanes* (1590; STC 21240)
Ross, C., *Richard*	Charles Ross, *Richard III* (Berkeley, Calif., 1981)
Ross, C., *Wars*	Charles Ross, *The Wars of the Roses: A Concise History* (1976)
Ross, L.J.	Lawrence J. Ross, 'The meaning of strawberries in Shakespeare', *Studies in the Renaissance*, 7 (1960), 225–40
Rossiter	A.P. Rossiter, *Angel with Horns and Other Shakespeare Lectures*, ed. Graham Storey (New York, 1961)
Rous	John Rous, *Historia Regum Angliae*, ed. Thomas Hearne, 2nd edn (Oxford, 1745)
Rozett	Martha Tuck Rozett, *The Doctrine of Election and the Emergence of Elizabethan Tragedy* (Princeton, NJ, 1984)
RP	Richard Proudfoot, private communication
RQ	*Renaissance Quarterly*
Rutter	Carol Chillington Rutter, *Documents of the Rose Playhouse*, rev. edn (Manchester, 1999)
SB	*Studies in Bibliography*

Scot	Reginald Scot, *The Discouerie of Witchcraft* (1584; STC 21864)
SEL	*Studies in English Literature*
Seneca	Lucius Annaeus Seneca, *Seneca's Tragedies*, trans. Frank Justus Miller, 2 vols (1917; rpt. Cambridge, Mass., 1929)
Seneca, *Tragedies*	Lucius Annaeus Seneca, *Seneca, His Tenne Tragedies* (1581), ed. Thomas Newton, 2 vols (1927)
Seward	Desmond Seward, *Richard III: England's Black Legend* (1982; rpt. 1997)
Shaheen, *Biblical*	Naseeb Shaheen, *Biblical References in Shakespeare's Plays* (Newark, Del., 1999)
Shaheen, *History Plays*	Naseeb Shaheen, *Biblical References in Shakespeare's History Plays* (Newark, Del., 1989)
Shannon	Laurie Shannon, *Sovereign Amity: Figures of Friendship in Shakespearean Contexts* (Chicago, 2002)
Sher	Antony Sher, *The Year of the King* (1985)
Sidney	Sir Philip Sidney, *The Poems of Sir Philip Sidney*, ed. William A. Ringler (Oxford, 1962)
Siemon, 'Between'	James R. Siemon, 'Between the lines: bodies/languages/times', *SSt*, 29 (2001), 36–43
Siemon, 'Power'	James R. Siemon, 'The power of hope? An early modern reader of *Richard III*', in Jean Howard and Richard Dutton (eds), *A Companion to Shakespeare's History Plays* (Oxford, 2003), 361–78
Simpson	Richard Simpson, 'The political use of the stage in Shakespere's time' and 'The politics of Shakespere's historical plays', *New Shakespere Society's Transactions*, series 1, 1–2 (1874; rpt. 1965), 371–95, 396–441
Smallwood	Robert Smallwood, 'Shakespeare at Stratford-upon-Avon, 1992', *SQ*, 44 (1993), 343–62
Smidt, *Impostors*	Kristian Smidt, *Iniurious Impostors* (Oslo, 1964)
Smidt, *King Richard*	*The Tragedy of King Richard III, Parallel Texts of the First Quarto and First Folio with Variants of the Early Quartos*, ed. Kristian Smidt (Oslo, 1969)
Smidt, *Memorial*	Kristian Smidt, *Memorial Transmission and Quarto Copy in Richard III: A Reassessment* (Oslo, 1970)
Smidt, *Unconformities*	Kristian Smidt, *Unconformities in Shakespeare's History Plays* (Atlantic Highlands, NJ, 1982)
Smith, *Sermons*	Henry Smith, *The Sermons of Master Henrie Smith* (1592; STC 22718)
SPD	*State Papers Domestic*
Speaight	Robert Speaight, *Shakespeare on the Stage* (Boston, Mass., 1973)

Spedding	James Spedding, 'On the corrected edition of *Richard III'. New Shakespere Society's Transactions*, series 1, 3–4 (1875), 1–76
Spenser	Edmund Spenser, *The Faerie Queene*, in *The Works of Edmund Spenser*, ed. Edwin Greenlaw, Charles Grosvenor Osgood and Frederick Morgan Padelford (Baltimore, Md., 1932)
Spivack	Bernard Spivack, *Shakespeare and the Allegory of Evil* (New York, 1958)
Sprague, *Actors*	Arthur Colby Sprague, *Shakespeare and the Actors* (Cambridge, Mass., 1948)
Sprague, *Histories*	Arthur Colby Sprague, *Shakespeare's Histories: Plays for the Stage* (1964)
SQ	*Shakespeare Quarterly*
SS	*Shakespeare Survey*
SSt	*Shakespeare Studies*
STC	*A Short-title Catalogue of Books Printed in England, Scotland, and Ireland: and of English Books Printed Abroad 1475–1640*, A.W. Pollard and G.R. Redgrave, ed. W.A. Jackson, F.S. Ferguson and Katharine F. Pantzer, 3 vols (2nd rev. and enlarged edn, 1976–91)
STM	*Sir Thomas More*, ed. Vittorio Gabrieli and Georgio Melchiori (Manchester, 1990)
Stow	John Stow, *A Survey of London*, ed. C.L. Kingsford, 2 vols (Oxford, 1908)
Stříbrný	Zdenek Stříbrný, *Shakespeare and Eastern Europe* (Oxford, 2000)
Strobl	Gerwin Strobl, 'Shakespeare and the Third Reich', *History Today*, 47 (1997), 16–21
Stubbes	Philip Stubbes, *The Anatomie of Abuses* (1583; STC 23376)
Sutton & Hammond	Anne F. Sutton and P.W. Hammond (eds), *The Coronation of Richard III the Extant Documents* (Gloucester, 1983)
Tacitus, *Annals*	Cornelius Tacitus, *Complete Works of Tacitus*, trans. Alfred John Church, William Jackson Brodribb and Sara Bryant (New York, rpt. 1942)
Tarsitano	Marie Tarsitano, 'Sturua's Georgian *Richard III'*, *Theatre History Studies*, 9 (1989), 69–76
Tempera	Mariangela Tempera, 'Italian responses to Shakespeare's histories', in Hoenselaars, 115–32
Theses	*Theses Martinianae* ([1589], STC 17457)

Thirty-Nine Articles	*Articles whereupon it was agreed in the . . . yeere of our Lorde God 1562 . . . for the auoyding of the diuersities of opinions, and for the stablishing of consent touching true religion* (1590)
Thomas, K.	Keith Thomas, *Religion and the Decline of Magic: Studies in Popular Beliefs in Sixteenth and Seventeenth Century England* (1971; rpt. New York, 1997)
Thomas, S., *Antic*	Sidney Thomas, *The Antic Hamlet and Richard III* (New York, 1943)
Thomas Lord Cromwell	*Thomas Lord Cromwell* [1602], in C.F. Tucker Brooke (ed.), *The Shakespeare Apocrypha* (Oxford, 1908)
Thomson	W.H. Thomson, *Shakespeare's Characters: A Historical Dictionary* (New York, 1951)
Tilley	Morris Palmer Tilley, *A Dictionary of the Proverbs in England in the Sixteenth and Seventeenth Centuries* (Ann Arbor, Mich., 1951)
Tillyard	E.M.W. Tillyard, *Shakespeare's History Plays* (1944; rpt. New York, 1946)
Toole	William B. Toole, 'The motif of psychic division in *Richard III*', *SS*, 27 (1974), 21–32
Torrey	Michael Torrey, '"The plain devil and dissembling looks": ambivalent physiognomy and Shakespeare's Richard III', *ELR*, 30 (2000), 123–53
Treatise	*A Treatise of Treasons Against Q. Elizabeth, and the Croune of England* ([Louvain], 1572, STC 7601)
TRHS	*Transactions of the Royal Historical Society*
TRKJ	*The Troublesome Raigne of John, King of England* (1591), ed. J.W. Sider (New York, 1979)
Troughton	David Troughton, 'Richard III', in Robert Smallwood (ed.), *Players of Shakespeare 4* (Cambridge, 1998), 71–100
True Tragedy	*The True Tragedy of Richard the Third, 1594*, ed. W.W. Greg (Oxford, 1929)
TxC	Stanley Wells and Gary Taylor, with John Jowett and William Montgomery, *William Shakespeare: A Textual Companion* (Oxford, 1987)
Ulrici	Hermann Ulrici, *Shakespeare's Dramatic Art*, trans. L. Dora Schmitz, 2 vols (1891; German edn 1839)
Union	Edward Hall, *The Union of the Two Noble and Illustre Families of Lancastre & Yorke* (1548; STC 12721)
Urkowitz	Steven Urkowitz, 'Reconsidering the relationship of Quarto and Folio texts of *Richard III*', *ELR*, 16 (1986), 442–66

Van Laan	Thomas F. Van Laan, *Role-playing in Shakespeare* (Toronto, 1978)
Vergil	Polydore Vergil, *Three Books of Polydore Vergil's History of England*, ed. Henry Ellis, Camden Society, vol. 29 (1844)
Vickers	Brian Vickers (ed.), *Shakespeare: The Critical Heritage*, 6 vols (London and Boston, 1974–80)
Virgil	Virgil, *The Aeneid*, ed. and trans. H. Rushton Fairclough, Loeb Classical Library, 2 vols (Cambridge, Mass., 1860)
Walker	Alice Walker, *Textual Problems of the First Folio* (Cambridge, 1953)
Walsham	Alexandra Walsham, '"Frantick Hacket": prophecy, sorcery, insanity, and the Elizabethan Puritan movement', *Historical Journal*, 41 (1998), 27–66
Walton, *Copy*	J.K. Walton, *The Copy for the Folio Text of Richard III* (Auckland, NZ, 1955)
Walton, *Quarto*	J.K. Walton, *The Quarto Copy for the First Folio of Shakespeare* (Dublin, 1971)
Watson, D.G.	Donald G. Watson, *Shakespeare's Early History Plays: Politics at Play on the Elizabethan Stage* (Athens, Ga., 1990)
Watson, R.	Robert N. Watson, *Shakespeare and the Hazards of Ambition* (Cambridge, Mass., 1984)
Watson, Thomas	Thomas Watson, *The Hekatompathia* (1582), facsimile edn, S.K. Heninger, Jr (Gainesville, Fla., 1964)
Whetstone	George Whetstone, *The English myrror* (1586; STC 25336)
Whitaker	Virgil K. Whitaker, *Shakespeare's Use of Learning: An Inquiry into the Growth of His Mind and Art* (San Marino, Calif., 1953)
Wiggins	Martin Wiggins, *Journeymen in Murder: The Assassin in English Renaissance Drama* (Oxford, 1991)
Wilks	John S. Wilks, *The Idea of Conscience in Renaissance Tragedy* (1990)
Willen	Diane Willen, 'Women and religion in early modern England', in Sherrin Marshall (ed.), *Women in Reformation and Counter-Reformation Europe* (Bloomington, Ind.,1989), 140–65
Williams	George Walton Williams, 'Scene indivisible: the battle of Birnam Wood', *Shakespeare Newsletter*, 55 (2005), 33, 36
Willis, *Nurture*	Deborah Willis, *Malevolent Nurture: Witch-Hunting and Maternal Power in Early Modern England* (Ithaca, NY, 1995)

Willis,
'Witch-hunts'

Deborah Willis, 'Shakespeare and the English witch-hunts: enclosing the maternal body', in Richard Burt and John Michael Archer (eds), *Enclosure Acts: Sexuality, Property, and Culture in Early Modern England* (Ithaca, NY, 1994), 96–120

Wilson, *2H6*

William Shakespeare, *2 Henry VI*, ed. John Dover Wilson (1952)

Wilson, *Three Ladies*

R[obert] W[ilson], *The Three Ladies of London* (1584; STC 25784)

Wilson, *Three Lords*

R[obert] W[ilson], *The Three Lords and Three Ladies of London* (1590; STC 25783)

Wing

Donald Wing (ed.), *A Short-Title Catalogue of Books Printed in England, Scotland, Ireland, Wales and British America and of English Books Printed in Other Countries 1641-1700*, 3 vols (New York, 1945–51)

Wolfit

Donald Wolfit, *First Interval* (1954)

Wood

Alice I. Perry Wood, *The Stage History of Shakespeare's King Richard the Third* (New York, 1909)

Yamada

Akihiro Yamada (ed.), *The First Folio of Shakespeare: A Transcript of Contemporary Marginalia in a Copy of the Kodama Memorial Library of Meisei University* (Tokyo, 1998)

Young

Bruce Young, 'Parental blessing in Shakespeare's plays', *Studies in Philology*, 89 (1992), 179–210

INDEX

The index covers the Introduction, the commentary notes and the Appendices; it excludes references in the textual notes and references to the OED. Page numbers in italics refer to figures. The abbreviation 'n.' is only used for footnotes in the Introduction and Appendices; it is not used for commentary notes.